FOOD IN EARLY MODERN ENGLAND

Food in Early Modern England
Phases, Fads, Fashions 1500–1760

Joan Thirsk

**hambledon
continuum**

Hambledon Continuum is an imprint of Continuum Books
Continuum UK, The Tower Building, 11 York Road, London SE1 7NX
Continuum US, 80 Maiden Lane, Suite 704, New York, NY 10038

www.continuumbooks.com

First published 2006

British Library Cataloguing-in-Publication Data
A catalogue record for this book is available from the British Library.

ISBN 978 0 8264 4233 88

Typeset by Egan Reid Ltd, Auckland, New Zealand
Printed and bound by Biddles Ltd, King's Lynn, Great Britain

Contents

Illustrations

Between Pages 188 and 189

Styles of cooking

Styles of eating

Putting the food together

Commercial and domestic breadmaking

Preface

Since food and drink are the mainstay of life, there is not a soul on this planet who does not have interesting views and information about it. So the final shape of this book, with its emphasis on phases, fads and fashions, distils ideas that are an inseparable mixture of my own reading, observation and reflections, and those of my family, friends and colleagues. I would like to give special thanks to my sisters-in-law, Jean Blackburn and Betty Thirsk, who have always kept me in touch with the food of Northern England and the Cotswolds; and, among historians, to thank John Broad, Elizabeth Griffiths, Richard Hoyle, Brian Moffatt, Hassell Smith, Lena Orlin, Mary Prior, Malcolm Thick and Jane Whittle for many insights that have enriched this book in countless different ways. My husband has given unstinted help with the bibliography of the subject, and my son Martin has been endlessly patient in making the technology of computers and digital cameras available to an ignoramus. As for the long years that I have spent in this study, I realize now how much I have learned of food history that gives a fresh dimension to my thoughts when I am cooking in the kitchen.

Acknowledgements

I acknowledge gratefully the permission given me to study and cite the Sidney manuscripts of Lord De Lisle on deposit at the Centre for Kentish Studies, Maidstone; also the Hampshire Record Office, of access to the Sherfield MSS (Document: 44M49/L48/134) in the Jervoise of Herriard Collection; and the Royal Society, London, for use of its Domestic MSS. The help of Fiona Lucraft was invaluable in enabling me to use at home the collection of culinary texts which wee assembled by Alan Davidson, and which now form *The Old Culinary Text Project* for the assistance of all students of food history. It is a most precious resource.

I also give warmest thanks to my publishers, most of all to Tony Morris, the Commissioning Editor for Hambledon and London, who has for so long spurred my endeavours, and Anya Wilson, Jane Rogers, Ben Hayes, Jane Olorenshaw and Jonathan Styles who toiled so carefully to produce this book.

The author has endeavoured to find all copyright owners of the illustrations, and wishes to thank the following for permission to use their images: Mr George Leonard, Leonards, Kirkwall, Orkney (for no. 1); Getty Images (no. 2); the Folger Shakespeare Library, Washington DC, USA (nos. 5 & 12); the Duke of Marlborough, Blenheim Palace, Woodstock, Oxon. (no. 8); the Earl of Pembroke and Trustees of Wilton House Trust, Salisbury, UK. (no. 10); the British Library, London (no.11); the Shetland Museum, Lerwick, Shetland (no. 13).

Introduction

What persuades a historian of agriculture to turn to food history? I studied the history of farming and regional differences for nearly 60 years, and often asked myself how farming changes affected people's diet. As time went on, I became increasingly dissatisfied with my shadowy image of women cooking in the kitchen and serving their families at the meal table. My curiosity sharpened as I cooked for my family, travelled somewhat, and found my knowledge of farming and food in the past constantly confronting current daily news items about food fads and fashions. I wondered whether, in that respect, past and present matched each other. Some ten years ago, a chance question put to me at a lecture in the Folger Library in Washington DC started me on deeper research into our food history.

I stand on the shoulders of my predecessors, and pay the warmest tribute to their researches. But I also know that my knowledge of farming history gives me different insights, and these will become clear in the text that follows. I also realized as I worked myself into my subject that diet in the past was continuously changing, not as fast as it does nowadays, of course, but nevertheless at a pace that people consciously noticed in the course of one lifetime; they certainly recognized fashions in food. So I have constructed my book in a way that gives a distinctive shape to chronological phases, dividing time roughly into 50-year periods (but making an exception for the Civil War and Interregnum), examining in each one the food that farmers and gardeners produced, the changing public image of foods as the market developed greater commercial expertise, and noting the way authors commented on food in their changing world and enunciated their latest views on what was a healthy diet. At the same time I have kept my eye on the cookbooks, and have searched for every clue to show me the cooks in the kitchen; I know that they were affected in varying degrees by what they read, saw and heard in the public world, while still following the food traditions of their individual families.

My task, perhaps, could have been better tackled by ten people rather than one, but I hope that I make a useful contribution to our food history that will stimulate others. Over and over again, my searches among the archives have made me revise and refine my viewpoint, sometimes driving me to despair at my arrogance in ever claiming to generalize. As we know from looking at shoppers' trolleys in the supermarket, every family, indeed every individual, has different food preferences; it has always been so, and every assertion can be proved wrong by another example.

I have learned finally to see two food worlds, and to accept that they existed alongside each other. The one was inhabited by food writers who, throughout the period with which I am concerned, pontificated about food and were happy to pronounce authoritatively, though none of them knew as much about food throughout England as they liked to think. The other world of the kitchen was inhabited by women and some men cooking food according to their social, local and family traditions, while adapting them in each generation to suit changing tastes and circumstances. The two worlds interacted all the time, but coexisted and were recognizably different.

When analysing the world of private families, it should, of course, be subdivided into classes. The food eaten by the well-to-do is reasonably well known, but that eaten at lower social levels is not. For most of my period, a curtain screens more than half the scene from view. But things improve somewhat in the course of the 260 years studied here, and I have done my best to peer through chinks that let some light into dark places.

I finish with the conviction that the food world was a lively place undergoing continuous change; and that sense of swirling movement is sharpened by some emphatic comments by contemporaries along the way, showing how keenly aware they were themselves of changing food habits in their lifetimes. Some of the changes were modest, but they were, nevertheless, memorable in the experience of individuals. The improved recipe for an apple turnover bears eloquent witness to one such exciting experience; it earned praise in an ode of 77 lines by Leonard Welsted which he composed in 1704, and I have printed it in full. Other changes in the food scene prompted no specific comment, for the domestic routine was a commonplace that rarely attracted interest. So some changes have to be inferred or guessed at, relying sometimes on somewhat slender clues. Thomas Moufet in 1600, for example, had firmly stated that ducks were not edible food unless they were farm-fed since they fed on frogs, toads and water spiders. Yet at the very same time duck decoys were beginning to be set up, which would soon bring thousands of wildfowl, including wild ducks, to the market and provide bountiful food. Arthur Standish, in a tract of 1613, maintained that 40 years before, in the 1570s, even 'the poorest sort scorned to eat a piece of meat roasted with seacoal'. Thus did the prejudice against coal surface in print, but people had to learn to accept the changed flavour, and silently they did so. A striking alteration in morning routines was wrought by tea-drinking for breakfast, yet surely no historian would ever have spotted it. The working man's drink of ale was gradually superseded by tea, and much later on William Cobbett vividly depicted the consequences. When getting up in the morning, a kettle had to be boiled before tea could be made in the labourer's home; so it resulted in an entirely new explanation being offered by workmen to their employers whenever they arrived late for work in the morning.[1]

We are not then surprised to read the verdict of Eliza Melroe in 1798, viewing things across a wide canvas, and concluding that the system of living in the last 20 or 30 years had 'almost undergone a total change'. His remark had particular significance in relation to food, for Melroe was a naval man and physician who showed an unusual interest in the details of food preparation. I have come to realize that a similar remark could have been made in every earlier generation.[2]

So the first part of my book sets food within the context of a changing economic, social, political and religious world. The second part takes a closer look at some individual foods in order to pull together facts that have been scattered in the first part, and gives a sharper outline to the changes that affected the content, quality, quantity and status of each food. Some very different influences were at work, altering, for example, the breads, meats, fruits and cheeses that were eaten. It is instructive to see more clearly how many facets of change impinged in some way on single foodstuffs. It has become a conventional assertion among historians who have not studied food history in any detail to say that our forebears ate a monotonous and boring diet. I hope that my account will put an end to such a mistaken conclusion. Food is universally recognized as one of the main pleasures of life in all cultures: a Chinese proverb tells us that 'for the people, Heaven consists of eating'. Is it conceivable, then, that human beings, resourceful, ingenious, inventive as they are, would have settled for drab monotony all through the ages, when they lived in a countryside overflowing with animals, birds, fish and plants in the greatest variety? Through aeons of time, women have made up the majority of cooks in the world, and I have learned to admire and respect their originality, ingenuity, and resourcefulness. The variety that people enjoyed in the past was different from ours, but that obliges us to see it on their terms. A recent writer on nutrition has told us that human diet once contained 225 different foods, whereas today 90% of our average calorie intake comes from only 18. We surely do not want to boast of that achievement.[3]

The food regime of the early modern period shows our forebears eating a multitude of plants, animals and birds that we neglect. Among cereals, they ate not just wheat, but rye, barley and oats, and, moreover, differentiated the flavours with such discrimination that separate varieties of the four grains were used for different dishes. We, in contrast, have settled on wheat flour almost alone. Among meats our forebears relished kidneys, livers, cheeks, tripe, noses, bone marrow, as well as the muscle meat of beef cattle, sheep and pigs. Crisply roasted sheep's heads were a special treat. Hardly a bird in the sky was not eaten – quails, plovers, sparrows, cranes, bustards, herons, woodcocks, blackbirds, larks – they were routine food, and many were there in abundance. Tiny birds like wheatears, found in large numbers on the South Downs in Sussex, made a veritable feast. The best contemporary account of this bird, which was described by one writer as 'just a lump of fat', comes to us by accident, because in hot summer weather the birds could not be sent to London to arrive fresh; normally, they were speedily despatched to serve the select few who could afford such treats; in hot weather they had to be sold nearer to hand, in Tunbridge Wells, and a Kentish informant describes the trade.[4]

We have less difficulty in believing in the plenty and variety of fish in the past, since we have ourselves watched the range of choice in our shops shrinking in our own lifetimes; some once-plentiful fish have almost disappeared. But in this case we know by actual experience what we have lost, and so can understand the relish with which people once ate fish in greater variety, some of it fresh from their rivers, dykes and ponds, or, for those living at the coast, straight from the sea. For greenstuff people either went into their gardens or looked anywhere in 'nature's storehouse' – the title of a book by a contemporary writer, J.S., in 1684 – on the edges of fields, in hedgerows, in woodland, and on commons. Green leaves of all kinds went into the pot. In contrast, I can remember in my childhood in the 1930s we relied on only three basic herbs for flavouring: parsley, thyme and sage. Fortunately, that lean phase ended around the 1960s (and warm thanks to Elizabeth David for that). A lively interest in other herbs has been revived, and some of the almost endless list of greenstuffs eaten by our forebears, such as sorrel, rocket and purslane, are again being savoured with appreciation, as they were in the past.[5]

A blinkered view of food in history is readily understandable, since it rests on ingrained assumptions and conventions built into our own experiences. Our upbringing accustoms us to accepting one food style as pleasant and satisfying, and it is not easy to appreciate the grooves of habit that run deep across those assumptions. They shape our expectations, and make it difficult for us to appraise the diets of the past in terms of their own time. I have had less difficulty than some in displacing old food assumptions with fresh insights as this work has proceeded, but I suppose that half the battle was won for me by my being an agricultural historian, already immersed in a story of changing farm crops. Nevertheless, I recognize that other insights, as yet barely visible on the horizon, lie waiting for fresh experience to reveal their relevance. The news headlines in September 2005 told us that a diet rich in beans could mean more protection against cancer; my pages on beans in our past diet, therefore, acquire a deeper significance than when I wrote them.[6]

We used to lean to the view that insufficient quantities of food were much to blame for poor diets. But keener observation these days of the diets and performance at work of people in Third World countries, plus the growing problem of obesity in the western world, has produced some unexpected headlines in scientific journals advising us to avoid illness by eating less. Some journals are even bold enough to specify the illnesses, like tumours and cancer, that could be avoided by following a more abstemious regime. So as present-day food styles further illuminate the past, it may well be that we shall empathize with the old writers who, while condemning the gluttony of the rich, also began in the later seventeenth century to applaud the frugal diet of labourers.[7]

Of course, people's different routines and scale of physical effort called for a different balance between the basic ingredients than that which we require to work efficiently. Few of us nowadays exert the enormous physical energy that was once demanded of almost everyone. The duties of ploughmen and farm women were more strenuous than we can easily imagine, taking them into the fields to lift and pull heavy loads day after day in all weathers. The sixteenth-century diaries of the gentry show clearly how they too were constantly on the move, riding on horseback from home to attend courts or quarter sessions in the local town, to London on business, to perform duties at court, or to attend Parliament. They were out in all weathers, often riding over difficult country; it is quite sobering to read their list of engagements and to realize how little time some of them had to spend at home.[8]

The physical stamina needed for all this activity depended on the consumption of sufficient, sustaining food. Not surprisingly, then, a good bean and cereal pottage, bread, dumplings, puddings and pies made up a large proportion of food on the table of those who did not have access to large quantities of meat. I myself can remember delicious sponge and suet puddings and dumplings in the food of the 1920s and 1930s, which were always appreciated for supplying the energy that I needed to walk to school and to keep warm at home in winter.[9]

Another assumption that has to be firmly placed in our reconstituted scene from the past is the aspiration of most people to be self-sufficient. Even the gentry hearkened seriously to that lesson when Xenophon's work *Of Household* was published (in Latin) for their benefit in 1508 and reissued five times by 1526. To know that one could supply from one's own land enough food for the household for most of the year conferred the kind of satisfaction that requires insurance policies today. But insurance calls for the spending of money. In the early modern period, the manager of the household sought above all else to avoid spending money on food. So a diet that was home-produced gave satisfaction that suppressed many hankerings for exotic items. The same sentiments are alive to this day in some parts of Europe. An attractive recent book about country life in Spain depicted a peasant in Andalusia totally shocked that his English acquaintance should go off to the town to buy food when he had all he needed to fill his stomach on his own farm.[10]

When Gervase Markham was farming and writing books of instruction in the early 1600s, he took it for granted that his fellow husbandmen would strive to supply from their land all the food needed in the household. This was obviously not possible for all townsfolk, nor for those involved in daily journeys around the country. But the majority of the population lived in the country, or in towns whose inhabitants had daily access to the resources of the countryside. To prepare a meal they expected to have foods stored in the house or waiting to be gathered in gardens, fields and hedgerows. So in the sixteenth century, when imported items came to be regarded as desirable ingredients in cooking, and they had to be bought – currants and raisins, for example – people who could afford them had to accustom themselves to a new experience, making a deliberate effort to stock up by a special visit to a market town or to London. It could require an expedition over many miles, or at least the services of a local dealer; such goods were not last-minute purchases from the shop down the road for, except for those living in the very centre of towns, that convenience did not exist. We should not be surprised then that many folk were perfectly content with accessible local substitutes, and never thought of it as a hardship to be limited to using them.[11]

The striving for an economical supply of food within the home and household comes out vividly in the pages of William Ellis's *Country Housewife's Family Companion*. Admittedly, it was written at the very end of our period, published in 1750, but it contains many reflections that belong to the whole of the early modern period, expressing the basic tenets of generations of good housekeepers. By closely questioning neighbours and others, William Ellis, a Hertfordshire farmer, showed his informants cheerfully devising tasty food, whatever the constraints of a meagre larder. His is an outstandingly satisfying account of what self-sufficiency meant in practice, out of the mouths of the women themselves. It has taught me to judge the food of our forebears in a positive, respectful mood, rather than deprecating it. So many were resourceful and inventive, and worked wonders without spending. This does not, of course, mean distorting reality, forgetting those who died of hunger on the roads or lived painfully through days and weeks of acute food shortages. Nor does it forget the many cooks who were ignorant or slovenly in their cooking procedures. William Ellis encountered some of them; Eliza Melroe expressed special concern for the ignorance of the poor, 'chiefly bred in London', he said, choosing bread and butter or bread and cheese that required ale to wash it down, rather than nourishing soups. In a graphic phrase he described foreigners making their soup in a pot while the English made it in their stomach. Thus his troubled comments on working people's ignorance of food values alert the historian to the significance of the recipes for cheap but healthy dishes that began to be printed after 1700 in the magazines; they are difficult to find, but deserve to be carefully perused.[12]

Another consideration, lying in the background of this account, and needing to be incorporated when weighing up the satisfactions of food of the past, concerns flavour. The bulk of food eaten by our forebears was fresher than anything we taste nowadays. We know that flour tastes and nourishes best when freshly ground between millstones, and not in a roller mill. But most of us have lost the opportunity to savour that pleasure. We have no idea how long ago our flour was milled, grateful though we are that it is free of insects, weeds and gravel, and that it has been hygienically prepared and packed. We have gained but we have also lost by modern technology. The housewife took her grains to the miller in a mixture chosen by herself; it was ground for her in small quantities, to use immediately, and it exactly suited her family's tastes. Milk similarly came fresh from the cow and, in the countryside at least, the ordinary family reckoned to have at least one cow of their own. They also had their own pigs, and had a routine for securing and storing pork and bacon to be ready as needed. Vegetables and herbs moved straight from the ground to the kitchen, and were always fresh. Moreover, they had a stronger flavour in the past because the improvement of varieties, frequently for commercial reasons that have nothing to do with flavour (for easier packing, for storing over longer periods, for uniformity of size or shape or for more attractive colouring) have diminished the strong flavours of the plants tasted by our forebears. More on this score will be said below, but my favourite quotation is from Thomas Moufet describing carrots around 1600 as aromatic and spicy. Plainly, that vegetable was different from the one we taste nowadays.[13]

The flavours of fresh, and often stronger tasting, foods gave satisfaction to the eaters, as contemporary descriptions sometimes reveal when a writer exclaims with pleasure at the relish of very simple foods – gruel or flummery, for example, consisting of nothing more than a cereal with lashings of creamy milk, those apple pasties taken out to the fields for a midday meal, or cheese cake, described by an old lady around 1900 as 'food for the gods'. Finicky attention to flavour is revealed in many of our writers' throwaway lines. Thus is the cook depicted for us at a pig-killing, hovering in wait for the moment when she can throw a sprig of rosemary into the melting fat to give the pork lard that special flavour. She was one of many thousands of women making the best of food to please her family.[14]

Contemporary literature conveys a strong impression that we have lost some of the sensitivity to flavours our forebears possessed, for we do not experience so many subtleties in the same food items as did people in the past. It is a loss that has to be built into our imaginative reconstructions here, while we also acknowledge gratefully being spared from eating the disasters of the worst cooks. People distinguished between the taste of well water, spring water and rainwater. (I myself have observed these strong sensitivities among my peasant neighbours in southern Spain.) People differentiated the meat of geese fed on grain dropped in the harvested fields, and those fed through the summer on the grass of the commons. One of Robert May's recipes defines the goose needed for his recipe as 'a stubble or fat goose', silently implying that the grass-fed one was leaner and had a different taste. This immediately deepens our understanding of the reasons why the thousands of geese, described by Defoe walking to the London market from the fens of East Anglia in the early eighteenth century, set off at one particular season, between August and the end of October. They could eat *en route* the grain lying in the stubble fields and arrive in good shape at London's market. Again and again, contemporary writers on food at the table conveyed the sensibilities of discerning eaters. Londoners above all showed themselves to be sharp observers and astute buyers of the best quality.[15]

If we shed the notion of a limited selection of ingredients making up the diets of the past, we also need to recognize the basic human need for variety from meal to meal and from day to day; it was as strong in the past as it is today. One nineteenth-century housekeeper and food writer, Eleanor Orlebar, took it for granted that 'change and variety – in food – are natural instincts of our humanity'. In Robert May's cookbook of 1660 (admittedly written for an upper-class clientèle) the need for variety was writ large on his pages: one basic recipe was followed by others slightly different 'for variety', 'for a change'. But when William Ellis questioned his far less affluent informants, they similarly offered different versions of the same dish.

Another kind of variety was also greater than it is today, for cookery books gradually introduced more uniformity. Every cook in the early modern period gave free rein to variations of her own devising: they may have been inferior, of course, but they could have been better or ingeniously economical. We shall encounter below cooks who did not have the conventional ingredients to hand, and cleverly made do. All of us will recognize that last constraint: we can so readily picture the breadmaker seizing the flours that she happened to have in the house, a bit of barley, a bit of rye and some wheat, or wheat with rye alone (since these two grains were often sown in the field together). I myself like the taste and consistency of a bread mix of wheat, barley and rye, and I like to think that some housewives in the sixteenth century would nod in firm agreement with me, if they could read these lines. The historians, then, who tell us that wheaten bread was the main bread eaten in the sixteenth century are out of touch with the world of the past. Their thinking is dominated by twentieth-century lifestyles, when the majority of people buy a standard loaf from the baker made with standard wheaten flour.[16]

In the early modern period, people who regularly moved outside their native parish took for granted a world of strong local differences, and it is an enlivening experience to encounter those who stubbornly refused to tolerate so-called 'foreign flavours'. William Ellis in 1750 described the traders coming from Lancashire to Hertfordshire to sell their wares and bringing their own oatbread with them. They could not stomach the wheat bread of Hertfordshire, seemingly because of the stronger flavoured yeast that was used in those parts. Travellers on the road likewise frequently complained of unfamiliar regional foods, though we can never be sure if it was because they were badly cooked or because they were simply unfamiliar flavours; and sometimes people were pleasantly surprised to find how unjustified were their prejudices. The taste for cider will appear below as one example of a new experience for some in the middle seventeenth century, turning what had once been despised as a peasant drink into a fashion and then into a substantial commercial trade. At the end of our survey, we recognize that monotony was certainly not the salient feature of contemporary complaints about food.[17]

The present-day traveller, moving around the globe more freely than ever before, has learned many lessons about the diets of others who live a totally different lifestyle from our own. They teach obvious truths that have been learned many times over in the past, yet seem always to have to be learned again. As a result, I have often found myself endorsing the words of Eglantyne Louisa Jebb when struck by the prominence in diets in Austria of one group of prolific local plants: rye, maize, gherkins and cabbage. Her characteristic woman's comment was that 'I must know what people eat if I am to understand them'.[18]

Studying food, then, is one way of getting to the heart of a people's culture. But when historians are at work, they cannot take it for granted that food patterns are regionally uniform. Humbly and inadequately, therefore, this book tries to differentiate some regional diets. Counties are too large for such a study, since the landscape of England changes over much shorter distances, and in every district the natural resources of the land shaped a distinctive diet that made the best of the local foods. We can be sure that they fostered loyalty and pride among the locals, even if some mixtures seem humdrum in the classificatory system of the gourmets; but they could well have had a distinctive local flavour. The truth of this constantly thrusts itself to prominence in other places across the world. In southern Spain, for example, a dish of 'migas' makes use of little more than stale breadcrumbs, but flavoured with spices, and cooked with painstaking care, even to the point where the aroma of the wood used on the brazier counts in the pleasures of the final dish, it emerges as a local delight. In the same way, a Slovenian mining town on the border with Italy takes pride in its special kind of ravioli, relying on pasta and potatoes for its main ingredients, but flavouring it all with parsley, marjoram, chives and sautéed bacon fat. The local people insist on boiling and eating it without delay, for that is to them essential if the correct humidity of pasta and filling is not to be lost. These 'zlikrofi', as they are called, were once the food of high days and holidays. Now they have become everyday items on restaurant menus, and the local people bewail the loss of much delicacy of flavour and fragrance. The kneading machine for the pasta, the food mixer for the filling, and the freezer to keep everything stored for days on end, have, they say, destroyed subtleties in the taste that were achieved in that slower-moving, more trouble-taking world between 1500 and 1760.[19]

I have sought in this work to assess the food of the past on its own terms, believing that people relished it as much as we do our own foods today. It was a lively, bustling world of talkers, cooks and eaters, who have taught me far more than I expected about its phases, fads and fashions. I hope this account of it will open up some pathways that others will follow in the future.

Joan Thirsk
16 September 2005

Sources and Abbreviations

I set great store by giving readers the sources of my statements, for they come from many scattered places. I have grouped my notes of them at the end of paragraphs, in order of argument. Only where I have used the same book more than once in a single paragraph have I placed the page references from the one source together.

Abbreviations used are as follows:

AC	*Archaeologia Cantiana*
AHEW	*The Agrarian History of England and Wales*, ed. H. P. R. Finberg, later Joan Thirsk
AHR	*Agricultural History Review*
BL	British Library
CCA	Canterbury Cathedral Archives, the Precincts, Canterbury, Kent
CJ	House of Commons Journals
CKS	Centre for Kentish Studies, County Hall, Maidstone, Kent
CSP	Calendar of State Papers
CSP Ven.	Calendar of State Papers Venetian
CSPD	Calendar of State Papers Domestic
DNB	*Dictionary of National Biography*
EcHR	*Economic History Review*
EETS	Early English Text Society
Folger	Folger Shakespeare Library, Washington DC, USA
GLC	Greater London Council
Hartlib MSS	These are in Sheffield University Library, and are also fully transcribed on a CD-ROM, ed. J. Crawford and others (1995)
Hartlib, *Ephemerides*	This is the Diary of Samuel Hartlib, in Sheffield University Library, and also on the CD-ROM
Hants. RO	Hampshire Record Office
HMC Rutland	Historial Manuscripts Commission, Rutland MSS

Invs.	Probate Inventories
John Rylands Univ. Lib.	John Rylands Library, University of Manchester
KAS	Kent Archaeological Society
Lancs. RO	Lancashire Records Office, Preston
L&P, Hen. VIII	Calendar of Letters and Papers, Foreign and Domestic, of Henry VIII, ed. J. S. Brewer and others, 1862–1910
NA	National Archives, Kew
NRO	Norfolk Record Office, Norwich
ODNB	*Oxford Dictionary of National Biography*
OED	*Oxford English Dictionary*
Phil. Trans.	Philosophical Transactions of the Royal Society
PPC	*Petits Propos Culinaires*, ed. Tom Jaine, Prospect Books, Totnes, Devon
Prussian Report	Typescript of a Prussian account of a visit to England, 1765–6, in author's possession, from Berlin archives
Roy.Soc.	Royal Society, London
T&C	Joan Thirsk and J. P. Cooper (eds) (1972), *Seventeenth-Century Economic Documents*, Oxford
TED	R.H. Tawney and E. Power (eds) (1924), *Tudor Economic Documents*, 3 vols
VCH	*Victoria County History of England*

Setting the Scene before 1500

Since mankind has to eat to survive, our food history goes back thousands of years to an age before any record was written down. Selecting, preparing and cooking food were skills passed on by word of mouth and by practical example. We learn only a little about the oldest practices by digging up seeds and bones of animals and fish, and finding traces of braziers and pots used for cooking and storing food. Then a fresh age begins around 1300, when administrative documents mention crops and animals on farms, and writers record stories or ballads that mention feasts and sometimes even everyday foods. By the fifteenth century more documents accumulate, testifying to the existence of table manners that were expected in rich men's houses, and naming the luxury dishes served at rich men's feasts. The basic food allowances given to labourers when working in the fields are also enumerated in estate accounts.

We can readily picture the medieval scholar of this time inscribing and reading his parchments, turning to food to sustain him as he worked, but giving not a thought to the idea that food might be a subject for scholarly study. The change of attitude had to wait for the coming of the printing press, in the 1460s on the Continent of Europe and ten years later in England. Books now circulated far more plentifully than ever before, and as a result a multitude of fresh ideas passed around among more readers, and suggested subjects for discussion in more books. After 1500 we engage with a new age, when food would be seriously discussed by scholars, prompted at first by their concern to discover the best foods and food style for preserving health, and then commenting on the food they saw being eaten around them. We must be prepared for some highly varied, individual opinions at that time on what were good and bad foods for health, but at least these ideas were written down, and we can begin to match some of the theories with some of the practice, even though they stemmed from people viewing the scene from a rather elevated social viewpoint. We shall also begin to pick up some notion of changing food regimes, for merchants now ventured more boldly on new trading enterprises, carrying the foods of one country to another.[1]

Around 1500, however, we must be content with a misty scene that is based on very limited evidence, aided by some allowable, reasonable guesswork. Even so, in a few respects it has similarities with the situation that we still encounter at the supermarket today. Our forebears all had different tastes just as we have, different foibles and prejudices about a healthy diet, access to different foods, and different amounts of money to spend. But in one respect they were very different in 1500. Knowledge and opinions had not yet submitted to the discipline of a majority view, spread abroad through publications in print. So our verdict on food at the beginning of the early modern period has to accommodate an even greater variety of tastes and food habits than those familiar to us today. Knowing as we do the lively, distinctive cultures of our many regions in the kingdom, stretching from the south-west to the north-east, from coasts to mountains, through woodlands and fens, from temperate to less clement climates, from fertile to hard, unyielding soils, we can be certain that all regions nursed individuality and ingenuity, and these affected cooking as much as every other human activity needed to make a living. Our generalities can hardly scratch the surface of a hidden story. We have to accept with resignation our ignorance of all but a small fragment of the many individual ways in which our forebears handled their food.

Nevertheless, we can strive to sketch a very general picture of food belonging to this age. Certain salient features stand out because of national influences so powerful that they affected the whole kingdom. Food supplies throughout the realm had come under heavy pressure from a rising population in the twelfth and thirteenth centuries. That phase dramatically ended with plague in 1348–9, killing nearly one half of the population. Circumstances then imposed a different farming strategy for the next 150 years, during which time the quantity and quality of food available to ordinary people actually improved. With fewer people to work the land, and fewer people needing the basic foods, the reduced demand for cereals allowed more land to be put under grass. Meadows and pastures produced more meat, and since the wool industry prospered at the same time, it is reasonable to guess that mutton became the commonest meat. But that was only true in some parts of the country. Regional differences have to be allowed for, and are firmly underlined in two unusual household accounts from the first half of the fifteenth century. Cited by Christopher Dyer, they show two households, including guests and servants, eating far more beef than mutton; in one case beef comprised 48% of all the meat eaten, in the other 56%, compared with 14% mutton. Two samples are tiny indicators, but they remind us to be cautious in generalizing, and to beware of reducing the variety of foods enjoyed by our forebears. Pigs could be economically kept if nuts were available in the woods to fatten them in autumn. In the two households already cited bacon and pork came second to beef in the ranking, comprising 28% and 17% of the households' meat. Poultry made up another 6% and 9% of the meat diet, and rabbits, wild birds and deer 1% and 7%. The meat of goats did not enter these kitchens, but in some parts of the country where rough uncultivated land gave these animals a living, kid meat was also eaten and goats were milked. The choices listed here allow for many permutations across classes and places.[2]

The rules for fasting on two or three days a week and for six weeks in Lent gave fish an almost equal place in the diet alongside meat. An established trade ensured the supply from the Baltic and North Seas of plentiful sea fish, mainly herrings that were salted or smoked, or cod, ling and other fish that were salted or dried. All could be transported far inland and lasted for weeks or months. At the same time, our island situation enabled all coastal parishes and a remarkable number of market towns in the hinterland to get sea fish fresh, including shellfish, though in some deeper countryside it was doubtless no more than a special treat. Another noticeable development in the later Middle Ages was the construction of ponds by middling farmers, or the use of moats round farmhouses, in which freshwater fish were kept that could be served at a moment's notice. Roach and tench were the commonest, pike and bream were luxuries in 1500. But people were always on the lookout for more variety still; carp, in fact, was a new arrival from the Continent between 1450 and 1500. In some parishes that had rivers running through them, and even better in fenland areas, local people enjoyed a supply of fresh fish with much less effort. The thousands of eels owed in tribute to monastic houses in the East Anglian fens testify to a plenteous supply for all inhabitants of a delicious food that has all but disappeared from England now. It is still a treasured luxury in the food of Japan, reminding us of what we have lost.[3]

The bread most generally eaten underwent some change, at least in eastern and southern England, in the course of the fifteenth century, almost certainly as a result of a long run of good harvests between 1440 and 1520 (following upon a severe famine in the late 1430s). Barley bread had long been the mainstay, but now contemporary writers bemoaned the excessive expectations of labourers for better bread, which meant wheat, as well as for more meat, and for ale instead of water, when they took part payment for their work. Since they were not always working on their lord's land but worked for others too, they might well pick and choose between employers offering them better food. As a generality, however, the observation about bread needs to be carefully defined regionally and perhaps also classwise, for people in the north harboured a distinct preference for oatbread that persisted for centuries. Barley bread also, having been the staple bread of the past, held its own, since it was a useful all-purpose cereal and a liking for its sweet taste lingered on. It is true that barley bread lacks gluten and does not rise, but people must have been accustomed to its dense consistency. Since bread was so often crumbled into pottage to thicken it, or was laid on the table as a trencher or thick slice on which pottage and other food was heaped, its density was an advantage in absorbing liquid. The Archbishop of Canterbury's tenants, when performing labour services for him, always received barley bread in their meals at work, and these must often have been eaten while resting outdoors in the fields. But oily herrings often went with the bread, so again its density might be softened by fish.

We may reasonably look for the increasing prominence of wheat at this period, but we should not overstate the situation. It did have the highest social status, and on the loams of eastern and southern England it seems to have become, at an earlier date than elsewhere, a familiar bread among some people, especially in the towns. But a great variety of bread preferences continued throughout the period studied here, and diversity was still the order of the day in 1500.[4]

Dairying efforts also seem to have undergone some significant changes after the Black Death, though our class-biased evidence makes it difficult to uncover all the ramifications. Dairy goods in general had a lowly status in the food hierarchy, being regarded as pre-eminently poor men's food, and given the derogatory name of 'white meats'. Country people generally expected to have a cow or two to satisfy their family needs, and thus had milk, curds, whey and cheese ready to hand. Butter was almost certainly not much made or eaten by ordinary folk, for pork lard and beef dripping were far more plentiful and less trouble to obtain. Cheese, however, was another matter. For working men, it was an everyday food, especially convenient in the field. It is true that in Christopher Dyer's tabulation of harvest diets at Sedgeford, Norfolk, between 1250 and 1430, at a time when meat consumption by ordinary folk was rising, cheese-eating, particularly in the early years of the fifteenth century, appears to have been falling. But we should not assume that that represented the true state of cheese-eating when calculated over the whole year; at harvest time, the work was hard and the demand for workers pressing. In competition, employers who were known to offer better food – meat rather than cheese and herrings – had the edge over others, and might get their work done faster. A kindly viewpoint was expressed in the eighteenth century that could have operated in any age: harvest workers deserved something different from their everyday fare.[5]

In grand households the status of cheese wavered between tolerance and disdain. But it was not always treated as poor fare, for it was eaten for supper in 1265 in the royal household of Eleanor de Montfort, sister of Henry III; the cheese pies were evidently popular, and the cheese was clearly served to men above labouring rank. As for butter, it is generally assumed that in high-ranking households at this period, when great quantities of butter were used in cooking, it was kept in the kitchen and not seen at the table.[6]

Since milk and cheese were conspicuous ingredients in the diet of plain folk, and economic circumstances turned the relations of landowners, tenants and servants upside down following the Black Death, we may expect some repercussions in the cow-keeping sector, which was the small farmer's speciality. Cows' milk did not dominate the scene everywhere. We can safely assume that ordinary folk mostly used cows' milk, but the milking of ewes was customary on some monastic estates before the Black Death. Indeed, on the lands of the bishops of Winchester the bulk of the cheese was made from ewes' milk. Labour was presumably abundant at that time, and people had a taste for sheep cheese. When the deaths resulting from plague altered the labour situation, keeping sheep for their wool became less trouble and probably more profitable. The time-consuming job of milking ewes was brought to an end on many estates, noticeably in the years between the 1360s and the 1420s. It is logical to suspect in that economic context that some small cowkeepers seized their chance and stepped in to fill a gap in the market. The suspicion hardens when we witness the expansion of cow dairying that began to emerge quite noticeably by the later sixteenth century. It was a slow development, but it resulted in a considerable growth in peasant dairying and the size of dairy herds among prospering farmers rose faster still in the seventeenth century, in some areas to 40 and 60 cows per farm. That trend is much better understood if we posit this earlier step along that road. Cow dairying would grow into a substantial branch of commerce, and the milking of sheep would gradually die out altogether. By the middle eighteenth century all memory of it had faded, and when Prussian visitors arrived to study English farming in 1765, they were told that English farmers never milked their ewes.[7]

Another significant new trend drifted in shadow-like before 1500 affecting greenstuff, herbs and fruit. It involved changing opinions and fashions, which, as in the case of dairy foods, cut across class divisions, and is not a simple story. Ordinary folk routinely ate greenstuff from fields and gardens, and the countryside gave them a bountiful supply in great variety. Worts, that is simple leafy plants from which leaves were plucked, were the mainstay. But all this was regarded by the well-to-do as a minor accompaniment to meat and fish dishes, and it played only a small part in the total array at their tables. Like dairy produce, it was classed as food for the poor and meek, not unreasonably since so much could be gathered freely. But the poor and meek, theoretically at least, included monks and nuns in whose diet mean food featured prominently. So they too ate vegetables, herbs and fruits, and they also fastidiously cultivated them as medicines in their gardens. Much professionalism, therefore, entered into those labours, and fresh stimuli were regularly administered by visitors from home and overseas, since botanical curiosity and enthusiasm for exchanging plants was gently growing.[8]

Among such scholarly and observant men and women the first glimmerings of a rising interest in the potential of herbs and green plants emerged in the fourteenth century. It started modestly as an esoteric concern among churchmen with an interest in scholarly botany, but it was encouraged by wealthy patrons, and foreign influences are also likely to have propelled it, as such pursuits became fashionable.

Echoes of this surge of interest evidently sounded down the next century: in 1577 William Harrison claimed that a plentiful supply of herbs, fruits and roots had existed in the fourteenth century that came to be totally neglected in the fifteenth. We have to allow for distortion in that sweeping statement since it concerned a time long before Harrison's own experience. But notable physicians and botanists were certainly at work in England in the fourteenth century as collectors of plants, translators of foreign texts about plants, and compilers of their own lists. Their activities denoted a step forward in horticultural investigation that would pave the way for a major shift in attitude to greenstuff and fruits that Harrison perceived in his own day.[9]

The newly introduced herbs and other plants that came into England in the later Middle Ages were prized first and foremost, of course, for their medicinal virtues. Indeed, at no time before the late nineteenth century should we separate food from medicine, for throughout all ranks of society they were regarded as one and the same. It is possible that the heightened zeal for finding new plants is partly explained by the hope of finding more protective agents against the plague. The fear of infection already hung over the first half of the century before the great epidemic befell. People were already searching for a defence against infection, and when they found a herb that they believed in, they also found a food to be included in their cooking ingredients.

So in scattered places, and certainly among the intelligentsia, among physicians, people in high places at court, and among the well-to-do, a gently revitalized interest in garden plants stirred in the fourteenth century that would eventually lead on to a golden phase in the sixteenth and seventeenth centuries. Unusually well attested is the introduction of saffron and rosemary into the kingdom, both of which were acclaimed first as medicines, and then as flavourings in the kitchen. Hakluyt in the sixteenth century gave a graphic story of saffron (*Crocus sativus*) arriving in England from the Levant, secreted in the hollowed-out staff of a pilgrim in 1339. This was just before the worst bout of plague struck with the Black Death. No one else repeats that tale, but Ralph Holinshed, c. 1577, believed that saffron arrived in Edward III's reign, that is some time between 1327 and 1377, the dates matching well enough the other story. The plant succeeded so well that Walden in Essex took the name of Saffron Walden, and chose saffron as the emblem of the town; eight saffron flowers are inserted in the spandrels of an arch between the nave and the south aisle of the church, and the will of one Saffron Walden resident shows saffron growing there in 1457. By the end of the fifteenth century saffron was growing in Essex and over the border in East Hertfordshire, while a composition for tithes shows it growing also at Thriplow, south of Cambridge in 1474, implying in a tithe agreement that the plant was being grown for a commercial market. By 1520 it was also being tithed in Norfolk.[10]

Rosemary was another fourteenth-century introduction, brought in 1340 by Queen Philippa of Hainault, wife of Edward III, as a gift from her mother in the Low Countries. Friar Daniel, a dedicated botanist and physician who came to England as a Jewish convert, was an expert in growing it, and wrote a treatise on rosemary between the 1380s and 1390s, having spent some effort in acclimatizing it in England.[11]

These two medicines and flavourings plainly did not add much substance to late medieval food, but they did add flavour, and are signposts to a qualitative change in horticultural effort in the fourteenth century. John Harvey, who examined the subject deeply, associated it with a longer, specially favourable period between 1250 and 1400, stimulated by a great flowering of interest on the Continent of Europe, and particularly associated with the Italian, Pietro de Crescenzi. It trickled through to England under the influence of foreign wives of English kings and some much-travelled English laymen.[12]

Through the marriages of two English kings with women from Provence and Castile, a fresh delight in gardens was noticeable in court circles in the thirteenth century. Henry III married Eleanor of Provence in 1236, and one of the gardeners at Windsor from 1268 to 1277 was Fulk le Provincial, plainly one of her countrymen. Eleanor of Castile, who married Edward I, likewise showed a great love for gardens, and as the lessee of an estate at King's Langley, Hertfordshire she procured the planting of a new garden with vines and fruit trees. Grafts of a special apple variety (the Blandurel) were bought in 1280, and the queen had evidently brought Spanish gardeners from Aragon to work in England, for in 1290 they took their leave to return home. Queen Philippa of Hainault (d. 1369), who married Edward III, was another keen gardener in England, making a 'herber' (a pleasure garden) at Odiham, Hampshire, whence she passed special plants to that other dedicated botanist who at one stage had a rich garden of plants in Stepney, Friar Henry Daniel.[13]

These royal associations with new food plants have to be counted alongside contemporary evidence of monks and clerics enjoying a wider variety of greenstuff than is documented in earlier times. For example, in 1321–2 the gardens at Lambeth Palace were supplying not simply leeks, onions, worts and garlic to the kitchen, but skirret, cress, cabbage, cucumber, spinach, lettuce and parsley. It is not unreasonable to postulate some impact on the diet of ordinary folk in the neighbourhood, watching this changing scene.[14]

Most country folk and many townsfolk had garden land next to their houses for the convenience of having greenstuff at their elbow for the kitchen. Moreover, in the thirteenth century, signs are found of gardens being enlarged. John Harvey also noticed references to 'garden beans and peas' rather than just beans and peas from the field, a sign perhaps of some delicacy in handling their growth for the food table. This would become conspicuous in the seventeenth century when early garden peas would be ready in May or early June, and became a fashion in London, commanding a fancy price. The first wine from Bordeaux is a parallel modern example of the way the frenzy of fashion could work on the food scene.[15]

In all ages and cultures, individuals have nurtured in their gardens special treasures that they have dug up from the wild or have been given by others. Thus garden cultivation set these plants on their way to becoming cultivated varieties. The skills of specialist gardeners were most notable in monastic houses and on the estates of queens and great lords, and it was always they who gave most attention to exotics from abroad. But we should not overlook the improvements of wild plants by plain folk bringing them into their gardens from the woods and fields. The more readily accepted stories inevitably focus on the gardeners working for rich men, but the discoveries could equally well be those of women working in their kitchen gardens, and sometimes tending gifts from the gardener at the manor house. Whenever gardens were renovated in one neighbourhood, we can be sure that they were noticed by someone living nearby. What new ideas, for example, circulated between Odiham in Hampshire, where Eleanor de Montfort kept house for two weeks before Easter 1265, and Kemsing in Kent where she had another manor? What gossip, and what exchange of favours, occurred when the royal gardener was at work at Everswell, Woodstock in 1264–8, planting 100 new pear trees? We can be certain that local people watched exactly what was going on. Moreover, gardeners were and are an international and cooperative fraternity giving generously to professionals and village neighbours alike. Knowledge and plants trickled out from the many royal gardens that were scattered all over the kingdom. While the fruit trees and vines were being planted with unwonted enthusiasm on royal estates and were adding new foods and flavours to rich men's tables, we can be sure that ideas, know-how, plants and cuttings were circulated in the neighbourhood, and slowly but surely notions about food and potential new ingredients seeped out into a wider world.[16]

These remarks are not meant to exaggerate the advance of horticultural expertise in the fourteenth and fifteenth centuries. Our examples in the fourteenth century all relate to people at a high social level, and we should not expect the trend to be noticeable far beyond the south-eastern quarter of the country. When John Harvey made a list to show the main vegetables consumed by the well-to-do in the fifteenth century, it was still a modest collection. It contained onions, leeks, garlic, worts and some cabbage, sometimes broad beans and peas, always parsley, and hyssop for further flavouring. But it would be unrealistic to depict islands of improved gardening and the eating of greenstuffs and fruits that were totally insulated from the surrounding population. We can reasonably assume that in scattered places some better and more varied garden vegetables were entering into the diet of ordinary people in a modest way because rich men locally had set the example. It is more than possible, if we tone down Harrison's general assertion in the later sixteenth century, that lords did lose interest in gardening in the fifteenth century, since for them the labour costs of land cultivation also deterred many of them from direct farming. But rich men's withdrawal from the scene could well have spurred some family farmers into more energetic gardening; the circumstances of the fifteenth century certainly had this effect in sending them in other directions. So the cabbages that are mentioned along with the simpler colewort in the fifteenth century, the parsnips that are actually described before 1500 as belonging 'more to meat than medicine', carrots and skirret, which were being eaten c. 1450, and celery, which was known in the fourteenth century, could well have become familiar to some country folk in the course of the fifteenth century. Some fruit may also have been improved in variety and quality; by the fifteenth century fruits and nuts went well beyond the homely, native ones of Chaucer, and included mulberries, gooseberries, walnuts and filberts. A stirring of enterprise in the growing of garden produce is thus faintly sketched across the contours of the fifteenth century, and we need always to remember that whatever enthusiasm for gardening was aroused among rich folk, the actual work was done by their servants, labouring men and women on their hands and knees, with enough intelligence to absorb some lessons from the work they were doing for others. Some of their efforts could have brought a taste of interesting new foods to their own tables from time to time.[17]

The basic daily dish of cooked food for plain folk was pottage, giving scope for infinite variations according to the season and the plants growing in the locality. It is a pity that the word 'pottage' conveys such an unattractive image, since it was a most nourishing dish of cereals, pulses, greens and herbs, with sufficient meat to give a satisfying, meaty flavour. Older Scottish and Irish people still recall it with great warmth and affection, and some of us come near to the same experience with our substantial home-made soups, even though we do not use all the wild food and do not savour the strong flavours of wild plants of the past. Nor should we forget that much of this food was free for the taking, for the majority of the population lived in or close to green fields and woods. We are too urban-minded these days to enter imaginatively into that world without long training. The author of this book will strive on every page to bring it closer.

Another theme of this book will be the continually changing food scene over these two and a half centuries. It requires another effort of the imagination, running against the grain of historical conventions. Our textbooks usually depict a monotonous food regime in the past, prevailing until some time around the coming of the industrial and agricultural revolutions. In fact, we have to accommodate many new branches of overseas trade starting (and sometimes stopping) from the Middle Ages onward and continually bringing new foods into England to enlarge and change Englishmen's food tastes. Currants from Corinth, for example, were first brought into northern Europe in Venetian vessels sailing to Bruges in Flanders, and unloading at the port of Sluys. A vessel that had paused to take on more cargo in Andalusia (almost certainly raisins from Malaga) stopped in London in 1410, and another stopped in Southampton in 1427–8.

Thus were dried fruits brought to England in increasing quantity until we ate so many that by 1600 the Italians asked themselves if we used currants for dyeing. English cooks were adding currants and raisins to innumerable dishes, and by the middle of the sixteenth century Londoners, at least, also took for granted a regular supply of oranges and lemons.[18]

Some early customs accounts recently examined leave us astounded at the foods that arrived in Sandwich, Kent as early as 1300. It should be noted, of course, that Sandwich was within very easy reach of Canterbury, so that churchmen and others of their class were at this date almost certainly the chief beneficiaries. The documents examined on this subject cover a period from 1299 to 1304, and then from 1428 to 1479. Around 1300, almonds arrived regularly in ships' cargoes, and so did cumin, which was evidently then the main spice, though most of it was probably destined for the apothecary. Saffron was also very occasionally imported for medicinal purposes, a quarter century earlier than the date given above, between 1327 and 1377, when it began to be grown in England. Figs, raisins and some dates were fairly often in the cargoes, though there was no sign as yet of currants. Gradually more sugar came in as well. Sandwich's other imports were basic foods like onions (especially from France), salt, cheese, herrings and, once or twice, Thames mackerel.[19]

Three or four generations later, between 1428 and 1479, trade was quickening from the Netherlands and France and also from the Mediterranean. Many enterprising Italians were now unloading figs, ginger, currants, raisins and capers. Others brought oranges, dates, pomegranates, not to mention all the now familiar spices like turmeric, ginger, cloves, cinnamon, cassia and cumin. Merchants with Flemish names (Mardelyns Picarde, for one, in 1444) landed onions (84 barrels of them on 4 October 1428), garlic, 100 cabbages, lettuces and apples, and in 1469–70 Sandwich received what may have been its first case of prunes. Sandwich was undoubtedly benefiting from its position not far off the main sailing route from the Mediteranean to Flanders, and Flanders at this time had a vibrant sector of vegetable and fruit growers with an appreciative eye for new foods. But at the other end of the country, along the Devon and Cornish coast, other places were equally well placed to receive Mediterranean luxuries like figs, saffron, and cumin. Indeed, saffron was imported into Exeter in 1312/13, 26 years before the legendary bulb arrived concealed in a pilgrim's staff. It leaves us guessing how many other ports on the south coast gave occasional anchorage to foreign vessels, allowing the locals to enjoy an early taste of the same foreign foods. We can only speculate on these matters, but we can be sure that the merchants, as always, were seeking fresh markets. New food experiences were entering England from many directions by 1500, with the promise of more to set the cooking pots stirring.[20]

2

The Food Scene Captured in Print, 1500–50

This chapter attempts to capture a first notion of the way food was talked about, written about and procured by different classes of people, once printed books began to appear. The subject now entered a new phase with the much wider distribution of facts, ideas and opinions. There were, of course, as yet no established conventions among writers about the range of topics on food that would interest readers. But the evidence encourages some reasonable guesses by taking hints from the priorities that they themselves observed. As for food preferences, we learn something from their comments of surprise or distaste when encountering food habits abroad. Which practices were actually new in this period and which were familiar is another problem for the historian, for we have so little information about all the variations, regional and class-related, before 1500. But knowing already what a transformation in food patterns occurred later, we are at least alerted from the very beginning to the notion of a continuously changing scene. So while some suggestions about novel food practices will be made in this chapter that may be judged in the end to be idle fancies, others will be proven valid by the way things turned out subsequently.

Being a new subject in print, the first books on food to be published in England offered guidance on catering in royal and other large households. We enter a high-ranking circle of people where feasts abounded, and tasks like meat carving and meal serving were on a scale that needed expert instruction. The first known book was *A Noble Boke of Festes Royalle and Cokery. A Boke for a Pryncis Housholde or any other Estates* in 1500, and the second (in 1508) dealt with carving and sewing (i.e. serving). A third, *A Proper Newe Booke of Cokerye*, dated 1545, dealt with meats in different seasons, and their dressing and serving.[1]

Some knowledge of foreign books on food was also circulating by the 1530s, dressing the subject in a distinctive guise, as the means to promote health. The Italian, Bartolomeo Sacchi, librarian at the Vatican, usually known as Platina, in 1475 wrote a book on good food and healthy living. His *De Honesta Voluptate* appended recipes by the cook, Martino. Then Giovanni de Rosselli published in 1513 *Epulario*, also using Martino's recipes; and in 1549 Cristiforo di Messisbugo published *Banchetti Compositioni di Vivande*, of which several editions appeared up to 1626. Foreign influences, through these books and conversation, thus reached literate men in England, and are the most reasonable explanation for the book of Sir Thomas Elyot, entitled *The Castel of Health*, in 1539. It was not a cookery book, but a guide to the treatment of illness that also offered opinions on diet. Elyot was an experienced, travelled diplomat and scholar, who had already published *The Book called the Governor* (1531), setting down the desirable education for children who were marked out to be statesmen and governors. He had twice been overseas, attending as ambassador on Charles V, and on the second visit was in Barcelona and accompanied Charles on the expedition to Tunis, returning to Naples in 1535. His book on health was thus backed up by a traveller's meetings, conversations and observations while abroad. A first edition is claimed to date from 1534, but no copy is known, and the first survivor in our libraries dates from 1539. It was reprinted many times in the second half of the sixteenth century, a fact that reflects, along with Messisbugo's experience, the interest aroused by that time for such a theme.[2]

Elyot (1490?–1546) was brought up in Wiltshire and, while a student, had had the works of Galen read to him by a physician, possibly Linacre. As an adult, he settled near Woodstock, and as an intimate in Wolsey's circle and then of Thomas Cromwell we can be sure that he became thoroughly familiar with courtly food styles. His public biography dwells on his problems when confronting all the religious and marriage controversies of Henry VIII's reign, which clearly did not make his life easy. For a more peaceful life, he turned to scholarly pursuits. In this occupation he held one plainly modern view, favouring the use of English rather than Latin. Thus he wrote on diet and health in English, and his work stands as our first guide to opinions that were held by educated people in England, and to some extent no doubt in Western Europe as well, in the first half of the sixteenth century. We must also expect his views to have influenced others for another two generations at least. But since views on food are never unanimous, his should be read as a stimulating introduction to varied opinions rather than as a statement of one universal doctrine.[3]

Elyot saw the healthy human body holding a balance between the four principal humours: blood, flume, choler and melancholy. Different foods engendered different humours, so a correct balance was needed or sickness followed. He allowed for different temperaments and different personal food preferences; one learned by experience about one's own body and what it liked best. Elyot also thought that Englishmen had a different constitution from those studied by the classical authors. So, having read the relevant texts of his forebears, he finished up with his own opinions. Bread flour containing bran, for example, nourished little or not at all (though, in fact, the bran contains the most protein!). Certain meats in his list made good juices, others ill juices, though the reader in the twenty-first century will be struck rather by the great variety of meats that were named. The list gives no idea of the way contemporaries ranked them, however, though one clear opinion evident in Elyot, and repeated by others, rated mutton as the meat above all the rest to be prescribed in illness. Fish was inferior to meat because it thinned the blood. Butter was nourishing, while cheese was the enemy of the stomach. As for fruit, he admitted that before corn was 'invented', people lived on fruits, but our bodies had changed since then, and now fruit engendered ill humours, rising to putrefying fevers if eaten continually. On greenstuff and vegetables he had read the classics, and knew that formerly coleworts and cabbages were the medicine against all diseases. This was averred by Cato, he said, though he might just as well have cited Columella, who devoted many pages to the merits of cabbages. Referring to roots, Elyot expressed a strong view in favour of turnips, since they were thought to augment the seed of man; parsnips and carrots also were nutritious. We see here the stirrings of a deepening interest in cabbages and roots that will feature prominently after 1550. Finally, Elyot plainly had a strong prejudice against spices. It is surprising to read his strong words concerning the avarice of merchants who had caused spices to be brought to England 'to content the unsatiableness of wanton appetites'. They mingle with a noticeable preference for simplicity and restraint in food consumption, which surfaced at many points in Elyot's text. He had observed the great strength and long life of people in Cornwall who seldom drank anything but water. He had noticed that men and women brought up on milk and butter were extremely healthy looking, a lot less sickly than those who drank ale and wine. A mixture of different meats at one meal was also the enemy of health. Finally, he concluded that gluttony was an abuse that was rife in the kingdom. Clear hints are contained in these opinions of opposing dietary styles, and variations between classes and regions.[4]

At much the same date and with much experience of life on the Continent, Andrew Boorde wrote his *Dietary of Health* (1542). He came from a different part of the country, being born sometime before 1490 at Borde Hill in Cuckfield parish in the Sussex Weald. But he was brought up in Oxford, and subsequently collected wide experience in other parts of Britain and abroad before publishing his *Dietary*. We cannot, therefore, rely on him to voice any locally based food preferences. He became a Carthusian monk at a young age, but was officially 'dispensed of the religion' in 1521, went on to study medicine, at first possibly in Oxford, then certainly in Montpellier. He practised medicine in Glasgow in 1536 and lived in Montpellier between 1538 and 1542. Another book of his entitled *A Breviary of Health*, also dating from about 1542, was a physician's advice on the cure of different diseases, written to help the layman. Yet another, *The Fyrste Boke of the Introduction of Knowledge* (also dated to 1542) had started out as a work on physic but ended up describing his travels. Judging by its lively details, he had spent time in the Netherlands, Denmark, Germany, Spain, Italy, Greece, and Turkey, and in 1538 had visited Jerusalem. Different food habits regularly caught his attention; he even sent Thomas Cromwell seeds of rhubarb out of Barbary in 1535, writing that 'in these parts it is had for a great treasure'.[5]

Boorde's views on food were, like Elyot's, a mixture of domestic and foreign experiences, laced with much good sense and practical wisdom learned during his career as a respected physician. Among his patients he had numbered the Duke of Norfolk. But he was far from pompous about the professional use of obscure drugs and potions: he sometimes recommended that the body be left to heal itself. His ingredients for a long life were honest mirth, a merry temperament, and good company. Finally, the cook in the kitchen was for him the chief physician. His writing is extremely sympathetic to the present-day reader.[6]

Boorde's opinions emerged from a different pattern of life from Elyot's, and they draw our attention to several different facets of the food scene that determined people's verdicts. Plainly, the scale of values of all contemporaries was different from ours. In Boorde's first statements about any region he was visiting, he remarked on whether food was plentiful or scarce thereabouts; he then enumerated the principal ingredients in local diets, and commented on the skill in cooking them; the flavour of the dishes was a fourth issue, but this was discussed in connection with the fuel that was used in the cooking, not in relation to the herbs and spices it contained. Herbs and spices in his inventory were judged by their medicinal virtues. Food tastes, in other words, rested on different standards. We see the way one contemporary handled these four criteria in Boorde's varied comments.

But we should note straight away that Boorde and Elyot did not always agree. Boorde did not have Elyot's prejudices against spices; he positively recommended mace and ginger for comforting the heart. He saw distinctive virtues in nutmegs and cinnamon, cloves, cardamon (the interpretation the editor, Furnivall, gives to 'grains'), saffron and pepper. On the other hand, he did not warm, as did Elyot, to the simple diets of country folk. He did not look favourably on milk and whey as healthy drinks, for example; seeing them much drunk in Wales, he remarked on the poverty of the country and its 'many rude and beastly people'. When he encountered much drinking of water, as in some mountainous districts on the Continent of Europe, he was obviously surprised: he himself differentiated very carefully between sources of water, choosing rainwater as the best, tolerating running water, but giving careful instructions for straining all standing water before use. He exercised extreme caution when travelling abroad, as he explained in his account of a journey to Santiago de Compostela, when he was accompanying pilgrims whom he wanted to protect from danger on the way. They all died on the journey home, he said, through drinking water and eating the local fruits without restraint. He studiously refrained from both, and counted himself lucky to return alive. In another place writing of drinks, he declared yet more positively that 'I do leave all water'.[7]

Boorde's frequent comments on the plenty of food in some places and scarcity in others draws our attention to the great contrast between thickly populated urban centres and a more thinly settled countryside. He made a kindly comment on the good victuals, good meat, wine and competent ale that he met in Welsh market towns in contrast with the country. This difference was noted again on the Continent. In the country districts in Biscay and the wide plains of Castile, 'we could get no meat for money', he said, but in Santiago de Compostela, the pilgrims' goal on that journey, he found 'plenty of meat and wine'. These were contrasts in places that were not so far apart from each other geographically, but where the difference has to be absorbed into our picture of the age. It will especially illuminate our understanding of the situation in times of famine. Yet another related assumption about living standards lay behind Boorde's reference to the cheap living in Scotland. It was cheap, so long as you accepted 'the country fashion'. In Venice, where luxury and high fashion set the tone of the place, victuals were expensive.[8]

Some of Boorde's adverse comments on food were concerned more with the skill shown in cooking than with the foods themselves. When he commented on the simple diet of country folk in Cornwall, his harsh words about their meat, bread and drink were accompanied by the remark that they were spoiled by bad preparation. The ale was especially vile, white and thick as if pigs had wrestled in it, he said. Then in the same lines Boorde remarked on the use of furze and turf as fuel; it is fairly certain that it was the flavour these imparted to the food that prompted his dislike. Others would later express a distaste for food flavour when coal was used as a cooking fuel.[9]

Boorde's naming of the ingredients in regional diets not only discloses some silent assumptions, but reveals also some novel encounters and surprises. He made standard reference to meat and fish, which he plainly regarded as the basic foods everywhere, and in some cases that closed the subject. But in travelling around north European countries he emphasized the plenty of fish as against meat, sometimes naming particular kinds – the sturgeon and tunny of Brabant, for example, and the herring, salmon and eels in Zealand and Holland. In Spain and Navarre the sardines were plainly a new experience, for he went out of his way to describe them as resembling pilchards. His mention of the abundant wildfowl in Flanders, Denmark and France had yet deeper significance. Here was meat, but not of standard farm animals. When he came to enumerate wildfowl in England, he wrote of pheasants, his first choice, and second of partridges, 'soonest digested'. His other wild birds were woodcocks, quails, plovers, cranes, bustards. He did not commend wildfowl that live by water, and their exclusion deliberately expressed a prejudice of his age. It is certain that some of the wildfowl he saw in Flanders, if not in Denmark and France, were waterfowl, and they were not conspicuous as a source of food in England in Boorde's day. It would not be true to say that no local people, in the fenlands, say, ever ate wildfowl. They almost certainly did. But among people like Boorde, coming from outside the fens, it was not a familiar or acceptable meat. So wildfowl caught his eye when he was abroad in the 1540s, and he noticed it there for its being an acceptable food. The remark would stir a new idea in the minds of many book readers, and it would mature into a fresh attitude in the next generation. Under Dutch influence, wildfowl decoys were introduced into England at the end of the sixteenth century, and it was not long before thousands were caught in a season. Thus we perceive the observations of an Englishman in a foreign land alerting his readers to the commercial potential of a new foodstuff.[10]

Another new food idea filtered into England when Boorde and others noticed the generous use of butter in the Low Countries and in Low Germany around Cologne. It was evidently unfamiliar to Boorde, and drew from him several comments of surprise. Indeed, it seemed to him that the Dutch ate butter at all times of the day – 'Buttermouth Fleming' was the name for men of Flanders – whereas Boorde preferred to eat butter in moderation, on its own in the morning before other food, or mixed with other foods. This comment on butter was another foretaste of an imminent change in food customs. Butter-eating would grow markedly in England in the next century, initially stimulated by this Low Countries example, but finishing with consequences that would not only change the look of dishes on the table, but would transform dairying into a substantial branch of commercial business.[11]

Cheese-eating also drew Boorde's attention. He had already noticed the Welsh liking for toasted cheese, and his comment on this novelty joined the decidedly ambiguous attitude that was common elsewhere to cheese in all its forms. It was generally regarded as the food of the poor or a food to be avoided altogether. Boorde identified five sorts, among which he considered soft cheese to be the best. On curd cheese he was unwilling to pass judgement since it depended on every dairywoman's individual skill with herbs, and he did not know the range; it sounds as if the herbs determined the nourishment. Cheese in general was tolerated by Boorde rather than spurned, but not warmly. Cheese with worms, on the other hand, astonished him. When he encountered it in High Germany, he was astounded to see people's liking for it. 'They will eat maggots as fast as we will eat comfits,' he exclaimed, adding by way of explanation that 'they have a way to breed them (i.e. the maggots) in cheese'. When cheese did become more acceptable in England in the course of our period, the prejudice against cheese with worms persisted.[12]

Moving southwards on the Continent of Europe, Boorde noted the increasing use of fruit and nuts in the diet: in High (i.e. southern) Germany it was apples and walnuts; in Bohemia it was unnamed fruit and herbs; in Naples, Genoa, southern Spain and Portugal it was the great number and variety, including figs and pomegranates, that struck him most, and in Castile the fact that the apples were used to make cider. All these remarks on the fruit of Continental countries gain in significance when coupled with Chapter 21 in his *Dietary*, in which he again expatiates on fruits but devotes almost all the space to the exotics of warmer climes: figs, raisins, currants, peaches, grapes, dates, pomegranates and oranges. Home-grown fruits like pears, apples, quinces, plums, damsons, medlars, the fruit of the service tree, strawberries, cherries and whortle berries were commended, but without enthusiasm; Boorde's comments were brief and conveyed none of the pleasure or care for cultivation that would be manifest in England by Elizabeth's reign. Indeed, a reference to strawberries struck a positively sour note, being prompted by a reference to strawberries with clotted cream, which he thought gave little nourishment, satisfying rather 'a sensual appetite'. The strawberries in this case were undoubtedly the wild ones, for they were described as 'a rural man's banquet', and Boorde had known such banquets to put men 'in jeopardy of their lives'. He allowed nuts, which were always ranked along with fruits in this period, to be nourishing. Walnuts, filberts, hazelnuts and chestnuts were named in that order. Almonds, surprisingly, also appeared in the list, not as a foreign import but as a food as familiar in England as the others. Does this mean when we find medieval cottages in southern England named after the almond tree that the trees were already growing here and the nuts were ripening? It is difficult to believe this, unless we class their owners among the brave ones who were making the first trials. All the other evidence from Boorde and Elyot suggests that the fruit-growing renaissance in England was as yet a world away, and did not enter their imagination.[13]

We have already noted approving remarks by Elyot on the subject of roots and greenstuff. His only named roots were turnips, parsnips and carrots. Boorde, on the other hand, knew the roots of borage, bugloss, alexanders, elecampane, parsley, fennel, radishes and rapes as edible foods, and added leeks, onions and garlic. The green shoots of some of these roots were also eaten, and so parsley, borage, bugloss were named again, together with other greenstuff like rocket, chicory, purslane, lettuce, sorrel and more. Colewort and cabbages were not mentioned at all, a strange omission that may have been inadvertent. Every other root and greenstuff was credited with some particular effect on the body without any plant being elevated above any other. The ordering of a scale of preferences, and finicky choices between varieties of brassica, turnips and carrots awaited another generation.[14]

Drinks deserve a brief reference here, although they receive attention later, for Boorde made one general comment on the liking for beer in place of ale which had current significance. It was a cold drink, he noted, drawing attention to the fact that in this respect it was unfamiliar when compared with ale. Posset ale, for example, was a comfort in fevers, being a drink of hot milk mixed with cold ale and herbs. Boorde was sharply aware of the relentless beer-drinking seen in the Netherlands and Low Germany, and was affronted by drunkenness. But he could see beer even then winning favour in England, anticipating a change that proceeded steadily in the next half century. In the meantime, other drinks in England were known. Mead was honey and water; Boorde knew the Welsh habit of drinking metheglin, i.e. water and honey with herbs. He also knew those in England who drank cider; some people were accustomed to it, and he judged that it did little harm as a harvest drink, but it was not one that physicians favoured. Here was another liquid that was destined to surge in popularity after the mid-seventeeeth century, being transformed from a poor countryman's taste to a modish urban and upper-class drink.[15]

Finally, Boorde upheld temperate eating and condemned gluttony. Two meals a day were sufficient for those leading a gentle life, three for a labourer. Moderation meant restricting the variety of meats eaten at one meal to three and no more, and curbing variety of drink. The lessons of a man who had sat through many banquets seem to shine through his ironic observation that meats light of digestion were the most nutritious, and yet, he said, they were the ones reserved for the servants.[16]

Yet another author of the 1540s was John Hales, who had digested Plutarch's advice on health, and wrote a book on his precepts. He was particularly concerned with preserving the health of officials who wore themselves out on affairs of state. They above others, he thought, needed to take care of themselves. His career would not lead us to expect a book on diet, so further details on his life need to be set in the background. He was a politician, MP for Preston, and author of a searching treatise on the state of the economy in 1549, *The Discourse of the Commonweal of this Realm of England*. He was as much exercised by the sight of gluttony as was Elyot, claiming that more men died from intemperate eating than from the sword or plague. Those were strong words that deserve to be pondered. The concern of two writers with gluttony and Boorde's urgings on temperate eating arouse the suspicion that some knowledge of food habits in courtly as well as political circles at Westminster lay behind these remarks; it could well have featured in gossip in London, and spread disapproval, even disgust, in casual talk. Indeed, details about Henry VIII's lifestyle could readily have leaked into a far wider public domain since he was always on the move from one gentleman's house to another. His insatiable greed for globe artichokes, for example, is documented, and public knowledge of this can be inferred from the Privy Purse expenses recording many gratuities given for artichokes brought to his door. The sight of his fat, ungainly body, and his generally unhealthy physical state drew public notice in his old age; it was almost certainly a talking point much earlier among physicians, frowning on this example of overeating by their sovereign.[17]

What is worth pondering in Hales's work is the innuendo that he tacked on to his strong condemnation of gluttony. He first urged his readers to accustom themselves to simple foods so that they would be ready to swallow them without distaste when they were sick. But he went further: in his view, eating strange and dainty meats when no hunger required it stirred up dissension in the nation: 'make no sedition in the commonwealth', he commanded. Are these words loaded with a particular meaning? They were written in the 1540s, when food prices were rising sharply, and they were the words of a man who was an Enclosure Commissioner and in 1548 was actually blamed by the Earl of Warwick for the anti-enclosure disturbances in Buckinghamshire. Did he attribute riot and rebellion to men sickened by the contrast between the lives of the rich and the poor? Hales's other concerns with social unrest that showed up the contrast between wealth and poverty make this a plausible suggestion.[18]

In commending 'moderate and mean fare' to statesmen serving under the pressure of a busy life in government, Hales was basing his advice on the precepts of Plutarch, as summarized and interpreted by Erasmus. Hales's reading of this classic work offers an insight into ideas about food that were circulating among literate men from about 1530 onwards, opening their minds to a fresh viewpoint on the consequences of gluttony. Hales's stereotype of poor men's food was what he called 'food sodden', pottage of some kind, frumenty, bread sops (bread soaked in a broth) and cresses, that is, greenstuff which he dubbed 'common fare', washed down with water rather than wine. Some soul-searching about the eating practices of different classes was evidently in progress among thinking people in London circles in the 1530s and 1540s. It would expand the imagination further in the next half century.[19]

So what, in fact, were people eating? The diet of large noble and gentle house-holds is moderately well documented in this period, but we should not imagine that the food of the rich was unknown to the rest of the nation. Rich, middling and poor did not live in separate worlds. Many, indeed most, ingredients in food at the castle and in the manor house were grown, reared or trapped by ordinary folk living as neighbours in the same place. The women cooked the food, or saw it cooked, before it was served at grand tables. Ordinary folk in the countryside had their chance to taste some of the same foods in the plentiful season. Their knowledge of food went far beyond the basic cereals, simple greenstuff and white meats. The Privy Purse Expenses of Henry VIII between November 1529 and December 1532 afford a view of rich men's food that obviously touched the lives of all classes. They show innumerable payments for foodstuffs that arrived in the royal kitchen, all dependent on the toil of labourers, tradesmen and the intermediaries who handed them over. Goods were either bought for the king, or they were brought to him unasked by loyal citizens or by messengers, these last receiving a gratuity that denoted the perceived value of the gift. They give us an idea not only of the foods that the king was known to appreciate, but also of the many, often ordinary, folk who produced them. Some of the higher-ranking senders knew the king personally, and had perhaps entertained him, so they developed a regular routine of sending the food they knew he liked whenever available. Lady Sidney specialized in fruit, and sent pies – orange pies in April 1532, for example, presumably made with imported oranges, though they might, just conceivably, have been home grown. She also sent quince pies. Birds were also gifts from nobility and gentry: shovelards from Lord Cobham, who was at home in Kent; pheasants, and on one occasion wildfowl in mid-December from Sir Edward Guildford, also at home in the same county. In other cases the food came from modest local people who took pride in presenting to the king some seasonal speciality of their district, the opportunity often being seized when he was making a visit nearby: hence the pears that the mayor of Northampton presented to the king when he was at Grafton in the Northamptonshire forests, or the sturgeon and lampreys for which the Severn estuary was famed, and which required a carrier to make all haste to London from Gloucestershire. They were sometimes baked first, and Lord Berkeley's messenger once received a generous reward of 20 shillings for delivering his parcel. One gift to the king came from a Spanish lady who had another way of preserving them, by salting; she also went away with the same especially large reward of 20s.[20]

Food items could be a fashion that burst suddenly upon people in the courtly circle, who later exerted their influence in a wider world. It is not easy to trace the vital steps in any such story, but we may have an example in the domestic breeding of pheasants. This seems to have been a practice seriously inaugurated in Henry VIII's reign. The first reference to any such attempt occurs in a footnote in the eleventh edition of the *Encyclopaedia Britannica*, referring enigmatically to the artificial breeding of pheasants at Upton in the fifteenth century; it does not give the county in which Upton lies, or any further details. That the pheasant was a bird of high standing in the early sixteenth century is evident in Andrew Boorde's *Dietary of Health* (1542), describing it as, of all wildfowl, 'most best'. This high praise may reflect a heightened interest at that time, and be connected with a move in Parliament in 1533 'on the king's behalf' to present a bill 'for' (presumably meaning 'to punish') 'partridge and pheasant takers'; time-wise the references cluster around one item in the Privy Purse Accounts in 1532. Henry was returning with Anne Boleyn from a visit to France in November in the days before their marriage. It records royal authority for a payment of 9s. 4d. to a French priest, described as a pheasant breeder, at Eltham. A month later, in December 1532, the French priest was again described as 'the pheasant breeder', and was given a further 40s. to buy a gown and other necessaries. Was this the moment when a pheasant breeder was brought from France to set up a breeding enterprise in a royal palace, prompted by something seen on the visit there? It is not a preposterous suggestion, since Anne had lived for years in France as a child and had the eyes and ears to notice such details on this royal visit. After December 1532, our Frenchman disappears from the record, but the breeding of pheasants evidently entered into the routines of nobility and gentry thereafter: by 1607 the Earl of Rutland at Belvoir Castle in Leicestershire was paying widow Welborne to feed milk and cheese to young pheasants and buying scissors for her to clip their wings. Pheasants caught wild, of course, remained a delectable food, but pheasant breeding was now an art, painstakingly mastered in the households of nobility and gentry, that would supply these birds more regularly as food at the table. At Rainham in Norfolk Sir Roger Townshend in 1630 was seemingly thus provided, judging by a document referring to a yard 'to keep young pheasants'.[21]

Among other foods brought to the king that belong to the newfangled, newly fashionable category were plants that were either imported or grown in the royal gardens. Such were the deliveries by James Hobart, a London dealer, who imported fruits, and supplied the pomegranates that had been made fashionable by Catherine of Aragon: she had used pomegranates as her heraldic emblem, which was rapidly cleared away from the palaces when Anne Boleyn became queen. Hobart also sent dates, lemons and oranges, sometimes having to transport them some distance to reach the king wherever he lay, once to Hertford, often to Hampton Court. Hobart, incidentally, was one of several dealers who handled 'sweet lemons' in the sixteenth century, a mysterious variety that we no longer know. Other foreign fruits were unexpected surprises, like the one and only melon, presented by an Italian when the king was at Abingdon, and the figs of Portugal, presented by a Mr Worsley. Were these fresh figs? Dried figs would not have been anything special, being imported routinely by this time.[22]

The king's gardeners were expected to grow the latest plants in vogue, and they were highly successful in the gardens at Greenwich, Beaulieu in Essex, and Richmond. Regular deliveries from these places give us a glimpse of the herbs, greenstuff and roots that were specially favoured by the king at that time: they included lettuce, surely to please Queen Catherine, who has the credible reputation of having introduced the taste for (improved) salad greens from Spain; cucumber, which was once transported from Beaulieu in Essex to Hertford for the king's pleasure; radishes, which, because they appear only once in the whole list of Privy Purse expenses, may still have been a novelty in the late 1520s; and early peas, delivered once as early as 31 May, and so likely to have been a gardener's special pride and joy. Early peas became the modish aspiration of many fastidious gardeners in the seventeenth century.[23]

Certain cultivated fruits were also newcomers on the food scene in Henry's reign, being improvements on the wild and indigenous varieties. The strawberries arriving from Beaulieu on 25 May and still being harvested in the months of June and July were surely cultivated, not wild. Cherries of the sweet kind were new on the scene in Henry's reign, so when the mayor of London sent them as a gift to Anne Boleyn as early as 1530, it is possible that they came from the Netherlands. We cannot be entirely sure of this, however, since gifts of cherries are noted on 14 occasions in the same record; and cherry trees do take several years to bear fruit. Early as it is, in 1530 a harvest from home-grown trees has to be contemplated. The royal garden at Richmond also furnished grapes and peaches.[24]

Some of the foods reaching the king were luxuries as yet known only to a few, and hardly heard of outside the charmed circle of court nobility. But a great many other foods coming to the king were donated by ordinary folk, proud of their local specialities, and doubtless hoping for a generous royal reward. They were not out-of-the-way foods that local people could not themselves have enjoyed. The list usually describes the bearers as 'poor women', but we can safely judge them to have been working people rather than paupers. They brought foods that they had gathered wild or grown themselves and which they expected the king to enjoy as seasonal pleasures – damsons, quinces, medlars and filberts, for example, as well as apples and pears. Fruit was especially noticeable as gifts whenever the king travelled through Kent to Dover.[25]

Poultry was another gift to the king, and it was always women who brought the hens, chickens and capons. Women were clearly the keepers of the poultry at home. When cheese arrived, it was also brought by women; and we may guess at some local pride when a cheese was sent to Greenwich by Old Lady Oxford. She was Elizabeth, daughter of Sir Richard Scrope, and wife of the 14th earl of Oxford, of the De Vere family; the family home was Castle Hedingham, in the Colne valley in Essex, where Suffolk cheese was the chief product. Suffolk cheese is usually referred to in deprecating terms by contemporaries, but in this case a relatively large sum of 18s. 8d. was given as a token of thanks. We may suspect that this cheese came from a family recipe that put this Suffolk cheese in a different class; it was not always regarded as an abomination. Another specialist cheese from further afield came routinely from Llanthony in Wales.[26]

The foodstuffs arriving for the king, and itemized in Privy Purse Expenses, might convey the impression that fruit and cheese featured conspicuously in the royal diet. But it is more likely that they featured often in this list because they were eminently suitable as personal gifts, easily transported without deterioration or damage. As dietary items, they were special treats for the king, for they ranked behind the basic ingredients of meals that consisted primarily of meat, fish, bread and drink. They were still miscellaneous extras at this date, rather than having a secure place in family menus, and different households acquired them in different ways, not always expecting to have their own home-produced supply.

While our picture of kitchen supplies in Henry VIII's household remains incomplete, it is helpful to seek further clues about rich men's fare from another pattern of supply: the household of the Earl of Rutland at Belvoir Castle between the early 1520s and 1540s. Supplies from the home farm doubtless satisfied most needs in this case; we know that the Earl had a keeper of the dairy, of the poultry, and of the garden. But gifts or solicited supplies flowed in from local sources, bringing a crane and peacock in 1525, a boar at Christmas and another for New Year. Fresh fish arrived regularly from other people's ponds, adding to those fished out of the lord's own. A neighbour, Lady Markham, the windows of whose house looked onto Belvoir Castle, on one occasion sent lamprey, pike and salmon trout. For large quantities, however, during Lent in 1541, fish was brought from Boston in Lincolnshire. The source of wildfowl was a provisioner in Crowland in the fens, and seagulls and other birds came from Holderness in East Yorkshire. Food was varied because it came from many different sources, and no trouble was too much to get fresh food and delicacies.[27]

The Earl of Rutland's accounts show clearly that in the later 1530s people around Belvoir were growing cherries and strawberries, and deliveries were made to the Castle that look like gifts from friendly neighbours; Lady Markham sent strawberries in 1539, and the parsons of nearby Waltham and Ropsley both sent cherries, conjuring up a picture of orchards attached to parsonages, and parsons with a gardening interest that had put them a step ahead of the rest. How our clerics acquired their cherry trees in the first place is another question, though we might guess at a supply contrived through friendship with the gardener at the manor house.[28]

A more satisfying summary of the food scene between 1500 and 1550 should encompass the foods of varied classes and varied regions, rather than focusing only on the well-to-do and a few places with grand houses. But at this date writers engaged with food only at a very general level, and when they considered basic food it was mainly meat, fish and bread. Still, meat and fish did encompass a large number of alternatives, ranked according to geography and class and the prevailing fashion. Venison, thought Boorde, was nowhere in the world so esteemed as in England; nevertheless, he deemed it gentlemen's food, and poachers were warned off. However, we know it was a fairly familiar meat in forest country; Thomas Cromwell investigated deer-stealing in the parks of the Kentish Weald in 1538 and found poaching to be the light-hearted recreation of many young men on dark nights in good weather. Geese and ducks, in Boorde's estimation, were valued not for their meat but for their feathers. But he was not speaking for the peasant farmer who frequently kept one or two at his door. Sturgeon was unusual, and when caught in the Severn estuary the king in London was a first recipient. Fair enough, but other fish, just as tasty, were inordinately plenteous. Flounders, sole and plaice were so abundant on the Cornish coast that at low tide in some seasons they could be scooped up by handfuls close in shore. Eels absolutely filled the dykes in the East Anglian fens. Along the river Medway in Kent, the locals caught hundreds in their weirs. Fish was a free food for large numbers of people, and they did not have to wait for days of abstinence to get it.[29]

Herbs and greenstuff were so abundant everywhere in fields, hedgerows and woods that they scarcely drew any comment from sixteenth-century writers, and it is only later in our period that we shall meet botanists explicitly describing the way countrywomen gathered them as family food. Upper-class interest in differentiating so many common, lowly plants built up quite slowly from the fourteenth and fifteenth centuries. So only as new plants, new varieties and foreign influences were absorbed did any discussion appear in print. It took a long time for this flowering of scientific and intellectual interest to mature, but when it did, the botanists at last took notice of the daily routines of country folk in gathering their food for free. We historians can do better than they and will not underrate people's powers of observation and effort in vegetable improvement. A mid-fifteenth century document, for example, explained how 'to make round cabbage', by setting them one yard apart on well-dunged land, and regularly picking off the lower leaves until the upper ones started to roll inwards. The plant would then grow round. The first observers of that opportunity will go for ever unnamed, but we shall later hear of a woman in the middle seventeenth century who did exploit commercially a similar chance discovery, only publicized because the intellectuals had learned after long years of blindness to respect the wisdom of country folk. Many fragments of information about food in these years had the potential to set a small fire ablaze; somehow the time was ripe.[30]

Roots were living at this time, like colewort, in a twilit world that we can hardly penetrate. Carrots, turnips and parsnips were differentiated, but they were not elevated above parsley and bugloss roots, so all were probably small, misshapen and as yet unimproved. We have already suggested that the single reference to radishes in the Privy Purse accounts indicates a relative newcomer, though the botanist William Turner did name them in a matter-of-fact way in 1538. The total absence of any references to cauliflowers, asparagus, Jerusalem artichokes and mushrooms (except for Boorde's special note that they were eaten in Lombardy, along with frogs, adders and snails) reminds us that more new vegetables were waiting in the wings to make their mark before the century was out.[31]

Every gentle family had its own food preferences and conventions, and no generalization could cover all their kitchen practices, let alone those of ordinary folk who had to make do with what lay around them. In the case of the Percy family of Northumberland, we can suspect a precocious interest in herbs and the distilling of essences for health and medicine, but that is only because they had an early book of herbs in their library. A household book of 1511–25 actually contains an instruction that no herbs be bought henceforward since the cooks would have enough from their lord's garden. How typical the Percys were in Northumberland or Sussex, it is impossible to say.[32]

Beyond the work of the few writers already named, references to the food of ordinary people are sparse until after 1550. Few probate inventories survive from this time to shed any light on the contents of peasant kitchens. Wills yield little information beyond bequests of cereals and animals to kinsmen, coupled with very rare references to fruit and herbs, or, more likely, bequests of orchards and herb gardens. Pottage still featured largest as the cooked food, and it is graphically represented in some early illustrations. For cold food eaten in the fields, barley or wheat bread, herrings and cheese were the most serviceable alternative. We should not, however, entirely ignore clues given in the *Dialogues* prepared by the Spaniard Juan Vives a few years before his death in 1540, when he composed exercises for Latin translation by the pupils attending his private school in Bruges (a considerable town, be it noted), and introduced meals into his subject matter. They do not depict English life, but they do not totally exclude experience of England, for Vives spent time in England – he became an Oxford professor and was tutor to Princess Mary – and one of his dialogues refers to English cheese. He gives us the expected view of the cauldron hanging over the fire on a pothook, and the broth inside, made from bones, sometimes meat, whether salted beef, veal, lamb or chicken, plus cereals, rice, turnips, coleworts, peas, beans and lentils. The pupils in the dialogues informed their questioner that they got as much bread as they wanted, and it was made of the whole grain, not sifted. But they were expected to eat moderately of the pottage. On certain days they ate a little roasted meat, sometimes veal, sometimes kid meat. On days of abstinence, they had fresh fish if it was cheap in the market, or, if not, salt fish which had been well soaked, and so made perfectly good eating. Alternatively, they ate eggs, either cooked hard in the fire (for which a ration of two per person was allowed), or fried or made into an omelette. On days of lighter food rations, they might also have cheese and nuts. In summer they had a second course of radishes, cheese, pears, peaches or quince. For tea, in addition to bread they ate almonds or hazelnuts, dried figs or raisins, and in summer pears, apples, cherries or plums. They drank fresh water or weak beer and, rarely, watered wine (though that would have been unheard of in England). Other drinks mentioned were milk, buttermilk and whey.[33]

This was food using the simplest ingredients, but it was not totally monotonous, and it allowed flexibility on fast days to satisfy the healthy appetites of growing boys, and variety in summer when fruit was available. Almonds and cherries sound more like a Flemish rather than an English boy's rations at this date, but hazelnuts and apples were perfectly possible alternatives. We can reasonably imagine much the same menu served from the kitchen of any resourceful English housewife, varying the food according to the season in much the same way. No cook needed relentlessly to serve pottage on every meat-eating day in the week; she could easily use her skillet or posnet, both pans with long handles, or one of many brass pans, available in all sizes, to make a batter of flour, eggs and milk, mixing in roots, greens and herbs, and a fragment of meat cut from the bacon joint hanging from so many kitchen roofs; she could make a satisfying hash in a pancake or omelette; or, on another day, she could put similar ingredients into a pasty, and by covering it with a pot bake it in front of an open fire. Those of us who cook daily know how to use much the same ingredients while introducing some changes to achieve variety. Vives's *Dialogues* also give us a brief glimpse of seasonal and local variety that all classes could exploit and enjoy. People did not have to be rich or to engage in lavish expenditure to savour changes in the daily menu. The seasons, the alternation of fish and meat days, and the variety of England's wild plants and animals over short distances, drove away monotony.

The talking points among writers between 1500 and 1550 depict a fairly lively food scene, shot through with more appreciation than complaint. Meat and fish were plainly the menfolk's major concerns, but they did not overlook the many extras contributed by the women's efforts in supplying wild greens, dairy foods, eggs and poultry. Regional differences only came the way of those who travelled, but seasonal variety was everyone's experience. Some of the class differences vanish when we take account of the abundance of free foods for all, and other local differences were softened by neighbourly sharing or poaching. An impression lingers of many people's ignorance in the right handling of good ingredients, and that would persist throughout our period of study. Ignorance also existed, alongside a lack of interest in some, but that is found in cooks of all ages, including the present. For the majority of human beings, the enjoyment of tasty food is a powerful urge to effort, and we shall, in fact, end our story in 1760 with a most convincing account from one writer testifying to the assiduity of women in preparing pleasing meals for their families, and their originality in coping with straitened supplies. In all walks of life and in a multitude of different ways, we shall encounter people in this early modern period getting their chance to enlarge their experience of food. In 1550 they stood at the beginning of a new era of opportunity.

3

The Widening World of Food, 1550–1600

The food scene took on some significant new characteristics in the years between 1550 and 1600, differentiating it from the previous half century. The surrounding circumstances require scrutiny since people's diets were being altered by external influences, which broadened the range of food supplies, changed attitudes to certain foodstuffs, and started fashions among the well-to-do that would ultimately affect everyone else. In the first place, the debate about the relationship between health, food and medicine deepened, and involved not only physicians who came to hold scientific views that separated them into different camps, but also laymen bringing varied experiences from places far apart in the world. We are in a good position in the early years of the twenty-first century to understand how the tone of these discussions could change over the years, for we see the same thing happening in our own day. We have become conscious of industrial processes altering the natural ingredients in our basic foods. Scientific research turns up new discoveries about the content and merit of such changes, and people then notice significant linkages: how, for example, once rare diseases have become common. They may be struck by the loss of flavour in their food; anything may spark a new animated debate, and our perceptions of the relationship between food, health and medicine are balanced out afresh.

So the debate concerning food, health and medicine assumed a lively, serious tone in the second half of the sixteenth century. Physicians, chemists, alchemists and intellectuals all joined in. They argued about the merits of different medicines and the rules for a healthy life. Not a few of the men whom we nowadays rank as pure scientists wrote books about food, though the present-day scholars who investigate the scientific debate may well pass over in silence the same authors' work on food in order to concentrate on their other topics. For the food historian, of course, they are key texts, and we shall read them with care. They greatly help us to get into the minds of contemporaries, and poke around among the innumerable bits of intellectual baggage that lay cluttered in the background of people's opinions, explaining at least in part their food regimes.

We, for example, put sage into our sage and onion stuffing for the sake of its flavour; our forebears valued sage for comforting and sharpening the brain. So they chopped it in butter, and sage butter was a main item for some at breakfast,

clearing the mind for the rest of the day. Sir John Harington translated, and
perhaps embroidered, an ode to sage in 1607.

> 'But who can write thy worth (O sovereign sage)?
> Some ask how men can die where thou dost grow ...
> Sage strengthens the sinews, fever's heat doth swage ...
> Since then the name betokens wise and saving.
> We count it nature's friend and worth the having.'[1]

So I always toss sage from my garden into my soups, hoping to benefit from
this ancient wisdom! As all food was also medicine, certain foods loomed large
on everyone's food list if they promised to preserve against plague. One writer,
Henry Buttes, Master of Corpus Christi College, and later Vice-Chancellor at
Cambridge, believed that tame pigeons, bred in dovecotes (definitely not the wild
variety), were a preservative in time of pestilence. It is a factor to bear in mind
when observing the status of dovecotes at this time, and the fact that manorial
lords lost the exclusive right to keep them in the mid- to late seventeenth century.
A Welsh gentleman, William Vaughan from Carmarthenshire, where dovecotes
were less conspicuous, was emphatic that sorrel leaves, eaten fasting, were an
equally effective preservative. Other remedies were walnuts in vinegar, a roasted
onion, and mugwort (*Artemisia vulgaris*). Most noticeable of all was the fact
that the medicinal properties of herbs stood above their value as flavourings.
Spices were the prime ingredients to add for flavour, while herbs plainly added a
blend of mingled, but not distinctive, tastes. Yet more subtlety was imported into
his viewpoint by Thomas Moufet, the physician, distinguishing what he called
'physic herbs', which cured disease, from 'wholesome herbs', which promoted
health. If this was a widely held assumption, it must have made a difference to
the choice of herbs used in the kitchen.[2]

In medical circles an increasingly lively issue after 1550 was the division of
opinion between the disciples of Galen and Paracelsus. The authority of Galen's
teaching, dating from the second century AD, had been confirmed and strengthened by humanist physicians earlier in the sixteenth century. Paracelsus, on the
other hand, was a man in close touch with the culture and folklore of country
peasants and miners in south Germany, and he advocated a different system
of medical treatment. He made use of medicines from, among other things,
precious stones, metals, minerals and chemicals. The alchemists had received
licences to practise with these materials in the fifteenth century, and their procedures were subsequently sanctioned by the physicians. Paracelsian doctrines
won substantial support from English physicians in the years 1570–90, with the
result that a thin thread of interest in distillation expanded into a broad skein in
the second half of the sixteenth century. A translation into English in 1527 of a
German work on distilling by Braunschweig, first published in 1500, worked its

way slowly into gentlemen's libraries, followed by distilling equipment that was installed in manor houses and eventually even into some yeomen's farmhouses. The result in this period was a host of essential oils distilled from minerals, spices and plants, to be consumed by the connoisseurs for their medicinal virtues and then appreciated as food flavourings.[3]

The transition can be more closely followed in books clustering around the same date. John Hester, a London apothecary, was intent on explaining in his 1575 book the medicinal uses of distillations from spices, seeds, roots and gums (though without giving much help to the beginner on the use of the distilling apparatus). In 1582 he moved on to translate the work of the Italian Leonardo Fioravanti on cures from herbs and minerals; distillation was becoming a distinct vogue. The shifting viewpoint was even better illustrated in another textbook. John Fitzherbert had published useful advice on farming procedures in 1523. When his book was newly corrected and amended for a fresh edition in 1598, not only was the importance of garden produce for health and profit underlined, but 29 new pages were inserted on distilling essences. In the same decade Hugh Platt, the son of a London brewer, was also experimenting with distillations, and published two books in 1594 and 1602 full of practical advice on the yield of oils and the best equipment for distillation. Purchases of distilling equipment now featured regularly in the accounts of expenditure by the gentry.[4]

We may well speculate on the intensity of flavours that people experienced as a result of all this experimentation. The essential oils prepared by Hester and his like used spices like mace, cinnamon, ginger and coriander as often as herbs. Did their strong flavours creep into cooking? On that score, we can only guess, but all the practices of the day point to adventurous trials with all things edible; food was being explored in a confident spirit, seeking for new flavours.

Not surprisingly, flavour became a matter for quite finicky analysis in some table conversations. One dialogue, in a Huguenot teacher's textbook of Elizabeth's reign, shows us this when it compared the turnips of Caen with traditional English turnips, the French ones triumphing because they were 'of much better taste'. Thus we reach a sharper understanding of the fine differences that could determine choices in people's food buying. The household accounts of gentry reveal, without explaining, the liking for particular cheeses and particular meats. All we can do is acknowledge without testing the variety they experienced in the flavours of locally produced foods, not to mention the variety achieved by cooking them in different ways.[5]

What is underlined in all the documents is the heightened interest in food in general, both in conversation and in experiment. Moufet described how Francis Drake brought back a strange kind of bread from his journeys across the Atlantic and offered Moufet some to taste. Moufet himself looked at the fish stalls as he walked round London, and described how, on his way back from a visit to

Barn Elms (probably to see Francis Walsingham, who lived there), he spotted an unfamiliar fish, bought it, and had it cooked for supper. Drake's men noticed in port crustaceans that had attached themselves to the woodwork of their vessel; they ate them appreciatively, and reported the fact to others. Raleigh brought back potatoes from his voyages, and left some tubers in southern Ireland where he paused on his journey home. Plainly, they were planted by local people showing an active interest in new foods, and as a result they found their first congenial habitat in Ireland, long before they settled in England. We shall refer below to Hugh Platt's experiments in London with pasta; they were sparked off by his contacts with Italians in London, and were prosecuted energetically because of the interest that mariners showed in this convenient victual to take on sea voyages. Pasta became one more talking point in London circles.[6]

A host of different currents of conversation flowed through the capital in those years, and food was among them. Ideas on the subject prompted trials by interested, curious and inventive people. In a small world it is not difficult to visualize how it happened, for we see comparable sequences today in a much larger world, but one which benefits from a fast rate of communication. When an idea seemed to meet a current need, it fired people's imagination, and in a climate of public interest it was sure to be picked up somewhere by individuals with intellectual curiosity and enthusiasm for adventure. It might or might not blossom into a large enterprise, but it got the best chance to do so. Food ventures were as exciting as industrial projects and they were at the height of fashion. New thinking was, of course, being stirred by the wealth of foreign foodstuffs arriving in London and other ports like Bristol, Southampton, King's Lynn and Newcastle. From there imports trickled out to rural areas in a haphazard fashion. But, sometimes with remarkable speed, they reached the homes of nobility and gentry, who had developed a taste for foreign foodstuffs either abroad or at rich men's tables in London, and wanted to enjoy the same at home. Enterprising merchants were always alert to chances of expanding their provincial trade. So German miners prospecting in the north of England enjoyed oranges that were carried for them all the way from London to Newcastle in February 1569. The Earl of Rutland was quickly recognized as an appreciative potential customer, and received oranges in quantity at Belvoir castle: 500 in 1553; 120 in 1585; 250 in 1586. He even enjoyed 'marmalady suckett', carried to Berwick-upon-Tweed by a London merchant when the earl was Warden of the East and Middle Marches and was campaigning in the north in 1549–50. The fairs in famous centres like Stourbridge catered for all comers, and were notably well-patronized distribution centres for fish and spices, attracting purchasers on a regular basis from far afield. The Shuttleworth family of Gawthorpe Hall, near Burnley in Lancashire, shopped for certain things at Stourbridge in Cambridgeshire.[7]

Above all others, the London food markets overflowed with delicacies from abroad, and well-to-do families regularly fitted shopping trips to London into their calendar. The results are portrayed indirectly in the London portbooks, one year's return in 1567–8 showing us sugar and treacle that came from Barbary and Genoa via Antwerp, fruit in a ship from Spain that contained nothing apart from its 40,000 oranges, prunes coming from Rouen in December, presumably having been dried in the autumn from the harvest of local orchards in Normandy. Apples and onions arrived in September from St Omer, figs for Christmas from Portugal, almonds from Malaga and Barbary, and huge quantities of eastern and West Indian spices via Antwerp and Amsterdam. From Scotland and northern Europe came fish.[8]

Behind all this foreign trade lay the influence on English eating habits exerted by the well-to-do who travelled abroad and had frequent contact with foreign visitors in England. In the last 40 to 50 years, we have again become familiar with the effects of world travel on our own food regimes, so no great effort of the imagination is needed to conjure up a similar scene in the later sixteenth century. As more and more Englishmen travelled on the Continent of Europe and even further afield, the food habits of others were among their first subjects of conversation. After all, they had to find food to eat as soon as they set foot on foreign soil! We have already noticed Andrew Boorde's abiding memory of the drunkenness and butter-eating that he saw in the Netherlands, and his extreme caution, born of harsh experience, towards the drinking of water and overmuch fruit-eating in Spain. But he had learned to be broadminded about other people's food regimes, and added appreciative remarks on the good sense of Jewish, Saracen and Turkish physicians who, in his view, had 'as much wit, wisdom, reason, and knowledge for the safety of their body as any Christian man hath'. Others were just as observant, tolerant and ready to be persuaded as Boorde of the virtues of different food habits: Moufet noted that the Italians were in love with veal; the Italians and French, he said, taught the English to eat burdock (i.e. burr roots), enabling them to enjoy a flavour similar to asparagus. Olive oil in salads seems to have been a rich man's taste adopted from the Continent at the beginning of the sixteenth century, and it gradually spread among the gentry class. Its progress cannot confidently be measured, but bottles of salad oil appear in the household shopping lists of country gentlewomen by 1600 that would have been uncommon or unseen before 1550; often they were sent from London.[9]

Among the stay-at-homes were those who gathered fresh ideas about food from reading books. These multiplied remarkably in this period, some written by English authors who combed the ancient classics and mixed old ideas with their own current opinions, others being translations of foreign works. An example is Thomas Twyne, an alchemist and associate of John Dee, whose book on diet was entitled *The Schoolemaster or Teacher of Table Phylosophie*. He summarized the work of many ancient authors including Galen, the ninth–tenth-century

Persian physician Rhazes (whose work had appeared in many Latin editions between 1497 and 1555, as well as in French in 1566), Avicenna (980–1036/7) and Averroes (1126–98), noting their advice on diet without adding any opinions of his own.[10]

Italian authors had led the field with the earliest books in Western Europe on food, but it is important to acknowledge the slow pace at which their ideas at first percolated into England. Their books had made a quiet entry in the late fifteenth and early sixteenth century, and lay around for decades, known only to a few. Now they slowly gathered more readers, responding to new impulses in a changing world. By the period between 1550 and 1600 English readers were absorbing foreign notions, particularly from Italy, with lively interest.

The best known pioneer among the Italians, as we briefly noted above, was Bartolomeo Sacchi de Platina, writing in the late fifteenth century *De Honesta Voluptate*, including *The Art of Cookery* in ten books. The presence in the British Library of more than a dozen Italian editions of that work (in Latin), running from 1475 to 1503, plus an Argentinian edition of 1517, plus German translations from Cologne, Augsburg and Strasbourg, and two French editions in Latin from Paris and Lyons between 1529 and 1548, tells us how the work reached English readers in different languages, and gradually opened their eyes to the potential interest of food as a subject. A modern bibliographer, Lord Westbury, calls Platina's book a cross-section of contemporary (Italian) food, but it was not translated into English until 1998, so it did not attract the widest readership. But it did contain food recipes, taken from another book by an Italian cook, Maestro Martino; his work has survived in only one known copy in the Library of Congress in Washington. Plainly, these Western European pioneers in food books were not immediately proclaimed by their contemporaries. They were followed, at a long distance, by three more Italian writers, Cristiforo di Messisbugo, writing in 1549 on banquets, Domenico Romoli, publishing in 1560, and Bartolomeo Scappi in 1570. Then the favourable moment for food books arrived, and their work, now written in Italian rather than Latin, ran into many editions.[11]

English readers about food now took notice and began to translate more and more of these Italian authors, starting in 1558 with William Warde's translation of the work of Alexis of Piedmont (working from a French version, though he claimed to be in personal touch with the author, who yielded him more information for later editions). This work, *The Secretes of the Reverende Maister Alexis of Piemount*, contained remedies for disease (for Warde was a physician and lecturer at Cambridge), but also included thoroughly practical advice on food matters. Interest in his book is suggested by the five further editions that had appeared by 1615. Another Italian, the Calvinist Gulielmus Gratarolus, fleeing religious persecution in Italy, wrote books between the 1550s and 1570s. One of these gave particular advice on food for magistrates and students, insisting that diet was the best cure for sickness. It was translated from the Latin in 1574 by an Essex parson, Thomas Newton, who plainly found translating a congenial diversion from his clerical duties. Many other translations appear under Newton's name in the library catalogues, including a book in 1580 by an unknown author, in which the modern reader will be struck by the many essential oils that were recommended medicinally, and by the distinct differences in the virtues attributed to the same plant when wild or when cultivated. This draws our attention to a subject that prompted frequent expressions of emphatic opinion in this half century, until the controversy faded away, presumably for lack of hard evidence either way. Yet another more weighted culinary, rather than medicinal, work by an Italian author was *Epulario or the Italian Banquet*, translated into English in 1598. Two Venice editions of 1549 and 1562 reached England, plus two later versions of 1606 and 1649, all now in the British Library. It gave many readily understood recipes for meat, fish, pottage, and sweet tarts with egg and milk fillings or fruit. Reading this work, the English housewife must have been struck by the frequent use of cheese in cooking, whereas in England it was usually eaten cold and uncooked, and in consequence normally went unnoticed in the cookery books. Another surprise was a matter-of-fact reference to pasta, described on one page as a paste of flour and water, rolled around a staff, cut in pieces, and boiled in water or broth. It was entitled 'A devised meat after the Roman manner', and on another page the paste was to be broken into pieces and dried in the sun, after which it would keep for two or three years. The appearance of this book was one event that doubtless stirred the curiosity of Hugh Platt, for he in turn experimented and exchanged ideas with mariners seeking a food that would keep well on board ship. A further novel idea in this stimulating text was for mustard balls that could be dried and carried around as a ready flavouring for use wherever the jaded traveller found himself confronted with a dull, tasteless platter. The idea of having a portable spice has surfaced again recently in the work of a modern traveller describing his routines in remote regions; it makes one wonder if the drovers at some time also found it a useful and unobtrusive piece of baggage, to accompany the oatmeal that they generally carried in their pannier bags.[12]

The dominance of Italian authors on the food scene in England was strengthened in this period by the many English visitors to Italy, including those who studied medicine at the university of Padua. For them the connection between food, medicine and health was a major preoccupation. Remedies for the plague commended by Fioravanti were translated as *A Joyfull Jewell* in 1579, and since the definition of health extended to improving the memory, this concern resulted in another work by Gratarolus, translated in 1563 as *The Castel of Memorie*.[13]

Because books on health and food passed through so many editions, we can safely assume that some found readers beyond the circle of gentlemen and scholars. John Partridge, writing first in 1573 on *The Treasurie of Commodious Conceites and Hidden Secrets*, almost certainly as a physician, expected his advice on 'the good housewife's provision for the health of her household' to reach the wives of farmers and craftsmen, and since his book was reissued in 1580 and 1584 (this last being called the fourth edition), and yet again in 1586, 1591, 1594 and 1596, and since it cost a modest fourpence, the author's hopes were surely not altogether frustrated. When the work was enlarged in 1600, yet more editions followed, in 1627, 1633, 1637, 1653 and 1656.[14]

So far we have discussed food in its positive aspects, underlining an expanding array of ingredients made available by the growing volume of national and international trade. But pressure to find food from fresh sources also came from another direction. While this half century saw long spells of plentiful food, they were interrupted by crises when severe food shortage threatened local famines. One loud alarm had sounded in 1527, impelling Henry VIII's government under Wolsey to search out grain supplies all over the kingdom. Two worrying years in the 1550s, 1550 and 1556, prompted another search for food stocks, though on a more modest scale. After that, for almost 30 years no crippling harvest failure broke the calm and people were lulled into a sense of security. A whole generation became accustomed to adequate food supplies, until suddenly they were again brought up short. Serious harvest failures struck in 1585 and 1586, prompting sharp measures by the Privy Council in 1586 to supply cereals to needy areas. The crisis passed, but then returned more alarmingly with four consecutive years of bad harvests between 1594 and 1597, which proved traumatic. A national index shows deaths in 1597 rising by 52 per cent above average and births falling by 19 per cent; plainly starvation haunted many, many families. It set writers thinking on new lines. Their books actually discussed how to survive starvation, in novel ways that had not been discussed before. Hugh Platt published in 1596 *Sundrie New and Artificiall Remedies against Famine written ... uppon the Occasion of this Present Dearth*, in which he offered advice on making various plants palatable in emergency. Among those he named were beans, peas, beechmast, chestnuts, acorns and vetches, and his detailed instructions revealed his own many practical experiments, some of which were entirely sensible, like cooking out the bitterness of acorns before mixing the pulp with flour, grinding more bran into meal than was usual, or adding herbs to disguise a disagreeable taste. Richard Gardiner, a burgess and dyer of Shrewsbury, described in his treatise of 1599 how he had grown 700 close cabbages and carrots, and managed to feed poor people in his town for 20 days before the cereal harvest relieved their hunger.[15]

Henceforward, brassicas, and roots like turnips, carrots, parsnips and succory would be viewed in a fresh light, as the life-saving foods that could insure against starvation. People grew roots on dunghills outside London, and public officials urged local authorities to promote their growing by the poor. The well-to-do, in their turn, also heeded the importance of growing 'cabbages and roots' as an insurance against lean times, and looked more appreciatively at those vegetables. Characteristically, though, they sought out the improved varieties that were coming from the Continent, and made finicky choices about which variety they would serve to guests at their tables.

Meanwhile, hunger was pondered from another viewpoint by adventurers planning their voyages to the New World; we can be sure that the realities of starvation had become common talk among mariners who counted their good fortune in returning home alive in those years. William Vaughan, who actively promoted settlement in Newfoundland published one book of *Directions for Health* in 1600, which he greatly enlarged in 1617; in the second version he inserted a new section entitled 'Shew me a way to preserve my life if perhaps I be constrained to straggle in deserts'. Vaughan's ideas for meeting such perils were far from reassuring, but at least they set more people thinking and talking: chewing liquorice or tobacco was one suggestion; mixing suet with a pound of violet leaves was another (this was said to preserve life for ten days); sucking alum rolled in the mouth was alleged to keep you alive for a fortnight. This last was a piece of wisdom emanating from Turkey, showing over what long distances food information now travelled between inquisitive investigators.[16]

In the first half of the sixteenth century we noticed some authors exploring ways to ensure good health, but digressing now and then to remark on variant food customs in their experience. In the next 50 years, recorded views of the subject broadened greatly, partly because of the changing conditions of economic life and trade that spread so many new food experiences, and partly because people travelled more, and with the help of printed books were exchanging information and ideas in a new spirit of enquiry.

THE CONTEMPORARY VIEW

We should not then be surprised to encounter in 1587 someone writing a wide-ranging survey 'Of the Food and Drink of the English'. This was William Harrison, a long-time rector of Radwinter in Essex, next door to Saffron Walden. He gives a most illuminating picture of the general food scene, viewed by an intelligent observer who picked on the features that had struck him most forcibly in his lifetime, but he coloured them with some knowledge of the historic past. He spread himself boldly over a long period, starting from classical times, and continued through the early English period until the Normans. Finally, he reached his own day, when he screened his view through a national and then a social prism. He remarked usefully on differences between English, Welsh and Scottish eating habits. Then he focused on the food habits of the different social classes in England. Plainly, Harrison was most conversant with the life of London and the south-east. He had sat at the tables of noblemen, and he had also travelled. But despite his long life as a cleric, he showed little or no intimate knowledge of the lives of the poor.[17]

In arranging his topics for discussion, Harrison was not particularly logical, for he left bread and beer to the end. But both did ultimately receive detailed attention, the varied mixes in bread flour and the size of loaves being set out with some care, while on the preparation of beer he filled nearly five pages. Seemingly this was because he had a maltster at one elbow and his wife at the other, the latter insisting that he include details of her careful routine in the preparation of her household brew. Beer brewing generally will be discussed below. What is important here is the glimpse of one person's survey of food and drink in general, representing the verdict of a thoughtful scholar, knowing most about southern England but with a care to particularize as well as generalize.[18]

Harrison was struck, not to say oppressed, by the quantity and variety of meats, including wildfowl, plus fish, seen at the tables of the nobility in his day. If the diner had eaten something of everything, he said, he would have yielded to 'a conspiracy ... for the speedy suppression of natural health'. In practice, of course, no one ate from every dish on the table, and Harrison explained that the sumptuous spread sprang from the need to be sure that all members of large households, plus all the unexpected guests ('many times unlooked for', he noted) received enough to eat. At the end nothing was wasted, for the leftovers went to the poor.[19]

On meat, Harrison showed a prejudice against the meat of wild animals, ranking it in nourishment below that of tamed farmhouse animals. We have noticed this prejudice already in another writer's reference to tame versus wild pigeons. Harrison would cheerfully have banned the keeping of deer and rabbits, thus repeating one opinion, on rabbits, at least, that had been expressed in a disquisition by Christopher Langton in 1550. Langton, however, had such highly individual views on many other foods as to put him in a class of his own. But adverse opinions on wild meat were not uncommon, contrasting with another, also current, and held by Thomas Moufet, for example, positively relishing the taste of meat from totally wild creatures. They underline just one of many sharply conflicting opinions on food at this time, dispelling any notion of our finding one hardened majority viewpoint. A commercializing food market was striving to secure larger quantities of food to serve more people, and some new practices among provision merchants were fostering new prejudices or hardening old ones. Ambivalence towards wild versus tamed meat was one of several controversial topics in this period, serving to light up commercial pressures in the background. We are thoroughly familiar with the same circumstances in our own day, and can readily imagine the scene.[20]

Descending the social scale, Harrison grouped the diets of gentlemen and merchants together; plainly he was thinking of substantial London merchants rather than provincial ones. Both groups fed very well, in his view, seeking out dainty foods from all over the country, and decorating their tables with all kinds of fanciful confections. They did exercise moderation, however, restricting the number of dishes at one meal, and reducing them further when dining at home without visitors; this group did not expect guests every day of the year. Next he named artificers and husbandmen, both, he said, needing food that could be procured and cooked quickly. Clearly, Harrison was not totally remote from the practicalities of working people's lives. Artificers' wives bought in the market, but used as much as possible from what they had to hand on their land or could be gathered free. But on convivial occasions, both groups were as generous as their means allowed, and they rose to the occasion magnificently when celebrating such events as bride-ales and the churching of women. Of the poor Harrison had almost nothing to say, deciding that they had no regular routine but ate and drank whenever and wherever the chance came. The poorest of all, of course, were regularly on the road, begging at doors.[21]

Harrison saw the world as consisting, for the most part, of reasonable people who ate with restraint, resisted excesses, and did not linger long hours at the table forever eating. He recognized that in our cool climate, compared with some other countries, the English needed more food than others, especially in the winter. Beyond this satisfied verdict, Harrison gives glimpses of further assumptions and changing perceptions of the kind that are generally difficult to recover from the past when so much of daily life was simply taken for granted. The first to deserve closer investigation concerned dairy products.[22]

Harrison believed that dairy foods had once been the mainstay of British diet, but now had been socially downgraded, being regarded as food 'appurtenant only to the inferior sort'. The wealthy ate all kinds of meat and fish, but this trend had developed, he claimed, along with a great rise in the price of dairy products. This to us seems an odd conjunction of economic facts; it may be possible, however, with the historian's hindsight, to weave them into a more complex tapestry of other current changes of which Harrison was not fully aware.[23]

The main farming effort in Harrison's day was concentrated on producing more cereals for bread and more meat. So a comparative neglect of dairying as the population rose might sufficiently explain the rising price of dairy goods. A supplementary reason would be general price inflation, which was substantial in Harrison's day, and could account in part for Harrison's words claiming that dairy produce was 'never so dear as in my time'. But at the same time we should notice that Harrison lived in Essex, where dairying was a speciality. Essex looks across to the Netherlands where dairying was a markedly expanding branch of commerce. Moreover, Harrison was aware of an accelerating pace of commercial dealings in butter, the buttermen coming to farmhouse doors 'faster than they can make it', he asserted. Indeed, he had seen the price of a gallon of butter rise from 18d. to 3s. 4d. and even 5s., and attributed this to the dealings transacted on farms rather than in markets, by which free competition was suppressed. In the face of these Essex experiences, the most convincing explanation for Harrison's remarks about high prices may well lie in the emerging first signs of a transformation of the dairy market, now beginning to get under way in London, and already affecting Essex. It would spread in the seventeenth century and affect many other regions, resulting in much differentiation in the qualities and flavours of dairy foods, and affecting both rich and poor. When Harrison described dairy produce as the food of the poor, he was voicing the current conventional view, but in fact fashions were changing on his very doorstep, and would come clearer after 1600. By the later seventeenth century, complaints about the machinations of wholesalers of cheese and butter would reverberate in Parliament and lead to corrective legislation.[24]

Evidence at this same period gives several other glimpses of new trends affecting dairy foods. The rising demand for cheese must have increased the quantity of whey the poor always drank, to their benefit; it was something farmers gave away without charge, thinking it worthless waste from the dairy. Cheese, on the other hand, which had hitherto been a poor man's food, had become expensive. How then could the poor any longer afford it? Considerable differences in price between soft and hard cheeses explain in part how the poor managed to eat it cheaply, probably eating more of the soft cheese quickly prepared, while the rich ate the hard, long-maturing cheeses that cost more. As for the price rise, fashion also partly explains it. A taste developed among the rich for fancy cheeses, especially if they were brought from far away. The Privy Council, which was composed of the highest dignitaries in the land and met for dinner in law terms in Star Chamber, saw no cheese on the menu in 1567. But by 1590 a change in attitude had begun. Three Cheshire cheeses were served in Michaelmas term, four unnamed cheeses were bought for Trinity term in 1602, and more for Michaelmas term in 1605. Among foreign kinds Angelot cheeses from France, or English copies of them, were particularly modish. So were 'Holland cheeses': the Earl of Rutland's household accounts show payment to Mr Peet's son in 1600 for bringing two cheeses out of the Low Countries. As the Earl had gone to the Netherlands in May 1600, we may guess that he took a fancy to what he tasted there. Other remarks, recorded below, show the esteem in which all hard cheeses from Holland and France were coming to be held among the well-to-do.[25]

More butter-eating was also creeping in as a fashion, and, as we have noticed already in recording Andrew Boorde's comments, it was explicitly attributed to the example set by the Dutch. Judging by the quantities of butter featuring in the accounts of manorial households, gentry families made their own butter in summer but in winter bought in extra supplies from local family farms, where it was a speciality. The difficulty of keeping it fresh meant that quality varied. We can reasonably guess, then, that the poor quality reached the poorest; and since some writers gave instructions on how to disguise a sour taste, we can be sure that a poor quality was always on sale somewhere. Rancid butter was the very worst, and was sold to grease wheels.

Regional differences in the dairying scene became more conspicuous at this time of change, and one of these is highlighted across Essex and Norfolk. A number of Dutch immigrants, fleeing religious persecution in their homeland, settled in the east and south-east of England. We can readily imagine them among those mentioned by Harrison joining in the clamour for butter at the doors of dairy farms in Essex. But at much the same date a different situation prevailed in Norfolk. In 1567 one Flemish settler in Norwich wrote to his wife in Ypres telling her how his fellow countrymen were making their own butter, 'for here it is all pig's fat'. If he really was well informed on what his English neighbours were eating and selling, then plainly he was standing on the threshold of a major change in cooking habits in the Norwich area; a generation later, butter would come to play a much larger role in diet.[26]

Some regional differences that thrust themselves on our notice here will be stressed again and again in this book, for diversity was increasing. Yet it has left few signposts in our documents. It makes all generalizations hazardous and every single one is likely to be audacious and imperfect. Our Flemish commentator on Norwich people's food habits would tempt us to dub East Anglia an immature dairying area, but, in fact, at least in central Suffolk, this was assuredly not the case. It already boasted some dairies that were as professionally specialized as those in Essex. Evidence comes from a remarkable, indeed unique, narrative, published in 1588, the date itself offering another sign of rising commercial interest in dairying at this time, as Harrison hinted. An account of dairying procedures was inserted as an annexe to a wholly different work – a translation from the Italian, by an unknown author named T. K., of Torquato Tasso's *Householder's Philosophy*. Tasso's main subject was 'The True Economy and Form of Housekeeping', giving advice on aspects of family life. The dairy book comes as a total surprise at the end of such a masculine text, being a dialogue between a Hampshire woman and one Bartholomew Dowe, a resident in Hampshire for some 47 years who had been born in Suffolk. Dowe proves to be one of the most sympathetic spokesmen of his age, strenuously denying any desire to teach experienced dairywomen how to keep a herd of cows. But, as he explained to his readers, he was an old man, lacking the strength for physical labour, yet not wishing to be idle. So he responded to his neighbours who 'earnestly' plied him with questions about dairying practices that he had watched as a child in Suffolk. Some full and circumstantial answers ensued.[27]

Bartholomew Dowe's mother, with her milkmaids, had once upon a time managed more than 140 cows, reckoning that each maid could handle 20 cows. His questioner was astonished at so few maids to so many cows; they must have been 'very long in doing', she said, for in Hampshire they always reckoned on a maximum of eight to nine cows per maid. But the Suffolk dairymaids rose before 4 a.m. every day, and so even on Sunday they arrived at church as early as everyone else. The Hampshire women were learning the first of many instructive lessons. Responding to the dairywoman's persistent enquiries, Dowe described the special features of Suffolk's cheese presses, salting troughs and churns (all slightly different in form, and for good reasons), their method of milking the cows (quickly and forcefully to produce thicker milk and more cream), the churning of the butter (it must be a continuous effort without a break), the several changes of cloth-wrapping needed for the cheese, and the supreme importance of cleanliness. In response to one question he agreed that a dairy house should have a chimney, for it was essential to have hot water at hand to clean all vessels. A picture emerged of highly professional women in the dairying district of central Suffolk, closely watched by this young boy with a keen memory. He never made butter or cheese himself, he insisted, but he memorized many details, and here he faced Hampshire women hungry for tips to help them in their own dairies.[28]

The ways in which practical skills in food preparation and cooking spread across regions come vividly to life in these brief exchanges between Suffolk and Hampshire. Chronologically, they tell a slowly developing story, for it turns out that Katherine Dowe was the chief dairy woman at Sibton Abbey, near the market town of Saxmundham, from 1507 until at least 1513. She started with 66 cows and ended with 140, as her son averred. Young Dowe evidently then went to farm in Hampshire and built up more experience: he learned, for example, that some cows liked dairymaids to sing to them while they milked; he had known one cow that stubbornly refused to be milked by anyone other than her regular singing maid. Now in the 1580s Hampshire women were pressing to know more of dairying practices elsewhere. The consequences can be judged by the first half of the seventeenth century, when butter and cheese were markedly prominent in some Hampshire farmers' probate inventories, which listed their stocks in hand at death.[29]

Thus Harrison first sheds light on an aspect of a changing world of food in this half century, and on closer investigation yields precious local detail. But still the picture is partial. Much clearer evidence in the seventeenth century will trace dairying developments when they had become inescapably obvious. Meanwhile, other changes in food habits were gestating, prompting some forceful comments from Harrison concerning the eating of herbs, roots and fruits. He believed them to have been grown and eaten in plenty in the late thirteenth to early fourteenth centuries, then neglected until the beginning of the sixteenth century, around 1510; in the intervening period they had come to be regarded as food suitable only for pigs and wild animals. Now, however, they had turned extremely fashionable; they were served as dainty dishes at the tables of merchants, gentry and nobility, who obtained seeds for their gardens from abroad, and were even venturing to eat aubergines and mushrooms. The particular vegetables and fruits named by Harrison were melons, pumpkins, gourds, cucumbers, radishes, skirret, parsnips, carrots, cabbages, turnips and all kinds of salad herbs. The beginning of this trend was dated in Henry VIII's reign, and we have already noticed the evidence confirming the truth of that judgement. Harrison had seen the transformation of gardens as a result, especially in London, and our historians have since sketched in further detail from the record of some great houses with gardens, refurbished or new built. The purchase of seeds from abroad was one of the foreign influences that drove this horticultural revolution. But it also involved the hiring of many foreign gardeners to work in great houses, who introduced ever more sophisticated gardening techniques. Peaches and apricots were ripened against sheltered, even artificially warmed walls; ambitions ran even higher in the competitive world of aristocrats tending gardens that one day expected a visit from Queen Elizabeth; they needed to shine more brightly than any she had visited before.[30]

In the midst of all this gardening effort, Harrison judged the old style of garden as 'a dunghill' when compared with standards achieved in his day. His strong words underline the refining process in horticulture that had gathered such speed since 1550. We shall see it reflected in household accounts discussed below, and in the recipe books. But at this point we must turn from Harrison as our prime informant to read other writers of this time who expressed appreciation of other aspects of their food.[31]

Harrison said nothing about the subtlety of flavours that people enjoyed when so many foods of the same kind now came from different countries and regions of countries. The gourmets, however, were constantly being provoked to discriminate. One eloquent spokesman on this score was Henry Buttes, who became Master of Corpus Christi College, Cambridge in 1626 and Vice Chancellor of the university in 1629. He published a witty book about food in 1599, *Dyets Dry Dinner*, which described his many likes and dislikes. Surveying prunes, for example, it was those from Damascus that were most commended, though the French prune was acknowledged to be much in request in England for special use, he said, though he did not say what that use was. He differentiated the dates of Egypt and Judea from those of Italy (where they never ripened properly), and from coastal Spain (where they were sour and unsavoury). Spanish olives were bigger than Italian; and the best capers came from Geneva. (Surely he meant Genoa?) Moufet was similarly fussy about English flavours, contrasting that of salmon caught in the Upper Severn with that from the Lower Severn; the fish caught high up the river were the best.[32]

Flavours in food were being made yet more subtle and varied by the pressing of oils from plants and by distillation to intensify them. Male apothecaries remained in charge of medicinal preparations for sale, but a zest for this activity manifested itself on the domestic front and became a task firmly allotted to women. Purchases of rosewater and sweet waters were invariably attributed in household records to mistresses rather than the masters, and by the second half of the seventeenth century some women were paying enormous attention to distilling and storing large numbers of essences.

The aspect of this trend that was distinctly innovative in this period concerned the recovery of oil from plants, a quiet development that got under way without any clear statement at this stage of its prime purpose. It was fairly certainly sparked off by irksome shortages of olive oil, used in the first instance to serve industrial needs, notably in the processing of woollen cloth. The publication of a book in 1551 on 'a lately invented oil' is a sign of thoughts stirring on the subject, and it was followed by two more books on oils, by Francis Cox in 1575, and in the same year John Hester's *True and Perfect Order to Distill Oyles out of all Manner of Spices, Seeds, Rootes and Gummes*. These two works appeared shortly after the first signs appear in our records of rape being grown as an oil crop, in the 1560s, again responding to the need for an industrial oil. In the event, it was rapeseed that achieved the best success when grown by the Dutch in the newly drained fens. That development benefited from French skills in the use of oil mills, of which one model was imported from France expressly for use in the finishing of cloth. So industrial uses seem to have stimulated these first efforts. Then oil from olives began to be used in salads, copying the eating habits seen in Italy, and rapeseed oil thereafter found its way into the kitchen. Apart from London, towns like Wisbech in Cambridgeshire were fairly certainly the first users of rapeseed oil in cooking, for a notable number of oil mills were early concentrated in fenland areas that were growing rape. By 1660 that high-class cook, Robert May, was using rapeseed oil for deep frying fish, and later still it was used in quantity to pickle cucumbers.[33]

Stillhouses became a routine facility in manor houses, adding a further refinement to the preparation of medicine and food, aided by published books of guidance. The purchase of new equipment featured often in household accounts: the Shuttleworths near Wigan sent to Manchester for their 'stillatory'; the Earl of Rutland at Belvoir sent to Nottingham for glasses to distil waters, and to Newark for further items to make damask water. (He paid for his herbs to be gathered in July 1540, and received from Lady Markham distilled waters as a gift in 1541.) Especially informative was John Partridge's book, *The Treasurie of Hidden Secrets* (1600), which gave precise rules about the gathering of herbs and the setting up of the still: do not wash the herbs, he said, just wipe them dry, and make sure your still is very clean.[34]

HOUSEHOLD ACCOUNTS

Information, now sometimes appearing generously in household accounts, encourages us to scrutinize them intently for more detail about the domestic food scene, day in, day out. We may also perhaps discern some of the effects of fashion, for it was only partially disseminated by the books. The accounts do not, of course, relate to ordinary families; they were kept only by nobility and gentry, and not until a later date by hands-on farmers. But even so, much can be learnt indirectly about the facilities for shopping, routines for ensuring home-grown supplies, and cooking procedures; the kitchen of the manor house was not a closeted, secret place: ordinary folk were resident servants eating every meal under the same roof as their masters. Other servants lived out but came into the manor house to prepare and cook food for their grand neighbours; and when they themselves bought food, some of it came from the same markets as those of the gentry. So all classes shared to some extent in the dealings that were the routines of the age, and all would adopt and adapt some of the practices seen in their neighbours' homes. We can build up some details with regard to regional preferences and the availability of certain foods, despite the fact that ordinary folk never wrote a word about their diet.

For the later sixteenth century household accounts survive for the Earl of Derby at Knowsley in Lancashire, and a fine set for the Earl of Rutland at Belvoir Castle in Leicestershire. Robert Dudley, Earl of Leicester, has left us so-called household accounts but these give hardly any glimpse of a domestic scene, showing rather how much of his life was spent gadding about between royal palaces, staying in other people's houses, eating out, and paying for his servants to find their meals somewhere else. Gifts of food were presented to him as to all noblemen and gentlemen, but we can only guess what he did with them; perhaps he passed them to whichever hostess was closest at hand. A much more revealing household account derives from a gentry family of Lancashire, the Shuttleworths at Gawthorpe. They did not live a showy life, but ate well, show signs of being affected by some fashions (they took pride in building themselves a new house at the end of this period) and, fortunately for us, they employed painstaking stewards to keep their records. Meat, fish, cereals and drink feature conspicuously in the record for, despite being home produced, they were mixed with a considerable quantity of bought items. Some of the less frequent purchases were of vegetables, fruits, eggs and dairy produce, and that is why those items raise so many questions about their place in diet. But the truth is that they were all partly produced on the estate and partly not. Seasonal shortages were filled by buying in, but as far as possible the household relied on food that came to hand without spending money.

One significant fact is noticeable among the items for occasional purchase (vegetables, fruit, eggs and dairy foods); they were mostly produced and traded by women. So, when bought, they were acquired not through an organized structure of markets that lay in men's hands, but through women's much more informal associations. In many cases in the country they were neighbourly arrangements, and in nearly all cases they reflected the small scale of business favoured by women. This conclusion is markedly obvious in the record of a major feast at Oxford in 1570, when Robert Dudley, Earl of Leicester, was Chancellor of the University. Male suppliers were named for flour, beer and wine. But when it came to the butter, seven different women furnished separate qualities and quantities, ranging from 28lbs to half a pound, another three supplied cream and milk, while eggs came from two women, 250 eggs in one case, 32 in another. Just as eggs were women's concern, so was the supply of poultry. To obtain ten capons four women were called on, and similarly to get chickens and pigeons. The contrast between the scale of women's and men's dealing was not absolute; Mrs Cogene sold butter, turkeys, peacocks and fat mallards. But others conformed to the pattern. Nor were all the women based in Oxford: Goodwife Peers sent two capons from the village of Radley; Goodwife Addowes sent chickens from the village of Kennington; the home of some butter wives was not stated, but their milk had to come from cow herds living in fields, so they too came from within Oxford or villages around.[35]

So the meagreness of the details in household accounts about the source of eggs, dairy goods, vegetables and fruit has not one but two explanations. Much was produced on the estate. When it was not, then local women came to the rescue, but by a male convention these foods were ranked as secondary, and the record was minimal and informal. Significant changes were under way, however, in the London area, giving special significance to William Harrison's general comment on the accelerated pace of trading. It brought benefits, he believed, 'for the better furtherance of the commonwealth'. We would use another form of words, describing it as 'the commercialization of food'. Men were intruding on the butter market in London, supplanting the women, and as trading horizons expanded, merchants established contacts with a wider world, not just in London but also overseas. The more commercialized structure of the market for dairy produce eventually became clear, and historians have explored it in recent studies. Even then, it was not always the dominant form in more distant parts of the country.[36]

What basic foods, then, decked the tables of nobility and gentry in the half century 1550–1600? Harrison was conscious of merchants searching all over the place for tasty delicacies and novelties: they hunted out 'all the secret corners of our forests for venison, of the air for fowls, and of the sea for fish'. They sought new-fashioned wines in Spain, Italy, Greece, even Africa and Asia, thereby lowering current satisfaction with French wines. Harrison, anchored in the south-east, was acutely conscious of a changing scene. But when focusing rather on regional diets elsewhere, what do household accounts reveal about all this?[37]

We take bread first. The favourite bread among all the rich was manchet, made with the finest white flour. This fancy for the whitest possible bread even influenced the choice of wheat variety, for some produced a yellow or reddish meal. But in the household of the Earl of Derby we find that ordinary bread was made of equal quantities of wheat and barley, and his domestic regulations actually specified that these two cereals should be 'mingled together indifferently'. Only when the earl was at home was manchet made; it disappeared when he was absent. The Shuttleworths were slightly lower in the scale of landowners, and though they also lived in Lancashire, they had different preferences. The content of their bread was not precisely explained, but their home-grown cereals were almost entirely oats and barley. When meal was mentioned it seems to have been oatmeal. Occasional small purchases of wheat bread were a deliberate decision, but apparently only when visitors were staying. Signs of wheat being grown or bought were few, so that everything suggests the family's adherence to Lancashire's local traditions, eating oatcake, oatbread and barley bread.[38]

As for meat, every household account shows what a remarkable variety its residents enjoyed, just as Harrison had asserted. Meat followed a seasonality of supply that brought far more variety than anything familiar nowadays. The home farm yielded much, and gifts from friends and neighbours flowed in all the year round. Additional purchases were made locally. There was absolutely no sign as yet that the beef of old England was the meat favoured above all others. It is true that André Simon, when analysing the meals served to Privy Councillors in Star Chamber at Westminster between 1567 and 1605, judged that more beef was provided than any other meat. But that was far from being the typical domestic scene. At Belvoir the Earl of Rutland was served from a magnificent array running far beyond the usual meat of cattle and sheep from his fields. He enjoyed venison, turkey, partridge, hare, capons, kids, swans, wildfowl and larks, and even when he was campaigning in Scotland his rank ensured that plenty of these succulent wild meats were brought to his tent. When he was in London, delicacies like baked stag and deer pasties were sent from Belvoir, and he even took the powdered (i.e. salted) carcase of an ox with him to the Netherlands. Was this to advertise English beef abroad, or only because a salted whole animal would travel best?[39]

The clearest picture of seasonal variety and family preferences comes from the Shuttleworth papers. Beef featured hardly at all in their diet; the listing of half a buttock of beef, bought in 1585, comes as a surprise. The family ate a lot of mutton and lamb, but seemingly an even greater quantity of veal, regularly buying a quarter, a half or a whole fat veal along with calves' heads and calves' liver. This meat was certainly not regarded as a penance since a fat calf was bought in December 1598 'against Christmas'. In the Earl of Derby's household, on the other hand, veal was reserved for occasions when the earl himself was at home or visitors arrived, and not when family members were few and were living more frugally. It may be that, unlike the Shuttleworths at Gawthorpe, this family (the Stanleys) at Knowsley were not living handily among small dairy farmers with a lot of calves for sale. But at one festivity, when Lady Strange was being churched after giving birth, 13 veal were bought in one week and seven in the next; plainly it was for them a celebratory meat, and one could get hold of it in bulk for special occasions. At Haddon Hall in Derbyshire, the Vernon family's accounts seem to mix the conventions of the Lancashire families. They bought in veal regularly between April and June, again almost certainly from local dairymen when they were selling their male calves, and they also celebrated at Christmas with veal.[40]

Dairying was a speciality of Lancashire, as commentators observed when commenting on its liking for milk gruels. The eating of veal, therefore, reflected sound practicalities. The dairy produced too many male calves to be fattened for beef, whereas they could be fed for a few weeks or months and profitably sold young. We shall encounter the practice spreading elsewhere in the later seventeenth century, as soon as dairying took firmer hold in other areas. It prompts reflection on the reason why the taste for veal later faded from England whereas it has remained strong on the Continent of Europe. Recently publicity was given to a farmer intent on reintroducing veal to our tables. He was, perhaps unwittingly, planning to revive a piece of long-forgotten English history that might have ended the killing of many calves at birth and the shipping of live ones overseas. But, sadly, veal continues to be a rare and expensive sight in the shops.

The Shuttleworths did not need to buy any pork since they fattened their own pigs at home, buying half a dozen in March or April. They were plainly pleased with the result, for a flitch of bacon and two pork gammons were sent to someone in London in May 1589. They also bought goslings to fatten, killing them as green geese when fed on summer pastures, or as stubble geese when fed on corn gleanings after harvest. Venison, rabbits, chickens and pigeons all featured on their table, while a first reference to the purchase of two turkeys and a hen in April 1592 raises the possibility that this was a new venture in their family's housekeeping.[41]

Wildfowl were regularly brought into Lancashire kitchens during the autumn and winter, and on one occasion in November 1588 a man was paid for the birds 'and his pains', possibly signifying a deliberate commission to shoot them. It points up in a fresh way how mistaken is the notion that fresh meat was never available in winter! Among the wildfowl that were plentiful on the moors and in the forests of the Pennines, a favourite was woodcock, which were trapped in nets in autumn. The calendar reminded when nets were to be repaired or newly bought in autumn, and woodcock pies and puddings were regularly sent to someone in London. Six puddings in May 1587 weighed 16lbs, and when the birds were sent uncooked, yards of canvas were bought to wrap them in. In September 1584 an ounce of pepper was packed for the cooking; evidently it had something special about it, but we do not know what.[42]

The variety of fish at these same tables matched the variety of meat, and it is more than likely that a careful scrutiny of the many fish eaten regionally and seasonally would produce a distinctive pattern. The Earl of Rutland had his own ponds and took great trouble to stock them. On one occasion, pike were brought from West Deeping in Lincolnshire, and bream and tench were 'rowed' from Crowland to Market Deeping and then put in a barrel to get them live to Belvoir. A pamphlet of 1615, *The Tide's Increase*, tells us that good fishing of cod and hake was had from the coast of Lancashire between Easter and Midsummer, and this should have benefited the Shuttleworth family. But these are not the fish named in their accounts. They received a lot of smelt caught in the Mersey (half a hundredweight was bought around March 1585): this fish was appreciated for its slight smell of cucumber. They also regularly tapped other sources for sea fish; they were always buying at Preston salt eels, red herrings, white herrings, cockles and mussels, as well as making occasional purchases at Bolton, Manchester, Wigan, and Bold on the Mersey. Sometimes they got men to catch freshwater fish for them for two days on end. Thus pike, bream and freshwater trout were bought, seemingly at Formby, in February 1596. The men took fish with a net from the dam, involving them in a trip that lasted two days and two nights.[43]

Visits to buy salt at Northwich in Cheshire were probably combined with some of these fish-buying trips, but the distances were modest compared with the trip to Stourbridge in Cambridgeshire, to which almost every substantial household resorted, no matter how far away they lived. Lord Derby patronized this fair for 'Lent stuff'. The Shuttleworths went to Stourbridge in September 1589, and the Earl of Rutland in October 1604. Others from February onwards observed their own convenient date in readiness for Lent, and ling, cod and stockfish were their standard purchases. When the Earl of Rutland made the singular choice in 1602 of getting his fish at King's Lynn, through the good offices of Mr Jessup of Grantham, we may wonder if plague had raised an alarm.[44]

The fourth basic ingredient among household needs was drink. My lord and his kin both at Belvoir and Gawthorpe drank a lot of wine, and most of all claret, but white wine and sack featured also in the Shuttleworths' purchases, carried from Chester or more often from London. Ale and beer were always brewed in house for the servants, and hops were bought from London. Lord Derby's beer and ale was made with barley and oat malt, a choice that was far from unusual all over England, and it was the Stanleys' custom to add a little ground wheat as well. Everyone had their special tricks of the trade, as we note in the case of Mrs William Harrison's instructions, while the choice of grain was constrained by the local farming regime.[45]

Under the heading of drink we must add distillations, although they were usually drunk at this date in modest amounts medicinally, or used sparingly for their aromatic flavours in food. The household accounts give tantalizing clues to the increasing vogue for sweet waters without proving absolutely that it was a new fashion. But we note that the Shuttleworths bought glasses in July 1589 to contain rosewater, and a 'stillatory' was specially ordered from Manchester in October 1590. Both events make a first appearance in the accounts at this time and tie in neatly with the modish interest seen elsewhere in the nineties for distillation.[46]

Vegetables, as explained above, made only a modest appearance in our accounts, for the gardens supplied most household needs, and hence neither the Earl of Rutland's papers nor those of the Earl of Derby vouchsafe any information. But in the case of the Shuttleworths the prominence of root rather than green vegetables is noticeable, and was almost certainly typical of all the northern counties. The Shuttleworths grew onions on a sufficient scale to sell some, and turnips and parsnips were two other favourites. Carrots appeared in their accounts only when they were in London: perhaps they savoured the improved varieties that had come in from the Netherlands? More intriguing is a reference to a maid bringing artichokes in August 1589, followed in April 1592 by artichoke slips being brought from London 'for my lady'. Did these represent an introduction to the family table after an encounter with metropolitan fashion? They were a novelty at court in Henry VIII's reign, and they may well have taken 50 years to spread successfully to the climate and soils of Lancashire.[47]

Similarly, it is possible that some of the fruits named in household expenditure in the nineties were a novelty. Apples and pears were familiar enough, and pucelle pears were an old Lancashire variety named casually in the accounts. Oranges evidently reached this part of Lancashire, though in small numbers only – in sixes or sevens, not in hundreds – but cherries could have been a special treat in July 1594, and possibly plums, or a new variety of them, in 1597 and 1598.[48]

Dairy produce presents another problem of qualitative change without offering any firm evidence in the accounts of the Earls of Derby and Rutland. Their families will almost certainly have relied on their own dairies. The Shuttleworths tell us more: they certainly had a dairy, but they seem to have engaged dairywomen on short-term contracts, for only a few weeks or for half a year extending over the summer months. It sounds like a logical system, winding down in the winter. They were clearly proud of their cheeses for they sent two to a brother in London in May 1588, and another four in March 1589. But production was calculated to meet normal domestic needs only, and after 1600, when great building work was under way, they had to buy in lots of butter and cheese, presumably to feed their hungry workers. We can guess that they were confident of a plentiful supply from all the family farmers in the neighbourhood.[49]

Other foodstuffs, which varied much more noticeably in importance between households, were spices, dried fruits and sugar. The Shuttleworths, like most gentry, got their spices from London, except on one occasion when someone was conveniently in Chester on another errand, and once when they bought in York, though they were probably chastened to find that the carriage home cost them 58s. 6d. Mustard seed, being a home-grown spice, was not a large purchase for them. Dried fruit was bought by the Shuttleworths in considerable quantity from London, especially currants – 18lbs at a time. Sugar also varied in importance in different families: the Shuttleworths never bought any sugar, but had hives and relied on honey. Only once did they buy treacle and since they also needed a pot to put it in, it sounds as though it was for them a novel experience. But in other families sugar was a major necessity, further confirmed for us by the very large quantities that were imported into London. It may be that sugar was much more entrenched in cooking in the south than in the north.[50]

RECIPE BOOKS

The first strivings towards the making of recipe books began in this period, but they were tentative and unsystematic. Notions of nourishment and medicine were so entangled with each other that most books mingled the two without a thought for any system of classification. Some gave far more attention to physic than food, though a careful search even through those books produces information on cooking customs, some of them unexpected, as well as hints about changing fashions.

An early hint of ideas on food and physic coming in from the Continent of Europe was offered by William Warde, already mentioned for translating the work of the Italian, Alexis of Piemount. Warde was translating from a French version, was aware of an existing Dutch translation, and was in touch with the author himself, and so supplemented his first translation in 1558 with more tips in 1562–3 and 1569. We are thus introduced to the network of physicians corresponding with each other across Europe, and can visualize the exchange of food fancies as well. Warde's prime concern was to make public more knowledge of the physic that used herbs, being evidently oppressed by the multitude of illnesses afflicting humanity in his day, and believing that more 'strange and unknown' diseases than ever before were circulating. Never before, he felt, had mankind had so much need of physic as now, a sentiment that would subsequently be expressed by others, and can now be validated by our own current experience. More people travelling across the world do, indeed, spread new and unfamiliar diseases.[51]

Although both Warde and Alexis of Piedmont were preoccupied with physic, *The Secrets* did offer practical help to the housewife in the kitchen. It confronted aspects of food preparation that later became significant main themes, some of them developing into high fashion. It gave advice on keeping meat fresh in summer by seething it first, potting it in vinegar with juniper seeds and salt, and keeping it in a cool cellar. More practical ways of preserving meat would be publicized later. It also urged gathering herbs and leaving them to dry in the sun, giving more emphatic and systematic attention to the right season for collecting them, and to collecting them in the right condition. Finally, in 1569, in the last addition to his translation, Warde referred to distillation, the making of comfits, and fanciful decorations with sugar paste – all tasks that would inspire great enthusiasm in kitchen quarters in subsequent decades.[52]

Among surviving books of English origin, the first to give recipes appeared some 15 years later in the 1580s, when food became a focus of special interest and alarm because of scarcity in 1586 and 1587. One example was *The Widowes Treasure* (1585), naming no author beyond saying that it had been written by a gentlewoman for her private use. It gave first place to medicines, to induce sleep, ward off plague, ease aching feet and so on, but other simple cooking directions were included that carry us straight into the kitchen of any ordinary housewife. Meat stews were cooked in a pot, using mutton or chicken, hare or rabbit. Fair water was used for the broth, with salt and pepper, adding root vegetables in winter (carrots were specifically named) and herbs in summer (those mentioned being hyssop, thyme and parsley). A stuffing was suggested for hare and rabbit, using dates, cream and sugar, but with other meats bread was the simpler choice for thickening the liquid. Verjuice or vinegar were sometimes used to sharpen the flavour. One of the most noticeable features of its otherwise straightforward meat dishes was the infrequent use of onions, vegetables which are constantly present under our cooking regime. The author gave a cake recipe that sounds odd for it began by baking the flour in the oven, but presumably that was in part at least designed to kill any weevils. After that the procedure was familiar enough, sieving the flour and mixing it with butter, sugar, cream and egg yolks, and adding flavourings of cloves, mace and saffron. The third interest in this book lay in preserving fruit: damsons and quinces by cooking them in sugar to make a syrupy purée; pears by drying.[53]

In another book of the 1580s a similar mixture of food and physic appeared, though it put food first and physic second. Its title gave its purpose clearly enough, *The Good Hous-Wives Treasurie, beeing a very Necessarie Booke Instructing to the*

Dressing of Meates (1588), and its first page more succinctly still abbreviated the title as *A Book of Cookrye*, though again no author was stated. This work showed its first concern for a good broth, a subject that loomed large with nearly all subsequent writers. It was started with a piece of beef, plus marrow from bones (a prized delicacy that was often served as a dish in its own right), dates, a flavouring of mace, pepper, salt and, if wanted, sugar, with verjuice as well, and possibly, but not necessarily, wine. The broth was thickened at the last moment with egg yolks. For white broth herbs from garden and field were the flavouring – endive, succory, marigolds, marjoram, parsley, thyme and rosemary – and again dates. Broth for fish used water and yeast with herbs, mace, and prunes, verjuice, vinegar and butter. Pies were on this author's menu for meat, fish and fruit, but with very slight clues to the content of the pastry, though more than one kind was envisaged, one being called florentine and rolled so thin that you could blow it up from the table; it sounds like filo pastry. Variety in meat included a haggis pudding, black pudding and sausages, and sauces were prepared to go with different meats.[54]

This author's choice of subjects was individual, for it included vinegar-making that was started by buying in six gallons of vinegar from St Katherines, adding elderflowers, putting fresh ones in each year while leaving the old, mixing in strong or small beer, and using old barrels and the remnants therein to accommodate it all. Outside London, housewives did not start making vinegar in this way. They began with their own sour wine or ale, using it for vinegar rather than throwing it away. But whatever the starting point, these details assure us that the flavour of vinegar in every household was distinctive. The distilling of rosewater was also explained in this book, and the resulting oils were expected to last two to three years. The next recipe was for cakes of damask or red roses, but they were not edible ones; they were aromatic cakes to lay between clothing in the cupboard, and they were expected to keep their fragrance for three or four years. The preserving of fruits was another major concern in this book, using a sugar syrup (one pound of sugar to one pound of fruit, the same proportion that we use for jam) to cook cherries, gooseberries, damsons, pears, plums, bullace, barberries, quinces and oranges. Distilled damask rosewater was added to the pears and red rosewater to the black plums and barberries. Sugar for the syrup had long been available in the markets, but this substantial section of the cookbook vividly conjures up for us the difference it made to housewives to have this simple means of preserving fruit through the winter. Most of us can only guess at the delicate flavours introduced by the use of distilled flower flavours. It is an art that has been continuously maintained over the centuries in countries like the Lebanon and Afghanistan, but that disappeared from England some time after the sixteenth century and was forgotten. Curiously, it is being practised again these days by a few connoisseurs, using lavender flowers in Provence, violets around Toulouse, and by one devotee in England using violets. So a fashion from the sixteenth century has returned again in the twenty-first century and, if it should get itself established, it will enable more of us to appreciate the subtlety of floral flavours known to our forebears.[55]

The foregoing books alert us to fruit preserving and flower fragrances in food as some of the keen interests of cookery writers in the 1580s. These were emphasized in a work by John Partridge entitled *The Treasurie of Commodious Conceites and Hidden Secrets Commonly Called the Good Huswives Closet of Provision for the Health of Her Household*. It is dated 1584, and is called the fourth edition, but only one earlier edition of 1573 was known to the bibliographer, Arnold Oxford, when compiling his bibliography of cookery books, and he did not explain where that copy lay. It passed through many more editions and its content was altered, so that this work is of special value in yielding clues to shifts of fashion in progress. Conserves, marmalades and sweet waters featured prominently in 1584, even though the book started conventionally with meat – baking a capon, a pheasant, chickens, woodcocks, making a sauce for rabbit, as used for Henry VIII, and baking ox tongue. Then Partridge moved swiftly to marzipan, vinegars of roses, violets and elderflowers, fruit preserving, sugar pastes and sweet waters from herbs, though without giving any instructions for distilling. The herbs and flowers were inserted in glass bottles and laid in the sun, and for vinegar they lay there all summer long. Another edition of 1600 rearranged and enlarged things and now started with marzipan, fruit cooking and preserving, vinegars and comfits, but this time, significantly, gave rules for distilling. This seems to mark the moment when housewives who already grew and collected herbs were officially welcomed into the stillroom. They were advised to use glass equipment, to take earthenware as second best, and avoid lead as the worst of all. More advice was given on timing when gathering herbs, and on selecting the best places. Herbs grown in fields were better than those grown in towns and gardens, and for medicines the best were to be found on hills in the fields. Physic was consigned to the end of the book, and recipes for everyday food disappeared. It would be interesting to examine yet more editions of Partridge in the 1630s, but by the time of the 1659 edition, when the subject matter of the book ostensibly remained the same, the advice on herb gathering survived, but the rules for distilling had gone. Judging by other evidence in the 1650s, it seems that women continued to prepare physic and some perhaps had a stillroom, but the excitement of distilling as a household novelty had evaporated.[56]

A better-organized, more balanced recipe book, published in the 1590s, was *The Good Huswifes Handmaide for the Kitchen* (1594), giving a fairer conspectus of a whole variety of foods, prepared without great extravagance. Admittedly, the cook used dried fruits and bought spices freely but these were well within the purse of housewives of the middling sort in London. They could always buy small quantities: cloves cost about 5d. an ounce, but they weigh so little that you got a large number for one ounce; currants only cost between 4d and 6d a pound, and raisins and prunes cost about the same. As for the country housewife, she could adapt these recipes readily using the stock of plants and fruits from her own garden and neighbourhood. In other respects, she would have found all the recipes entirely practical.[57]

The most favoured meat in this housewife's kitchen was mutton and lamb; beef was unusual, and capon and veal came somewhere in between. Most of the vegetables were thoroughly familiar, like turnips, carrots, colewort and cabbage, and there is one reference to spinach, a vegetable that had become known only in the past 30 years or so. Herbs for boiled mutton were described as 'any kind that may serve', conjuring up the style of a resourceful cook using what came to hand without searching far afield or spending any money. Parsley and fennel roots were used, endive, borage and lettuce, plus other herbs expected to be grown in the garden or found growing wild. Sometimes meat quantities were extended by turning them into stuffings or cooking the same stuffing mixture separately in a bag, and for a broth the flavour was sharpened with ale, verjuice or vinegar more often than with wine. Sometimes the old-fashioned trencher survived in the serving of what were called 'sops', moist mixtures of vegetables with sour fruit like gooseberries, laid on a bread or toasted base before the main meat was placed on top. Meat roasted on a spit was served with tasty sauces.[58]

Recipes that used calves' and pigs' feet, tripe and salted beef featured along with the joints and whole capons, and dried fruits were routinely mixed together with herbs as a flavouring in the one dish. The value of wild birds, especially woodcock, and of rabbits for meat in winter was underlined in the assertion that both were at their best from October until Lent. For us it is an important reminder of all the meats that were free to anyone who made the effort to catch them.[59]

Pastry featured in some recipes, encasing meat, fish and fruits, but again with no directions to suggest that any firm rules for making pastry were as yet generally recognized. Sometimes the flour and butter were mixed with ale, or almond water or salad oil, rather than water, and whole eggs or egg yolks were generously used as well; one recipe used four handfuls of fine flour and twelve egg yolks, with saffron, but no butter. These instructions were the forerunners of far more precise pastry recipes that would appear in recipe books in the course of the seventeenth century. Only then would notions of conformity in kitchen practice take stronger hold.[60]

Fruits like apples, pears, quinces and oranges (with a single peach recipe) were either stewed on their own or put into pies in this recipe book. Even medlars and rosehips were put into tarts. Cooked cheese (Banbury cheese) also featured in a tart, betokening perhaps the middle-class origins of this author, who had forsaken the prejudices against cheese of some of his contemporaries. Several milky dishes were to make manchet bread. A recipe for shortcake relied, like *The Widowe's Treasure*, on baking the flour first in the oven.[61]

Another author in the same decade was Thomas Dawson, who published *The Good Housewife's Jewel* (1596–7), using earlier books without acknowledgement, but adding his own touches that help us build up a firmer notion of standard cooking routines. He allows us to understand why so much paper was bought for kitchen use. Not only were cake mixtures laid on paper, with metal shapes on top to keep them enclosed, but paper was wrapped around parts of joints that were in danger of burning in front of an open fire or on the spit-ends of joints. Some meat was so finely chopped or pounded, it must have entailed very long, hard labour in the kitchen. But it is noticeable how the majority of meat meals went into earthen pots with a variety of green vegetables, roots and flavourings. In other words, the kitchen hob would have looked much the same to a visitor today, whether entering a mansion or cottage. A pottage would be cooking, which could be dressed up or down.[62]

The first move for Dawson in preparing dinner required the making of a broth, and again it did not necessarily include onions. Green leaves were separately distinguished, as endive, cabbage, lettuce, spinach and sorrel, these being among the most common. Carrots, turnips and parsnips were the usual roots, less often skirret. The meats were more varied than we eat nowadays, and included the entrails of animals, and some bone marrow. Juan Vives's *Dialogues* had bewailed the careless cooks who did not seal up the ends of bones, thus allowing the bone marrow to boil out. Herbs and spices were mixed in the same dish, where we would nowadays keep the flavours separate. The books already summarized above prepare us for the commonest herbs named here: thyme, rosemary, marjoram, pennyroyal, hyssop, savory and sage. The recurring spices, apart from salt and pepper, were ginger, mace, cloves, cinnamon, nutmegs and, much the most expensive, saffron. Liquids in broth were vinegar and verjuice and if these were too acid, then sugar remedied them. The blood of the meat was saved and used. Many separated egg yolks and whites were needed for different purposes: yolks thickened the mixture; whites were used to clarify; once they were used here to line a bladder so that they would set hard and give a white egg shape to a stuffing – fanciful cooking, indeed, for 'a good housewife'. Yeast was used noticeably in some fish broths, as when cooking pike, for example. Salt was most often mentioned by Dawson towards the end of cooking rather than at the beginning, but in the use of butter, he was no different from the rest, using it lavishly to melt in a flavoured broth, 'half a dish' being a common quantity. In a pie this would set firmly when cold, and by sealing the contents from contact with the air it allowed the pie to keep for some time.[63]

Sharp fruit, such as barberries, gooseberies and green grapes, was regularly used in meat dishes by this author, but he also used dates, currants, prunes and raisins. Lemons and oranges were expected to be always at hand. His meat was regularly served 'on sops'. In other words, the contents of the pot gave a moist mixture that was put on the bread trencher, which soaked up the juices before the meat was laid on top. In baking a red deer, Dawson part-cooked it, and then put it in a 'coffin', a pastry case oozing with butter; in this, it cooked in the oven all night. Vinegar was poured in the morning to neutralize some of the fat, and it was ready to eat for dinner that day. Not all pastry cooked for so long was destined to be eaten by illustrious guests; it may well have been passed to the poor at the gate. Rye was often the cereal chosen for such pastry since it kept well. A neat's tongue, for example, was baked in rye pastry, and was in the oven for four hours, when vinegar was poured in and the pastry closed for longer cooking. Some dishes cooked for many hours on a slow heat, sometimes for as much as 24 hours in what was effectively a steamer. They required their water to be topped up at intervals as it boiled away, leaving us to picture the poor soul who slept fitfully in the kitchen that night.[64]

The meats in Dawson's book showed, like the others already inspected here, a preference for mutton and lamb and little reference to beef, except for some beef sausages that used salted beef. This accords with another comment at this period that more mutton than beef was being eaten, a fact of life that one might have guessed in any case, since sheep farming was deemed at this time so much more profitable than cattle, and so much public outcry centred on enclosures for sheep. Dawson's so-called steaks turned out to be of mutton and not beef.[65]

Like the other authors already mentioned, Dawson was intent on preserving fruit such as pears, apples, damsons, cherries, strawberries and rosehips, and a whole section of his book was devoted to this subject. But he conformed to the usages of his time in paying small heed to cooked cheese, save in one recipe for fish days when he rolled out pastry as a base, put vegetables and eggs on top and allowed for 'a little cheese fine scraped'.[66]

True to current form, Dawson's way with pastry was not carefully described when he was making 'fine paste': it was a mixture of wheat flour, egg yolks and butter, without any clue to quantities. But he did give a more helpful account of puff pastry that described the many rollings and foldings that were required. Having started his book conventionally with meat, Dawson then let his subjects escape any orderly scheme, in order to accommodate points of husbandry for husbandmen, medicines and ointments, and distillations.[67]

CONCLUSION

In the period between 1550 and 1600, recipe books became more familiar, but none yet followed an orderly or comprehensive plan. When surveying them all, we may be emboldened to separate old cooking conventions from incipient change, but without placing too much faith in their validity, here, there or anywhere. Individualism reigned among women in the kitchen even while they constantly borrowed recipes from each other and passed them on to friends; our examples are far too few and the background too hazy to allow us to pronounce confidently on any current fashions. Yet we know that they would have been instantly recognizable to diners when sitting down as guests at someone else's table.

Where we can be confident is in saying that the world was changing around our cooks in the kitchen. Their news of food, of access to it, their sight of it in the market, and their ingrained attitudes towards it were all undergoing a subtle transformation. People living in London caught first sight of the latest opportunities and gimmicks. If you visited London occasionally, then you noticed some of them too and they might alter your shopping and cooking routines: you might start to buy sugar, or more sugar than before, in order to preserve fruit for the winter; you might give your family a taste of Banbury cheese that was now often cited for its good reputation; or you might buy some cherry tree stocks for your orchard. You did not need to belong in the gentry class, by the way, to have a modest orchard: many parsons as well as farmers had them, and so did smallholders in a favoured county like Kent. At the same time, another substantial section of the population dwelling far from London lived unaware of this changing scene, content with its old eating habits and relishing its local specialities.

A highly diversified picture, in short, comes closer to reality than any generalization aspiring to describe one English diet. But we can add refined shading to every single scene by pointing out the beginnings of new trends, even though they were only scattered here and there – in eating and cooking cheese, say, in buying imported fruit, in growing certain vegetables with more deliberation, or sprinkling oil on salads. The spread of these practices was totally haphazard, starting from gossip in the alehouse, a traveller's casual comments at an inn, or an initiative launched in the house of the manorial lord after the family had been travelling elsewhere. Thus people who never set eyes on Thomas Dawson's recipe book might still see and taste skirret for the first time. It was destined to become a candied delight in the seventeenth century. They might watch pastry being made with many eggs instead of just butter, and wonder which was best. Experiments afoot would by the 1630s cause one commentator to complain about everything in his day being wrapped in pastry. Or they might be struck by the many comfits newly displayed in London shops. These sugary sweetmeats were already known by name in the 1480s but now they were seen more frequently because Spanish confectioners had arrived to demonstrate the Moorish way with them. Variations in the dissemination of general food knowledge alongside eccentric cooking habits can only be guessed at. But as books multiplied and ideas spread more vigorously, they spread information about food, and that was one prerequisite for a little more conformity between regions and classes. What we can see clearly is incipient change.

4

Science and the Search for Food, 1600–40

The food scene in the 40 years between 1600 and 1640 wore yet another face, taking on features that distinguished it significantly from the period between 1550 and 1600. Some fresh currents of thought figured prominently in discussions among thinkers, gossips and writers, meeting from time to time in London, while some older interests were infused with a new liveliness as the study of ways to health and the actual tasting of more varied foodstuffs enthused people and stimulated their efforts to search for more. As before, our sources of information show us only the gentry class as the main writers and talkers. Published books reveal their network of contacts as they lent books to each other, exchanged food plants to grow in their fields and kitchen gardens, exchanged recipes and served enticing new dishes at their tables. But, as we have seen, villages with resident gentry were sprinkled far and wide, and their food enthusiasms enlisted the efforts of local dealers, grocers, merchants and nurserymen. Knowledge passed to parsons, gardeners, and so to all villagers; the word and the foods spread. We shall meet two particularly informative authors in these years, a physician and a botanist, the physician reporting on general topics of discussion in his circle, and the botanist indirectly telling us about food novelties on their way to becoming a fashion. Both took notice of the life of all classes of people, and vividly conjure up common scenes in everyday life. At this date we cannot hope for more than that.

PHASES OF FOOD SCARCITY

The whole period starting in 1600 is noticeable for the sharp shocks regularly administered by cereal shortages. The scarcities of 1586 and 1594–6 were but a foretaste of crises that recurred in every decade between 1600 and 1650. In 1585 William Cecil had publicly rejoiced in the fact that the kingdom had enjoyed some 27 years without food crises, though he bewailed the consequences; people had forgotten the possibility of food scarcity and were blithely using wheat for making starch. They were abruptly reminded in the very next year, when the harvest of 1586 failed. Still worse misfortune befell between 1594 and 1597, and things then ran on in the same vein throughout the next 50 years. Peter

Bowden, surveying the longer period from 1500 to 1640, concluded that the 1620s, 1630s and 1640s 'were probably among the most terrible years [of food scarcity] through which the country had ever passed', and the early 1650s added more. In the background of this half century, then, we have to recognize a sense of unease and uncertainty, which offers one explanation for the significant efforts to increase basic food resources by improving land (resulting in a lot more enclosure). We also encounter further discussion in the books about alternative foods for use in emergencies.[1]

But how did cereal scarcities affect people from day to day in different classes and different regions? Because the government took more trouble at this time to investigate the local scene, we see more clearly than before that some shortages, deemed to be widespread, show on closer enquiry strong differences in their timing and local intensity. Generalities relating to England as a whole are therefore suspect, for experiences could vary markedly in different years and different places. We are given an insight into this phenomenon between 1607 and 1610. A royal proclamation sounded an alarm about food shortages in the second half of 1607, just after the Midland Revolt had taken place. The revolt aroused much fear locally, being a serious public outcry against enclosure in a relatively small number of villages clustered on the borders of Leicestershire, Warwickshire and Northamptonshire. The government claimed that it had not been provoked by famine or the scarcity of corn. But in fact the general price index of arable crops did rise in that year from 443 to 584, the harvest in the west of England is known to have been bad, and one pamphleteer, Arthur Standish, part of whose family lived in exactly the area of Northamptonshire where the Midland Revolt occurred, was deeply affected by the episode; he wrote of 'the extreme dearth of victuals' at that time as though it had been a contributory factor in the revolt, and in his view – he had London connections – prices in the previous six years, 1605–11, had been higher than in the 20 years before. Standish's concern for food shortages was so great that he spent the next four years travelling all round England to find out more about the situation and ways of improving food supplies by diversifying them. In the end national measures to improve the supply of wheat and barley for bread ran on for three years after 1607.[2]

Regional differences in the stress of food shortages illuminate many subtle nuances in people's experience. When reports came to Westminster from local JPs, responding to the Privy Council's questions about local grain stocks, the different counties and also different districts within counties told separate stories. In some places the shortages were dire, in others there were none, and in others the JPs were confident of remedying a threatening problem by grain imports from abroad. On the other hand, at certain moments, the tables were turned, and a spell of low grain prices was blamed on the scale of grain imports; they were impoverishing farmers when conditions made them unnecessary.

Another alarm sounded in late 1612, which persuaded the government to act in January 1613: it apprehended worse food scarcities to come because 'the weather continued so strange and unseasonable as it giveth no hope of amendment'. Grain exports were prohibited, though in the event the harvest of 1613 was nearly a quarter higher than in previous years.[3]

Two good harvest years in 1618 and 1619 brought low prices, which threatened to ruin farmers. Norfolk wanted grain imports banned, and an unusual proposal was put forward to set up magazines of corn to store the surplus and maintain prices. It produced some candid, sceptical responses from the counties, which showed some to be without any fear of scarcity, so confident were they of foreign imports solving all problems, while other counties did not grow enough to find any surplus to fill a storehouse. A significant statement from Nottinghamshire explained that its residents did not fear scarcity since other counties came to them for coal (via the Trent) and brought grain in return. But by September 1621 a cold summer – 'no one seems to remember anything like it', wrote the Venetian ambassador – and a poor harvest changed the situation entirely, driving the Privy Council to send out a circular letter asking for ideas to remedy the grain shortage, while it resorted to its usual strategy, banning grain exports. This harvest was especially bad in northern England in 1621 and by the summer of 1622 shortages were more alarming still. York reported a scarcity 'greater than ever known in memory of man'. In 1623 things were much worse and many people died in Cumberland, Westmorland, Lancashire and the West Riding. In Devon they were not immune, as an order at Barnstaple to make malt with oats rather than barley bears witness.[4]

Official anxiety about food supplies eased off in 1624–5, only to be replaced by plague in London and southern England in 1625–6. There followed a lull until December 1630 when high grain prices were again reported. Whereas they had been regarded as reaching very high levels in Portsmouth in 1608, when wheat was 3s. 4d., even 5s., a bushel, now in 1630 wheat in Newbury, Berkshire, was 7s. 6d. a bushel, and the price index, which had stood at 666 in 1621 in the last crisis, reached 1064. That year was particularly remembered in Northampton as a traumatic experience when people ate unimaginable things to survive. The trouble continued into March 1631, when even Westminster suffered, the citizens having to pay 13s. 4d. for white wheat (so that their smart folk could eat manchet), and even 11s. 6d. for red wheat, whereas in at least one part of Kent, 6s. 6d. a bushel, almost half the price, was the going rate in February 1631.[5]

In the north people suffered in 1631, but not severely, and as the Privy Council multiplied its watchful enquiries of JPs in every county, the pronounced local character of grain shortages became ever more noticeable. Ports along the south and east coasts, and the countryside inland from these ports that was accessible by river, were confident of foreign supplies, evidently not envisaging the possibility that the Baltic countries or France might also be struck by harvest failure at the same time. At Dover fortuitous aid rescued local people, when the French offered to sell them the wheat captured from a prize vessel. In March 1631, Bramford in east Suffolk on the River Gipping was confident that the Eastland merchants would bring corn to remedy their scarcity. Yet circumstances varied greatly over short distances: Ipswich had enough grain in February 1623, but there was not enough in 28 surrounding parishes. Hull was tolerably well supplied in February 1623, but its imported grain was not sufficient to serve parishes in the hinterland. Towns obviously seized the first supplies that arrived, leaving the rural parishes to struggle for the residue; geographical situation counted for a lot. Rural Herefordshire in March 1623 knew different fortunes between parishes, some having enough grain, while others went short. Kent in 1623 reported good experiences along the Thames estuary, in the Dartford neighbourhood, but these people drew on the richly productive arable lands of the Isle of Thanet and the downlands. The lathe of Shepway, on the same corn-growing downlands, was also adequately supplied in February 1631, so much so that it was able to send wagonloads of wheat to Ashford market. Local people were paying only 6s. 6d. a bushel for wheat (this was in February 1631) whereas, in contrast, a month later the citizens of Westminster were paying 13s. 4d. a bushel.[6]

In these different places we light up extremes of experience in urban and rural neighbourhoods, moderated by the strength and proximity of local grain-growing specialities. Social structures, and concentrations of industry or its absence in different communities, also made a large difference. One social situation was graphically described by the JPs of Surrey in relation to parishes in and around Godalming and Wonersh in 1630. They were populated by poor textile workers who, if they could not work and earn wages, were entirely without food, it was said. The authorities reckoned on at least 1,100 people in this category and in parishes further afield they calculated that the number could rise to 3,000. These round numbers were plainly guesswork, but the central significance of this statement lies in the assertion that these people had 'no other means of livelihood than their dependency on trade of clothing'. Another social/industrial situation was conjured up by the clerk of the peace in the West Riding of Yorkshire in May 1638, describing a countryside that was partly barren, he said, but was being newly replenished with clothworkers creeping into closes and settling on parcels of waste land as well as in the local towns. They too subsisted on their trade and scarce one of them, it was said, brewed their own drink. This clear statement about a population of recent immigrants relying for its drink on alehouse keepers and alewives poses the further question how they obtained their bread. Did they buy all their cereals too? We can accept the convention of the time that bread and cereals were the largest element in the food of the poor, and that they did not themselves grow cereals, but had to buy them or obtain them in exchange for labour. But did industrial populations with a roof over their heads devise no dependable food stocks, trap birds, rabbits, grow greenstuff in their gardens and gather food from the countryside? We need to ponder these public statements more deeply and question the silent convention that ignored such sources of food in official pronouncements.[7]

For ensuring a supply of drink when barley was needed for both bread and liquor, official orders went out commanding oats to be brewed in beer, thus leaving more barley for bread. But again we must question the reality lying behind some of these official pronouncements. One message from the Privy Council to all JPs everywhere in October 1622 boldly said that in scarce times barley was the usual breadcorn of the poor. We know this to be a view of England from the south-east. So some scepticism is needed when weighing public pronouncements in their local context; in many parts of the country oats were the usual breadcorn, and in a few places rye.[8]

Official assumptions about clusters of people in the kingdom wholly dependent for food on money earned in industry is a half-truth that needs to be scrutinized critically. Clusters of wholly committed industrial workers doubtless did exist in the sixteenth century, since our account of general economic development allows for a very substantial growth in the cloth industry. In the absence of serious food shortages between 1560 and 1585, we may well guess that in that period the plight of an industrial force going hungry did not impinge as a serious governmental concern. So it may not have loomed into public consciousness until some time in the 1590s or later, when concurrent food scares and industrial fluctuations constituted a novel experience, taxing the authorities in unprecedented ways between 1600 and 1650. A rhyme that lies in the State Papers among those defining the crisis in 1630 lights up the background to one food scene.

> 'The poor there is more
> than goes from door to door.
> You that are set in place,
> see that your profession you do not disgrace.'

In other words, not all the poor and hungry were vagrants on the roads.[9]

A new onus of responsibility was placed on the gentry in Elizabeth's reign; they were expected to probe more deeply into the problems of poverty and hunger in their communities. In response to this criticism in the early seventeenth century, JPs could truthfully reply that they conscientiously attended markets and took some tough action. In December 1622 one suggested remedy was that farmers selling corn should sell one quarter of their grain at underrates to the poor. In Huntingdonshire in March 1623 the instruction was differently worded: farmers and corn sellers were asked to sell their grain to the poor at a conscionable price and wait for two hours while the poor were supplied before free market conditions were allowed. JPs in the Rape of Arundel in Sussex also ordered in December 1630 that the poor be given the sole right to buy grain in the first two hours of the market's opening. These were purposeful measures to deal in a practical way with the hunger of people who were not wandering the roads but were suffering less visibly at home. It relied for its effectiveness on accurate local knowledge about who was poor and who was not.[10]

After the dire year of 1630, sufficient harvests eased grain prices until 1637, when another harsh time of scarcity befell.[11] But after that cereals remained at a moderate level and lasted through the first years of the civil war. In 1640, indeed, low rather than high grain prices were the complaint in Hatfield Chase, reflecting perhaps the progress that had been made in the 1630s in draining fenland thereabouts and creating more arable land for grain growing. A more grievous period of food scarcity at the end of that decade remains to be described in the next chapter.

FRESH THINKING ABOUT FOOD REGIMES

This period of about 50 years, representing generously the lifetime of one individual, showed food shortages every seven years. So when Arthur Standish in his treatise of 1612 stated exactly that – high grain prices came around every seven years – he was expressing hard personal experience since 1585. We may not forget the regional differences that qualify the generalities, but food shortages recurring regularly impinged strongly on current experience between 1600 and 1640. So it is no surprise to find writers continuing to ponder the provision of food in emergencies. In Chapter 3 we have already given Hugh Platt his place in that roll of honour, being the remarkably practical experimenter with food in time of need, and publishing in the mid-1590s his treatise on remedies against famine.[12]

William Vaughan, a Welshman living in Carmarthenshire, was the next writer with the same concerns. He wrote a first little book on diet and health in 78 pages in 1600, *Naturall and Artificial Directions for Health*, when he was recovering from a grievous illness. His approach was general, dealing with essential meat and drink, saying something on vegetables and fruit, only a sentence or two about bread, nothing on cereals, and moving swiftly on to exercise, bathing, mental tranquillity, sleep and temperate behaviour. But in 1617 he published again (though he had, in fact, written this piece in 1613), expanding his remarks this time to over 300 pages. Now he was thinking of his friends settling in straitened conditions in Ireland, but he was yet more deeply involved in settling colonists in Newfoundland. So he viewed diet and health from a different standpoint, being much more specific about individual foods, but dealing most significantly of all with the means to preserve life 'if perhaps I be constrained to straggle in deserts'. The chewing of liquorice and tobacco to keep alive for a few days were evidently current ideas in the worst emergencies.[13]

The subject was also broached by Gervase Markham in his book on *Hunger's Prevention* (1621). The subtitle narrowed its subject to the whole art of fowling by land or water, but Markham directed his work at those who travelled by sea and came into uninhabited places as well as those 'that have anything to do with new plantations'. In other words, he was thinking of Virginia, and dedicated his treatise to Sir Edwin Sandys and other adventurers there. Markham knew fowling as a pleasurable recreation in England, but he was also acutely aware of its role in different circumstances overseas. As we shall see below, events, springing from quite different circumstances, were conspiring at this time to put wildfowl on the agenda as a satisfying and tasty food that could be successfully caught in large quantity for a commercial market. Birds would secure a new place in diet hereafter.[14]

In 1622, a year after Gervase Markham had made his contribution to preventing hunger, William Vaughan went to Newfoundland and further enlarged his experience. A work by him entitled *The Newlanders Cure* appeared in 1630. Its full and lengthy title implied that people now recognized an increase in the variety of illnesses 'in these latter days'; travel was seen to be spreading disease, as we too have realized in the last half century. Vaughan had named scurvy and the sweating sickness in earlier writing, but now he added fevers, coughs, gout, colic and more. Moreover, he was convinced of the connection between mind and body in determining health, and he was troubled by the excessive eating and drinking of some, that he had seen of late years. New lines of thought had entered his head, resulting in particular from an encounter with a Jesuit, Leonardo Lessius, a Fleming, and Luigi Cornaro, an Italian, from whom he had collected 'an admirable diet'. It was not a harsh, tasteless food regime, but it set a measure of food and drink allowing about 12–14 ounces per day of flesh, bread, gruel and eggs (this being the prescribed amount for sedentary folk), which was varied in flavour at different meals by butter, honey, sugar, oil, currants, saffron, ginger and so on. Vaughan had followed this diet for three months to his benefit, forcing him to think positively about a food regime that was, in fact, not far removed from that of his peasant neighbours.[15]

The wider influence of the theories of Lessius and Cornaro now threaded its way through the next 10 to 20 years on a course that deserves more investigation. The hopes and chances of living longer had been heightened by the fact that Queen Elizabeth lived to the age of 70, far exceeding the next longest-living Tudor monarch, her father Henry VIII, who died at 55. Cornaro set the most glowing example because he was believed to have lived for 102 years and was still a sprightly horse rider at 95. His *Discourse on the Sober Life* (1614) upheld his conviction about the virtues of eating sparingly, and while Englishmen first read the essays of both Lessius and Cormaro (1613 and 1614) in Latin, their message spread more widely when translated in 1634 by Nicholas Ferrar, that singular man who spent his later life in an ultra-pious household of family members at Little Gidding (later caricatured as 'an Arminian nunnery'). Ferrar was helped with his translation of Lessius by George Herbert, poet and neighbour. It was much read from the 1640s onwards when the editions multiplied in French, German, and other languages. Indeed, it is still considered by some to offer wise advice.[16]

Prescriptions for new diets were now passing through a fashionable phase and, not surprisingly, they prompted some to exploit the commercial possibilities of selling certain foods and drink as miracle foods. We begin to see in shadowy outline a new branch of trade developing out of what might be called the commercialization of diet, cashing in on hopes of a longer life by eating proprietary food preparations; the growth of that branch since the late nineteenth century has been phenomenal. William Folkingham devised one such food, though he is much better known as the author of *Feudigraphia* (1610), a well-thumbed practical text book on surveying and measures of land improvement. In 1623 he offered the public his own brew of ale and herbs, called 'panala ala catholica'. It was announced to the world in a book of that title, and as a compound ale it was advertised as a medicine for all infirmities. Its ingredients were not given in detail, but they included yeast, raisins and ale, to which a 'composition' was added, which Folkingham supplied. This was left to infuse for three days or more and was drunk cold. As a medicine, it was specially recommended for spring and autumn to cleanse the body of impurities, but it was also to be drunk routinely. It is worth noting, in parenthesis, that Folkingham also explained in 1628 how he had been involved in a project to promote the commonweal, by improving the River Welland at Stamford. This had embroiled him with 'unseasoned and improvident agents without control to abuse noble intentions and bury bounteous contributes [sic] in ill-pondered pursuit of fond addle plots'. This, of course, was the age *par excellence* of projects, and our foodies lived in the midst of all such schemes to secure patents and monopolies.[17]

Folkingham and Vaughan both explained that they had learned to value good health above beauty and wealth, an avowal that had special meaning at this time when the world was overflowing with disreputable schemes for making money; monopolies in public discourse had become a byword for the most odious means of getting that wealth. We can adopt a cynical stance and say that the striving for good health rather than corrupt wealth was only a clever but different way for projectors to dip into the pockets of the well-to-do. But too many varied currents of thought flowed through public discussion of food for any one connection to be given more or less significance in the later outcomes.[18]

Another theme of discussions in literate circles in this period was the notion that people belonged naturally in their native places, and if they stayed there then they were assured of good health. If they forsook that place, then they had to face disease. This assertion was made by William Vaughan in his *Directions for Health* in 1617. It is apparent again, indirectly, in James Hart's statement of 1633 that some physicians sent their sick patients back to their native places to recover. Supposedly, such thoughts were in part nourished by experiences of colonizing ventures in the New World. When serious attempts at permanent settlement were projected, adventurers had to preserve their health while eating food that was far from familiar. There hovered in the background of all these ponderings a widening knowledge of regional food differences to which we shall return below. Among certain professionals, these notions were mixed with a curiosity to know more about regional foods, and even strong competitive urges to be the discoverers of new foods. These were years of food investigations that carried people in many directions.[19]

So far we have pursued currents of thought that were concerned with finding a diet that would promote health. Foreigners' views mingled with those of the English. The same mixture was apparent in a different current of ideas flowing through the botanical and gardening fraternity. They were intent on propagating and fostering a more sensitive appreciation of fruits and vegetables. Among these must be numbered the Italian, Giacomo Castelvetro, a Protestant sympathizer out of tune with his native Italy. He was a resident in England from the 1580s, actively promoting Italian culture, publishing Italian literature, and in 1592 living in Edinburgh as tutor to James VI of Scotland, the future king of England.[20]

Castelvetro was not continuously in England but roamed Europe, so he saw many different food styles. But in 1613 he was back in England living at Charlton near Greenwich in the household of Sir Adam Newton. Here he wrote *A Brief Account of the Fruits, Herbs, and Vegetables of Italy* (1614), placing health in the forefront of his concerns, but showing himself to be botanically well informed on different varieties of food plants, and knowledgeable about varied ways of cooking them. His eating experiences in England had plainly left him dissatisfied with elaborate concoctions dominated by meat. His task was to praise simplicity and vaunt the pleasure of vegetables, herbs and fruit, setting them in higher esteem. He recognized that the climates of Italy and England engendered different attitudes, but he hoped to persuade the English to handle their vegetables, herbs and fruits in the kitchen with the subtlety shown by the Italians, grow better specimens, and so enjoy them more. In some cases he hoped they would eat plants that grew in England but were neglected as food; mushrooms were one of these, about which he introduced novel ideas at variance with earlier views. Thomas Newton had in 1580 been emphatic that many were poisonous and the whole lot were to be feared.[21]

Since Castelvetro addressed his work to Lucy, Countess of Bedford, we have to assume that she was sympathetic to his ideas, having, like other noble families, a garden that was already professionally cultivated by a dedicated gardener. And while Castelvetro wrote down his advice in order to raise the standard of greenstuff and fruit, grown and eaten at the tables of the well-to-do, we can be sure that other Italians voiced the same opinions, politely, we hope, when face to face with their hosts in other gentlemen's houses scattered through the land. The whole subject was being turned into an upper-class topic of conversation that lights up a network of like-minded people, and would lead to action.

A BOTANIST'S VIEW OF VEGETABLES AND FRUIT

Nowhere was the message of Castelvetro and fellow Italians more cogently, if indirectly, urged among Englishmen than in the books of John Parkinson. His origins are unknown: the old DNB suggested possibly Nottinghamshire, but the new *ODNB* ventures no opinion; what is certain is that he was born in 1567 and apprenticed in 1585 to a London apothecary of the Grocers' Company. Apothecaries resented their lowly status among grocers, and he readily joined the separate organization of the Society of Apothecaries when it was set up in 1617, and was at first active in its administration. Then he withdrew to devote his time principally to his garden in Long Acre which was stored with rare plants. In the long term he was to be most celebrated as a botanist with a consuming interest in identifying all plants capable of being used for food, physic and decoration. In distinguishing and precisely naming their many varieties, he conjured up more vividly than anyone else the eagerness among professionals at this period to find, identify and enlarge knowledge and skill in the range and use of plants then known. Thus, he serves us admirably as a historian of food, even though he disclaimed any intention of writing 'a treatise of cookery'.[22]

Parkinson's first work, published in 1629, *Paradisi in Sole Paradisus Terrestris* is a mine of information on the efforts expended in these years in growing tastier varieties of accepted food plants and trying out new ones that came from abroad. He dedicated his book to Queen Henrietta Maria, and was rewarded by Charles I with the title of 'botanicus regius primarius'. He is much the best of our informants on the foreign influences that drove botany forward, indirectly by naming the plants with their place of origin, and directly by his remarks on the way the Dutch, Flemish and French settlers in England had taught the English to eat new foods; living in London he was in a good position to observe the process. In fact, he described a situation markedly similar to that experienced by the present author around 1939 when German and Austrian refugees, fleeing Nazi persecution, clustered in the Swiss Cottage district of London, and profoundly altered the food scene there. Like the sixteenth-century refugees they brought their food habits from the Continent, and these in due course have spread all over the kingdom. The best illustration of this has already earned an allusive reference above: the English had a traditional curd tart in the sixteenth century, made out of milk curds, with the addition of currants; from the Continent around 1939 came another kind of cheese cake made with a cream cheese and additional sultanas or other fruit. That cheese cake has now become more familiar than the traditional kind, though the first retains its loyal clientèle in Yorkshire and the north.[23]

On the food scene, one of the marked foreign influences that Parkinson noticed in his day was the Dutch and Flemish use of herbs with a stronger flavour than that to which the English were accustomed. To understand his comments fully, it is important to remember that all herbs, vegetables and fruit had a stronger flavour then than now. They have been 'improved' by centuries of cultivation and the introduction of new varieties, the result being in most cases a milder flavour; the same trend in our own day can be observed in the weakening flavour of garlic. Thus we may, for example, understand Parkinson's otherwise puzzling opinion when describing chervil. The French and Dutch liked salad herbs with a stronger flavour than the English, he said, whereas we do not nowadays regard chervil as having an unsavoury strong flavour. Similarly, a strong taste, not appreciated by all English people, was attributed to tarragon and cress, the difference in our present-day cress being further illustrated by Parkinson's statement that in his day it grew two feet high.[24]

Parkinson moved in a circle of like-minded botanists who shared his burning zeal to find ever more novelties, acclimatizing them in their own gardens, advertising their virtues among their friends, and giving away cuttings and grafts. One close colleague of Parkinson was John Tradescant the elder: he passed on to Parkinson some fennel, with directions for growing it, that the diplomat Sir Henry Wotton had sent him, probably from Venice. Matthew Lister, Charles I's physician, sent Parkinson 'monks' or 'bastard' rhubarb from abroad. (According to Culpeper this was a dock, with some purging quality.) It enabled Parkinson to grow something equivalent to rhubarb in his own garden before anyone else did. In conversation with the Italian ambassador in London, Parkinson encountered sweet parsley in the latter's private garden for the first time, and found it sweeter than any of the other three kinds. In these asides Parkinson introduces us to the network of friends who spurred each other on, though cooperation was not without its fiery competitive edge. In a later work, *Theatrum Botanicum* (1640), Parkinson praised the singular judgement of another collector, Guillaume Boel, but complained sourly when Boel, travelling in Spain in part at Parkinson's expense, gave some chickpea plants to an Essex collector, and so robbed Parkinson of his claim to make the first trials in England. 'While I beat the bush, another catcheth and eateth the bird,' he wrote sourly. Parkinson had been the one who 'with care and cost sowed them yearly, hoping first to publish them'. He 'had their descriptions ready for the press', he said. These botanists might be friends, but they were also keen rivals; and we have still failed to acclimatize chickpeas in England![25]

Encircling this group of London-based quasi-professional botanists we glimpse in Parkinson's work another group of individuals with a less earnestly focused interest in plants and food, scrutinizing gardens, neighbouring fields, hedgerows and woods for edible rarities or 'curiosities', as Parkinson called them, and positively relishing the eating of vegetables and fruits at home alongside their flesh and fish. His many references to 'those that take delight in eating of herbs', or 'those whose curiosity searcheth out the whole work of nature to satisfy their desires' conveys the image of club members subscribing to a new faith. Indeed, in the 1620s some contemporaries seem to have been positively carried away by their enthusiasm for fruit and vegetables, for the clustering of events promoting them is quite astonishing. It is in this decade that we identify the first English artist, Sir Nathaniel Bacon (1585–1627), to choose still life as a subject, painting 'ten great peeces in wainscoate of fish and fowl, etc.', a still life of game, and one canvas now in the Tate Gallery, London, of a cook maid standing among luscious-looking vegetables and fruit, and dated between 1620 and 1625. Bacon had visited the Low Countries in 1613, had been in Antwerp where lived Frans Snijders, a major artist of the genre, and is thought to have received some training there. As well, his letters show his enthusiasm for horticulture and care for his health. It is also around 1625 that a project for planting fruit trees to promote cider-drinking, as an alternative to beer, was presented to government. The nagging thought persists, moreover, that the fruit frenzy, further detailed in Chapter 9 below, was also stirred up by stories told by the English who watched the feasting in Madrid in 1623 when Prince Charles and the Duke of Buckingham arrived, expecting Charles to pledge marriage to the Spanish Infanta. The documents record some spectacular meals. Thus horticulture received its accolade in the 1620s, and that would lead on to the emergence of a few dedicated vegetarians in the 1650s, recruiting more disciples by the 1680s. It would then take another turn of the wheel in the mid-nineteenth century before those seeds flowered into a formidable display, with the founding of the Vegetarian Society in 1847.[26]

Alongside people with botanical expertise was another coterie of upper-class snobs who set store by vegetables and fruits just because they were rare. The food table was the place for them to display their skill in growing rare fruits and making a flourish. In other words, while diets were undergoing change in this period, individual foods were being stuffed with class prejudices. 'Far-fetched and dear-bought' was a catch phrase for foods that were much sought after just because they were rare and expensive; they ceased to appeal when once they became plentiful, cheap and accessible to all. John Partridge in 1584 had given the same words a strong class emphasis, saying 'quainty and dainty, far set and dearbought is good for great estates'. One food of snobs in Parkinson's generation were globe artichokes, some having recently been brought into gardens from the wild, while one, a French kind, was plainly still in an experimental stage. Deeper meaning can be read into Parkinson's remarks about globe artichokes when we recognize the many references in the garden accounts of gentry to their setting up artichoke gardens. They were modish and unusual. In contrast, another vegetable that was relatively new on the scene at the same date, Jerusalem artichokes, were at first regarded as 'dainties for a queen', but when they grew so prolifically, and became plentiful in the markets, 'even the vulgar despised them'.[27]

Other references by Parkinson to dishes that were fashionable in his day point us to the signs that would have had clearer meaning for contemporaries than for us when surveying an elegant food table. Clove gillyflowers (i.e. carnations) that had been pickled between layers of sugar and covered with vinegar made a winter salad that was recognized as the latest foible among high-ranking gentlemen and ladies; cauliflower likewise would have attracted attention since it was known that few people then could propagate them successfully. In contrast, melons in a former time had been enjoyed only by kings and nobility, having been nursed by gardeners brought from France, but now they were being eaten by 'the better sort of persons', and thus were descending the social scale. Pumpkins also were losing their social ranking, being pounced on by the rich only when the earliest arrived at the market; after that they were left for the 'meaner and poorer sort'. Red beetroots, however, were now much appreciated in upper class circles, being cleverly cut into artistic shapes and arranged decoratively on dishes of meat and fish; anyone seeing these on a table would have recognized the touch as something having 'grown of late days into a great custom of service'.[28]

Many conventions and assumptions of Parkinson's generation shone beacon-like through his factual statements, sketching out a distinctive profile of these decades when some eternal truths were mingling with passing phases of fashion that would be gone by the 1650s. Parkinson also peered discerningly across a wider geographical landscape and down longer passages of time. He was fully aware of long-standing regional differences in diet, governed by different local soils and climates; he knew that many different varieties of the same plants were scattered through the kingdom, some yielding better, and some poorer, food flavours. He was also conscious of historic changes in the appreciation of food, some going back to classical times, some recalling the situation no more than a century past when the monks cultivated fine kitchen gardens. All these experiences differed from what he called 'late days' and the present. Recent landmarks for him were John Gerard's *Catalogue* and his *Herbal*, published in 1596 and 1597, giving food plant lists that were for Parkinson 30 years out of date.

Understandably, his head was full of more recent introductions, none perhaps more striking than the new variety of apricot which John Tradescant had brought from Algiers, having voluntarily joined a naval expedition to suppress piracy in the Mediterranean, and using this chance to look for new plants. Other foods which Parkinson emphasized for their novelty in recent years – 'new conceits' was one of his terms for them – ranged from musk melons (not all trials of these, he said, were proving successful) to cucumbers coming from several different sources and being fastidiously differentiated. The number of known varieties named by Parkinson is, in fact, for us one guide to the vigour with which growers and grocers were experimenting at this time. Six varieties of cucumbers were listed, including a French, a Danzig and a Muscovy kind. The Danzig was the one that was pickled, and the Muscovy was the smallest, no larger than a lemon. At this date pickled vegetables were becoming highly valued winter food, and the cucumbers for this purpose were all imported; Englishmen's attempts to pickle them produced nothing so tender, firm or savoury as the Danzig ones, said Parkinson. In the event, provision merchants had to wait until the second half of the seventeenth century to discover the know-how and finally satisfy their customers with something home grown.[29]

The food scene, in short, was teeming with novelties and experiments that might or might not produce lasting results. Every part of every plant – whether leaves, roots, stalk or seed – was tried out in the search for a palatable food. Eleven or 12 varieties of lettuce were known, of which some bore names indicating a foreign origin – Romane (i.e. Italian), Virginia, Lombard, Venice and Flanders or Bruges croppers. How dramatically the scene had changed since the days when Catherine of Aragon had married in England, asked for lettuce, and found nothing to satisfy her! Two varieties of potatoes were now recognized, one from Virginia and the other Spanish, though this last was not flourishing on English soil, and so was recognized as more expensive when seen on the table. Nor had the English yet settled on the best way to eat them, for the comfit makers were candying them. Spinach had been made familiar by the Dutch, who cooked it in its own moisture and ate it with butter, but ingenious gentlewomen had other ways, like cooking it in tarts. Yet just how quickly new varieties of familiar plants could sometimes take hold was made clear in the case of parsley. Only two varieties had been known, one with plain and one with curled leaves. But a Virginian kind arrived and now, said Parkinson, was 'almost grown common'; so that must have happened between 1607, when Virginia began to be settled, and 1629. It had spread remarkably quickly. Meanwhile another kind, the sweet parsley from Italy had been seen by Parkinson when it was still a novelty, and had found itself a niche served as a salad on its own. While some foods quickly grew fashionable, however, other old familiars fell out of favour in what Parkinson called 'this delicate age of ours'. These, apparently, included French mallows and pennyroyal as potherbs. More strangely, leeks had fallen from grace, and only the poorest people and the vulgar gentry of Wales remained loyal to this vegetable. It is fortunate for us that it did regain favour, and so has a firm place in our repertoire nowadays.[30]

Light was shed by many of Parkinson's asides on the food of ordinary folk and the poor, making clear their ready access to greenstuff in winter as well as summer, if they could bestir themselves to go out and collect it in the fields or plant it at home betimes. Garden plants were the handiest convenience, and often improved when hand tended, so everyone was becoming alert to the value of tending their gardens. But it was a routine among all to gather wild food as well, and much of it was dubbed by Parkinson equal or sometimes even better than the garden variety. Garden rocket, mustard seed, and goatsbeard were exactly the same in the wild as cultivated, he said; and in some places the wild parsnip seed was so plentiful, one could fill a quarter sack, as good as any garden seed. The roots of parsnip as food then lasted all winter long. Wild strawberries were plentiful in the woods, but it was readily admitted that they improved when brought into gardens. So people were being shown the rewards of gardening, and while only commercial gardeners or the gentry's gardeners used bell glasses to cover musk melons, there was nothing to stop anyone from hanging up a few cabbages by their roots in a winter store and planting them out as soon as the frosts had passed to ensure that they had early cabbage leaves in spring. This practice evidently produced branches on which grew edible green pods, seemingly the beginning of Brussels sprouts. Parkinson knew about the making of sauerkraut in eastern Europe, but significantly did not feel inclined to recommend it in England, almost certainly because the English did not suffer so severely from the lack of greenstuff in winter. But some other tricks of the trade were readily adopted: it was not unusual to see matting made of reeds forming a fence to protect radishes from the cold in winter, so that they could be enjoyed until Christmas. It was fairly certainly a device first demonstrated by market gardeners in London, but a hemp cloth on a frame would have been a cheap substitute for any housekeeper.[31]

While spring was the busy planting time for all, it was common practice to reserve some seeds for sowing later in order to have a winter supply. Thus not only could radishes be eaten at Christmas, lamb's lettuce, spinach and sorrel too lasted all winter, along with the usual onions, parsnips, carrots and turnips. Since the great majority of the population had at least a cottage garden, this meant that no one needed to be entirely without roots and greenstuff in winter, though one expected to run short and welcome the sight of green shoots in spring. Some gardeners with more energy than most even covered endive and purslane to whiten and remain tender and edible through the cold days. The professionals in this case were doubtless the exception, but it is an illusion to think that ordinary folk were wholly deprived of winter greens. Practically the whole population of

England absorbed countrymen's lore from their birth; they knew the routines of gathering foodstuff from the wild, and it was second nature to make the very most of nature's bounty.[32]

Parkinson's book contained a separate section on orchard fruits, but they were not so readily found in the gardens of ordinary folk as in those of the gentry. Fruit trees above all needed space, and some grew best when grown against walls, which the gentry possessed, if not other classes. Vines to produce dessert grapes were grown in that position 'without any extraordinary pains', said Parkinson. So, we can be sure that some others – parsons spring first to mind – took advantage of their shed walls for the same purpose. People also had a trick for keeping the grapes till Christmas, by packing them in layers in a barrel of dry, clean sand, sealed tight. So it was not beyond the means of resourceful yeomen and even some interested husbandmen to have dessert grapes, as long as they did not live too far north. Parsons often had small orchards, and occasionally we find a contemporary plan depicting village houses with enough ground to accommodate herb beds and trees as well. The fact remains that tree fruit did not grow in cottage gardens, and we shall need to pay heed to Parkinson's comments on the fruit that grew wild to remember that fruit (apples more than anything else) was available to the humblest folk.[33]

Parkinson's ordering of fruits had no obvious logic, starting with fig trees which were a gentleman's conceit and held out poor prospects of feeding many people in the future. He knew that a tree had been brought from the Algarve, but evidently the fruit did not ripen well in England. Yet to avoid any waste, which was anathema in this age, the unripe fruit was candied by the comfit-makers. Parkinson turned next to other unusual fruits: first, the pleasant-tasting berries of the wild service tree (alternatively known as the chequer tree), eaten when fresh and thoroughly ripe, of which Tradescant was intent on finding more varieties. The service tree has now become more rare than the fig, though it can still be found in old woodland in Kent. His other, to us uncommon, fruit-bearing trees were the lotus and the cornelian cherry, wholly forgotten nowadays as bearers of edible fruit, and the medlar, which is all but lost save in ancient orchards. When Parkinson reached the cherry tree, however, he embarked on fruit in a quite different class. Cherries were already high fashion in his day, having been favoured by Henry VIII, and greedily devoured by James I. Sweet varieties had by then been introduced and they were innumerable, their names revealing two kinds brought from Flanders, three from France, and more from Morocco, Naples, Spain and Hungary. Their place at the table when eaten fresh from the tree was before or after meals, though the recipe books were finding many more ways of serving them, in tarts and by preserving them for winter use.[34]

Plums were another well-known tree, producing a plentiful crop; again Tradescant was given credit for procuring new varieties. But English varieties growing wild in hedges had laid a foundation, and the French had obviously elevated the status of this fruit in the sixteenth century by establishing a trade to England in two of their own varieties, damask prunes – a sweet kind that was dried and sold at the grocers – and tart bullaces, which were known as French prunes. Yet another pleasantly tart kind, called pruneola (or bruneola), were dried and, with the stones removed, were packed in fancy small boxes to be sold dear as banqueting stuff. We see here finicky ways with food being taught by the French to English merchants who as yet lacked the same finesse. London caught the first wave of this fashion, and it is there that we shall later find more of the same stylishness by which other foods also moved first into London, and then out into the Home Counties and so to manor houses scattered further afield.[35]

The fruit with the most intriguing history at this time, and slightly more exotic than the plum, was the apricot. Judging by the numerous recipes for apricots in the cookery books, it was regularly home grown and a common sight in the kitchens of the gentry, and we shall encounter a still more goodly store of this fruit being harvested in the eighteenth century. Yet it has become a rare fruit among us nowadays, except when imported. So we may read, carefully though regretfully, Parkinson's words on the situation in his day. Apricot trees were best planted against a wall, and were known in six varieties, including the Algier apricot that Tradescant had brought back from his brave Algiers voyage in 1620. It was a fruit often used at banquets but not exclusively so, for Parkinson never suggested that it produced a disappointing crop. It was preserved, candied by the comfit makers, and dried. Present-day plantsmen bewail the diseases that strike the apricot, whereas the historian, viewing Parkinson's world, must wonder if or when resistant varieties were lost that might have served us today.[36]

Peaches were another favoured fruit, emphatically associated with the gentry only, and eliciting from Parkinson a comment that implied the recent arrival of several new varieties. He listed 12 named kinds, seemingly from Spain and Italy, and in addition described others, without naming them, which could well have totalled some 20 or more varieties. Nectarines were yet more recent arrivals, seemingly from Italy, more highly rated than peaches, and holding promise for the future since they were already known in eight varieties. They do not feature in recipe books, however, suggesting that after 1650 the optimism of the 1620s had already faded.[37]

In quite another category were the well-established fruits known to all: apples, pears and quinces. Apples were the commonest, causing Parkinson to make a special point about the innumerable regional varieties in existence, which differed in colour, taste, aroma, durability and fashion – yes, he himself used the word 'fashion'. Many were derived from wild varieties in the woods and hedgerows; in fact, some people, learning from nature, actually planted apple hedgerows. All in all, Parkinson painted a picture of apples in plenty for all, masters and men alike eating them stewed and in pies. Kent and Worcestershire were particularly well served, for they were noted for their many wild trees; also many trees were known in the south-west, possibly including many more imported varieties; it was here that cider was made in large quantity, some of it for sea voyages. The one doubt that Parkinson left with his readers concerned any quantity, let alone quality, found in the north country. Throughout his book he did not seem to be particularly well-informed about the north.[38]

Pears were the second commonest fruit in Parkinson's ratings, again available in infinite regional variety of which the full range had not yet been discovered. From abroad had come new varieties, their origins made recognizable in the place-names of Portugal and Spain, and one reference to Jerusalem. Parkinson's full list of native and foreign pears ran over two full pages, giving us several glimpses of the immense zeal among some gentlemen to secure fruits that would make them the envy of others. One was called the Hundred Pound Pear, because the proud owner had had to pay so much to procure it; his messenger had brought back nothing apart from certain grafts. On the other hand, ordinary pears, like ordinary apples, were plentiful in the countryside and all classes enjoyed them, eating them fresh, baked, stewed and dried. Even the most unpalatable were not wasted for they made a perry, close to a mild, pleasant wine.[39]

The last among Parkinson's commonest English fruits was the quince, prompting from him the surprising comment that no fruit growing in this land was of so many excellent uses in dishes for the table, for banquets, and for medicinal purposes. It startles us to read such commendation in the twenty-first century when the quince has lost this high place among foods. It is virtually never served alone as a cooked fruit, and is best known in a jelly. In Parkinson's day six varieties were grown, the English being apple-shaped, a Portuguese one also being apple-shaped and sweet enough to be eaten raw, a pear-shaped kind coming from Portugal that had to be cooked, a variety from Barbary, and another from Lyons.[40]

Among soft fruits sweet enough for desserts Parkinson named strawberries, the sweetest of them all, raspberries, white and red but described as somewhat sour, red and black currants, gooseberries and mulberries. For some reason, he was only mildly informative about these plants and said next to nothing of different varieties; had they perhaps not yet captured as much professional interest as the hard fruits? This seems to be the most likely explanation since he did not neglect other berries which were much used in savoury sauces. Of these, gooseberries came first, classified as three common kinds, and more of the less common. They were thoroughly familiar in sharp sauces for fish and meat, while some sweeter ones were eaten raw or cooked in tarts. Another common, even fashionable, berry at this time was the barberry (*Berberis vulgaris*), so highly appreciated for savoury sauces that the berries were pickled for winter use and sometimes the leaves were cooked. This foodstuff is now totally lost to us, posing a mystery, to which Maud Grieve alone has offered an explanation. In the eighteenth century, she says, the barberry bush was blamed for harbouring a fungus that spread spores through neighbouring wheat fields, and ruined the cereal crop with mildew. So the bushes were rooted out wholesale. Thus was lost a refreshing jelly for garnishing meat, and incidentally a precious anti-scorbutic.[41]

Nut trees were always the companions of hard fruit trees in orchards, and Parkinson named the wild hazel, transplanted from the woods, walnuts and almonds. Walnut trees were highest in fashion in Parkinson's day, partly because of the wood, but also because great quantities of the fruit were pickled. The nuts ripened successfully, and were eaten fresh, preserved and candied, as well as being stored in barrels and pots for eating around Christmas time. Almonds also featured prominently in the cookbooks, for Arab influences in the Middle Ages had familiarized cooks with marzipan, with ground almonds used as a thickening flour, almond butter and almond milk. Our almond tree house-names add further evidence for the growing of almond trees at this time. Again, Parkinson said nothing about problems in ripening the nuts. Does all this suggest the existence of varieties that flourished in our climate? Perhaps we should be sceptical in this case, for the trees were worth growing for their blossom alone, and a considerable quantity of almonds was imported from Spain, at least into London. These could well explain the assumptions of the recipe books that almonds were ready to hand. A port book for London for the year 1567–8, for example, shows them arriving from Malaga in quantities varying from 10 to 26 to 34cwt at a time. They were nothing like as common a cargo as Malaga's sun-dried raisins, but in London they were sufficient to supply the gentry class at a price that they found reasonable. For a banquet in Oxford, 1s. a pound was paid in 1570, and between 1s. 3d. and 1s. 6d. a pound was the price asked of a modest Lancashire gentry family in the vicinity of Preston in 1617–18. In contrast, a port book of Boston, Lincolnshire between 1601 and 1640 shows only one occasion when almonds (24lbs) were delivered in 1617; they came on a boat sailing from Rotterdam. Almonds were almost certainly an unusual treat in fenland Lincolnshire.[42]

Because Parkinson's survey of fruit was weighted down with trees growing in orchards, it was biased towards the fruit that reached the gentry, and so gives an optimistic picture of the variety that was available to all. But this was plainly a period when a very lively search for new edible plants of all kinds was under way, though some of the vital enthusiasm displayed at this time would fade. What does emerge from Parkinson's pages is a strong sense of networks of activists in and around London, almost certainly exerting as yet little influence in more distant counties, and yet disseminating ideas that would recruit a widening circle of devotees in the 1650s. By bringing wild fruit into their orchards, the gentry did undoubtedly set an example to country people who already knew what grew in their woods and hedgerows and could copy the same procedures, gathering wild fruit and transplanting wildings into their gardens. The gentry were setting an example of a modish taste for fruit that encouraged local people to pay more attention to growing and eating the same.

While the same influences affected the growing of greenstuff and root vegetables, the tasks involved were that much easier. More people had gardens than had ground for orchard fruits. But in the way that has been described already, they could collect from the wild seeds of herbs, greenstuff and roots, or collect the grown food itself. Parkinson spread the word about the good quality of much wild food, repeating in fact much of the traditional lore of country people. Even today that lore survives in isolated communities in Britain, and more still on the Continent of Europe, preserving ancient habits of collecting nature's bounty, especially in spring.

A MIDLAND FOOD REGIME

As a botanist and gardener, moving on from being first an apothecary, John Parkinson has focused our attention on vegetables and fruit in diet. Our second guide across a wider field at the same period must be James Hart, a physician. He was born in Edinburgh between about 1575 and 1585, and wrote a book about food ostensibly for the sick but in fact offering a sound diet to all. It was entitled *Klinike or the Diet of the Diseased* (1633), and was based on some 20 years' experience. He had travelled and studied on the Continent, graduated MD at Basle in 1608, and lived for more than two years in France, long enough to learn something of its provincial food habits. He had also travelled in the Low Countries, in Saxony and Bohemia, returning to England in 1610 to live out his life in Northampton. He never belonged to the College of Physicians or Company of Barber Surgeons, although his first two books had been on the subject of urine, one being a translation in 1623 of someone else's work, the other being a work of his own on *The Anatomie of Urines* (1625), condemning those who relied solely on urine when diagnosing diseases. His writing on food is in a different vein, incorporating wide reading, touched with humour and irony, flavoured with illuminating incidents from his own life, and infused throughout with strong Puritanical beliefs that made him uphold moderate eating and drinking, abhor gluttony, and strive for charity for the poor. His language became quite intemperate when condemning the profiteers who battened on poor people: he likened enclosers to cannibals, devouring the weak and helpless. But next in his list of evildoers were the quack doctors, also the parsons who meddled in medicine, and above all women healers, 'petticoated physicians' he called them, whose regimes for curing sick people were the very reverse of his own. What angered him particularly was their always overfeeding and overclothing their patients in bed.[43]

Hart's account of current food practices and opinions offers many invaluable insights. The year 1630 had been a year of acute food scarcity in Northampton, leaving sore wounds in the memory that had not yet healed when he wrote in 1633. For hunger, people had boiled cat with their pottage, a great many had died, and the churchyard of All Saints in Northampton and the church itself had overflowed with corpses, which he regarded as a serious risk to health: they should have been buried outside the town.[44]

In turning to food habits and the means to preserve health, he took a balanced view of English practices, having seen and read enough of life abroad to recognize merits and faults. His life had taken him into the houses of rich and poor: thus, he dedicated his book to Edward Montague, Baron of Boughton in Northamptonshire, whose wife had been his patient; and as a town physician he knew much of the food habits of labouring men and 'the vulgar' as he termed them. He was also aware that 'country ways' with food differed from those of townspeople, while occasionally he referred to habits that were common in both town and country.[45]

Hart regarded meat as the most nourishing and congenial food of mankind, but he started his discussion of foods with cereals, for these were 'the staff of life'; no meal was ordinarily served without bread, he maintained. He was plainly conversant with the difference in cereals used for bread in the south of England, the north, Scotland and Wales as well as the Continent and the West Indies – this last perhaps learned from books rather than actual experience. After cereals, he proceeded with roots, which he thought was the food eaten by mankind long before flesh (a shrewd and perhaps original observation), then herbs, greenstuff and fruit, before he arrived at meat and fish. He ended with seasonings, spices, sauces and drinks. More of his detailed remarks will be recounted below. Here we disentangle some of his fundamental beliefs and principles about diet, which summarized opinions shared by others in the 1630s, and pertain to an East Midland countryside.[46]

We have already noticed troubled comments on gluttony and drunkenness before 1600, which gave contradictory verdicts on the prevailing scene. In a broad survey published in 1587 William Harrison had not inflated the problem to scandalous proportions. Hart in 1633 was convinced that these evils had increased in his lifetime, and had spread from poor folk to gentlemen. Once upon a time these indulgences had been reserved for night revels that were particularly associated with beggars – hence the phrase 'drunk as a beggar'. But nowadays people were seen unashamedly reeling up and down the streets in daytime, including gentlemen assuming the right to 'grace their gentility' by the practice, he said. Our Puritan was plainly riding a hobby horse with these words, but some harsh truths doubtless lay behind it all.[47]

Hart was also sharply aware of changing fashions in food and drink in his day, and again as a Puritan he was highly critical. His sharpest jibes were directed at the womenfolk whom he thought responsible for most of the fads of the moment. They liked sweet things, and had taken such a liking to sugar that honey was now despised. His medical experience surfaced here when he warned his readers that sugar rotted the teeth. More significantly, perhaps, he suspected that the high death rate in London, as shown in the Bills of Mortality, was due to merchants whitening sugar with lees of lime. This sobering possibility is something our historians have yet to consider. Women also used a lot of cream in their dishes. They served it with strawberries and with apples; Hart frowned again.[48]

In eating meat, another fashion had developed, favouring young animals still at the suckling stage. Sucking lambs, for example, were evidently eaten under six weeks old, when Hart considered that two-year-old wethers were equally good. Young poultry were also a fad of the 'palate pleasers' whereas he thought that nothing beat a fat capon. That represented a change of taste since Elizabethan days when it was said that people never ate pullets. Among wild game, quails were the height of fashion – Hart saw this as another fad for something rare (their credit would quickly 'crack' if they became as common as capons) – and he saw the same folly in the high reputation of plovers, and yet more in a few women's practice of nurturing snails in their gardens, and serving them in milk broth. The snail remedy had insinuated itself into country ways, he asserted, being given to sick people in the countryside around Northampton. In roguish mood, he did not discount the possibility that snails and frogs, already eaten by the French, would become equally common in England, like French clothing fashions, he said.[49]

Hart was a traditionalist and out of love with novelties, which often came from abroad. The old proverb about some people's liking for food that was 'far-fetched and dear-bought' tripped off his tongue, and, having already expressed his prejudice against women nursing the sick, he added another on this score: expensive things were 'good for the ladies'. Was he perhaps more conscious in Northamptonshire than he would have been elsewhere of well-heeled gentry families living round about? They were certainly present in some number, more perhaps than in some other counties. So, countering such notions, he spoke strongly in favour of home-grown herbs. We had so many efficacious plants in England, he saw no need to pay heavily for costly herbs and spices that often arrived from afar in rotten condition. Some eloquent sentences fastened on sage, whose sovereign virtues Sir John Harington had recorded in verse in 1607. Hart reported the oft-cited adage asking why anyone could possibly die when he had sage growing in his garden. Hart shared that faith, adding that if it had been fetched from the East or West Indies and had become the fashion among 'our shagd or slasht mounsieurs', it would quickly have been picked up in the country 'for we are all now for the new cut'. His implied neglect of sage, however, runs against the evidence of other writers who plainly gave a high place to sage in their diet, starting the morning with sage butter to clear the brain.[50]

RECIPE BOOKS

Our picture of food so far in this period has come from the literate classes reporting their general observations. We now turn to more practical books for the recipes in use in literate, well-to-do households. Among authors of these books one figure towers above all the others at the beginning of the period, and that is Hugh Platt. We have already noticed him in the 1590s, describing emergency foods that could alleviate hunger in the years of serious food shortage between 1594 and 1597. He published this advice in 1596 in *Sundrie New and Artificall Remedies against Famine*. By 1602 memories of that food crisis were fading, and now he addressed a different audience, skilfully summarizing new trends in food preparation that he had watched as they developed into a fashion in the 1580s and 1590s until by now they had become established practices with the smart set. They were commonly seen in gentle households in and around London, and he wished to make them known further afield. *Delightes for Ladies* was his title, the book written in an attractive, chatty style, with asides that gave his women readers tips on shopping that would allow the more economical of them to indulge in the new food fashions. For us his topics signal the notable features in cooking procedures that would dominate food literature for the next 50 years. They were concerned with preserving food longer than ever before, conserving vegetables and fruits so that they could be enjoyed out of season, and candying with sugar, another way of preserving that was becoming ever more common since sugar was so freely available in the market and people were developing a taste for sweet things. Lastly, he offered what he called the 'secrets in distillation', giving practical advice on the use of the still, and showing how enthusiasm for distillation, which we have already noticed growing gently through the sixteenth century, was spreading further, yielding new flavours and fragrances in the making of flower waters and the extracting of essential oils. The skill in all this was being refined to the point where Platt could give a speedier method for distilling than those used before, and a way of storing rose leaves in a tightly closed pot in order to distil rosewater later – as late as Michaelmas. This, he explained, would enable you to buy roses in bulk in the market when they sold for only 7d. or 8d. a bushel. Some of Platt's other recipes offered new ways within old traditions, such as making brawn, or Polonia sausage, frying fish in rape oil instead of olive oil, or making good mustard sauce in the Venetian way. The practical good sense of the book must certainly have made it a delight for ladies, and its popularity is evident in its many editions: in 1605, 1608, 1609 and 1611; and in seven more editions up to 1636.[51]

Did Platt's work, in fact, diminish the need for more recipe books from others? The thought occurs because one might otherwise have expected to find their number expanding, following those that had begun to be published in the 1570s, 1580s and 1590s. In fact, things worked out differently. Instead, writers moved off adventurously to discover more about cooking styles on the Continent of Europe. Curiosity about foreign countries had been enormously stimulated in Elizabeth's reign, so cooks with foreign experience and an urge to write turned their energies in that direction. The most prolific author in this class was John Murrell, publishing in 1617, 1621 and 1631 books that boasted of his travels in France, Italy, the Low Countries, and elsewhere, and containing recipes culled abroad. His first two books in 1617, *A New Booke of Cookerie* and *Daily Exercise for Ladies and Gentlewomen* bore traces of Platt's influence in their emphasis on the latest fashions and the inclusion of foreign usages. But he also paid attention to English traditions in cooking meat, fish and fowl. He used spices and dried fruits in the old style, often used barberries to sharpen his sauces (and since some of these recipes were French they raise the question whether the taste for barberries, or perhaps for sauces in general, was partly driven from France). He used potatoes on more than one occasion, 'if you have any' – and if not, then skirret. He liked salads of flowers, and followed Platt in favouring the pickling of cucumbers. When he published his 1621 book, *A Delightfull Daily Exercise for Ladies and Gentlewomen*, his Epistle to the Reader promised to add at the end a treatise on cooking for the unskilful, but nothing of that sort was recognizable in the text. His foreign conceits seemed more prominent than in 1617; indeed, the title page promised the choicest dishes in French and Dutch fashions, and started with a capon cooked with cauliflower. John Parkinson has already alerted us to the rarity of cauliflowers, so we can imagine the puzzled grimace of some readers from the very first page. The next recipe used butter to butter a cauliflower, and the second advised on drawing butter thick as cream, another notion savouring at this date of Dutch more than English taste. Other recipes, like fritters to garnish meat and salad dishes, needed special metal moulds that could be bought from Thomas Dewe in St Dunstan's churchyard in Fleet Street, and these may well have been foreign imports. Other recipes, for French biskets, Italian crust, and candied fruit and flowers, savoured of Platt's recommendations, while the experiments with potatoes showed an individual touch in a recipe for tossing them in a candy height syrup and drying them on glass. Readers who had not already read Platt or kept abreast of London fashions may well have felt that this book belonged to a different world from theirs.[52]

Platt and Murrell were virtually the only authors of substantial cookbooks in this period. The only other author was Henry Grey, Lord Ruthin, son of the eleventh earl of Kent, whose recipe book, *The Ladies Cabinet Opened*, was issued in 1639, the year of his death. But his book is a puzzle. His recipes dealt with preserving and conserving in the mood then current, as well as embracing physic, surgery and general cookery, but his name does not appear on the title page. It is still attributed to Lord Ruthin and was issued again in 1654, though that was some years after his death. It is difficult to believe that Lord Ruthin really was the author of this cookery book, especially since his widow, the Countess of Kent, published her own cookery book, *A True Gentlewoman's Delight*, in 1653. The recipes must have emanated from the same kitchen, and certainly they yielded some very similar, though not identical, recipes: so the two works will be considered together as books belonging to the 1650s. They will leave us without any explanation for their being separately published, though one may suspect in 1639 some diffidence on the part of a woman of noble birth (she was Elizabeth Talbot, daughter of the seventh Earl of Shrewsbury) in publishing her own cookery book in a world that expected authors to be male. Did an opportunist publisher perhaps assist in 1639, whereas some dispute in the 1650s resulted in two slightly different cookery books being published in 1653 and 1654? By then, after 15 years without any fresh cookery publications, new cookery books were almost certainly in demand.[53]

FOOD MIRRORED IN HOUSEHOLD ACCOUNTS

Variety in diet was expanding at this time, as merchants going overseas spread their nets more widely, bringing back highly varied and frequent food cargoes, which inland provision merchants carried to towns far from London. Diaries and correspondence of the gentry give evidence of the wide circle of family and friends that was entertained in manor houses, and vividly conjure up a picture of the way food news was being spread. Our documents now allow us to watch individual families broadening their tastes, and picking up the latest food fads and fashions. We cannot, of course, see their cooks in the kitchen, nor the dishes served at their tables, but we may well spot changing food styles and changing habits through their menus and household accounts when they placed their orders with grocers and bought from other food suppliers. Our view of such things is still concentrated on the gentry class, but it is not unrealistic to envisage some middle-class families in towns following some of the same routines, since deliveries in quantity of fairly exotic foodstuffs were already reaching towns like Canterbury, York and Manchester.

Our first question must be to ask what sort of cook the fashionable gentry looked for in the 1620s. A lively portrait with significant detail is given by James

Howell in his *Familiar Letters* in June 1630, when Lady Cor [*sic*] asked him to recommend a cook who had seen the world abroad. He sent her a candidate, assuring her that he could marinate fish, make jellies, a piquant sauce and a haugou (was this a haggis?). He was also quite good at *olla podrida*, a Spanish-style stew, for which he knew all the ingredients to turn it into a gourmet's delight, namely, mutton, beef, bacon, cabbage, turnips, artichokes, potatoes, dates and more. In an amusing play with words Howell turned the *olla podrida* into a demanding matron, who also 'must have marrow to keep life in her and some birds to make her light'; moreover, 'she must go adorned with chains of sausages'. This was unlike the pottage or stew in traditional English style, but the eulogy suggests how fashionable were Spanish dishes at this time, the reason being that Prince Charles was wooing the Spanish Infanta for marriage and, as it happened, Howell was also in Madrid at the same time. In the event, the royal marriage plans fell through, and Howell travelled home from Madrid in convoy with all the jewels that Charles had intended for his wedding gifts. Nevertheless, Spanish food had been temporarily in vogue in 1624, and when the fashion faded, Frenchmen's skill in marinating fish, making jellies and piquant sauces were alternatives.[54]

When we next ask what the gentry actually ate at table, we turn to their household accounts as an informative source, and use these to fill in another section of our picture. One sixteenth-century Italian author assumed that the family's choice of food and flavourings represented the commands and preferences of the master of the household. We meet such an assertion with surprise and scepticism, though we can never know the whole truth of that matter. What is clear is that all families had distinctive food styles. Knowing more of the gentry than other classes, we can confidently say that they were not one uniform class in food conventions, but rather divided into several, even many, groups. They differed in their lavishness at table, and also in their regional customs and personal food preferences; and some of that was obviously dictated by the agricultural conditions under which their food was grown, bred and caught.

The Townshend family of Stiffkey in Norfolk offer a first example. They laid out an astonishing variety of meats at every single meal. Page after page in their chef's list of menus names the meats for dinner and supper. The greatest variety was reserved for the high table, embracing poultry, wild birds, mutton, rabbits, beef, venison, pork, fish and shellfish, while a more modest array sufficed for the 'board's end', where, presumably, the senior household officials sat. For them, mutton figured largest of all, but they also ate plenty of rabbit, capons, rather less roast beef and roast veal, and fish, but not wild birds. The only named accompaniments to the meat were salads, artichokes and butter. As the artichokes appeared more often at the board's end than at the high table, it is likely that these were Jerusalem artichokes. Jerusalem artichokes had been a rare, new delicacy in the sixteenth century, but in cultivation they spread so easily that they soon lost their status as a delicacy and became commonplace. They became just another root crop, and they would have helped to fill the stomachs of servants very satisfactorily. Sometimes, indeed, on a lean day the second course of meats at the board's end consisted only of rabbits and artichokes, though usually they had more choice than that.[55]

As for the lord of the household, he did not despise Jerusalem artichokes, but they appeared less often at his table, and it is always possible that his were globe artichokes. More distinctive were the many luxury dishes set before him, like roast mutton with oysters, a carp pie, roast swan and, seemingly verging on this category, roast pig, roast pullets, marrow bones, pigeon and pigeon pie. These were dishes that the household officials did not taste. Nor did they finish the meal with a tart, or a pear tart, as did their master and his family sometimes. It is possible that the tart was still slightly unusual among some families, though it was becoming more of a routine. We shall see below other evidence of the growing taste for sweetmeats and confections.

Another family offering a sight of their meals was the Shuttleworths in Lancashire. We examined their household accounts in the 1580s and 1590s in Chapter 3. But significant changes in their lifestyle overtook the scene in the next 20 years, between 1600 and 1620. Their records relate to household purchases rather than menus, so their meals are to some extent still guesswork. Even so, some conclusions are possible. In the first years of the century, they were building a new house at Gawthorpe, which meant that much food had to be given to labourers. This seems to account for large purchases of cheese and butter, not seen before, and going far beyond the quantities that their domestic dairy could supply. Womenfolk in the neighbourhood filled the gap, and only once was butter bought at Padiham market.[56]

As we noted in the late sixteenth century, the Shuttleworths' favoured meat was veal and calves' head, usually bought locally, often at Whalley; and evidently breast of veal was even more special, for this was a particular purchase when Mr Cuthbert Hesketh, their physician, came to eat in December 1605. The liking for veal, as we noted earlier, lights up the dairying speciality in Lancashire. When the family wanted beef, they bought fat oxen or cows in Clitheroe and Preston; mutton was also bought, once coming from Whalley nearby. Plenty of fish continued to reach the table, as we saw in Chapter 3, usually from Preston, where herrings were bought by the barrel, as well as salt fish and salt salmon, cockles and mussels. In the first years of the seventeenth century the absence of any sugar purchases persisted – the family bought honey instead, and their interest in spices and dried fruits seemed modest compared with earlier purchases in London – but now they sometimes bought in York, and so maybe they relied on smaller quantities ordered more often; the caterer needed only ½lb of currants,

1lb of prunes, and small quantities of aniseed, mace, and cloves for one Christmas preparation.[57]

Bread still consisted of oatcake, for they were always drying oats in the kiln and milling oatmeal and cut groats. (They also used oats in brewing beer.) The occasional purchase of 'wheat bread for my master', and on one occasion two loaves of wheat bread for household use, suggests a special concession – perhaps for a change, perhaps for a sick family member, since the physicians always sought more digestible foods to aid their patients' recovery. The idiosyncrasy, noted in Chapter 3, that made a special feature of pepper among the food provisions, persisted, and is made more mysterious by the entry in June 1602 when they bought two ounces of pepper 'against the rearing', preparing for a celebration when the building of the new hall had reached the roof. They also paid for a piper that day.[58]

The eating experiences of the Shuttleworth family underwent a profound change when they spent nearly a year renting a house in Islington, near London, between July 1608 and May 1609. The diet at home thereafter changed in many ways. While at Islington, they bought cucumber, radishes, parsley, carrots, lettuce, eight artichokes (these sound like globe artichokes) and pints of salad oil. Among fruits and nuts they tasted cherries, apples, oranges, plums, damsons, walnuts, hazelnuts and bullaces. We cannot know how many of these vegetables and fruits were a new experience; they had eaten oranges and cherries before, but none of these items appeared in the same quantity in the household accounts when the family was in Lancashire, and not all of them can have been home grown. It is reasonable, therefore, to argue that a qualitative change took place in the family's diet when in London that made a permanent difference. For one thing, they had to buy bread, and we can assume that it was wheat bread and not oatcake. Did they have a hankering for their favourite Lancashire cereal when they bought a peck of oatmeal groats in January 1609, which the editor of these accounts guesses was for black puddings? They developed a liking for Holland cheese, not having their local cheeses to hand. Most noticeable of all, they tasted sweetmeats. They bought comfits from Thomas Leaver the confectioner in February 1609, and when they journeyed back to Lancashire, Mr Leaver sold them 6lbs of sugar for 5s. 4d. Thus we can picture the changes that their London visit had wrought. Thereafter sugar was one of their regular household expenses – 6lbs in May 1610, 6lbs 12ozs in October 1612, and a box of sweetmeats which Mr Leaver sent particularly for 'my young mistress' in March 1613. A taste for cakes crept into the record around 1610; Halifax cakes were bought in May 1610 and Banbury cakes in March 1612. This last commission actually involved a journey to Warwick to buy them, for which the journey alone cost 30s! But perhaps the taste for sweet things was beginning to be met locally, since the family bought sweetmeats in Bolton in May 1612.[59]

Other finicky London tastes may be suspected to lurk behind the purchase (though perhaps for medicinal use) of two ounces of pomegranate flowers beaten to powder and two ounces unpounded in May 1610, costing 3s. 6d., and wine vinegar bought for 4s. 4d. Yet again, the order for spices and dried fruits subsequently represented much larger quantities than hitherto and included new additions. In September 1617 Mr Leaver despatched a large order for dried fruit plus 4lbs of Jordan almonds, 3lbs of almond comfits, 18lbs of powder sugar and many fruits, which were presumably candied for some were out of season – cherries, barberries, raspberries, gooseberries and plums. These were a special order since the lady of the house was in childbed. More comfits were bought in London in October 1617 and in November 1617 more spices and fruits – 4lbs of case pepper, 24lbs of prunes, 20lbs of two kinds of raisins, 18lbs of currants, and 18lbs of powder sugar. When the same items were ordered in March 1618, yet more fresh tastes were in evidence, for a barrel of olives was included, a barrel of capers, and 8lbs of figs. By 1617 we clearly have to envisage the tastes of a younger generation influencing the scene. Purchases from the London comfit maker continued in February and June 1620. Already in February 1619 spices were being bought in Manchester, including a new item – 2lbs of treacle – and sweeetmeats came from Manchester in June 1620. We can reasonably infer from this that the demand for these indulgences had reached Lancashire more generally. A new interest in custards may also be signalled by the Shuttleworths' purchase of eight custard pots in June 1620.[60]

We noted in Chapter 3 the sophistication that was signalled in some London circles when people recognized different varieties of turnip at the meal table. Perhaps that discerning eye for the quality of roots had arrived in Lancashire by December 1611, for the household accounts record buying not just turnips, but 'Manchester turnips'. Moreover, after the family had returned to Lancashire the mistress of the house took a much greater interest in vegetable seeds for planting in the kitchen garden. The family had always bought onion seed, but after 1616 were added lombard lettuce, clary, purslane, tarragon, thyme, French sorrel and more. Thereafter vegetable seeds featured more prominently still, being bought 'for my mistress'. They included radish seed, carrot seed, garden seeds sent from somewhere far away to be picked up at Colne, carrot and leek seeds in March 1621, turnip seeds, and garden seeds. Another sign of the times was the purchase of Rimbert Dodoens's *Herbal* in October 1621. The lifestyle of the Shuttleworth family had entered a new phase. It was firmly in contact with current cultural trends emanating from London, and certain fashions now affected goods on sale in Manchester. The beginnings of all this go back to a date shortly after the family returned from their stay in London. The Shuttleworth accounts come to an end in 1621 and we can follow them no further. Nevertheless, they embolden us to throw a bridge across the years of this decade linking the lifestyle of one

Lancashire gentry family with the trends that underlay the writings of the botanist John Parkinson and were not totally unrelated to the food scene that James Hart depicted from his Midland viewpoint. Local differences reflected distinctive local experiences, but food choices were broadening for this class of well-to-do people everywhere, along with travel and trade.[61]

THE WORK-A-DAY FOOD OF ORDINARY FOLK

In searching for more work-a-day food in the houses of middle class and labouring people before 1640, we lack any writers with sufficient curiosity to report on recipes at first hand, and so we are driven to comb the work of those who did not offer recipes but at least gave credible accounts of food seen on the table. Food had become a subject that was worthy of literary comment: poets and dramatists noticed it; writers on husbandry had food production at the centre of their concerns, and physicians, as students of health and sickness, had rules and opinions. Their descriptions, comments and advice offer some insights into the current scene. Among the dramatists one might hope for a glimpse of food in Shakespeare's plays, for they brim over with scenes of conviviality. But literary critics always notice how little interest Shakespeare took in the subject of food. He drank in alehouses, and doubtless ate in taverns and inns, probably writing some of his plays amid the hubbub of many companions exchanging raillery and ribaldry. But when we look for food in his plays, and surely expect to find a reference at least to 'pottage', the word does not make a single appearance. A 'pottle of sack' is there, and 'the pottlepot' for carousing; it seems that drink was more interesting than food.[62]

If Shakespeare disappoints us, then what of Ben Jonson? He showed a positive interest in food and where it came from. The best and most informative picture is given in his poem, 'To Penshurst', though it is a view of a rich man's generous hospitality to his friends and associates, which included Jonson and his like. It is informative, but sheds no light on the food of ordinary folk, except insofar as it implies that the Sidney family kept open house for all comers. When Jonson was at table at Penshurst, he was offered 'plentie of meat. Thy tables hoord [hoard] not up for the next day', he wrote; and no one counted how many cups he drank.[63]

In the same poem, moreover, we are given a sparkling account of all the food produced on the estate at Penshurst: mutton, beef, veal, rabbits, pheasants, partridges, fish from the river Medway and from ponds (carp, pike, eels), as well as fruit from the orchard (cherries, plums, figs, grapes, quinces, apricots and peaches). In addition, Jonson portrayed the lord's neighbours bringing more gifts of food, a procession of which we have already seen many examples: they brought capons, 'a rural cake', nuts and apples. Cheese was given by those who 'think they make the better cheeses' – a nice reference to ordinary countrywomen, inhabiting circles outside those of gentle folk, who plainly prided themselves on their own special recipes. Such gifts were really superfluous in these well-provisioned houses – they were 'far above the need of such', says Jonson – but still the neighbours brought them, cherishing their lord for his fine reputation for entertaining his guests with exactly the same food as he ate himself. The women bringing gifts were the producers of such food, so we can be sure that they occasionally tasted it.[64]

Among the poets of this age, the most rewarding writer on peasant food is undoubtedly Robert Herrick. He was another Londoner, educated, it is thought, at Cambridge university, and a one-time companion of Jonson in London's taverns. But then he moved to a parsonage deep in the Devon countryside, at Dean Prior on the edge of Dartmoor. Although he dropped remarks that are much quoted by the critics, fretting at his isolation from London, and 'this loathed country-life', constituting 'a long and irksome banishment', some of his poems show warm appreciation of the pleasures and contentment of country living, with which many of us will sympathize. His 'New Year's Gift' sent to Sir Simeon Steward contrasted London's political ferment unfavourably with a much more innocent and joyous country round; he offered his friend at the time of the Twelfth Night festivities 'no news of navies burnt at seas', 'no closet plot or open vent, that frights men with a Parliament', but rather 'winter's tales and mirth that milk-maids make about the hearth … [and] twelf-tide cakes of peas and beans … [along with] fired chestnuts' leaping from the hearth. So when Herrick was ejected from his living as a Royalist in 1647, and went back to London, swearing never to return, he plainly thought better of it and did return in 1662, dying at Dean Prior in 1674. A poem entitled 'His Content in the Country' in *Hesperides* describes the contentment, along with the food, with the conviction of an old man who had learned many lessons along the way:

> Here, here I live with what my board,
> Can with the smallest cost afford.
> Though ne'er so mean the viands be,
> They well content my Prew and me [this was his maidservant Prudence]
> Or pea, or bean, or wort, or beet,
> Whatever comes, content makes sweet:
> Here we rejoice, because no rent
> We pay for our poor tenement:
> Wherein we rest, and never fear
> The landlord or the usurer.[65]

More poems that are equally specific about Herrick's country meals conjure up a true-to-life picture of peasant food that was tasty and much relished. The weddings and funerals, the country festivals at May day, harvest home and Christmas all brought out a generous array of carefully prepared and home-cooked country fare.

> Ye shall see first the large and cheefe
> Foundation of your feast, fat beefe,
> With upper stories, mutton, veal
> And bacon (which makes full the meale)
> With sev'rall dishes standing by,
> As here a custard, there a pie
> And here all tempting frumentie
> And for to make the merry cheere,
> If smirking wine be wanting here,
> There's that which drowns all care, stout beere.[66]

The contentment of the simple life is yet again unambiguously stated in 'Content, not Cates':

> A little pipkin with a bit
> Of mutton or of veal in it,
> Set on my table (trouble-free)
> More than a feast contenteth me.

For the most vivid picture of the daily meal, however, we turn to 'Thanksgiving'.

> Lord, I confesse, too, when I dine
> The pulse is thine
> And all those other bits that bee
> There plac'd by thee,
> The worts, the purslain and the messe
> Of watercresse
> Which of thy kindnesse Thou hast sent;
> And my content
> Makes those, and my beloved beet
> To be more sweet.
> 'Tis thou that crown'st my glittering hearth
> With guiltlesse mirth,
> And giv'st me wassaile bowles to drink,
> Spic'd to the brink.

Here are the beans (an ingredient that recurs more than any other in the poems and was a basic item in poor men's pottage), the peas, the cabbage, the purslane, the watercress and the root vegetables, and since Herrick mentioned spice that went into the drink, we can be sure that his faithful maidservant, Prudence

Baldwin, included flavourings in the more solid fare that went into the pottage on the fire. Herrick saw his cook as a veritable treasure in his life, and when she died, he hoped that violets might blossom on her grave.[67]

The third writer shedding light on peasant food was Gervase Markham, who may seem oddly placed with the poets and dramatists, though he was, in fact, another poet *and* dramatist (momentarily likened to Shakespeare) until he turned to writing the books of husbandry for which he is best known. His guides to farming, horse management and hunting are practical, carefully phrased textbooks that were read to pieces in their time. So he fits conveniently here as a writer and farmer who also observed food on the family table of ordinary folk, and then was prodded to go still further and investigate procedures in the kitchen. His recipes and instructions on the preparation of food in *The English Housewife* are precise, and plainly spring from sound personal knowledge; they add much information on the way food was prepared, and many of the details will be further examined below. Here we confine ourselves to his general observations on food and foodways that shed light on the conventional assumptions and routines of unceremonious, everyday housekeeping. Markham did not claim the original text of the work as his own, but had edited and added to the work of someone else.[68]

Markham might at first be thought an unreliable authority on everyday food, for he came of a gentry family in Nottinghamshire, had a university education, attended at court and served overseas as a soldier. He was not peasant-born. But he then spent nine years as a working farmer, talking much with his fellow farmers, learning from them many different methods and prejudices and learning to respect them as well. He wrote careful books of instruction on farming, show-ing a keen eye for the practicalities of life. So when this work for the English housewife came his way, he deemed it worth publication, and set about editing it in a professional way. He described the owner of the manuscript as an honourable countess but did not name her; nor did he suggest that she was the author. Most probably it belonged to someone else working in her kitchen. Within the text, which he amended and reorganized, he directed his remarks at the housewife in 'every goodman's house' that can 'as well feed the poor as the rich'. Priority was given to the making of good pottage, while he sought outside help on the subject of medicine and wine, on which he plainly did not regard himself as a specialist. He distinguished firmly between everyday foods and dishes that he deemed fanciful or foreign, but by page 110 he had reached a point, quite reasonably, where he felt able to move to 'banqueting stuff', recognizing that while they were 'not of general use', all classes used them at festive times.[69]

Economical housekeeping was Markham's watchword, and that struck the right note with housewives of his day. It meant making use of everything edible that lay to hand, first for food, and, if not, then for feeding livestock and finally for fuel. One should not *buy* anything unnecessarily: that was a rule of life that Markham, along with others of his time, constantly urged. The housewife should ensure that her meals 'proceed more from the provision of her own yard than the furniture of the markets'. Simple recipes were thus the order of the day, and that meant that 'every goodman's house' would be more concerned with 'ordinary wholesome boiled meats' (using the word 'meat' to mean not just flesh but food in general). The everyday cook reached for a cooking pot, not for a spit or an oven.[70]

Markham emphasized this message in another way by urging the housewife to avoid rare, strange and foreign foodstuffs. In his fine 1986 edition of Markham's text, Professor Michael Best sardonically notes that Markham's recipes did, in fact, call for many imported seasonings. But while that doubtless reflected the style of the original manuscript compiled for a countess, by 1615, 200 years after spices had first been introduced from the East, we have to assume that merchants had made them familiar through the land, and some were accessible to all in small amounts. The Shuttleworths in Lancashire, for example, once bought pepper from a pedlar. This was almost certainly on an occasion when he wandered into the village, enabling other village folk to buy small amounts at the same time. We can safely assume that the everyday housewife occasionally bought spices like ginger, cloves and mace for special occasions. Though a gulf was apparent to contemporaries separating the rich, who caught on to any new fashion no matter how expensive or esoteric, and the ordinary housewife, who shunned new-fangled gimmicks, even she could sometimes afford a touch of luxury.[71]

Time was almost certainly reducing the price of some spices, though inflation makes it difficult to measure the change realistically among ordinary folk. Prices in household accounts, not allowing for inflation, show them, as one would expect, much more expensive in 1617 than in the fifteenth century. But Shakespeare offers us a neat phrase betokening the economical usages of country people in *The Winter's Tale* when the Clown is preparing a sheep-shearing feast – a country festival that might have allowed for some indulgence in spices. He picked and chose those for which he was prepared to pay. He would pay for saffron to colour the warden pies, he said (much saffron was by then being grown in England), but he would not admit mace or dates into the recipe for 'that's out of my note'; and to get a root of ginger he expected to beg someone for it.[72]

A further glimpse of the country housewife's priorities is vouchsafed by Markham's attention to the dairy. He registered its supreme importance by devoting a whole chapter to it, and described cow's milk as 'the main of a housewife's profit'. Its essential role among household provisions was yet more eloquently enunciated in 1594 in a play by Thomas Lodge and Robert Greene, *A Looking Glass for London and Englande*: 'My cow is a commonwealth to me, for first, sir, she allows me, my wife and son for to banquet ourselves withal: butter, cheese, whey, curds, cream, sod [boiled] milk, raw milk, sour milk, sweet milk, and buttermilk.' The expanding story of dairy produce at this period will occupy more space below, but everything points to a growing appreciation of its versatility, a readiness to recognize its value for health (thereby ending the prejudices that had confined it to the poor), and a growing commercial market that would further diversify its products. One major step was taken in that direction when the meat courses at gentlemen's tables were followed by a milky confection. Among those, the curd cheese tart must hold pride of place, for it turns up often in the sixteenth and seventeenth centuries among both rich people and farming folk. On Henry Best's farm at Elmswell in East Yorkshire it was a noontime treat for sheep shearers in 1642. A clear recipe is that of the Countess of Kent in her recipe book of 1653. Apart from its large quantities, it virtually reproduces the one that has been traditional in the family of my Yorkshire in-laws for more than a century.[73]

Markham's manuscript allotted no singular place to herbs, vegetables and fruit, and in no way highlighted the novelties that were changing the face of horticulture at this time. Rather, he took them for granted, noting first and foremost, as any farmer might do, that the housewife's 'first step thereunto [i.e to get a knowledge of cookery] is to have knowledge of all sorts of herbs belonging to the kitchen, whether they be for the pot, for sallats, for sauces, for servings, or for any other seasoning, or adorning'. In this respect, the housewife was expected to have the skills of a cultivator, knowing when to plant what, and so Markham gave a summary account of the skill she needed in the garden; he could not have given a clearer sign of the role of greenstuff in meals.[74]

CONCLUSION

A multitude of different trends have mingled in this survey of life impinging on the food scene between 1600 and 1640. In the background lay recurring food shortages, but they persisted alongside courageous endeavours to remedy the situation by improving the food supply through overseas trade, increasing home-grown produce, especially dairy foods, vegetables and fruit, and farming more efficiently with the help of enclosure, the draining of fenland, and the use of new crop rotations. An ingenious, lone planner, thinking along entirely fresh lines, was Richard Corne, a merchant who had spent 20 years in Normandy, and offered a scheme in 1625 for planting fruit trees all over England, as he saw them in Normandy. He wanted an Act to insist that every farmer of a ploughland planted 300 trees on one acre of ground. Thus the land now growing barley for beer would be released for wheat. He was sure that people in time would learn to like cider as much as beer, for it was more nourishing, and a year's supply was made in one season instead of employing, as now, servants every week to make a fresh brew. Keeping an orchard, moreover, was far less work than cultivating cereals. His was surely a far-sighted time-and-motion study, and unusual at this period. Meanwhile, other strategies improved the food supply. Better use was being made of existing resources like the seasonal wildfowl caught in decoys. Some gluttonous appetites may have been curbed in response to dietary theories spread by physicians, or by the lessons of experience. Some of the demand for food was eased by the emigration of settlers to the New World. Various of these trends would strengthen in the next two decades when civil war unsettled lives and stirred many fresh attitudes. Ranking the relative importance of these many tendencies is impossible, but the historian who focuses primarily on the food supply may reasonably vaunt above all others emerging skills in food preservation, because it has been so neglected in historical discussions hitherto. It held out great promise for the future, by improving the quantity of food that was available to all classes through all seasons of the year. It absorbed food that would otherwise have been wasted in seasons when the supply was more than sufficient for current needs. Then, the known success of preservation encouraged the production of yet larger quantities, just as our present-day use of freezers has encouraged us to grow and then store so many foods for months after their season has passed.[75]

In this connection, it is worth pondering the observation of Arthur Standish in 1612 in his treatise, *The Commons Complaint*: in his experience fruit in a plentiful year eased the price of victuals. Effectively, he was saying that the greater diversity of foods in certain months noticeably eased the demand for cereals and meat. These were early days in the history of food preservation, but by the eighteenth century it must count as one of the factors explaining how England managed to feed its growing population. It is a powerful argument waiting to be woven into the economists' explanation for higher food productivity, which so often focuses solely on the yield per acre of cereals and meat.[76]

The preservatives were salt, vinegar and sugar. The great increase in sugar imports is so conspicuous in our customs records in the seventeenth century that no one has yet sought to measure the trend. Vinegar was an ancient, home-produced preservative, which had many possible flavours according to the tastes and traditions of individual families, but again it has failed to arouse scholarly interest. Salt was the third preservative that evidently did stir enthusiasm and enterprise in this period, since four patents were registered for making salt between 1630 and 1635. But that may not have betokened any great increase in the use of salt, since, according to John Collins, a knowledgeable writer on the subject in 1682, its price had risen sharply in 1627 and 1628 because of the war between France and England. Perhaps that was the reason for the patents.[77]

More qualitative differences in the food scene will doubtless be uncovered in the future as we turn our gaze from the wide horizon and become more sensitive to localized and short-term changes on the food scene. We can already catch glimpses of women's efforts to expand supplies of poultry, for example, of men's efforts in increasing the number of warrens to supply more rabbits, and of the improved supplies of fresh and pond fish in southern England. But there is more to discover if we listen with sensitive ears to the gossip here, there and everywhere. The household accounts of Sir William Smyth of Hill Hall, Theydon Mount, Essex from 1633 onwards seem to show particular interest in roots, carrots and turnips, matching other such signs noticed above in other parts of the country. We may note the more frequent references in our documents, first to Parmesan, Angelot, and Dutch cheeses, and then to Cheshire and Banbury cheeses, supporting the suggestion that dairywomen in our own country were setting their sights on a larger trade; and we should perhaps ponder the opportunism of the second-rank playwrights, like Richard Brome and Thomas Nabbes, latching on to the latest modish words for the plays that they entitled *Covent Garden* (1632), *The Weeding of Covent Garden* (1632), and *The Sparagus Garden* (1635).[78]

5

War and a Renewed Search for Food, 1640–60

The 20 years between 1640 and 1660 call for discussion as a separate phase in food history, since the circumstances in which food was produced and supplied to consumers were unique. Civil war between 1642 and 1646 and again in 1648 caused the destruction of much food wherever the opposing armies engaged in battle; in villages where soldiers were quartered, they commandeered the food of local people. Butter and cheese were in demand on an unprecedented scale, being instant food, 'so ready a commodity' for soldiers wanting 'a bit(e) upon a march', that they counted it 'a sin martial' if they left any such food untouched. Even when the civil war in England came to an end, war broke out on other fronts, lasting from 1649 to 1652 and requiring soldiers to be sent to Ireland and then Scotland, and demanding the despatch of large quantities of provisions to sustain the soldiery, even though the army seized food freely from the Irish and Scots *en route*.[1]

FOOD IN NEW CIRCUMSTANCES: IN WAR; IN BAD WEATHER; UNDER A COMMONWEALTH

Our documents actually record the substantial quantities of butter, cheese and biscuit that were sent from Cheshire and East Anglia to Ireland and Scotland when once the Irish and the Scots were drawn into war. Cargoes with anything from five to 30 tons of Suffolk cheese, plus East Riding cheese, via Hull, went to Scotland in 1650. They conjure up a picture of dairying folk holding very mixed views on the respective merits of life in peace or war. War was an extraordinary stimulus to their kind of farming; and they must ruefully have faced many local customers who had to go short when the army took priority. We never catch sight of local food scarcities known to have been caused by such emergencies, but we can be sure that local people complained if they lacked their handiest cold food while working in the fields.[2] In other respects, the same story of varying local food supplies can be told with greater assurance. Some decisive battles were fought across the Midlands, devastating much food in the fields; one writer claimed to know of 3,000 sheep belonging to one man all killed by an encampment of soldiers in one night. The numbers were surely exaggerated, but when reduced to a more realistic 300 sheep, they are perfectly credible. So is the reporter's wry comment that the sad loser of the sheep was, in fact, a friend of that side in the war.[3]

Country people felt that their corn was safer than their animals, for animals could be swept away in a night, so they feared their worst cereal losses in war between July and September when the crops were ready for harvesting. Yet individuals could escape entirely from a misfortune that we as historians would tend to imagine being spread over a wide area, and encompassing everyone in sight. Plainly, it is dangerous to generalize. John Beale of Herefordshire stated authoritatively that in the late wars 'none of our poorest cottagers did see true want. In all our houses, they had the same number of meals, and the same constant fare'; and it is clear from another discourse in Hartlib's papers that even livestock farmers sometimes managed to save their animals from seizure by their timely removal to another place, when all around their neighbours suffered.[4]

Worse distress spread over all parts of the kingdom when a long spell of freak weather lasted for five years between 1646 and 1651 and destroyed harvests and animals year after year after year. It is most vividly depicted in the diary of Ralph Josselin, parson of Earls Colne in Essex, starting in September 1646 with a wet season when the harvest should already have been gathered but instead cereals rotted in the fields. The rain made the grass grow, yet meat and dairy foods rose sharply in price, and fruit rotted on the trees. The same unseasonal weather persisted relentlessly through 1647 and 1648, cattle disease spread, rye was killed by April frosts in 1648, hay rotted in flooded meadows between June and August, and corn was laid low. The disastrous weather continued through 1649, and although Josselin's own household evidently had sufficient food – 'we wanted nothing needful or fitting for use', he wrote in mid-April 1649 – by late November his family went without a meal a week in order to give food or money to the poor. Beggars were many, and especially in Cumberland and Westmorland it was said that 'the poorer sort are almost famished and some really so'. People died on the highways for want of bread, and many others were powerless to help themselves, having no seedcorn to plant and no money to buy food. The government received despairing petitions, and took action in April 1649 to secure corn from Hamburg. But we know how long such cargoes took to arrive; death from starvation became an all-too-familiar tragedy.[5]

Five years of precarious food supplies verging on famine in some districts lasted until the harvest of 1651. The misery was compounded by other dark forebodings about the future, for the execution of the king in 1649 and war in Ireland and Scotland extended political anxiety into the distant future: was not God punishing a sinful people, and for how long?

When confronting these dark thoughts, there nevertheless arose among some Parliamentarian supporters a spirit of almost messianic hope for a different future under a republic. This harnessed a fresh energy among landowners and farmers, eager to create a new commonwealth, improve agriculture, increase and diversify foodstuffs, and thus improve the condition of all classes. At that moment, the right man appeared, to harness this energy in a constructive way. Samuel Hartlib, a native of Poland living in England, and tireless in pursuit of his ideals to promote the commonweal, brought to his task strong international contacts and wide cultural and economic interests. He wove a web of correspondence among landowners, farmers and writers, intent on discussing and experimenting to produce more food, improve its quality, and extend its variety. No better mirror of all these conversations could be found than Hartlib's personal diary, *Ephemerides*. His circle of informants did not restrict their attention to cereals and meat, but passed information to each other about all kinds of other food – dairy produce, rabbits, poultry, bees for honey, vegetables and fruit. The large archive at Sheffield University incorporates Hartlib's remarkable letters, as well as the diary recording his visitors. It lights up a rural scene peopled with keen, innovative farmers and experimental food producers, including many women. Measured against the whole population of the kingdom, of course, they were a minority, but they successfully made contact with each other, through hearsay, chance encounters and books. Admittedly, their letters, treatises and other writings reveal little more than aspirations at this time, but the casual comments of travellers, titbits of news from observers in the countryside, and farmers' working notebooks show how the books actually influenced practice. The aspirations as regards food were grandly expressed in the anonymous work *Archimagirus Anglo-Gallicus* in 1658, promising to teach the reader a better art of cookery, which was 'none of the lowest requisites in a well-governed commonwealth'. It is worth noting alongside this that Nicholas Culpeper's remarkably successful herbal promised in its title health for the rich and poor *by diet without physic*.[6]

Thus the ten years between 1650 and 1660 were rich in constructive thought about improving food supplies and the health of all. It is noticeable how older authors were re-read: Arthur Standish's treatise of 1611, having been written in the hope of increasing supplies of meat, fruit and fuel, was circulated again, and read in a fresh light. The works of foreign authors, French and German, were passed around and digested. Foreign friends sent to Hartlib plants and livestock that represented new varieties and breeds: they promised tasty food from abroad if it was once transplanted to England; Van Mussig promised in 1648 to get a new sort of apple and send the kernels to Cologne for onward transmission to England; a year later he was commending Borsdorf apples as the best in Germany. Knowing the English love affair with cherries that had begun in Henry VIII's reign, Frederick Ludovick sent large black ones from Flanders in 1650. Did these, by any chance, play any part in the evolution of the large black cherries for which Hertfordshire was famed in 1750? Then Hartlib's son, Clodius, told his father of yet better cherries than the English in Holstein, and another correspondent praised highly the great black cherries of Pomerania and Mecklenburg. Turnips having become a fancy of the English gentry, Grundmann sent news in 1648 of a fine Brunswick variety, and Clodius recommended in 1651 another kind – sweet turnips from Mark Brandenburg. A Paris correspondent passed on information from a lady in Rouen describing how calves in France were fed on boiled turnips. It is, of course, true that through time immemorial plants and livestock have been exchanged across countries, but traffic at this period was more than ordinarily purposeful.[7]

Hartlib, for his part, published in his own book, *Samuel Hartlib: His Legacy*, the most useful proposals and opinions that came his way from all correspondents, revising its contents twice over in the second and third editions. He also constantly urged others to publish books. John Thomas, a gardener in St Albans, hoped to put his wisdom into a book that would sell for 6d., though our libraries show nothing to suggest that he succeeded. Other authors who did publish were Walter Blith, writing the very best book yet on arable farming and new crops in the 1650s, Ralph Austin writing on fruit trees, John Beale on fruit for cider- and perry-making, Robert Sharrock also on fruit, and Ad. Speed in *Adam out of Eden* (1659), aiming for more variety in food than anyone else with his instructions on rabbits; on the domestic rearing of birds, including pheasants and partridges; on keeping bees; and on growing more varied vegetables. As regards greenstuff and fruit, Speed focused on items that had become better known since Elizabethan days, including pumpkins, musk melons and roots. Roots, in particular, helped all classes, for it was clear that anyone could grow them.[8]

The full list of authors' topics at this time underlines the diversity of foods, both new and improved, that came under discussion and experiment. The practical questions about improving and spreading them were receiving many new answers. Cressy Dymock, for example, was intent on feeding poultry more cheaply, and had benefited from reading a French treatise on the subject. A Polish way of cramming capons was noted alongside different English ways that used meal with turnips and carrots, or bread soaked in ale; oats were evidently used by poor people to feed hens, but that was thought expensive, and these alternatives were deemed cheaper. To get hens laying more eggs, spurry was recommended. Rabbits were the subject of many experiments, after Mr Slegger's writings of 1588 were re-read, thought to be 'still valid', and acted upon. Breeding rabbits in hutches rather than in warrens was described, and the costs carefully calculated by one writer; some experiments of Sir Richard Weston were also referred to, and may possibly have followed the same lines. It is significant that recipes for rabbit pie in the 1650s prescribed 'conies, wild or tame' in the ingredients.[9]

John Beale's enthusiasm for roots, herbs, pulses, especially kidney beans, and salads for a healthy diet went beyond all bounds, and drew him towards complete vegetarianism, at least in summer. His children accepted his regime cheerfully, though he did not impose it on his servants. (We shall meet a more vehement campaigner for vegetarianism later in the century.) For drink, he was content with good water plus, of course, the home-made cider which he laboured tirelessly to improve: it 'danced in the cup', he claimed. Ad. Speed gave advice on storing root vegetables successfully in cellars, or hanging them in strings, ready for use at any time; clearly, opinion had undergone some change since the days around 1600 when the storing of roots in London cellars had been condemned as an evil practice. Its success was now accepted, and was being widely advertised.[10]

Innumerable other practical details featured in Hartlib's correspondence, revealing a tiny fraction of the great wealth of advice on food improvement that passed in conversation from place to place. Among the purveyors of this news our documents show almost none but gentlemen, but they were carrying knowledge that was constantly being picked up in amiable chat and confirmed in observation at the markets, especially in London. Gentlemen put these ideas into practice on estates that were scattered all over the country, and so the news rippled out into a wider world. William Petty carried information about potatoes and rapeseed into the East Anglian fens. John Beale advertised his obsession with cider among his west country neighbours, and in his letters to Hartlib. Cheney Culpeper in Kent learned from Cressy Dymock in Yorkshire of a better than common way of fattening a pig. Somewhere in southern England, the Earl of Southampton planted many thousand fruit trees in the hedgerows, demonstrating the current strong enthusiasm for fruit as food for all.[11]

We can legitimately guess at a host of other conversations spreading ideas beyond and outside gentry circles. From Oxford came more news of scientific fruit-growing as Ralph Austin worked on the improvement of cider and perry; he was dedicated to the proposition that these drinks ensured health and long life, and claimed credit for having saved a valuable nursery of 15,000 young fruit trees in Oxford from destruction by the soldiery some time before 1652. From Durham came news of a special variety of oats that local people guarded appreciatively, and another account of raspberries growing plentifully there for wine. From Wadworth, near Doncaster, Cressy Dymock sent many long letters bubbling over with fresh theories and experiments. More letters passed between London and Ireland, revealing the transfer of plants and other foodstuffs in both directions: Lord Strafford had earlier taken partridges to Ireland, which were now breeding successfully; English apples were transplanted to Ireland; apricots were carried to Belfast by Lord Chichester. Amid this flow of information in all directions came word in 1657 from as far away as China, via the Jesuits, telling of a novel kind of plough. Knowing Chinese skills in horticulture, we are alerted to the possibility of yet other food-growing tips coming at this early date. Almost a hundred years later, in 1748, Pehr Kalm dropped a hint that the practice of

keeping birds with their wings clipped to eat pests amid vegetable crops might
have come to England from China. Pehr Kalm saw the practice in use in Essex in
Mr Warner's kitchen garden, where four seagulls were kept, two common ones
and two from Newfoundland; they had originally been tamed by being fed with
meat and bread. The lurking suspicion of a possible lesson from China lies not
so much in Pehr Kalm's remarks as in the fact that the Warner family had over
generations been long-serving traders overseas.[12]

The salient themes in public discussion about food between 1640 and 1660
centred on increasing the food supply by diversifying diet. This meant expanding
the production of items whose potential had already begun to be perceived in
the second half of the sixteenth century, and which was further demonstrated
in practice by gentry, parsons, farmers, and gardeners in the early seventeenth
century. It was now being given a fresh boost in the 1650s, inspired by the ideals
of the commonweal under the new republic. Lurking in the background were
botanists and herbalists assiduously identifying plants and different varieties
of the same plants, spreading information about their favoured habitats, and
slowly but surely enhancing appreciation of their uses, first as medicines, and
secondly as enjoyable foods. Admittedly, it was knowledge that dripped out into
the world in a random manner. Nicholas Culpeper comes first to mind because
of his great popularity ever since, and his sympathetic message, insisting on using
home-grown plants rather than fetching them from the other side of the world.
But another distinguished botanist was William Coles (1626–62), who died at
the early age of 36, but earned for himself the title of 'the most famous simpler
or herbalist of his time'. He slipped into his pages many scraps of information
about current food practices, and the way wild plants were being moved into
gardens and closes nearer home.[13]

In this more informative age, events allowing for the spread of food in greater
variety emerge in a clearer chronology. We can now, for example, record the
slow but ultimately substantial progress of rosemary, which had been newly
introduced into England in 1340, but by 1657 was dubbed 'no stranger here in
England'; it grew in most gardens, and was known in many varieties. A shorter
timescale for the first successful phase in growing potatoes had resulted from
accidental circumstances. Potatoes were brought to England in single samples
by seafarers in the later sixteenth century, and early seventeenth-century recipe
books refer to them casually, suggesting that some were being home-grown,
mostly in London, although some were also imported from Spain. But they did
not thrive readily in the English climate, whereas a few had been left in Ireland
in the later sixteenth century, where they flourished. When campaigning there
in the early 1650s, therefore, English soldiers were startled to see whole fields of
them. So the English imported specimens of the better acclimatized potatoes
from Ireland, and they finally appear clearly in the 1670s growing in Lancashire

and Somerset. By 1711 they were spreading around London, notably at Hackney. A third example concerns the taste for cider, which was thoroughly embedded in the traditions and country lifestyle of Herefordshire, Worcestershire and Somerset. But it was only during the civil war that cider-drinking spread more widely because many battles were fought in the West Midlands, which meant that soldiers tasted cider as a staple drink for the first time. Some took a distinct liking to it, and relatively quickly – by 1700 – it had become a successful commercial export from Bristol to London.[14]

FOREIGN INFLUENCES AND CHANGING VIEWPOINTS

Thus varied developments shaped knowledge and attitudes to food between 1640 and 1660, forming a background to the 1650s, when recipe books began to be published again. We need also, of course, to allow for some fresh English percep- tions of the food that was eaten in Europe, for many Royalist sympathisers fled overseas to France and the Netherlands, ate regularly at foreign tables, savoured their food styles, and returned to England in the 1650s. Hartlib's archive shows his correspondence with foreigners, notably those living in the German states. In the second half of 1648 he sought among his friends a copy of Bartholomaeus Carrichter's *Kraüter und Arztenenbuchs*, knowing that it was rare, but plainly wanting to read more about what the Germans were eating as well as what they were growing. The first edition of this book in the British Library dates from 1575, so it was not entirely unknown to English readers well before 1648. But by 1615, and possibly earlier, a third part had been added to the same work (which does not always survive in library copies), devoted to German people's daily diet when healthy and sick, entitled *Der teutschen Speisskammer*. Food was divided seasonally; thus the readers of Hartlib's generation learned in some detail of the measures taken to store food through the winter. They doubtless took notice of German procedures with root vegetables and the practice of storing cabbage as sauerkraut.[15]

An observation by Sir Cheney Culpeper in undated correspondence with Samuel Hartlib deepens the significance of his concern to read Carrichter's work. Culpeper was aware of Sir Hugh Platt's efforts, allegedly successful at the turn of the century, to promote food preservation, by managing to keep artichokes for a whole year and cherries until Michaelmas. But he feared that the secret had died with him. If more heed was paid to the art of preserving, he believed, it would be possible to turn winter into summer. Hartlib's generation, in short, looked farther ahead than we usually imagine, and it has taken another 350 years for their dreams to become reality.[16]

Other shifts of fashion were also recorded by contemporaries who were not interested in food recipes, but alert us to watch for general trends. Sir William Coventry, looking back on the civil war period from a vantage point in 1670, remarked on 'the increase of the use of fruits, herbs and roots, especially near all great towns, whereby an acre of garden will maintain more than many acres of pasture would have done'. John Beale, who was so energetic in the 1650s promoting vegetables and fruit, declared in 1675 that 'within my memory they are become the chief relief of England'. Walter Blith, in a book on farming in 1653, numbered among his six improvements 'orchards and garden fruits'. And when Thomas Moufet asserted in *Health's Improvement* that fruit maintained long life, as was seen among the peoples of India, Africa, Asia and some parts of Europe, where they fed wholly or principally on fruit, we may wonder if that was really what Moufet wrote before he died in 1604, or, more credibly, was an insertion by Christopher Bennet, editing the text in 1655, and hearkening to his, by then, vociferous contemporaries.[17]

Out of contrasting experiences of food shortages, buoyant new aspirations, and foreign food customs, came a crop of recipe books from varied authors, filling a long gap of time since about 1600 when little had been published or has survived. Nothing was to be expected in wartime during the 1640s, but a more hopeful world for some now opened out, and authors brought some refreshing experiences and insights to the food scene. Eight books on food and cooking appeared in the 1650s, five by members of the nobility and gentry or servants and cooks in their households, one by a physician, and two were anonymous. We shall also briefly revisit Moufet's careful work on food, written *c.* 1600, for it was not published until 1655, and then it was edited by the physician Christopher Bennet, whom we suspect of altering the text to fit the new age; so a second reading is rewarding. In content some of these works were more preoccupied with medicine than nourishment, others interested in candying and preserving, some concentrating on daily dishes, and some combining all three interests.

Some long-established conventions persisted in these works, harking back to an old food style, while new views also made their mark. The books' tables of contents still roamed in a random, unordered way among meat, fish, bread, fruit, milky foods and some drinks. It was still usual to serve meat with raisins, currants, prunes, dates and bone marrow, together with the most favoured spices, cinnamon, mace, cloves and ginger. Rosewater continued to be much used, and many oranges and lemons. Meat and fish mixtures were still commonly served on sippets of bread.

The first recipe books in the 1650s were by a husband and wife: Lord Ruthin, the heir to the earldom of Kent who died without inheriting the title; and his wife, the Countess of Kent. The circumstances of publication, as explained in Chapter 4, are a puzzle, but the books make an appropriate beginning to this decade, for both forge links between past and future culinary themes. Lord Ruthin's work of 1639 was entitled *The Ladies Cabinet Opened*, and when re-issued in 1654 was renamed *The Ladies Cabinet Enlarged and Opened*. Since Lord Ruthin died in 1639, it is not certain how much he had to do with his first book and he certainly had nothing to do with the second. When it was reissued, it was enlarged from 58 to 226 pages to accommodate more daily dishes, and became much better known. Its preface then claimed Lord Ruthin as a learned chemist, engaged in extracting oils, waters, etc. Thus was he associated with the lively interest in distilling essences for medicinal and food purposes that had become a particular fascination among menfolk since the mid-sixteenth century, and which was most famously manifested when Lord Percy and Sir Walter Raleigh were imprisoned in the Tower of London early in James I's reign and used their time in chemical experiments.[18]

The recipe book by the Countess of Kent appeared in 1653, a year before her husband's enlarged work in 1654, but two years after she had died. The copy used here, labelled a second edition, did not name an author, though it is attributed to the Countess of Kent in the library catalogues and is so attributed here. It was divided into two parts, the first being entitled 'A Choice Manuall or Rare and Select Secrets in Physick and Chyrurgery ... as also Most Exquisite Wares of Preserving, Conserving, Candying, etc.', and the second 'A True Gentlewomans Delight, wherein is contained All Manner of Cookery, together with preserving, conserving, drying, and candying'. It was published by 'W. I., gent.', and the recent *ODNB* inclines to treat him as the author. In fact, W. I., gent. introducing the first part of the book, explained that he had heard that the Countess of Kent's manual was to be reprinted (the copy used here, it should be remembered, is the second edition, and libraries seem to have only this one), and he wanted it to include cordial spirits. These had come his way through his old school friend, Samuel King, who had them from Sir Walter Raleigh when they both spent time together in the Tower. The menfolk, and probably all opinionated foodies at this time, linked the distillation of essences with cooking, expressing an association that had been conspicuous in practice throughout the second half of the sixteenth century. After 1600, increasing numbers of probate inventories listing the domestic possessions of the gentry had named alembics and other distilling equipment, sometimes also books about distilling. The gentry's household accounts also showed their purchases of these items. Essences were in vogue and distillation had become an occupation of absorbing and serious interest to women and men for both culinary and medicinal purposes. So now the Countess of Kent's editor inserted in the first part of her book his own information on making cordial waters, and gave space for her recipes in the second half. It is fairly certain that contemporaries would have agreed with the proposition that cordial waters, also sometimes called diet drinks, had become a conspicuous fashion of the age.[19]

So we conclude that Lord Ruthin and the Countess of Kent shared an interest in cooking, and somewhere lay manuscripts of the family's cookery receipts, which were re-assembled by editor/publishers after both had died. The Countess's book printed verbatim some of the same recipes that had been in her husband's book of 1639, but in many other recipes she was her own woman, or gave ingredients and details that were similar but not exactly the same as her husband's. Both books signalled the current preoccupation with conserving and candying fruit and flowers, using large quantities of sugar. They reflected greater familiarity with these skills than was evident in the second half of the sixteenth century, when they had been emerging experimentally, and it would be instructive if we had some measure of changing imports of sugar in the century 1550–1650, possibly supporting this idea. However, the novelty of flower candying is at least conveyed in Lord Ruthin's account, for in the 1654 edition he claimed that it was an art 'newly used'. In 1639 he presented the recipes somewhat differently, calling the result 'a conserve' of roses, violets, cowslips, etc., but then adding that they were 'canded [sic] rather than conserved'. Then he gave a recipe for Spanish candy in wedges, in which the flowers were mashed unrecognizably, and when cold the mixture was gilded and boxed in pieces. This made 'a fine sort of banquetting stuffe and newly used', he said. We may wonder if Charles's train of courtiers visiting Madrid for the contemplated Spanish marriage, and banqueting in fine style during that unsuccessful venture in 1623, had first given the fashion momentum. At all events, candied flowers seem to have become for a while something of a time-consuming obsession in rich households. It is betrayed by one heading in the cookbooks about 'rare forms of sugar work', though at its height it seems to belong to Charles I's reign rather than the 1650s. Perhaps the skill did indeed undergo some modification, for by 1653 another anonymous work, *The Ladies Companion*, recommended more sober procedures: sprinkling barberries, grapes or gooseberries with sugar, which when dried in the oven would look like 'so many sparkling diamonds'.[20]

Looking forward to another food fancy, the Countess of Kent offered an attractive 'salad of all manner of herbs', using fresh herbs, in contrast with Lord Ruthin's, which were preserved or pickled. She set hers out as a separate dish, as did Archimagirus five years later, in 1658, garnishing his dishes with 'lettuce salads'. Recipes still incorporated flavourings that were prepared in bulk for the store cupboard, like pickled broombuds and preserved barberries. But the royal cook, Joseph Cooper, publishing his *Art of Cookery Refin'd and Augmented* in 1654, disparaged the pickling of flowers, seeds, and buds, regarding that operation as so commonplace and tedious that he did not deign to discuss it. In other words, pickling was now too well-known a procedure for a royal cook to boast about.[21]

Candying, preserving and drying (which in practice, as Lord Ruthin showed, seems to have meant something different from our understanding of the word; it meant cooking in a syrup) were some of the ways that afforded food in the dark days of winter. Other favoured means of preservation at this time were the liberal use of solidified butter to exclude air, pickling with vinegar, using airtight barrels, and storing some fruits like cherries in beds of hay and straw. Skill in food preservation did not yet satisfy Sir Cheney Culpeper but the recipe books suggest that it was mounting and ambitions were expanding. Pies of meat or fish that were filled to the brim after cooking with butter or a meat jelly, and were thus made airtight, kept successfully in a cool dark place for weeks, even months, and in some cases for more than a year. The cookbooks regularly emphasized these keeping qualities.

Admittedly, housewives could only learn the tricks of the trade from others or by reading the books. But our documents show how knowledge filtered out from London and the south-east, opening little pockets of country where Londoners' know-how was adopted in other towns, and in some country houses. James Hart, the physician who wrote eloquently about current food opinions around Northampton in 1633, plainly had a keen sense of the differences between country ways and those of London. He also held some firm prejudices in opposition to current fashions. He thoroughly abhorred the taste for excessive sugar, and would have had no time for the counter-argument, that candying gave scope to the cook to demonstrate her artistry in shaping, decorating and colouring. When fruit, even carrots too, were mashed into a paste that could be moulded into interesting shapes, one had to have servants to spend time on such fancy food; the Countess of Kent, when describing the preserving of angelica, told her readers that the task 'will ask you a whole day's work'. So the satisfaction of this creative work could only be defended by those who produced spectacular table displays to delight their onlookers. The menfolk generally fastened disparagingly on the taste for sugar as the women's foible. The women, clearly, were the queens of candying, and thus it was a woman in *The Ladies Companion*, 1653, who gave practical explanations of what was meant by boiling sugar to candying height and *Manus christi* height, when the sugar finally ran in the thinnest string off the spoon.[22]

Another prominent characteristic, in the food texts of the 1650s, in addition to preservation, was their discrimination about types of pastry. Earlier cookbooks had given recipes for pies, without any details about the pastry mix. Now cooks were finicky about the right pastry for different dishes. Puff pastry was made as we make it nowadays, and is the type most often cited. But other kinds were used, which sheds light on a more varied scene. Because pies could be made that preserved food over a long period (Cooper claimed three months), they were becoming popular in a new way, and the explanation for this interest in pastry therefore has wide ramifications. We can only understand it fully if we also look at cooking methods over a longer time-frame.[23]

CHANGING COOKING METHODS

In the Middle Ages cooking in one pot over an open fire was the most usual method, as our illustrations of medieval kitchens show. One pot, large or small, accommodated a great mixture of ingredients that made by itself a satisfying meal of pottage. In addition, by the sixteenth century more humble households usually had one spit for roasting, but it was not used regularly, being brought into use for special occasions. As for baking food, the watchful cook could always bake food beside an open fire, and that is how bread was often made. Common ovens in village communities served that purpose better, though English documents do not shed much light on where and how often common ovens were kept in use in villages; they were more common in towns. In the later sixteenth century, when inventors were busy with new projects, vague references occur in the documents to more economical ovens on sale, suggesting that the so-called Dutch oven, a dome of metal placed over a metal or stone base, was available, but we cannot at this date be sure how common it was or how widely distributed.

What was much more revolutionary on the cooking scene resulted from the construction of chimneys, either built on to the ends of houses, or constructed within the house by taking some room off the hall to make a chimney alcove, or purpose-built from the outset in new houses. Chimneys enabled more and more people in the course of the seventeenth century to have ovens, and that greatly enlarged the opportunities for cooks in quite ordinary homes, not just gentry in grand manor houses, to make pies. The seemingly growing taste for pies may have been one such result. Three claims for patents were made in 1635 and 1636 for ovens, two claiming to save wood and one in 1635 designed for bakers and cooks using coal and promising not to let the fuel spoil the flavour.[24]

We catch sight of the growing popularity of pies from another prejudice of the Northampton doctor, James Hart, in 1633, deploring meat dishes that were 'smothered and suffocated in pie crust'. He thought this dish 'for health worst of all others', and when contemplating a venison pie, he deemed the crust to offend the body more than the venison. We can imagine some of the excesses in using pastry, for the recipe books dealt with large quantities, and often ordained thick pastry on the sides and base of pies to keep them from collapsing. Cooked for several hours in the oven to ensure that the contents were tender, some pastry must have been unappetizing, and some assuredly was not eaten except by the poor at the gate.[25]

The cookbooks of 1653–4 explained more generously than ever before, then, the different kinds of pastry that were possible. Puff pastry was named first. Another for florentines was named but without a recipe: it had to be rolled so thin that 'you may blow it from the table'; it sounds like filo pastry. Other types were still less familiar. Mrs Medgate offered a recipe in the anonymous work, *The*

Ladies Companion, which required butter to be first boiled in water, into which the flour was then mixed, presumably while hot; if the dough was not stiff enough then egg yolks were added. The cold handling of pastry, which is an axiom with us, was evidently not then a firm rule. In other recipes in the same book, pastry was fried, when making apple turnovers, for example, and in two cases the fat for frying was suet. In the work of Archimagirus, the pastry was made with oil, but you had to take away the scent of the olives, the method not being explained.[26]

A 1654 recipe book by Joseph Cooper was still more fussy about types of pastry, and since Cooper had been cook to Charles I it is not impossible that a French influence had been exerted by Henrietta Maria that explains some of his fancies. His recipes for pies ran from pages 90 to 113, continued with tart recipes, and then returned to pies from pages 129 to 131. His pastry was of five kinds, starting with puff paste which required ten or twelve rollings and turnings; next came a cool butter paste requiring 'a great deal of elbow grease'; then another pastry for thin bake meats (this one also boiled the butter as did Mrs Medgate's in *The Ladies Companion*); then came custard paste, again using boiling water but no butter (was this perhaps the kind that was not intended to be eaten but only to contain food or be decorated?); and finally another pastry for cold bake meats using rye flour. This was well known to other writers; rye pastry was always valued for keeping a long time. It evidently held up well in raised pies, like our pork pies. Does anyone use it nowadays?[27]

Other foods that featured newly in these recipe books of the 1650s draw our attention to novel tastes, some plainly having diversified the array on offer at the grocer's, or that handled meat differently and introduced a new vocabulary of named dishes. One word that took on fresh connotations in this decade was 'bisket'. It is first noticed in the *Oxford English Dictionary* between 1555 and 1600, when it denoted a twice-cooked bread, without yeast or salt. It was convenient as a food on sea voyages and for soldiery in war. By the 1650s it had been decked up for more pleasurable eating as a sweet and flavoured crispbread. Basically, it was made of bread dough with yeast, egg yolks and flavourings of aniseed, coriander seeds, and sometimes caraway and rosewater as well. Most books offered at least one recipe, and some more. After the first baking as a bread loaf, it was left untouched for two days, then sliced, and sprinkled with sugar for a final drying in the oven. We encounter it first in Thomas Dawson's recipe book of 1597–8, when it was called bisket bread. His recipe was elaborate in containing damask water, musk, and wine or muscadine for the liquid. In the years between 1600 and 1640 it gained favour among the gentry, who bought it ready made from the grocer as a sweetmeat along with comfits, though in sparing quantities at first. A pound or two often lasted several months with the Walmsley family of Dunkenhalgh in Lancashire, though their order did occasionally increase to three or four pounds at holiday times or when entertaining. Even so, it was not an expensive treat, as were some comfits: when they first bought it from their Manchester grocer in January 1614, the Walmsleys paid 22d. for one pound. But cooks also made it at home; James Hart in 1633 knew it, containing fennel seeds. Indeed, he thought that so few gentlewomen were ignorant of its preparation by then, that he did not need to elaborate further.[28]

By the 1650s bisket had a firm place in the cookbooks, and its varied names and ingredients pointed to some foreign influences that had made it more popular still. Henrietta Maria's cookbook explained how to cook 'almond biskets, and you could choose between French biskets, Spanish, Italian, Lorain, and Naples biskets'. The physicians had even found a reason for sick people to choose it in place of bread, commending it to those with weak stomachs who, after suffering some chronic disease, could not digest an ordinary loaf.[29]

So a food that had started as lowly fare for soldiers had been upgraded to something enjoyed by gentry and perhaps nobility as well. We may even guess that it created a new occupation in London; surely, we shall one day find 'a bisket maker' somewhere, leaving a will or inventory? At all events, it had a promising commercial future, for bisket also remained a basic food among soldiers and sailors. It was a godsend when Cromwell's soldiers had to be fed during their campaign in Ireland, and supplies were sent of *cheese, butter and bisket*. We can assume that the mixture was more austere than that for the gentlefolk, lacking any coriander seeds and aniseed, even perhaps without the dusting of sugar. But it kept well in barrels and boxes.[30]

THE FRENCH INFLUENCE

Other lesser changes in food taste seem to be attributable to foreign influences. Signs of French traditions lurk in the sudden occurrence of a dish called 'a fricassée'. The French word was used to mean minced meat cooked in a sauce, though it is first found in a translation from the Spanish in 1568, next in an English cookbook of 1597, and not again, according to the *Oxford English Dictionary*, until 1656 and 1657. In fact, the Countess of Kent used it in 1653, and the Earl of Kent and Joseph Cooper both did so in 1654. None of them seemed to know how to spell the word or pronounce it. Lord Ruthin settled for 'frigasies' and Cooper for 'frikese'. It was commended in recipes for a loin of veal, chickens, pigeons, rabbits, lamb and sweetbreads.[31]

In other pages of Cooper's cookbook, foreign influences stand out more distinctively still and may well have originated in the fact that Cooper had been chief cook to Charles I, and so presumably hearkened to, and concurred with, food preferences expressed by Charles's French wife, Henrietta Maria. Cooper wrote much the most sympathetic book of the decade – its conversational style was so friendly, and its philosophy so open-minded, one would like to have met him in person. He did not heavily underline any French rules, but let them slide in unobtrusively here and there; for example, he often urged the cook to rub the cooking or serving dish with garlic. But his was a singularly cautious use of the flavouring, betokening his awareness of English prejudices, for in another instruction to put a clove of garlic in a barrel of pickled oysters, he cautioned the cook to do this only 'for those that like it'. The anonymous author of *Archimagirus*, who repeated some of Cooper's recipes without acknowledgment, followed suit in his own book, in one case giving his cooks the choice of using garlic or not as it pleased them, and in another substantial dish using only one clove of garlic, and urging the cook when serving up to remove it entirely! Other French influences were revealed in Cooper's use of pickled and fresh mushrooms in sauces. This was at a time when most Englishmen warned against them, but a coterie of mushroom-eaters was already forming. John Beale had dined at Sir Henry Wotton's table at Eton and taken a liking to them, commending them to Hartlib.[32]

One of Cooper's comments in his recipe book suggested a consciousness of fashion in food, of which he is likely to have been particularly aware at the Stuart court: thus, to decorate one dish he commended 'what other garnish you fancy or is in fashion'. At the same time, some of his practices were distinctive but not necessarily of foreign origin. He used potatoes as a matter of course. He had a keen eye for attractive colours on the plate. Other usages that were unfamiliar in the recipes of his contemporaries may have struck those who cooked for less exalted personages than the king as strange or foreign; but they have to be considered against a wider background than that found in England. He often used pistachios, pine kernels, and occasionally chestnuts in meat dishes. He minced lemons in meat dishes and sauces, and he also preserved them, both unusual practices among English cooks, then as now; he also cooked lettuce, and used something that he called 'hard lettuce'. But in the 1650s the French cook François Pierre de la Varenne began to influence the food scene, and he must now be accommodated in our narrative.[33]

The publication in English in 1653 of the French cookery book by François Pierre de la Varenne, *Le Cuisinier François*, is generally thought to have marked a new, strong phase of French influence on English food styles. Some immediate interest is to be inferred from the fact that the translation appeared within two years of the first French edition, but its impact may have been greater in other Continental countries, and did not register noticeably in England until after the Restoration. In many respects, Varenne's style chimed in with the style already current among fashionable English cooks; in others the English could well have considered themselves to have equally good recipes of their own. Their own cookery books had since the 1580s been cultivating preferences that matched Varenne's, in using many vegetables in pottage and casseroles, and varied meats that were roasted and braised in tasty sauces; it is also possible that the English surpassed the French in their zeal for pastry of different sorts, and for cooked fruits. A reading of Varenne when one has become familiar with English cookery books of the same date inclines the reader to moderate some of the exaggerated claims for Varenne's originality in breaking with centuries of old traditions, and shaping the course of cooking in a new way. English recipes were already moving in the same direction, and it may be that Varenne seemed a great deal more innovative to readers in other European countries. Greater familiarity with that literature is needed before any firm judgement can be passed on that score. In any case, it is possible, indeed probable, that the English liking for more vegetables, herbs and fruits in cooking stemmed from earlier contact with French cuisine and, if so, one would have to include in that generalization the influences of Italian and Spanish cuisines as well. Even the details surrounding the English reception of Varenne's book seem to support a moderated view of his novelty. The English chose to translate the second edition of his work and not the first, for that had an extra section on preserving, whereas the first edition did not. English cookbooks had already shown a keen interest in that subject, and clearly people were looking to compare their own methods with Varenne's. Moreover, when the English published larger second and third editions of their translation, they added, not more French recipes, but English ones, prepared 'by a prime artist of our owne nation'. In the 1673 edition these extras numbered 244 recipes! The English were plainly not dazzled by the French style. In Hartlib's correspondence, it may be significant that Varenne was nowhere named, though that may simply be because cookery in his circle was seen as a different operation from food production, in which Hartlib was far more deeply interested.[34]

In his book, Varenne addressed the reader as one concerned for the most ordinary housewife's dishes, avoiding undue expense, and using the innumerable herbs and legumes found plentifully in the countryside. In that respect, he spoke a familiar language, no different from that of Gervase Markham. When he offered a number of Lenten dishes containing single vegetables, his English readers may well have seen that practice as something of a novelty, though they had encountered it among the Dutch, as noticed by Parkinson, when eating chervil and spinach. Individually, the reader would undoubtedly have found among Varenne's pottage, meat, fish and egg recipes, dishes that contained some interesting variations from the known English ones. But these were mixed up with many others that were much the same, and some of Varenne's recipes omitted details that by the 1650s would have been expected in English cookbooks. He prescribed 'a bundle of herbs', for example, without itemizing them. He used pastry but did not, until towards the end of the book, give any recipes or explain the different terms for it. When he described puff pastry, which incidentally he labelled 'after the English' manner, he gave such a jumbled account that many readers must have felt utterly confused. Where he surprised English readers most was perhaps in his emphasis on sauces; he drew attention by using them so often, listing them and almost constantly using them in his entrées. This was almost certainly the origin of the English prejudice against sauces which, when featured by foreign cooks, were more complex than simple English sauces.[35]

Perhaps we can reasonably posit a European circle of foodies, gradually mingling their food conventions, and learning continuously from each other in the early modern period. The group included many diplomats, physicians and merchants, so that one never knew how or where their enthusiasm for foreign dishes would spread the word and galvanize cooks to imitate foreign models. Some of Varenne's recipes, for example, are noticeably similar to those of Joseph Cooper, who served Charles I and published his own cookery book in 1654. So while various explanations are possible for these coincidences, it might be safer to call Varenne the publicist of his like-minded contemporaries, rather than an innovator, in the same way that Turnip Townsend in the early eighteenth century publicized but did not introduce turnips into English fields, though that is how his fame has endured.

THOMAS MOUFET RECONSIDERED

With the same networks of information and fashion in mind, we may speculate on the circumstances surrounding the appearance in print in 1655 of Thomas Moufet's comprehensive general book on food, *Health's Improvement*, which he had written a generation earlier in 1595. It had doubtless circulated in manuscript among Moufet's contemporaries, but Moufet had died in 1604. So 'for the common good', Christopher Bennet, a physician with a high reputation in London for his practical experience and research interests, was prompted to correct, enlarge and publish it. We have already discussed the text as a work reflecting the scene in 1600. But it calls for a second reading in the light of changing attitudes and access to food in 1655. Did Bennet alter the text at any point to mirror a different scene? Moufet had had plenty of foreign experience on the Continent of Europe, in Spain, Italy, Switzerland (where he received his MD at Basel in 1578), the Low Countries, Denmark and Germany. So we must allow his foreign experience to shine through some of his personal opinions. But another set of qualitative differences in the food scene separated Moufet's life from Bennet's 60 years on. Can any of these be reliably identified?[36]

With regard to vegetables, a statement by Moufet that globe artichokes had been made so common by industry and skill that the poorest man now possessed these princes' dainties sounds distinctly premature in 1600. Gentlemen were assiduously planting out artichoke gardens in the 1620s; they were then the height of fashion and certainly not yet old hat. The remark that asparagus was now being served at every board also sounds distinctly out of place in 1600, though credible at the tables of gentry and the middle classes in London by 1655. Similarly, the assertion that potato roots were so common and well known that every husbandman bought them to please his wife was a gross exaggeration in 1600, and, indeed, still highly suspect as a generality in 1655. It could readily be accepted, however, if it reflected everyday scenes in Covent Garden market in London. It is also possible that the appreciative reference to stubble geese belongs to the 1650s. They became much more common as a commercial item, walking from East Anglia and reaching the London market in large numbers in the second half of the seventeenth century; so it is not impossible that the gooseherds had begun to make their mark by 1650, but not so easy to believe that this was happening in 1600.[37]

Two other arguments in Moufet that strike a false note in 1600 concern meat. All sixteenth-century evidence suggests people's strong liking for capons. Moufet's published text, on the other hand, argued that birds should have plenty of exercise to improve their flavour. It condemned cramming for producing an unwholesome meat and being 'a bad procedure'. Birds feeding abroad for themselves were better than those crammed or cooped in a little house, and, if they were crammed, then 'by your leave Mr Poulter', says the text, a middle fat hen was preferable to the fattest. This opinion, repeated three times over and unusually underlined by the writer, sounds anachronistic in 1600 and belongs rather to 1650. Another opinion out of tune with 1600 was that in favour of eating a variety of different meats, while still eating moderately. It was extremely strongly worded, and did not accord with Moufet's gentler, more tolerant style; it was also at variance with the common statement in the sixteenth century that too many different meats were undesirable and made for poor health. But in the 1650s the cookbooks took a great variety of different meats for granted when listing ingredients, and the production of meat in greater variety is one of the general conclusions drawn from surveying the wider food scene between 1600 and 1640. It is also noticeable that the forceful sentences on this score are followed immediately by another passage supporting the use of compound medicines. These were preparations that mixed different herbs and essences in one potion. A very considerable controversy built up in the mid-seventeenth century for and against compound mixtures, whereas it was not a problem or debating issue around 1600. Since both come together in this text, it strengthens the suspicion that Bennet, a conscientious physician, had been emboldened at this point to interpolate his views on one score and could not resist airing a prejudice on another. Speculation is enticing, but we can push the suggestion no further.[38]

JOAN CROMWELL AND COUNTRY COOKING

Another publication, out of the common run but reflecting on the food scene at this period, was a book of recipes ascribed to Mrs Joan Cromwell, the Protector Oliver's wife. They were said to have been given to the author by one of Mrs Cromwell's near servants, though we have no clue to the date when the recipes were assembled, beyond that of publication in 1664. The author was an inveterate enemy of Parliament, purporting to represent the tastes of Mrs Cromwell when she kept house for the Protector in Whitehall. In the author's view, she was a niggardly housekeeper, and nothing more than 'a brewer's wife'. The book warrants careful examination as a mirror of the food that might have been typical of parish gentry, as well as middle-class families of yeoman status. The author's venomous prejudices burst out on every page: he described Mrs Cromwell as living at home in a Huntingdon brewhouse, whereas in fact the family had the status of modest gentry. Indeed, the recipes sound authentic enough for that class, following a prudent, far from showy regime of kitchen management. Mrs Cromwell plainly prided herself, as Gervase Markham had urged, on feeding her household from her own yard, while nevertheless ensuring that her family enjoyed variety every day. Her recipes shed light in country places that are usually obscure.[39]

The hostility of Mrs Cromwell's biographer stemmed from the fact that she did not change her modest catering style when her husband held court in London as the ruler of the kingdom. She was economical and sober, refusing, for example, to serve orange sauce with veal to her husband when the war against the Spaniards in the West Indies made them expensive. She had evidently not disguised her opposition to his foreign policy, whereas he had plainly failed to think through the kitchen consequences. Viewing her historically as a lady brought up among parish gentry in the dairying country of East Anglia (she is referred to at one point as 'a rustical lady', once entertaining her friends impromptu with a cream cheese, dusted with sugar and nutmeg), we, in contrast, can enjoy this intimate glimpse of a housewife's regime so deeply engrained that Mrs Cromwell would not cast it off when she moved to Whitehall Palace. Her recipes used quite a lot of cream, compared with some others, and she evidently expected to keep charge of her own dairy, as she had done at home in Cambridgeshire. She kept two or three cows in St James's Park, and was much commended by her cronies for her fine butter. She also planned, as was her custom at home, to brew her own ale, but in the event a new ale called Morning Dew appeared in the London market and, as it won general favour, she settled for that. Incidentally, we see here the male brewers of London striving to win greater control of the market by offering new flavours with new names; thus they hoped to persuade ever more of the moneyed citizens to forsake home brewing – a thoroughly familiar marketing strategy that lives on with us today. In its time the manoeuvre lifted London beer supplies onto a different plane from the conventions still prevailing outside the capital; in the country, however, the women continued to brew their own beer for another century at least.[40]

The author of this scurrilous but revealing book described Mrs Cromwell's menu as 'spare, not curious'. Suppers were simple snacks, only 'some slops' or eggs, since dinner at midday was expected to offer the main sustenance. Cromwell himself, it said, never indulged in any luxurious or epicurean excesses, either in meat or drink, 'except sometimes in his cups', when he excused his copious drinking as a means to clear gravel from his kidneys. In other words, he feared the stone with which 'he was continually molested'. So were many, many of his contemporaries; it is the result of urinary tract infections, prevalent in places without flushing toilets. As for Mrs Cromwell's cooking style, her reporter classified it as 'thrifty baseness', 'fitter for a barn than a palace'. But her ingredients showed her using a goodly supply of vegetables, including cabbage, cauliflower, winter savory, skirret, spinach, carrots and turnips; and when these were less plentiful in winter she used samphire (presumably pickled) and capers. She made liberal use of bought lemons and oranges, as did all other cooks in cookbooks, and disposed of all the usual spices: nutmeg, cinnamon, mace, ginger and cloves. She sprinkled barberries generously on most of her meat dishes, and she expected to eat a great variety of meats, ranging well beyond beef, mutton and pork. She showed a special liking for veal (fillets of veal being 'almost her constant dish'), and this was a significant preference, which would come to epitomize the century as a whole; as dairy production expanded, a use had to be found for more and more unwanted male calves. Mrs Cromwell also served venison abundantly, her enemy explaining that Cromwell's policies cheapened this meat and made it available to everyone. Did this mean that hunting fell out of favour in a world ruled by Parliamentarians, or was it rather that more assiduous agriculturists put parks to other uses? Mrs Cromwell's recipes also included many alternative meats, allowing for increasing variety from wild birds, poultry, ducks (but, significantly, not geese), hares and rabbits. At the head of the fish list came eels, as was to be expected from a fenlander, next oysters (because they were so often added to meat dishes), and then, only once mentioned in each case, came trout, perch, carp, cod, flounders and scallops. A sour note by the author at the end explained that fish days were not observed, all days being alike. But since policy-making was an awesome business in these years, and fasting was ordained for certain occasions in which Cromwell's friends joined, old habits did not entirely die; fasting was merely distributed differently through the year.[41]

The author attributed to the Cromwell family a strong prejudice against foreign foods. Mrs Cromwell, he said, sought 'a ready and natural, not forced or foreign relish'. We can surely credit that caution to many other countrywomen across the kingdom. Nevertheless, quite a few of her recipes were labelled, Dutch, French or Italian, and she was credited with three recipes for fricassee (though the meat in them was not cut small). In short, Mrs Cromwell did not eschew all current food fashions, some of which, we may guess, were no longer actually recognized as foreign. She used Naples biscuit and pistachios, and she once used an unusual mixture of coriander seed, aniseeds and fennel seeds, together with cloves and cinnamon – a mix that was called in Italian *tamara* – to make a dish of stewed beef. It was also used by Archimagirus with a fillet of veal, and was so unusual that it may well have been instantly recognized as a new fashion. Mrs Cromwell used mushrooms in her dishes without comment, rubbed the bottom of a dish of woodcocks with garlic, inserted garlic in stewed carp, and in another recipe suggested two cloves 'if you please'. Two or three times she put potatoes into recipes, again without comment, and made syrups and candied fruits, though not perhaps with the verve and dexterity of some of the women confectioners noted above. She was also deemed to have succumbed to the craze for eating the first green peas in spring; the author narrated with relish an episode in 1654 when a countrywoman walked to London to delight the Lady Protectress with her first basketful of green peas. She expected a handsome reward for her pains, but instead was offered only a crown. She threw it back in disgust, for *en route* through the Strand she had already been offered five shillings more by a cook near the Savoy.[42]

Mrs Cromwell's menu may be said to have maintained a traditional English style, while adding here and there fashionable touches from a foreign source. She made conventional fruit pies, but did not suffocate everything else in pastry, though she did know how to fry it. She noted how to make puff pastry but not other kinds. Her sauces were markedly simple, containing little more than butter, vinegar and lemon, and sometimes wine. (This was the simple sauce to which the English were accustomed, quite unlike the elaborate French ones.) Our sneering author simplified it further by describing 'the chief court sauce' as nothing but onions and water. Like all the English, she favoured mustard for piquancy, and that was a home-grown herb (especially in East Anglia) that had the highest place in all English sauces. When she used small beer or ale in a sauce, we may guess that her guests smiled knowingly, recognizing this as a sign of someone from a modest home who always improvised with things to hand, even though she was not exactly a brewer's wife. Finally, she was a fan of curd tart, and thought she knew 'the best way'.[43]

The cookbooks of the 1650s identify a mixture of tastes that discerning contemporaries would almost certainly have divided between the new and the old-fashioned, thus distinguishing the cooks who belonged to the smart set from those who rejected all novelty, while others devised a tolerant mixture of both new and traditional routines. Mrs Cromwell's author acknowledged the world of fashion, when describing the Dutch way of boiling pigeons, by allowing also for an alternative 'modern way'. He saw the differences more sharply than we can, though our better sources in these years do lift more of the veil. Judging Mrs Cromwell's style overall, we can deem it to have been an economical middle way between modernity and tradition, reflecting fairly the choices of the middling sort as they slowly enjoyed widening access to news and the new products arriving in vibrant trading towns.[44]

A BOTANIST'S VIEW FROM THE FIELDS

This period yields few insights into the cooking of ordinary folk. During the war, we learned more of food deprivation and food destroyed; thereafter, a run of failed harvests in the years from 1646 to 1651 prolonged food shortages. But when the mood changed, it was the aspirations of the gentry to improve the food supply with enterprises launched on their own estates that produced the documents that have best survived, and set the tone of the next eight years. Nevertheless, we can pick up some information from William Coles, the young botanist who roamed the fields in search of plants at this time and so had plenty of opportunity to see country folk gathering and eating food from the fields. He poked around all over the country reporting on the precise sites in which he found edible and medicinal plants, around Ramsey Mere in Huntingdonshire, on Sheppey and the Isle of Thanet in Kent, and around Oxford in his native county; he even named the exact field in Mawdesley, Lancashire, north-west of Wigan, where wild rosemary grew in abundance. Does any grow there now, I wonder?[45]

Coles had a scholarly training at Oxford, graduating in 1650, and cherished many scholarly friends, as his thanks to fellow plantsmen bear witness. His uncle, significantly, was John French, the physician who wrote books on distilling, and doubtless deepened the interests of his nephew. But other remarks in Coles's books suggest that when he explored the hedges and fields, he also listened out for people who would reveal their local food traditions. He seems to have kept a homely eye on their doings, showing an interest in the way they used plants in the kitchen, remarking at one point that not a day passed without their picking herbs for their pottage to give 'an admirable relish and make them wholesome for our bodies'. He plainly knew the ways of country housewives in the dairy (using nettles to wrap their butter) and in the kitchen (preferring to cook colewort and cabbage when it had been touched by frost and had a better flavour). He may have come near to being a vegetarian in diet himself, for he commented regretfully on the way meat had now come to the fore as the superior nourishment, and yet Pythagoras, he reminded his readers, had lived on vegetables and lived longer than people did nowadays. He even urged gentlemen and their ladies to dig and weed their gardens, for he knew 'no better way in the world to preserve health', an eternal truth that has been rehearsed in recent times.[46]

Had Coles not died at the early age of 36 we would doubtless have learned much more about the everyday plant food of ordinary folk. But in his two books of 1656 and 1657, *The Art of Simpling* and *Adam in Eden* he brought some country ways, and the special content of food in different localities, vividly to life. Around Iver, they had whole hedges of barberries for supplying them with sharp sauce; it was the leaves that were used for the sauce, he said, not the berries, as we might have thought; the berries were used to make a conserve. People elsewhere without such hedges brought barberries into their gardens and orchards and cultivated them there. In the north country valerian was always put into pottage for the sick, being 'the poor man's remedy'. Oats were the chief bread corn in Lancashire, he noted, and Lancashire people enjoyed as good health and strength of body as those that lived on wheat only. He revealed several routines that yielded greenstuff in the winter months. Chicory was buried to whiten it and was used in salads through the winter. Lamb's lettuce, which grew in cornfields as well as in gardens, often lasted all through the winter months for salads, and if not, then it was the first greenstuff to be picked in February and March. He was the one and only person to report the stories of soldiers seeing fields of potatoes growing in Ireland. He obviously talked to everyone and thus learned much about local plants and local foods.[47]

At the national level Coles became sufficiently well informed to generalize about some significant features on the wider food scene. He knew how strongly the London market exerted its influence over gardeners, stimulating them to produce fine fruits that brought most profit. Peaches, he said, were nursed by gardeners living near the City of London who were certain of a ready clientèle to buy them. (In such remarks we learn in the end to understand how Londoners' diet could differ significantly from the provincial.) He seems to solve for us the mystery of how so many recipe books took for granted the cook's ready access to apricots in the kitchen. The trees, he said, were planted 'in almost every gentleman's garden', and they ripened when protected by a wall. He was alert to fashions in food that came and went: they had made leeks now unacceptable to the snobs, and caused Jerusalem artichokes to be despised by those who thought nothing was good unless it was dear; they grew too plentifully, as we well know. He was keenly conscious of the market forces that drove growers to concentrate on the items that sold dearest. He had known liquorice when the gardeners were keen to plant it because it was so profitable, but now too many had followed suit and the profits were diminishing. The same had happened to saffron. Gooseberries were particularly noticeable in gardens round London, he said, and he explained why: because the demand for gooseberry sauce was insistent, and people had a ready sale for the fruit at Cheapside and elsewhere.

Among common eating conventions he knew the routine for serving parsnips on Wednesdays and Fridays, and he was thoroughly outspoken about the folklore and the market demand for globe artichokes – they were much sought after by 'luxurious persons', but the people who needed them most were those who had failed to have children and needed to enhance 'bodily lust'.[48]

No other writer of this age so well illustrated as did William Coles the many facets of food habits – the changing phases, the fashions and the local preferences. But no other writer also revealed so many small details in the routines of ordinary folk, illustrating how intently they sought out herbal flavourings that cost nothing. It was this that gave them as much opportunity as the rich to add varying relishes to staple foods. Writing of dried peas, he remarked that they were 'no inconsiderable food in poor folk's houses'. But then, revealing to us his eye for detail, he further observed that peas were used to make pottage 'wherein mint and parsley and other herbs are put to give it better relish'. As a plantsman *par excellence* Coles appreciated the role of herbal flavourings in transforming humble ingredients into enjoyable and infinitely variable dishes. We shall understand this better still if we incorporate the strong suspicion that many plants had a stronger flavour then than now. Cooks who cared to prepare enjoyable food to feed their families, and that is a strong human urge everywhere, found ingredients lying all around them. In the twenty-first century we live in a different world, where a large proportion of the population lives in towns and has lost contact with country ways. It is because we fail to understand those other circumstances that we find historians dubbing the food of the past dull and monotonous.[49]

FOOD FOR THE POOR

Before concluding this account of food between 1640 and 1660, public efforts in feeding the very poorest hunger-stricken people in the nation should not be passed over in silence. Hartlib's correspondence reveals so much debate in his circle about all aspects of economic life that one must expect to find some thought being given to luckless poverty and ways to alleviate it. In fact, one such pamphlet by Hartlib himself does exist, dated 1649/50, prepared in 'these dear and hard times' of food shortage when hopes were yet raised for better government under the Commonwealth. Entitled *London's Charity Inlarged*, it focused particularly on London's problems in employing poor children and educating them. Since the children had to have bed and board alongside jobs and schooling, food was one of its concerns, requiring the author to express a view on the basic diet needed to maintain life.[50]

Hartlib's poor children, when accommodated by the authorities, must, he declared, have three meals a day. Real life obliged him then to consider other categories of poor children, those living at home with poor parents who had insufficient food to feed them. Parents had to send them out on the streets to beg for bread and pottage, so he envisaged them also receiving rations of food three times a day while going home to lodge with their parents at night. Another group of poor children were those of poor parents who were not sent out to beg but who lived hard. Their fare for the most part, he said, was bread and pottage, plus roots in winter and herbs in summer, or radishes and salt with a piece of bread without butter or cheese. Their drink for the most part was fair water from the pump. Despite their hard rations, he thought they lived long and were healthy: this may have been true, though not in all cases. What is significant is the diet of the poor that he took for granted: bread, pottage (which we know to have consisted of bread, grains, pulses and vegetables), with the addition, he said, of roots in winter and greenstuff in summer. Our knowledge of all the foods seasonally eaten at this time should not allow us to dismiss this fare as totally monotonous or unpalatable, or a starvation diet. He then prescribed standard rations: for breakfast in winter three ounces of household bread, a portion of pottage and half a pint of something to drink; for dinner five ounces of bread, one pint of beer, and pottage, made sometimes of meat, sometimes of milk, and sometimes of water gruel (and that would include oatmeal), one herring or other fish and a turnip; for supper four ounces of bread, half a pint of beer, a herring with a turnip, and sometimes broth in cold weather. Since the author was intent on encouraging the fishing industry, he wished the children to eat fish four times a week, and meat on Sunday and Thursday. In short, the content of this diet was not badly balanced, every single item was nourishing, and the whole ensured a reasonable allowance of starch, protein, fats, minerals and vitamins. In passing, the author remarked that at Christ Church Hospital the allowance of meat for children on meat days was a quarter of a pound of beef, and on Tuesdays they had a little dumpling of pudding fare 'that so oft children delight in'. In summer, he added, provision was cheaper than in winter. The details hinted at a kindly attitude lurking under the formal discipline, gainsaying our usual assumptions about the hard diets meted out to the poor. Hartlib was writing a pamphlet about 'charity inlarged', and it would be reasonable in this age, when luxury for one class was being enlarged, to allow for some qualitative change to have taken place in attitudes to the poor that sometimes gave the hungriest children a treat.[51]

CONCLUSION

This survey of the food scene between 1640 and 1660 lights up several different strands in a multicoloured skein of qualitative changes. The evidence points to an increasing variety of food ingredients, which became better known around the country as merchants spread both their home-grown and imported goods along well-tried trading routes. Biskets are a good example of the process: we saw in the 1620s how that fashionable grocery speedily reached Manchester, and was bought by the gentry. Thereafter biskets not only spread to other markets, but the recipes were varied in order to produce different qualities and prices to suit different classes of people. Cider underwent much the same transformation when it ceased to be the routine lowly drink of country folk in Herefordshire and Worcestershire and began to be known and drunk around London. Other changes had their own ramifications. Cheese became more plentiful in the market, and many hitherto local cheeses were more widely advertised. The intimate connection of dairying with veal production meant more veal for sale, particularly in the south-east where London offered a strong demand. Again, we know that greater plenty also meant greater variety in its quality, for some calves were fed on mother's milk for months, some only for weeks. So the price varied.

None of these trends in the food market can be measured precisely; they command notice by virtue of the scattered allusive comments of contemporaries. In the background, attitudes to food were subtly changing, and that helped to spread information and encouraged people to listen with more interest when food was discussed, and to try out new recipes. Vegetables and fruit were being urged by their most fervent advocates as equivalent in nourishment to bread and meat. That conviction had been expressed by Arthur Standish in 1613 in his *New Directions of Experience to the Commons Complaint*, after he had toured all over the country in search of ways to increase the food supply. He had learned by questioning others that when fruit was plentiful, people noticed a lowering in the price of victuals in general: Londoners had observed the phenomenon, and even the cattle drovers had told Standish how they had 'felt the smart of the plenty of fruit'. We can only speculate on the practical consequences of all this gossip in changing attitudes towards fruit and greenstuff, but some shift of opinion may be guessed at from the remark of John Beale in 1675, claiming that 'within my memory' vegetables and fruit 'are become the chief relief of England'. That was plainly an exaggeration, but John Parkinson's botanical history of fruit in 1629, and its second edition in 1656, had shown where the seeds of a transformed viewpoint were being sown. Some of the results were now visible.[52]

Another highly significant shift in people's expectations of food concerned their ability to preserve it. The scope for preservation was being recognized from at least 1600, but it was in these years that Sir Cheney Culpeper, in one of his frequent communications with Hartlib, expressed the idea most imaginatively: if more attention were paid to preserving food, he said, it would be possible to turn winter into summer. We managed to do this in the twentieth century, but here in the 1650s the idea dawned, as so many different methods of preservation were being made better known in books, gossip and market displays. Sir Hugh Platt had been a pioneer in this endeavour 40 years before. Now the various methods were becoming more conspicuous to shoppers: the French were known experts in drying apples, pears, pippins and prunelles; they sold their fruit neatly packed in boxes, according to Frederick Lodovick, and it was eagerly bought in England from the comfit makers, those specialists in expensive delicacies. The Dutch were more expert than the English at keeping butter fresh, and in 1655 firkins of more long-lasting butter were sent from Leyden for 'English housekeeping', a turn of phrase that suggests that the connoisseurs were an elite group in exploiting this information; it was not known to everyone. We shall note below the suspicion that the Dutch taught the English how to keep butter longer in barrels. As for cheese, it is possible that the English gradually shifted the weight of their commercial effort from fresh soft cheeses, that were made and eaten in a matter of days or at most two weeks, to matured cheeses that were kept for months. It is hazardous for historians to speculate on such a gradual process as a shift in the popularity of soft versus hard cheeses, but the hints are there.[53]

A diversification of diet was under way, resulting from several different trends that built up in these years. The merchants persisted, as ever, in supplying more varied foodstuffs from whatever quarter; improved skills in preservation allowed summer foods to be kept for winter eating. A more commercialized dairying industry was the direct result of war. Information about the variety of other foods eaten in England also circulated more widely because the war sent people to parts of the country they would never otherwise have seen. Thus they saw the varied natural conditions prevailing locally, learned much about the diet and recipes of one neighbourhood contrasted with the next, and perceived how every locality had a different range of choice. Books spread this information more widely and stimulated further curiosity. We may guess at, but not prove, some practical results when William Coles told his readers that buckthorn (i.e. buck's horn plantain (*Plantago coronopus*)) was grown as a salad herb in Italy and France but not in England; yet the plant did grow in England, and positively asked to be used for dinner since the leaves stayed green all through the winter. In fact, we can be fairly sure that people somewhere in England already knew this plant locally and were in the habit of using it in salads. But Coles's remark was interesting enough for others to try it. Another green plant, more widely advertised by Coles, was hops, of which the tops were eaten as a spring vegetable in Kent. They are still known in Kent for that purpose, and, indeed, were recently publicized as a special delicacy by a Herefordshire grower in that other hop-growing county. Information like this spread food tips and diversified diet in countless hidden ways. Turnip tops that had run to seed were another of Coles's recommendations; they ate like asparagus, he said. Young nettle tops were another suggestion, sometimes revived nowadays if you want a really vivid green soup, though townies grimace at the very idea.[54]

A relish that was seemingly first made known to the English in the time of Thomas Moufet, *c*. 1600, and regularly used in Germany, was horseradish, put into a sauce. It was already favoured by some few gentlemen in England, said Moufet, though others thought it too strong for most stomachs. In this instance, it is possible, as before, that the reference to horseradish was inserted by the later editor, Christopher Bennet, in 1656, for it was only in the 1650s that horseradish gained much notice in the recipe books. The more general prejudice against sauces as a foreign fancy will surface again in the period after 1660, when it was more frequently ventilated, but horseradish counts among the novel ingredients for a sauce with a doubtful beginning either around 1600 or more probably in the 1650s. Without knowledge of horseradish, however, ordinary folk had another plant long used as a sauce with meat, saltfish and in salads. That was garlic mustard, also known as 'sauce alone' or 'jack by the hedge'. With this familiar wild plant (*Alliaria petiolata*) they achieved an equally satisfactory tasty flavour. As another alternative, of course, they always had plenty of wild (or cultivated) mustard.[55]

More variety in food and better knowledge of food diversity modified some of the principles on which the theorists had insisted in former days. The principles of a good diet, enunciated tirelessly in the sixteenth century, had maintained that health was best preserved by 'a few dishes of good juice and nourishment', and this was reiterated in 1658 by William Higford in his *Institutions or Advice to His Grandson*. We have seen how the Jesuits early in the seventeenth century commended still more restraint. The rule at that time was more urgently directed at the well-to-do, who were so often seen to gourmandize. By the 1650s homilies against gluttonous eating were far less common, and a variety of meats in moderation was commended, suggesting that experiences in the previous 50 years had made an impact on public opinion and the rules of eating.[56]

As for current perceptions of a distinctive English dietary style, change among the whole population should not be exaggerated. The process was always slow and patchy. It is worth pondering the words of John Beale in 1658, when summarizing the English diet in contrast with Italian practice. In his view, the Italians ate well, relishing bread, with salads and sauces, oranges, lemons, salt, spices, vinegar and old cheeses. (By old cheeses we should probably understand matured cheeses: Parmesan was one of the best-known Italian cheeses in England at this time.) Englishmen, on the other hand, were depicted by Beale eating current broth (by which Beale meant the broth on the hob that day), plum bread (this was called plum cake in Hertfordshire), a substantial cake of flour, yeast, currants, raisins, milk, a little cream if possible, nutmeg and caraways. It was evidently fairly common food already, and in 1750 Hertfordshire housewives were said to bake it twice a week for their harvest men. For the better-off it was decked up by including butter, eggs, cinnamon, cloves and rosewater. Beale's summary account of English diet continued with cheese cakes, fat ale, hoppy beer, sugared wines (foreigners had often commented on the way the English put sugar in their wine) and luscious sauces. The notion that sauces were an English staple comes as a surprise, since so many English were positively prejudiced against sauces as a foreign notion. But, as we have learned above, the word 'sauce' to the English signified two different kinds, and it is likely that Beale was using it in the sense of a simple gravy, an innocuous liquid made from the juices that fell into the roasting tray with additions such as vinegar, lemon juice and mustard. Cheese cakes, as we have seen already, were a widely appreciated English food both in the fields and in the most elegant manor house, and comprised a pastry base and a cheese made from fresh curds that were quickly drained from the whey as soon as the cows were milked.[57]

Beale's account of the English diet suggested something more starchy than the Italian, focusing on cake and pastry rather than salads, and did not mention vegetables or fruit. So it is a cautionary tale, a warning against our giving any over-grand role to greenstuff for all. Beale might well have painted a more optimistic picture of greenstuff and fruit in diet, for he was a fervent, almost fanatical, advocate of these foods for himself and his family. Moreover, he was summarizing English diet from a desk in Herefordshire or Somerset, both noted fruit-growing counties. Yet he did not see these items bulking large in the general picture, when compared with Italian food habits. Another cautionary indication against overmuch emphasis on vegetables and fruit eaten by the population at large may be drawn from the words of Beale's nephew, Peter Smith, writing from Dyffrin in Wales in 1655, this time in response to an exhortation to plant an orchard of cherries. He thought such a project more appealing to London palates, which valued delicacies above necessaries, than to the palates of his neighbours 'that esteem nothing but bread and beef'. Local diets and class diets were still poles apart from one another, and evidently Welsh tastes were seen to be far removed from those of Herefordshire or Somerset, let alone London.[58]

6

Food in a Quickening Commercial World, 1660–1700

In the 40 years between 1660 and 1700 food settled into yet more fresh grooves; most surprisingly of all, it took up an accepted place in the fashionable conversation of scientists and intellectuals, and was treated as a serious matter alongside gravity, optics, metallurgy, and all the many other fresh interests of the time. This movement in the background of kitchen routines served as a stimulus to experiments and new explorations of food that galvanized merchants at home and abroad. An accumulation of many influences were brought to bear on current diets.

CHANGES IN THE BACKGROUND

We should not, of course, expect the changing scene to have made any speedy, practical difference to people in provinces far from London. In fact, almost certainly, the gap widened in this period between the eating habits of those living in London and those people living more than 80 miles away in the Midlands, the north and the south-west of the country. Even so, the influence of London did filter through in a slow trickle. We have seen how gentry living in Lancashire in the early decades of the seventeenth century learned in a matter of 20 or 30 years to rely on Manchester to provide spices and other delicacies instead of getting them from London as they had done in 1600. Gradually Manchester grocers introduced more local folk to food items from the capital so that they could buy them near at hand. The less affluent will hardly have noticed these London food fashions, but, nevertheless, some will occasionally have had chance encounters, in the open market or in manor house kitchens, even if they paid little heed to them. Information and tasting trials of food did slowly spread into new channels.

In the world of lively public discussion in London, however, in the new coffee houses as well as the old inns and taverns, food and drink became an ever more engrossing subject for gossip. Opinion and enthusiasm for fresh food experiences fed on the opportunities that burgeoned in London because of widening internal and foreign trade. A very small but perplexing glimpse of this trend emerged from the Countess of Kent's cookery book of 1653, *True Gentlewoman's Delight*, in a recipe that called for Irish butter. She lived in Bedfordshire; how did she taste Irish butter, unless she had occasion to spend time with her husband, Lord Ruthin, in Ireland? We may guess that Irish meat appeared at her table, for it certainly commanded a conspicuous place in the London meat market after 1660. Thus, many young beef cattle began to be imported from Ireland for fattening in England with the result that English farmers and landowners mounted loud protests against this unfair competition with their home-bred animals. But was much Irish butter imported too? Contemporaries do tell us that Dutch butter of high quality arrived, and the Dutch contrived this by keeping their poorer quality to eat at home. Perhaps the Irish were doing something of the same, but, if so, what was special about their recipes for making it?[1]

General commentaries on life in the 1660s and 1670s still dwelt on the spirit of optimistic enterprise among farmers growing food, confidently expecting that the energy and drive that had been shown in the 1650s would be maintained. Dr John Beale, who had corresponded assiduously with Hartlib in the 1650s, was still writing animatedly in 1675 about 'bold adventures in horticulture and agriculture', and the letters of John Locke in the 1680s conveyed the same excitement. Indeed, the continuity of themes in published treatises between the 1650s and 1670s is noticeable, especially with regard to promoting fruit and garden crops, including root vegetables. The discussion then spread from farming to food, thereby elevating what might have been regarded as the humble practicalities of the kitchen to an equally high place in the world of intellectual endeavour and debate. It might have been expected to happen in the 1650s among correspondents in the Hartlib circle. But it did not; their letters did not begin to discuss food quality, flavour, or recipes from the cook's point of view. Instead, that interest waited until after 1660, and then it startles us with examples of scientists and members of the Royal Society actually inscribing cooking recipes amid writings on quite different political and scientific themes. The Georgical Committee of the Royal Society, for example, initiated enquiries in 1664 about how to dry fruit; Lord Brereton was asked to communicate what he knew of that subject, and Dr John Pell, the mathematician, evidently expressed willingness to explain cheap and easy ways used in Switzerland. If it happened today in the work of august members of the Royal Society, we would think it incongruous.[2]

INTELLECTUALS DISCOURSING ON FOOD

JOHN LOCKE

John Locke is one of the personalities in this group of intellectuals who had such diverse interests. His writings on political economy are ranked first in his life story, but food historians owe him a place in the network of food discussants and improvers. His patron was Lord Shaftesbury, a keen farmer who espoused new ventures and had many acquaintances among influential administrators, scientists and policy makers, such as Benjamin Worsley, Henry Slingsby and Robert Boyle. Locke's letters show his practical interest in useful plants and the exchange of seeds, and include many references to the appetizing foods they were intended to supply. They show how firmly farming and gardening were now connected to food choices in the kitchen. While living in Holland, Locke supplied his friend Edward Clarke in England with seeds for a variety of root vegetables from the Low Countries – three kinds of turnips, three kinds of carrots, one of parsnips, one of salsify and two of skirret roots. They were sent with advice on the way to eat the skirret roots – buttered like turnips, or in a salad dressed with oil and vinegar. Locke wrote to Mrs Clarke in January 1684, anticipating a walk with her 'in the turnip grove next summer', promising moreover, when she visited him next, the sight of 'new fashions, new housewifery, new cookery'. He was clearly familiar with the notion of fashions in food. Indeed, Locke was consciously helping one food fashion on its way, by sending to Clarke, in October 1686, Muscovy or Russian cabbage seed plus blood-red cabbage seed, this last being regarded in the Low Countries as the most wholesome of all, being a remedy for scurvy. It was either boiled or eaten raw in a salad, and it was handy in winter, since cabbages could be stored in cellars, and be brought into use whenever needed; one simply peeled off leaves as required for one meal and dressed them with oil and vinegar.[3]

Locke's words suggest that red cabbage was a novelty in England at this time – not totally unknown perhaps to connoisseurs, like botanists, but unfamiliar in London markets, and he lightheartedly envisaged the possibilities of turning red cabbage salad into a fashion. If he had been in England, he said, he would have been tempted himself 'to bring it into use under some fine new name'. Fashions in food had provoked scorn at an earlier period, but contemporaries now accepted the phenomenon without demur. We see another of them in the same letter from Locke to Clarke referring to the importance of drinking spa water. This touched on another vogue of the time that was beginning to produce quite a few treatises. It sent many well-to-do people to socialize at up-and-coming spas around the country, and left its mark in their household accounts: the Duke of Rutland paid out £7 6s. 8d. in 1674 for water to be fetched several times from Quarndon in Derbyshire to Belvoir; and more water came in 1675 from 'the spaw'. Another fad of the age, now in vogue, was for tea drinking, and sure enough we also find in the Duke of Rutland's shopping list in 1670 half a pound of tea costing him 10s., and a tin box in which to keep it cool on journeys. By 1694, tea known as Regal Tea had been invented, and featured in a matter-of-fact way in Ann Blencowe's cookbook. Yet another fashion of the time was created when cocoa beans arrived in the market, and almonds were coated with chocolate. In 1667 they duly arrived at Belvoir for the pleasure of Lord Roos.[4]

JOHN COLLINS

John Collins (1625–83) was another intellectual of the day who had an interest in food, mixing this with a professional study of statistics and saltmaking. He is commonly described as the inventor of political arithmetic, but he also moved around kitchens in high places with a discerning eye. He once worked for John Marr, who was a clerk in Prince Charles's kitchen, and he married a daughter of William Austen, head cook to Charles II. All this was mingled with an interest in government policies on trade, on which he wrote pamphlets (1680–82). He became a Fellow of the Royal Society in 1667.[5]

One of Collins's pamphlets described English and foreign ways of extracting salt, accompanied by careful information on methods of salting and cooking meat and fish. The information had been collected just as carefully as for any scientific experiment, for he consulted Mr William Martin, who was a saltworker in Cheshire and Staffordshire, obtained Italian recipes from a Mr Richard Alcorn, and asked saltworkers to correct any errors. He relied for his fish recipes on John But, who had been a cook for 30 years, and he further expounded on the significant differences in kinds of salt when used on various foods. Eel recipes followed, ways of salting and drying fish and flesh for long keeping, and ways of pickling vegetables. His was a very full story of salt in its many aspects, even including concern for the sad condition of saltworkers, accommodating their livelihood to an excise on salt, and Scottish and French competition.[6]

SIR KENELM DIGBY

Another child of this age, indefatigably pursuing health through food and the tastiest recipes, was Sir Kenelm Digby, who lived until 1665, and wrote a book, published posthumously in 1669, that was brimming over with recipes. Digby is conventionally described as an author, naval commander and diplomat, and was, in addition, Chancellor and confidant of Queen Henrietta Maria. But his *Closet Opened* reveals yet another side of his life. Plainly, he talked to all he met among his own class about food and the favoured recipes used in their households, asking about fine details, writing it all down, and even getting demonstrations by the experts. He took for granted the whole variety of common ingredients from field and hedgerow that was familiar to ordinary folk, plus, of course, the luxuries that his class alone could afford. He of all writers on food underlined the truth of that discerning remark by an earlier writer in the 1650s that basic foods were the same for all classes; it was only the extra adornments and refinements that made the dishes different.[7]

Digby devoted some 50 pages to pottages. They started simply, with a broth of bones with meat attached (beef, mutton or veal in his 'ordinary pottage').

The bones were nothing special: at one point he described those for jelly broth as the butcher's bones which otherwise were thrown to the dogs. The meat was in one case a knuckle of veal or scrag end of mutton. Bread was added, seasonal root vegetables and herbs (a generous list that in deep winter comprised parsley roots, white chicory, navets (i.e. turnips) and cabbage), or in another recipe onions, roots or cabbage, and herbs. The prime ingredients were thus thoroughly ordinary and accessible to all classes. It was only when Digby came to the extras that refinements appeared that were available only to a higher class of cooks; he acknowledged that 'it mendeth a bouillon much to boil in it some half roasted volaille [poultry] or other good meat'. Another pottage of Lord Lumley started with a base of dried peas, the same as was used by any cottager, and was flavoured with equally ordinary plants from the fields and gardens: onions, mint, parsley, winter savory and sweet marjoram, the only refined extra being coriander seed. At the far end of the food chain lay yet more exotic ingredients, as in Lady Monmouth's broth, which used a capon, plus endive, skirret or parsley roots, and to which were added chestnuts, pistachios and pine kernels, of which the last two items must have been foreign imports.[8]

A very simple water gruel was another item in Digby's diet that would have been found in any labourer's food regime; indeed, it was named in Hartlib's diet for poor children in London in 1649. The basics were water and oatmeal, until Digby added mace, nutmeg, sugar, butter, and rosewater, egg and white wine, thus relying on these last additions to make the gruel delectable in upper class circles. The oatmeal and water that settled at the bottom of the cooking pot he described as 'good water gruel for the servants', so we can assume that some flavouring lingered there too. But in the cottage we can be sure that a resourceful cook could make as good a flavour simply by adding a few herbs from the garden.[9]

More could be said about Digby's recipes, but here we fix attention on inflections in the general tone of the food debate that belong peculiarly to this half century. Cakes, notably seed cakes and plum cakes (already mentioned as part of a routine diet by John Beale in the 1650s), seem to have become more common items of food, with yeast being in the large ones but not in the small cakes. Digby likened the small ones to those sold at Barnet, presumably Barnet fair, so they were well known to all. Digby did not have a cake tin, but for the larger quantities he placed the mixture in a tin hoop to keep it in shape, laying it on two well-buttered sheets of paper. The decoration of the plum cake in Digby's recipe (using 12 pounds of currants!) was an icing consisting of a meringue mixture with rosewater, spread over the cake and returned to the oven to dry out. Earlier use of egg whites and sugar had not so clearly suggested this whipping up of meringue, and may have been an improvement copied from French cooks. Digby's marchpane recipe, on the other hand, fitted under a heading that had long been familiar. But his version made use of a pan containing hot coals, which was laid on top of the mixture to dry it – but not, he emphasized, to burn it. This made the exterior crisp but kept the interior moist, seemingly a new detail in procedure that we still use if we put marzipan on top of a simnel cake. In changing a sweetmeat that had not formerly been exposed to heat we may be observing a slight alteration in cooking practice that discerning contemporaries would have registered as something new, and confidently given it a date in their own lifetime.[10]

The old prejudice against cheese was evidently fading, judging by Houghton's clear statement that it was a nourishing food, kept well, and could be carried to most parts of the world without damage. The toasting of cheese, formerly dismissed as a vulgar Welsh practice, was now perfectly acceptable, for Digby gave a recipe for a slipcoate cheese, comparable to that made by the market women, taking only eight days to be ready, and served after it had been scorched on top with a rough and ready fire shovel. This was peasant food turned into respectable fare for the rich. William Rabisha, a cook with a rich clientèle, went further in cooking cheese and made a kind of substantial omelette with grated Parmesan cheese, grated bread, egg yolks and caraway seed. Parmesan cheese had long been a routine import.[11]

Digby had a remarkably keen eye and open mind for innovative cooking practices, and they sometimes concerned quite small matters. When spit roasting, for example, flour was sometimes sprinkled over the meat to make a thin crust, but Queen Henrietta Maria had an original method of her own, using the yolks of eggs. Digby mentioned Lady Lasson's unusual way of making pastry, producing something short and light, but not using hot water or melted butter. Her method sounds like the procedure for puff pastry, which was the most usual kind mentioned in the cookery books. But Digby's directions made a point of melting the butter in water and then skimming it off for use with some water clinging to it.[12]

Foreign ways with food were always worth notice: Digby gave two ways, including one from Holland, of dressing stock fish. A recipe of the Countess of Penalva for making Portuguese eggs for Queen Catherine of Braganza, Charles II's wife, reminds us of likely Portuguese influences on food ways. Indeed, we shall meet Portuguese varieties of beans being grown in England, which may well derive from first encounters when they were eaten in food at someone's table. Portugal broth, as made for the queen, also appeared in his pages.[13]

Health drinks had been a modish interest since the end of the sixteenth century, but for Digby the subject was an obsession. He concentrated on mead and metheglin, for which he cited 109 different recipes, running from page 8 to page 83. One recipe came from Russia, another from the Muscovy ambassador's steward, and altogether they used a host of different herbs. The water in one case came from a conduit, in another from Hyde Park, and the metal of the containers in which it was prepared was also deemed significant in determining the final flavour.[14]

FOOD PRESERVATION AND COMMERCIAL GOALS

Many references to methods of preserving food showed the ever-increasing importance attached to keeping all cooked foodstuffs for more than a few days – sometimes as much as three months, even a year. Butter was used lavishly to seal the cooked food from contact with the air, and, in order to ensure that no cracks appeared in the sealing, many pounds of butter were used in large households. To cook a dozen woodcock, for example, 7–8lbs of butter were prescribed, and another 3–4lbs was allowed for in order to seal the pot after baking. The meat was expected to keep fresh for two months. The tricky job of pouring the melted butter into the pie was helped by the use of a funnel, inserted before baking, and was first mentioned by a helpful lady author, Hannah Woolley, who gave more practical details than others. In Digby's recipe for venison pie, the butter seal was further reinforced by binding the whole in a piece of sheep's leather to make the exclusion of air doubly certain. We glimpse in all this, along with the use of butter when serving vegetables at the table, a most satisfactory explanation for the rapidly expanding dairying industry at this time. The French traveller, Henri Misson, in the 1690s gave a memorable description of all the heaps of cabbage, carrots, turnips, herbs and other roots at table, 'swimming in butter'.[15]

Yet more rarefied ways of storing meat were now tested and introduced. One method used in the Prince of Wales's boiling house, the Inns of Court, and in some colleges, called for the meat to be laid in a brine for a day or two, from which it was then lifted out, rubbed with salt, and hung in a warm kitchen. This salting was enough to keep the meat in good condition for a long time. Another method involved putting the meat in a liquid in barrels, rather than in layers of salt, and this became a highly popular method. Lady Portland ventured half way with this method by pickling capons in a white wine broth for four days, then adding vinegar to keep it for a longer period. Using vinegar was, of course, already known for preserving vegetables: a variety of vinegars of malt, wine or verjuice were used, and flavourings such as elderflower were added. Yet another flavour was introduced with rape vinegar, which used rapeseed, a new farm crop of the seventeenth century. Now the method of pickling in a vinegar liquid was being used on pork meat, and it won such favour that some housewives turned away from drying and smoking bacon. It was known as wet pickling and was quicker than dry salting, which took some 8–11 weeks for the meat to be ready to pack into casks, and which always involved some waste when the contents of the barrel neared its end.[16]

More purposeful methods of fattening chickens were also publicized now, not only as regards feed (barley meal, with milk and sugar, plus raisins and broken beer was one mixture) but also by keeping the birds tightly closeted in a confined space to prevent them moving around, even leaving a candle burning all night in the coop to keep them eating. This was Lady Fanshaw's way of fattening them in a fortnight, and would nowadays be called a hen battery. But at least she was humane enough to vary the flavour of the feed, alternating water with milk and ale. This poultry-fattening style plainly lent itself to commercial use, and matched the mood of the age as the food business in London fastened firmly on quicker financial gains as a major goal.[17]

In short, amid all the small changes in food handling and cooking methods revealed by the food writers, we see some sharper calculations of profit and loss heading the agenda of food merchants as they strove to supply food in greater variety and quantity to their clients. The population was increasing, and some people were well-heeled and becoming ever more discerning and demanding. One glimpse of a wholly new commercial opportunity seized by food producers comes into view in the treatise by John Collins on salt, decribing cucumber pickling on a large scale by 'the oilmen'. The very profession of 'oilman' was new in the seventeenth century, brought into existence when rapeseed became a considerable farm crop, notably in the newly drained fens of eastern England, and large acreages were sown after about 1650 producing seeds that were pressed for their oil. A scattering of small oil mills sprang up where the crop was grown around the Wash, while two larger groups clustered in Wisbech, Cambridgeshire and in London. The oil had originally been intended for cloth finishing, in place of the more expensive imported olive oil, but subsequently it began to be used for lighting and in fact allowed for some early street lighting in Wisbech itself. Inevitably, it also suggested itself as an oil in food. As John Collins explained, 'the oilmen' found themselves a profitable by-employment pickling cucumbers. For one batch, they bought a thousand cucumbers, layered them into a barrel with dill and fennel for flavouring, added a small quantity of rock alum, and left them for three to six weeks. The liquid was boiled again, skimmed and returned to the casks, where the cucumbers, kept close covered, were now ready for sale. One salesman was Joseph Pierce, oilman at the Sign of the Swan, Holborn Bridge, who also sold rape vinegar and red herrings in vinegar as well as cucumbers. Outside London's shops, we have no way of gauging how much rape oil was used in food, but John Evelyn, in a private recipe book, named rape vinegar for pickling cucumbers, and one recipe in Robert May's cookery book of 1660 chose it for frying fish. When rapeseed was grown again in the twentieth century, the oil was considered carcinogenic, and had first to be modified by the scientists, so we can only hope that our forebears did not consume too much. For historians, this story has special interest in illustrating how a farming innovation was begun for industrial purposes and finished up in diet.[18]

FOOD AND JOURNALISM

The lively opportunism that was being nurtured in the food world by a quickening of trade continued to be mirrored throughout this period in the activities and writings of scientists and intellectuals. Between the 1680s and 1703 it was best personified by John Houghton, a journalist who broke new ground by publishing a fortnightly *Newsletter* from London, and chose foodstuffs as a major topic of interest for his readers. His letters ran from 1681 to 1703 (he died in 1705), and obeyed the same rules as those observed by earlier writers like Digby and Collins. Careful research was carried out in informed quarters, questionnaires were in vogue, letters to correct or add information were invited, and much importance was attached to the dissemination, far and wide, of accurate factual knowledge. The *Newsletter* was delivered to Londoners for one penny a week, or sent outside London by penny post; some copies reached further afield, as far as Amsterdam. One of the most arresting instances of precise factual information was the vivid, first hand account, published in August and September 1703, of the way Shetlanders collected birds and eggs for winter food from some of the wilder neighbouring islands like St Kilda, Boreray and Soay. The information came originally from Sir Robert Moray, one of the founders of the Royal Society, who had died in 1673.[19]

Houghton's driving urge to disseminate information is conveyed in many interjections in his news-sheet. He had started with information on farming procedures and hoped 'by degrees we shall get all the husbandries that are in Europe'. He moved on to food and expressed strong support for hawkers and pedlars selling perishable foods in the streets, for 'a great trade is better for any country than a little one'. He was keen to publish news of any books that gave practical information. He even published individual recipes, and when his readers made themselves 'merry with my receipt of cakes, hasty-pudding, etc.', he rounded on them by naming august figures like John Evelyn and John Ray who were concerned with the same things. He drew attention to people's ignorance of practices in one neighbourhood that would have benefited the folk next door, if they had known of them. Thus Robert Plot gave the example of cereal varieties growing around Thame and Watlington that were unknown further north, in Burford and Banbury, though they lay in the same county. So Houghton was eloquent in favour of increasing consumption in London, for its effects rippled out to encourage 'the breeders of provisions and higglers thirty miles off'; if the incentive could work its way to 80 miles distance, it would create ever more work. His imagination was fired as he contemplated better sales of fresh fish from the sea; horses should carry fish on the day it was landed to more inland towns, just as it was at present carried from Hythe, Hastings and Chichester to London. Looking yet further afield, Houghton made frequent references to food for the plantations; he was contemplating a much wider market in which to sell English food, and clearly the improved skills in preservation greatly expanded these possibilities.[20]

Thus, Houghton's schemes envisaged a much larger trade in woodcock pies to be carried overseas. At home ordinary country folk had their fill of them, for they were caught in plenty from autumn onwards through the winter, and we have seen what a favourite they were at well-to-do tables in the early seventeenth century. Houghton wanted to promote a closer integration of the food trade in country and town so that woodcock pies, thousands of them, sealed in pots with butter, could be transported to the plantations! The cheapness of the birds and of the butter in the countryside would, he said, easily pay the cost of the transatlantic passage. In another bold flash of the imagination he wanted oranges coming from Spain to be landed at the outports as well as going to London. He reckoned that in one year, 1694–5, nine million oranges and lemons were imported into London, averaging out at one per head of the national population. Ordinary folk in London were seen munching them in the streets; they should be made available for a much wider population to enjoy.[21]

Houghton's readers were alerted to innumerable commercial opportunities through the information in his news-sheet; the revolution under way invites comparison with that wrought recently by eBay auctions on the Internet. He listed the current prices of basic commodities and annual imports of foreign goods, and printed personal advertisements from individuals offering goods or services. The information he purveyed was varied and totally random – the cargo of a vessel newly arrived from Surat, for example, or the condition of the cornfields in a piece of country where Houghton happened to find an informant. Husbandry and trade were his proclaimed news topics, but these abstract nouns were promptly converted into practicalities that would inform ordinary folk about ways of making bread, pastry, puddings and cakes. Ways of brewing and fermenting introduced a train of thought that led him on to a well-informed re-port on life in Derby where fine malt was made, and among other things he gave a valuable summary of the varied diet enjoyed by people in north Derbyshire.[22]

DRINKS AND JOURNALISM

A summary of Houghton's news items on food and drink can be trusted to give us a fair idea of the latest gossip in this London world of chattering people meeting in the coffee houses and taverns or entertaining at home. Fine water came high on their list of desirables in this period, doubtless because of the rising population living in towns. In London six pipes had already been laid from different conduit heads outside the capital, and water was now being led from these through lesser pipes into named streets in the city and West End, reaching as far as Leicester Square and Piccadilly. The water was at first, in December 1694, advertised 'for washing and other uses', and householders wishing to be connected to the supply were invited to treat with the contractors 'at reasonable rates'. A year later the water was described as fit for drinking.[23]

Some new drinks, all needing this good water, were establishing their popularity. A long account, spread over nine issues, told Houghton's readers about cocoa, and showed up-to-date knowledge of the special place that drinking chocolate had come to occupy (and still does) in the Spanish diet. The English were still experimenting with it, but some coffee house proprietors already offered a chocolate drink that was advertised in Houghton's news-sheets in 1698 and 1700. Lately, the coffee houses had also found a good reception for their water gruel: Frank's coffee house offered it from 5 a.m. onwards. Another of Houghton's articles claimed to have unusual detail about the very first introduction of coffee into London; since the story sounds authentic, it is printed in full in Chapter 9. The coffee bean, too, was the subject of experiments, for an advertisement appeared in 1697 for coffee in powder form; Nescafé has its precursor.[24]

Drinks with medicinal virtues were numerous. Sassafras, made from the boiled roots and bark of a tree that was brought from Virginia, was offered as a diet drink, and was commended for curing pox and scurvy. The coffee houses were experimenting with their own concoctions for other remedies: Houghton had tasted a pleasant reddish liquid, made from sassafras sweetened with sugar, called 'bochett', and alleged to cure sterility. Asses' milk for convalescents was mentioned in this period rather more often than earlier; the Lord Chancellor of Ireland, John Methuen, claimed to have been greatly assisted in his illness by asses' milk, and Houghton's news-sheet informed readers that they could hire an ass for a week if they wished.[25]

MORE INGENIOUS FOOD VENTURES

The preservation of meat had gradually acquired a leading place in the cookery books in the course of the seventeenth century, and now led into discussions of the different kinds of foodstuffs fed to animals, which affected the flavour and keeping qualities of meat after butchering, and the different kinds of salt that were recommended. Collins's treatise on salt had sparked a keener interest, and Houghton made use of that work, plus the comments of others, to expatiate on the separate merits of rock salt and sea salt and the places in England where salt was mined or evaporated. Housewives were acutely sensitive to the attributes of different salts in cooking and preserving.[26]

Among meats that were singled out for special mention in this period by Houghton and others, veal stands out as the one that was plainly playing a more prominent role in the London market than ever before. We noticed how conspicuous it was in the diet of Lancashire gentry in the early seventeenth century, being associated with a sensible use of male calves in a county that was already noted for its interest in dairying and for its liking for milky dishes. Some highly detailed accounts were now given of Lancashire's admirable regime in rearing male calves; they were suckled for several months by an older cow as a nurse mother before they went to the butcher. In Essex and Hertfordshire, the feeding regime also became quite famous, and Tring was given special mention. Some dairymen found that they could not compete in the milk business because their land did not have a sufficient supply of good water, nor did they have all the hands needed to make butter and cheese. So they turned to veal production, their nearness to London placing them at an advantage. In fact, of course, this speciality could sustain many a poor cowkeeper anywhere, and contemporaries bore witness to some who had only two or three cows, but bought in male calves at 7–10 days old from their neighbours. In this way, they reared 20 calves a year, fattening them in a matter of nine weeks, and keeping the meat white by giving the calves a piece of rock chalk to lick.[27]

The food market in London plainly stirred the most opportunist enterprises in accessible districts. In 1694 it was said that Mr Harrad milked 300–400 cows at Hoxton for the Londoners' milk supply, and when they dried off, he fattened them for the butcher. But ingenuity was not the attribute of near-Londoners alone; the village of Over, 8½ miles north-west of Cambridge became celebrated as a dairying centre, supporting some 1,000 milch cows. The Cambridge colleges were the beneficiaries in this case. The inhabitants contrived to buy in cows at Michaelmas so that they would have cows calving every month through the winter; thus, they were able to supply almost as much butter in winter as in summer to the university dons.[28]

In the course of producing news-sheets over 20 years, we can readily imagine Houghton casting about for new topics. When he had run through the basic foodstuffs, he turned to novel and sometimes exotic foods, hoping to add variety to the spice of life. An Essex man was growing caraway successfully, and he thought it had commercial possibilities; he was less sanguine about dittany and scammony. His advertisements showed that vermicelli was being imported, mangoes, yams, caviar, lime juice and Bologna sausages. But this last food was taking a circuitous route from producers to consumers: the middle guts of the ox were sent from England to Italy, and were put into Bologna sausages. We are only guessing at the next step when they returned to England, but it seems reasonable to suggest it, since Houghton advertised some Bologna sausages as 'lately imported'.[29]

Whether the clustering of such novel foods in London in the middle 1690s betokened any qualitative change in the scale of overseas food trade, markedly boosting the diversity of luxury imports, is unclear. But if so, it is a subject worthy of more exploration. In the event, any flow of fancy foreign foods must have been interrupted, since a lean time followed in 1698. But as luck would have it, at that very time, a most important famine food was waiting in the wings.

In Houghton's sequence of news about food, he gave a summary account in December 1699 of the introduction of potatoes, expanding somewhat on that told by William Coles in 1657. It was probably the story that by then circulated conventionally, but its exact words deserve to be quoted, for it illuminates the circumstances more vividly:

> I have been informed that potatoes were brought first out of Virginia by Sir Walter Raleigh, and he stopping at Ireland, some was planted there, where it thrived very well and to good purpose; for in their succeeding wars, when all the corn above ground was destroyed, this supported them, for the soldiers, unless they had dug up all the ground where they grew, and almost sifted it, could not extirpate them; from thence they were brought to Lancashire, where they are very numerous, and now they begin to spread all the kingdom over.[30]

As London had a much larger array of foods than anywhere else, it is not surprising that potatoes appear to have been readily available there in the 1650s (we have interpreted Moufet's remarks to this effect as being an interpolation by Bennet in 1655); they were also at this same time being named without comment as ingredients in the recipe books. In the 1660s Sir Kenelm Digby relied on getting his from the seed shops; so did John Collins, who wrote so knowledgeably in 1682 about salt, and told his readers that potatoes could be got from seed merchants all the year round. That, of course, was the London scene, but the situation in the countryside was not the same. Potatoes were not yet a familiar vegetable in the country at large, and that was borne out in the early 1660s by the considerable efforts of the Royal Society to spread the word; Mr Buckland and Robert Boyle were two members who attended its meetings then, and expressed a readiness to supply seed potatoes themselves to interested growers. Even in 1700 it is not always clear where seed potatoes and cooking potatoes could be bought in the provinces.[31]

By the 1690s, however, potato pie was a familiar dish in the recipe books of gentle folk, though it was still not firmly associated with savoury flavours. Diana Astry's potato pie (*c.* 1700) was called Spanish, using imported Spanish potatoes that were longer in shape, said to be 'more luscious', and certainly more costly, so that made the dish suitable for the better-off. It had puff pastry at the bottom and on top, cinnamon as the chosen spice, and a glass of sack was poured in when serving. In another recipe of Ann Blencowe's the potatoes were mashed with much butter (1lb to 1lb of potatoes) and nutmeg was used to flavour it. She dubbed this 'a good potato pudding, the best', and it was certainly rich, for it also contained ten eggs and half a pound of sugar. It is noticeable in this and other recipes that no firm convention as yet introduced onions as the foremost partner of savoury potatoes.[32]

Other potato recipes suggest that experimentation was still the order of the day, and interesting variations were tried. Rabisha's recipe for a pie again used Spanish potatoes, sliced thick and laid in a pastry coffin with nutmeg, cinnamon, sugar, ginger, marrow bones, raisins, dates and citron. A liquid containing vinegar, sack, butter, sugar and egg yolk was poured in when baked. A very similar recipe was given by Hannah Woolley.[33]

Food tips were eagerly and routinely picked up by English travellers when abroad, and as more people were venturing as far as India and China, some practical hints may well have come from the other side of the world. Houghton's urgings warn us to watch for these foreign influences seeping in, particularly through the Jesuits, who were sending back reports to Europe from Asia about agriculture and food habits. Somewhere their remarks were bound to fall on receptive ears, for clusters of curious people were scattered everywhere. John Beale, in correspondence with John Evelyn, desired to see the Jesuits translating books on the herbs, trees and stones found in China, those remarks being prompted by the publication of Jean de Thévenot's *Relation of China*, which described, in French, his journeys through Turkey, Persia and the East Indies to China. Beale had obviously encountered its first volume promptly after publication in 1666; the English translation followed in 1687.[34]

COMMENDATIONS FOR A SIMPLER, EVEN VEGETARIAN, DIET

In general, a thoroughly open-minded attitude towards a good diet was visible in Houghton and others, whether publicizing foreign food ways or commenting on the diet of people in classes below their own. At an earlier time writers would have shrunk away with distaste from the lowly food of the poor. Now a wider knowledge of food eaten abroad and closer observation of the physique and health of other classes taught the intellectuals to look more carefully at diets and their consequences. They saw merits in a simpler food style, for it manifestly enabled the labouring classes to enjoy good health, work hard, and not fall prey to the diseases caused by rich foods and gluttony. Richard Baxter, the Presbyterian pastor of Kidderminster in Worcestershire, had entered many a poor man's cottage and come to respect their slender diet in promoting health. Its main ingredients he listed as brown bread, milk, butter, cheese, cabbages, turnips, parsnips, carrots, onions and potatoes (he was writing in the 1680s), whey and buttermilk, peas pies, apple pies, puddings, pancakes, gruel and flummery (a mixture in milk of wheat flour and oatmeal, and similar to frumenty, which was hulled wheat, boiled in milk, with sugar and spice). In due course, we find John Houghton himself commending coarse bran bread as eaten by countryfolk, comparing it favourably with the over-refined bread of Londoners. We are left wondering if this revised notion of what was healthy bread resulted in part from French experience, for John Evelyn wrote in Houghton's news-sheet on bread, noting the bread of Rouen, from which no bran at all was removed. At first eating, it seemed rough and harsh, he thought, but he found it pleasant when he got used to it, and the health of Frenchmen assured him that it was wholesome and strengthening.[35]

The most eloquent defence of the simple diet was delivered by William Temple, asserting c. 1680 that 'health and long life are usually blessings of the poor, not of the rich, and the fruits of temperance rather than of luxury and excess'. His further observation was made from his own personal acquaintance with people who had lived to a ripe old age, most of whom came from the pastoral counties of Derbyshire, Staffordshire and Yorkshire, and none being 'above the rank of common farmers'. Temple wrote soberly and incorporated much experience when writing in his early fifties. 'From all these examples and customs,' he concluded, 'the common ingredients of health and long life ... are great temperance, open air, easy labour, little care, simplicity of diet, rather fruits and plants than flesh which easier corrupts.'[36]

'Rather fruits and plants than flesh' were words briefly summarizing the merits of a vegetable diet. Already, Thomas Fuller in 1662 had suggested that 'in some seasons the gardens feed more people than the field'. Now came the moment when some opinions hardened a little more in favour of a vegetarian diet, after nearly a century when opinion was building up slowly in that direction. It had shown signs of converting some intellectuals in the 1650s; we noted above the vegetarian regime that John Beale enjoined on his family, but not on his servants; John Milton, Isaac Newton and John Ray, the botanist, have all been cited as vegetarians. John Evelyn circled around the subject: in *Acetaria* (1699) he gave instructions for a salad and was satisfied that his discourse had 'advanced in favour of the herbaceous diet'. He also expressed himself well aware of other people in the world living on herbs and roots and thriving 'to incredible age, in constant health and vigour', though he refrained from becoming doctrinaire.[37]

A firmer posture was adopted by Thomas Tryon, a thinker/doer of very mixed experience, proclaiming the merits of strict vegetarianism in several books published between 1682 and 1706; he died in 1703. Personal experience in Barbados, where he saw the physical effects of a vegetable diet on workers in the sugar plantations, no doubt strengthened his convictions. So he imposed a tough regime on himself, eating no meat or fish, no live creature that had to be killed, and relying for his sustenance on herbs, fruit, grain, eggs, dairy produce and water; and he lived to be 67 years old.[38]

The public world as revealed by writers, philosophers and journalists up to 1700 mirrors a food scene in London that was vigorously responding to strong commercial urges among merchants, and conveying a stimulating message to good effect among some growers and livestock producers in the neighbourhood of London. Already in 1653 Hartlib's contacts had described fields around London being turned into gardens – that is to say, market gardens – and that was followed by the next phase when the same vegetables sold so well that they were planted out in fields. Commercial drive after 1660 resulted in more ready-prepared foods being put on sale: pickled cucumbers and biskets of many different kinds are two well-documented examples. Meanwhile more recipe books were published, and women kept their own private collections, which have survived in considerable numbers in our archive offices. We turn to these sources of information for food eaten at the table.[39]

THE RECIPE BOOKS

Not surprisingly, more recipe books were published in these years than in the previous 20. Men still featured most often as authors, but they acknowledged women as informants and/or devisers of some recipes. William Rabisha's recipe book (1661) was actually dedicated to five women, all members of the nobility or bearing the title Lady. The author described them as upholders and nourishers of the mystery of cookery. Moreover, Rabisha and other cooks explained how they themselves got their wide cooking experience, through the endeavours of women instructing them, or else sending them away to be instructed. Significantly, perhaps, the one woman who stands out from this masculine group, Hannah Woolley, who wrote several books on food and womanly behaviour, entitled one of her works *The Gentlewoman's Companion or, A Guide to the Female Sex.* She seemed to wish to separate the women's distinctive viewpoint, and in some ways she did so by her clear style in writing instructions and her liking for simple recipes.[40]

Hannah Woolley's introduction to authorship in 1661 was a work on the 'curiosities of preserving and candying both fruit and flowers', but she moved on to write *The Ladies Directory* in 1661, re-used old material and added more in *The Cooks Guide* (1664), adding still more in *The Queen-like Closet* (1670).

More routine cookery followed in *The Gentlewoman's Companion* (1675), though she disclaimed authorship, while not denying her hand in it; the publisher had evidently altered her text against her will. She died around 1675. Woolley was joined on the shelf of cookery books by Mrs Mary Tillinghast, who published a recipe book in 1678; she ran a school, and wrote in thoroughly practical terms for middle-class readers. Women at home, meanwhile, were assembling innumerable manuscript notebooks, of which a rich assortment has survived in our local archives.[41]

Taking the first three authors who published substantial works after the Restoration, we notice how quickly they launched themselves into print. They were evidently aware of a keen demand, Robert May issuing his work in 1660, and Hannah Woolley and William Rabisha in 1661. An alluring array of recipes resulted, covering all the main types of dishes, and ingredients that featured regularly in the repertoire of those cooking for gentle folk. By the 1680s and 1690s there had emerged out of this assemblage a certain familiar pattern, revealing the favoured dishes eaten in comfortable households, at least in and around London. We may safely assume that the women who prided themselves on their cooking skills read some of these printed recipe books, while taking many other ideas from their friends, as their own notes inform us: manifold trends of the time were nourishing publicity and sharpening commercial acumen, and all this fostered uniformity in diet among gentle and professional people. Menus that they saw when dining away from home taught them what was generally modish. From Diana Astry's notebook recording meals that she had eaten outside the home between 1701 and 1708 we can compile an almost standard list of dishes which were likely to turn up wherever you dined. They set the tone of the age, as it was experienced in and about London.[42]

MEAT RECIPES

If we attempt to summarize the eating habits of the better-off, we see a great wealth of roast *and* stewed red meat and birds in roughly equal amounts, together with a variety of fish still eaten in accordance with old customs in observing days of abstinence. Despite the abandonment of fish days during the Interregnum, old habits died hard. In any case, the selection of meat and fish was still generous enough to allow for the serving of different meat and fish dishes on the same day at two successive courses, even though some people still murmured about the prejudice to one's health when eating more than one meat at a meal. John Evelyn was of this mind, and translated some Latin lines in *Acetaria* as a warning: 'For different meats do hurt; remember how, when to one dish confined, thou healthier wast than now.'[43]

Straightforward roasts and stews sat alongside many different fricassées, showing by their frequency how this newly modish dish of the 1650s had become a routine by 1700. For Rabisha, it was a very fancy food with asparagus, pistachios, lambstones, etc.; 'a rare frigacy', he called it. Other people's fricassées were often composed of rabbits or chickens that were cooked with oysters, anchovies and herbs in a broth thickened with egg yolks. Wild birds, small and large, were still plentiful; Hannah Woolley served lark pie, and made up for their small size with bone marrow. Calves' head, which had always been a favourite, remained as popular as ever; it was sometimes baked in a pastry coffin and eaten cold; sometimes it was more elaborately contrived by cutting the head in half and putting it back together again on the dish. Now, however, the standard way of eating calves' head was to have it hashed: the bones were broken into small pieces, and the whole was cooked with anchovies, oysters, meat balls, bacon, cockscombs and ox palates.[44]

One striking feature of the meat recipes lay in the number containing instructions that invited the cook to preserve the finished dish for weeks and months if she chose. It accords with expectations that we have already formed from reading more general books about diet: pies sealed with butter were one method, cooked meat sealed on its own in pots with butter was another similar recourse. In one recipe for sausages the meat mixture was stored in a gallipot after cooking, and when needed, pieces were rolled into sausage shapes and cooked again. Sausages 'in the Dutch way' were boiled in their cases, and then stored from Michaelmas to May. The details about pouring in butter to exclude air seem to have been taken for granted by Woolley, since she omitted them from her instructions. I consulted my niece who watches the process nowadays on the Greek island of Andros. Her Greek neighbours seal the pot with pork fat, sometimes including a fragrant herb. Otherwise the sausages are smoked and kept in a cool building, an alternative used also by our English cooks. Another recipe by Woolley for Polonia sausages used the smoking method, but her unusual flavouring contained cloves, mace, ginger, nutmegs, cinnamon, aniseed, caraway and coriander seeds, kneaded with muscadine. The sausages were smoked for one night in the chimney, further dried near a warm fire, and then kept in a barrel of sifted wood ash, for 'as long as you please'. Yet another unexpected method of Woolley's suggested keeping them in oil, claiming that then they would last for seven years. This recipe almost certainly came from a foreign source, but it adds to other evidence showing how experiments in preservation were the order of the day. Indeed, John Collins, writing on salt in 1682, and remarking incidentally on the increasing number of salt springs recently discovered and opened in Cheshire, Worcestershire and Staffordshire, assumed that more experiments were in progress, and encouraged his readers to impart them to all.[45]

PICKLING AND OTHER MEANS OF PRESERVATION

Among new methods of preserving at this time was the pickling of meat and fish in a liquor. No precise description has been found explaining how the process evolved, but the pickling of vegetables probably suggested that trials might be made with fish and flesh, and two patents were obtained in 1691 for preserving fish, flesh and fowl in liquors, implying that it was something of an innovation. It was introduced in print as the method used with beef in the Prince of Wales's boiling house. That was Collins's information, imparted in his book of 1682, practised also in the Inns of Court and some colleges. The meat was soaked in brine for no more than a day or two (though it was also sometimes soaked for as long as eight days); it was then taken out, rubbed with salt and hung in a warm kitchen to dry. People preferred this method to the old dry salting method, presumably because it was quicker and more economical, since the brine was boiled and used again. The novelty of trials with this method of meat and fish preservation will make more sense when we find the method further elaborated after 1700.[46]

Other preservative measures for meat involved cooking it in the oven and pounding it in a mortar to make a pâté, though the French word pâté was not then used for it, 'paste' being the usual term. Yet another dish made to last but not reduced to a paste was 'coller of beef', which remained as a roll of meat, flavoured with herbs and spices, and was simply wrapped in a cloth and kept in a cool upstairs room. It was expected to last for three months, though it is likely that some other detail in its preservation was omitted from the recipe book.[47]

The individuality of cooks makes it impossible to span all the various methods that they used to feed their families, but it is worth noticing Rabisha's sardonic comment on this score when he burst out uncharacteristically in Book VI under the heading of 'Hot Boiled Flesh Meats', while setting out a recipe for a 'bisk'. It was originally a French dish, said Rabisha (presumably bisque, though when used in English in the first OED reference of 1647 it was described as an Italian rarity, and meant a rich soup made by boiling down birds or, secondarily, crayfish). But, he added, it had been much mended by the English, who never thought a thing well nor rich enough but must augment it, while turning away from 'unnatural compositions'. What he meant by unnatural compositions he did not explain, but his prejudice against bisk was shared by Hannah Woolley. She regarded it as a fancy French concoction, 'put together with all this cost and trouble ... by some rare whimsical French cook'. As far as she was concerned it was 'a miscellaneous hodgpodg of studied vanity', and certainly the long list of ingredients made it formidably elaborate. The terms used by Rabisha and Woolley suggest that the French style of cooking would have to overcome much opposition from English cooks if it were ever to prevail. Yet the English were not altogether logical, for they claimed to prefer things simple, while in practice, according to Rabisha, they were altering every foreign dish to make it accord with their own style.[48]

Sauces were now more prominent in the recipe books, sometimes featuring as a separate item. In practice they remained of two kinds, and only one kind nurtured deep prejudices. John Evelyn was deeply hostile. They were for him a wanton and expensive luxury, debauching the stomach, and taxing the digestion with difficult concoctions. 'The most simple has ever been esteemed the best,' he declared. The word 'sauce' had had a connotation in the past as a simple gravy or liquid flavouring to moisten otherwise dry food. Rabisha's sauces, for example, included mustard for beef and brawn, and mustard and sugar for pheasant; another author's sauce for quail was only claret wine with gravy from the cooking, plus salt and fine breadcrumbs, and for mutton the sauce was just boiled onions. Woolley offered many sauces in a seventh edition of *The Gentlewoman's Cabinet Unlocked*, with varied flavourings in each case, but they could still be called simple.[49]

STORAGE AND SEASONS FOR VEGETABLES AND HERBS

Vegetables and herbs were now routinely pickled for storage. May put them in a strong saline liquid and covered them; even ash keys were pickled. Green stuff was more welcome when fresh, and for the well-to-do it was all grown in their kitchen gardens. But reading the list of salads in the recipe books shows us a very familiar countrywoman's mixture of green plants that she could gather wild – lettuce, sorrel, purslane, borage, nettletops and all spring flowers. It was equally accessible to any who went out to gather it wild in the fields. Plainly, country folk could not get the same variety for as long a season as their wealthier neighbours, but variety was theirs, sometimes more than that served to the rich, and flavour too was sometimes more intense in plants gathered from the wild.[50]

Some of the recipe books now included what was called a 'grand salad', which assembled a large variety of greenstuff and was a flamboyant display to celebrate the coming of a new season. Robert May, on the other hand, carefully kept each salad plant separate on the dish. Attitudes to seasonal differences were almost certainly a personal matter, as they are today, and we may even guess at some expressions of regret at the loss of distinct seasons, such as we also hear today. The seasons were already being mixed together by the arts of preservation. Rabisha insisted strongly on seasonal differences in his seasonal bills of fare and his Epistle to the Reader, yet his final dish did not exclude foods that belonged to other seasons: his 'grand salad' for spring laid out fresh green plants – lettuce, spinach, alexander buds, watercress, cowslips, violets and much more, but then added olives, capers, raisins and currants. Incidentally, he also had on the dish a pastry centrepiece shaped as a castle with balconies and statues holding cruets of oil and vinegar. When all the guests were seated, the cruets were unstopped and the oil and vinegar ran onto the salad. Rabisha was a Cornish cook who had served kings and nobility, so he delighted in such elaborate conceits. But Hannah Woolley also made a grand salad with the same full array of sweet herbs plus capers, dates, raisins, almonds and currants, and set it off with a centrepiece of pastry, which she did not describe. A last-minute addition of hard-boiled eggs offered a contrasting colour in her dish, but plainly authors of recipe books will have watched and copied each other.[51]

FRUIT, CREAMS, CHEESES AND CAKES

Fruit that could be similarly preserved or pickled was also a thoroughly well-established favourite by this time; alternatively, the fruit was turned into wine. Indeed, so many fruit wines were now described in the recipe books that we may wonder whether the London importers of foreign wines noticed a falling demand for their wares! Certainly, we can reasonably infer indirectly from all this a larger harvest of fruit, including some of good quality for dessert and pleasurable eating. The many recipes for apricots continued, firmly demonstrating how successfully apricots were grown, at least in southern England; they came as readily to hand as plums. At the same time, much advice was now being given for keeping raw fruit in good condition so that, if one had the storage space, it called only for care rather than expertise to have some fresh fruit lasting until March and April. Alternatively, since the cook in the kitchen could preserve it in sugar syrup, we may take it for granted that some fruit was eaten throughout the winter.[52]

Preserving, of course, also resulted in a host of pickle jars standing in the store cupboard. Preserved barberries, used to sharpen savoury dishes, remained as popular as they had been in the 1650s. Some cooks, like Susanna Avery, had a special liking for pickled plums and peaches. Ann Blencowe treasured a singular recipe for an Indian pickle, called *pickle lila*, which was surely piccalilli. It contained the authentic ingredients – cauliflower, cabbage, celery, radishes, French beans, asparagus – plus one pound of ginger, one pound of garlic (with the consoling extra note that half that quantity of garlic would do), mustard seed and turmeric. The mixture was sufficiently unusual to sound authentically Indian; and since the recipe had been given by Lord Kilmorey, we may suspect that his name was known in India.[53]

Flavourings that went into meat dishes still included a variety of different home-made vinegars; gooseberry vinegar, which had to be kept for two years before it was ready, featured in Ann Blencowe's cookbook, and much trouble was also taken in preparing the basic broth. Blencowe used a leg of veal that she cooked down until it cut like a soft cheese. It received seven hours' cooking on the first day and 2–3 hours on the second, and produced a jelly that kept for a year and could be spooned out in small quantities at any time. A knob as small as a nutmeg was strong enough to flavour half a pint of broth, she said, and its consistency was indicated by the fact that she called it veal glue. The name was unattractive but it was doubtless superior in flavour to our stock cubes.[54]

A markedly stronger interest was shown by this time in the sweet course, which was served as part of the second course, when alternative meat dishes also appeared. The choice included fruit pies and tarts and fruit syrups, milky creams using almonds (Spanish custard was one), and cream caramels; by 1700 a chocolate cream had made its appearance, as well as chocolate cakes and slab chocolate, and in the Earl of Rutland's household at Belvoir castle in 1667 chocolate almonds were a treat. Recipes for making cheese still appeared in the recipe books, but they were rare, and were for soft cheeses, quickly made.

Public discussion about the machinations of cheese merchants strongly suggests that cheesemaking in the home was dwindling, and many small cow-keepers may well have confined their efforts to soft cheeses. Hard cheeses, at least around London, were becoming a food made by specialist dairy farmers, for housewives could rely on access to a lively network of cheese merchants. The situation was different in country areas distant from London; all market towns had a stall for cheese sellers, who were often countrywomen coming in for the day to sell from their small home dairies. But even their cheesemaking may have been dwindling as large cheesemakers outbid them. Finally, the cook was busier than before in making cakes: plum cake, caraway cake and cheese cake featured regularly.[55]

MEALS FOR ALL CLASSES

The recipe books were most successful in instructing gentle folk, but they also reached a growing class of professional people who were near-gentry, many members of whom ate at the same dining tables. Authors, moreover, took pains not to stand aloof from ordinary folk. Robert May, for example, was far from snobbish. While he knew all the fanciful dishes that could be contrived by those with bottomless purses, and he also had enough foreign experience to open his mind to the tastes of other countries, he was also intent on describing 'what is ordinary in this art'. He gave dishes that were easy to prepare, 'most pleasing to the palate, and not too chargeable to the purse'. His many variations on a single recipe 'for a change', and 'for variety' are pointers to the way ordinary dishes could be varied and decked up, but they show in their foundations basic ingredients that were the stock of the simplest kitchen. Thus we have a golden opportunity to pare them down to fit into the simpler dietary routine of ordinary folk, and gauge meals they ate that called for little money to be spent. We have already noticed several times our anonymous author of 1652 describing diets. His remarks are worth recalling yet again: he was a cynical satirist, but shrewdly perceptive; he had had experience in the world, being a physician who had studied in Padua, and had now arrived at some simple basic principles about diet. He did not hold with fancy foods. Intemperance and gluttony were for him the path to sickness, mirth was a better path to health, and hunger was the best sauce. His special interest lay in promoting diet drinks, and some were fancy: but he quickly recognized 'a lady-like nicety' when the same item turned up among serving men. ''Tis all meat which you have already tasted of,' he scoffed, 'the difference is only in the dressing, the which is rare and exquisite.' This basic truth underlies many of May's recipes. They were decked-up versions of dishes that were dressed down in the homes of ordinary folk.[56]

Pottage was on May's menu in several different versions. One in the English fashion contained oatmeal and the most ordinary herbs, like thyme, sweet marjoram, parsley, chives, marigold leaves, sage and pennyroyal. Several botanists in the seventeenth century compiled long lists of plants growing in England, noting the places where they had seen them in abundance, and sometimes remarking on their use in food. So we learn from their compilations (those of William Langham in 1633, William How in 1650 and Christopher Merrett in 1666 are the ones used here) of some of the plants that made flavourings and more substantial foods and were growing wild all over the place. Among the plentiful herbs were marjoram, mint (in six varieties), chervil 'everywhere in hedges', sage and caraway stalks, this last being singled out by Langham for making 'a sweet and well-smelling pottage'. Plainly, no one needed to search around for a variety of flavourings in pottage when so much was there for the picking.[57]

For meat in pottage May had a rack of mutton and a knuckle of veal, whereas many an ordinary housewife had only a bone and a slice from her bacon flitch. But she could also add dried beans or peas from the fields for extra protein, plus carrot roots growing wild, which Langham thought pleasant and wholesome and, significantly for our understanding of this distant world, superior in their strength of flavour to the carrots that were cultivated in gardens. Caraway roots were another good vegetable, and in Langham's view superior in flavour to parsnips. Other remarks of the botanists about root vegetables, and referring particularly to parsnips and turnips, tell us that farmers and gardeners made a point of growing them in the vicinity of towns and cities. Here we have a sharp insight into the commercial stimulus that was expanding the array of foods laid before townsfolk at their markets.[58]

Thus many versions of pottage were possible, all making nourishing and tasty dishes, and capable of a considerable variation in flavour around the seasons,

whether the housewife spent money on spices and extras or not. Among the
additions used by May, apart from onions, carrots, turnips, and parsnips, was
seasonal greenstuff, which our botanists also observed growing plentifully in the
wild. In the hedges they noted milk thistle, which one botanist deemed superior
to the finest cabbage, and sow-thistle (of the *Sonchus* family), which Merrett
saw growing between Woolwich and Greenwich, and which, in the smooth-
leaved variety, was deemed as good as spinach. If a little more meat came into
the hands of poor folk, it did not consist of expensive joints of muscle meat,
but it gave satisfaction – perhaps an ox cheek, an ox palate (they used to cost
6d. each, said Houghton, and now they sold for one penny), a calf's head, the
feet or tails of an animal, a rabbit or a wild pigeon. If the meat did not go into
pottage, it made a meat hash that was cooked slowly in a pipkin over the fire. In
London, and doubtless in other towns too, the poor got meat from charitable
butchers. John Houghton described poor women in London buying from the
market bits of rump steak after the butcher had cut out the best four pieces for
the rich. The poor made pies with them, or the meat was stewed or boiled and
sold ready cooked to poor folk. According to location and season, other foods
going into pottage or hash included hop buds, mushrooms, barberries (or their
leaves), sorrel and, in place of capers, which were imports, broom buds. The list
of alternative flavourings in stews was endless. In gentle households, the whole
mixture was likely to be served on sippets, whereas it would appear on plain slices
of stale bread in the ordinary home. Yet the dish for all classes would have been
recognizably similar; it was May's meat hash, dressed up or down, and when
made by a resourceful cook in a simple kitchen it could be just as satisfying as
in the rich man's hall.[59]

The dressing of meats received considerable attention from May, for it stood
for the coating of meats before cooking, the use of stuffings, and the pouring on
of sauces at the end. In all recipe books, stuffings were used in surprisingly large
quantities, far more than we use them nowadays. The basic ingredients were
simply bread, butter or suet, eggs and a choice of flavourings. Authors of recipe
books used many spices, such as cloves, ginger, mace, nutmeg and cinnamon,
and since these were plentiful and moderate in price, they may well have been
used almost daily in middle-class households too. In 1616 ginger cost less than a
penny farthing for an ounce; a full survey of spice prices over the century would
shed more light on what ordinary folk could afford. The basis of sauces was
similarly modest, using bread, butter and onions, plus vinegar, which was easily
made at home with crab apples from the hedgerows, or with ale tinged with yeast
to get it started. Poorer households simplified their way of adding substance to
whatever meat they had, not by making stuffings but by adding dumplings. As
for the poor housewife's sauce, she had a multitude of flavourings off the land,
mustard seed if it grew locally on the wayside, otherwise charlock seed which was

reckoned a good substitute for mustard, or 'jack by the hedge' (*Alliaria*), often called 'sauce alone'. This last, according to Merrett, was found everywhere in the hedges.[60]

Fish was plentiful in all places round the coast. In fact, in some estuaries people waded into the water in some seasons and took the fish by hand. Inland, the sharp eyes of the countryman exploited every chance in the same way. Eels, for example, were known to be especially plentiful and cheap in winter between Lamport and Bridgwater in Somerset: on frosty mornings people walking along the river banks and spotting a green patch of water knew that it meant heaps of eels lying there. In some rivers the locals could fish freely at any time; in others they were allowed to take fish only on fish days. We cannot be sure how much fish came the way of people living inland away from rivers. Some contemporaries claimed that sea fish was carried into all parts of the country, but it did not mean that all could buy it, or that our authors had accurate knowledge of conditions distant from London. Saltfish was available at any time in large shopping centres, but not everyone will have made the effort to obtain it. Middle-class people, as their diaries bear witness, received gifts of fish from friends who had lakes, and resourceful villagers made money by fishing and trading locally with their neighbours: but we cannot be sanguine about fresh fish regularly reaching village kitchens. But then it does not do so nowadays.[61]

Fresh salads featured regularly in all middle-class cookbooks, but again our botanists knew a list of wild green plants that were just as tasty in salad – the leaves of *Eringium*, for example, 'sweetish, with a slight aromatic, warm pungency', according to Linnaeus, though the fashion-seekers were concentrating all their attention at this time on candying the roots as comfits. Caraway stalks made another tasty dish, 'wonderfully pleasant in salad', said Langham. Winter cress, also known as *Herba Santa Barbara*, was treasured for salads in the cold months. Purslane was another welcome salad plant, often cultivated in gardens, but also found growing wild, as it was by Christopher Merrett when prowling about Ramsey mere; it was growing along footpaths by the rape mills. This may be an example of a plant newly arriving on the scene where old ground had been disturbed. People were constantly alert to this happening. One such newcomer was a plant called a water houseleek, which grew in Holderness and in the fens of Lincolnshire, but, according to William How in 1650, found also 'in new ditches of the Dutch works at Hatfield [Hatfield Chase in the Isle of Axholme] within 3–4 years after they were made'. The identity of this plant is unclear, but according to Grieve one variety of the houseleek known as 'stonecrop houseleek' bears leaves and young shoots that are still used as a salad in Holland. It sounds as if the Dutch drainers may have brought this plant, deliberately or inadvertently, from home to Axholme.[62]

Wild fruits attracted comment from only one of our three browsing botanists, namely Christopher Merrett, and their names and small numbers suggest that their habitats, and knowledge of them, was highly localized, thus preventing the botanists from drawing up any long list. Even nowadays small shrub fruits like whortleberry and bilberry are geographically localized and unknown to many people living outside the areas where they flourish; the blackberry stands alone in being universally familiar nowadays. The blackberry was called by Merrett in 1666 the bramble bush, and was then widespread, found all over the place, he said, 'in hedges and thickets'. But Merrett also referred to a mulberry bramble, so-called by country people at Sutton, Essex (was this Sutton, near Southend?), leaving the reader unclear whether it differed from the blackberry, or was just an eccentric name. Another berry-bearing shrub was called by Merrett the raspis bush or hindberry, in other words the wild raspberry, which he knew in the north of England and in Wales. But it was also as common as brambles, he said, in the woods of Chesham Bois, Buckinghamshire. This scattered distribution of the wild raspberry makes it sound like another highly localized fruit at this time, though raspberries were on the way to being transformed into a cultivated, commercial crop. They were already being assiduously tended by London market gardeners, setting an example that invited imitation. Before long, its cultivation by the professionals would be transferred to Scotland, and we have the letters of a Scottish gentleman writing from London to encourage his gardener to grow them, to show how it happened.[63]

Among tree fruits, apples were always named as the most plentiful, and were clearly available to all classes; labourers took apple pies to the fields. Pears were less common, but were already regularly mentioned by writers who visited Herefordshire, Worcestershire and Somerset. The service tree, which Merrett encountered in woods and hedges, especially in Sussex, bore another edible fruit, but he did not make clear whether he saw the true, domestic service tree or the wild form, the domestic form having by far the pleasanter fruit. (The tree is still treasured in Kent, where it is also known as the chequer tree.) Wild cherry trees were known to Merrett, growing plentifully in Petersfield, Hampshire, and in a wood near Bath, while another variety of black cherry was known to him growing in several places in Kent; we may well wonder if this last was derived from a Dutch/Flemish original that had been imported a hundred years before when cherries first became the rage in fashionable circles. In the end, we build up a picture of many highly localized wild fruit centres, the fruit being eaten by the poor in season, most of it doubtless impromptu when gathered off the trees. But apples reached the kitchen in most quantity, as apple pies were so often named as everybody's fare, and they were relatively easily stored. As for the pie crust in which labourers took their apples to the fields, it could be made extravagantly or economically. We shall learn more in the next period about the housewife's ingenuity in devising a host of different recipes for making her bread and pudding mixtures to suit her circumstances. We can be sure that the same individuality marked every housewife's pastry.[64]

Custards, creams and blancmanges made another category of food which featured at the tables of gentle households and often used almonds imported from abroad. The more economical cook used milk thickened with eggs or flour or a clot of milk and cream on the way to becoming butter. Many a modest family had one if not two cows, hens were so commonplace that they frequently went unnoticed in the record, and eggs, if bought, were cheap. Omelettes were a common dish, for which May offered 21 recipes in his book, filling the simple ones with green vegetables, like spinach or sorrel, or fragments of bacon or cheese, or making them fancy with pine kernels and pistachios. Such a simple basic recipe positively asked to be varied with other ingredients, and any housewife could have found something suitable on the shelf, operating no differently from the gentleman who sent Houghton his recipe for adding cream to his eggs, while another cook flavoured her omelettes with sugar and orange juice. Pancakes and fritters were made with yet another simple mixture that was popular with all classes and gave variety; these sometimes incorporated fruits like apples, barberries or gooseberries from the hedgerow.[65]

Puddings were more likely to appear than pastry on the tables of ordinary folk, for pastry required more careful preparation and cooking than pudding, which was easily boiled in a pan of water, required no oven, and no close supervision when cooking on the hearth. May had a section in his book on several sorts of puddings; at its simplest was bread pudding made of penny loaves grated and mixed with eggs, cream, spices, plus herbs as common as strawberry leaves or primrose leaves; fruit could always be added if any was available. The homely housewife could use left-over bread, as did May, milk or whey as a substitute for cream, add suet or whatever fat lay to hand, plus some sugar, throw in May's pennyroyal and rosemary but omit his rosewater, and have a tasty pudding in prospect. To this she could well have added a few currants, for in 1693 two ounces would have cost no more than a penny. Alternatively, not using lemons or oranges, as did May, she could have reached for more herbs, lemon balm, sweet cicely, rosemary or mint, and, copying May, she could have boiled her pudding in a bag over a pan that contained other food. Thus was many a substantial dish made for the ordinary family. The possible variations on pudding were innumerable: hasty pudding, quaking pudding and shaking pudding; and a savoury pudding could include pig's liver or lights, goose blood, or cheese.[66]

Thus, while the well-to-do reached for foodstuffs that were bought with money, a frugal housewife found alternative ingredients that cost her little or nothing. Yet none of these women went down in history for their skills in domestic economy; they were just following a normal routine that was taken for granted. So we women can perhaps be grateful that one tribute has survived (and more may perhaps be found in future when we read personal memoirs to get a better view of the womenfolk). It was uttered by Samuel Clarke, the martyrologist (1626–1701) describing his wife's prudent management of her kitchen, despite some hard times when he was ejected from his living in 1661. 'She would have divers dishes of meat with little cost, yet so dressed and ordered as made them grateful and pleasing unto all. When they were alone, she had such variety of dishes and dresses as prevented nausciousness.' Many other husbands and children would have said much the same.[67]

CONCLUSION

In a world of heightened commercial opportunities and endeavour, at the same time as news and knowledge about food was spreading more effectively than before, it is difficult to summarize all the many trends. The pursuit of profit in the food trade was conspicuous in London at least, and some people even sought patents to make them rich. Walter Underhill in 1668 wanted a patent for his method of bringing salmon live from Newcastle to London. John White in 1691 had devised a liquor that would preserve flesh, fish and fowl; it was evidently a pickle that was different from those of others (though they all used vinegars while adding their own individual extras). Other experiments were under way that would come to nothing: a spirit was being distilled from carrots and parsnips, tasting most like French brandy; Lord Wharton had successfully grown pomegranates. Changing fashions and foibles surrounded people's choice of foods, and these were more obvious now that so much news about food circulated in print, and in coffee houses and taverns. As usual in such lively circumstances, beneficial and regrettable consequences followed, sparking enthusiasm among those who saw a brightening future if things went on in that vein, while turning others to despair for what was being lost. John Evelyn emphasized the losses. He saw market gardeners forcing plant growth in hot beds, recognized that they achieved 'miracles of art', but preferred to eat food that had not been tampered with, the purer produce of 'the countryman's field and good wife's garden'. We all understand that sentiment. He ran on over pages in *Acetaria* in favour of the simple diet, having become convinced that 'husbandmen and laborious people [were] more robust and longer lived than others of an uncertain, extravagant diet'. He commended herbs and fruits 'for temperance sake and the prolongation of life' and regarded all meat-eating as part of the luxury of the present age, which certainly shortened life. The appendix of *Acetaria* contained vegetarian recipes given him by a housewife. Seeing life from a different viewpoint, as a Presbyterian minister in the West Midlands, Richard Baxter shared some of the same views.

He did not campaign for a vegetarian diet, but, as we have seen, he visited many a poor man's home and saw them eating their food.

At the other end of the spectrum stood the journalist, John Houghton, actively working to spread knowledge about the variety of food that was available, and how the recipes used them. He was sharply aware of the ignorance about farming and food practices between localities that were geographically close to each other, and while establishing a better flow of information between the regions of England, another of his ambitions was to learn about husbandries in Europe, and to persuade visitors to India and China to bring back their news. In assessing the success of all this effort, we constantly have to bear in mind the fact that Houghton's achievements were more significant in and around London than anywhere else. Admittedly, he had many correspondents who had travelled as far afield as Shetland, but most people and most cooks in the more distant counties quietly continued their traditional routines, knowing nothing about Mr John Houghton and his news-sheet. Celia Fiennes arrived at a sober understanding of the detached provincial life when travelling through Derbyshire, saying that 'the common people know not above two or three miles from their home', while in Yorkshire and further north, 'they live much at home, and scarce ever go two or ten miles from thence, especially the women'.[68]

Nevertheless, many people would have been aware of the content of their food changing, some of it in quite small ways. A major change, according to Evelyn, was the diminishing taste for sugar, not when preserving fruit, of course, but in savoury dishes; people appreciated more acid flavours. According to Houghton, mackerel and oysters had won unaccustomed favour in recent times, but presumably he was referring to the better-off, since among ordinary folk both were a routine food among those near the sea. Lesser changes were registered simply by watching what was for sale at market stalls: the wealth of cheeses almost certainly surprised people, and possibly the variation in price. John Oxton, a cheesemonger in St Martin-in-the-Fields in 1679, had cheese at 27d. a pound and another kind at 17d. Was this wide variation a recent development compared with the past? We have reason to suspect that different qualities of butter were certainly an ever-enlarging experience. Sugar peas and then potatoes must certainly have surprised shoppers when they first appeared in their market, at any date from the 1650s onwards. Those who took an interest in cooking styles would instantly have distinguished a currently modish one from a traditional one; pickled mushrooms in the 1670s, say, would have signalled a cook in the latest fashion. Yet not everyone identified the innovations correctly. Evelyn mourned the loss in 1669 of walnuts and chestnuts in food, and wondered why they had fallen out of use. But he may have been judging prematurely or in ignorance of other ways then current, for Robert May put chestnuts into pies and pottage in his book in 1660; and John Houghton in 1700 was under the firm impression that the French had taught the English to cook chestnuts in stewed meat and pies, changing the ways of the English, who had been in the habit of eating them as sweetmeats, boiled and sold by pedlars. William Westmacott (1694) bewailed the disappearance of ladythistle, which used to be boiled and eaten as a spring herb, 'but as the world decays so doth the use of good old things and others more delicate and less virtuous brought in'. This means that when Joseph Cooper, once cook to Charles I, used ladythistle in a pie, and gave the recipe in his cookbook of 1654, he signalled to his contemporaries his sympathy with an old tradition. But it had passed away 60 years later.[69]

One of the assumptions of the age, which we find impossible to work into our reconstruction of food at this time, was the difference in flavour that marked every dish eaten in a different household. We are accustomed to a considerable uniformity of flavours because so many of our basic foods have been standardized. Without standardization, much greater variety in flavours obtained, and this expectation lay behind all the many conversations and writings about food at this time. The individuality of every home-brewed drink shines out from Sir Kenelm Digby's collection of innumerable recipes for mead and metheglin; his had been collected from Lady Gower, Lady Morice, Sir William Paston, Sir Baynam Throckmorton, Lady Bellassise, Sir John Fortescue, Lord Gorge, Lady Vernon, Sir John Arundel. The list ran on, leaving us gasping at the many hours that Digby must have spent in gathering them. Cheese was another hot topic at this time, for many different generic types were discussed, and the dairywomen themselves produced individual flavours. It is enough to explain why the first Lord Ailesbury, or rather his wife, sent a man from their home at Ampthill, in Bedfordshire, in September 1678 to buy cheese far away in Marlborough. But it does not explain why in November she paid for a dairywoman and maids to come out of Leicestershire. Had the family taken a liking to Stilton cheese, which was made in Leicestershire, and was now in vogue? Speculation is idle, but it reminds us of the individuality of housewives and cooks throughout the kingdom. In the next 60 years our sources will shed further light on their ways, each and all of them convinced that they knew the very best ways with food.[70]

7

On the Edge of the Next Food World, 1700–60

By 1700 the publication of news-sheets, improved conditions for transport and marketing, and the more intent study of human health as well as that of plant and animal life in the kingdom were some of the notable features in everyday life that heightened knowledge of food and diet. Clearly, not everyone's perceptions were altered by these developments, but information was being spread more widely than before, and as historians we benefit from the fact that the volume of printed material broadened and deepened. Our commentators tell us more than before, and give us a better chance to identify customary food practices, and separate those that were genuinely new in this period, like pickling meat, from those of long standing, like the gathering of nettles as a vegetable in spring.

CHANGES IN THE BACKGROUND

Our informants on food still clustered in and around London, while lifestyles in the provinces continued to be different and various. But our writers became increasingly conscious of the fact that different diets bred some equally well-nourished, long-lived people, so variant opinions about rules for a healthy life continued to proliferate while local conventions held their ground. When we end this survey in 1760, the tides of opinion and changing practice continue to ebb and flow just as before.

Since food had become an accepted and absorbing intellectual theme, people from more varied backgrounds wrote cookery books. Some of the highest nobility and gentry taxed their servants hard to produce exotic foods on their estates, lengthen the growing season, and contrive original and sometimes spectacular dishes to impress their visitors at table. Among medical men, the search for dietary rules for a healthy life became an ever-more serious, scientific and practical investigation, and while the claims of well-to-do patients weighed heaviest upon them, some also began to give more deliberate thought to the diet of the poor. Finally, the zeal for experimenting with all food, whether from plants, fish, birds or mammals, in order to find tastier ways of handling them, lurked everywhere, and people were stimulated more than ever before by their access to news-sheets and advertisements. So whenever someone published anything about new cooking procedures, correspondence from readers brought in corrections and variations, and revised practices were advertised and carried off into a wider world. Information about food circulated ever more effectively, with the result that some contemporaries waxed quite eloquent on improvements that they had seen in their lifetime.

A remarkable poem published by the Hertfordshire farmer, William Ellis, in 1750 extolling the delicious taste of a new-style apple turnover alerts us to the way contemporaries registered memorable improvements in their food. The apple pie or turnover, said the poem, had once been just 'homely food', but now with its delicious puff pastry, eating 'exceeding short', with a quince to add fragrance to the apple, plus cloves and candied peel, and with cream poured over it, it had become the richest of repasts; yet it remained a convenience food to carry out into the fields. The poem had been written by a Mr Welsted and ran over two and a half of Ellis's pages, and while it described the making of the pie, it did not really explain what was so different about it now compared with the past. It may be that the mystery is in part solved by a letter from a Mrs Peasly, responding to one of Professor Richard Bradley's articles in one of the current journals, the *Lady's Director*. She wrote about pastry-making, distinguishing that which was made 'according to the old fashion' from that made nowadays. Old-style pastry, she said, was made with eggs and it came out of the oven hard, tasting 'like sticks'. But when using flour, butter and water alone, without eggs (in fact, as we make it nowadays), 'your pastry will melt in the mouth'. She even had a further refinement: for sweet pastry, she sometimes added sugar, and instead of water, she used milk, sack and brandy. Here, in short, is an unusual illustration of historic trials with pastry. It was publicized in print, and so exemplifies a multitude of other experiments with food that were increasingly defining rules, promoting conformity, and lifting cooking standards. The information revolution in the eighteenth century greatly accelerated the pace of these changes.[1]

Another prominent feature of this period was the toughening spirit of commerce in general, which stirred ambition, fresh ideas and a stronger sense of competition among provision merchants. The evidence is most obvious in and around London because those who commented on the subject were mostly settled in London and the south-east. Information about other parts of England is far less plentiful, and gives us no more than a misty picture of the varied life of the provinces. Nevertheless, we see enough to know how widening circles from the whirlpool of London business spread irregularly into other parts of the kingdom. A greater volume of trade in the provinces is implied by the river and canal improvements at this period, and while it brought more food and drink to London (cheese and cider from the West Midlands are notable examples), we can reasonably guess that shoppers in West Midland markets also benefited from a more ample display of the same foods in their shops. Other provinces in the land would remain untouched by that trend, but would benefit from another. The fact that Yarm in Northumberland gained recognition in places far afield at this time as a notable butter producer is one of the commercial successes implying some change in food supplies locally. We remain tantalized by our ignorance of the stages by which Yarm built up that reputation, but a remarkable expansion of its exports of butter (from Wensleydale) is documented between 1638 and 1665 and it continued to hold on to the trade into the later eighteenth century.[2]

Amid a variety of local initiatives, however, the food scene in London remained distinctive. Indeed, the food supplies available to Londoners seem to have diversified more than ever, so that two food worlds existed, one serving people in London and the nearer parts of the Home Counties, and another everywhere else. If you wanted peppermint, for example, you were told that it was not easy to find, but it was cultivated in some physic gardens in Mitcham. Houghton's news-sheet enumerated a goodly list of exotic foodstuffs imported into London, reporting promptly on the latest cargoes to arrive. A trickle of information then flowed through the houses of townsfolk and gentry in the provinces, yielding them some of the same luxuries when they went to London, or ordered their grocers to obtain them. Alternatively, they sent their servants to shop for them in large towns nearer home. Villagers only heard about all this through hearsay among their neighbours; they continued to rely mostly on their local resources. But we should not overlook their locally grown, seasonal delicacies that arrived in their kitchens in a quantity that townsmen and Londoners could only envy.[3]

The special privileges enjoyed by Londoners yield vivid insights into the more commercial world that was evolving. By 1724 London enjoyed fresh fish, which was carried regularly in waterbutts on wagons from as far away as the East Anglian fens between Whittlesea and Ramsey. The water was changed every evening on the journey. Greenstuff, which had formerly been grown by gardeners, spread out into fields, where farmers grew the same on a much larger scale. This development was now regularly noticed by contemporaries immediately outside London, singling out for special remark the garden beans and globe artichokes that were grown in fields. Richard Bradley estimated that the 10,000 acres of market gardening land serving London in 1688 had grown to 110,000 acres by the 1720s. Complex consequences flowed from all this, and it did not always redound to the sole advantage of London. Nor did it always win approbation as a sign of progress. The lessons are brought home in two contrasting illustrations, concerning fish in the London market, and fruit and greenstuff, grown first for Londoners, but then profitably copied in Scotland.[4]

The government had long supported fishing, not only for food but as a training for the navy. Two compulsory days per week of abstinence from meat in 1548 rose to three after 1563, and remained in force until the rules were abolished under the Commonwealth as a Popish observance, though people's old habits persisted; indeed, some of us still eat fish on Friday. Other official regulations were enacted to improve fish supplies, by prohibiting the sale of undersized fish and the use of small-meshed nets; overfishing even then was a sufficient concern for the need for controls to be accepted. But the market at Billingsgate watched a war raging between traders and fishermen at this time. The fishmongers were intent on guarding a monopoly over sales, while fishermen were equally determined to break their stranglehold; so fishermen sold freely at landing stages, and only dribbled their very fresh supplies onto the market to keep up the price. Walter Stern, peering at the scene more closely than most, has given us a short, sharp glimpse of the ingenuity of salesmen's schemes; the monopoly at Billingsgate provoked others to set up another fish market at Westminster. It all mirrored a world of fish selling in London that was becoming more aggressive and fiercely competitive. Meanwhile we can picture countryfolk in Cornwall, Lancashire and Northumberland getting their fish in an atmosphere far removed from this fevered manoeuvring.[5]

In the commercializing world of fruit and greenstuff, some gentler but nevertheless significant commercial influences were operating to the same end. They are illuminated in faraway Scotland, in the letters of John Cockburn, writing from London to his gardener at Ormiston, near Edinburgh, between 1727 and 1744. An editor of Defoe's travels described this particular Scottish estate in 1732 as 'a perfect English plantation', warning us at the outset of an English lifestyle that had been carried north of the border. The letters show how it happened. John Cockburn, the landowner, lodged in Tottenham, a suburb now absorbed into London, but then a noted centre of market gardening. His gardener had also spent some time training there, and this gardener's brother continued to work as a market gardener near Hampstead. Cockburn gathered up seeds and know-how in order to transport the same standard of vegetable- and fruit-growing to his estate at home. Through his letters he kept almost daily control over the work carried out by Charles Bell in Ormiston. In his very first letter Cockburn reported sending cabbage and turnip seed, white and green savoy seed, and onion seed; this last he could not with certainty identify, but it was Strasbourg, Spanish, or a mixture of both. He was interested in growing all the modish things that were finding favour in London: asparagus, walnut trees, filbert trees, prickly cucumbers, cherries, mulberries and sweet herbs. He was equally vehement that his gardener should grow larger quantities to sell at a lower price rather than small amounts at a high price, as was currently the convention in the neighbourhood. He knew that customers had to be coaxed into developing a taste for 'garden stuff', but he was sure that success would bring his gardener financial reward. At one moment he wanted a wild barberry hedge removed so that raspberries could be grown instead, in order to make scarce, but lovely, raspberry brandy. He urged his gardener to cultivate people with a discriminating taste, citing the lessons he had learned at Covent Garden and in Tottenham. His explanation for the lack of ambition among Ormiston growers was peculiarly his own: we would attribute it to the lack of any pressing demand from a relatively small number of buyers; he attributed it to their weak intellects. The 'low diet both in eating and drinking' of his neighbours, he had decided, gave 'little strength to either body or mind', and their malt drink was 'the most stupefying stuff ever was contrived' [sic].[6]

Cockburn was an unusually ambitious property owner in lowland Scotland, but the enthusiasm of just one man could make a difference in the neighbourhood. It may have done in this case, for one hundred years later, in 1841, this valley was sending 200–300 Scots pints of strawberries every season to Edinburgh.[7]

In theoretical discussions about food at this period, the more scientific study of anatomy among medical men in the seventeenth century had already tended to shift food debates away from theories of the humours to focus more simply on the health properties of individual food items. As we have seen, it had resulted in a modest cluster of vegetarians winning publicity for their food regimes, their diet, in fact, coming close to being a decked-up version of the traditional diet of poor folk. This fact did not escape those who had often noted the strength and good health of labouring families.

SIMPLE FOOD STYLES COMMENDED

A cogent expression of this last viewpoint was published in 1724 by a physician, George Cheyne MD FRS, in *An Essay of Health and Long Life*. He had written medical texts on fevers, gout and the waters at Bath, and towards his last days responded to the request of an august personage, the Master of the Rolls, no less, to give him personal instruction in leading a healthy life. Having written at length on the subject, Cheyne deemed his text worthy of publication, and gave some revealing reasons for his decision. He had seen many people intent on living healthy and long lives, he said, but in practice they had suffered 'mortal agonies' following their self-inflicted rules. If better instructed, they could have 'passed their lives in tolerable ease and quiet'. So he assembled his own experience and observation to give his readers more dietary freedom. His principal article of faith lay in eating simple foods in their natural state. He abhorred the practices of London foodmongers cramming poultry, feeding animals in stalls when they should be grazing in fields, and forcing vegetables in hotbeds. In other words the commercializing food market was sufficiently obtrusive, at least in London, to command notice, and to Cheyne it was anathema. Perhaps it explains his decision to retire to Bath and live there to the end of his days; in that way he could escape the artificial food practices that offended him in London. As for rules of cooking, he favoured plain roasting (on a spit) or boiling, no high sauces, and no smoking, salting or pickling, which were the undesirable inventions of luxury. Food quantities also had to be restricted, and in this discussion, while recognizing the varying needs of individuals, he cited Cornaro from the early seventeenth century for his recommended meagre measure of food (12–16 ounces only). Closer to home, he offered more recent examples than Cornaro of people who lived long; noticeably, some of them lived in the north of England, eating coarse food, especially oatmeal, and drinking whey. In summary, he advised moderate eating and exercise, consonant, of course, with maintaining the bodily strength needed for different occupations. While not urging strict vegetarianism, he favoured more vegetables than meat, and expressed an unexpected prejudice against pork and sea fish.[8]

For drink Cheyne recommended water, watered wine or small beer, and in particularizing, expressed dismay at the liking by the better-off for 'high country wines'. He plainly did not mean by this wines made from country fruits, though they feature prominently in the cookbooks of this period. Brandy and strong waters seem to have been intended; he pronounced firmly against punch made of rum, brandy and malt spirits. We may wonder, therefore, whether the many fruit wines in the cookbooks at this period – they had become singularly conspicuous compared with former times – represented a positive movement against strong waters that encouraged drunkenness. It is true that fruit wines were an ancient country tradition among families of all classes, and it had long been a convention to insert a recipe or two for fruit drinks in cookbooks. But they had never been as numerous as now.[9]

FOOD FOR THE POOR

Cheyne was not one of the physicians who showed an interest in recommending food to the poor. But external influences were leading others in that direction, for a debate on fresh ways of relieving them through formal parish support had run on steadily since 1660, and many pamphlets had flowed from the press. In proposing work for young and old, and requiring parishes to build workhouses, a great web of bureaucratic red tape had been spun around poor law officials, entangling them in some heavy duties that fell on every parish in the kingdom. Officials had to decide exactly which parish was responsible for helping which individuals in need. Sometimes this meant not just moving them on but personally taking them many miles across country back to their home bases where they could rightfully claim food or money for food. In 1757, it required four poor law officials, for example, to accompany a pauper family over 70 miles from East Hoathly, near Uckfield in East Sussex, to their official place of residence in Thatcham, Berkshire. It was a short step from these concerns to a more realistic calculation of the cost and content of essential foods to keep the penniless poor alive. That led some to give advice to those not totally penniless who lived precariously, but were ignorant when choosing the most suitable foods.[10]

One of these advisers with deep care for the poor was Dr Theophilus Lobb. Not surprisingly he was a man of the church, born in 1678, who became a nonconformist minister in Guildford, Surrey, then in Shaftesbury in Dorset, next in Yeovil in Somerset, and finally at Witham in Essex. He had an interest in medicine that had been apparent from an early age, and his profession in the church gave him plenty of scope to practise it. After 1736, when he was 58 years old, he devoted his energies entirely to medicine, and published a number of books on religion and physic. Two volumes of his lectures to medical students were published in 1771 after his death, and the copy of Lobb's work in the British Library is the one that belonged to George III.[11]

Most pertinent to our concerns is Lobb's treatise, published in 1763, giving *Advice to the Poor with Regard to Diet*. It plainly circulated beyond the narrow medical world, for it was reprinted in a volume of 1767, entitled *Primitive Cookery: or the Kitchen Garden Display'd, containing a Collection of Receipts for Preparing a Great Variety of Cheap, Healthful and Palatable Dishes without either Fish, Flesh or Fowl*. No author of this collection was named, but the cook plainly had vegetarian sympathies, without being doctrinaire; ingredients for some dishes included bone marrow and sauces based on veal broth. The book started with eight pages of directions for picking and preserving fruit. Then followed Lobb's advice on a diet for the poor, covering six pages. The remainder, comprising 80-odd pages of recipes, was designed for workaday families, concentrating on vegetables and fruit, avoiding the expense of meat or fish, but insisting on tasty flavourings to make palatable dishes. It ended with a bill of fare for 70 meals that would cost not more than twopence each.[12]

Lobb's advice assumed that the food cupboard contained cereals, beans and peas along with other vegetables from the garden, milk, butter and cheese, salt, ginger and pepper, and only sometimes meat or fish. For drink he named strong beer or cider, but only 'when the poor could afford it'. He must have assumed that they normally drank small ale or water. Significantly, Lobb's thinking about a 'nourishing and healthful diet' had been influenced, as he acknowledged, from his reading of a book by the Revd Edward Terry containing first-hand comments on Indian diets. Terry had set off to India as the chaplain to the East India Company in 1616, and on arrival had found himself begged to become chaplain to Sir Thomas Roe, ambassador to the Great Mogul, whose own chaplain had recently died. Roe could not contemplate the life of an atheist, he said, so Terry accompanied him on his journeys up country, finally returning to England in 1619 with a fascinating story of his experiences. Among other things, he had learned to appreciate the merits of the Indian food regime. People had flesh and fowl in plenty but ate very little meat on its own, and never dressed it in great pieces. They cut it up small, adding onions, herbs, root ginger, other spices and butter. It was food that pleased all palates, and was washed down with water. Poorer people ate rice, flavoured with ginger, pepper and butter, and as bread they ate a thick cake of a grain which he did not name, baked on an iron plate. People carried this plate with them when they travelled: doubtless some of Terry's readers recognized the similarity of this practice with that of the cattle drovers trudging across Britain, carrying oats in their panniers together with a cooking plate. On this diet, Terry had seen the Indians 'as strong as they could be if they had their diet out of the king's kitchen'.[13]

Lobb's advice on diet for the poor was not offered as a routine to be followed all year round, but was intended to give pleasant, cheap and nourishing food when provisions and work were scarce, notably in winter. He assumed that shortages of food would disappear in summer, and food would be more varied and sufficient for all. Bread should be of barley or rye, or a mixture of both, and if not made into loaves, the dough could be made in the shape of muffins or oatcakes. (Since the barley did not rise well, we can understand how cakes cooked on a griddle and eaten fresh would be a special treat.) In general, people were urged to eat grain, pulses and vegetables, little meat, and to drink little strong liquor. Health and strength came from food, said Lobb, rather than drink, though he did favour porter as beneficial. For the main meal at dinner he specified a broth made from bones with two quarts of dried peas, rice or bread, flavoured with onions, herbs and ginger. The meal should finish with a small, nutmeg-size piece of Cheshire or Double Gloucester cheese to correct flatulence, this last discomfort presumably being caused by the peas. For children with scorbutic itching he recommended a tea made of the bark of elm with milk.[14]

We shall further stress below the significance of the large quantities of pulses prescribed for workaday folk throughout this book on *Primitive Cookery*. They yielded protein as a substitute for meat, and were mixed with a great variety of green vegetables, much endive, plus roots, such as parsnips, Jerusalem artichokes, carrots, onions, skirret and potatoes. Some of the greenstuff was expected to be available in gardens, but one plant at least was to be found wild in the fields. Cardoons, fried and buttered, were specially singled out as a wild thistle, 'growing in every ditch and hedge'. Lobb found himself in this book in the company of a cook who shared his care for the poor, relied on things they could get from their own yard and the hedgerows, and counted the cost of meals in pence.

HUNGER-SUPPRESSING FOOD

When we find writers on food giving advice about nourishing, simple diets drawn from faraway countries like India, we begin to appreciate the widening perspective of the thinkers (though not all cooks) at this time. Their thoughts roamed further still when they started to search for plants that might actually kill the pangs of hunger. It is an interest that has revived again at the present day, but this time round as a means to combat obesity. An article in *The Times* in 2002 reported on a cactus used in a remote part of Kalahari, on the South Africa/Botswana border, where no rain had fallen for ten months and hunger loomed, and where the xhoba plant was traditionally used to stave off hunger and thirst. The local people regarded it as 'just part of life', and had routinely relied on it to sustain them without food for three days at a time when out hunting. Now, in the search to control over-eating in the modern world, it is being investigated for pharmaceutical use. In fact, our researchers might equally well have looked for an equivalent plant nearer home for, like so many problems of humanity, we have been over the same ground before, and could benefit from harnessing local wisdom from the past.[15]

A search in Britain for just such a hunger-suppressing plant first comes to light in our documents in the 1660s in Royal Society circles. On a day in 1662 when Mr Buckland at the Royal Society was urging members to support the planting of potatoes, and Robert Boyle promised to supply some for trial by fellow members, Boyle also mentioned an author who had written more generally about food for scarce times. But Boyle had mislaid the paper bearing his name, conjuring up for us a vivid picture of a scholar's cluttered study with which some of us are also familiar. Nevertheless, he promised to communicate the information when he found it so that it could be reprinted. The idea was clearly in mind, waiting to be further stimulated.[16]

In the early 1680s, a fresh impulse came from Scotsmen reflecting on the classical writers, such as Pliny, who referred to such hunger-suppressing foods that had been used in the ancient world. Further references were found in Scottish writings, which mentioned the usages of the ancient Britons and highlanders, and actually named Scottish plants. It all resulted in some positive experiments focusing on the heath pea or caremyle, otherwise known as bitter vetch (*Lathyrus linifolius*), colloquially known in Scotland as 'knappers'. Valuable correspondence on the subject was preserved by the Revd Robert Woodrow (1679–1734), a Glasgow cleric and museum curator, writing first to Dr James Fraser (1645–1731) (another Scotsman, who became Secretary of the Chelsea Royal Hospital and was a bookdealer in London), and second to Sir Robert Sibbald (1641–1722) (co-founder of the Royal College of Physicians of Edinburgh and of the Botanic Garden). Fraser experimented on himself, likening caremyle to liquorice, and cheerfully going without food for 66 hours as a result. Evidently, more people further afield were stirred by the enquiry. Charles II and others at court encouraged it, our three correspondents engaged others in experiments, and Sir Robert Sibbald published a pocket-book treatise of 24 pages entitled *Provision for the Poor in Time of Dearth and Scarcity, where there is an Account of such Food as may be easily Gotten when Corns are Scarce and Unfit for Use.* This essay was first published in 1699, ran to a second edition in 1703, and survives in a reissue of 1709 in the British Library.[17]

Information about bitter vetch or caremyle was part of a longer text giving much more information on sustaining food in hard times. It was prefaced with remarks about people in the East Indies surviving on vegetables alone, and, significantly perhaps in the light of other changes in English diet that actually occurred at this time, it went on to name the Romans who fed much on pulses, the Egyptians who fed much on peas, lentils and white cicers (chickpeas?), the Turks and Persians on rice, and the Irish on potatoes. The particular year of hunger in the forefront of Sibbald's mind was the great scarcity of 1674, when a root similar to parsnip roots had been eaten. Then followed his own long list of wild and garden plants that made nourishing food, plus birds and fish, wherein more than once he singled out as illustration the food eaten on the Faroes. He thus revealed linkages in his thinking with his reading of the publications of the Royal Society for they included a vivid account of the way wildfowl eggs were gathered on the Faroes, a narrative that Robert Houghton then reissued in 1703 in his news-sheet.[18]

Thus we glimpse the remarkable network of like-minded people, living many miles apart from each other, who were drawn into these debates and experiments in search of foods to satisfy hunger. Some of the general dictionaries of plants at this time – Philip Miller's, for example – name bitter vetch without showing any knowledge of its worth in combating hunger, but it would be interesting to establish areas in Scotland and England where it grows freely, for it is said to be ubiquitous in the British Isles, and may in the past have been known locally in some places for fending off hunger. Sibbald had picked up his reference to it in the work of Doctor (Robert) Morison, a Scotsman, who became head of the Oxford Botanic Garden and wrote a history of Oxford's plants. (It is not mentioned by Richard Mabey in *Flora Britannica.*) The information on egg-collecting on the Faroes and Shetland islands had come from Sir Robert Moray, conventionally described as a soldier and politician but also known for his interest in natural phenomena.

COUNTRY HOUSEWIVES OBSERVED

Another precious workaday view of cooking at this time was sketched in 1750 by a writer who did not, like Lobb, mingle with the very poorest souls, but who talked genially with country housewives, wives of yeomen, husbandmen and day labourers. This was William Ellis, a farmer in Hertfordshire with an insatiable curiosity, first to discover the systems of farming adopted by fellow-farmers, and then to investigate the secrets of cooking by country housewives. His viewpoint was entirely different from working cooks writing recipe books. As a farmer he employed many farm servants whom he had to feed at his own expense every day of the year; and in much larger numbers he engaged workers at harvest time when they lodged on his farm for one to two months. As they were expected to give him their best efforts, he and his wife had to plan well ahead to secure a continuous supply of food and varied menus to keep them fit and cheerful. His book, which was entitled *The Country Housewife's Family Companion*, makes plain their philosophy of household management, to be efficient and reasonably economical in providing meals for everyone; at harvest they fed their men five times a day while ensuring variety and quantity, plus little treats from time to time.[19]

In describing his own procedures, Ellis assembled a wealth of information from housewives in the neighbourhood and from people he met anywhere and everywhere on his travels. He talked with gentlemen customers buying his farm goods, he questioned women on their ways with pastry, and when he despatched a young man to Devon whom he had recommended as a farm servant, the lad was enjoined to send him news of all interesting food habits that he met in the south-west. We can imagine the jokes that were made behind his back by people who knew Ellis's quirkish ways of interrogating everyone in sight. The fact remains that he was a sympathetic character, totally unpretentious. He obviously had respect for the resourcefulness of women in the kitchen, and took a highly practical interest in details of their cooking. Indeed, for the food historian he is one of the most precious informants of his age, shedding much light on the cooking routines of working folk, including the families of farm labourers. He was, for example, well aware that a recipe could be dressed up with expensive additional vegetables and flavourings for the rich, but made a perfectly tasty though more economical dish for the labourer without them. Women were always having to make do with less than the full assortment of desirable ingredients, and he told his readers how they coped. Some made pastry by mixing barley with wheat flour, and found it made a pleasant, crisp crust. Describing this manoeuvre Ellis was recording the practice of a yeoman's wife in Hertfordshire, but it must have been an obvious economy in hard times among poorer folk when, as on one occasion, he said, wheat cost 4s. a bushel and barley only 18d. Other women, without enough fat for pastry, used the same mix of barley and wheat flour but added warm skim milk with a little touch of yeast. It ate short and sweet, they said. Another woman poured the milk boiling hot onto the wheat flour and got the same satisfactory result. To make her bread, a day labourer's wife mixed barley and wheat meal together, and having sifted it to suit her taste, she prided herself on using the coarse bran that was left over to feed her pig. Women's devices to make the best of the food they had were just as individual and ingenious as they are nowadays.[20]

Barley alone, of course, made a coarse, hard loaf, and since it does not rise like wheat, it has long puzzled me how it was made palatable. Ellis gives us some answers. Barley bread, he said, was made with half wheat and half barley meal. Other tips collected from women in Devon were to put in more yeast than usual, mix the dough with scalded skim milk instead of water, and knead it less than usual. So it was called barley bread when it actually contained some wheat, as well as incorporating other tricks to lighten its density. Another device divulged to Ellis by a baker was to add some fine oatmeal, soaked overnight. It sweetened and lightened the bread, and made it taste like a wheaten loaf. It is worth reminding ourselves also that the Devon women baked their bread on the hearth, rather than heating an oven. They fitted what Ellis called a large iron kettle closely over the loaf (in other words, a Dutch oven), and covered this dome with damp straw or horse litter plus a few hot ashes. The straw burned, and the loaf was thoroughly baked on top as well as on the bottom. This method economized on fuel, and the women were pleased with the result; they called it 'a sweeter method of baking'.[21]

Ellis's enquiries brought to light a host of slightly different recipes used by the ordinary housewife to give variety while still feeding her family at modest expense. Bread was not always the essential basis of the meal. They had ways of using cereals other than bread without having to heat an oven. Pancakes made good meals, for then one could use barley flour without wanting it to rise; milk, salt and a little ground ginger were added to make the batter. If milk was not available, they used ale or beer. When the pancakes were fried, apples were chopped up for the filling, and three pancakes per person made a satisfying plateful. The pancakes were equally handy if wrapped around other food, like a slice of bacon or some cheese, and so taken to eat in the field. This was yet another case of dressing food down for working folk, while the recipe books just as regularly dressed it up for the rich. Ellis described the rich cook's recipe for pancakes, which used spices like cinnamon, nutmeg, mace and cloves in the batter, added sack and rosewater with, or instead of, milk, pouring on melted butter and cream when cooked, and finally strewing sugar.[22]

Barley was also made into puddings, which were either moulded into cakes and baked on a griddle, or boiled in a pudding cloth. For these the mixture of barley meal with salt and water again included a touch of yeast to make it rise, and the pudding was then sliced at the table with melted dripping and salt poured over. Those of us who remember the delicious taste of bread and dripping can understand the relish of this simple meal. Ellis's family ate a pudding with their pickled pork almost every day, he said, while others mixed the apples and pork into the pudding before boiling it.[23]

Equally appetising was a pudding with apples alone, covered with a sauce of melted butter or milk, with sugar sprinkled on at table. No wonder that Ellis praised puddings as an essential item in English diet and regarded the plum pudding at harvest as the celebratory festival dish. A festive pudding to serve six harvest men contained between a half and three quarters of a pound of raisins, half a pound of suet, and was cooked for three to four hours. It was obviously a close relation of our present-day Christmas pudding.[24]

Ellis knew women's ways in the kitchen exactly as we know them still, ingeniously contriving good meals with the ingredients that lay to hand while keeping within their income. The dull monotony, which is often ascribed to the food of the past, represented the failures of dull housewives without interest in food, who are found in every age including our own. But at the same time, there were women among all classes who strove to please their families with tasty meals. In contemplating their ingenuity we may ponder Ellis's story of two women living near him who made two puddings. One put in two eggs with flour and salt, the other dispensed with eggs but used hot water in which she had already boiled some bacon and turnips. The second pudding, he said, turned out far better than the first, being 'full of little holes and light'. (Had she, perhaps, included a touch of yeast?) 'So great a difference there is', exclaimed Ellis, 'in good housewifery and management!' Yes, indeed. Judging by Ellis's discursive, gossipy book these lively, resourceful housewives were everywhere, and Ellis had no difficulty in finding them.[25]

MAJOR DIETARY CHANGES

The breadth of Ellis's leisurely book on cookery directs our attention to some conspicuous changes in this period in the content of diet. In fact, he defines the most important developments better than anyone else, for he commented on them all. He deemed the most significant change with regard to meat to be the practice of pickling it rather than salting and drying it. Hitherto, the conventional method of keeping meat for a long period had been to salt it over several weeks in a trough. The trough was a regular item listed in probate inventories at death. Meat taken from the salting trough was dried and smoked in a chimney, and later hung in the roof of the hall. Pieces were then cut off as needed, the salt was soaked out of them, and it was ready to be cooked in a pottage or braised in a pan with other ingredients. Keeping the meat this way entailed a considerable amount of waste: if it had come too near the heat, it developed a rust (the bane of rust even in rich households with plenty of labour is indicated in instructions by Patrick Lamb in *Royal Cookery* (1710), when making soup santé: add a bit of bacon that is not rusty, he said); alternatively, it might taste sooty, sometimes even rank; or it might be attacked by the hopper fly or maggots. Invariably, over time, it would develop a thick rind that had to be thrown away.[26]

The pickling of vegetables had made great strides in the seventeenth century, and so it was inevitable that in due course experiments would be tried on meat. Pork was the first choice, and it proved highly successful. Ellis was eloquent on the subject: the method had first reached perfection in Kent, he claimed (had it been introduced by immigrants from the Continent?, one wonders); and by the time he was writing in 1750 Kent people ate very little bacon at all. Everyone, from the peer to the peasant, he said, preferred pickled pork; the common ploughman's favourite meal at midday was a piece of pickled pork with an apple dumpling – a satisfying meal, you could say, having a fair mixture of protein, carbohydrates and vitamins.[27]

The author of *Tusser Redivivus* (1710) confirmed Ellis's remarks on the merits of pickled pork, and expressed them more crisply. The meat kept its natural taste and sweetness, far less was wasted, and it saved salt. Moreover, it was a simpler, quicker procedure. When killed, the pig was hung overnight, and in the morning the meat was cut into square pieces, spread out for a day and a half for the blood to be drawn out, and sprinkled with salt and saltpetre. It was then packed tightly between layers of coarse sugar in a glazed clay pot or powdering tub, which was firmly closed to exclude the air. A brine formed, which was carefully watched from then on, and might need to be boiled again and replenished. The meat kept for as much as a year.[28]

The recipe books still referred sometimes to smoked meat (the rich man's cook, Charles Carter, still used smoked meat in his recipes), and York ham was still cured in the traditional way by salting and smoking, and upheld its fine reputation in London. But pickling gradually became the common practice. According to Ellis, Suffolk enthusiastically followed the lead of Kent, and farming families ate no other meat. The pickling of beef and mutton was also practised by London traders, and others as well, but pickled pork was the favourite.[29]

It is tantalizing not to know more exactly when the practice of meat pickling was introduced. John Mortimer, a writer on agriculture, but also a merchant and Essex landowner, wrote in a matter-of-fact way about pork pickling in 1707. In 1750 Ellis declared that his family ate 50lbs of pickled pork for every 1lb of dried, smoked bacon. It does not seem to feature in cookery books before 1700, which suggests that it first became known around that time. As it was quickly apparent that this method used meat more efficiently and the end product tasted better, in some places the practice spread quickly in the next 50 years, aided by all the new publishing media. It was one of the major improvements in diet that was memorable for this generation.[30]

PEAS AND BEANS

Another significant change in the content of meals, and one of great importance when we consider its nutritional value, was the increased eating of peas and beans by all classes. Historians focus their attention on the eating of potatoes, which began to spread at this time, but only because they know what came after. In fact, peas and beans also came to occupy a larger place in diet, and before 1750 the weight of contemporary comment suggests that their consumption, at least around London, surpassed that of potatoes.

Peas and beans as a more substantial item in diet had a prime advantage over potatoes in not having to carve out a wholly new niche for themselves in the fields; they had long had a firm place in farmers' arable rotations as a fodder crop; they had also long been grown in small quantities in gardens for household use. Garden peas and garden-grown broad beans were already appreciated by all classes in summer: green peas featured often in soups; and Mrs Matthew Parker, the wife of the archbishop of Canterbury, when they were living quietly and frugally in disfavour in Mary's reign, has left us her cookbook of 1557–8 in which she used broad beans in two recipes, one savoury with onions, and the second sweet, in a tart with sugar and cinnamon. That beans stood low in public esteem, however, is obvious in all the early writings about them; William Harrison, for example, described peas, beans and lentils as horse corn, and immediately followed with a reference to the labouring poor putting pulses into pottage, and sometimes, in years of bad harvest, putting beans into bread. Underlying such remarks lay the assumption that such a recourse was a desperate measure, used by poor people in hard times. On the other hand, as peas and beans dry well and last long, they had long been invaluable as victual on sea voyages.[31]

In the mid-seventeenth century, when Parliamentarians under the Commonwealth devoted so much effort to improving agriculture, and correspondents with Hartlib endlessly discussed current foods and drink with an eye to all chances of enlarging and varying choice, pulses began to be seen in a new light. The reading matter and the European contacts of the intellectuals in Hartlib's circle ranged widely, and it is significant that in the autumn of 1648 Hartlib was searching for the German book about plants, *Kraüterbuch*, by Bartholomeus Carrichter, 'very hard to be gotten', he was told, which contained a whole section on the food that was commonly eaten daily among German people, both healthy and sick. This included beans and peas, eaten by the Germans fresh in summer and stored for use in the winter.[32]

Carrichter's book was a successful publication on its home ground, and the British Library has a good range of editions in its collection, running to six between 1575 and 1597 and another six between 1615 and 1673. So the book must have reached some English readers even before Hartlib's day, but it was still evidently little known. It had started as a guide to plants, particularly those with a medicinal use, and a major theme had been the influences on them of the phases of the moon. By 1615, and perhaps in earlier editions too, a new part had been added about the daily food of German people, and we may perhaps infer some especially lively interest in this part since a number of library copies lack this section; it had been removed by readers for closer reading. At all events, Carrichter's book showed the daily and seasonal cycle of foods eaten and stored by German families, and since it named not only the green peas and beans eaten in summer, but the beans and peas stored for winter, it may well have stirred reflection among the intellectuals. It was, after all, being read in the midst of other discussion about pulses in the Hartlib circle of the 1650s.[33]

Hartlib's files show some pertinent correspondence about growers propagating new varieties of peas and beans. John Parkinson had written in 1640 about beans being picked up off the Cornish coast whenever ships were wrecked, and these are likely to have been new varieties that caught the attention of the locals and were planted. Robert Boyle was conversant with one experiment to distil spirits from peas and make wine from beans. John Beale, the near vegetarian, wrote more aptly still from Herefordshire: his long accounts of his efforts to improve cider were intermixed with another aspiration, 'God willing', to bring the use of kidney beans and Roman beans 'into familiarity in all these parts'. He had found them to be a prolific crop on his own land, multiplying every bean sown five hundred times over. Furthermore, a kinswoman of his had got the same rich harvest from some peas that she had found, seemingly growing wild, when she was picking currants. Planting them at home, she possessed in the second year a considerable plantation of such sweet-tasting peas that the birds threatened to take them all. A local minister, Thomas Swift, a sequestered Royalist, of Goodrich in the Wye valley, who had served his flock faithfully from 1628 until he was ejected in 1649 (incidentally, he was the grandfather of Jonathan Swift), was the celebrated grower of peas, this time sugar peas, which until then had been a rarity. His efforts in propagating them had enabled him to fill the (local) markets, so he claimed. Cressy Dymock, in his turn, reported in March 1653 on his obstreperous farmworkers when he was trying to grow beans, probably by some new farming method such as drilling, for novel methods were his *forte*, though he did not say how he intended to use the beans. William Coles, a fastidious botanist writing his *Adam in Eden* in 1657, compiled a careful list of nine varieties of peas known to him in England (observing, conventionally, that dried peas were much used as victual on long sea voyages, and were 'no inconsiderable food in poor folk's houses'). He named four varieties of beans, declining to bother with the endless other kinds coming, he said, from the East and West Indies. He also added the significant remark that 'even the better sort feed on them', hinting that change was in the air. In the light of this stirring of interest in peas and beans, we should also read some words in Thomas Moufet's manuscript on food in a questioning frame of mind. As we noticed above, it was originally written around 1600, but we had reason to suspect it of having been altered in places to suit the views of a later generation, when it was published for the first time in 1655. So Moufet, or more probably his editor, expressed appreciation of more delicate garden varieties of beans and peas that were then being grown in England. Beans, he said, had once been a field crop (in other words, an animal fodder crop) but they were now being grown in gardens to make them more 'sappy'. It is more than likely, though the author or editor did not say so, that they belonged to a new variety. The field bean situation was highly fluid and was well understood by growers, but neither our author nor editor had full knowledge of the details which a botanist might have explained to them.[34]

Thus, we catch sight of the enthusiasm spreading at this time among clerics, and also among gentry and other country people, for propagating new varieties of plants that would make good food. The botanists had helped to make the subject a talking point and a practical hobby, and interest would spread, gently and slowly, until it significantly affected this vegetable in diet by the early eighteenth century. A decade after Thomas Swift had taught his neighbours in Herefordshire to appreciate sugar peas, another gardener, John Thomas, on the other side of the country, in St Albans in Hertfordshire, was publicizing another pea variety, called Hastings peas; they were commended in a document of 1659/60 that actually found its way into State Papers. Admittedly, Thomas described this variety as food for pigs, but by 1704 peas that were called white, and green Hastings peas, which were presumably related, were growing in gardens as food for the table, and were praised for their sweetness. By that time other varieties were accepted as food, including the Hotspur that was ready in six weeks from planting, and was now also called a sugar pea. The anonymous author of *Tusser Redivivus* (1710) believed that peas were much more eaten than formerly, though he was probably registering an impression only of the previous 30 years or so. But by 1750 Ellis was devoting nearly four pages of his book for housewives to the use of peas in family food, differentiating white peas, also called dwarf marrow fat peas, that had to be soaked overnight, from blue peas, seemingly the same as *non pareil* peas, the *great union*, and the large hollow grey pea, this last variety being said to be 'lately propagated'. By 1750 William Ellis grew all these kinds, not in his garden but in his fields, and went on to write four pages on peas pudding, giving the recipes of Hertfordshire farmers' wives, who flavoured theirs with bits from the family's pork carcase, and boiled them in a bag. In some circles, dried peas now had higher status still, judging by one of Ellis's recipes from a gentleman at Gaddesden who boiled his peas with a leg of beef, cooked the meat to rags (a current phrase for long cooking), and then gave the meat to the poor, while he treasured the peas. He flavoured them with pepper, mace, cinnammon and celery, and enjoyed his peas pudding as a veritable feast.[35]

Pulses had long been recognized by farmers for their value in improving arable land between cereal crops, though this knowledge came from practical observation, not from any scientific understanding of their role in fixing nitrogen in the soil. But they were not yet understood to be a significant source of protein. That knowledge waited on discovery by the chemists in the late nineteenth century. Nevertheless, Ellis and plainly many others had learned by experience to appreciate in practice their role in filling the plate alongside meat, and satisfying hunger. They also knew from growing pulses as fodder that they were easily dried and kept through the winter. So in these decades between 1700 and 1750 some of the new varieties, which had first been introduced into gardens, were being moved out to be grown on a larger scale in the fields. Over and over again, writers referred to the spread of vegetable crops into the fields around London, underlining how noticeable it was. The Swedish traveller, Pehr Kalm, journeying through the countryside of Essex and Hertfordshire with a sharp countryman's eye in 1748, registered the same impression, remarking on whole fields of beans (a variety with small and narrow pods, he said), seen growing between Gravesend and Rochester for sale in London. The main thrust of this significant change in eating patterns seemed to centre on London and the Home Counties.[36]

The absorption of peas and beans into the diet of all classes was thus a noticeable development at least in the south-east at this period, not heralded by any trumpets, but constituting an improvement in the protein content of the diet, which we should not ignore just because we cannot measure it exactly. By the mid-seventeenth century the eating of early garden peas had become a compulsive fashion, judging by the lady who carried some early peas from the suburbs of London to Joan Cromwell in Whitehall in the 1650s. She clearly knew the craze among the well-to-do for getting them and serving them at table before anyone else. She had expected a good reward, and was indignant at the small sum given her for her pains. A veritable frenzy subsequently developed among market gardeners for producing garden peas earlier in spring than anyone else. These peas, of course, were tenderly raised by gardening methods, some even in hotbeds. Then the intellectual debate about improving both peas and beans for human consumption attracted livelier attention between 1650 and 1700. In 1675 the varieties grown in the field for drying and use in the winter were thought so many by John Worlidge – white, grey, and green – that he did not deem it necessary to enumerate them. John Mortimer in 1707 named white peas, garden Runcivals (grown in Staffordshire, but in fields, he said), Henley greys, red shanks, Vale greys, Hampshire kids, an unnamed, early-ripening kind, and the Cotswold pea. As for beans, Mortimer still only knew of horse beans growing in the fields in 1707. Yet a generation earlier, in 1675, John Worlidge had regretted that what he called 'the larger sort of beans' were not more grown in the fields rather than in gardens, since they yielded such a large increase. He was writing of them as food for people, and since he was also urging that they be sown in rows, he was suggesting a method of cultivation that was exactly in tune with the time. Row-husbandry was on the agenda of progressive farmers, following Jethro Tull's precepts, and a suggestion for a suitable crop as human food that would be grown in this way would certainly attract notice. Worlidge also recommended the French kidney bean, sweet-tasting and 'lately brought into use among us, and not yet sufficiently known', he said. John Houghton, another commentator in 1699, picked up the gossip and asked why kidney beans were grown only in gardens and not in the common fields.[37]

Some of the tips about beans and peas were plainly taken up by farmers reading the current literature, though we are at a loss to discover which varieties won most attention from them. Nor can we always pick our way reliably between contradictory accounts. The Swedish visitor, Pehr Kalm, who met William Ellis personally and spent time in Essex and Hertfordshire, Ellis's own county, declared in 1748 that beans and peas, other than fresh green peas, were seldom eaten at English tables. Yet he also commented repeatedly on seeing them growing in the fields; they grew in passageways between asparagus, and between cabbages, clearly not intended for livestock feed. In any case, the bean fields and large pea fields were conspicuous all over Essex, though he recognized the fresh green peas as the strongest English fancy, persuading some farmers for their best profit to grow nothing else. Broad Windsor beans particularly, and others as well, were the ones that fed people. So we finish in 1750 by relying more on Farmer Ellis's accuracy of observation than on Kalm. Ellis wrote appreciatively of broad beans that eked out meat, and were eaten with relish at harvest time by his workers; these, of course, were the ones that were eaten fresh in August and went well with fat bacon and salt pork. Ellis did not say if the beans at his meal tables were grown in fields, but we can be confident that they were, for his peas were certainly planted there. He listed his varieties and explained his method of cultivation, in enclosed fields, he said. He also gave instructions for drying them, and hinted at a recent, warm popular verdict on the white beans almost as though they had become a fashion. When cooked, they were now being cried for sale about the London streets, he said; and the poor were urged in winter and spring to cook and eat them with melted butter. If the poor added salt, and perhaps some parsley, acting on a memory of their former country ways, they were filling their stomachs with good, tasty nourishment.[38]

So while we cannot quantify this change in the content of diet, the casual and scattered comments by contemporaries add up to a quiet transformation taking place in the growing of beans and peas that made a significant, cheap addition to the nutritional content of food for all classes. Comments in print focused noticeably on their being grown for eating fresh in summer, and this attention by the market gardeners also resulted in a lengthening of the growing season, an achievement from which Londoners probably benefited more than anyone else. But news of the methods spread; we even find gentry accelerating the seasons by growing beans for summer eating in hotbeds. Nicholas Blundell in Lancashire hastened the growth of his French kidney beans to be sure of getting them ready early in 1728. Stephen Switzer was precise in describing the results. The gardeners were stimulated by the price advantage of bringing their wares to the market before anyone else. So now kidney beans were sown in January and February instead of April, and were eaten early in April instead of mid-June. They lasted as 'a constant and most useful dish for every week in the year between that and the beginning of October'. When reading that last bold claim, however, we must make room for class distinctions that did not allow such benefits to all.[39]

The full dimensions of the pulse revolution conceal themselves in the manifold individual efforts of curious botanists bringing in new varieties from abroad, growers in the market gardens and fields, and the cooks. But the deeper questioning about beans by John Ray, the botanist who published between 1670 and his death in 1705, and who has been called 'the father of natural history', further stirs the imagination on this subject, for he asked himself whether the beans now being grown were the same as those of the ancients in classical times. He was clearly aware of a changing scene, and his remark prompted Thomas Hale, writing in 1756, to ruminate in the same vein as he took his walks around Chelsea, Fulham and Battersea and saw garden beans fast moving into the fields. Hale pruned in print his list of peas because there were so many varieties, he said, and they were 'every day increasing'. But he did print his list of bean varieties, and it was one of the longest of any, illustrating in some of the names the scale of foreign connections in transmitting them across the sea. Apart from the common field bean, he listed the Portugal or Lisbon bean; had it perhaps come in as a novelty in Charles II's reign, since his marriage to Catherine of Braganza in 1662 brought Portuguese cooks to London and some Portuguese recipes entered the cookery books? The bean had to be protected from the cold by being set against a reed hedge, and was not thought superior to others; it did not sound as if it had a glorious future. But it lit up a picture similar to that depicted by John Parkinson between the 1620s and 1640s, when his botanist friends were already combing Europe for interesting medicinal and food plants and bringing them back to appreciative collectors. Another variety in Hale's list was the small Spanish bean, in favour for its sweetness, and a broad Spanish bean for maturing early. A home-grown Sandwich bean was still among the best liked, but other varieties named were toker beans, blossom and mazagan beans, the mazagan having been brought from the African coast by Portuguese traders. In the end, we notice, Hale named the Windsor bean as sweet and tasty, undoubtedly the best of all for the table. It was also judged the favourite variety in the Chelsea area when Pehr Kalm visited in 1748. Finally, Hale affirmed two economic truths that exerted the greatest power over the market: beans yielded heavily, seven to one, he reckoned, far more than any cereal; and both peas and beans were financially profitable crops.[40]

RECIPES FOR PEAS AND BEANS

Turning from the evidence of people growing the many new varieties of beans and peas, we look to the recipe books for more clues to the way they became acceptable in diet to all classes. The stirring of interest in pulses as a respectable food for all is first noticeable in the 1650s, and apart from associating it with the discussions and experiments in the Hartlib circle, it is just possible that it was further encouraged by the publication of the cookery book of La Varenne, in French in 1651 and in English translation in 1653. This Frenchman's book is thought to have exerted much influence on western European cooking generally, and it certainly included a remarkable number of variations on peas soup, though peas never bore the same strong stamp of being food for the poor as did beans. In addition, Varenne made much use of what he called a peas broth: peas that were partly sieved, as a thickening (with bread added as well) and put into dishes with meat and other vegetables. Garden peas had long before shown themselves to be acceptable to the English, and so any French influence may have been virtually imperceptible to contemporaries. Robert May in 1660 recognized peas pottage as a respectable rich man's dish, served sometimes with meat, sometimes without, and on sippets; he even suggested a sweet tart of green peas with saffron and sugar. But he had no truck with beans.[41]

The next stage in the progress of pulses comes into view after 1700. The royal cook, Robert Smith, writing in 1725, made soup with peas (one recipe even pounded the shells in a mortar; these were possibly mangetout). He did not offer any pottage, but he did pickle French beans, like the ones that we know today, to be used, he said, before they became stringy. Another cook to the nobility, Henry Howard, writing in 1726, also accommodated peas soup, sometimes mixed with other vegetables such as spinach, sorrel and lettuce, and peas pottage. He also pickled French beans, and suggested a not very appealing way of preserving fresh peas by sealing them in a jar of mutton fat, and keeping them until Christmas. Charles Carter, another cook in noble households, writing in 1736, used peas as a broth and a soup, offered a French recipe for *peas françoise*, and then signalled his own distinctive style by allowing three recipes for beans into his repertoire. In one of these, beans were recognizably fresh broad beans, served whole, with thin slices of ham or bacon and plenty of butter, while there were two versions, savoury and sweet, of a bean tansy, baked with egg yolks in the oven. He also included French beans in his recipes for pickling. But still, it seems, fresh beans rather than dried were the rule.[42]

Among cooks who moved in less exalted circles, Elizabeth Cleland wrote a cookery book in 1755 for young ladies studying cookery in her school in Edinburgh. Following La Varenne she cooked pease in a soup on their own or mixed them with meat and/or other vegetables. She used mashed peas in a 'cullis', or paste, for soups and sauces, and she made pottage. But she was another cookery author who did not cook beans. Thus the cookery books bear out the statement of other writers that peas were much more commonly eaten than beans; indeed, we could say that dried beans remained unusual in cookery recipes for the middle classes even while they were much enjoyed eaten fresh in the fine days of spring to summer, Switzer having stretched the season from April to October and Thomas Turner in East Sussex listing many meals in his diary when he ate fresh beans for dinner. William Ellis, however, gives the clearest view in 1750 of farming folk who regularly ate beans as well as peas, while Londoners enjoyed hot beans, originally dried, from the street traders. So beans were firmly on the menus of food for the poor and for less affluent working folk, and this is further made clear by the cookery author in 1767 who printed Lobb's diet and then added a generous array of bean recipes. Significantly, these began with 'beans dressed the German way' (at which we may guess that Bartholomew Carrichter would have smiled approvingly), then moved on to bean tart using green beans, then bean tansy in savoury and sweet versions, then a ragoo of kidney beans, next a harricoo of kidney beans using dried French beans, and finishing with a dish of pickled beans, which had been stored in an earthen pot and had been kept for a whole year.[43]

Another set of recipes for poor people in a time of scarcity was devised in the spirit of Lobb but published a little earlier, by the Revd. Sir James Stonhouse, a physician in Northampton for 20 years from 1743. Surprisingly, he did not use dried beans at all, which might suggest that the vogue for such food had not yet travelled to all places north. Instead, split peas featured in a first recipe, then alternatively garden broad beans (presumably fresh) in the second, and split peas or blue peas in the third (both possibly dried). Stonhouse was intent on keeping costs down, but seemingly beans were still held on the fringes of his world. In this seemingly fluid situation, generalizations about the eating of peas and beans in districts far from London would be hazardous. But we may still nurse the suspicion that they became a routine ingredient in broths and pottage that were regularly noticed in workhouse diets by Sir Frederick Eden in 1797.[44]

POTATOES

Historians give more space to potatoes than to peas and beans when writing about diet after 1750, and with good reason. But between 1700 and 1750 it is likely that peas and beans were eaten in greater quantity. The evidence seems to point to an incipient pulse revolution that was cut short by the arrival of potatoes. Potatoes, like all other new foodstuffs that diversified diet in the early modern period, advanced very slowly, taking a long time to find their right geographical and social niches, and only attracting the comments of writers through accidental encounters that we cannot trust to give us a true picture of reality. Raleigh and his men in Elizabeth's reign probably took the first potatoes to Ireland, while they and many others delivered more to curious botanists, friends and family in London. From the 1650s onwards they featured as an ingredient without any special remark in recipe books that circulated in and around London. The authors of cookery books knew them by then, but like, say, skirret, scorzonera or purslane, they were almost certainly regarded as a vegetable with local affiliations only, not available everywhere; cooks who had them handy took them into the kitchen without comment, while others never had a chance to buy them. Patrick Lamb, the royal cook, was conversant in 1710 with such situations: he prescribed vegetables for his dishes quite vaguely, leaving his readers to select what was available in the neighbourhood; he was plainly familiar with a varied local scene, and as a royal cook was probably more aware than most of gentlemen's gardeners producing some surprising and unusual vegetables according to the eccentric whims of their masters. We should read one or two recipes for potato pie and potato pudding that appear in the cookery books from the 1650s onwards in that spirit: they might have struck some readers oddly while attracting the interest of cooks who had seen potatoes for sale in London. No one as yet asserted any firm view on whether they were for sweet or savoury dishes; marrow with sugar and spices often accompanied them in pies that were covered with pastry.

Potatoes attracted far more notice during two bouts of severe food shortage in the early eighteenth century, at a time when potatoes were spreading, and people now observed in practical terms what a lifesaver they were. Two especially severe winters occurred in 1714–15, when the Thames froze for ten weeks, and in 1728–9 when Richard Bradley conducted an enquiry into the sickness and mortality that ensued and published a whole essay about it. Unusual consequences accompanied this second experience: in the Home Counties north of London large flights of snipe appeared in the sky. These usually solitary birds were seen in flocks of four to five hundred; so boys knocked them over the head and, though the birds were thin, sold them by the dozen as welcome food in London. Wild geese similarly were unusually plentiful, and wildfowl decoys filled up three weeks earlier than usual.[45]

As starch to fill empty stomachs, potatoes proved a significant lifeline at this time, as one Lancashire gentleman explained to Bradley. Potatoes for an emergency were already a practical possibility in the north for they had found their first congenial habitat in Lancashire and Cumberland in the 1670s and 1680s. Ireland's trade with Lancashire had established the effective link between a country where potatoes had already by the 1650s shown themselves to grow successfully, and the mainland where, so far, they had not. John Forster who had in 1664 published a treatise, *England's Trade Increased*, commending their food value, carried them into Somerset, where he lived on the north side of Mendip. John Houghton in his news-sheet told the world in December 1699 that potatoes were abundant in Lancashire and Cumberland, and were beginning to spread all over the kingdom; and although we may judge him somewhat too optimistic about the future, he was probably well informed on one or two localities in the north where they had taken root. One Lancashire gentleman, who had urged people around him to grow them, reported to Bradley in 1729 his satisfaction now that they had shown their worth in his neck of the woods; he saw them as a kind of boiled bread.[46]

Elsewhere, potatoes spread haphazardly, our documents tending to highlight the names of individual gentlemen, like Mr Buckland who carried them to Somerset, but without giving any credit to the labourers who were digging them on their own small plots and telling their friends. Irishmen are thought to have planted them in Essex, for example, and that story is credible when we read the words of a surveyor in 1711 bemoaning the lack of labour to mend the turnpike road between Enfield and Shoreditch. He blamed the shortage on the many small farmers who had switched in the last ten years to planting potatoes, and carrying them to market in horse panniers.[47]

We are not likely to learn much more about the many other resourceful individuals who acted to great effect by growing potatoes on single plots, cooking them in their kitchens, and chatting about them to friends and neighbours. But we can see the patchy results by 1750 and the surge in their popularity soon after. They had found a home in Staffordshire by 1722, for they were by then being tithed in the two parishes of Sedgley and Caverswall; that was a reliable sign that sufficient were being grown to leave some for sale outside the parish in excess of domestic needs. Another four parishes were added to the Staffordshire list of tithe-payers in the 1730s and another four in the 1740s and 1750s. By 1750 they were growing in Devon, Cornwall, Shropshire, Nottinghamshire, the Vale of York and Nidderdale, and a German visitor was particularly struck by the quantity of potatoes being grown around Leeds when reporting home in 1766. A patchy geographical pattern dominated William Marshall's more general statement that they were not much grown until after the 1750s, while by 1798 a dramatic turnaround was depicted in Somerset by John Billingsley, who said that one acre of potatoes in one man's possession was an extraordinary sight in the mid-1760s, whereas nearly 40 years later many parishes had 50 acres; the writer himself had grown 30–40 acres, and once 100 acres. When a nationwide crop return was taken in 1801 the haphazard distribution of potatoes in the fields was yet again confirmed.[48]

Thus we can understand why potato recipes, destined only for readers of books, increased in these years from one per cookery book to four or five. More revealing still are the two and a half pages which William Ellis wrote about them in 1750. Farmers' wives whom he encountered in and around Hertfordshire had assembled a variety of interesting ways of serving them. They simply boiled them and served them with butter as a separate sauce, or having boiled them first, they put them under roast beef or mutton to catch the dripping fat and gravy; this was also the way Pehr Kalm ate them in Essex, having noted them growing conspicuously in the fields. Alternatively, Ellis described them being fried with onions or garlic, stewed in a pot with meat and vegetables in ale, layered between herrings or pilchards, baked or boiled with saltfish and more butter, or mashed and eaten with pork or bacon. They might also be roasted in the fire in their jackets, mashed in a pudding cloth with currants and pork fat, or turned into a sweet pie with raisins, suet, butter or bone marrow, sugar, and sometimes apples.[49]

Our housewives had arrived at an array of dishes far greater than those described by the writers of cookbooks, and all were economical. They are a lesson to be heeded when we appraise other cookbook recipes in relation to the unseen doings of women at home in their kitchens. Only in this one case can we set the cooks' bookish prescriptions beside the actual working practices of ordinary women. But the comparison obliges us to give the women in the kitchen much credit for their good sense and their fund of original ideas.

In gathering information about potatoes Ellis had learned enough to regard those grown in Lancashire as the best quality available; and so he selected those in particular for planting in Hertfordshire. Someone had also described to him the Manchester market, noting the numerous sacks of potatoes that were bought by the rich as well as poor. The Irish had also taught the Lancastrians how best to preserve them through the winter, and so they stored them in straw-lined trenches or dried them briefly in a kiln. Kiln-drying presented no problems to Lancashire folk, for they were already thoroughly conversant with drying oats in a kiln, oats being, as we noted in the sixteenth century, their prime bread cereal. Potato growing still had a long way to go before everyone in the kingdom accepted them as the first vegetable of a main course at table, but plainly Lancashire people had pioneered the way for others to follow.[50]

We have so far discussed pickled meats, peas and beans, and potatoes as innovations in their different ways on the food tables of this age. They were outstanding in adding quantity and variety to the diet of all classes. But did other modest shifts in taste and fashion take place at the same time? We know that changing fashions would have been instantly recognized by contemporaries, just as we recognize such shifts of taste in our own day, in our much increased eating of pasta and pizzas, for example, and in the declining taste for shepherd's pie and date pudding. So while the question is not easily answered, it is worth uttering, since the documents are more abundant at this time. The cookbooks multiplied in number, and drew in authors from more walks of life. More cooks working in royal or noble households took a fancy to compiling recipe books, and so did some women who ran eating houses or schools of cooking for young ladies. Between them, they broaden our picture of current cooking styles.

RECIPE BOOKS BY RICH MEN'S COOKS

A recognizable pattern of dishes was emerging since books undoubtedly promoted standardization. The authors read each other, and appropriated some of each other's recipes. Workaday cooks, in their turn, read the books and spread the same recipes more widely, and weaker influences flowed as news-sheets appeared, mustering yet more readers.

Upper-class tastes are reflected in the books of three authors in this period, whose work passed into several editions. One was Henry Howard, one-time cook to the Duke of Ormond, the Earl of Salisbury and the Earl of Winchelsea. The first edition of his *England's Newest Way* appeared in 1703, and passed through four impressions before he issued another in 1726, the one that is used here. In this he added further recipes from the manuscripts of several unnamed ladies. Another author was Robert Smith, claiming 30 years of cooking experience, having worked for 18 years under Patrick Lamb as a cook to William III. He had also served as cook to the Duke of Buckingham, the Duke of Ormond (causing us to wonder if he had worked alongside Henry Howard), and the Duc d'Aumont, the French ambassador. His *Court Cookery, or the Compleat English Cook*, which covered all branches of cooking, appeared in 1723, and a second edition in 1725. The 1725 edition, used here, omitted one whole part on confectionery, which may possibly be significant in indicating a somewhat fading interest in sweetmeats, which had been such a strong fashion in the earlier seventeenth century.

Patrick Lamb, who had supervised Robert Smith in the king's kitchen, also published a book entitled *Royal Cookery* in 1710, and that too sold well, running on to a second and third edition in 1726 and 1731. His experience went back considerably earlier than the others, for he had cooked for four monarchs from Charles II onward. He was criticized by his younger pupil, Robert Smith, for errors, and for old recipes that Smith deemed 'impracticable at this time', so we may interpret such remarks as showing how conscious were young cooks of changing food fashions. Patrick Lamb had evidently included recipes that were already unfamiliar to his younger colleague, and Smith did not expect or want them to be recorded now that they were no longer in current practice.[51]

Our three cookery authors give a fair conspectus of the bill of fare that contemporaries considered customary and up to date in the most well-to-do households. To start with, they set great store by the preparation of a strong broth as the basic essential for all meat and fish dishes and soups. In Smith's directions, 8lbs of fillet of beef, a marrow bone, and half a calf's foot were cooked down for 8–10 hours to the consistency of a syrup. In another of Smith's recipes he boiled a leg and shin of beef for 12 hours, in another he cooked beef and bacon 'to rags'. Howard prescribed plenty of meat, though less cooking time in one recipe, but he used 4lbs of coarse beef, 3lbs of mutton, and seven quarts of water to boil a white soup broth. In another he made a broth that was kept in liquid form 'one week under another'. Extending this procedure for making a broth, it became one of the fads of the day to boil down a broth to a glue, which, when cold, was cut into pieces, wrapped and stored, like a stock cube used today. One could carry it on one's travels.[52]

Among meat recipes the first striking feature in Robert Smith's collection is the preference for boiling and braising rather than roasting on the spit. Fricassées and ragouts (spelled ragoo by Smith and ragow by Howard) had become favourite cooking styles, and even when these words were not used in a recipe, the meat was nevertheless cooked in much the same way. It was simmered in a pot on top of a fire, and highly varied sauces were added to embellish it at the end. An alternative method was to part-roast the meat on a spit, and then cut up the meat for longer braising. It is possible that this would have been identified in upper-class circles as the sign of a new fashion, for Pehr Kalm, in contrast, visiting lowlier farming folk in the country in 1748, still regarded roast beef and pudding as the basic English diet, implying that everyone ate meat off a joint; that notion was reinforced by his saying that every kitchen had a spit. Spiced flavourings like nutmeg, mace, cloves and ginger still featured prominently with salt and pepper in the braised dishes, but more bread was now used for thickening and less use was made of sippets on which the food had often been laid when served on the plate.[53]

Another very strong favourite, noted already between 1660 and 1700 in adding bulk to the meal, was what contemporaries called forcemeat, a stuffing of minced meat mixed with other ingredients. It featured repeatedly, inserted either in the cavity of a bird or animal, or between the skin and the flesh, and sometimes rolled into balls and cooked alongside. The meat might even be pounded to a paste (now called a cullis, a modish term in the cook's vocabulary), and it was mixed with herbs, other greenstuff, spices and colouring. A great variety of extras, such as mushrooms, capers, anchovies, oysters and even truffles, might be added to the paste, though we can picture the more economical housewife adding cereals and stale bread, as we do nowadays. The use of sugar had virtually disappeared from savoury dishes (John Evelyn had already noted this trend in the later seventeenth century), and a generous mixture of vegetables went into the pot, including turnips, a lot of endive, and sorrel. The liberal use of lemons and oranges for adding juice to sauces continued as before, and barberries remained in demand for their sharp flavour, though barberry sauce was less often chosen than in the mid-seventeenth century and had further faded from favour by 1750.

Veal was as conspicuous among the meats as in the seventeenth century, which accords with the many references by farming writers to the popularity of calf-fattening in the Home Counties. Veal was in high demand in London, and all commentators stressed the commercial profit of calf-fattening that accrued to farmers in Essex and Hertfordshire who could readily transport their meat to London.

Evidently, competition between them was strong, and was reflected in yet more strenuous efforts to make their meat white: they had in the past fed the calves with chalk; Kalm in 1748 even noted the practice of bleeding dying calves overnight, so that the meat was white for market next morning. It is noticeable that farmers in Surrey and Kent, in contrast to those of Essex and Hertfordshire, were never mentioned as producers of veal.[54]

The salting and drying of meats, being one of the oldest arts of preservation in the kitchen, did not need to be described in these cookbooks, but advice was still offered on the fuel to be used, for it affected the smoke in the chimney and hence the taste of the meat. Polonia sausages, for example, had to be hung in a chimney where wood was burned. Grilling always had to be done over charcoal and not over seacoal. The potting of all kinds of meat and fish may still have been relatively unfamiliar, for its procedures received much attention from both Robert Smith and Henry Howard. The method was to cook meat and fish with flavourings in a lot of butter in an earthen pot in the oven. The butter was then poured off, and the contents put into a fresh pot and sealed with at least an inch of more fresh butter. A bladder and a piece of leather were then tied on top, to be sure to exclude all air. In this way Smith potted pork, beef, pigeons, rabbits, hares and venison, as well as lobsters, salmon and lampreys, and recommended a storage place that was neither moist nor dry. Howard recommended a cellar.[55]

The pickling of meat has already been described because William Ellis gave it so much prominence. The usage was also plainly accepted in well-to-do circles.

Smith's meat for pickling included pigeons and pork. Howard dealt with the pickling of meat to keep 'for a pretty while', and exhorted watchfulness over the pickling liquid, for it needed to be boiled up 'as you find occasion'.[56]

The prejudice that was voiced in the earlier seventeenth century against overmuch pastry probably no longer aroused strong feeling, since the cutting up of meat into small pieces was in vogue for ragouts and fricassées, and if it went into pies, the pastry did not need to remain so long in the oven. Precise ways of making pastry, and the different kinds, received little attention either from Smith or Howard, the principal types in use now being puff pastry and 'paste for a pasty', presumably a short crust. What was more important, at least to Smith, was the 'lear' or liquid that was poured into the pie, when lifting the lid after it was cooked. For a kid pie, he made a liquor of Melton oysters fried brown, white wine, gravy, barberries, thickened with eggs and butter. The meat for the pie was sometimes parboiled beforehand or, if not, was cut into thin slices beforehand, to cook in a short time. Even so, some pastry was still cooked hard and long: a pie containing a quartered chicken was expected to take three hours to bake, and in that case the pie crust must surely have been a coarse flour mixture that was not intended to be eaten. Calf's head pie featured in both Smith's and Howard's recipes, but was different from the calf's head dish that later achieved almost legendary status. With this last the head was first boiled, and all the bones taken out before the meat was cut up and laid in the pie dish.[57]

Fish dishes ranged over the greatest variety, for all fish were evidently expected to be readily available to well-to-do households. Carp, eels, pike, barbels, plaice, tench, salmon, flounders, turbot, halibut, roach, smelts, lampreys, mullet, all featured in Smith's recipes, and all were either poached and given a savoury sauce with more delicacies added (such as shrimps, capers, anchovies), or the fish was pounded (like meat) and put into puff pastry patties. Fish pickling was now taken for granted along with meat pickling, and Smith's fish for this purpose included oysters, herrings, mackerel and smelts, the latter exceeding anchovies in flavour, so he claimed.[58]

Innumerable fresh vegetables were available to royal cooks, some of them now quite exotic. But what engaged attention in the cookery books was the art of pickling, because it was not yet so ancient a tradition as to be known to all. Among cooks with the space to store barrels, earthen pots and glass containers, it opened up a new world of possibilities for expanding their menus between November and March. Stone jars were recommended for pickled vegetables by Smith who then gave recipes for mushrooms, cauliflowers, cabbages, samphire, French beans, gherkins, beetroot, turnips, onions, asparagus, red cabbage, barberries, walnuts – the list was seemingly endless. Howard's list was much the same but added French beans, plum buds, and elder buds, all of which were expected to keep for a year. Among pickled vegetables, at least in London circles, cucumbers unquestionably came first in favour, and the more often they were boiled in vinegar, the greener they became. One recipe promised 'a regalia of cucumbers', slicing twelve of them, beating and squeezing them dry, then frying them brown, and adding gravy, claret, butter, flour, cloves, nutmeg, mace, pepper and salt, to make a sauce for lamb, mutton or veal. Professor Bradley, sharing the same gentlemanly taste, gave similar attention to pickled cucumbers with three different recipes in his book for country housewives. In one of these recipes, from a Buckinghamshire gentleman, the cook was told that they had to be of the smallest size if they were to be brought to table 'among people of the first rank' – a fine point that we onlookers might never have noticed.[59]

Turning to sweet puddings, we notice in Henry Howard's cookery book, of which the first version was written early in the century (in 1703, though it was still current in 1726), he used no exotic fruit and sometimes no fruit at all. Oatmeal pudding was one of his suggestions, flavoured with cinnamon, nutmeg and mace. Other puddings relied on a lot of cream as a base and used flavourings like lemon, or were thickened to make blancmange. One dish in Smith's book was a chocolate cream which contained 'a spoon of scraped chocolate' and was served in 'chocolate cups'. Other novel flavours were Howard's sage cream, made with red sage juice and rosewater (or any other healthful herbs for that matter), or green walnuts cooked in sugar after the husks had been peeled off. This last was an eccentric use of walnuts, which were more usually pickled when their husks were still soft.[60]

When using fruit, Howard made apples his first choice – Kent pippins were the best in his view – or carrots, in a sweet pie with cream topped with puff paste. Apples were in fact the readiest fruit at all seasons of the year, so that apple pies and apple fritters could appear at any time in the winter months. Sample bills of fare that were inserted in Smith's and Howard's books did not give great prominence to fruit dishes, but they did form a considerable group in the actual recipes, emphasizing the veritable revolution that had taken place in the art of preserving summer fruit throughout the winter. The first method was the same as that which was revived among us in the war years between 1939 and 1945, by bottling and sterilizing the fruit in the oven, then sealing it. Alternatively, Smith dried the fruit, giving recipes for cherries, apricots, gooseberries and barberries. He also candied fruit, though his pages given to candying had diminished when compared with some of the seventeenth-century cookbooks; the earlier craze was ebbing away. An alternative way in the making of fruit purées, favoured by Howard, who described them as a conserve cooked to a jelly. Made with equal quantities of fruit and sugar, purées could be stored in glass containers and would preserve their flavour indefinitely, until needed in tarts. The scale of the seasonal transformation in fruit dishes served at the table may be gauged in one of the bills of fare in Robert Smith's book, prescribing apricot tarts in January, and, in Henry Howard's book, serving a raspberry cream in February. But in any case, the maturing of fruit was brought forward by a month or two in many rich men's gardens. Stephen Switzer, the expert gardener who in 1727 wrote in *The Practical Kitchen Gardiner* of his memory over the past 25 years, had seen melons, which formerly were not ready until between the middle and end of June, being ripened by the end of April or the beginning of May. Using glass frames, some strawberries were ready at the beginning of April, were plentiful during May, and continued through to July.[61]

Cakes were now a standard item of food among the well-to-do. They did not appear in bills of fare and so were presumably eaten at other times with tea, coffee or wine, though tartlets and cheese cakes did appear in May and July in Smith's menus. Cakes usually had some yeast put into them, as, for example, in plum cake, which contained currants, raisins and almonds. Caraway cake contained 3lbs of flour and 1lb of caraway seeds. Gingerbread had 2lbs of treacle with 3lbs of flour, and 2ozs of beaten ginger. Seedcake, queen's cakes and Shrewsbury cakes were other favourites. Sweeter cakes in Smith's repertoire were called ratafias and were really meringues, given the ratafia flavour by beating apricot kernels very fine with orange-flower water.[62]

Cheese cake remained a routine item among all classes, but cooks catering for rich folk could not resist elaborating on the basic recipe of ordinary folk. They usually put in currants like everyone else, but Smith added some grated Naples biscuits, rosewater and sack. He also offered another unusual orange cheese cake recipe, using orange peel in the butter/eggs mixture, by boiling the peel well to remove the bitterness, then mashing it in a mortar till it was 'as tender as marmalade'. This careful treatment of orange peel to be eaten was not unusual; Howard used it to make orange tarts. In one of Smith's other recipes for 'an extraordinary orange pudding', even the pips were mashed and included – one of many illustrations of the way edible food items that we discard were put to good use in the past. We should also notice the hard work that was involved in pounding with a pestle in a mortar; it must have developed strong wrists.[63]

According to Pehr Kalm, the Swedish visitor to England in 1748, cheese was regularly placed in a large piece on the table at the end of the meal, and people helped themselves. We may suspect this to have been a middle-class, and not necessarily an upper-class, practice. Cooked cheese dishes were still a rarity despite the growth of dairying and the much higher quantities of cheese produced on farms. In Smith's book, cooked cheese was not mentioned at all, and in Howard's it featured once only as toasted cheese, using Cheshire cheese mixed with egg yolks, butter and breadcrumbs, which was spread on white toast and toasted again. The Welsh custom of toasting cheese had once been regarded in modish circles as an abomination, and this concession in a book compiled for noble households may only have become acceptable because the practice was here connected with Dutch usage; Howard told his readers that the dish could only be done 'in a Dutch stow', presumably a Dutch oven.[64]

Nevertheless, rich men's cooks cannot be said to have set themselves apart from the middle-class women who also published recipe books. Or perhaps we should turn the argument around and say that the middle-class women had no practical problems in following the lead of more august cooks. As a royal cook, Patrick Lamb, for example, had not been extravagant in the use of expensive or exotic ingredients. Among fruits, he did not once mention strawberries or raspberries, and seemed to put apples first; among vegetables he mentioned asparagus infrequently. He used carrots and turnips freely, and, when no summer vegetables like celery or endive were available, settled for Savoy cabbages, cabbage lettuces and dried peas. More than once he urged the cook to use 'such herbs as the country where you are will afford', and in selecting bacon, he was quite as accustomed as any homely housewife to discarding bacon that was rusty.[65]

MIDDLE-CLASS AUTHORS

The three middle-class women compared here prepared much the same dishes as the rich men's cooks, while paying perhaps rather more attention than they to the building up of a store cupboard; but that might just be a womanly trait. Diana Astry, later Mrs Orlebar, lived in Bedfordshire, and published 375 recipes, partly collected from among her friends, c. 1700. She preserved a multitude of fruits, including apricots; she pickled cucumbers and cooked Spanish potato pie, though whether the potatoes were grown in England or imported was left unclear. She made many fruit wines, pickled barberries for her sauces, and along with all her contemporaries she made peas pottage, pickled pork, and prepared Westphalia ham. She liked fricassées of chicken and rabbit, shared with everyone else at this time a liking for calf's head, ate veal regularly, and still served fish on Friday. Favoured desserts were fruit fools and creams rather than more solid puddings; cheese cake was a standard item. She was somewhat individual but not alone in using chocolate in a cream and in cakes.[66]

Mary Kettilby, our second middle-class cook, revealed nothing of herself beyond a concern to help cooking maids in country inns. She published 300 recipes in 1728, showing much the same tastes as Diana Astry, starting with peas in a soup in three versions, and following with meat, which she preferred to boil, braise, or bake rather than cook on a spit. She also pickled pork, cooked veal, stewed carp and herrings, made the same Spanish potato pie as Diana Astry, enlivening it with bone marrow; she preserved barberries and made puff pastry. She used butter lavishly: one pound went into a sauce for stewed carp.

1. This living room in Kirkwall, on the Isle of Orkney, in the 1920s-30s, shows a cooking pot on a fire with no chimney. It would have been a familiar scene all over England before 1700, cooking the main family dish of the day.

2. Cooking for a large household, probably of a nobleman, and depicting vividly the hot, heavy work, and the many people performing varied tasks at close quarters.

STYLES OF EATING

3. At a royal table with onlookers. This engraving shows James I and Prince Charles honouring Don Diego Hurtado de Mendoza, the Spanish ambassador, and others at York House, London, in 1623. He had accompanied Prince Charles on his return from Madrid, where Charles had intended, but failed, to settle his marriage with the Spanish Infanta. On such public occasions, a railing would be put in place to prevent the crowd from approaching too near the table.

4. A lady of the gentry class, eating alone. Note the bare furnishings in this room.

5. Eating, or rather waiting to eat, in sober but mixed company. The trenchers are in place on the table. Note how warmly clad are the diners, with their hats on.

6. Eating in a Family Circle. This is a well-to-do family, but they have a bed in the corner. Note the servant scouring a pot next door.

PUTTING THE FOOD TOGETHER

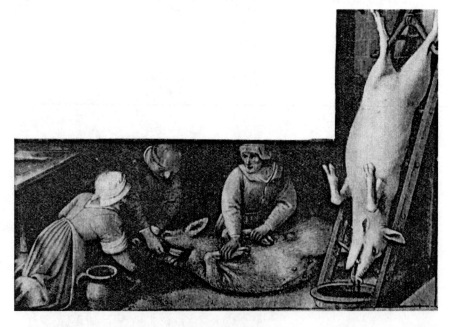

7. Killing and cutting up the pig. This was usually a task for the autumn, allowing some feasting and sharing of meat with others on the days after the slaughter, but mainly providing a store for winter.

8. Getting in the water. In towns many people had water near at hand from wells or fountains, or better still had it in the house, but we do not know what proportion of people were so blessed. This is Marcellus Laroon's image of a man crying New River water for sale in a London street.

9. Taking in the eggs. One would normally expect a woman to be delivering her eggs locally. Was this man perhaps a casual trader?

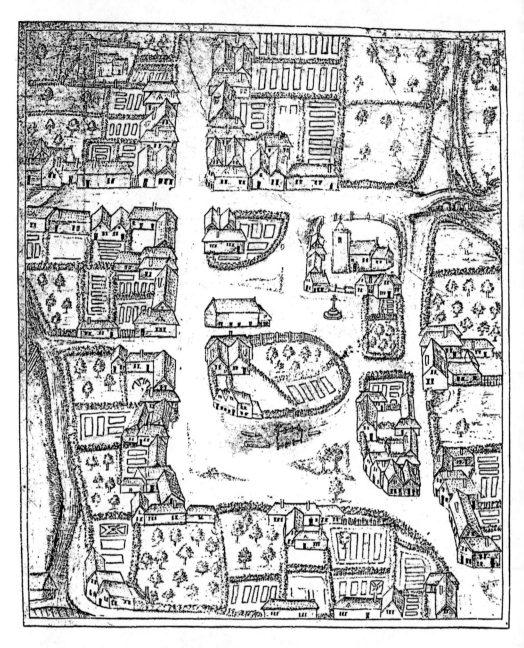

10. Growing your own vegetables and fruit in 1565, in Wilton, Wiltshire. This plan of Wilton clearly shows vegetable beds in the back gardens of the village houses, and fruit orchards.

11. These thirteen pictures of the different stages in bread making show every operation from grinding the grain, seasoning it, and stoking the fire, through mixing in the raising agent, shaping the loaves and weighing them, dividing the dough into loaves and setting them to rise, putting them in the oven, closing the door and, finally, drawing them out when cooked. This baker must surely have been working for a shop.

The pictures surround the title of a book by John Penkethman entitled *Artachthos, or a New Booke declaring the Assise of Weight forth by the right Honble the Lords and Others of his Majesties most honourable Privie Councell, London, 1638.* The earliest version was printed before 1532, then in 1544 (?), and in seven more editions.

12. When baking bread at home, the women saw things differently. This drawing best portrays the real-life experience of mixing bread dough!

Below: 13. Milling flour without a miller near at hand. This is a quern, turned with a handle, in use in Shetland for milling grain, and also malt for beer. In a smaller version the quern was much used for milling mustard seed and other spices. Querns are so common in probate inventories, that it suggests that most at this period were used for milling malt. But in the countryside, not a few country folk must have lived beyond comfortable walking distance to a mill, and sometimes ran short of flour. They will have used a quern, as did others who resented paying dues for using the manorial mill, and were fined in court for the offence.

To make ham from pork, she adhered to the conventional recipe for Westphalia ham; this meant hanging it for two days, rubbing it with saltpetre and common salt, adding coarse sugar, basting for three weeks, and then drying it like bacon. Everything possible was pickled to give variety in winter – walnuts, mushrooms, neats' tongues and pigeons. Her recipe for cheese cake was the standard one, but with puff pastry at its base. Custard creams were a common dessert. She relished a lavish plum cake (which we would call a fruit cake) that was prescribed by a friend; and she was proud of English wines, including birch wine (as made in Sussex) and cherry wine (as made in Kent).[67]

In choosing meat, these women showed no great preference for beef or mutton, but used a varied selection of animals and birds. Diana Astry's recipes, it is true, used more beef than mutton or lamb (her 13 beef recipes compared with four for mutton and lamb). But 14 others used parts of the pig and nine used veal, while hare featured in five recipes, chicken in three, and other birds in five others. In a word, the meat coming into her kitchen was as varied as in any rich man's kitchen. In a separate list Diana Astry recorded the dishes served when she went out to dinner between September 1701 and September 1708, and we may guess that on those occasions her hostess did not offer everyday food, but selected special treats. So that list was, indeed, different: venison featured 16 times, rabbit ten, mutton nine, beef only four times, and veal only three. Meats featuring in a middling number of dishes were chicken on eight occasions, wildfowl on seven, turkey on six, calves' head on five, and lamb on four.[68]

For a family living in Bedfordshire and not near the sea, there was a reasonable selection of fish, judging by the recipes at everyday meals, but more eels (from the neighbouring fens?) and oysters (from Essex?) were used than anything else. Carp, pike and tench no doubt came from local ponds, whereas less often she served salmon, and sea fish like whiting, herrings and shrimps. When eating out, Diana did not always name exactly what fish she was eating, and perhaps she did not always know, but sturgeon was clearly something special. Nicholas Blundell of Little Crosby, Lancashire in his *Diurnal* also offered the same assessment in a reference in 1707 to 'a treat of sturgeon'. Ranked behind sturgeon, when Astry ate out, came salmon and oysters. Only once was lobster served.[69]

Our third cookery author, publishing in 1755, was Elizabeth Cleland, a lady running a school of cookery in Edinburgh and wishing to help her pupils. She might have been expected to show a distinctive Scottish style, but in fact she followed much the same usages as royal and middle-class cooks who worked down south. When her soups were ready, they did have meat of some kind placed at the centre of the dish. Her pottage 'in the French way' had a distinctly vegetarian flavour, using herbs, vegetables, oatmeal, egg yolks and a whole pound of butter, and was served on toast. Another soup, with only vegetables and herbs, was called a meagre broth. She availed herself of as much variety in greenstuff as any southerner, including celery, endive, sorrel, lettuce, purslane and spinach, marigold flowers, and strawberry and violet leaves. She dried and pickled vegetables and fruit like her contemporaries; she also made wines and cordials. She made forcemeats for meat and fish, potted fish in butter, and pickled meat. She made ragoos and fricassées, and plenty of pies with pastry, sometimes boiling them in a pudding cloth as others did. Potatoes went into a sweet apple pie with dried fruit, and barberries went into her sauces. She offered lots of puddings, some of sago, millet (this imported cereal was an unusual item) or fruit, pancakes, and dumplings. There were so many custards (with different flavourings), blancmanges and creams that her recipes for these ran on for five pages; she had a trifle recipe, one of the first to be so named. Cakes, like seed cake and plum cake, and biscuits were routine, and some still used yeast. She also made cheese and found Welsh rarebit perfectly acceptable.[70]

Finally, one author stands on her own, awaiting research to identify others of her kind. She introduces us to what is at present a shadowy world of flimsy, cheaply printed cookery pages, appearing in weekly parts. She was Sarah Jackson, publishing in 1754 *The Director: or Young Woman's Best Companion ... a Book Necessary for all Families, Collected for the Use of her own Family and printed at the Request of her Friends ... being One of the Plainest and Cheapest of the Kind*. It was a cookbook of 112 pages and over 300 recipes, printed for J. Fuller 'at his circulating library in Butcher-hall-lane, near Newgate Street (London) and S. Neale, bookseller at Chatham'. It could be regularly delivered to your door from the local bookseller, or you could borrow it from the publisher's circulating library. Sarah's book title clearly proclaimed her intention to offer straightforward recipes to the average housewife; and since the many recipes in this periodical were assembled over a period in book form, it has by good chance survived in the British Library, and shows us how faithfully she kept her promise. Recipes prescribed exact quantities, but were far from listing innumerable fancy ingredients as did the royal cookbooks; she used only a few, very ordinary items like carrots and 'brockley', and often required no more than ten or fewer lines for her explanations. The foods taken for granted in this run-of-the-mill kitchen are significant, especially as regards wildfowl. Jackson's publication plainly reached out to a reading public of ordinary housewives not only in London but also in Chatham, Kent. In Chatham, some fortifications enclosing a dockyard and barracks were being built in 1758, so it sounds as if it was then a bustling place with some lively young women visiting its shops.[71]

Excluding Sarah Jackson as a singular author from our generalizations, we can see the assemblage of other recipe books moving towards a conformity. Not only did the cooks watch each other closely, so did the food producers and importers. An information network had come into existence that relied on a professional literature, as well as travellers' keen observations. Two hundred and fifty years on, we notice many dishes and ways of cooking then that were moving towards a standard pattern which remained familiar into the mid-twentieth century.

CONCLUSION

With the benefit of hindsight, we can identify this period of 50 years as a significant turning point, when pulses (notably beans) and potatoes were in competition with each other, vying for a bigger place in the diet. Potatoes would in the end emerge triumphant. When examining the local history of food in a separate chapter below, we shall see the battle continuing between 1750 and 1800. But as potatoes took far less time to cook and used much less fuel than beans, and women, being called away from the house to work in factories, could not watch the hob as carefully as in the past, we can postulate a frustrated bean revolution, while the potato revolution forged ahead. Beans and peas had to wait another 200 years before they won more favour in the 1960s and 1970s, along with vegetarianism. Their protein content was then better understood and they ceased to be called, as I remember them, 'second-class protein'.

When historians wonder how the greatly increasing population of the kingdom was fed in the later eighteenth century, they look first at wheat production, seeking evidence for an increase in the volume produced as a guide to all cereal production, and so explaining England's success in filling so many more hungry stomachs. Our food history, on the other hand, shows that many other food items contributed to that achievement.

One factor not discussed here or anywhere else, but not to be ignored entirely, was the lively concern for the latest methods in preserving grain. We have not yet looked to see how successful in fact were the various practices that followed discussion of this problem in this half century. A treatise on the subject in 1753 by Duhamel du Monceau is usually cited as a milestone, but doubtless a long preamble led up to this pronouncement. It was made in a period that showed much zest for innovation, and it has to be weighed alongside the many other factors improving cereal quantities.[72]

Other ingredients in diet added bulk and enjoyment as well. We see numerous strands of fresh enterprise, innovation and lively debate in this period that diversified the situation in many directions. For one thing, commercial pressures were more intense, and new avenues of opportunity opened up through the growth of world-wide trade and the greater ease of transporting foodstuffs internally. Success in preserving food grew remarkably, and ways of publicizing food facts through printed matter, gossip in the coffee houses of London, on the roads, and in the growing number of foodshops all over the kingdom spread the word more effectively.

Examining more closely the food at the table, we see after 1700 the eating of peas and beans supplementing nutrition with more protein, while all the arts of preservation of meat, vegetables and fruit added extra nourishment to winter diets. Pickling meat, instead of salting it, made the meat supply go further, and the remarkable expansion of dairying produced butter and cheese in many different regional types and qualities to suit all purses. In some special circumstances, as for example in the case of the Cambridge colleges wanting a continuous supply of butter in winter, the achievement was heroic. The dairymen of Over in Cambridgeshire became celebrated in the cowkeeping world for their system of selling off their cows when they were drying off at Michaelmas, and buying in others that would calve every month through the winter. Meanwhile, the gardeners and farmers extended the growing season of many vegetables and increased the many different varieties of each kind to suit different climatic regions; so they were no longer the luxuries of a rich upper class but reached a larger public who bought them or grew them for themselves.

Focusing on wheat production as the explanation for a remarkable increase in the food supply after 1750 represents a very narrow view of an achievement on a far more adventurous scale. It lies quietly embedded in our farming and local history, as does the ingenuity of the womenfolk who devised a multitude of different ways of cooking their food. Admittedly, pickling and preserving were procedures most easily handled in the roomy houses of gentry, yeomen and prosperous traders, but they were available to any resourceful woman who had the interest and took the trouble. Ellis referred to a woman storing apples for months in straw in a chamber. We catch one fleeting glimpse of herbs being dried at a window. For generations, many widows made money by malting barley in the corner of a chamber. As women were never encouraged to blazon their doings abroad, we have to use our imagination to construct a fairer picture of their ingenuity in exploiting the agricultural revolution to benefit the family eating food at the table. William Ellis is a generous commentator in recording their resourcefulness. But the superlative words of an eloquent poem on the apple pie or turnover also deserve a place here, defining the many steps in the making of one food item. It seems relatively simple food to us, but it became a delight. In William Ellis's words, it was 'a main part of a prudent, frugal farmer's family food' and went into the pocket of the ploughman and ploughboy in the field.[73]

Of Apple Pyes
Of all the delicates which Britons try,
To please the palate, or delight the eye;
Of all the several kinds of sumptuous fare,
There's none that can with apple-pye compare,
For costly flavour, or substantial paste,
For outward beauty, or for inward taste.

When first this infant dish in fashion came,
Th'inredients were but coarse, and rude the frame;
As yet, unpolish'd in the modern arts,
Our fathers eat brown bread instead of tarts;
Pyes were but undigested lumps of dough,
'Till time and just expence improv'd them so.
King Coll (as ancient annals tell)
Renown'd for fiddling and for eating well
Pippins in homely cakes with honey stew'd,
Just as he bak'd (the proverb says) he brew'd.
Their greater art succeeding princes show'd,
And model'd paste into a nearer mode;
Invention now grew lively, palate nice,
And sugar pointed out the way to spice.
But here for ages unimprov'd we stood,
And apple-pyes were still but homely food;
When god-like Edgar, of the Saxon line,
Polite of taste, and studious to refine,
In the dessert perfuming quinces cast,
And perfected with cream the rich repast;
Hence we proceed the outward parts to trim,
With crinkumcranks adorn the polish'd brim,
And each fresh pye the pleas'd spectator greets
With virgin fancies and with new conceits.
Dear Nelly, learn with care the pastry art,
And mind the easy precepts I impart;
Draw out your dough elaborately thin,
And cease not to fatigue your rolling-pin;
Of eggs and butter, see you mix enough;
For then the paste will swell into a puff,
Which will in crumbling sounds your praise report,
And eat, as housewives speak, exceeding short:
Rang'd in thick order let your quinces lie;
They give a charming relish to the pye;
If you are wise, you'll not brown sugar slight,
The browner (if I form my judgment right)
A tincture of a bright vermeil will shed
And stain the pippin, like the quince, with red.
When this is done, there will be wanting still
The just reserve of cloves, and candied peel;
Nor can I blame you, if a drop you take
Of orange water, for perfuming sake;
But here the nicety of art is such,
There must be not too little, nor too much;

If with discretion you these costs employ,
They quicken appetite, if not they cloy
Next in your mind this maxim firmly root,
Never o'er charge your pye with costly fruit;
Oft let your bodkin thro' the lid be sent,
To give the kind imprison'd treasure vent;
Lest the fermenting liquors, mounting high
Within their brittle bounds, disdain to lie;
Insensibly by constant fretting waste,
And o'er inform the tenement of paste.
To chuse your baker, think and think again,
(You'll scarce one honest baker find in ten;)
Adust and bruis'd, I've often seen a pye
In rich disguise and costly ruin lie;
While the red crust beheld its form o'erthrown,
Th'exhausted apples griev'd their moisture flown,
And syrup from the sides run trickling down.
O be not, be not tempted, lovely Nell,
While the hot piping odours strongly smell,
While the delicious fume creates a gust,
To lick the o'erflowing juice, or bite the crust;
You'll rather stay (if my advice may rule)
Until the hot is temper'd by the cool;
Oh! first infuse the luscious store of cream,
And change the purple for a silver stream;
That smooth balsamick viand first produce,
To give a softness to the tarter juice.
Then shalt thou, pleas'd, the noble fabrick view,
And have a slice into the bargain too;
Honour and fame alike we will partake,
So well I'll eat, what you so richly make.

8

Regional and Social Patterns of Diet

We are accustomed to a lifestyle in which almost all our food is bought in the market. So it requires long, hard effort to think ourselves back into a totally different world of assumptions. In the early modern period it was an axiom of life that people should 'lay out seldom any money for any provision, but have it of their own'. These are the exact words of William Webb in 1621, writing of Cheshire farmers, and we have already quoted advice to the same effect by Gervase Markham at much the same date. Another commentator on self-sufficiency was Sir Robert Wroth, who was commemorated in a poem of Ben Jonson because he preferred to eat at home 'with unbought provision blessed'. These utterances, all from about the same date, give cause to wonder if it was a recent fashion to write thus. In the Middle Ages few people could have given a thought to any other situation. All but a privileged few took it for granted that they had to produce their own food. Were these aspirational utterances, clustering around 1600, by any chance sparked off by an intrusive reality showing a swelling quantity of food imports like dried fruits, sugar, oranges and lemons? The first arrival of figs and raisins in northern Europe from Genoa seems to date from the 1380s, when vessels were heading for Sluys and Brussels in Flanders. Such voyages slowly increased in frequency into the 1420s to 1440s, when they started occasionally to stop off at Southampton. A new traffic like this could well have made a disturbing intellectual impact on some, giving birth to prejudices against any dependence on imported foods. Does it perhaps partly explain the special sympathy among book-readers for Xenophon's treatise *Of Household*? This was a highly fashionable classical text in the early sixteenth century, commending self-sufficiency among householders who had home farms, and it was taken to heart by many gentlemen, when they resumed active farming on their estates. As a train of thought, self-sufficiency may indeed have represented a quietly pervasive mood in the sixteenth century, running out of steam as housekeeping settled into a new routine in the seventeenth century, accepting novel foods, some imported from far away, and more varied and better supplies of the familiar ones, without threatening to destroy all the comfortable old traditions. Certainly, self-sufficiency was not mentioned as a noble aspiration by 1760; and some of us historians find ourselves startled by people in comparatively remote places at the later date already buying, and no longer making, their own bread.

Such thoughts can only be highly speculative, however. In this chapter attention
is centred on a related but different issue, namely long-lasting local differences
in diet. The bulk of people's food was grown locally, and dietary regimes were
regionally distinctive.[1]

A picture of strong local diversity fits well with the remarks by contemporaries
about regional cultural differences in general. John Barclay put it clearly in
1616: 'There is a proper spirit to every region which doth in a manner shape the
studies and manners of the inhabitants,' he proclaimed. The same assumption
lies behind the writings of John Leland, John Aubrey, Celia Fiennes and Daniel
Defoe. Indeed, it may even have been a dogma: Richard Bradley described in 1729
the trial of a man in the Weald of Kent accused of poisoning his wives because
he had buried fourteen in twenty years. He defended himself by saying that he
married women from hilly countries, and attributed their deaths to the change
of air and change of diet in the Weald. The physicians supported him, and he
was acquitted! So when investigating food history, we may not fix firmly on one
characteristic English diet before the nineteenth century, for there were many.
Climate and soils laid the first and strongest impress on local food patterns.
Natural conditions dictated which wild plants grew best, and yielded certain
foods that were free to all in that locality. Farmers learned from nature what
grew best on their land, and duly selected those crops to grow in their fields.
Finally, that produce passed into the kitchens of local people and instilled food
preferences that lasted throughout life.[2]

Regional variety is the first theme of this chapter, then, but two other themes
concern variety of another kind. Class differences have already been emphasized
many times, but they will be better illustrated here by sources from the end of
our period that shed more light than before on the labouring classes. A third
theme will broach notable differences in the diets of people living in coastal
ports, when compared with inland markets and country villages. The contrast
between food in London (the leading port in the kingdom) and elsewhere has
already been strongly argued in this book, but the recent publication of probate
inventories between 1475 and 1625 of people living in Southampton, the port
that lay on the route of all sea traffic from the Mediterranean to the Netherlands
and northern Europe, show what foreign luxuries and food flavours came the
way of Southampton's citizens long before they reached places inland. They
strengthen the suspicion already aroused by medieval evidence of food from
the Low Countries coming across the North Sea to Sandwich in Kent and so to
Canterbury, making diet in coastal areas qualitatively different from those inland.
The whole subject merits closer investigation, but at least it is introduced here.

Taking geographical differences as a first theme, it is most directly mirrored
in the types of bread eaten across the kingdom. Historians have generalized
about the preponderance of wheaten bread by the sixteenth century, but that

statement is only credible for southern and south-eastern England; elsewhere it relates to the better-off classes and not to the majority. It is certainly not a correct description of bread eaten, say, in Lancashire, where oatcakes were the rule, in parts of the Vale of York, where rye bread was common, or in the Midlands, where barley bread was most usual.

Other foodstuffs that become conspicuous in our documents in the Tudor period had plainly entered local diets because they were growing abundantly in the wild. They had found the soil and climate congenial, and had been left to grow freely in the hedgerows and on waste land. Writers described fruit growing in every hedgerow in Kent, Sussex, Herefordshire, Gloucestershire and Worcestershire, for example. These counties formed two regions that became known as specialized areas for better-quality fruits in the sixteenth and seventeenth centuries, when once a change in the scale of commerce and in food fashions took place and farmers chose to exploit their perceived natural advantages. Hops were another crop that grew wild in the Kent hedgerows, and when a cultivated variety was introduced from the Netherlands in Henry VIII's reign, they enjoyed lasting success there. Reynold Scot, who learned the skills of hop-growing in Flanders and wrote a book to help his neighbours, advised those who wished to grow only enough for family needs to take them wild from the hedgerow. He differentiated the appearance of the wild plant from the cultivated one, but did not urge one before the other when making beer. Interest in hops spread to Sussex, Essex and East Anglia, Worcestershire, Herefordshire and Gloucestershire, but Kent remained the most favoured county for centuries, accommodating until recently the Hop Marketing Board, which governed hop-growing affairs throughout the kingdom. A tradition of eating hop plants as a spring vegetable survives to this day in Kent and Herefordshire – an apt reminder of the way some characteristics of local diets survive even now.[3]

A knowledge of native plants and their most congenial habitats shines a beam of light on many local foods, singling them out from the basic ingredients eaten by everyone. Samphire, for example, once grew freely along parts of the east and south coasts of England, and it still survives in some places. It was a vegetable plant that featured prominently at a certain season in local diets in the Elizabethan period, and was sufficiently well known to become a commercial product, pickled in barrels to last for years. Shakespeare knew it, and his contemporary, Sir William Petre at Ingatestone in Essex, procured it that way. Local diets were being diversified by the commercial efforts of merchants, and so the references to samphire from around 1580 onwards may well mean that commercial sales were quickening.[4]

CORNISH DIET

Our regional recipe books are mostly of twentieth-century origin, but from the early modern period we can recover some of the hidden local story in inventories of farm and personal goods, household accounts, and reminiscences in miscellaneous books of the time. Cornwall, for example, was seen as a poor county in the sixteenth century, subsisting meagerly on its own resources, but that was an outsider's judgement and not necessarily that of its inhabitants. Much long-distance trade impinged on coastal communities as fishing fleets went out from Devon and Cornwall to Newfoundland, and victualled beforehand in those two counties. The demand for such supplies spurred local farmers to respond, and gradually shifted certain emphases in their own local diets.

In the first place, the county's long coastline guaranteed a very rich haul of fish and shellfish, yielding a long list of varieties, which made it unnecessary to store any in ponds. Pilchards came high on the list, and, though they are small and fiddly, no class despised them. The household accounts of the Reynell family in Devon show the large quantity bought for their genteel table, while Carew revealed the pressures of commercial fishing, when describing how 'drovers' trailed nets athwart the tide and caught large numbers of pilchard before they entered the havens. Fishing on that scale diminished the chances of small fishermen catching them closer inshore; so their complaints have a familiar ring. The French came to buy pilchards pickled in barrels, the Spanish and Italians bought them ready smoked. As a result of these overseas sales, pilchards, which had been the cheapest food for Cornish people, rose in price, though Carew faced this fact with equanimity, believing that plenty was left to meet all demands. Flounder, sole, and plaice followed the tide up fresh rivers, and at low water country people simply waded in to take them in their hands or catch them with a spear. No wonder Carew believed that no one, at least on the coast, needed to fear starvation.[5]

Cornish farmers bred cattle and sheep, so it was possible for the better-off to eat beef and mutton, but these meats were not the mainstay of the rest. Cows, pigs and eggs served them best. The inhabitants kept cows before all other livestock to supply the family with milk and dairy products, and farm outbuildings regularly included dairy houses. Cowkeepers with a surplus of milk sold it locally, and parsons settled for a special rate of tithe, on milk 'set out to dairy'. They also had pig houses, and pigs supplied pork and bacon. People also kept hens and quite a few geese, and whereas in other areas the documents ignored poultry, here the hens seem to have been more highly valued, for they were even counted, and in one parish geese were tithed, signifying a trade in this item. In rocky places people grazed goats, which were rarely seen in other parts of England.[6]

Cereal crops were not extensive, and although wheat-growing had increased by the 1630s, oats were an easier crop to grow, sometimes exceeding the acreage of wheat or barley, and serving for oatbread and for beer. Frequent references are made in the documents to kilnhouses, alias dryhouses, where grain and malt were dried. Carew in his lifetime observed a gradual increase in barley which caused more barley to be used in beer. The growing of hops is a hidden story in these parts, but between 1680 and 1727, somewhat late in the day, the parson at Lamorran made himself a hopgarden.[7]

A salient characteristic of Cornish diet was the importance given to herbs and fruit. It was routine for small cottages to have gardens and orchards, and some rectories increased the number of their gardens and orchards from one to three in the course of the seventeenth century. One parson's two apple gardens had some 50 trees in 1680; and as for herbs, Carew particularly drew attention to the fine flavour of some growing wild on the seacliffs, like wild hyssop, sage, marjoram and rosemary. Among greenstuff he mentioned salads and roots and had a special word for Cornwall's large quantities of samphire and 'seaholm root', otherwise known as eryngo (*Eryngium maritinum*), which was candied or kept in syrup. It is a seemingly casual reference here to something that became a highly fashionable confection shortly afterwards in London, and as the Cornish people favoured honey over sugar and kept many beehives, we may speculate on whether they had long used honey for candying eryngo and influenced the vogue that developed in London.[8]

Carew's attention to herbs and roots was a significant pointer to people's appreciation of their role in Cornish diet. Some were actually washed up on their shores, coming they knew not whence. Cornwall might be remote from London, but it was situated on a busy seaway carrying plants and people from Ireland, France, Spain, the full length of the Mediterranean, and the New World. The watchful locals plucked seeds and beans from the sea, grew them on, and the soft climate gave a home to many novelties without any trouble. New arrivals were continuously diversifying Cornwall's stock of wild herbs. It is tantalizing that no one names actual examples.[9]

Food gatherers, in addition, had golden opportunities to trap wild birds, greatly outnumbering the store from the dovecotes that some parsons were building at this time. New references to dovecotes in the glebe terriers suggest an increase in the course of the seventeenth century, but common folk could still rely on wild birds in their season. Among these, Carew named the wild quail, rail, partridge, pheasant, plover, snyte, wood dove, heathcock and powte. But above all the woodcock was the favourite, flocking in great numbers, said Carew, to the north side of the county, settling in every hedgerow, and then moving south. They could be trapped anywhere and everywhere in season.[10]

As for drink, whey was the cowkeeper's choice. But most of the water was crystal clear, and one did not need overmuch beer. On the eastern side of the county, under the influence of Devon people, cider was made, and was definitely

not despised by the gentry. It is shown in the inventory of Josias Hobbs, gentleman, of Orchard in St Stephens, near Saltash. He had 18 hogsheads of cider in
store in 1641; 50 years later, in May 1691, Nicholas Hewitt of Stoke Climsland,
status unknown, had ten hogsheads.

Andrew Boorde denigrated Cornwall's food and ale, and overall it might
well have looked like a poor country to outsiders when judged by its domestic
furnishings and poor markets for fancy goods, but its countrymen did not suffer
from a monotonous, dull diet. It included an assured supply of fish, much milk
and dairy produce, wild birds in plenty when caught on their seasonal movements
across Britain, and pigs (not just one or two in the sty but often many more).
Much greenstuff, many herbs, and wild fruit were picked in summer; garlic was a
speciality of Stratton Hundred, and was sold far away. Oatbread was commoner
than wheat bread, though strangers sniffed at it; Ralph Norden in 1607 deemed
it the bread of squatters on the commons, living 'very hardly on sour whey
and goat's milk and dwelling far from any church or chapel'. But we have seen
elsewhere how people brought up on oats preferred it to wheat, and as the main
cereal food of the Scots it was later deemed the prime explanation for their health
and vigour. In any case, the Cornish also had barley bread for variety.[11]

On the neighbouring Isles of Scilly, a parliamentary survey from the early 1650s
gives similar attention to fish and meat, showing a fishhouse on Annet Island, and,
in addition, rabbit warrens – though these lost their rabbits when the soldiery and
others ate them all during the Civil War. But sea fowl quickly learned to breed in
the rabbit burrows and gave another foodstuff; it's an ill wind that blows nobody
any good. On other islands were more warrens, sea fowl and goats.[12]

NORTH LINCOLNSHIRE DIET

In another part of the country, one of the finest accounts of local food, and
thoroughly convincing when depicting the diet of the labouring class, is Eileen
Elder's study of Lincolnshire food. It is drawn from the Parts of Lindsey in North
Lincolnshire, a district that stretches from west to east across fenland, clay vales,
limestone and chalk upland, and finishes in the marshland lapped by the North
Sea. Elder's details of diet record nineteenth-century traditions, many of which
can be shown to have gone back centuries.

Bread was a mixture of three cereals, wheat, barley and rye, and local lore
insisted on the virtue of that mixture, wheat for strength, barley for sweetness,
and rye to keep the bread moist and sound for longer. In the fens some bread was
made of peas and oats. The same cereals were used to make gruels with water,
milk or ale, and puddings were another routine filler, using flour, some fat, eggs
and milk, that could have a variety of forms and flavours. They could be savoury

with meat, vegetables and herbs, or sweet with fruit and sugar or honey, or with spices. They could be fried, steamed or boiled, and if no eggs were to hand, the flour and fat mixture was lightened with yeast; recipe books have already made us familiar with that routine.[13]

Milk lay at the base of many country labourers' diets if the family had pasturage for a cow. Sometimes in Lincolnshire pasture was allowed to labourers by their masters, or they used common grazing, which could be supplemented by the grass on roadside verges. A volume of probate inventories for one parish alone, Clee on Humberside, between 1536 and 1742, reinforces this statement through its many references to milkhouses, milk bowls, cheese vats, and butter and cheese in store. An early nineteenth-century commentator on the north Lincolnshire poor thought them living comfortably because they could keep one or two cows, 'milk being itself almost both meat and drink', and with bread 'perhaps the most wholesome diet in the world'. Better-off farming neighbours gave away buttermilk and whey to those without cows. So among Lindsey people curd cheese cake was as familiar as in East Yorkshire, and Eileen Elder gives in her book the recognizably standard recipe.[14]

Most meat for the labourer came from the family pig, the favoured Lincolnshire breed having been bred specially for hardiness and for growing quickly; it fed to a weight of 30 stone in 9–12 months. Eileen Elder dubs beef and mutton as something that was bought at most once a week from the butcher, because of the labourer's isolation and poverty. It is a perfectly reasonable generalization for that class, and Eileen Elder admits the possibility of veal as a labourer's treat at Easter when cow calving produced a surplus bull calf. We can modify the statement somewhat when considering husbandmen and yeomen in our earlier period for salting troughs were regularly listed in their probate inventories.[15]

Inventories for Clee on the Humber also show that geese was a local speciality. In other places rabbits that escaped from warrens were a wild meat, and wildfowl were evidently still plentiful in Lincolnshire even in 1872, when woodcock, snipe, peewits and more were listed in a school textbook that was used in the county, evidently assuming that children knew them well. Yet other birds were recognized in the fens, and the breasts of thrushes and blackbirds were still relished food in 1915, eaten with hard-boiled eggs and bacon, making 'as glorious a pie as man or woman could desire to taste'.[16]

Fish was another source of protein, both in coastal Lincolnshire and still abundant in the rivers in 1873, according to a Lincolnshire parson who listed many kinds, including eels; they were easily kept fresh until needed in watery captivity (in our earlier period too), while people living on the coast took crabs and cockles in plenty.[17]

Cottage gardens were highly valued for growing root and green vegetables, herbs and soft fruits. Wild plants supplemented this store in season, and every place had its local amalgam of customary flavours. One distinctive food in Lindsey was annual mercury, a leafy plant like spinach, which the herbalist, Maud Grieve, described as a troublesome weed, difficult to eradicate when once it had been introduced into gardens. But growing wild it was food for free, and Eileen Elder gives a recipe for it. Other 'weeds' eaten in Lindsey were nettles (in spring), chickweed (a green food that goes back into prehistory, and is nowadays being collected by professional foragers to supply some of London's restaurants), leaves of ground elder (a pest in my garden that I would like to remove by eating it!), and samphire, another old favourite nowadays elevated to a luxury. Among edible fungi, morels grew plentifully round Brigg and Scunthorpe, and were warmly appreciated by country folk well-schooled in knowing which fungi were which. Among fruits, gooseberries, currants and raspberries were grown in gardens, gooseberries in pies being regularly flavoured with elderflowers, or 'coddled' and eaten with bacon. Cottage gardens also usually had one or more apple trees, of which the apples were stored in lofts or dried as apple rings. Apples and crab apples made verjuice.[18]

The North Lincolnshire diet gave its own distinctive emphases to different foods. In the south of the county a native is needed to tell the full story. But I lived there briefly in 1939–40 and was struck by its many pork-based foods, like haslet and pork chap, that were unknown to a Londoner. They reflected old traditions of pig-keeping that are deeply ingrained.

LANCASHIRE DIET

The diet of Lancashire had some similarities with that of Lincolnshire and yet was different again. Everyone noticed the prominence of milky foods, Cogan remembering in particular oats put into whey. Milk troughs, cream pots, cheese and butter were prominent in the kitchen whenever appraisers compiled inventories, and quite humble householders had one or two cows. Oats were the main bread cereal; oatcake was cooked on a girdle or griddle, sometimes called a bakestone, and made a delicious gruel with milk; I too knew the delights of such gruel in my childhood. Farmers in west and south central Lancashire devoted themselves ever more purposefully to dairy farming rather than cattle breeding, and that suited the many small farmers admirably. Contemporary sightings of women milking the cows in Lancashire explain the county's success in breeding higher milk-yielding animals than any other county; the women observed milk yields closely. Admittedly, Samuel Hartlib did not give the county overmuch praise for its farming, but he did let that skill stand out, along with 'some few northern counties', giving attention to Lancashire's selection of the best milkers, unlike the rest of English cowkeepers. The dairying speciality also shines through in the noticeable level of veal eaten in Lancashire. As we have seen, veal featured prominently in the household accounts of the Shuttleworth family in the first half of the seventeenth century, spreading thereafter as a fashion in London. In Hertfordshire and Essex it drew public comment over and over again, for their dairymen delighted in finding this market for male calves.[19]

Lancashire countryfolk obviously set store by their root vegetables, for they were actually named in inventories – onions, parsnips, carrots, even potatoes in one inventory in 1640 of a vicar in Bolton-le-Sands. This is a very early reference to potatoes growing in the north, and lends support to the general proposition that clerics were significant pioneers in new-style gardening; they spread the word, along with cuttings and seeds, among their neighbours. Ducks, geese and turkeys were also conspicuous in Lancashire inventories, furnishing eggs and meat, feathers for beds, and quills for writing, while an owner of 'birdnets with cords and staves for them', worth 40s., shows us a professional wildfowler who offered birds for sale. Beehives tell of a supply of honey that reduced purchases of sugar from London.[20]

THE PENNINE DALES, NORTHUMBERLAND AND CUMBERLAND

In the north of England in the Pennine dales the inhabitants enjoyed a mixture of foods in other proportions: plenty of salmon trout, venison, oatbread as in Lancashire, honey, and milk products – milk, whey, buttermilk and cheese. We can be sure that their pottage was flavoured with wild garlic, for its green shoots in spring are abundant in the woodlands still. A Westmorland cookery book compiled by the Women's Institutes in 1937 mirrored the plentiful foods of another northern county, where people ate oatmeal in biscuits, parkin and bread, used barley flour to make scones, ate eggs very freely, favoured beef above lamb, and found a use for all their hedgerow fruits, like blackberries, damsons, elderberries and sloes, in pies and drinks. A memory of Lake Country food in 1864 illuminates the use of barley meal in making porridges that were called 'kitty slipdowns', 'serious grand things for making banging bairns', it was said, and when eaten with fresh cream considered to be 'the real luxuries of the north'.[21]

In Northumberland and Cumberland, bigg and haver were the principal cereals, bigg or bere being a primitive barley, and haver the local word for oats. Even the inventories of gentry showed little wheat growing. The bread of the cottager was likely to be oatcake cooked on a girdlestone, while those who made loaves of bigg could have cooked them under a pot on the hearth. Pigs were unusual in these two counties (and they appeared only occasionally in Lancashire, in contrast with Cornwall), but since the salting trough was called in the inventories a beef trough, we may be sure that beef was the commonest meat. Memories of people living in Northumberland in the 1890s claimed still that 'everybody had a cow', and the keep of a cow was included in servants' wages. A plentiful milk supply is betokened in the house of one gentleman, Sir Arthur Gray of Spindleton, who in 1636 had 50 cows. An absence of references to butter in store suggests that milk was used more for making cheese, and that beef suet provided the cooking fat. The probate inventory of Elinor Woddrington of Choppington in Bedlington in 1592 showed 37 goats, an unusual number, but perhaps she was renowned locally for her singular interest. Ale brewing at home was usually done with oatmalt, some people brewing in the loft, some in the backside.[22]

MIDLAND ENGLAND

A substantially different meat diet held sway in the forest country of Midland England, as, for example, in east Northamptonshire, where poachers were not much bothered by authority. Dr Moufet decided that venison was a most wholesome meat, having seen the young children of park wardens feeding on little else and remaining healthy and active. His observation carries conviction, for he himself lived in Wiltshire under the patronage of the Herberts, earls of Pembroke, so he saw their deer parks and the local people's lifestyle at close quarters. In another Midland county further west, in Cheshire, the inventories so regularly showed 'bacon, beef, butter and cheese' in store at death, that these words wrote themselves like a chant on one inventory after another. Quite a few people still made their own bread and so had a kneading trough. To fill their dripping pans, they probably relied on pig fat above all.[23]

SOUTHERN ENGLAND

Southern counties settled for yet another mix of basic foodstuffs, exploiting some fine grasslands, and a milder climate for fruit and vegetables. On the chalk downlands of Kent and Sussex local people particularly enjoyed tasty herb-flavoured mutton from their hill pastures, or fed more humbly on broth containing bits of meat from a sheep's head. Rabbits were common meat from many warrens. Wheaten bread was here the most usual, for wheat was grown in plenty, so that barley was reserved for beer or feeding livestock. In the Weald of Kent and Sussex, however, oats were a major crop and were there used to make malt, while cider was another common drink because of the fruit trees – so much so that William Lambarde was beguiled by living in the Weald himself mistakenly to call cider the chief drink of Kent. In another part of Kent, on the varied soils of Thanet and along the Thames estuary, farmers' inventories suggest a more richly varied diet than anywhere else in the county, containing much farm-fed poultry, always wheaten bread, and lovely cherries, strawberries and other fruits.[24]

Another southern county of England boasting some varied and plentiful food was Hampshire, with poultry galore – hens, capons, ducks, mallards, geese – and many hives of bees. Many pigs were almost certainly driven to the New Forest in autumn to fatten. Bacon and beef regularly hung in the roof, cheese vats and butter churns pointed to the many owners of several cows apiece (32 cheeses and 40lbs of butter in store were not unusual); many people had apples and onions in store, and they made their own verjuice. The inventories convey an impression of good eating in Hampshire, and among those living near Southampton that impression will be strengthened by evidence below of luxuries coming from France, Spain and the Mediterranean, which were landed at the port. Hampshire people, it seems, enjoyed quantity and variety.[25]

A PORT TOWN

This is the appropriate point at which to underline the array of foods available in one large port town. We have already emphasized a distinctive food style in London, which benefited so much from foreign imports. But London was not the only port to enjoy this advantage. Probate inventories, showing the possessions of Southampton people who died between 1447 and 1575, shed a bright light on the dietary delights and novel kitchenware that came their way as a result of a burgeoning sea-going trade. A remarkable number of the more substantial folk possessed distilling equipment in order to distil essential oils from plants, either as medicines or as food flavourings, or both. Their shops also sold special crockery including spice plates, both square and round; so-called 'cardinal's hats' (flat broad-brimmed dishes that we do not encounter elsewhere but that became commonplace in Southampton houses); and Venetian and French drinking glasses. Garlic mortars featured here that were totally unfamiliar elsewhere. Were they actually new on the market at this time? It is noticeable how writers of cookbooks made a point of referring to the English distaste for garlic. Two interesting stories must surely lie behind the ownership in 1564 of a 'Spanish pan' by a Dutch merchant, John Lughting, who lived in Southampton; and a silver gilt bowl, specially for fruit, weighing 25 ounces, in the house of Thomas Mill, gentleman, in 1566. Mill was plainly a connoisseur of kitchenware, owning separate cruets for oil and vinegar, a board for chopping herbs, and three stew pots with iron legs 'which have been whited with tin'. Merchants stocked many barrels of salad oil, most likely coming from Spain, all the now familiar spices (cumin, coriander, mace and ginger), along with sugar candy, Flemish treacle, rosewater (seemingly in a green Venice pot) and marmalade; would that we could know just how Southampton citizens reacted to the appearance of all these items in their midst! Comfits of many kinds were on sale, almond comfits costing 1s. 4d. a pound, clove comfits, musk comfits, and others priced at twice as much. Conserves of roses, prunes, cherries and barberries, and syrups of violets, quinces, succory and hyssop were almost certainly designed to go into medicines, but in the seventeenth century they would move on to flavour foods. We can only guess if the 9ozs of saffron valued at the large sum of 11s. was an import or home grown, and also whether the tank to water fish in, and so keep them alive until needed by the cook, was an imported foreign gimmick in 1573 or home made. Some Southampton residents were from the Channel Islands, and in several cases their house contents also hinted at some distinctive tastes, as well as a liking for their own home-made bread. But which grain did they favour?[26]

Southampton's display of fancy food items went along with luxurious furnishings in their houses, such as Venice, French and Turkey carpets, Flanders coverlets, walnut beds, tables and cupboards, and Spanish chairs. A comparable examination of probate inventories for, say, Bristol might well come close to matching this picture of high living standards in another port town, sending a trickle of influences that flowed out into gentlemen's houses locally. We cannot further explore this dimension of changing food patterns, but it could be a rich vein for researchers in the future. The port books for Sandwich in the mid-thirteenth to mid-fourteenth centuries have already shown another much more modest port town close to the Netherlands receiving cargoes that contained onions and cheeses, bunches of garlic, juniper berries, and in 1433 confectionery, needlework cushions, painted cloths and papers, for some of the local people to enjoy. Did it all go straight to Canterbury, we ask? And how were all the thousands of imported bakestones used, starting with a delivery in 1370, and bringing thousands more from 1442 onwards? They seem to have been real stones, not girdles made of iron; were they just ballast or were they as much used in Kent as in Lancashire, but for cooking pancakes rather than oatcakes? Such questions lead on to the subject of cooking methods, which cannot be allowed to divert us here. But in returning to food, one phase and fashion appeared in the early seventeenth century that brought oatcakes onto the tables of the nobility and gentry at court and in London, and may well at that date, though not earlier, have set up a demand for girdlestones as well. The accession of James I to the English throne in 1603 brought in a vogue for oatcakes, when many Scots courtiers with a firm taste for them arrived in the royal retinue. We see the signs in a special order for oatcakes 'against the coming of Lord Burghley' to Belvoir in February 1608; and the taste for oatcakes was still being readily met in London in the 1640s. We may judge this from the regular purchases of oatcakes by Rachel, Countess of Bath, when she stayed for a spell in London in 1642 and 1646.[27]

THE SOCIAL PATTERN OF DIET

While the history of food has a strong geographical dimension, it also had a social dimension which calls for a different kind of analytical subtlety. It involves some imaginative speculation, since poor folk did not write their life stories or describe their daily foods. Beyond a high level of generality, our knowledge of England's social geography is deficient, but we can start to paint in a background by examining the spatial distribution of houses and social classes, some in villages and hamlets, some in isolated places without near neighbours, and some in towns with close neighbours in the same street or the same house.

The standard village had several different classes living together, over whom a manorial lord presided from his manor house near the church. But a variant type of village had several resident squires, while yet others had no resident landowner at all, and for the most part the community was left to fend for itself; people learned to be independent. Yet another group lived in scattered places, pretty well untouched by outside influences, their lives shaped rather by their own family traditions. In towns, of course, people of all classes lived at close quarters, and could not fail to observe each other's routine of life. We observe the results in some of the sixteenth- and seventeenth-century comments about the food customs of the Dutch when they settled in streets alongside Londoners.

When we consider the diet of people living under such different conditions, we can reasonably infer some considerable differences in their food styles. It can be guessed at in one situation when a gentleman moved into a settlement where no gentleman had lived before, or at least none had lived in the recent past. Changes in people's perceptions of food and in their eating habits were bound to follow. Many examples can be found in the early modern period of gentry colonizing new districts, particularly in the forests and fens, and plainly introducing a different lifestyle and food style from that of the long-time residents. Gentlemen expected to make themselves as self-sufficient as possible, working demesne farms, creating fish ponds, building dovecotes, and renovating or creating from scratch orchards and kitchen gardens. Ben Jonson's description of the Sidney household at Penshurst depicts the scene at the highest level of perfection. But lesser gentlemen made an equally strong impression on the local landscape. A survey of the lordship of Northenden belonging to Robert Tatton (on the river Mersey, west of Stockport) depicts in March 1657 a household with its 'Hall of Withenshawe', a home farm, a banqueting house of brick, two large orchards, of which one was said to be lately planted with choice fruit trees, several gardens with many 'outlandish' fruit trees, other trees, plants, vines, flowers and, finally, herbs. Not all this was totally strange to the locals, for some tenants on the estate also had orchards and small gardens, but we can be sure that the content of the plantations and the scale of the lord's provision set different standards and a qualitatively different scene.[28]

The novelty introduced into a community where a gentleman planted himself as a newcomer is vividly depicted in the diary of Sir Arthur Throckmorton, building himself a new house in the Northamptonshire forest at Potterspury in Elizabeth's reign, intruding on a community of forest dwellers who had usually seen gentlemen at a distance hunting the deer from a royal palace or hunting lodge like Grafton. He had to have servants cultivating his orchards and kitchen gardens, and others cooking in the kitchen. His diary shows him taking a finicky interest in his food supplies, negotiating with a milller to work his mill, noting down when his goats had kids, and when six of his cabbages were stolen. He planted vines in 1611. He lent *The Book of the Onion* (a work no longer found in any library) to his neighbour, Sir Thomas Denton, and he bought for himself a copy of William Turner's *Herbal* in 1587. He also built a pond and a dovecote, though none of this has survived on the ground. A not dissimilar social whirlwind blew when Roger Townshend set up a new house at Rainham Hall in Norfolk in 1628.[29]

We can imagine the scale of the social revolution wrought by such gentlemen in many other scattered villages and hamlets. Historians have counted the rise in the number of gentry families between the sixteenth and seventeenth centuries, and although their figures are rough and ready, the orders of magnitude are startling. Michael Havinden has analysed the numbers of gentry in Somerset, showing 98 resident families in 1501–2, 168 in 1569, 377 in 1623, and probably between 415 and 460 in 1642, an increase of roughly four and a half times. In Suffolk, Gordon Blackwood has reckoned that the county had 166 families in the 1520s, 406 in 1603, and 689 in 1642, falling back to 577 in the 1670s. In some families we can perceive the personal circumstances that produced this situation. Certain gentry in the Vale of Tewkesbury in Gloucestershire, for example, managed to rear a remarkable number of sons to manhood, and most will have hankered for a landed estate. If they did not find one in a village, they settled for something more modest in a hamlet. But since they all needed servants, we have to envisage a broadening of everyone's knowledge of other food styles and some changes in diet that gradually affected the whole population. Gentlemen hired gardeners who had new skills, and brought some from abroad. Local workers in those gardens soon learned new tricks of the trade, received cuttings and seeds, grew some of the same foods themselves, and finished up having to pay tithes to the parson if they sold some of the resulting foods to their lord or to others. We can be sure that they also enjoyed some of it themselves, even though it might only be the blemished fruit or the misshapen vegetables. An exchange of knowledge and skill was in progress between the classes that made everyone familiar with new foods and tastes. In a later age, exactly the same influences were at work when women went into service for well-to-do families in the nineteeenth century, learned to cook stylishly and well and to be thrifty managers, and their grandchildren are still alive to tell us their tale. Nor was it one-way traffic. Village women working in the kitchen of the manor house passed on their kitchen routines as well as absorbing those of their mistresses. We glimpse the two-way traffic in Lady Dorset's cookbook of 1649, which cites recipes that she got from Goodwife Wells for rennet, Goodwife Rivers for liver cake, and Goodwife Cleaves for hog's cheek. These were plainly homely dishes made by homely neighbours, not recipes passed on by grand ladies. In another cookbook, entitled *The Ladies Companion*, of 1654, recipes are attributed to Mrs Medgate for broth, Mrs Hayden for a white broth, and Mrs Atkinson for a pudding for Friday; they stood alongside other recipes from ladies with titles like Lady Butler, Lady Goring and Lady Throckmorton.[30]

Gradually the diet of a whole local community would be enlarged and move towards certain conformities, without ever eliminating all the differences. We finish up with a picture that includes many local foods and dishes that were common to all classes, and that were dressed up or down according to the status and resources of different families. Curd cheese tart affords my favourite example. It makes a tasty dish with simple ingredients: fat, flour, and water for the pastry base; and milk curds for the content, made by adding rennet to the warmed milk, dripping the whey out of it through a muslin, and adding an egg. Mrs Henry Best sometimes made one for her harvest workers, to go with their bread and cheese at lunchtime as an extra treat. The ingredients were of the plainest and most ordinary kind from the farm and housewife's store, and most husbandmen's wives could have made the same dish without considering it an extravagance. Yet it was virtually a classless dish, for the great Sidney family at Penshurst ate cheese cakes at the master's table, both for dinner and supper, on 29 and 30 April 1629. Moreover, their record about supper on 9 May 1629 tells us that Mary Pilgrim supplied five cheese cakes containing currants, sugar, cloves, mace, eggs and pastry; it sounds as if she made them at home and delivered them to the great house. The same dish turns up in another work, claiming to record Mrs Oliver Cromwell's recipes, with slightly richer ingredients added. What she regarded as her 'best way' with cheese cake used some butter with the curd cheese, and some thick cream, currants, cloves, nutmeg, mace and rosewater. Socially cheese cake still ranked high, for it also featured in the recipe book of 1653 of Elizabeth Grey, Countess of Kent. She too used cream rather than milk, but did not add rosewater, and her only spice in the curd was nutmeg. But it was the same dish as Mrs Cromwell's, and it was recognizably also the farmhouse recipe, enriched with more costly extras. Present-day cooks making curd cheese tart practise similar variations, but when currants are added the tart most resembles the farmhouse version. I follow my mother-in-law's recipe and add a tablespoon of sherry, but doubtless the bakers in Beverley, Yorkshire, who sell it daily, do not.[31]

Pottage gives another example of a food that was familiar to all classes. Robert May's cookbook (1660) represented the experience of a cook for upper-class families (including the same Countess of Kent mentioned above) and it included both the simplest version and the more elaborate ones for those with money and time for extras. Many variations on a simple theme show Robert May seeking something for a change, in contrast with cooks having less time or less interest in their job, who lived with the same recipe week after week. But William Ellis's questioning of housewives (1750) showed many women devising their own slightly different styles and recipes, so that the same basic dishes varied in detail from house to house, and every meal, no matter how ordinary the ingredients, could taste different when handled by different cooks – as it does to this day. At the heart of any summary of class-based recipes we still recognize a kernel of truth in those words of that anonymous author in 1652, saying that we all eat the same food, 'the difference is only in the dressing'.[32]

LOCAL CLASS DIFFERENCES

So it is a bold author who generalizes about diets when every single person preserved individuality in the matter. Nevertheless, some class differences within the framework of local differences are not totally illusory. The well-to-do plainly expected a great deal more meat on the table than the labouring class, and chose from many more dishes. Quantities on the table were expected to be large, to express the hospitality and generosity of the family, even though individuals might eat moderately. Taking the Sidney family at Penshurst in Kent as an example, we find plenteous meat served at every dinner in the late 1620s – neats' tongues, mutton, veal, chicken, beef and rabbits all laid on for one ordinary dinner on 28 April 1629, though plainly individuals can only have sampled one or two and pecked at the rest. This meant that some food passed to the servants in the hall, and while their own planned menu for dinner already allowed for a different array – beef or pork for dinner and, for supper, cold beef, pork or mutton – it may be that some of the leftovers from the master's table added more variety still. Other luxuries served only at the lord's table were asparagus (at both dinner and supper in the month of April), while the kitchen provisions that fed others recorded fish and, as greenstuff, cabbages, lettuce, radishes and herbs. We cannot know how the spices, almonds, dried fruit, olives, oranges and lemons, and local fruits that were used to make apple pies and gooseberry tarts were divided between the classes in the household. But we note that the cook seems to have had instructions to ration the sugar carefully in 1629. However, when one of the ladies of the house went to London, comfits were on her shopping list.[33]

While class differences in diet obtruded in the great houses, it should not be thought that the sight of plenteous food was totally alien to the rest of the population; William Harrison marvelled at the sumptuous layout whenever the common folk were celebrating. At their feasting, he said, it was incredible to tell 'what meat is consumed and spent'. In addition, the conventions of the day allowed for more food and luxuries for working people at certain seasons and tasks. Considerable trouble was taken by some farmers and their wives to show appreciation for the efforts of their harvest workers and to keep them toiling cheerfully. We are given some idea of the scale of the food supplies prepared by the Spaine family of Knowlton, near Sandwich in Kent in 1629, though we do not know the number of workers involved. One week's provision included 31 cheeses, 50lbs of butter, 82lbs of beef, two flitches of bacon, honey, pears, vegetables, wheat, malt, and hops for brewing. The preparations for feeding workers on this scale began early in the year; William Ellis in Hertfordshire planned the meat supplies for harvest in the spring.[34]

RICH MEN'S DIETS

Exotic ingredients that had to be fetched from far away were, of course, a distinguishing feature of the upper classes' food provisions. Unstinting efforts were made to procure extra delicacies from great distances. Servants travelled far and wide to obtain the specialities of other regions, often provoking acid criticisms from commentators at the folly of the gentry in pursuing certain fashions at inordinate expense. The Sidneys served crab at one meal that must have made a long journey from the coast to Penshurst. The Earl of Rutland's household accounts show his steward seizing his chance at every due season to command someone to fish a river or shoot wildfowl and lay in supplies for the next weeks. When the earl went to Ireland in 1599 a great stock of spices accompanied him, presumably to make the same flavoured dishes he expected at home. When he went to the Netherlands he took a whole ox with him, leaving us wondering if he was expecting to entertain a dignitary and impress him with English meat. We have already noticed how Lord Leicester, the Chancellor of Oxford university, giving a great feast in Oxford in September 1570, had a supply of quails brought from Brill in the Bernwood forest of Buckinghamshire. Even some of the root vegetables may have come from there too, for although the carrots, parsley roots, fennel, succory and parsnip were supplied by an Oxford retailer, Michael Hearne, one of the protestations against the disafforestation of Bernwood Forest in James I's reign came from the University of Oxford, fearing the destruction of the herbs and roots there, which were described as some of its 'blessed commodities'.[35]

In other cases, the food items themselves proclaim their class association. A shopping list of provisions that ran to 2lbs of capers, a gallon of Genoa olives, a gallon of great olives and 3lbs of anchovies was plainly destined for a gentleman with refined food tastes; in fact, the order came from Sir Arthur Throckmorton at Potterspury, who was in the habit of entertaining honourable personages. Some of the same delicacies are repeated in the household accounts of Lord Howard of Naworth in Cumberland: he ordered one gallon of olives, a one pound case of nutmegs, and 6lbs of capers. Does this, by any chance, suggest that capers and olives were in high fashion at this time? It could do. If so, should we also notice that anchovies were on Throckmorton's list but not on Lord Howard's? Did that have something to do with their taste? Moufet, writing around 1600, described anchovies as originally coming from Sardinia and Provence and being barrelled in origano, salt and wine vinegar, but now, he said, they only tasted of salt and wine and were nothing like so pleasant. The remark could well pertain to events in Moufet's lifetime that affected the years when Throckmorton and Lord Howard were also dining; if fashion had set up a large demand for anchovies, it could well have encouraged the suppliers to adopt economies that spoiled them. Alternatively, this may be one of those observations that we suspect to have been inserted in 1655 by the editor, Christopher Bennet, and to relate to a date some 50 years later. Either way, it hints at the mass production of one foodstuff that resulted in deteriorating quality, an entirely credible outcome since we are all too familiar with it in our own day.[36]

COUNTRY GENTLEMEN'S DIETS

An insight into the food enjoyed by more modest country gentry is given in the household accounts of the Reynell family of Forde in south Devon. Like the Sidneys they ate lots of meat, but probably more wild birds than the Sidneys and certainly much more fish. They killed their own sheep and cattle, but also bought in some beef and mutton and sometimes a pig, though they did not often eat pork; it was very cheap by comparison with a side of mutton or a side and head of veal. They seem not to have kept hens and chickens but bought all poultry, including capons, and frequently eggs; almost certainly, local women supplied these. But their home farm must have supplied their vegetables, fruit, herbs and dairy produce, for none was bought; and they clearly made bread at home since barm was one of their purchases. When they went to Exeter, however, staying for days or weeks, carrots, turnips, onions, cabbages, salads, cucumbers and radishes, and fruit including pears, apples and plums were regular purchases. They also paid out for considerable quantities of bread on these visits, plus milk, cream and butter. They even ate oatmeal at Exeter, once with milk. Does that mean that a taste for oatmeal was instilled from childhood in all classes in Devon and Cornwall? Probate inventories show conspicuous quantities of oats growing (also rye); and general references to oats in Cornwall have recurred in this exploration of local diets. For drink they had claret at breakfast, and at other times wine and beer. Casual women knocked on their door in Exeter to sell them delectable items like salmon, but at home they had their own standard routines for getting snites, blackbirds, larks, plover, woodcocks and partridges, venison once when a red deer was brought to the house, and large quantities of sea fish – pilchards, flounders, red herrings, dory, mackerel, poorjohns (i.e. dried salted fish) in winter, and once Newfoundland fish. Their purchases of dried fruit and spices were noticeably concentrated in bulk just before Christmas, often when they themselves were in Exeter. They were conspicuous buyers at frequent intervals of mustard seed, and one recognizes in this the truth of the statement that mustard was an ancient condiment, used long before pepper took its place; it was probably grown locally. Salt was bought in bulk, and once four bushels came from Totnes; it may have been imported from La Rochelle.[37]

DIETS OF THE MIDDLING SORT

The diet of people of the middle class, town craftsmen, small merchants, and country yeomen and husbandmen is more difficult to gauge. We can assume that in all towns the variety of meats, fish, vegetables and fruit was far greater than in the neighbouring countryside because of the regular weekly markets. Some towns, sufficiently close to long-distance trade routes, could also readily obtain foreign imports, like spices, oranges and lemons. But we can also be sure, as the accounts of the Oxford feast in 1570 testify, that some close personal links were maintained between food traders and victuallers in the towns and suppliers and consumers in the immediate countryside around. A local network of food suppliers conferred certain characteristics on each district.

One cookbook of 1585 seems to depict a modest food style that would have been found among people of this class when meat was available. It was entitled *The Widowes Treasure*, and was a manuscript that came into the hands of a male author who could not resist turning it into an orderly work for publication, describing it condescendingly as a woman's collection of working recipes, 'not orderly set down as many of better skill might have done'. (I fear he would have said exactly the same of my cookery recipes!) The widow was described as a gentlewoman, and so pottage does not feature in her recipes. Medical recipes were largest among her concerns, and also many cordials, for she had flowers and spices to hand. But she was a widow, and her food recipes speak of economical procedures and ingredients. She always boiled meat; only once did she suggest baking fish, presumably by the fire if she did not have an oven. Her recipes for stewed mutton, hare, rabbit, chicken all used a cooking pot to which she added water, salt and herbs, and, in the case of mutton, carrots. Onions were not included automatically in her recipes, as they usually are with us, but for the mutton she did add some at the end. Bread was added to thicken the gravy, and often the stew was served on sops. Cooking for this widow was relatively frugal; only for rabbit did she indulge, with a stuffing of dates, sugar and cream. Her favourite vegetable was spinach, and her named herbs were our common ones such as marjoram, thyme, parsley and sage, but also hyssop, winter savory and pennyroyal. She often used cloves, mace and cinnamon, and currants and raisins in savoury dishes, but some of these items were used to dress up a modest dish of spinach with poached eggs. She baked cakes, baking the flour beforehand in a closed pot. Once mixed, she doubtless baked the cake itself in the same way, putting a domed cover over the top of a baking tray, with hot embers heaped around. It is noticeable that she never mentioned cheese in any of her cooking, and while herbs may have included greenstuff, she never mentioned cabbages, lettuces or the improved root vegetables of the time (apart from carrots). A guide to plain cooking lurks in this book without grand pretensions.[38]

Several glimpses of the food of countrymen, if not of townsmen, light up the role of the cow and the variety of dairy produce that it yielded. John Taylor, the water poet who died in 1653, visiting an old Shropshire farmer, Thomas Parr, asked him for the secret of his long life, and was told that it was green cheese, with an onion, coarse maslin bread (of wheat and rye), and for his drink milk, buttermilk, water or whey and whig (a pancake soaked in ale, whey or milk). Sometimes he drank metheglin or ale. Another recommendation for dairy produce came from Alice George, visited by John Locke when she was an old lady living in the Oxford area (she had been born in Elizabeth's reign). She described her diet to him as bread and cheese, or bread, butter and ale. A third view of the common man's diet comes from Richard Baxter in 1691. He had spent many a social hour with weavers and craftsmen in Kidderminster, and held very firm views on the healthiness of the husbandman's diet. 'Your whey and butter-milk possets is [sic] much more healthful than their [the rich man's] sack and claret; and your whey, curds, and milk, and cabbage and turnips and parsnips and flummery and such like than their venison and costly fowls and fish.' His references to their meat picked on the parts of the animal that have already featured as the ordinary housewife's economical choice. 'When you must have flesh a sheep's head of sixpence or a beef's cheek will give you a better broth and stronger nourishment than most of their costly preparations; or sheep's feet are a wholesome meat … well-made pancakes and puddings are more nutritive than quails and larks.'[39]

Within the different classes of society were occupational groups with access to certain foods that played a larger role in their diets than in those of their peers.

Some warrens at this period were rented out to farmers and were no longer a gentleman's monopoly. This meant that warreners and their friends had plenty of rabbit meat. Henry Soane of Otford, yeoman of Kent, had a stock of conies in 1688 worth £15, along with crops and livestock worth another £79 10s.; he was plainly comfortably provisioned. Park keepers had easy access to all the venison they wanted as the Revd. J. E. Linnell, vicar of Pavenham, Bedfordshire, and native of Silverstone, Northamptonshire, knew from his first-hand experience in the late eighteenth century.[40]

We remain in ignorance of labourers' foods, let alone that of the very poorest, though the well-to-do held firm opinions on what was suitable food for them, Moufet being especially outspoken. They could tolerate gross foods, because by their labour they would digest them, whereas those less physically energetic could not. So he assigned to labourers salted beef, bacon, goose (remember that goose did not become a fashionable meat until the seventeenth century), swan, saltfish, beans and peas, turnips, hard cheese, and brown and rye bread. When discussing fish, Moufet commended salt herrings to labourers, but not to refined people, whereas all classes, including the richest, evidently savoured fresh herrings.[41]

DIETS OF THE LABOURING CLASSES

We do not know how far labourers in Moufet's time obeyed his rules. But we have one golden chance to see their diet more clearly at the end of the eighteenth century. We have already noticed among physicians signs of an interest in labourers' food at the start of the eighteenth century. More public concern for their welfare built up in the following decades, as the legislation concerning poor relief bears witness. Then, in the 1790s, it inspired a remarkable investigation by Sir Frederick Eden into *The State of the Poor*, paying close attention to the food they ate. Although it carries us on some 40–50 years beyond the date at which this study of food history ends, it is still highly relevant because it dealt with the past as well as the present, and it was extremely careful to identify counties, and actual towns and villages, when citing the sources of its evidence. It amalgamates a view of local and social food patterns that focus firmly on poor folk. As we have sought high and low throughout this study, without finding more than a few crumbs of information and resorting to guesswork, it is an opportunity not to be missed.

Sir Frederick Eden was a benevolent businessman, born into a gentry family, who became a founder and later chairman of an insurance company. He was a man with an enquiring and scholarly mind. Stirred by concern for the high price of provisions in 1794 and 1795 (he was then only 27 years old) he harnessed the help of many local informants, including parsons, visited some parishes himself, and hired one researcher to tour the country for over a year with questions that he framed. We can only guess how he chose his sample parishes, and how personal were his contacts with his local informants. They obviously differed in the care that they gave to their replies: some resented the questions, others thought, with regard to workhouse diets at least, that they delved into private matters; on the other hand, in Kendal, Westmorland, a conscientious reporter gave an unusual number of personal food budgets. Somehow or other Eden secured a remarkable amount of information from varying numbers of towns or rural parishes in every county. It enabled him to describe briefly the state of the local economy, often adding a comment on the progress and effects of enclosure, enumerating standard food prices, and defining the customary diet of the district, the diet of the labouring poor, and the foods that were provided in the local workhouse. In many cases where Eden obtained sample budgets, he added his own judgements on the reliability of his informants, for their arithmetic was sometimes weak. His report, which he published in 1797, brought him lasting fame.

Eden had a strong historic sense; indeed, the title of his published results actually promised *A History of the Labouring Classes from the Conquest to the Present*. For us, its details of food patterns focus on the central theme of this book, and sufficiently separate the past from current circumstances to allow a view of long-term economic and dietary differences between regions as well as giving first-hand accounts of the meals of the poor. It lights up some dark corners in food history.

Significant features in local food regimes, as well as the composition of poor people's diets, emerge most clearly by taking the different items of food in their local setting, separating town experience from rural, the pastoral from the arable regions, and both from the coastal areas. Some factors to which we do not normally pay heed will be shown to have played a considerable role, if only temporarily, in determining family diets. Obviously, it was the locally grown produce over centuries of time that shaped local tastes, but so did people's varying access to foods traded in markets. The differences in diet between a town and its surrounding rural parishes were especially underlined by one informant writing about Carlisle in Cumberland. It had an industrial population and busy markets, and he noted how 'the diet of these people is very different from that in the surrounding countryside'. Townsfolk drank tea and ate butcher's meat, while country folk ate hasty pudding, butter, milk and potatoes, plainly having good access to dairy products which townsfolk did not.[42]

With regard to bread we can identify several different clusters of custom and prejudice. If we ask first how usual it was for women still to bake their own bread, then we do not get a clear answer, for Eden had no interest in that matter, and made no deliberate reference to it; we have to rely on our own inferences. We can do this by noticing the places where the weekly cost of bread in budgets was given in loaves, rather than in the price of a stone of flour. The absence of a loaf price was noticeable in the case of a spectacle maker in Wolverhampton, Staffordshire, for example. His wife was said to use about 14lbs of flour a week to feed their family of four children; plainly, their bread was being baked at home, so we can imagine their distress when in August 1795 they had to pay 5s. for a stone of flour compared with the previous year's price of 2s. 3d. In contrast, the weekly purchase by a gardener's wife in Epsom, Surrey, was given in quartern loaves, thirteen of them, telling us of a lady who did not bake her own bread. We finish up reasonably guessing that farmers' wives in rural areas baked their own bread regularly; so did many labouring people, but certainly not all. Reporters said that most did – it was said of Herefordshire labourers, for example – but that was contradicted by much of the evidence from budgets. In populous towns all classes had bakers near at hand, and the price of fuel, local custom and personal preferences mixed several factors in the final choice. In one family home bread-baking was said to have stopped because of the current high price of fuel, and since more than one informant commented on the many family meals that consisted largely of cold food, especially bread and cheese, the implied importance of fuel costs has to be taken seriously; the occasions for eating hot food were limited, and in some homes depended on a local baker cooking it in his oven, especially on Sunday. We can reasonably guess that fuel constraints on home baking were stronger in towns, without access to woodland or peat beds, than in the countryside, while in villages local differences in bread-making habits could depend on the presence, or not, of a baker. Did every village have one? We cannot be sure in all cases and at all times. Routines did exist among neighbours of bread-making using a communal oven, and they feature in the local history of many Continental countries: indeed, ovens in gardens still survive in many villages in southern Spain, for example. But in our English documents such routines leave hardly a trace.[43]

As for the dominant cereal used in bread, historians have been inclined to assume that by 1750 wheat was the dominant cereal. That seems to have been the case in the Home Counties but not by any means everywhere else. In Surrey, the usual labourer's diet in Reigate was said to be wheaten bread, almost always in Sussex, in Kent, and in Hertfordshire. Kent bakers around Ashford had gone one stage further and stopped using unsifted flour, and this had allowed a prejudice to become entrenched that brown bread disordered the bowels! As a result, the farmers' wives around Ashford, who were still in the habit of baking their bread from unsifted flour, using it exactly as it came from the mill, were plainly thought to be living in the backwoods. Our Kent informant dated the switch to fine sifted flour only to the last 20 years, however, the local sense of opulence going back evidently to the mid-1770s but not earlier. A custom of eating none but fine wheaten bread seems to have taken hold a good deal earlier in Ealing, Middlesex, for when prices rose high in the late 1790s the local officials intervened to give help to distressed families by arranging for bakers to make a browner bread specially for them, using flour without sifting out the bran. The measure was ungraciously received. People found it so coarse and unpalatable that they rejected it, and opted to pay one-third more for a white loaf. Another very strong wheat-eating area was Norfolk, not surprisingly since it lay in the supremely fertile arable quarter of the kingdom; wheaten bread there was said to be universal.[44]

One significant change in the general economic conditions under which people got their cereals ground at the mill found a place in Eden's survey, and his explanation was exactly repeated by David Davies, in a pamphlet published in 1795. Davies's work was entitled *The Case of Labourers in Husbandry Stated and Considered*; it regretted the fact that householders could no longer buy small quantities of cereal for domestic use from their local miller. The Eden report, from Herefordshire, explained the circumstances: the labouring class 'usually bake their own bread', but now they had difficulty in getting small quantities of whatever cereal they liked best from the farmer, for millers and mealmen reckoned to deal in large quantities and expected consumers to pay them something more than the miller's charge to give them as much profit as they had from the wholesalers. The personal relationship that had once existed between farmer and labourer, and between local miller and labourer, had gone: wholesalers, mealmen and shopkeepers now occupied places in a chain of dealers, each of whom took their cut from the final purchaser. It was a situation with which we are only too familiar in commercial developments in our own day, and it is more than likely that Frederick Eden and David Davies personally exchanged sympathetic views with each other on this score. In the end, of course, we have to recognize how these same commercial trends obliged the public to settle for bread wholly made from one cereal, thereby losing all appreciation for the taste of the other single or mixed cereals that housewives had taken for granted in the past. We have recently been reminded of what we have lost by a rising taste in the 1990s and 2000s for sourdough and rye breads.[45]

Rye bread was the commonest kind eaten in Northumberland, and pitmen in Newcastle bought their rye cheaply from their masters, according to Eden's reports, though, when boiling one of their favourite dishes of gruel, whether crowdie or hasty pudding, the cooks in the workhouses, at least, used wheat. In Durham and some Midland counties including Shropshire (at Ellesmere), wheat mixed with rye was a favoured bread. But rye was plainly the least-used cereal, surviving only in small pockets of the country.[46]

As for barley bread, once the commonest bread of the peasantry, it is surprising how rarely it was now mentioned. Only in Cumberland and Cornwall was it still the bread of the peasantry. In Cumberland, it made an unleavened or leavened cake rather than a loaf, half an inch thick, 12 inches in diameter, and it lasted 4–5 weeks in winter and 2–3 in summer. Plainly this was a bread that had to be softened by being dipped into soups, but a discriminating taste is implied by the various thicknesses of cake that were given different names. The local reporter gave the cheapness of fuel as part of the explanation for people's preference for it in Cumberland, but the explanation was indirect. People liked hot soups and a hard bread went well when dipped in the soup. The liking for barley was further strengthened by the view that it was extremely nutritious. Elsewhere barley in bread featured unexpectedly. We can infer from the budget of a widow living at Seend, near Melksham, Wiltshire, that she baked barley bread simply because she liked it. It was the usual diet of working people in Great Driffield in Yorkshire, but no explanation was suggested for that idiosyncrasy. Mixtures with barley were favoured in other places: in Empingham, Rutland, labourers' bread was made of wheat and barley; in Nottinghamshire opulent farmers liked a mixture of wheat, rye and barley, but it was firmly rejected by their labourers. An attempt in Westmorland to introduce it in place of oatcake when oatmeal prices soared failed miserably. When once oat prices fell somewhat, people returned to their old favourite. Local tastes were set in a mould and did not easily change, so in many cases we can only explain them as conservative survivals from the past. We can, however, offer some observations in defence of barley that may in part explain its local use. It had a sweet taste that was liked. It was an unusually versatile, multi-purpose cereal, so that where it grew well it had the strong virtue of serving many uses: it made beer and fed livestock, it made a tasty gruel, known as frumenty, and made enjoyable broth and barley milk. However, when once commercial trends drove men towards one cereal only, it could not prevail for ever against wheat. In the 1790s farmers regarded wheat as much the most profitable crop at the market, and if the local environment and agricultural improvements favoured wheat-growing, barley took second place. A once wider choice of cereals for bread was being hemmed in by economic considerations. Moreover, barley does make a denser loaf, and since labouring people were now eating so much cheese as the main protein for dinner, it is not surprising that they preferred it encased in a softer bread.[47]

Oatbread, or rather oatcake, remained a great favourite in the north of England. William Ellis, the Chiltern farmer, had remarked on the Lancashire men's strong attachment to oatcake when he was writing in 1750, and the same sentiments were echoed in other reports from Lancashire and Westmorland. The liking for oatcake extended further, into parts of Yorkshire, and also into parts of Derbyshire; and since it made lovely gruel as well – crowdie and hasty pudding were favourite supper and breakfast dishes – great quantities were bought in labouring families. A Kendal family with six children at home used 150 stone of oatmeal a year. That meant handling some 46lbs a week (counting 16lbs to a stone, though it may have been 14lbs), so the cook who made oatcake must have been grateful to have a less tough physical task in making the mixture than the maker of a bread dough.[48]

Dairy foods tell a story of other constraints on labouring diets, and are of particular interest when focusing on the distinctiveness of regions. We have traced a minor revolution in commercial dairying between 1500 and 1750, and it had an intricate local history. Eden's account in the 1790s showed that there were still parishes in the countryside where people were able to keep a cow or two for their domestic needs. Miners at Stanhope in Durham, for example, kept a family cow. In Bury, Lancashire, labourers took small lots of land as farms to keep a cow or two. At Empingham in Rutland, cottagers had land to keep a cow or pig, and in Louth, Lincolnshire, the small man's keeping of cows in summer and winter was taken for granted. At Hothfield in Kent, a common allowed the poor to keep a cow, and it was then blamed for attracting poor people into the parish. This was not perhaps surprising since Kent did not have much interest in dairying, and so milk was generally scarce in the county. Indeed, one bold reporter generalized about the whole south of England, saying that cowkeeping was not usual anywhere because grassland was too expensive. Where it did survive, in short, the facility was explained by the presence of extensive commons, or a local tradition allowing labourers to lease small pieces of land cheaply. At the same time several stronger economic trends in the commercialization of dairying narrowed the chances for country people who did not have a cow to obtain dairy produce. In time long past there had been no such difficulty, for dairy produce had been dubbed the food of the poor, and was disdained by the rich. Farmers who made butter and cheese had no use for curds or whey and gave it away. But by the 1790s dairy produce had moved up in the world socially, and become a desirable food in upper-class circles. A discerning appreciation of distinctive local cheeses spurred the ambitions of small dairy farmers who in the past had catered only for local customers; now they set their sights on distant markets, some even overseas. Butter was used ever more lavishly in sauces and as a sealant to exclude air in cooked pies containing fish and meat. Finally, the public perception of dairying as a commercial business changed attitudes to everything connected with it, spawning cheesemongers, many grand wholesalers, and parliamentary legislation to control them.[49]

In the north of England the strong liking for whey, buttermilk, skim milk, or milk and water, as drinks, persisted among the poor, harking back to a former age when dairy foods were generally acknowledged to be their food. But Eden's survey referred to many parishes where now very little milk was available for sale. What did that mean? The explanation in some cases lay in its being fed to calves for making veal; this was the reason given for the scarcity of milk in Gloucestershire, and we can guess that the same applied throughout the specialist veal-producing areas in Essex and Hertfordshire. Alternatively, farmers concentrated on making butter and cheese, and apart from again having no milk for sale in consequence, they greatly valued their curds and whey for feeding their pigs. Fattening pigs had become another substantial commercial pursuit.[50]

The price of milk in towns ran high. In Ellesmere in Shropshire, in an expanding dairying region, very little milk was sold, and when it was, it was not inordinately dear, being 1d. a quart. But in London we gasp to read that it cost three and a half times as much, threepence halfpenny a quart. In consequence, in many places labourers drank no milk at all or almost none. This was said of Kibworth Beauchamp in Leicestershire, also of people in the Weald of Kent, and of one family in Portsmouth. Since labouring families, or at least the women and children, were mostly addicted to tea by now, they drank it without milk.[51]

The account of butter- and cheese-eating gave no sign of these foods being made in the homes of labourers, and indeed little sign of much butter being used at all. It probably meant that whatever fat was saved came from meat, especially the pig, and sometimes the poor bought fat in shops, for servants collected it from the kitchens of big houses where they worked and sold it on. The rise in butter consumption was led by the middle and upper classes. Cheese, however, played a large part in working people's daily meals, and in workhouses it was one of the staple foods on days when no meat was served. Almost always it was bought in (though some workhouses did keep cows), but while some commentators thought it an expensive item in working family's budgets – it was clearly costly in Cobham, Kent, which was said to pay prices that followed the London markets and resulted in cheese costing 5d. to 8d. a pound – it was nevertheless regarded as a convenient food that had to be afforded. Fourpence a pound was cited as the price of common cheese in Devon and that meant that it was less expensive than meat, and used no fuel in preparation in the kitchen. Many working families ate a daily diet of bread and cheese and only tasted meat on Sunday.[52]

Workhouse rations of cheese varied greatly: in Wirksworth, Derbyshire, no cheese was allowed except at Christmas, but this was exceptional and may reflect some odd prejudice of the warden. In most places rations were not ungenerous, allowing anything between 3ozs and 8ozs a day. Such quantities strongly suggest that cheese played a far larger role in labourers' diets than in those of the middling sort, and if a bold generalization has any meaning in this context, then the greatest demand for common cheese came from working people in the south rather than the north.[53]

A varied picture of meat-eating by working people has emerged from this study, moderating the more sweeping generalities of historians that allow for hardly any meat at their tables. Geographical situation and local farming specialities made a lot of difference in determining whether meat was cheap and relatively plentiful, or scarce and dear. One document discussed more fully below asserted more precisely in 1770 that butchers' meat bought for the poor in Leeds cost one-third of the price prevailing in London. None of Eden's reporters referred to the labouring poor catching rabbits, hares or wildfowl in season, even though we know that in all ages there have been, and still are, families making the most of such opportunities. The silence of commentators on this subject can only be explained as a convention, or due to pure ignorance, for at the same period parsons and gamekeepers told stirring stories of another lifestyle among those enjoying food for free.

Eden's informants dwelt on the relative prices of beef, mutton, veal and bacon, and showed how regionally varied they were. Beef and mutton ranged between 3d. and 6d. a pound; in some places veal was cheaper than beef and mutton, in others more expensive. Pork prices were often not given at all, on the assumption, as a few reporters confirmed, that labourers kept pigs at home. Bacon was always considerably dearer than any raw meat, at 8d. to 10d. a pound, and very occasionally pickled pork was mentioned as labourers' food, costing much the same as bacon. In one well-managed workhouse, and one only, at Petersfield, Hampshire, inmates ate pickled pork on three days a week, but the price quoted at Reigate of 9½d a pound and the rarity of other references to it suggest that this innovation of the early eighteenth century, while representing a considerable economy in the handling of meat, was not yet economical enough for the poor to benefit.[54]

Meat-eating in labourers' own homes varied between two extremes. Miners in Newcastle ate meat three or four days a week. In Ashford, Kent, it was boldly stated that the poor in most of the county had eaten meat daily in the mid-1780s, but hard times had stopped that unless they went into the poorhouse. All workhouse reports suggested that the poor ate more meat as inmates than they would at home, and that was the impression of those who made explicit comparisons. Inmates had meat for dinner on three or four days a week and quite often every day. The quantities were generous, ranging from 6ozs to 8ozs per person, and sometimes no rationing at all was imposed, allowing inmates as much as they could eat.[55]

Patchy references to 'garden stuff' leave many doubts about the quantity of vegetables in labouring diets. It was not mentioned as a universal food, as was bread, and in the workhouse at Ashby de la Zouch, Leicestershire, potatoes and vegetables were treated as a substitute for bread when bread prices were high. Only in certain counties, like Hampshire and Herefordshire, were vegetables named as a regular accompaniment to meat. In other cases one is left in doubt as to whether they were silently taken for granted or not. Roots, cabbages, peas and beans were the vegetables most frequently mentioned, and some hint of a prejudice against greenstuff seems to lie behind a reference at Empingham in Rutland to labourers 'beginning' to use vegetables very generally, and learning very fast to discard prejudices in favour of other diets. We may suspect the influence of a benevolent gentry family at work in that village: the Heathcotes ruled there, and allowed cottagers to have land to keep a cow or fatten a pig; in the workhouse, moreover, the poor were said to have 'good eating'. Other workhouses had good gardens attached which supplied the kitchens. These examples hint at a deliberate effort in some places to increase the eating of greenstuff by the poor. That same opportunity might seem to be implied in the report on Ealing, Middlesex, where market gardens were said to number 250, and Eden's informer went out of his way to describe the women, mostly Welsh, carrying heavy baskets of fruit from Ealing or Brentford to Covent Garden, sometimes covering the nine miles twice a day. Yet the report on the workhouse diet in that neighbourhood made no reference to vegetables or fruit. Indeed, apart from an occasional apple pie, no workhouse anywhere seemed to serve fruit at all.[56]

Among vegetables, potatoes stood out from all others in sparking the interest and comments of reporters. Both growing and eating potatoes were far more prominent in the north of England than in the south. They were mentioned in budgets in the south, but no strong appetite for them was evident except in scattered places: very few were sold in Bedfordshire, for example; they were very seldom grown or used in Streatley, Berkshire. The patchy picture tallies with the impression drawn in East Sussex by the diary of Thomas Turner, the shopkeeper, covering the years between 1754 and 1765. Potatoes were familiar to him but were only occasionally eaten. On the other hand, the reporter from Cobham in East Kent thought them 'a principal diet in large families', and we may suspect this to have been true in parts of Essex near to London. Far away in Cornwall, around Penzance, they also received much attention, though the phraseology of the local report suggests that potato-growing was a more serious, commercial operation selling in distant markets, since two crops a year were gathered; it did not necessarily allow local families to eat many. Northerners, in contrast, ate potatoes in great quantity, had many different ways of cooking them, and were thought to like them because they also had plenty of fuel for cooking them. They were described as 'a very general article for dinner' in Kendal, Westmorland, 'the chief diet of labourers' families' in Tanfield, Durham, and in Cumberland they were 'the principal part of a labourer's diet' along with oats.[57]

Finally, among this array of general observations on local differences, it is salutary to be given some hard evidence of price variations. They were so considerable in one case that they surprised the investigator, and must have made a great difference to the quality of workhouse diets from place to place. A revealing document on this score lies among Arthur Young's correspondence, clearly marked as being 'private not for publication'. The document is undated and does not divulge the name of the writer, but he was writing from London. It was addressed to a Mr Smart and told him to allow Mr Young to use it. It described the writer's visit to a workhouse in London when food was in preparation. The sick had flesh meat on three days a week, peas soup on one day, and cheese and bread on the other three days. The visitor was present on a cheese day, and the Dutch cheese looked good. Each person in the workhouse cost 3s. 4d. per week in food, and he considered that that figure represented very good management when considering prices thereabouts. But he had been in Leeds in 1770, where food costs were exactly half – 1s. 8d. per person per week – and butchers' meat was little more than one-third the price of London; to that he added the remark that in Leeds they also ate a lot of oatcake. In Liverpool in 1776 he had seen the food of the poor costing even less, 1s. 6d. per week, and there the governor 'bought immense quantities of potatoes at extreme low price, that root abounding in the neighbourhood and of the best quality in England, it was said'. Obviously, workhouse conditions varied greatly between regions.[58]

Certain basic items in diet that prompted little comment call for a moment of reflection. Almost no reference was made to eggs. They were given a price of a halfpenny each at Chesterfield in Derbyshire, and in Kendal six cost only 2d. But that was all that was said of them. Of poor people's access to grassland only once was reference made to a commons, in Hothfield in Kent, where the poor could keep a cow or poultry, and that was blamed for attracting the poor from afar. Poultry were ignored, but that may have been an old convention; compilers of probate inventories scarcely gave them a look when valuing property. Yet it leaves us guessing how many labourers in towns and country still kept hens. Fish also were cursorily mentioned as being abundant and cheap all round the coast; in Workington in Cumberland, cod in season only cost a halfpenny a pound! But no one added further details, nor was any clue given to the value that local people attached to their river fish.[59]

One item in diet that was common was pudding, clearly a filling ingredient in labouring families, and on some days for children it served as a main food. It often consisted of dumplings in a stew or else was pudding dough encasing meat and vegetables. Occasionally in the workhouse a pudding was served sweet with a sauce or treacle. One would be inclined to guess that puddings were a working-class rather than a middle-class food, since their ingredients were few and cheap, and they cooked happily on the hearth without a lot of supervision. Yet it is surprising how many cookbooks gave recipes for dumplings. They were everybody's satisfying way of making meat go further, though the middle-class cook might well spend more time on making a stuffing, which looked different but served the same purpose.[60]

For drink, habits were regionally varied and surely class-biased as well, since wine was out of reach of labourers, and even beer was sometimes deemed expensive. Northerners still drank a lot of milk, in the form of whey, buttermilk, skim milk or milk and water, all of which sold cheaply when compared with whole milk; and they were staunchly loyal to milky gruels with oats. In the south people had become addicted to tea, and the habit was strong among the middle as well as the labouring classes. The East Sussex shopkeeper, Thomas Turner, followed a regular routine of tea-drinking in mid-afternoon, while Eden's survey and workhouse rules showed the prevalence of tea-drinking among women and children, even when milk was scarce and they drank tea without it. One reporter judged that everyone drank tea in 'astounding quantities', though this did not mean the absence of all prejudice in the north, judging by the lady living in Cumwhitton, Cumberland, who had never in her whole life had a teapot in the house![61]

A. G. L. Rogers, who summarized Eden's survey, concluded that beer-brewing at home was still being done on a considerable scale, and judging by other evidence that seems to be a valid generalization. But viewing things more closely, local reporters saw it as a dying practice, and that was surely equally true. Like cider-making and cider-drinking in Somerset, practices that received only one reference in Eden's report, they were sustained by local loyalties, whereas investigators seem to have been blind to them. A tide of uniformity was gently washing away at the edges of such regional distinctions.[62]

In summary, the most striking differences in diet remarked by reporters in the 1790s separated the north from the south, and said little about east and west. The contrasts were attributable to many different factors working together, notably climate, crops, animal husbandry, and local customs that had become established over many generations. Hot meals were most welcome in the north and they required a liquid to wash them down, so soups and pottage (though it was rarely called pottage by this date) reigned supreme on the table. Rogers summed up the southern diet as showing an insuperable aversion to broths and barley meal soups, citing an outcry against 'washy stuff that affords no nourishment'; 'we will not be fed on meal and chopped potatoes like hogs' was cited as the exact words of the poor. We can readily credit a remark like that coming from a Londoner who had watched rich men eating in the taverns; and the sentiment might well be picked up and spread fast among an unthinking multitude who had lost contact with country life.[63]

Reporters mostly observed more economical housekeeping in the countryside than in the towns, and that was not surprising since urban amenities had enticed town dwellers to do more shopping and less cooking, and these influences as yet touched fewer country folk. The editor of Eden's report in 1928 also underlined this final verdict, after laboriously summarizing the parochial reports on labourers' diet for a new generation of readers. He phrased his explanation differently, and was fully sympathetic to labourers' aspirations for a better life. But he could not accept that the southern labourers' monotonous diet of dry bread and cheese was wholly due to their scant income; rather, he suggested, it was due to ignorance, custom and prejudice. The historian with a longer and broader view of economic change would certainly include those factors in the explanation. But others have to be added. One may be inferred from comments on the more diversified food of the north when compared with the south, even though the southern labourer enjoyed a higher cash income. It is summed up in the description of a standard soup in Northumberland and Cumberland: the reporter started the list of ingredients with meat, oatmeal and barley, and finished with potherbs, onions, chives, parsley, thyme etc., finally adding potatoes. The countryman still drew on the fields for many varied flavours without incurring any expense. Eden's reporters did not make any specific comparisons between town and country lifestyles. They did not seem to reflect on it at all, perhaps being so certain of other merits in town life that they did not see the losses alongside the gains. In the different climate of opinion prevailing some two hundred years later, we have to posit the town dweller's loss of much free food, the loss of country lore by which free food increased the nourishment of daily meals, and almost certainly the loss of the larger meat rations that were customary in country places. Wild meat was seasonally plentiful everywhere, and livestock-keeping and neighbourliness in village life was always at hand, yielding many offcuts of meat informally from the village slaughterhouse to feed the poor. Some of the parish reports on meat in diet named bullocks' or sheep's heads, and bullocks' cheek. They remind us of the food routines that are so well attested in earlier documents, ingeniously using every scrap of meat from carcasses. The poor could often get pieces of meat cheaply or were given them free in villages where they were known as neighbours. Amid much larger numbers in towns, the poor would have been turned away from town butchers, as old traditions of generosity slowly died.[64]

CONCLUSION

In a chapter that has feasted on a varied amalgam of food prevailing in different regions and classes, a few crisp generalities in conclusion do not carry conviction. But one observation must surely hold attention, insisting on the many different patterns of diet that contented those who were accustomed to them, even while they might provoke criticism or distaste from those who viewed them from the outside and were not already trained to appreciate them. Our judgements should not settle for agreement with the adverse critics while dismissing those who expressed satisfaction with the local diet. Taste preferences are undoubtedly established by long usage, as our many modern-day travellers are learning by experience. We have to resist the notion that the food of the past was dull and monotonous for all but the rich. Every class and every region relished its own seasonal calendar of foods, and every class showed ingenuity and resourcefulness in making the best of what lay to hand. Moreover, when we choose the word 'class' to differentiate food styles and particular dishes, we should be more specific and see the people doing the cooking: in other words, men in the large kitchens of the rich, and women everywhere in the kitchens of the rest, the majority of them representing the middling and labouring sort. Improvisation was to them second nature, for mouths somehow had to be fed daily. A memorable picture of this resourcefulness was given to Sir Frederick Eden by a friend calling on a Scottish woman in her highland cottage in Lochaber. To feed an unexpected visitor, and while her kale pot was already boiling, she rushed out to her croft, cut down some barley, thrashed and winnowed it by throwing it into the wind, and ground it in a hand quern; some she used to thicken the kale soup, the rest she made into bannocks, baking them by laying them upright against a stone next to the fire. 'Thus in less than half an hour, an excellent repast was smoking on the table', he said. Note the use of the word 'excellent'; the scene comes vividly to life before our eyes.[65]

Scottish people have been more eloquent than the English in proclaiming their pleasure in their local diets, and for illustration of this we can turn to *Granny's Cookbook*, published by the Tay Valley Family History Society in 1994, in which present-day residents recalled their grandmothers' recipes. Carragheen pudding was one, a favoured sweet course using carragheen moss (a seaweed collected from the edge of the sea), and soaked overnight in water, to which one pint of milk was added warm in the morning; it was then strained, flavoured with cocoa or chocolate and possibly coloured. They described a recipe for potato scones as 'mouth-watering', after a hard day working in the jute mill, yet it was simply and quickly prepared, and economical in cost. They recorded one proud memory of a Scottish lady who made a new life in Canada, but 'never let the family forget their Scottish heritage'.[66]

Pride in the distinctiveness of local foods is best illustrated in England in the cookery books that have been produced by the Women's Institutes, some precious ones dating from the 1930s. A series of county cookbooks, edited by Pippa Gomar, also recently picked out the same theme. The series was most successful in defining some of the salient features of food in the counties, like Gloucestershire's elvers, fished along the Severn and celebrated at eating contests in April and May; its lampreys, which the local abbots sent to London for Henry VIII; the whortleberries and crowberries of Herefordshire that make delicious puddings; and the sorrel soup of West Herefordshire, exploiting a plant that yields bounteously on the acid soils of its meadows. Worcestershire boasted its Pershore plums for a sweet/sour sauce, and Wiltshire its graylings from the rivers Avon and Kennet, and its 'souse' for pickling the belly of its famous pigs.[67]

Our judgement on food has to accommodate innumerable local traditions, acknowledging that they were variously experienced by different classes of people. Eliza Melroe, with his deep interest in local food traditions, aptly summed up this rich regional variety: 'the bulk of the English', he said, 'are not all of one nation or under the same laws and government'. In other words, one should not attempt to write just one history of English food.[68]

9

A Closer Look at Some Foods

The study of food thus far has examined it over 50-year periods, and in each phase has uncovered significant changes in the demand and supply of some items and in the quality and quantity that became available as the market responded. Such changes are to be expected in the course of 260 years, though, in food history, it has not so far been usual to track them over such short phases. Our own experience in the last 70 or 80 years, however, has clearly demonstrated how conspicuous such changes could be in one lifetime. We have seen the consumption, quality and flavour of our milk, for example, transformed out of all recognition in that time. Our bread has passed through several phases to satisfy changing tastes, first favouring brown rather than white bread when Hovis bread became a favourite, then favouring white bread cooked in a rectangular shape and sliced to make sandwiches, so displacing all cottage-shaped loaves, and now exalting a multitude of Italian breads containing various flours and other ingredients such as tomatoes. As for our meat, we have seen beef, mutton and pork making room for poultry; we have lost rabbit almost entirely; we may gradually eat more venison. We rarely see liver, hearts or kidneys for sale, and we cannot any longer buy bones for broth. Among vegetables, I never tasted nor heard of sorrel or rocket in my youth, and today's sprouts and broccoli look quite different from those sold in the 1920s and 1930s; white turnips do not have the taste that I remember from the past, and the same can be said of small, so-called new potatoes, now available all the year round. Among fruits our strawberries are larger than of old and enjoy a much longer season, and varieties of apples in the shops are quite different from those of yore. The cheese counter at one time made a little room for French cheeses, but now finds space for many more as well as English kinds, some of which revive old traditions, while some are quite adventurously new.

Admittedly in the twenty-first century we live in an age of greatly accelerating change, and things move much faster than they did between 1500 and 1760. Yet our study has shown foods undergoing similar changes, though they developed more slowly, representing distinct phases, fads, and fashions that have been more realistically measured over periods of fifty rather than ten or five years. In the following pages the course of change is summarized with respect to individual foods, in order to give a sharper outline to the chronology, and in the hope that food historians in the future will be sufficiently intrigued by some of the puzzles to explore in further detail. We may also persuade some cooks to recover some of the foods and flavours that we have lost, for we live in an age that is interested in alternatives, and our forebears give us much food for thought.

BREAD

We have become familiar in this study with different regional food regimes, and the differences are especially pronounced with regard to bread. The notion that refined white bread was the most desirable goes back a long way, and is well illustrated in the will of Peter Fromond, inhabiting my parish of Hadlow (in a far from affluent period and part of the Weald of Kent), and contemplating death in 1462. He bequeathed two bushels of wheat to be distributed to the poor on the day of his burial, and it was for making into *white* bread; by the sixteenth century, white bread featured so prominently in London that historians have often claimed that it was by then the commonest bread in the kingdom. Such, however, is a fanciful exaggeration. Londoners lived in their own distinctive food world that was unknown elsewhere. It had bakers galore, as well as cookshops and food stalls that reckoned to offer food to travellers at all hours of the day, and probably at night as well. It had a food regime that was poles apart from that of people in, say, Cornwall, Nottinghamshire or Cumberland.[1]

The way contemporaries looked at their bread is a novel experience for us who are accustomed to conformist standards. People obviously expected every piece of bread in their hands to taste differently, and so they scrutinized it critically. This is strikingly brought home in the conversations put together by Juan Vives in *The Dialogues*, published in Basle in 1538 as exercises in the Latin language. Vives was a humanist scholar, originally from Spain, who spent time in England, Scotland and France, and set up a school in Bruges. His pupils were given these dialogues to translate into Latin, and their subject matter concerned domestic, everyday scenes. A visitor, Simonides, sitting down to a meal, immediately commented to his host on the fine white bread: it weighed less than a sponge, he said; the flour was well sifted, and he decided that his host must have a good miller; 'why don't you put him in the bakehouse?', he asked. Polemon joined in but criticized the spongy bread for having too much water in it; and he liked it kneaded more. Criton liked the bread spongy so long as it was not cooked too quickly; but this bread had bubbled in the baking (did he mean that it was full of holes?), and that happened, he thought, because it was baked on the hearth. But this bread was baked in the oven, they told him. Polemon thought this household bread bitter and acid, for which Escopas blamed the workers who mixed chaff with the wheat and added other cereals as well. Acidity in the bread came from too much yeast, he claimed, whereas Criton believed that this bread had little yeast in it. Simonides asked for common bread, made of rye, and explained that then he ate less for the bread did not taste so good. What a range of opinions was revealed by this conversation! But it showed how varied, for a host of different reasons, could be the quality of bread, making everyone hypercritical in a way that is unfamiliar to us. In another scene in the schoolroom, a pupil explained that they always ate for breakfast bread of unsifted flour (i.e. containing more bran), and pupils were ordered to bring out their knives and clean the crust of any coal or cinders. The expectation that coal or cinders would be in the crust almost certainly explains an eighteenth-century recipe which puzzled the cookery writer, Elisabeth Ayrton. She found directions to rasp the crust all over with a knife when cooked, and thought that perhaps people did not like a crisp crust. More likely they were removing the specks of ash.[2]

These dialogues show people's familiarity with the details of bread-making, and lead us on to the aspects that were undergoing change in the course of our period. Cereals offered a choice between wheat, rye, barley and oats, and we have already drawn attention to the use of all four, each on their own, or in varied mixtures that were favoured according to class and region. In the Middle Ages barley bread was commonest among ordinary folk and wheat among the well-to-do. But in some areas barley bread remained for far longer the first in favour. In 1694, for example, John Houghton reported that the mill at Wycombe in Buckinghamshire ground 17 quarters of corn per week, of which 16 were barley. Rye bread was singular in the Vale of York and a few other scattered places, and was appreciated for keeping moist for two to three weeks. But more often rye was used in a mixture with wheat. Oats was the most favoured cereal in the north and in some other districts of England, including the south-west and Wales, and even in 1758 it was estimated that nearly 40 per cent of the inhabitants of Cheshire, Derbyshire, Nottinghamshire, Lincolnshire and Lancashire ate oat bread. Moreover, it was handled in a host of different ways, either made into a fermented bread loaf or, more often, into a batter that was cooked into something like a pancake. In colder seasons, beans and peas could be added to wheat or barley breads, and of necessity in periods of grain shortage.[3]

So our generalizations about bread eaten in the early modern period have to be extremely cautious. Every housewife chose her favoured cereal, influenced perhaps most of all by the varieties that were grown in her locality. Silently, she also knew that there were different varieties of each cereal, and that each one had a substantial effect on the resulting bread, though she was rarely in a position to fuss about that. Under strict manorial rules, she had to go to the manorial mill for her grain to be ground, though in isolated places she might grind it in a quern by hand. Querns appear surprisingly often in probate inventories, though many seem to have been used mainly for grinding malt, and smaller ones for grinding mustard. Our housewife herself then chose between sifting the flour coarse or fine at home (though the miller would already have made a certain choice when milling it), and to start the dough rising she normally relied on a sourdough that was already lying around in the unwashed bread trough, adding salt and water. 'Leaven' was the usual word for this spontaneously fermenting starter dough, though the word was not always used in that strict sense. A yeast, usually called 'barm', and consisting of the froth that forms on fermenting malt liquors of ale or beer, was also used to make bread rise, but it is impossible to know how often it was actually bought and sold for use in bread before the sixteenth century. It is unstable, and beer yeasts, in particular, could taste bitter. Our documents show barm being freely sold in the sixteenth century, and debates are recorded in the seventeenth century for and against its merits for health, so it may not have been until some time after 1500 that ale barm was used on any large scale in bread-baking. But that, at present, has to be a guess. Finally our housewife heated her oven at home, or baked her bread under a dome by the fire; alternatively, she used a common oven or paid for the use of the baker's oven. The flavour of the bread would then vary again according to the fuel used, whether wood, peat or coal.[4]

Every single operation in this bread-baking routine underwent change in our period, so we can be certain that the resulting appearance, texture and taste of the bread were affected. To begin with, the cereal varieties became more numerous as a result of foreign imports and farmers' personal choices of the best bread corn for their land. Some grains produced a whiter bread, some a yellow bread, some a brown bread that was quite unsuitable, we are told, for manchet, and some that were better for pastry and biscuits. The sifting routines also varied according to the housewife's financial means and family tastes. The relative use of natural yeasts or ale barm changed in course of time, as we noted above, and we have earlier demonstrated the popular prejudice against the growing use of coal on the fire because it affected food flavours.[5]

BREAD-MAKING PROCEDURES

Details of bread-making routines that are set out in books of the time show that mixing the flour and water was started the night before, and on seeing the degree of fermentation the next morning the breadmaker added the remaining flour, waited longer for the dough to rise more or hastened things by adding some ale barm. One of our most informative writers on this subject is Gervase Markham in the early seventeenth century, and it is noteworthy that he prescribed barm for manchet but sourdough for ordinary household bread. As manchet increasingly became the favoured bread of the well-to-do in the sixteenth century, and Markham, himself a gentleman, called manchet 'your best and principal bread', it is worth speculating on the role of manchet in raising the demand for barm.

We are totally ignorant at present of the bread-making conventions that must have existed among neighbours, but a keener search by local historians will almost certainly produce more clues in the future. Adam Maurizio, who did so much to record peasant practices on the Continent of Europe, noted one convention whereby the person using the communal oven for a big baking was duty bound to leave a piece of the dough for the next user of the oven. The habit of sharing yeast with neighbours was mentioned by William Ellis in 1750. Whenever housewives brewed ale, he said, they passed on yeast to neighbours, so saving one another the expense of buying it; in towns, yeast could cost dear in times of shortage. As for the sharing of ovens, hardly anything is known of such neighbourly routines in this country; it awaits an observant researcher.[6]

Women were the main brewers of ale in the Middle Ages, and while their role diminished in our period, they remained considerable sellers of barm at the market, which yielded them one of their extra sources of income. But ale barms are temperamental, unstable and sometimes bitter. So we can be sure that many women remained loyal to sourdough. The strongest prejudice against ale barm was brought out into the light of day in a debate in Paris in 1666, when the medical men in a dispute decided that it was harmful to health. They did not prove able to stop its use, however, though in 1670 they insisted that bakers in Paris should at least get it fresh and not buy it in from the countryside. This controversy across the Channel prompts us to wonder about similar prejudices in England, and to focus on the sixteenth to seventeenth centuries as the period when the subject might have become controversial. Ale barm appears in household accounts, like Lord Petre's at Ingatestone, Essex, in Elizabeth's reign, showing him cheerfully buying barm to bake with. But it did not appear as a purchase in the accounts of Lord Howard at Naworth, though he did buy yeast to bake bread for the horses. Robert May's recipes (1660), on the other hand, show him using it freely. More significant conclusions might be drawn if the frequency of references were more carefully studied. Thomas Tryon, the principled vegetarian at the end of the seventeenth century, thought barm harmful and disagreeable to the stomach, so he firmly recommended natural fermentation.[7]

Some cooks insisted on making yeast from their own beer vat rather than buying it from the brewers, so that indicates some preferences on the grounds of health, flavour or possibly cost. When they did get barm from the brewers they washed it several times over to drain off the bitterness. Elizabeth David, our English authority on all this, says that we have lost the taste for barm yeasts, because we now buy a commercial, compressed distillery yeast, but people always said that barm yeast had a more interesting flavour. We confront the vexed question of how we can ever recapture flavours that have been lost. By the beginning of the nineteenth century brewer's yeast had vanquished the use of sourdough on the grounds that it was a much quicker operation. However, interest in sourdough has returned in recent years, spreading news among us of families from the Continent who are proud to have kept their flavoursome sourdough for decades, if not generations.[8]

PROFESSIONAL BAKERS VERSUS HOME-MADE BREAD

Another question entirely, though we shall never find a reliable answer, concerns the role of bakers in taking over the baking of bread from the housewife. Some towns had many bakers in the sixteenth and seventeenth centuries. Derby, for example, had 20 in 1693, seemingly one for every 35 households. Relying on the evidence of ovens in houses, and looking at the construction of chimneys in kitchens, one might guess that people in our period did not generally bake bread at home. But they could have mixed the dough at home and baked it on the hearth, or else taken it to a common oven, or got the village baker to bake it for them. A visitor in Winchcombe, Gloucestershire in 1678 watched the women carrying bread and puddings to the bakehouse, knitting as they went, though he did not specify the status of the bakehouse. One of the few historians to address this question is John Goodacre in his study of the Lutterworth area between 1500 and 1700. The manorial monopoly had at one time insisted on people baking their bread in the common ovens, and in the mid-sixteenth century in Lutterworth 20 men and women or more were presented in the manorial court for baking at home. In other words, the attempt was still being made there to keep the monopoly going, though a few of the more important householders did have their own ovens, as did the common bakers. When using the manorial oven, c. 1600, you paid for the baking by giving one penny and a piece of dough for every strike (half a bushel) baked, and by the 1640s you were giving twopence plus dough or twopence halfpenny without dough. The manorial monopoly seems to have broken down in Lutterworth around 1600–30, and two yeomen bakers, possibly more, were supplying the town and were also named as the common bakers of two neighbouring villages (Kilworth and Gilmorton). Nevertheless, the court records show a tussle still going on, as people were setting up their own mills, or using querns, and being ordered to cease. Of the two common ovens existing in Lutterworth, one closed down in the mid-seventeenth century, suggesting perhaps a victory for the commercial bakers. That conclusion is reinforced by the fact that Lutterworth c. 1650 had seven common bakers, and in some villages around Lutterworth the bakers were actually taking their bread to Lutterworth to sell on Thursday market days. It may be that home baking was in decline there, for only 16, or at most 20 to 30 of the 'better sort of housekeepers' were said to have private ovens (Lutterworth households numbered 248 in 1670). It looks as if professional bakers were taking over in the course of the seventeenth century in that modest market town, though it certainly should not be thought to represent the situation in all towns and villages. We have no idea how many villages lived without any baker at all, and were too far from a peddling town baker. Historians will perhaps show further interest in this question in the future.[9]

FANCY BREADS

Another topic of interest in this increasingly commercial age concerns the types of bread that were put on sale. The assize of bread regulated standard prices for ordinary household bread, but we can be sure that bakers in the larger towns devised their own fancy kinds. Many names for different breads are mentioned by Ann Rycraft in an essay about food in late medieval York. Yet by the sixteenth century all those bread names had already gone out of use, and something called 'York maynebread' was in high fashion. Its composition is unknown, but it was the kind always chosen for presentation to visiting dignitaries. That too showed signs by 1552 of falling out of favour, prompting orders to the bakers in 1552 to continue baking it. By 1595, however, it had failed to survive, the explanation being that spiced cakes had taken its place. Yet its reputation still resounded, for in 1617 when James I visited York for the second time, he asked for it. His airy royal statement that 'he would not have so ancient a thing to discontinue' failed to influence the food market, and so the maynebread of York disappeared from the scene. We can be sure that this short, vivid story of a special bread that came and went from York was familiar in many other towns of England. Every populous town, every port, and every town that attracted foreign immigrants nurtured the right environment for other such ventures to prosper among the bakers of a staple food. It puts our local historians on their mettle to find more. Meanwhile, we can acknowledge as proven that people in every generation saw their bread changing in some way in accordance with phases, fads and fashions.[10]

THE MEAT OF FARMYARD ANIMALS AND RABBITS

Just as meat production on the farm underwent considerable change in this period, so did the context in which it was viewed and handled as food. A brief resumé is attempted here, highlighting changes in the relative importance of the different meats in response to altered supplies, changing opinions about their status, and a guess at the quantities that came within the reach of working and poor people.

The Englishman's love affair with meat drew regular comments of surprise from foreigners visiting England in the sixteenth century. Coming nearly always from the Continent of Europe, they were convinced that Englishmen ate far more meat than they did. Foreigners did not, of course, form this judgement from encounters in the deep countryside, or by entering the houses of ordinary folk. They based it on London, or places *en route* to London, perhaps being entertained in gentlemen's houses on the downlands of the south-east, or when pausing in some of the populous villages along the Thames as they travelled between Canterbury and Greenwich. Some ventured as far as Oxford and Cambridge, but they did not penetrate into peasant country; we never find them in, say, the deeper Weald of Kent, though some did get as far as the rim of the Weald, at Penshurst, to the grand home of the Sidney family; but they certainly never reached Cornwall or Westmorland.[11]

Londoners in the late Middle Ages were already familiar with meat that had come long distances to their meat market; store beasts walked from Wales, Scotland and northern England, and were then fattened up in the Home Counties. But extravagant accounts of English meat-eating gave a one-sided picture, for London life was one thing, and provincial life something else. Doubtless it was satisfying for the English to live on a legend, and hear the average plain country fellow described as 'a terrible fastener on beef'. When gossiping in the alehouses everyone enjoyed the notion that our nation fed on a far richer diet of meat than anyone on the Continent. But the actual quantities in daily consumption among ordinary folk were far more modest.[12]

The middling sort served one kind of meat at a meal, and pieces of a carcass that we would not nowadays regard as prime cuts. Sheep's heads and calves' feet, for example, were far more common at the tables of ordinary folk than muscle meat. Peering into the cooking pot on the hearth of the husbandman, one would often have seen no more than a slice of smoked bacon cut from a joint hanging in the roof, or a meat bone thrown in to give flavouring. This is not to say that the resulting meal was not tasty and satisfying. Far from it, for it would have included a variety of vegetables, both roots and green leaves, cereals to thicken it, and herbs galore. The delicious smell of stews, simmering all day in a cooking pot on the stove, ready to comfort hungry workers when their work ended, is still a warm memory among some old people. It was at festive times, at holidays, which were more frequent than we enjoy today, when ordinary people appreciated meat carved off joints. William Herrick's poem graphically depicted the harvest home when beef, mutton, veal and bacon all appeared.[13]

In provincial towns, where many people made their living from trade and manufacture, our records show a goodly number of meat suppliers, as their work gave them much to do, since they pastured animals as well as butchering them, and every morsel of the carcasses was used. Spalding in Lincolnshire, for example, had a population of 443 adult males in 1642 (representing perhaps roughly the same number of families), and it had 12 butchers (as against seven victuallers, and 21 bakers) to feed them. One butcher per 37 households does not sound like an excessive number for one tradesman to satisfy.[14]

THEORIES AND CHOICES

As for food theories, everyone paid lip service to the notion that meat was the most desired food of all, and among alternative meats, beef was put at the head of the list for giving strength. Its red colour probably seemed to confirm that assertion, whereas mutton was regarded as best for the sick and the old. As enclosure proceeded in the sixteenth and first half of the seventeenth centuries, and its purpose was often enclosure for sheep, people ate more mutton and lamb than beef. But countrywide that is only a guess; one author who showed a familiarity with the counties of Oxfordshire, Northamptonshire and Buckinghamshire, claimed this as a recent trend around 1550: 'the most substance of our feeding was wont to be on beef, and now it is on mutton', he said. That assertion was supported 30 years later by Thomas Cogan (1584), deciding that mutton was eaten more than any other meat both in sickness and in health. It is noticeable also that when Henry Best, a farmer in the East Riding, prepared harvest meals for his workers in 1641, he always provided a joint of roast mutton as one of five or six dishes, for, he said, that was what they always expected. It is nevertheless true that in some farming regions of England, one could safely assert that more beef cattle than sheep were produced. Yet it would be erroneous to postulate a high consumption of beef everywhere; it is more likely that beef was conspicuous among the well-to-do in London and in gentlemen's houses elsewhere, and that was the origin of the legend. Given the trend of agrarian changes overall, more mutton than beef was produced and eaten through the sixteenth and up to the mid-seventeenth century, while beef remained the supreme meat for high occasions.[15]

BEEF

After the mid-seventeenth century, a gentle drift towards more beef is likely; a somewhat strident public debate focused then on the growing cattle trade from Scotland, Ireland and Wales, and the scale of such droving plainly increased. It yielded more information concerning the routes of drovers, the pressure of their demands for overnight grazing *en route* to the south, and it even yielded a picture of the drovers' lifestyle. A victualler might lodge them, but they always carried in their saddle bags a girdlestone and in their pouches oatmeal to cook with water into nutritious oatcakes, sometimes enriched with animal blood. Thus they got modest nourishment from their animals. In the first half of the eighteenth century, when the meat market was becoming a serious commercial business, production of both beef and mutton rose, and sales of sheep meat are said to have increased by over 50 per cent. We do not have any comparable figure for the increased eating of beef. So no generalization about trends in the relative consumption of the two meats would be safe, though it is likely that opinions about beef still gave it the highest place in common estimation.[16]

Meat was eaten from animals of all ages and from all parts of the carcass. Long, slow cooking was the norm in the kitchen, and beef of any age could be made succulent and tasty by gentle cooking for hours. Fast frying was virtually unknown; indeed, judging by the remark of John Byng some time in the 1780s or 1790s it was possible to hold a firm prejudice against it: Byng positively objected to meat that was fried in butter, and insisted that meat be boiled. As for flavour and their handling before slaughter, many writers debated the merits of old versus young animals, wild versus tame, gelded males versus females. Virtually all agreed that animals that had had strenuous exercise in the plough or in draught made more flavoursome meat than others that had had none, an observation that is commonly still held to be true. The search for distinctive flavours also led to considerable lengths as is illustrated in one of Hollyband's conversational *Dialogues*, describing a wild sow that had been taken alive in France and from which two of her litter had been sent to England. One lady serving one of the precious pigs at the table said to her guest: 'Cut some of that wild boar pig, it is better than our tame pigs'. Bull baiting with mastiff dogs ('baiting almost to death', said John Houghton) was another practice, still used in the later seventeenth century, which not only made entertaining sport, but tenderized the beef.[17]

Traditional butchers to this day affirm the virtue of grazing beef on pastures for at least two and a half years, to get the best flavour. In the early modern period, beef of three years and older was the norm, and if older still or not hung long enough, then slow cooking was the solution. But it was not the only cooking strategy: a most ingenious method used by French soldiers who could not wait for their beef to hang was described by Thomas Moufet. He had seen it in camp in the Low Countries when he was accompanying 'that flower of chivalry, the Earl of Essex'. The method was used by French soldiers from Normandy wanting to tenderize the meat of a cow, presumably an old one, to make an instant meal. They killed it with an axe, turned it on its back, made a hole in the navel to receive a swan's quill, and then blew it up till the whole skin swelled like a bladder and the beast seemed to double in size. While this went on, two or three others beat the animal hard with cudgels, never bruising the flesh because of the air between flesh and skin. It made the skin into better leather, said Moufet, and the flesh ate better and was more tender. The episode is a fine illustration of the many resourceful devices used in the past for making the best of available food in whatever circumstances.[18]

Another delicacy from a cattle carcass was the bone marrow. Everyone treasured it. Its value was clearly set out in the sixteenth-century *Dialogue* of Juan Luis Vives. A school usher complained because 'we always have brought to us here bones without marrow in them'. The excuse given him in that case was that 'bones have but little marrow in them at the new moon', whereas at full moon they had plenty. In later years another explanation was more usual: the cook was blamed for the way she cooked the bones, causing the marrow to escape or the flavour to be drowned by the use of excessive herbs and spices, like ginger. Robert May (1660) used marrow bones in stews, and in one case garnished a shoulder of mutton with it. Marrow was still relished as a delicacy in the nineteenth century, and Mrs Beeton showed how to cook the bones without letting the marrow escape. They were boiled for two hours, upright in the pan with the ends sealed. As for getting the marrow out of the bones, a special piece of cutlery was made in the eighteenth century for retrieving it.[19]

Readers may wonder what marrow looked like, for it has totally disappeared from our ken nowadays. It is a light, digestible fat that was eaten in both savoury and sweet dishes. It was often served on toast with honey or treacle, and Joan Cromwell obviously liked it, for she had it for breakfast in a pudding with almonds, sugar and rosewater; it is no use grimacing at the thought of marrow on toast for we have no idea how it tasted.[20]

Other palatable foods of the age included not only bone marrow but calves' and pigs' brains ('in great esteem with us', said Dr Hart in 1633), offal, and the nether ends of animals. Robert May gave recipes for neats' udders, palates, noses and lips of steers, oxen and calves, and these recipes were the ones written first in his book before he turned to consider fillets of beef. But by the time that John Houghton was writing, 35 years later, admittedly as one who was relatively detached from the practicalities of actual cooking, a deprecatory attitude towards offal and other small pieces of beef carcass had crept in. The lips and palate of steer and ox had plainly fallen in esteem. Whereas Robert May, serving as cook in the houses of nobility and gentry, had offered in 1660 several quite elaborate recipes for the palates and lips of beef animals, John Houghton in 1695 described the best use for the lips of cattle as food for dogs, and the palate of the ox for pottage, hashes and 'lumber pyes'. The palate had once cost sixpence; now it cost only a penny. Liver was by some reckoned good meat, but 'tripe-folk' were said to boil it for dog's meat, and when cut small it was given to feed ducks, geese and turkeys. The greater quantities of meat now being sent to the market had evidently resulted in a new ranking of the parts of the animal, a shift of opinion that we may simply term 'changes in taste', but which slid over a complex story in our farming history. Falling prices at least gave the poor the chance to buy more of the cheaper cuts.[21]

The meat from the beef animal that we have virtually lost nowadays is veal. It was much eaten in Lancashire in the late sixteenth and early seventeenth centuries, as the Shuttleworth family table bore witness. In other slowly emerging dairying areas, quantities for sale by the butcher gradually rose, since male calves had to be put to good use. Killing them at birth as we do now would have been an unthinkable waste. Andrew Boorde in 1547 had claimed that many thought veal the best meat, and some clues to its comfortable status alongside mutton are given in two records: one shows the meats served to the Oxford martyrs, Latimer and Ridley, in gaol for two years (1554–6) in Oxford, before execution; they received 57 meals of veal compared with 53 of mutton and 25 of beef; and according to the household accounts of the Walmsley family at Dunkenhalgh in Lancashire, their visiting actors were fed on veal in 1617–18, incidentally costing the family substantially more for veal than the Shuttleworths paid. One veal cost the Shuttleworths 7s. 4d. in March 1583 (though in March 1585, a lean year, they did pay considerably more – 11s.); the Walmsleys in 1617–18 paid 10s. 6d. But by 1691 veal had become more plentiful, though the Revd Richard Baxter did not see much chance of a farm tenant's family eating veal often. That comment rested on observations in the Kidderminster area of Worcestershire, and might well say more about the scale of dairying thereabouts than about people's preferences.[22]

Nearer London the stronger commercial trend persuaded farmers to catch the eye of buyers by whitening their meat. Around Tring in Hertfordshire in 1681 this was done by bleeding the calves every week or ten days and giving them chalk licks as well. Essex men fed them with rice, malt, flour and cream instead of so much milk, sometimes topping up the feed with a touch of brandy to make the calves sleep and fatten faster. Oscillating profits between cheese and butter and veal were closely watched by farmers who chose to specialize. The veal itself also ranged in quality, from that of calves that had run with their dams until they were killed, to the meat from others that had been crammed in stalls. Thus rich and poor could pick meat at different prices. Veal as an item in the meat market soared onto a much higher plane in the eighteenth century, and would rise even higher in the nineteenth. That much is evident in the 35 pages devoted to it by Mrs Beeton. It is a sobering lesson for historians to consider why they have neglected it.[23]

MUTTON

Mutton was probably the commonest meat in the English diet, if all classes are judged together. It was deemed by one writer, William Vaughan in 1600, the most nourishing meat of all when boiled and eaten with cordial herbs. The plentiful supply was a visible fact of life since so many farmers across the whole class spectrum were likely to have sheep, some counting more than 500, others grazing no more than half a dozen. It explains the statement of Moufet c. 1600 about lamb's flesh being, through God's blessing, 'an ordinary meat amongst us in mean households'. Its classlessness shines through the fact that the sheep's head was a favoured dish at the table of all classes. The account book of Richard Latham of Scarisbrick, near Southport in Lancashire, shows him routinely buying a sheep's head that cost him only 2d. in the 1720s. Though an inexpensive meat, it was greatly savoured, most of all perhaps in Scotland where it was set to simmer, the longer the better, on the Sabbath, and provided a hot meal 'between sermons'. Dorothy Wordsworth was one of the appreciative eaters when she was in Scotland, and Olive Geddes describes the traditional way of serving it hot with the head taking pride of place in the middle of a bowl. Served cold, it was equally well received, judging by Robert Southey's comment on how good was the skin and the flavour given it by singeing.[24]

Commentators on meat differentiated the different types of fodder given to meat animals for its effect on meat flavour, and in the sixteenth and seventeenth centuries this was a particularly lively subject with regard to sheep meat because of changing farm practices. Sheep grazing on the short, fine grasses of chalk and limestone downlands made the sweetest meat, and these were not threatened by the plough until after the early modern period. But enclosure did alter the feeding of many sheep that had formerly grazed on commons and fallows, for they were now moved onto enclosed pastures where they fed on long, lush grass, and often at the end were fattened on peas. Peas-fed mutton was welcome for being ready in spring, whereas grass-fed mutton came later in the year. The animals were doubtless heavier but their meat was not as tasty. In the northern counties, in contrast, many agreed that sheep fed on holly made the most delicious meat of all, though another competitor for that honour came from the Herdwick breed. Herdwicks were the smallest of hill sheep and, it was claimed, the purest of British breeds; their wool was coarse, used more often for carpets than for clothing, but their meat has been called 'the sweetest mutton in the world'. So Northerners might be considered poor inhabitants of a benighted country, but they ate some of the best mutton.[25]

PORK

The meat animal giving the most bounteous supply of meat was the pig, since it produced many piglets (8–12, even 18–20), and that twice a year. There is no hint in the documents of this period that the pig was regarded as the poor man's meat. It had been commended by the ancient physicians, and that rule prevailed still, though some, like Henry Buttes, the Cambridge don in 1599, and Dr Hart of Northampton in 1633, qualified their judgement, deeming it best for those who took exercise, i.e. labourers and the young, and less good for scholars, the old, and those living a life of ease. Evidently people much relished the roasted crackling, as we still do, and some of Hart's reservations were due to this indulgence, which he thought caused indigestion in weak stomachs.[26]

The association of pigs with the poor seems to have taken hold only later when potatoes became plentiful and the skins and, indeed, the whole potato gave a source of food from kitchen waste after about 1750. That gave the poor the chance to keep more pigs than before. But in the sixteenth century, when pork and bacon were deemed nutritious and worthy meats for all classes, pigs were easily fed in woodlands, some grazing there in all seasons, and having food taken out to them at lean times, or being fattened in the woods on nuts and berries in the autumn. Other refined strategies were elaborated by Gervase Markham in 1623: bringing them home after six to eight weeks of feeding them on berries and acorns in the woods (acorns in Walter Blith's opinion (1653) produced the longest-lasting bacon), and finishing them off with 10–14 days in sties, fed on old dried peas; or, if woods were lacking, shutting them in sties to feed on peas or beans, whey and buttermilk for four to five weeks. In common field counties like Leicestershire, another device was to turn them out among pea ricks in the fields, near furrows that let water into the stackyard. Then, morning and evening, a slice was cut from the stack and spread among the swine; small porkets then fattened in three to four weeks. That was a novel device growing out of the commonest routine in Leicestershire, whereby the pigs fed on pastures and commons, but also had a spell eating the beans that were grown in the arable rotation. The local people boasted of the fine bacon that this produced throughout Leicestershire, calling it 'the food of kings'.[27]

Leicestershire was widely recognized as a specialist in pig-keeping; some 40–50% of its peasants may well have kept pigs. It stood out prominently in this regard when compared with some other parts of England where pigkeepers were far less numerous; in Low Furness and in Rossendale, their numbers could fall very low, showing only one-third of country folk owning a pig, and in the Pennines more generally and in the west of England they were relatively uncommon.[28]

The light and shade of this picture changed continually, however, particularly when dairy farmers kept more pigs by appropriating the whey formerly given free to the poor. Thus Baskerville, viewing the dairymen bringing veal to Norwich market in 1681, assumed that in season they would bring pork and hog meat as well. But another change on a different scale resulted from the growth of urban industries like soap-boiling, starchmaking and brewing, when their waste products were fed to pigs without anyone worrying about its effects on flavour. The victuallers of ships depended much on this pork because it was cheap, but, of course, it was nothing like as succulent as 'country-fed pork'. By the end of the eighteenth century, we watch a food business being coaxed into feeding a growing population of townspeople, and cheerfully sacrificing subtleties of taste.[29]

RABBIT

Another meat, which rose to greater prominence in the early modern period, though it is usually passed over cursorily in our textbooks, was rabbit. Having been introduced by the Normans soon after the Conquest, rabbit was at first a luxury meat in the Middle Ages and lords claimed to themselves the privilege of setting up warrens. But as rabbit numbers increased, some escaped into the wild, poaching increased, and the lord's sales of rabbit meat made it available to a wider circle. By the sixteenth century, warrens were recognized as the financially rewarding projects of gentlemen (in one case, paying the rent of the whole home farm), and in some places the rabbit population was allegedly huge; Moufet reckoned c. 1600 that Alborne Chase, north of Brighton, supplied more than 100,000 a year. In the later seventeenth century yet more new warrens were created as a way of using poor land to better profit.[30]

Rabbit meat circulated in some quantity in the markets and it was as classless as wildfowl. It is, of course, impossible to measure the quantities eaten, but it would thoroughly distort the historical picture if the rabbit were ignored when describing the meat content of diet of the different classes. It was available cheaply to middle- and working-class people; indeed, it remained so into the 1920s and 1930s, as some of us can still testify, while we mourn its virtual disappearance from the menu nowadays. Rabbit as food faithfully mirrors a significant phase in our history of diet that has passed. Will it perhaps return?

Among documents reliably illustrating the argument that rabbit constituted a routine meat, one is the list of 327 meals of meat eaten by the Oxford martyrs, Latimer and Ridley, between 1554 and 1556: 53 were of mutton, 57 of veal and 56 of rabbit. The cookbooks also always included rabbit recipes, but not usually as many as those for wildfowl; that could be because it was such a straightforward meat that cooks needed no recipes to demonstrate their spontaneity and originality; they could add any ready-to-hand herbs. Rabbit hash was plainly a favourite; Joan Cromwell had three recipes in her repertoire; Robert May (1660) offered rather more, and in his monthly bill of fare treated rabbit as a seasonal dish not only in February, June and September, but as fitting food for Christmas Day and New Year's Day as well. Professor Bradley singled out praise for the flavour of rabbit because the animals ate so many sweet herbs.[31]

Sarah Jackson, a credible guide towards the close of our period (1754) in advising young housewives on their cooking routines, did not show as much interest in rabbits as in wildfowl, but she did give three recipes, plus instructions on cutting up rabbit, while recommending it in February in her Bill of Fare. We need to remember, of course, the scattered distribution of warrens across the countryside, which must have governed the chance appearance of rabbit in local markets. But while rabbit was not a new food in the early modern period, it underwent a qualitative change in its status as more warrens were set up and it became a commonplace meat. While the cookbooks suggest a greater plenty of wildfowl than of rabbit, it is probable that people on the whole took rabbit as much for granted as bacon.[32]

MEAT HANDLING AND PRESERVATION

One of the serious debating points about meat at this time concerned its preservation. It was not just a question of preserving it when cooked, but about the best procedures before and during slaughter and when salting it, that would ensure good preservation later. The flesh of a stall-fed north country bullock would keep for two years after salting, they said, whereas a grass-fed ox would not salt so firmly and, in dressing it, more would go to waste. Some long and careful observations and experience lay behind these maxims.[33]

Slaughtering occurred whenever necessary during the year, though the killing of pork in the heat of summer was usually avoided. So-called Martinmas beef was the meat from animals slaughtered in the autumn, if the farmer knew that he could not feed them through the winter. While many were thus killed, many were overwintered to supply fresh meat whenever needed. Of more concern in the kitchen was the handling of meat in the salting trough. This stood in the hall or buttery, and some of the humblest country folk had one. It was generally salted ('powdered' meant the same thing) for at least a few days before being cooked, one to two days in spring and summer, two to three in autumn, and four to five in winter. But when meat was to be preserved for weeks or months, two weeks of salting, and often more, were usual. The actual salt used for salting, whether from English pits, or French sea salt, made a difference to its keeping qualities; according to one opinion, Northwich salt allowed beef to be kept in prime condition for 14 months. After that it might be smoked in a chimney, then removed and hung indefinitely in a less confined space, like the roof of the open hall. Some 20 years ago, Kay Coutin of East Grinstead corresponded with the author about smoking chambers found in Devon and Somerset houses, which she guessed might have been copied from the Low Countries and were dated from the late sixteenth to early seventeenth centuries. She had written an article on the subject in *Devon Life* in 1976, having found such smoking chambers in existence without their being recognized in old Devon houses. (They were large enough for six to eight people to stand inside them and were on the right-hand side of the fireplace, separated from a spiral stone staircase rising to the floor above.) The subject should perhaps be pursued further. Salted, smoked meat would last many months and, though distinctly inferior to fresh meat, was perfectly appetizing if well handled. In Shetland 'reestit mutton' is known to this day, prepared in a distinctive way; it is laid in salt water for three weeks, hung outdoors to drip, and then hung to cure indoors. When the salt is properly washed out (and this involves soaking it for three to four hours), it is dried, and cooked slowly for two hours; friends say that it is delicious.[34]

The method of long-term storage that required cooking was called potting, and was explained by Hugh Platt as though it were experimental late in Elizabeth's reign. Platt set great store by its future use at sea in storing meat without the use of salt. The meat might be parboiled first, and was then baked. It was next packed tightly in well-leaded stone pots on a good bed of clarified butter, with more melted butter poured round, and another inch of butter set on top. The air was thus excluded, and the pot was made yet more secure by a tight-fitting lid; the meat kept sweet for three months. Potted neats' tongues evidently won favour, drawing Houghton's attention in the 1690s when they were prepared in the distinctive Newcastle way, and sent 'where you please'. The process was akin to that of storing meat by long, slow cooking in a pie crust that would not be eaten. When cooked, melted butter was poured in to fill the interstices, this meat, kept airtight and in a cold, dark place, remained wholesome for several weeks, as the recipe books explained. Robert May (1660), for example, using rye flour pastry for the best keeping quality, even reckoned that a pie of wild boar kept for a whole year.[35]

Pickling meat, however, was the outstandingly new way of preserving meat, which began to be better known around 1700 and did not involve cooking the meat first. Raw pieces were cut up and carefully covered in salt, saltpetre and sugar and then packed very tightly in glazed earthenware pots or wooden tubs (gaps being packed with more salt). The lid was then tightly fastened. The salt and moisture in the meat quickly dissolved into a brine, and this was watched with varying degrees of care during storage, sometimes being re-boiled to freshen it. Meat pieces were lifted only from the top as needed, and the contents as a whole lasted for years (in fact, it was said to need a year to come to perfection); by this method no meat was wasted in contrast with smoking, which left unsavoury bits at the end, attacked by insects or hardened by long exposure to the air. The perfected method of pickling was thought by Ellis to belong to Kent, from where it had been adopted in Suffolk. Ellis in 1750 thought that all Suffolk people ate their pork that way, and from there it spread to Hertfordshire, which is how Ellis knew it. It enabled pork to be prepared in summer (ignoring the prejudice against the killing of pork in hot weather), and so afforded meat all the year round. It greatly reduced meat bills by cutting out all waste, and it was an economy for another reason – farmers were able to feed their harvesters on pork rather than the more expensive beef.[36]

The origins of pickling remain obscure; it is tempting to associate it with Continental influences, since pickling generally was a stronger early tradition there, and Kent and Suffolk absorbed foreign ideas readily. But nothing found so far gives firm support to that idea. Its history was extended by a remark of John Mortimer some 40 years before Ellis, saying in 1707 that pickled pork could be eaten in spring when other meat was dear; he evidently knew the method already, though we know not how; he was born in London and bought an estate, which he greatly improved, in Essex. Another author of a revised edition of Thomas

Tusser (the Essex connection here may also be significant) claimed in 1710 that the method was so well established that smoking was being discontinued in favour of pickling. Bradley was delighted with the taste of pickled pork in 1721 and published the recipe, and when Eliza Melroe reported on the same subject in 1798, he claimed that both pork and beef were pickled in Suffolk, and as a result no one ever cured bacon. In Kent pickled pork was preferred to bacon and was the principal dish of middle-class farmers and tradesmen. Melroe admitted having eaten pickled pork previously in the navy but never since, and implied that those who continued to cure flitches of bacon in the old way did so out of prejudice, thinking pickling unwholesome. So pickling seems to have come in gradually around 1700, perhaps even started in the navy, where it would have been more useful than anywhere else, but it was geographically restricted either in knowledge or popularity. Mary Kettilby, publishing a cookbook in London in 1728, offered one recipe for pickling, saying the meat would keep and was very good, but Elizabeth Cleland, publishing in Edinburgh in 1755, did not mention pickling, though she did favour potting. Ellis made one oblique reference that possibly implied more pickling in the south than in the north, so it not clear how popular preferences finally balanced out.[37]

FUEL AND SPIT VERSUS OVEN COOKING

Another lively debating point of the time concerned the type of fuel used to smoke or cook meat. When smoking meat in the chimney, the Dutch were said to screen it from coal fumes by wrapping the joint in 3–5 sheets of brown paper. In the London area the English had to put up with coal increasingly after 1600, but they fared better for wood in other parts of the realm, and the flavour of meat smoked or cooked over a peat fire was still a coveted experience in Lancashire: smoking over peat gave a pleasant tang to the meat, said Ellis, and fussy customers even paid for such meats to be sent considerable distances. Sensitive tastebuds, as we have seen many times, are a strong theme running through the literature on food in the early modern period.[38]

As for keeping fires burning correctly for cooking, we have lost touch with the skills of our forebears. It was not only the fuel that mattered; it required care and attention to keep the fire burning with the correct radiance, and for different joints this required experience. Mrs Beeton was eloquent on the subject, and cited a French writer who thought that you had to be a born roaster to judge the heat aright. Her remarks on the difference between roasting and baking in an oven are illuminating. Baked meats, in her view, were less savoury and less agreeable than roasted meats, and she had learned this when travelling in Germany and France where fuel was scarce and expensive and meat was mostly baked in an oven. In consequence, it had, she said, 'a singular uniformity in flavour, or want of flavour'. Another criticism had been passed by a Mr Lewis, a scientific author, noting that baking did not produce the gravy of English roasts. In any case, he said, foreigners shuddered at the thought that the gravy consisted of blood, and hence they favoured the serving of meat with some kind of sauce. This remark may shed some light on the English prejudice against, or lack of any need for, sauces; in the seventeenth century they were deemed a foreign nicety and were routinely sneered at. The fashion for, and aversion to, sauces swirled through printed commentaries in the seventeenth and eighteenth centuries; it is worth reflecting on whether varied sauces in fact originated in the need for a liquid with flavouring to combat the dryness of baked meats, whereas the need in England was satisfactorily met by roasting and savouring the consequent gravy. In the event, of course, the controversy died away, and elaborate sauces became an entrenched upper-class fashion.[39]

By Mrs Beeton's day, the choice between roasting and oven cooking was thoroughly familiar, for iron ovens were common in the kitchens of ordinary folk. But in the sixteenth and seventeenth centuries, ovens were far from ordinary and it is not easy to judge how and when oven baking in the home became commonplace, perhaps not until well after 1750. In the 1660s, when the hearth tax was introduced as a measure of national taxation, ovens were distinctly unusual; houses had to be relatively new to have chimneys already included; otherwise, they had to have had one added at the end of an old house. The tax was laid on both open fire hearths and what were called private ovens, but the records do not distinguish the two. In the town of Ashford, Kent, a chink of light is afforded by some idiosyncratic detail in 1662. Most people reported only hearths. But there were exceptions like Henry Kingham, who admitted to two hearths, of which one had 'a private oven in it'; Thomas Robinson, who had six hearths, of which one had an oven; and Robert Gibbs, who had six hearths, of which two had private ovens. As Gibbs also had a tenant, presumably she used the second oven. We cannot be sure that these few private ovens in Ashford reported accurately on the whole scene; it could have been a quirk of the hearth tax collector in one district only to record them thus. But at least in this part of the town, it suggests that most other people still boiled their meat or roasted it in front of an open fire. Alternatively, of course, and in towns particularly, people relied on taking their meat to bake in the baker's oven, at times when it suited his routines.[40]

The simplest cookbooks in print in the sixteenth century give the impression of meat usually being boiled. One with the modest title of *The Widowes Treasure* (1585), and another called *The Good House-Wives Treasurie* (1588), both show pieces of meat cooked in a pot with herbs and roots. The stew in a pot was the dish for all classes, and it could be dressed up with many extras or remain simple with vegetables, herbs and cereal. But many probate inventories in ordinary houses listed spits, and rods for spit roasting; they were extremely common, for example, in probate inventories of Clee in Lincolnshire. So we cannot yet say how conventions differed locally. Judging by complaints about the shortages and cost of fuel, one would expect those items to have exerted strong pressures on cooking methods. The very smallest hint of this concern emerges from a letter to William Ellis in 1748, written by someone who had gone from Hertfordshire to Devon and was pleased to discover a way of making a beef-steak pie that saved the trouble and expense of heating an oven. The pie became what we would call a beef steak pudding since it was cooked in a pewter basin covered with a cloth; we are still left wondering how far different cooking procedures reflected class and/or geographical location, and if further analysis would yield more refined conclusions.[41]

As our knowledge stands at present, all we can say is that oven baking was a cooking method available to aristocracy and gentry and was spreading during the early modern period to well-to-do yeomen and townsfolk. These assertions rest at a very simple level and await further local investigation. Baking was also available to whole villages if they possessed a common baking oven. But this facility usually represented something provided by manorial authority and tenants paid for it, so we do not know how usual it was. Some of Tressell's plans of houses round a courtyard in London hint at such a convenience between neighbours, or it may reflect a cooperative arrangement between modest commercial bakers of bread and pies. Other documents of the later sixteenth century hint enigmatically at trials with novel methods of baking using portable ovens; we would expect many domestic experiments at this time of heightened fuel scarcity. But the Tudors and Stuarts were also caught up in warfare on several fronts on the Continent of Europe, in Scotland and in Ireland, and the problem of provisioning armies must also have stirred some interest in portable ovens. References in English documents to ovens that were economical in fuel, and ovens 'in the Spanish style' need one day to be compared with facilities used on the Continent if the experiments of the time are to be fully understood.[42]

CONCLUSION

At a highly general level, historians have reckoned that meat consumption among ordinary folk in Europe rose in the later Middle Ages, when the population was reduced by the Black Death and much land fell back from arable to pasture. They then judge that meat-eating fell in the sixteenth century as population rose again, and bread then became the prime necessity. More cereals were, indeed, produced, so that by the 1660s the adequate supply of cereals allowed more attention to be paid to meat.[43]

This tentative judgment passes over all consideration of the quantity and variety of alternative meats, particularly wild birds and rabbits. But it generally serves as an introduction to the much-quoted judgment of Gregory King that half the population never ate meat, those receiving alms ate it not above once a week, while others ate it not above two days in seven. King's experience included a spell when he worked at Eccleshall, Staffordshire, a parish with a large number of poor living in scattered dwellings over a large parish. So he was not a Londoner without provincial experience; he had also been at school in Lichfield. On the other hand, not so long after, in 1729, Professor Bradley of Cambridge expressed a totally contrary view, that the poor customarily used a great quantity of flesh in their diet.[44]

It is fitting that this discussion should end in ambiguity, for that is the only honest verdict to which we are driven at present. Our increasing knowledge of local history gives hope of more informed discussion in the future. We can safely generalize about Englishmen's aspirations for meat, and we can put beef at the head of the list of desirable meats, lamb and mutton next, and pork as the food of the cottagers. But this study has shown many changes taking place in the local supply of different meats, and changing quantities available undoubtedly influenced by taste and fashion, which then affected prices and altered farming specialisms. None of this can be quantified. The qualitative evidence sheds light on local and class differences, changes in the use of the land, and, indeed, differences in the enthusiasm with which farmers and merchants seized their chances; all this was mingled with taste preferences that we can never fathom, knowing that flavours at the table were based on soils, feed, and the handling of food in the kitchen by innumerable individualist cooks. Finally, we have to allow for the ingenuity and strivings of innumerable sorts of people wanting, or not particularly wanting, much meat. A colourful story of life in the Northamptonshire forests was told by a parson living in Silverstone in the late eighteenth and early nineteenth centuries. Three out of four tenants of his father's cottages, he said, lived chiefly on what they picked up at night. He was sent to collect the rent but seldom got any, though he could have had the money in rabbits and hares almost any Saturday night. 'I verily believe that [one cottager] ... carried more deer over its threshold every year than ever found their way into royal larders,' he wrote, and when one tenant left, more than a dozen doeskins were found in the garden, many of them fresh. 'Yet that man was one of the most sober and hardworking men in the parish and a regular chapelgoer withal.' Meat is the most difficult subject of all in allowing general conclusions; it is not likely to yield any one bold generalization covering the whole kingdom.[45]

EGGS AND BIRD MEAT, FARM-FED AND WILD

Nowadays, the phrase 'bird meat' conjures up a picture of four birds bred on the farm – chickens, ducks, turkeys and geese – and among wild (or semi-wild) birds only three kinds – partridges, pheasants and grouse. The scene was entirely different in 1500. Farm-bred birds first and foremost meant chickens, and especially capons (gelded birds which were often crammed in their last days to make them fatter still, and were always expected at festive meals). Ducks and geese were regarded with suspicion, for they fed on frogs and worms and were not deemed healthy food. No one had yet heard of turkeys.

In contrast, every wild bird in the sky was regarded as a source of meat. Some were obviously more palatable than others, and some were firmly associated with class: at the two extremes lay rooks and rook pie for the poor, and at the other, pheasants for the rich. Nevertheless, the full list of birds routinely named as acceptable food was very long indeed. Wild birds of different kinds clustered in defined areas of the country, were plentiful in some places, scarce in others, and migratory birds were available as seasonal food. Thus every housewife had her own personal list of possibilities on the menu, dictated by her place of abode and her class. But wild birds of some kind were within the reach of all, and we can be sure that everyone caught them from time to time. Some menfolk had fowling pieces listed among their possessions, while some were specialist fowlers, and kept a variety of nets for trapping them alive. They fed them up for a week or two at home to put more flesh on them and enhance their flavour, and either ate them at home or sold them profitably. Some very simple contrivances that anyone could assemble were used to net or trap wild birds in woods and fields; everyone had access to birdlime, could learn to use fire or a dull-toned bell to attract them, or could imitate bird calls. In short, resourceful families everywhere could enjoy bird meat in their pottages and casseroles, families with adventurous teenagers probably enjoying more than the rest.[46]

Between 1500 and 1750 a qualitative change took place in the supply and ranking of all these various bird meats. It resulted from converging changes in the world around, from discussion in books, treatises, and gossip in the alehouse, which spread knowledge on ways of handling birds, both tame and wild. Practical methods of management as well as changes in fashion and taste extended country skills; and these fresh trends were reinforced when larger quantities of bird meat arrived in the market and sold well, for country people quickly spotted chances to augment the supplies on sale. Writers tended to report on the London market rather than any other, for London was the prime stimulus to commercial poultry production. So our best information comes from the capital, and it was doubtless there that the most spectacular transformation was wrought by the early eighteenth century. People became accustomed to seeing thousands of migratory birds, caught in wildfowl decoys, arriving by cart and carrier in London, plus hundreds of geese and turkeys walking from East Anglia.

HENS AND CHICKENS

Domestic poultry deserve attention first, however, for in 1500 they were the commonest birds of rich and poor, seen in every yard, on roadsides, and in fields, and valued most of all for their eggs. Harrison, in Elizabeth's reign, described them as being seen in 'great plenty in every farmer's yard', and, of course, they were always the responsibility of the womenfolk. We cannot know how much care was given to their feeding; we have to guess at wide variations between the careless and the careful women, and no doubt management relied on traditional lore.[47]

The later sixteenth century produces the first printed advice on keeping hens. The earliest to appear was in the pages of *Maison Rustique*, the French textbook by Estienne and Liébault, which was a most substantial book on all farming matters, much cited by English readers. First available in French from 1569 to 1570, it appeared as *The Country Farm* in English translation from 1600 onwards. Its authors wrote with noticeable respect for women and all the many jobs they performed on the farm, and its poultry section gave reliable instruction. Cleanliness and good feeding were urged as prime necessities, and some notion of the attention to detail when fattening birds for meat was conveyed in one tip: to put a dung heap near the henhouse which could be watered with beef blood so that worms would multiply for the hens to eat. The French reckoned to keep hens laying from February until early November, and with special feeding they would lay all through the winter. The same assertion was made by Leonard Mascall, when in 1581 he wrote the first book in English on poultry, relying on Columella as well as *The Country Farm*, and adding traditional lore and his own observations.[48]

Interest in poultry was plainly being enlivened by this time, as Leonard Mascall's explanation for his book makes clear. He was clerk of the kitchen in the household of the Archbishop of Canterbury, and was asked for instruction by Mistress Katherine Woodford, wife of Master James Woodford, clerk of the kitchen in Queen Elizabeth's household. She wanted information on keeping poultry, on the taming of wildfowl, and on keeping them for profit, that last purpose being, for the historian, a significant explanation. She came from a place that Mascall called Brestall; and it would make good sense if this was Burstall, near Ipswich in Suffolk, for Norfolk and Suffolk were later renowned for their poultry. It sounds as if Mistress Woodford had been deputed to provide poultry for the queen, and so was searching for more expertise.[49]

Another French text published in 1567 was in French by Prudent Choyselat, a practical poultry farmer. New editions of that work followed speedily, with an

English translation in 1580. Choyselat was a commercially minded egg producer with a keen eye on Paris consumers who wanted a fresh egg for breakfast, or, when sick, longed for the light nourishment of an egg for dinner. He was familiar with itinerant eggsellers walking the streets of Paris crying their eggs for sale; his treatise was possibly an eye-opener to the English, especially when he urged his readers to purchase 1,200 hens and keep them in some old rural building with stables outside Paris.[50]

In the next hundred years, little more was written on the subject of farm-fed poultry, as management was regarded as women's work, and the menfolk took little notice. Probate inventories usually named the birds perfunctorily as 'pullen', though hints of a more commercial attitude did creep into some counties, and hens, ducks, geese and turkeys began to be itemized separately, noticeably in East Anglia and Hampshire. Such attention pointed to a more careful management system taking hold in the background, as birds found a bigger commercial market. We know that they were being fattened on buckwheat in East Anglia and on vetches in Hampshire. Signs of improved management in East Anglia arouse the suspicion that Dutch, French and Flemish immigrants, who were settling as refugees there, had brought some new methods from home. Larger than usual numbers of ducks, geese and turkeys are found in some East Anglian probate inventories, and some of the testators bore foreign-sounding surnames. Anne Arminger, whose surname sounds Dutch or German, was a widow of North Creake in Norfolk in the early seventeenth century. She had 141 birds of different kinds, including 50 hens, two cocks, 30 capons, ten geese and ganders, 44 ducks and drakes, two turkey cocks, and three turkey hens.[51]

John Worlidge, writing from Hampshire in 1675, did not boast of any improved management of poultry in his neighbourhood (he lived in Petersfield), but then he showed no interest in women's work anyway, and would not necessarily have known how things had changed over the previous hundred years. To him, chickens were just the commonest poultry, rooting around in yards and fields, and generally shifting for themselves for most of the year. It may well be that this was the way a majority of the population got their eggs. But it was not the whole truth.[52]

EGGS

Plainly, some networks of women existed to ensure a large supply of eggs when needed. Well-to-do households bought large numbers at one time and used them very freely, if we may judge by their household accounts and recipe books. The Shuttleworths in Lancashire bought eight dozen on one occasion, and in December 1598, probably in preparation for Christmas, they bought 124 eggs. The chains of supply are never recorded, except in cases where tithe eggs were handed over by tenants to their landlords. But in supplying towns, and for ceremonial feasts feeding large numbers of people, we have to guess that Goody Brown and Goody Smith had a regular routine, locked into a network of small egg producers who supplied one local woman dealer. Thus, when Lord Leicester gave his sumptuous feast in Oxford on 6 September 1570, Mrs Gawene called on her band of suppliers to assemble the 250 eggs that were needed.[53]

At the end of the seventeenth century poultry keepers were confident of supplying eggs even through the winter. This was affirmed by one London poulterer of long experience in 1699. His method was to feed his hens on toast dipped in ale, and boiled barley. His account, like that of William Ellis, the Hertfordshire farmer, in 1750, showed what considerable trouble was taken to keep supplies going. Ellis reckoned to keep them fresh in store for two to three months.[54]

PULLETS AND CAPONS

Chicken meat had long been prominent in the household accounts of the well-to-do, and capons were routine at banquets. At Lord Leicester's feast in 1570, 32 chickens and ten capons were mustered along with seven turkeys and ten young, fat mallards. The suppliers were women, one producing four capons and another three women offering two each; they lived in Oxford and the nearby villages of Oseney and Radley. The taste for capons seems to have co-existed with a taste for crammed pullets, pullets being young hens that have started to lay eggs, but have not reached their first moult, so they are not yet mature hens. This taste was allegedly a novel development for, according to Barnaby Googe in 1577, there had been a time when pullets were never eaten in England. But now, said Googe, they were a dainty dish at gentlemen's tables, and the dining accounts of Star Chamber dignitaries in 1590 certainly bear this out.[55]

During the seventeenth century, the market steadily promoted specialist poultry keepers, and in London's orbit chicken meat became more plentiful. But phases and fashions interrupted some of the continuities. A liking for the cramming of capons faded. Henry Hart, the Northampton physician, pronounced against it in 1633, and Moufet in 1600 (or his editor in 1655) similarly preferred chickens to be fattened in the open air rather than crammed and fattened in coops. Capons, on the other hand, continued to be bought by all and sundry: by the Reynell family of Forde in Devon, for example, between 1627 and 1631; and the Earl of Kent took trouble with a recipe for capons in 1654. But for one reason or another the old way of caponizing did fall from favour, and it may be significant in this connection that a cookery text of 1658 commended a quick method of cramming in three to four days with a paste of flour, sugar and milk; Kenelm Digby noted in 1669 yet another practice of Lady Fanshawe, who fattened her poultry by keeping them drunk with ale and burning a candle all night to keep them eating. By 1750 the art of caponizing was being lost; William Ellis was bemoaning the fact that women with the skill were hard to find in Hertfordshire, though he still hoped to see the skill revived.[56]

Our documents in the seventeenth century point to other innovations involving new breeds of birds and new ways of fattening them. The Dorking breed became a favourite type, signalling a specialized location in Surrey for that development. A liking for Polish and Hamburg breeds was mirrored in a lively correspondence in the 1650s, whereby foreign experience was brought to England through the efforts of that great internationalist, Samuel Hartlib. As for feeding the birds, Hertfordshire farmers fed their hens on horse beans, hempseed, buckwheat, and a barley meal paste, and in consequence Hertfordshire hens won a high reputation, causing higglers in London to cry their eggs as a speciality.[57]

TURKEYS

Along with chickens, other birds were successfully reared on the farm for meat on a new scale, namely turkeys, geese, and ducks. All have their separate histories, revealing experiments in new ways of management and some false starts. Turkeys were an entirely new bird brought from Mexico and Central South America in the course of explorations in the New World. Their first introduction is dated to about 1523–4, one food innovation among many at this time that was introduced by seafarers, who were generally curious about new foodstuffs wherever they encountered new peoples. They brought back many an unknown tree fruit, animal and bird to show their friends in England, and so sparked off fresh food ideas; turkeys were an early success in being acclimatized. Turkey meat was not on the list of dishes that were served to Queen Mary and King Philip in the 1550s, though the price of birds was legally fixed in the London market in 1555, but the meat was prominent in 1570 at Lord Leicester's feast in Oxford, when seven turkeys were supplied by a local lady. Other references in probate inventories show turkeys on farms elsewhere in the same decade. We can safely guess at some early prejudices against this new meat: such were expressed by William Harrison, but his objection to their strong taste was removed, so he explained, when their keepers gelded the birds. It was a practice which William Harrison had heard about but never seen, when he wrote his *Description of England* in 1587. It enabled them to be led into the fields as tranquilly as sheep, and decades later they were docile enough to walk to London. By 1750 William Ellis claimed that some people preferred turkey before all other tame bird meat, and had decided that the castration of turkeys actually improved the taste. Keeping them was more trouble than other poultry, however, and it was gentry and yeoman farmers who made the effort.[58]

GEESE

In the first part of the sixteenth century geese were appreciated more for their feathers than for their meat. But their meat was described as a common food by Mascall in 1581, and by then they were plainly appreciated as giving little trouble to keep while yielding valued grease as well as feathers. The change of management by gelding them, hinted at by Harrison in line with the management of turkeys, made it possible to lead them quietly into the fields; and Moufet was familiar with Pliny's story of the geese of Brabant and Picardy being driven like sheep all the way to Rome. So it may be that this lore circulated in Europe first, becoming better known in England through the coming of the Flemings to eastern England. In the extensive fens of East Anglia in the seventeenth century, geese were allowed to graze on the commons in unlimited numbers, and in Lincolnshire we have a foretaste of their later importance, finding that in 1642 on the common fen in Whaplode and Holbeach parishes (reckoned to be six miles in compass), both inhabitants and residents had free common *without stint* for geese as well as cattle and swine. 'Inhabitants and residents' is a description that seems to embrace not only tenants but squatters too, a generous provision.[59]

When the first driving of geese to London took place is not something we are ever likely to be able to date firmly. Defoe described it as relatively recent, after a routine for driving turkeys that way had become well established. Perhaps we should date it to the years around 1700–10. We can then see it through other eyes in 1727 when Richard Bradley described how people living along the route could, from July onwards, buy geese from the gooseherds at 25–30s. a score, ready to put them into the stubble of their own cornfields after harvest; before that moment arrived, they fed them on garden waste, especially lettuce. By September they were being fattened for two weeks in a close place with barley and water, but it was important not to allow them to wander at that stage for they would lose more flesh in one day than could be regained in three. Experience had taught, moreover, that geese were gregarious, and were best fattened in groups rather than singly. For the highly commercial aspect of the droving system, William Ellis is our best informant by 1750, describing them going from Flagg Fen, near Yarmouth in Norfolk; he knew of a drove of 1,400 birds, which were sold at Stratford in Essex for local poulterers to fatten. Since this sale was arranged just outside London, it sounds as if some fattening proceeded on the outskirts of the city, just as market gardening for vegetables had settled itself in a similar situation.[60]

The droving route for geese allows us to assume that many people in Hertfordshire and Essex enjoyed goose meat in the autumn. But across the whole country, access to water and some commons allowed geese to be kept almost anywhere, for they fended for themselves most of the time. They needed extra care to get them laying early, before Christmas if possible; then green geese in the spring (i.e. young goslings, ready to eat in February and March) were a special treat. They also needed attention again when fattening in autumn, and that called for extra feed, if not in stubble fields, then sometimes in houses in the dark.[61]

A random sampling of probate inventories suggests that geese were kept mostly in the pastoral counties where commons were likely to be extensive; about one farmer in six kept them, sometimes as many as one in three, but the numbers in a herd were modest, two or three, less often as many as ten, and usually they were not even counted. An outstanding poultry farmer was William Dockray of Matterdale in Greystoke parish in the 1630s, who had 160 head of poultry; was Dockray, perhaps, of foreign origin? In the more densely settled arable counties, where common grassland was scarce and could only be kept wholesome by excluding geese (except, of course, on the stubble after harvest), they were few and far between. So a considerable contrast is visible between, say, Northumberland, Cumberland, Derbyshire, Devon and Cornwall, where people kept geese; and Somerset or Northamptonshire, where they did not; in fact, the appraisers of property in Northamptonshire barely bothered to notice any poultry at all, and when they did, they referred only vaguely to 'poultry in the yard' as though it were a convention not to notice them at all. All this suggests that goose meat became a more familiar meat in the south-east of England between about 1550 and 1750, because the London market stirred things into life, while in the more remote and more strongly pastoral counties, some (but by no means all) farmers carried on a quiet routine of keeping a few geese to feed their families, but did not stir themselves beyond that. The varied local history of food springs into sharp relief in glimpses like this.[62]

The breeds of geese were various, but details are vouchsafed only by one observer, caught up in activities around London: one cross between an English and a Portuguese breed sheds a ray of light on experiments that were continually under way. As for cooking your goose, we are told that in the Netherlands they were salted and dried like bacon and then boiled, but the English preferred to roast them fresh-killed, making the dish as familiar then as now, flavoured with sage and onions and apple sauce.[63]

DUCKS AND MALLARDS

Writers of books on food at the beginning of the sixteenth century did not relish the meat of ducks and mallards, and this distaste seems to lie behind the seemingly satisfied comment of Andrew Boorde in 1545 when he found that people in Bohemia also deemed them unpalatable. A prejudice against water birds was a convention, at least among writers, springing from a judgement that water birds fed on disagreeable frogs, worms and spiders. In 1607 Sir John Harington still held the view that mallard should not be eaten, though he accepted that it was good sport to see them killed in the course of hunting expeditions. Some country folk surely ate ducks without a qualm, but a changing attitude in the public world probably owed most to observation of the more regular domestic feeding of ducks in yards, coupled perhaps with increasing alarm at food shortages in lean years in the late sixteenth century when populations were noticeably rising and more meat was needed from somewhere. In Oxford some clerics showed no prejudice against mallard; the Oxford martyrs in 1555–6 occasionally ate mallard and teal while in prison. Lord Leicester's feast in Oxford in 1570 included ten fat mallards, their fatness presumably achieved by farmyard feeding, and Peachey's recipe book of 1594 contained two recipes for mallard. So by 1600 mallards were accepted fare, and Moufet in 1600 (or his editor in 1655) had come around to approving of ducks when they were farm-fed.[64]

A brave new venture in the rearing of ducks and mallards on a much larger scale was put forward by Arthur Standish in 1611 after he had seen them semi-tamed without any deliberate effort at his old family home in Standish in Lancashire. He saw these birds settling of their own accord on water round the house, and when once they were fed by the servants, they returned for food regularly at night and became so tame that they even followed staff into the courtyard and hall-house. Standish saw the chance of taming them systematically by erecting pullen plots by a river with a nesting house alongside. He urged that eggs be deftly taken from duck nests in the fens in spring, without disturbing the ducks, and be carried away to be hatched under hens. He knew of this as a regular practice by the locals in the East Anglian fens, showing how resourceful and opportunist were country people, uncluttered by theories, and relying rather on practical experience of success or failure. By 1750 William Ellis regarded ducks as 'dainty food for the nicest palates', as well as being useful birds for devouring pests in the turnip and rape fields. The commonest kind was the wild duck, but a Muscovy sort was also kept, and now the Normandy breed was in vogue with the gentry because of its bulk and delicate flesh. Plainly, people kept a constant watch for more succulent food from new breeds.[65]

Arthur Standish in 1611 saw the pullen plot promising more meat for ordinary folk, and more commercial profit than keeping a dovecote. In the event, his scheme did not attract support, because at much the same time the Dutch drainage of the fens was teaching the English how to set up duck decoys. But it is tempting to think that James I latched onto the idea, as he did to other new gimmicks, for several documents in the State Papers in 1624 refer to his concern for the preservation of fowl, which was his 'chief pleasure', and his wish to enclose some ground by the river at Newmarket, which he often visited, in order 'to feed young fowl for the increase of game'. A gamekeeper was being paid to watch over heron, ducks and mallards after the tenant had been persuaded to yield to the king's wishes to enclose some riverside land, and although the phraseology does not contain any reference to the Standish project, it came close to it in practice, and readers had already been told in Standish's published pamphlet in 1611 that it had the personal approval of the king.[66]

Methods of catching some wildfowl in the fens must long since have been devised by the fenlanders, but the setting up of decoys caught on and became a supremely successful way of trapping them in the autumn, as they followed their migratory paths from northern Europe across the fens. A full description of the method is given by J. Wentworth-Day in *A History of the Fens*, attributing the first constructed decoy to Sir William Wodehouse at Waxham, Norfolk, some time between 1603 and 1625. The author's other examples follow considerably later, in 1653, 1665 and 1670, and suggest a surprisingly slow start for this innovation that is not easy to credit, given all the other laborious attempts on manorial estates to increase the supply of wildfowl. A more systematic search of the records is likely to reveal many more decoys being set up between the 1630s and 1670s. All that is certain at present is that decoys spread eventually into almost every county of England, and at least 100 are known in the eastern counties alone. Prodigious numbers of birds were still being caught in the nineteenth century; Wentworth-Day guesses at 5,000 birds caught per annum in each of 100 decoys, while his own records show nearly 100,000 caught in the course of 35 seasons at one decoy in Ashby in Bottesford parish in Lincolnshire. In the seventeenth century London customers ate wildfowl on an entirely new scale.[67]

THE TAMING AND FATTENING OF WILD BIRDS

Decoys were not the only way of capturing wild birds. Outside the fens, in both woodland and open country, innumerable birds were there for the taking. Contemporaries, indeed, saw no limit to the numbers they could trap and the many ingenious means of doing it; they never begrudged the effort involved. A great mass of traditional lore already existed, and information now spread further through books and example; gentlemen's household accounts, moreover, show how much care was taken to follow bookish precepts. Thus Nathaniel Bacon's household accounts for Stiffkey in Norfolk show peewits caught in two different kinds of net, one net for those fluttering low and another for those fluttering high. Then came the challenge of keeping them at home and breeding from their eggs. As for their meat, Fuller, writing on Essex in his *Worthies*, described the peewit as poor meat, nothing but bones, feathers and lean flesh when young, he said. Yet through the years between 1600 and 1700 the professionals refined their skills, and by 1700 the London poulterers were feeding them with gravel to scour them and curds to fatten them in a fortnight; their flesh so prepared was deemed 'most delicious'. The tricks for fattening varied in detail for different birds, but were the same in general, requiring indoor boxes, straw and hiding places, plus a cover to prevent them flying away, and food in which the different birds delighted so that they fattened quickly. By taking this trouble, bird catchers were far from eating scrawny, meagre meat.[68]

Wild birds were a considerable source of meat, though its chronological and quantitative history eludes us. Sir William Petre at Ingatestone in Elizabeth's reign fattened quails in cages, and his household accounts show hempseed being bought to feed them. Quails were also caught wild, and it was doubtless the wild ones that were served at Lord Leicester's banquet in Oxford in 1570 when they were brought from Bernwood Forest, and possibly fattened *en route* by the fowler before he delivered them. Herons were a bird that Mascall dismissed as not worth the trouble of fattening – more expense than profit – but tastes differed, and one of the French teaching dialogues in Elizabeth's reign refers to the process, saying 'you need not fear that it tasteth of the sea for they are brought us alive, and we feed them in the house'. Larks were welcome in the kitchen of the Reynell family of Forde in Devon on several occasions in 1629–30, and evidently September to November was the season for catching them.[69]

A new urgency was given to the trapping of wildfowl when more and more colonists went to the New World, and later in James I's reign, Gervase Markham assembled for their benefit all he knew on the subject in a book entitled *Hunger's Prevention*. As a young gentleman mixing in court circles and roaming around the Northamptonshire forests as well as in the Weald of Kent, he knew a multitude of ways of catching wildfowl and told a full story of using nets, strings, birdlime, imitating birdcalls, laying out baits of hempseed, rapeseed and mustard seed, using stalking horses, and lighting flares at night. Many of the methods were truly simple, and were explicitly commended to poor men; if a fowler had no stalking horse, he could make shift with a piece of stuffed canvas, or cover his head with a hood, even just hold up a bush or branch. One man, he reported, painted an owl on wood and caught many birds that way. A sparrow net set against the eaves of a thatched house, barn or stables was an even simpler way of catching small birds, and no effort was required if the net was hung when men were flailing on the threshing floor. A whole flock of birds would descend together and be caught in a trice.[70]

When wildfowl were professionally caught they were placed in enclosures and coaxed to feed on wine and ale, which made them drunk; often they were mixed among birds already tamed to reassure the wild ones. That practice was used with thrushes, fieldfares and blackbirds. Partridges, quails, seagulls, peewits, pheasants, godwits, knots, stynts and plovers also submitted to this domestic feeding regime, even bustards, bitterns and curlews. They might bite the hand that fed them, but it was said to be worth the pain when they finished up as such pleasant food.

Individual tastes for different meats varied of course, but it was usual to argue that the meat tasted best if the birds had been caught in flight rather than in nets.

In the case of wildfowl, preference was expressed for eating the wings. But the same prejudice surfaced in the writing of John Ray, the botanist: when eating chickens, he preferred the legs for they had been continually in action. Finally, the merits of sweet herbs for close-feeding at the end were always emphasized, for that gave the flesh the most delicate flavour.[71]

We never catch a glimpse of birds in the cooking pot of common folk, but we can take them for granted in the countryside. Trapping wild birds was traditional country lore, and of all meat it was the one kind that was free to all. No laws prohibited the trapping of birds, so long as they were not taken on the lord's own land, on his demesne, in his warren, or in his own park, and a multitude of indirect comments confirm the fact that wild birds were a common meat. Gervase Markham relied on peasants and labourers to tell him all the tricks of the trade, and when John Worlidge in his book in 1675 added a few more tips, he urged his readers, if they wanted to catch partridges, to ask any carter or day-labourer, for they knew their haunts. Markham's account conjures up a lively picture of the fun enjoyed by youngsters on a night out, catching birds with flares and birdcalls, and we have noted already how carefully gentry families wrapped the food in yards of canvas when sending it to relations in London. John Worlidge's advice on catching woodcocks shows us the routine: woodcocks, he said, were known to 'take a great deal of pleasure in flying in the night-time through open places in tall woods, especially in a dim moonlight night'. So people cut a passage athwart the hill to lure them there, and laid a net before nightfall, making sure to be on hand when they were caught in the net. 'There is scarce any bird that flies', wrote Worlidge, 'but there is some peculiar way of discovering or ensnaring him, different from another.' So while it is impossible to measure how much wildfowl augmented the diet of different classes in different places, the evidence that we have shows the tide of news, example and interest sweeping people into an enlarging circle of well-informed and well-practised birdcatchers. We look below at the recipe books for more clues, while the gentry's household accounts show the quantities regularly supplied by fowlers, or given as gifts by neighbours; the trapping methods were perfected by observant country people. In short, plentiful bird meat was at hand for the resourceful countryman.[72]

The domestic rearing of wild birds, by hatching their eggs taken in spring, was another way of adding to the family's meat supply, and was a further skill practised by ordinary folk from time immemorial. Arthur Standish learned it in the eastern fens where nesting ducks and mallards were innumerable in spring. You took some eggs, but not all, going back regularly to the nest for about three weeks, but never touching any eggs in the nest with bare hands; so the birds continued to lay more. The East Yorkshire farmer, Henry Best, described the taking and hatching of partridge eggs in thoroughly matter-of-fact terms, whenever the ploughman stumbled on them while cutting grass. You cared for the eggs through various stages of hatching, until the birds were content to feed in an enclosure, and the family then enjoyed the meat later in the summer. It might all sound like food for gentry and yeomen's households rather than for common folk, but the account from the fenland shows the opportunism of all classes, when the birds were plentiful.[73]

Something of a fashion for breeding particular birds like quails and plovers (lapwings) seems to have taken hold around 1600, showing appreciation of their eggs as well as their meat; this is specially evident among gentry in the eastern counties. Nathaniel Bacon at Stiffkey in Norfolk kept both quails and plovers, and the breeding of pheasants at home may also have spread locally to more members of the same class, for Nathaniel Bacon was also thus involved. In general, however, pheasants were likely to have been viewed in a class apart. Signs of interest in that skill had been shown in the 1530s by Henry VIII, and we have suggested above that his enthusiasm was stirred by a visit to France at that time. The project involved a French priest coming to breed pheasants at Eltham palace, but how that royal project fared subsequently is unknown. Nevertheless, the French authors of *Maison Rustique* told their readers in the 1560s that it could be done, though only if someone were employed full time to tend the birds. As this French textbook on husbandry was assiduously read thereafter by country gentry, the breeding of pheasants was likely to be picked up as an exotic hobby from then on. We have shown above how the Earl of Rutland was certainly breeding them in 1607, paying a widow to feed them and buying scissors for her to clip their wings. That project was still under way in 1611, and we can only guess how many other rich men followed suit. Other gentlemen, meanwhile, caught their pheasants for the table by using a hawk or nets, and enjoyed the sport at the same time.[74]

Being women's work, the progress of poultry-keeping and game breeding continued to be a hidden story. But knowing the lively interest in producing more varied foods in greater quantity, and how strongly this thread runs through food history to the end of our period, we can guess that fresh opportunities stimulated positive responses somewhere. In the 1650s another small window was opened on the scene by Samuel Hartlib, collecting ideas and practical experience from all and sundry as he sat in London, and urged a more adventurous spirit in farming and food production on Cromwellian republicans. Arthur Standish's treatise of 1611 was circulated and studied afresh, though admittedly less attention was paid to his poultry project than to his others for fruit and fuel. These readers mentioned a French author, who was fairly certainly Choyselat. News came to Hartlib of the Poles cramming birds in a way that made them taste far better than others, and they were being transported in baskets in the many corn boats from Danzig to the Netherlands. Hartlib sent to John Beale in 1657 a book entitled *A Discourse on Hens*, now sadly lost, and other letters passed across Hartlib's desk, especially from Cressy Dymock, on the best foods for fattening poultry, including green plants, a mixture of chopped carrots, boiled turnips and bean meal; boiled livers were also recommended. Word of this last food evidently spread far afield, for in 1665 a man was charged at Quarter Sessions for annoying his neighbours in Reigate, Surrey, by keeping 200–300 hens in a barn and feeding them on livers and the fat from dead cattle.[75]

Other news circulated at this time about poultry specialists around London, including a Chelsea woman who was said to have hatched a thousand pheasant eggs, losing many, she admitted, but also saving many. Tales of this kind fed contemporaries with ideas, and alert us to changing perceptions of birds in demand at the market and in diet. Cressy Dymock summed it up by referring significantly to the need to 'breed abundance of poultry, as turkeys, hens, etc., in a more regular way than hitherto used'. Something like this had perhaps actually started by the 1670s, for Richard Blome in 1673 described Horsham in Sussex as 'the great emporium for capons' whence they were sent to London.[76]

One highly professional account by Adam Shewring, a London poulterer, which was put into print in 1699, explained his practices in fattening all kinds of birds for his customers, and as some of them are known to us from earlier writers, we may confidently believe that some domestic households practised them too. Shewring had different methods for fattening shufflers (like ducks but smaller), peewits, wheatears, quails, partridges, pheasants, godwits, knots, ruffs, curlews, blackbirds, thrushes and fieldfares, and he crammed capons as well. We know, moreover, that some of the usual food mentioned in all such advice, like hempseed and milk curds, was plentiful, wheat and barley were cheaper than ever, and livers were now being freely used to feed birds. Much varied information converges to support the argument that while the interest of male writers in poultry faded again after 1700, the topic retreated into the women's realm, and the literature tailed away, wild and farm-fed bird meat had established a far larger place in diet than it had occupied in 1500. At the same time, it is instructive to compare the bird meat market with dairy foods, which did not retreat into obscurity in the same way. It remained prominent on the male agenda, and the menfolk began to take charge of its production. A sign of the times was the way John Houghton's news-sheet in the 1680s and 1690s gave banner headlines to dairy foods, whereas it steadfastly ignored poultry-keeping.[77]

RECIPES FOR BIRD MEAT

Recipes for birds regularly appeared in cookbooks, supporting the notion that both tame and wild birds were a common source of meat. The various methods of cooking them enabled all classes to cook them satisfactorily, without elaborate cooking utensils. Of course, the choice of different vegetables and herbs made for many differences in the resulting flavour, and doubtless among contemporaries the flavourings were in or out of fashion as well as in or out of season. Thomas Dawson's recipe book (1596–7) used endive and spinach when cooking larks, which suggests a taste for exotic greens, since spinach was a newish vegetable at that date and endive was far from commonplace; ordinary folk at that time would more likely have chosen root vegetables, such as carrots and turnips, plus cabbage. Flavour also depended on the choice of wild herbs, which varied greatly according to the season and district.[78]

In the sixteenth century it was usual to serve all meat on sippets of bread. Then in the seventeenth century elaborate sauces began to be poured over meat. In 1736 Richard Bradley showed poultry dishes having a sauce poured over them, but sippets or sops on which the meat had once been laid had gone from his table. Bread was still used to thicken sauces, but mushrooms, which had been suspect as a food in the mid-seventeenth century, were now accepted, along with yolks of eggs popped in at the last moment before serving. Butter was used ever more plenteously in stuffings as time wore on. Richard Bradley's report in 1736 on the recipe of Mrs Lancashire of Manchester for curing woodcocks is memorable as an example: he praised it highly – 'a better dish is seldom met with'. When parboiled, the woodcocks were stuffed with butter, for which a dozen birds required 7–8lbs. Then they were covered tightly with paper and baked in an oven for about two hours. Next, the meat was packed afresh in the pot with another 3–4lbs of melted butter. Altogether, 10–11lbs of butter were needed, and the dish would keep fresh for two months.[79]

The few cookbooks that survive from the later sixteenth century show a substantial interest in bird meat, and the assumption that enormous variety would be available. But we can be sure that differences in the birds that were locally plentiful would have struck outsiders forcefully, for they varied so much between the fens and the Pennine moorlands, the forests and the coasts. But still bird meat of some kind was accessible to all, and that is silently acknowledged by the anonymous author of *The Good Huswifes Handmaide for the Kitchen* (*c.* 1594). The recipes spanned almost the whole gamut of birds, tame and wild, from capons, chickens, mallards, ducks and quails, to pheasants, partridges, plovers, snites, bitterns, herons, woodcock, sparrows, larks and more. Moreover, they offered three very different mixes of flavouring in the stewpot: green vegetables, roots, herbs and marrow bones, which the most ordinary housewife could muster; or dried fruits such as currants, dates, raisins, prunes and oranges (presumably for winter and for those with money in their purse); or a mix of summer fruits like gooseberries, barberries and damsons, which many people could gather wild. The book also offered as alternatives dishes that were roasted, baked, or baked in a coffin. The author plainly envisaged a wide range of birds coming into the kitchen; and while the instructions favoured some moistening of the innards of the birds with butter to keep the flesh succulent, butter was not prescribed in all dishes; the addiction to butter had not yet taken full hold in 1594.[80]

Thomas Dawson's book of 1596–7 belonged in the same tradition as the previous author. His recipe for stewing a cock was word for word the same as the earlier one, and his ingredients can be grouped in the same three ways, though he mixed them rather more often – dried fruits with lettuce, for example, and spinach or endive with currants. Ginger, cinnamon, mace and nutmeg were his routine spices, and many dishes were served on sops. He, like the earlier author, expected to be cooking tame and wild birds, but he also had a foreign repertoire: a Dutch recipe for chicken and mutton mixed; and a French one for pigeons with herbs, currants, cinnamon, ginger, cloves and mace.[81]

Robert May's cookery book of 1660 showed no effort to differentiate recipes in order to bring out the flavour of separate birds. But he expected to use plenty of flavourings, and made out a long list of possibles in his recipes. Middle-class authors likewise cooked all kinds. Diana Astry (c. 1700) listed the menus she encountered when eating out and regularly ate wildfowl between October and December, though she did not herself suggest any wildfowl recipes to her readers. On the other hand, Elizabeth Cleland (1755) certainly did, naming quails, larks, plovers, snipe and wild ducks. The likes of Astry and Cleland, admittedly, hint at a readership among people of the well-to-do middle class, but the answer to the next question about this meat being eaten by working folk is firmly given by Sarah Jackson, who published recipes in weekly parts for ordinary women to buy at the local shop. She was more informative than any of the other authors on the subject of wild birds, nurturing our suspicion that she was catering for a class that ate more wildfowl than the rest. It is, of course, true that a Chatham bookseller sold her periodical, and it is not impossible that she had a clientéle on the east coast that trapped wildfowl more readily than people living further inland. She gave an impressive list of recipes for wild ducks, pigeons, woodcock, bitterns, bustards, cranes, mallards, tern, partridges, quails, teal and pheasants, and in listing suitable menus she added knotts, ruffs, reeves, widgeon and easterlings. Here was a cook who knew and differentiated her local birds. Were people in other areas of the country as well versed?[82]

The same prominent place for wild birds in diet is conjured up in Eileen Elder's carefully researched book on *Lincolnshire Country Food*. Lincolnshire, with its long coastline and its place on a migratory route between north-eastern Europe and Africa, is another county that is likely to have enjoyed abundant wildfowl. Her evidence includes an 1872 Lincolnshire school book that expected pupils to be familiar with a host of wild birds. Mrs Elder did not believe that they ate much of this food by the late nineteenth century, but she was confident that their grandfathers and great-grandfathers had eaten plenty. So, in order to enter into that world with greater assurance and familiarity, we shall have to search our local archives more systematically. But ringing in our ears must be the words of a Lincolnshire resident in 1914, still relishing a pie containing breasts of thrush and blackbird, with hard-boiled eggs and bacon, and calling it 'as glorious a pie as man or woman could desire to taste'.[83]

FISH

Our food experience in the last 20 years has given us a new perspective on the fish-eating of the past. Compulsory fish days were once a routine, taken for granted by our forebears throughout the Middle Ages until the mid-seventeenth century. Among twentieth-century commentators such regulation is often treated as something of a penance, for we did not then envisage a scarcity of fish; it was more than plentiful in the shops. Overfishing in the seas has entirely altered our perceptions; fish is turning into something of a luxury food, and it is not cheap. We may justly look back on the early modern period with some envy for the enormous variety of fish that was then enjoyed by all classes: it allowed plenty of oysters, the frequent taste of herrings, and much food that was free to the takers. Healthwise, moreover, our forebears were consuming a highly satisfactory quantity of polyunsaturated omega-3 fatty acids, whereas people now consume far more omega-6 oils instead, not to mention other saturated fats that raise concerns for our health.[84]

As Thomas Cogan affirmed in 1584, half of every year in his lifetime was taken up with eating fish. Friday and Saturday were fish days until the late Middle Ages; Saturday was reintroduced by Parliament in 1548, and Wednesday was added in 1563 by Elizabeth. As for the regional pattern of fish-eating, it was more varied than was the case with meat, for the different coastal waters and rivers produced their own specialities. Pilchards were plentiful in the south-west, chars were a distinctive fish in Windermere, eels were abundant in the rivers and fen dykes, and many lesser specialities were treasured by local people that have now been forgotten: 'bleak', a small river fish, was found in the Thames in February, and in shoals in August, and was deemed by a Richmond connoisseur better than sprats and an excellent substitute for anchovies; he gave his recipe.[85]

Fish in some form was available to all, though we cannot be sure how far riparian owners across the kingdom effectively guarded, or wanted to guard, the fish in their rivers from others. Local customs differed. We learn in 1520 that people in Gloucestershire watched the Severn closely in the lamprey season to make sure that they had all they wanted before allowing people from afar to get near. Some Kent documents tell us how, along the innumerable wayward streams of the river Medway, the locals reacted with alarm when the Sewer Commissioners started to take stock of all the weirs in which they caught profitable quantities of eels. The river authorities were intent on clearing a deeper channel for larger boats to pass from Tonbridge to Maidstone, and they threatened the removal of all weirs. But in spawning time Yalding people said they caught two bushels in a night and reckoned to sell some. As for the rights of riparian owners and tenants, we have to assume that different local conventions were observed: the lord of the Isle of Axholme, for example, allowed *all tenants and inhabitants* to set bush nets and catch white fish on Wednesdays and Fridays. River fishing was certainly not as uniformly regulated as it is nowadays.[86]

What variety of fish was enjoyed by the different social classes is another question. Kings and queens tasted a grand array: a fish meal served to King Philip of Spain at some time in Queen Mary's reign between 1553 and 1558 saw on the table ling, salt salmon, fresh sturgeon, seal, porpoise, lobsters and more, together with freshwater fish that included pike, bream, carp, roach, fresh salmon and eels. One London portbook in the 1560s shows imported fish coming from Flushing, Amsterdam, Danzig and Hamburg, and names eels, herring, salmon grills, Scotch salmon in barrels (though coming from Flushing!), ling and cod's heads. Cargoes of fish in the early seventeenth century arrived in Boston, from Scotland, Emden, Bergen, Rotterdam and Amsterdam, thus conjuring up a lively picture of the fish that Lincolnshire people around the Wash could eat out of the North and Baltic seas, even though they already had eels from the fens in their thousands. From his vantage point in London and Essex, William Harrison in Elizabeth's reign professed to know little about fish, but nevertheless managed to fill two pages of text with the names of five categories and 36 kinds with which he was familiar.[87]

Not all parts of the country were equally well served, of course. But the efforts of the well-to-do in securing fish in variety and quantity in all seasons gives an idea of the esteem in which such food was held. The nobility and gentry sent their servants long distances to Stourbridge for dried fish in time for Lent. At other times, a well-heeled gentleman would set his heart on securing something unusual to impress his guests, and go to endless lengths to satisfy his desires, as when Thomas Throckmorton in inland Northamptonshire somehow procured lobsters and crabs in the summer of 1613 to entertain Lord Wootton, and brought a special cook from Oxford for the occasion.[88]

More remarkable still is the seeming ignorance of local fish seasons in the story of Henry Sherfield, at home in Salisbury, challenging his man in charge of household provisions to get him lobsters in January 1624, and causing Ambrose Prewett to visit the Isle of Wight; we can only hope that in the depth of winter he did not travel through a snow storm. There he learned that no lobsters could be had until June, after which they would continue for much of the summer. He returned to make enquiries 'of others which travel for transporting of fish from the Isle of Purbeck and other coasts near Exeter'. He learned that 'there is one Covent [*recte*, Corent] who is now an innkeeper at the Sign of the Lamb in Salisbury who hath himself heretofore been only a driver and transporter of fish from those western parts, but now keepeth servants and horses for that purpose'. This man was evidently willing to satisfy Henry Sherfield's every whim and charge modest prices; middle-sized lobsters in London could be supplied for about 14d. the couple, he said, though he was not yet certain in what quantity. He promised to go to the Isle of Purbeck (presumably from Salisbury) on Monday next to gauge the supply, and would also enquire about plaice and mullet. At the same time, Mr Prewett arranged to send a messenger to Gloucestershire to the river Severn for salmons 'if they shall be seasonable'.[89]

A rather different glimpse of a gentleman's personal interest in getting food and fish into his kitchen is afforded by Thomas Moufet, physician to monarchs and nobility, who was walking home to Putney from a visit to Barnes, probably to see Sir Francis Walsingham, some time before 1590, and saw a fish for sale called 'old wives', so-named, he tells us, because of its 'mumping and sour countenance'. He bought it, had it boiled at home with some thyme in wine and vinegar with salt, and never ate a more firm, white, dainty fish.[90]

Changing fashions in fish thread their way quietly through the story in these centuries. Fickle Londoners picked up one fad and dropped another, although all that may well have passed unnoticed among people living north, east and west. An unexpected account of James I keeping trained cormorants to catch fish leaves us guessing how new or old that practice was. A history of China by Mendoza had been published in translation in 1588, and it had described the method by which rings round the birds' necks prevented them from swallowing the fish; it is possible that gossip about this book, plus James's visit in 1608 to Thetford, where he saw three cormorants on a church steeple, started his interest in what he regarded as a sport. A much more significant interest in keeping fish in ponds rose to the surface of public discussion in our period. More and more ponds were dug or refurbished, noticeably in Surrey, Sussex and Kent. Already in the later Middle Ages, moats had been turned to good use for storing some fish, from which they were fished with nets; perch, described as a delicate fish by Harrison at this time, was said to flourish particularly well in moats. Then, as agricultural profit became a stronger gentleman's objective, the returns per acre from fish in a pond were calculated, and deemed superior to the profit from the same acreage of meadow. As for imported fish, a closer look at the cargoes landed at coastal ports would almost certainly differentiate the catches over time, and open up yet other views of ocean movements, changes in people's tastes, and more besides.[91]

Among passing fashions we have noticed above how carp and pike had so taken the rich man's fancy by the later seventeenth century that Evelyn was served with both at every meal when he stayed at the house of Lady Swallowfield in

1685; and they were of a size 'fit for the table of a prince'. In a French-teaching dialogue of Hollyband's about a century before, carp had been regarded as a very expensive food. Offered stewed carp by his host, the guest replied: 'You will put yourself to great cost.' 'Care you not for the charges,' replied the gallant host. But when Bradley was writing in 1736, his notion of fish for grand dishes had moved on, and the list featured turbot, fresh salmon, cod's head and pike. Cod's head had already been signalled by John Houghton in 1702 as 'a celebrated dish among our greatest gluttons', heading fish that for him included mackerel, much in request when it first arrived in London in season. Yet in Moufet's day, *c.* 1600 (or was it in the days of Moufet's editor, i.e. in 1655?), mackerel was said to have been much in request in the past but was now not much in favour.[92]

The quickening pace of commercial dealings in food generally is made evident in the way fish was transported over long distances, and doubtless this affected the quantities and kinds of fish that entered different markets. So people's changing experience of fish registered significantly in one lifetime. One family in Cumberland regularly sent salmon in barrels to their relations in London in the early seventeenth century; that meant a journey from Naworth in Cumberland to Newcastle, and a sea voyage to London, sometimes returning with saltfish. Would that we had stories of the adventures of the rippyers travelling fast with fish in their panniers from the south coast (from around Rye and Hastings), along recognized routes to London. They paused very briefly at Chipstead, near Sevenoaks, while others moved off to Worcestershire and Gloucestershire. They were known by local people to halt at Nimesfield at a common inn for one hour only every Thursday in the year at 4 o'clock in the afternoon.[93]

As for grading the fish for goodness, we learn from Moufet how the writers on food judged them by what they fed on, and the water they swam in. Sea fish came out sweetest and best because sea air was purest, the water was continually stirred up and never became stale, the salt washed away impurities, and the fish were constantly on the move, getting exercise. But particular coastal districts were distinguished as the source for different kinds of fish: sea mullet from the mouth of the Usk; small conger eels from the Severn between Gloucester and Tewkesbury; plaice of the best kind from Rye, Sandwich and Dover. Indeed, the pleasures of plaice prompted Moufet to dream of a time when, 'if we had plenty of such wholesome fish, butchers' meat would go begging'. As for scallops and cockles, he expressed himself more revealingly when thinking about those of Selsey and Purbeck; they were judged the best anywhere, he said, but then his mind wandered to the badge of pilgrims, and he uttered an extraordinarily fierce anti-Catholic jibe at the scallops caught off Compostela in Spain; they were thought by some to be the best, and so thither 'lecherous men and women resort to eat scallops for the kindling of lust and increase of nature under the name Pilgrimage to St James his shrine'.[94]

The hierarchy of fish put salt herring low on Moufet's list, giving no nourishment except to ploughmen, sailors, soldiers, mariners and labouring persons, to whom gross and heavy meals were most familiar and convenient. But a hundred years later, herrings were for John Houghton 'the king of fishes', because of their delicate taste and the great profit they earned. Why and how this happened remains to be explained. The poor were welcome to eat seal meat and red sprats in Moufet's day. Ladies and gentlemen, on the other hand, loved porpoise, and watched with amusement the way the prisoners at Newgate refused it. The care given to the cooking of all this fish is revealed in the recipes incorporating herbs like dill, vervain and fennel, with varied vinegars, while some were stored in barrels with wine and seawater to last half a year.[95]

Preserving fish and crustaceans alive was already an art among a few in the sixteenth century. Harrison in Elizabeth's reign knew people who kept oysters in pits, while Gervase Markham knew eels kept alive in home-made contrivances. John Taverner in *Certaine Experiments with Fish and Fruite*, strangely alleged in 1601 that fish-keeping (in ponds) was no longer so popular as in the past, but showed himself unusually sensitive to fish size, and the feed given the fish in ponds that affected flavours at different seasons. In small ponds he recommended owners to throw barley, peas, cheese curds and beast blood, indicating how much trouble was taken by some fish lovers who fervently believed in the health-giving properties of fish. The preservation of fish in pickle, copying the process devised for meat, represented a more significant development, and along with other ways of storage, fish preservation developed into a sophisticated art in the second half of the seventeenth century. It enabled Jos. Cooper, a royal chef, to pickle salmon that would last half a year, and Robert May (1660) to store cooked lobsters, wrapped in rags steeped in brine and buried in a cellar, to last for three months. Two patents were issued in 1691 to hopeful projectors who offered preserving liquors 'of their unique devising'; by that date preservation was all the rage.[96]

If John Taverner was correct in sensing a fading of interest in pond construction around 1600, it could perfectly well have resulted from early gossip about the more attractive returns from grazing sheep and cattle on pastures, saving all that labour in digging out new ponds. But by 1660 ponds were definitely again in favour, and pond fish too judging by the recipe books. In Robert May's cookbook of 1660 his first fish dish was carp, followed by 17 more pages of carp recipes. Pike also featured, whereas he had only six lines on broiling herrings, pilchards or sprats; was a tussle under way between the merits of, and fashion for, sea fish and pond fish? Around 1700 the best fish recipes were given by John Collins, writing first about salt, and then taking great pains to get good fish recipes (for all kinds of fish) from a cook with 30 years' experience, John Bull. His are the best of his age for straightforward instructions and economical flavourings, including one recipe that shows clearly how stockfish was made appetizing so long as one took trouble.[97]

Fish days were abolished under the Commonwealth as a Popish superstition, but it is not clear when abstinence from meat and fasting during Lent noticeably fell away. It is only mildly hinted at in *Tusser Redivivus* in 1710, when fish was still a cheap food in many parts of the country. But a changed world was dramatically proclaimed in Cobbett's angry outburst when he took his rural rides in the 1820s and 1830s, and bewailed the sight of decayed fish ponds; he had seen 500 since he left home, while he watched housewives buying all their food at shops and their dinners ready cooked. It is a thoroughly familiar sight to us now.[98]

DAIRY FOODS

The dairying business underwent some of the most profound changes of all foods in our period. In 1500 dairy produce was considered to be poor man's fare, and dairywomen sold their wares only in local markets. By 1760 it was a highly competitive business, conspicuously integrated into the national market, while dairy farms grew larger and larger, and butter and cheese were made, sold and exported in a wide range of qualities and quantities.

On the political scene, dairy food was virtually ignored in the sixteenth century. Parliament focused its efforts on stopping the conversion of arable land to pasture in order to uphold the plough and maintain cereal production. As late as 1652 Walter Blith summed up the general view of dairy farming as 'poor men's pursuits', though in fact 'poor women's pursuits' would have been a more correct description, for women did the bulk of the work apart from foddering and cleaning out the cowstalls. Our documents also show that it was women more often than men who sold the produce at local markets, though male cheesemongers were in charge in London. Hosts of families, in any case, provided for their own needs at home by possessing a household cow. In an unguarded moment in 1658 Kenelm Digby still believed that the meanest cottager had a cow to supply milk to his family, and while we can dismiss that as a grand overstatement, it was perfectly true that of all livestock a cow was the commonest possession of country people. When analysing specialist markets in the period 1500–1640, Alan Everitt found a markedly small group specializing in dairy produce: among some 800 market towns, only 300 specialized in anything at all, and of those nearly one half (133) were renowned for their grain, while only 12 concentrated on cheese and butter.[99]

THE RISING STATUS OF DAIRY FOODS

Things began to change slowly in the period between 1500 and 1650. William Harrison noted a defining moment around 1587 when the butter dealers began to swarm around farmhouses in Essex, straining to buy butter before it had even been made. Then in the course of the 1650s a dramatic qualitative change took place, when Parliamentary armies relied heavily on cheese, and rather less on butter, to feed the soldiery going to Ireland; Cheshire was the first county to be called on for supplies. Another army, going to Scotland, drew on supplies from Yorkshire and Suffolk, and some orders ran to 100 tons, even 300 tons at a time. Walter Blith showed his awareness of the changing scene by omitting from his book about agriculture the phrasing that he had once used, calling dairying 'poor men's pursuits'.[100]

So it is no surprise to find the conversion of farms to dairying gathering pace. Cheshire JPs in 1623 noted how much land in Nantwich Hundred had been converted to pasture for dairies, while shrill complaints mounted from factors and farmers about dishonest butter-packing (stones being put inside to weigh down the barrels), about rancid butter, poor-quality produce passed off as high-quality, and bullying by oppressive merchants. Whereas the export of dairy foods had been restrained in James I's and Charles I's reigns, it was positively encouraged after 1656, in order to dispose of the increased output when war gave way to peace. Finally, the ambiguous, grudging attitude among the upper classes towards cheese as a healthy food gave way to a surge of fashion in favour of milk, cheese cake and cheese. Samuel Pepys greatly relished a tankard of milk while sitting in his coach in Hyde Park in 1669, and on another occasion polished off a cup of 'new milk', no doubt freshly milked for him at the very moment he asked for it by milkmaids grazing their cows in the park. This was at a time when asses' milk was also much in fashion, particularly for invalids. By 1757 dairy products had risen further into modish favour, and a Cheesecake House had been opened near the park. In short, this all repeats, though in reverse, what some of us remember of attitudes towards milk between 1930 and 2000.[101]

Dairy food was high fashion by 1750, and a sixteenth-century observer would have gasped at the way things had changed. Philip Stubbes had referred to butter and cheese as 'naught', 'cheap trifles'; both were conventionally called 'white meat' and ranked as food of the poor. Bread and cheese were the usual foods in bequests to the poor in the fifteenth century. Thus were these bestowed by Thomas Grene of Creeting St Peter, near Stowmarket, Suffolk, in 1439, who also left all his milch cows to his wife; that bequest, incidentally, was no more than elementary justice, since we can be sure that she had done all the buttermaking in that family.[102]

Incipient change in the attitude towards dairy foods positively spills from the sentences in the little book cited earlier about dairying, published in 1588 by Bartholomew Dowe, and explaining his mother's highly professional procedures in his home county of Suffolk. Hampshire women were pressing him hard for precise information on the best practice that he had observed in his childhood. An enlivened cross-country trade was already stirring competition and setting high standards. Care for good management and pride in the quality of the product shone out of Dowe's account on every page; a little revolution was under way.[103]

MILK DRINKS

What, then, of the changing role of milk, butter and cheese in diet? Apart from the use of milk for a bath, evidently an indulgence of the Earl of Rutland in 1602, milk featured as a drink in the diet of all classes. But it was much more common among the poor than the rich up to about some time in the mid-seventeenth century, when, as Pepys's diary illustrates, it became a fashionable drink among the literati: Robert Latham, his editor, refers to 'a thriving trade in tankards of cold milk' in the 1660s at a milkhouse at the lodge gates of Hyde Park, and notes Pepys once taking a 'course' of milk in summer. Things were different in the sixteenth century. Thomas Platter, the Swiss scholar, travelling between Canterbury and Sittingbourne in 1599, was surprised to be offered milk to drink when he paused for refreshment on his journey to London. Probably, it was rarely offered as a staple drink in towns, but was usual in farmhouses. The poor did not often get whole milk, of course, but drank buttermilk, left after buttermaking. It is full of whey proteins and caseins, so it is nourishing and was an agreeable drink that was still being drunk regularly in the nineteenth century. William Cobbett deemed it preferable to beer in promoting heavy labour on the farm. Buttermilk curds made a still more solid dish if one added one third the quantity of warm, new milk, letting it settle, skimming off the curds, and eating it with cream, wine or beer. Whey left from cheesemaking was also drunk, though it is more watery than buttermilk, but can be much improved with additions. William Ellis in 1750 knew 'buttermilk curds' as a mixture of whey and buttermilk (not needing any new milk), to which breadcrumbs and sugar were added, and he regarded the result as 'fit for a king'. Another kind was described by Eliza Melroe as a common drink in Northumberland, where sugar, ale or wine, seasoned with nutmeg and ginger, were added to the liquid curds; it was drunk by these 'milk-diet men', as he called them, three or four days a week in summer at both dinner and supper, and Melroe too recognized that this sustenance explained some of the men's capacity for hard work in the fields. In short, these items made nourishing food and drink, and were given free to the poor by farmers who had too much and would otherwise have thrown it all to the pigs. It represented a substantial loss to poor people when the wheel turned again, dairy farmers took up commercial pig-keeping as well, and used the whey or buttermilk to make pork. The change was already discernible by 1760.[104]

When our documents refer to cream, curds, milk, buttermilk and whey as the five forms in which milk was consumed, we should not ignore the likelihood that yet more refined uses for milk were locally practised that have gone unrecorded and are now forgotten. The thought is provoked by a report in the late nineteenth century by Jessica Saxby, living in Shetland, and enumerating not five dishes using milk, but ten, each with its own distinctive name. 'Strubba' was a coagulated milk whipped to the consistency of cream, and in her day was eaten with pudding or with rhubarb (which grew abundantly in Shetland by the 1880s); 'klok' was a new milk simmered till it clotted and turned a yellowish brown, when it was flavoured with cinnamon and sugar; 'milk gruel' was the familiar porridge of oatmeal with milk instead of water, a dish that was equally well known in England; 'kirn milk' was the curd of buttermilk carefully strained till almost dry and eaten with cream; 'giola' was the curd of buttermilk only partially separated from the whey: 'blaund' was the whey of buttermilk, allowed to reach the fermenting, 'sparkling' stage, and then called 'soor blaund' – Saxby said that it 'used to be in every cottage for common use like water'; 'bleddick' was the local name for straight buttermilk; 'hung milk' was coagulated cream, hung in a bag until the whey drained off; 'klabba' was junket, thickened with rennet; 'eusteen' was hot milk separated into curd and whey by the addition of sherry or some acid liquid; 'pramm' was cold milk stirred in with oatmeal, and regarded as a handy dish for a hungry bairn or beggar; 'eggaloorie' was milk, eggs and salt boiled together, and traditionally given to women at childbirth when neighbours brought their congratulations. These ten dishes, all of milk, denoted foods with distinctive flavours and textures, and illustrate once again the ingenuity of cooks all through the ages in making the most of simple ingredients; we have a similar experience nowadays with crème fraîche, fromage frais, yoghurt and cream cheeses, all using milk to serve different tastes and purposes. Our knowledge of the individuality of local traditions is meagre indeed, and we rarely catch sight of them in their endless variety. But unusually revealed in this set of Shetland food customs, this account of multifarious milk usages gives deeper meaning to the exclamation of that rustic figure in the tragi-comedy of Thomas Lodge and Robert Greene in 1598, saying 'my cow is a commonwealth to me ... for she allows myself, my wife and son for to banquet ourselves withal'.[105]

Cream deserves separate notice, for while ordinary folk can rarely have indulged in the luxury of separating it from the milk, it was evidently an occasional treat even for them. Strawberries and cream, said Andrew Boorde, were a rural man's banquet, presumably (since he was writing in the 1540s) referring to wild strawberries gathered from the woods. But he also described cream as something 'undecocted', seeming to imply that it would ordinarily be further processed into butter or cheese.[106]

CREAM AND BUTTER

In better-off households butter was made from cream alone; indeed, Dr Hart in 1633 deemed cream and butter to be the same thing: cream 'which we commonly call butter', he said, was used for dressing meat. Colin Spencer detects among rich people a new passion in Elizabeth's reign for cream in fools, trifles and white pots, and certainly these dishes were by then firmly in place at the tables of the well-to-do, though for how long this had been so is unclear. Clues from banquets at court in Philip and Mary's reign, 1553–8, remind us also of other uses for cream. A list of ingredients for a fish meal included 12 gallons of cream for the pastry, and 15 gallons of cream was needed for a flesh meal. Cream was still being used to make pastry by Robert May in 1660, but this large quantity may have been needed for the custards as well. Certainly, custards were in vogue much earlier, for when Lord Leicester, as Chancellor of the University of Oxford, held a dinner there in 1570, local women were called on to supply cream, and one gallon came from Mrs Redding specifically 'for custards'. Another pottle was bought from Mrs Toneye for making white broth.[107]

Turning from milk and cream, we find in butter one of the two major explanations for the increasing demand for dairy products that spurred higher production. It seems fairly certain that before the sixteenth century butter was not spread on bread. It is a plausible assertion to make of a time when pottage was the main food and bread was either mixed in the cooking pot or laid out as a trencher to absorb the pottage at the table. It did not need butter to make it palatable. But around 1500 an Italian visitor of the Cappello family (probably Francesco) in London, noticing the many kites flying across London skies, was struck by their tameness, and observed how often they snatched 'out of the hands of little children the bread smeared with butter in the Flemish fashion, given to them by their mothers'. Francesco Cappello was extraordinary ambassador from Venice to England in 1501–2. Kites snatching food from children's hands was also mentioned by William Turner in *Avium Praecipuarum* (1544), though he may simply have been copying the earlier author. However, kites in London were also remarked on by the traveller Schaschek between 1465 and 1467 and their large numbers by Belon in 1560. (This must have been the red kite with forked tail, which is a scavenger and has recently (*c.* 2004) been successfully re-introduced into Oxfordshire.) Evidently, spreading butter on bread was not an English practice at that time but a newfangled Flemish one; it bolstered the reputation of the Flemings as great butter eaters. According to Andrew Boorde they were often called 'Buttermouth Fleming'.[108]

In the course of the sixteenth and seventeenth centuries, spreading butter on bread became an English practice too, so we find John Worlidge in 1704 in his *Rustic Dictionary* referring in a matter-of-fact way to butter 'eaten alone with bread'. The practice presumably followed naturally from a decline in the eating of pottage, and the convenience of bread and cheese as a meal, eaten in the fields and at home, sometimes for supper.[109]

The influence of the Flemish and Dutch on Englishmen's consumption of butter was exerted in other ways, for many of them came as religious refugees and settled in East Anglia from the 1560s; they brought their food customs with them. One of them living in Norwich in 1567 may not have gauged the English situation accurately when he declared that local people ate only pig's fat. But, in their turn, his English neighbours must have been struck by seeing at close quarters so much butter-eating by the Flemish.

It is also possible that the Flemish and Dutch taught the English how to preserve butter more successfully. The English reckoned to make butter the day before it was sold at the market, so that customers bought it fresh. The English criticised the saltiness of the Dutch butter; it was unsavoury to English tastes, and explained to them why the Dutch quaffed so much beer. Since the Dutch were already familiar with an export trade in butter, it is possible that their habit of salting it and storing it well was in some way superior to English methods of preservation. An allusive, though uncertain, clue on this subject is found in Gervase Markham's remarks in 1615 on English farming practices; he dwelt principally on 'sweet butter', i.e. fresh butter, which was stored in pots. The only big dairy farms, he said, were in Holland, Lincolnshire (i.e. in the fenlands), in Suffolk and in Norfolk, and there, because of the scale of their buttermaking, they stored it in barrels. This sounds like the Dutch practice having been transferred to East Anglia, and it could be explained by the fact that Dutchmen were living not only in the town of Norwich, but in rural areas as well; they were at work draining the fens from at least the 1590s. A later comment in 1655 seems to point again to Dutch success in storing butter: Hartlib's diary records firkins of butter, which was 'more lasting', being sent from Leyden for 'English housekeeping', a turn of phrase that suggests that an elite group of English connoisseurs was exploiting information about Dutch butter in special containers that was not known to everyone.[110]

A mixture of clues points to the high reputation of East Anglian butter in the Elizabethan period, and, taking a hint from Bartholomew Dowe, it is likely to have been Suffolk butter. Concentrated in the woodpasture region of central Suffolk, it could already have been something of a speciality in the area at the end of the fifteenth century, just waiting to be turned into a grander, trading enterprise. Flemish and Dutch settlers brought fresh ideas and assumptions on the subject and triggered more change. By the 1690s Robert Houghton was still proclaiming the superiority of Suffolk butter over northern butter, paying particular attention to its success in extracting all the buttermilk so that it kept better.[111]

In gentlemen's households astonishingly large quantities of butter were already being used in cooking in the late Middle Ages. But butter did not grace the table for, as Moufet pronounced in 1600, it was first and foremost food of the poor, and certainly not advisable for fit men of middling age, though all right for children and the old. But when vegetables became more interesting, were more varied, shapely and tasty, melted butter began to be poured over them at the table. By the mid-seventeenth century it was a routine to use butter as a sauce poured over all vegetables: William Coles in 1657 described carrots with butter, and parsnips with butter, served as a dish on their own on meatless days on Wednesdays and Fridays; Melroe commended a mix of melted butter, made tart with vinegar, to which pepper was added to make a good fish sauce. Butter sauces built up demand and the practice spread into more households. It was most memorably described by Henri Misson, a French visitor in the 1690s, seeing 'the middling sort of people' in England eating heaps of cabbage, roots and herbs, all 'swimming in butter'.[112]

A further use for butter was, of course, as a cooking fat in pastry. Our cookery books show pastry-making being carefully described by the 1650s, and the preference, at least among the upper and middle classes, was for puff pastry, which again uses a lot of butter. In connection with that, we have already cited the Northampton physician, James Hart, complaining in 1623 at the excessive making of pies.

The improved arts of preserving food also involved another use for butter, by filling pies after they had been cooked with melted butter to make an airtight seal, and filling jars and pots of cooked meat and fish in the same way. Thus they kept for days or weeks. Ten pounds of butter were used in the Saville household in Nottinghamshire in October 1637 to fill pots of 'baker's venison'; they sound like containers that had to travel to friends, perhaps in London, in the same way that the Shuttleworths in Lancashire had earlier sent their woodcock pies.[113]

A rising demand for butter has to be inferred from all this evidence, which was met by an expanding dairying industry and by ingenuity in devising ways of making butter more economically. This resulted in a lowering of some prices, and significant differences in its quality by the middle of the eighteenth century. In fundamental ways butter-making had needed to diversify in order to cater for the growing demand, so although we find no description of how the innovations happened, somehow or other a variety of different milk-mixing procedures emerged, and the price of butter varied likewise, putting it within the reach of more people. The finest quality was made from cream or whole milk, like the highly praised Suffolk butter. It could also be made from buttermilk after the first butter had been made, or from whey after the curd for cheese had been removed. Other procedures resulted in a list of butters that were ranked in a hierarchy, and so catered for people with more or less money to spend. 'After-butter' or 'back butter' was made from a second skimming of the milk after the first cream had settled and had been removed; the remaining milk was left for another twelve hours before churning. It was worth only half the price of the first butter, yet it was often sold in London to rich and poor alike who did not question its quality, and so were gulled into paying over the odds for it. Whey butter was worse than buttermilk butter, because it did not keep and ate 'rankish'. But it had its customers, and it could be improved slightly if a little extra cream was added before churning.[114]

Plainly, butter-making remained throughout this period a thoroughly decentralized operation. Housewives were past masters and all had their different procedures and different available mixtures, and showed varying physical strength in churning. So the taste of the butter was everywhere different, and we can be sure that multitudes of women shared Mrs Cromwell's preference for the butter that was home-made. Even the author of the scurrilous book about her was decent enough to admit that her butter was famous among 'the mushroom-zealous ladies of the court'.[115]

The flavours of butter were sometimes fancifully altered by adding rosewater, rosemary or jasmine, and it could be coloured with marigold flowers or saffron. But flavour became a more discussed issue around 1750 when it was affected by new grasses fed to the cows. From the 1650s onwards, experiments with new fodder plants were in vogue, and spurry was sometimes grown, following the example of the Dutch. It increased the yield of milk, and made a tasty butter that was preferred to May butter. Cows grazed the crop until Christmas, and the butter never tasted rank. It was still being commended to farmers in the 1690s. Around 1750, however, poor flavour became an issue of more concern for by then farmers were sowing clover, lucerne and sainfoin: their milk yield was increasing, but the flavour of the butter suffered. Burnet also became a favoured grass in the 1760s, but that did not give the disagreeable taste. Indeed, it caused Prussian visitors to visit David Lamb at Ridley in Kent, for his was the family that won a prize from the Royal Society of Arts for growing burnet. Even worse than artificial grasses was feeding cows on ground that had been limed. Then the butter did not keep at all well in summer. Yet, somehow or other, without any explanation being offered in the literature, the complaints died away. Housewives came to accept the changing conditions and the changing flavours; it may be that they simply got used to them.[116]

Developments in dairying resulted in the marked growth of butter as an export from England, starting from about the 1630s onwards. It went from the port of Boston in Lincolnshire to the Netherlands, Germany, France and Spain, and later from the north-east coast, where dairying on natural pastures made Yarm an unexpectedly celebrated centre for butter that kept well. Its exports of butter positively soared between 1638 and 1675, reaching a steadier state by 1745 when the bulk of it went to London.[117]

CHEESE

Cheese in this period had to overturn much deeper-seated prejudices than did butter, but half-hearted tolerance began to appear in the sixteenth century. Then came signs of appreciation in Elizabeth's reign, though it was directed at a very few specialist cheeses, mostly foreign, such as Dutch cheese, Angelot from Normandy, and Parmesan; even as late as 1660 Robert May's recipe book still favoured Dutch and Parmesan before all others. Towards cheese in general, Venner in 1620 and Dr Hart in 1633 were still voicing the old criticisms: cheese engendered ill humours, though the effects differed according to whether the cheese was new or old; cheese was really only suited to rustics who had strong stomachs (Hart described them as ostrich-like stomachs that could overcome iron), and Venner thought cheese tolerable so long as one took plenty of exercise. Several writers knew that 'some abhorr cheese' but were puzzled to explain why; Henry Buttes, that witty and knowledgeable academic at Cambridge, asked those among his readers who loved cheese best 'to write an apology in defence of the common dislike thereof, why so many love it not'. Plainly, the tide of opinion was turning, but it was still held back by strong currents of distaste.[118]

It is instructive to learn of a similar prejudice against cheese holding sway in France at much the same date as this. We learn of it in a book published in 1607, in which Elie Vinet, writing on rural life, included a treatise 'to discover if it is good to eat cheese'. He described an incident in France at a meal attended by a physician: he watched the servant bringing in the dessert with cheese, and then saw him snatching the cheese from his master's mouth, so anxious was he to protect him from harm. Some guests were astonished at his audacity, some praised him for his loyalty, and the physician was called to express an opinion. He prudently chose to say that some people could tolerate cheese, others could not.[119]

In well-to-do households in England the first references to acceptable cheeses hint, not surprisingly, at a snobbish preference for foreign kinds. Then early rankings of English kinds put Cheshire in first place along with Shropshire, next Banbury, and last Suffolk and Essex. These last two were noticeably grouped together, being both described elsewhere as hard and dry. It seems to have been a skim-milk cheese, and Emmison, noting its abundance, cheap price and heavy consumption in the household of the Petre family at Ingatestone in Elizabeth's reign, realized that it was bought for servants and definitely not for the master;

Camden had said that it served servants and humbler guests 'to fill their bellies with'. Another of its uses was on shipboard since it lasted without deterioration. A derogatory rhyme of the time said:

> Knives can't cut me, fire won't light me,
> Dogs bite at me, but can't bite me.

The worst cheese was said to be Kentish, an interesting assertion, for nowhere else was Kentish cheese mentioned in any league tables, and the centre of production at this time is not at all clear, unless it was the southern Weald. We should note also that the total number of English cheeses under discussion was still small.[120]

Well-to-do Englishmen who went abroad in the Tudor–early Stuart period, and sat at foreign tables must, however, have been startled to see cheese savoured in some places abroad among the highest ranks of society. Attending a banquet in Madrid in 1626, Cassiano de Pozzo, cupbearer of the Cardinal Legate, Francesco de Barberini, described the cheese on the table, 'cut into so many slices that they filled the plate'; plainly, the Spaniards enjoyed them. An anonymous Italian cookbook entitled *Epulario or the Italian Banquet*, translated into English in 1598, showed cheese being cooked in several hot dishes, in a stuffing, and in fritters. Grated cheese regularly topped other Italian meals or was grilled. What the English definitely did not like was cheese with maggots in it. Boorde saw it in High Germany, proving to him how 'grossly' the Germans ate, and Hart in 1633 described it as being 'greedily gaped after by gluttons'.[121]

Meanwhile, English cookbooks usually omitted cheese entirely. It seems not to have been considered as an ingredient in cooking, so when eaten at all it was eaten cold. The exception to this rule was the Welsh, who toasted it; indeed, for Andrew Boorde in the 1540s the identifying sign of a Welshman was that he loved toasted cheese, and that probably settled neatly with the general view of the Welsh as a rude, ignorant peasantry. Venner too was disgusted by toasted cheese, regarding it as only fit for the mousetrap, and long after that remark was made, the German traveller, Carl Moritz, thought toasted cheese quite unpalatable when he was served it at Tideswell, east of Buxton. Here he was in the Derbyshire Peak District, another countryside of upland moors; was our traveller already prejudiced to expect the same uncultured customs as in wild Wales?[122]

Meanwhile, as cold food in England, cheese was eminently convenient for people working out in the fields and wanting sustenance ready to hand. So we trace out a different story of cheese among working people. When the women found new work in the fields at this period, cultivating crops that needed careful weeding and hand-picking, we can reasonably guess that they made more and more use of cheese to feed themselves at dinner time, along with the children they took with them into the fields. William Ellis by 1750 regarded cheese as indispensable in farming families, and most of all at harvest time; he set out some varied recipes for dishes that pleased them, and explained how farmers laid in stocks of Warwickshire and Leicestershire cheese in February, buying at Baldock fair on 24 February, in good time for harvest. A century earlier, the Shuttleworth family in Lancashire also bought noticeably large quantities of cheese when once they started building a new house some distance from where they were living. Presumably this fed their building workers. They maintained only a modest domestic dairy at home, which obliged them to buy in cheese out of season; their dairy maids were employed only in the grass-growing months.[123]

In fact, the eating of cheese at this time was a good test of class in varied circumstances. For the sumptuous meal at Oxford, given by the Vice Chancellor of the university, Lord Leicester, in 1570, large supplies of milk, butter, curds and cream were laid in, but no cheese. In contrast, it was generously provided by a Yorkshire dalesman, to be served at his funeral, when he died in 1575 at Burton in Bishopdale. For this solemn occasion, Galfyd Calvert set aside 28 pounds of his home-made cheese, surely enough to feed 50 to 100 people? In the middle of these examples high and low, we may set Lady Fettiplace's Elizabethan recipe book, edited by Hilary Spurling, which gives her way of making cheese, but no cooked cheese recipes, and the cheese she mentioned, apart from one ordinary fresh cheese that was ready in a week, was the Angelot.[124]

Historians of agriculture have amplified this story of dairy foods by noticing in certain specialist areas of the country farmers gradually keeping larger dairy herds, and writers remarking with a new enthusiasm on local cheeses. In the longer term this development may conceivably have started with a shift of interest from soft cheeses to hard, though it took a long time to show commercial results. The speculation is prompted by a letter from Robert Wood to Hartlib in 1658, harking back to classical times, and saying that hard cheeses were not very ancient in the world, and soft cheeses, 'really curdled milk', he said, were most eaten. He was writing from Dublin Castle, where he had seen a little book by a Mrs Hill on hard cheeses, which he described as 'the art of hardening and so preserving of milk'. He deemed this a practice 'among better housewives', and commented that 'Irish eat that kind now'. Was he implying that hard cheeses in the 1650s, at least in his part of the world, were a novelty, whereas soft cheeses were routine?[125]

Be that as it may, the hard cheeses were attracting notice in the Elizabethan period, and the ranking of regional types was a talking point. Cheshire cheese seemed to rank highest of all, being acclaimed by John Speed as the best cheese in Europe. Demand accelerated remarkably in the 1640s and early 1650s because of the Civil War, and according to Charles Foster, the first shipload of Cheshire cheese arrived in London in 1650. Its significant role in food rations for the soldiers is seen in their daily allowance, laid down in 1654. Cheese was their major source of protein on four days out of seven; half a pound of Cheshire cheese with a quarter pound of butter was prescribed for those four days, and one pound of beef and one pint of peas on the other three. These foods were eaten with one pound of biscuit each day and a pottle of beer.[126]

Stimulated by a demand that built up for several different reasons, it is likely that an increase in the production of butter and cheese posed no insuperable problems to the womenfolk, for it did not require expensive equipment. Milk was processed quickly in small quantities, and, like as not, young women could be readily recruited as dairymaids in villages where small-scale farming was the rule. Some individual women became quite renowned, like Mrs Childs in the Isle of Ely, whose butter, 'far exceeding the ordinary way', and fine cheeses, enhanced by her method of making them, were all noted in Hartlib's diary. Locally, the womenfolk used their ingenuity or 'deep cunning', as the menfolk sometimes called it, and won great loyalty from their local customers. The Howards of Naworth rewarded one boy 13 times in one year for bringing them cheese from one local supplier. Nicholas Blundell at Little Crosby in Lancashire always turned to local women for his cheese, until he came to realize the profit in the business and made some of his own in 1708–9; 'brined cheeses', he called them, to be sold in Liverpool. As a talking point, cheeses and their recipes had become such a lively issue by the 1720s that Richard Bradley laid out the details for making many different kinds, as well as advice when making butter, in a book labelled *The Gentleman and Farmer's Guide.*[127]

As a more commercial operation evolved, more and more cheese was moved about the country by cart and by water, and people became familiar with the varied flavours coming from Derbyshire, Leicestershire, Warwickshire, Somerset, Gloucestershire and Wales. Carriers on the move from Cheshire to London in 1707 had a pleasant surprise when their cheese sold *en route* in unexpected quantity in Northampton and Dunstable. In December 1708 a shrewd factor saw a chance to sell Cheshire cheese in Flanders as the Flemish were flooding their land to impede the French army: Flemish cheeses would be scarce, he thought, and the English army would need cheese when they arrived there. He hastened to Cheshire to stock up in anticipation.

A strong commercial spirit swamped the dairying scene by the end of the seventeenth century; larger quantities at the markets gave much more choice of price to suit all purses, and encouraged people to eat more. It led to some quite sophisticated appraisals of the profit from cheap as opposed to expensive cheeses, and explains why the Suffolk dairy farmers switched from butter to cheesemaking round about 1708, so tapping into the London market for cheap cheeses that sold to the poor and to the navy victuallers. We only hear about this change of direction because it hit the Cheshire and Lancashire cheesemakers particularly hard. Producers and consumers were always and everywhere on the watch for price advantages and bargains. A good earlier illustration was given by John

Ivie, a town elder of Salisbury, devising his scheme to help the poor in the years of scarcity in Salisbury, between 1627 and 1628. When cheese was sold in bulk on market days, he watched for the slack times when the sellers found few buyers, and they positively begged him to take the cheese off them; thus he got it at 4s., 5s., and 6s., cheaper per cwt than usual. Ivie's scheme was kept going until 1640.[128]

At the other end of the social scale, a discerning taste for particular cheeses began to send some gentry long distances to obtain the cheese they liked: in 1678 Robert, Lord Ailesbury fetched a dairy woman and maids from Leicestershire to work for him at Ampthill in Bedfordshire, and in September of that year he sent a man to Marlborough to buy cheese. Was this, by any chance, because water meadows were being newly developed in that district, and the cheese from these improved, natural pastures acquired a high reputation in consequence? In the next generation a Leicestershire lady, Mrs Elizabeth Orton of Little Dalby, began to make Quenby cheese, using a recipe she had learned when working as housekeeper to the Ashby family. The Ashbys always called it Lady Beaumont's recipe, tracing it back to the Beaumonts of Coleorton or Stoughton. This in the end became the famous Stilton cheese, only because it was sold at the Bell Inn at Stilton in Huntingdonshire. That illustrious name has stayed with it ever since.[129]

The flavours of cheese were subtle matters that were as proudly and jealously guarded by dairy folk as the flavours of butter. So the same controversies filled conversation among farmers as among cooks wherever they turned to feeding their cows on artificial grasses, a move that was being strongly urged upon them after 1700. Clover was the main crop at issue, for it made cheese that was distinctly inferior in taste to that from natural grasses, and we must humbly accept the fact that our forebears knew what they were talking about; we have lost the ability to judge. When Prussian visitors came to England to study good farming practices in 1765–6, they learned from their Herefordshire hosts that that was why no cheesemaker there grew clover. Agricultural historians need to remember this thoroughly good explanation for the slow acceptance of clover, for our farmers are so often accused of being obstinate in accepting change.[130]

At many points in this narrative about dairy foods, the local history of particular districts has come to the fore without being pursued further. The recent publication by Dr John Broad of a history of the Claydon villages in Buckinghamshire, where the Verney family were the landowners, illuminates the importance of local circumstances in determining and changing farmers' specializations. The Civil War dealt the Verneys many hard blows through warfare, taxation, the sequestration of their lands, mounting debts and vacant farms. Already before the Restoration their policy had hardened in favour of enclosure and the conversion of land to pasture, and after 1670 it veered more positively still away from cattle keeping towards dairying. By the early eighteenth century the Verneys fostered a permanent grass system, avoiding the use of clover, be it noted, on large farms; and in the second half of the eighteenth century, farmers concentrated their preferences on butter rather than cheese. That last change is not fully explained by contemporaries, though Dr Broad attributes it to a change of taste, the lack of any distinctive branding for Buckinghamshire cheese, in contrast, say, with Cheshire cheese, and the profitable dovetailing of butter with the use of buttermilk for fattening pigs. That could well be the correct explanation, although an analysis emphasizing food rather than farming preferences still leaves doubts about other influences like prices, transport facilities, and the keeping qualities of butter versus cheese.[131]

THE LONG VIEW OF DAIRY FOODS

Dairy foods plainly travelled a long way in public estimation in the early modern period. We judge the developments in optimistic terms by focusing on certain aspects only. At the same time we should not overlook the adverse consequences for the consumption of milk. Many country folk, including cottagers, kept cows, and so did townsfolk, for we find references to people delivering hay to them. Even the very poorest, having no cow, commonly drank whey and buttermilk that was given them free. Then a notion among the intelligentsia that milk was good for health crept in as writers noted the fair complexions and good health of those who drank a lot of milk; it contrasted with all the maladies suffered by gluttons who devoured meat. So some adverse consequences followed when more and more milk was turned into cheese or butter, and the residue was fed to calves, to produce veal, or to pigs. Pigs became another highly commercial concern for producing pork and bacon, and so gradually a lack of milk developed into a local problem of no mean significance. It was identified with precision in particular villages when Frederick Eden's investigators carried out his survey on *The State of the Poor*. In Gloucestershire, because of veal production, wives and children had bread and water as 'almost the only diet'; very little milk was for sale in Dunstable, Bedfordshire, and at Humbershoe nearby. It was scarce at Cobham in Kent, very little was for sale at Kibworth Beauchamp (Leicestershire), Banbury (Oxfordshire) and Ellesmere (Shropshire). These were random scraps of information, not answers to any systematic questioning. But they give a vivid glimpse of the deteriorating diet of poor folk. Milk did not become so scarce in the north; and in some scattered places in the 1790s people still kept their household cow; perhaps, in such cases, the poor had managed to retain control of land allotted to them at enclosure. But the passage of time, particularly in areas where market pressures were most strongly exerted by dense populations, deprived some cottagers of grazing for a cow, despite the view strongly held by

John Houghton, and probably many others, about the high food value of dairy products. For Houghton, writing in 1695, milk was meat, drink and medicine, all rolled into one; his journal focused a bright light on its nourishment. The loss of milk among labouring people adds a seriously damaging element to those many other changes that accompanied industrial growth and the removal of people into towns. They lost contact with country routines, and their diet altered for the worse. It took another hundred years for the full scale of the damage to health to be recognized.[132]

VEGETABLES AND HERBS

Vegetables and herbs are here considered together since people did not make any clear distinction between them in the early modern period. Some authors, indeed, did not use the word 'vegetable' at all, but called all vegetables 'herbs'. Historians have long been exercised to assess accurately the role of vegetables in past diets, and the evidence adduced here explains why. It was a complex story, encouraging several different but equally valid judgements. Everybody ate at least some vegetables and herbs as a matter of course, while adopting varying attitudes towards this class of food in general. At the same time, changing opinions about particular vegetables and herbs threaded their way into cooking practice, influencing some classes more than others. One could doubtless penetrate the mysteries more effectively if the botanical and medicinal histories of each plant were explored, for the depths of explanation assuredly run as deep as in the present-day history of broccoli.

One marked difference between past and present practice is the way people took it for granted that all parts of a plant were edible – roots, stalks, leaves, flowers and seeds. So they handled each part separately, and if one part was not tasty, they tried a different method to make it so. They fully expected that every part would yield acceptable food, if not always in ways that we would expect. Parsley was valued for its leaves, but some, like Henry Buttes, valued its roots more; some parsley varieties must have yielded a larger root than those we grow nowadays. Coriander was valued primarily for its seed, but seemingly rarely for its green leaves.[133]

Some strongly positive views of vegetables and herbs in food are identified from the very beginning of our period in 1500. Among ordinary folk the age-old peasant tradition persisted, viewing vegetables and herbs as part of the natural world, in plentiful supply according to the season, and there to be gathered freely in woods, fields and hedges, and in lesser quantities in gardens. For winter use some herbs were taken indoors: a York man's inventory showed him with six herb pots in his buttery, while another from York in 1609 showed someone drying herbs under a coverlet at the foot of a bed by a window. Greenstuff, as we have already seen, was a basic ingredient in pottage, and when botanists once began to analyse plants individually and write about them more systematically – from the later sixteenth century – they offered a long list of those that were most regularly used. In spring the new shoots were particularly welcome and cheering, and ordinary folk gathered everything in sight, as peasants still do in southern Europe. They were all fresh and tender after a long winter, and we can readily understand how people felt the need to cleanse their digestive systems with as much greenery as they could find. Nettle tops and garden lettuce often came at the top of the spring list, but in the 1650s, when William Coles, the botanist, itemized many distinctive varieties and even some of the places where they grew, his list for pottage contained, alongside nettle tops and watercresses, some surprises, like buds of elders, clary and alexanders (or black lovage, *Smyrnium olusatrum*), also sometimes called 'black potherb'.[134]

Common folk ate greenstuff so regularly that it rarely attracted comment; historians are, therefore, grateful for the casual remark of any contemporary that accidentally lights up the scene. William Ellis did so in 1750, by describing a woman wanting some herbs to boil with her meat: 'It is usual with country women', he wrote, 'to gather them in the fields in the Spring time of the year.' Such a common sight of food being gathered for free may have fostered contempt among the upper classes; but for all we know, the cooks in well-heeled households might also have used them daily without comment, like everyone else. The result was that in sixteenth-century menus and cookery books, vegetables were hardly mentioned, and historians have doubted whether much greenstuff was eaten. For me, the most convincing testimony comes from William Coles in the mid-seventeenth century, describing the everyday scene, in his *Art of Simpling*. 'There is not a day passeth over our heads but we have need of one thing or other that groweth within their circumference', he wrote. 'We cannot make so much as a little good pottage without herbs, which give an admirable relish and make them wholesome for our bodies.' Thus the practicalities of life were made plain, though the intellectual argument about particular herbs and among different classes of people continued.[135]

The signs of certain named herbs being welcomed into upper-class diets go back to the fourteenth century. A fashionable interest was creeping in when some were imported from abroad and arrived with a high pedigree. This was true of rosemary. Foreign-born queens arriving in England expected to enjoy the foods and flavours they knew at home, and Philippa, queen of Edward III, is credited with publicizing rosemary, having received from her mother, the Countess of Hainault, a treatise commending its virtues. Faith and fashion spread so successfully that already in 1598 the German visitor Paul Hentzner was remarking on rosemary hedges at Hampton Court and in the gardens of the well-to-do. The shrub was nailed to the walls and spread in espalier fashion. In Henry VIII's reign Princess Mary's household accounts show one bill of £40 and another for £8, paid out for herbs, and as she was the daughter of Queen Catherine of Aragon, we may guess at her mother's influence on her diet. Catherine herself is known to have asked in England for salads, which had to be imported for her from the Netherlands. Another unusual insight into the taste for salads in noble circles is found in a petition from the Duchess of Suffolk to William Cecil, Elizabeth's chief minister, in 1550 begging him to expedite a lawsuit involving her servant, for until he returned to his garden, she could have neither salads nor sweet herbs.[136]

Foreign influences were highly influential in other ways in shaping the new scene in the sixteenth century. Religious refugees from the Netherlands and France settled in English towns and sought the foods they were accustomed to at home. Thus chervil was introduced to the English when they saw Dutch settlers eating it in Shakespeare's day. Lamb's lettuce, according to Gerard, was introduced to the English by both French and Dutch immigrants, and so began to be grown in gardens. Foreign influences also filtered in through opportunist merchants. In the month of November 1596 goods brought by Flemish traders into the port of London included 12,600 cabbages, 65 barrels of onions and 10,400 ropes of onions, and this was not just a luxury for Londoners, for port books show in 1593–4 that onions, carrots and roots were also imported into Newcastle. Thus people were made aware of new varieties and the higher quality of vegetables raised abroad, and we can be sure that some of these reached the table of Privy Councillors attending sumptuous dinners in the Court of Star Chamber; the master cook included among his expenses payment for his 'pains and travel going to market'.[137]

Thus, gardening and the status of gardens were gradually raised, and the search for good vegetables fanned out across the English countryside, much assisted by the botanists and the gentry exchanging gifts and seeds with each other. More and more edible indigenous plants were brought out of the wild into gardens where they were tenderly cultivated. Gardeners perceived how cultivation altered their size and flavour and launched a debate. Did they lose their medicinal and culinary virtues by being cultivated? Some thought they did; it is certainly likely that they lost their intense flavour. But the argument died out in the second half of the seventeenth century, because the convenience of growing a secure food supply in the kitchen garden overcame other considerations.[138]

Several different strands of action and changing opinion raised the status of vegetables and herbs until it was taken for granted that educated and informed people would devote attention to them. Sir Thomas Smith, who was Secretary of State in 1548 and became a Privy Councillor under Elizabeth, was deeply worried about his garden of medicinal plants and distillations when he was abroad; and it became common advice to urge such personages, for the sake of their health, to spend time working in their gardens.[139]

Plants already served two purposes, as food and medicine, and these two separate interests mingled instinctively in the minds of contemporaries whenever they sat down to eat. It was an assumption that we find difficult to absorb into our imagination now that we so regularly rely on bought medicines, made up by a pharmacist. When contemporaries recorded some of their sayings about herbs, they revealed the complex thoughts and hopes that lay behind their eating. Working people ate an onion in the morning believing that it defended them against the infectious air for the rest of the day. Sage butter was a favourite for breakfast among the upper classes, and innumerable august personages ate it, including Lord Mountjoy, accompanying his butter and sage with stale beer. It was a common saying to ask how anyone could possibly die if they had sage growing in their garden, in deference to which lore I regularly put sage leaves into my soups. Mustard was eaten in very large quantities, and featured prominently in some gardens. Sir Thomas Smith had a whole mustard seed garden at his Essex home, and maybe Sir John Harington did also. It was, of course, a major home-grown spice for adding flavour, but Harington, translating the wisdom of the physicians of the School of Salerno, was convinced that mustard purged the brain and expelled poison from the stomach; John Evelyn, in a later generation, valued it for reviving the spirit and strengthening memory. When mustard became a considerable crop in the East Anglian fens after drainage in the seventeenth century (some also being exported from there to the Netherlands), the locals no doubt expressed gratitude for the medicine as well as the spice.[140]

Alongside these positive views of greenstuff, of course, ran the deprecatory view describing it as watery, windy, and of no food value. It was a class view, thus expressed in 1620 by Tobias Venner, labelling colewort and cabbage as fit only for the common people because it filled the belly. But under the weight of fashionable attention these criticisms fell away in the seventeenth century, weakened further by a reading of the classical writers who had so obviously relished such foods in the past. Columella devoted many pages to cabbage as a cure for all ills, and when beans attracted more notice in the early eighteenth century, the classical writers were again cited in support of that food.[141]

The plants eaten in this period were far more numerous than anything we know nowadays, and they were highly varied locally. We have noted already how flexibly chefs responded to that knowledge. So a more sensitive reading of the literature in the future will almost certainly identify some fads and fashions for particular herbs at different periods and in different places. A moderately long list of common greens for the Yorkshire climate, giving 'sufficient for our country housewives', appeared, for example, in William Lawson's book on *The Countrie Housewifes Garden* (1617). The discerning eye would surely see something different there from a list of common vegetables in the south-east. Novelties also came into some areas and not others. Asparagus was one such, which Moufet (c. 1600 or, more likely, his editor in 1655), claimed was 'once food for an emperor' but 'now every board is served with them'. But that was a London opinion that was not likely to have been true of boards in the Midlands. However, no geographical precision was needed when discussing burdock roots (which Moufet, or his editor, called clot burr roots). They grow well on any waste ground, and were well known to Shakespeare. According to Moufet, they were eaten in April when young and tender, like young green artichokes; but it was the French and Italians who had found them out, so that now they were common in England 'through people who have travelled to other countries'.[142]

We have noticed earlier how 'cabbages and roots' became a kind of catchphrase around 1600, these vegetables having taken the centre of the stage when they proved to be life-saving food in a time of scarcity; and they both stored well in winter. So whereas roots had been thoroughly despised in the first half of the sixteenth century – in 1548 William Forrest had declared that 'our English nature cannot live by roots. By water, herbs, or such beggary baggage, That may well serve for vile outlandish coats' – they received official encouragement from JPs in the 1620s urging the poor to grow them. New varieties of turnips and carrots came in and overturned old opinions, and that trend persisted through the seventeenth century. The yellow Brunswick turnip was the talk of the Hartlib circle in 1648, and John Locke was a remarkably diligent collector of turnip, carrot and cabbage seed when he was in Holland, sending it to his friends, the Clarkes in England, and looking forward to a walk in their turnip grove in the summer of 1684. In something over a century, root vegetables had moved a long way up the social scale, while the common varieties had spread among ordinary folk to the extent that parsons in some parishes took tithe on them. As root vegetables increased in variety, skirret won particular approval, and since the name is thought to derive from a Dutch word, we can reasonably guess that it came to England from the Netherlands. It was in high favour with the Sackville family, earls of Dorset, at Knole in Sevenoaks in the 1630s. Some of their greengrocers' bills show one lot of skirret being delivered on Sunday, 18 December 1631, more on Monday, Wednesday and Thursday, and more to follow. It was still much appreciated in the early eighteenth century when Richard Bradley gave a recipe for it, but it had disappeared by 1800, seemingly because of the popularity of the potato. Mrs Beeton passed over skirret in silence.[143]

Rampions were another root hardly known until this time. This was a large white-rooted vegetable like a parsnip, not the radish-sized root known at the present day. It was eaten cooked, with the leaves served as salad. Moufet's comments on it imply, c. 1600, that it was beginning to be known 'indifferently well' in England under German influence. Yet another root, forging flamboyantly ahead at rich men's tables in the 1620s and 1630s, was beetroot, known in various colours ranging through white, green, yellow and red, and arresting attention by its colour and the decorative shapes into which it was cut. Its phase of fame and fashion was lit up by John Parkinson saying that all beets went into Englishmen's pottage, but the French boiled them whole and so 'in our country [do] divers that delight in eating herbs'.[144]

Among plants of the brassica family, many new varieties also came into vogue. Already in 1599 Henry Buttes was citing Master John Gerard on 18 sorts of colewort then known, while Parkinson in 1629 thought there was greater diversity in colewort and cabbage than in any other greenstuff. Some, he said, were 'wholly spent among the poorer sort', while others were dressed to delight the more sophisticated palate, urged on by Dutchmen who delighted in curiosities. People were developing curled colewort, a multi-coloured colewort that was 'beautiful to behold', another less curled kind, one of popinjay colour, and another deep green like Savoy. A headed cabbage had already been developed in the fifteenth century, and now an experiment was being tried in mild winters by gardeners: digging up cabbages, tying a cloth round the roots and hanging them in the house until the frosts passed, when they planted them out again. The cabbage then sent up a thick stalk, divided at the top into many branches with small four-leaved flowers which turned into pointed seed like turnip seed.[145]

The cauliflower also came from Sicily and Italy around this time, and was served at dinner to Privy Councillors in Star Chamber in November 1590. It was on sale to anyone in London markets by 1646 when the Countess of Bath bought them on a visit in June and July. In short, new varieties of greenstuff were being sought all the time, and some gentlemen kept notes in their commonplace books about them, one man reminding himself in 1684 of the great Zealand cabbage, Spanish lettuces and Italian cauliflowers. The red Russian cabbage caught the fancy of John Locke in 1686, and seed was procured and sent to the Clarkes in England. In 1727 broccoli was being cultivated with success in Holland, and had become known in England, though through mismanagement, according to Stephen Switzer, it had fallen into disrepute and he was trying to restore it to favour. He commended it cooked and eaten as a salad.[146]

Salad plants, eaten raw or cooked, made another group, and became an extended range as the Italian example of eating salad plants with oil and vinegar was copied. Parkinson knew 11 or 12 different kinds of lettuce, and did not think his readers would believe there could be so many. Using lamb's lettuce, one could have salad leaves all through the winter, or at least welcome them as the first growth in spring. Sweet cicely was evidently finding a place at the table in Elizabeth's reign, and William Harrison advertised a site at Crosby Ravensworth, in Westmorland, where it flourished. Purslane was mentioned for salads by Gervase Markham who had evidently taken a fancy to it, and added his own words of tribute when translating Conrad Heresbach's *Four Bookes of Husbandry* into English in 1631; in the mid-1650s William Coles identified wild locations for purslane in the saltmarshes of Sheppey, in the Isle of Thanet, and around Ramsey Mere. Many other salad plants named at this time by contemporaries were endive, cresses, burnet, rampions, clove gillyflowers, and goatsbeard (*Tragopogon*), and while these were all nursed in gardens, Parkinson, who was not nearly so intimately in touch with peasants as was William Coles, also acknowledged the wild ones that were used, referring to the many sought out by 'strangers' (meaning foreign settlers in England). Yet other collectors known to Parkinson were those 'whose curiosity searcheth out the whole work of nature to satisfy their desires'. Plainly, botanists recognized a vogue for finding new food plants, which influenced a certain circle of people around London and affected gentry in their country houses. One senses that the Sackville family was held in thrall at Knole, near Sevenoaks, since salad herbs were delivered almost daily, and sometimes twice in one day, in the morning and evening. On one day someone arrived with a rich mixture of lettuce, small salad, spinach, fennel, parsley, watercresses, nettles, sage, tarragon and comfrey, plus the routine parsnips, carrots and turnips. Artichokes (presumably globe) were delivered daily in season, two, three or six at a time on successive days, and 13 on Saturday. One undated bill showed cucumbers for the first time, another listed alexanders and watermelons. Our Lady's thistle or milk thistle (*Carduus marianus*) made an unexpected appearance in a pie in Jos. Cooper's cookbook of 1654, and was still cherished by some in 1783 when Charles Bryant described it in his *Flora Dietetica* as one of the best salad plants when boiled. But already a century before that, Westmacott was in 1694 deploring its neglect and the futility of fashion. Thus did leafy plants and flowers come and go in salads at table.[147]

It became a strong trend of the time to move greenstuff from wild habitats in fields and woods into gardens. References in print gave much evidence of this practice in the course of the seventeenth century, and it was more common still in the books about farming by the early decades of the eighteenth century. But the next step was to be the spread of the cultivated vegetables from market gardens back into the fields. That was heralded in one inventory in April 1691, of Peter Cornelius, having a surname that sounds as if it were of Dutch origin, and recording one acre of carrots and two acres of beans in Hinton St George, Somerset. Until we find more, that inventory can count as the defining moment of a new phase in market gardening history.[148]

We have seen above how peas and beans followed cabbages and roots to centre stage in the mid-seventeenth century, and when once they enjoyed wider publicity and their potential was seen, professional curiosity persuaded gardeners to seek out yet more varieties, colours and flavours. Lentils, which were still almost exclusively used as fodder for livestock, were discussed as possible human food, the editor of Thomas Moufet's manuscript interpolating his regret in the 1650s that they were not much eaten but ought to be. 'Let us for shame not discontinue this wholesome nourishment,' he wrote. The effort with lentils failed at this time, but beans and peas had more success. Matthew Parker's wife, living in straitened circumstances in 1557–8 under Catholic Queen Mary (though soon to be rescued when her husband, under Elizabeth, became Archbishop of Canterbury), was not too proud to cook beans, mashed with eggs, in a tart for her husband's dinner. A change in the status of pulses was on the horizon. A new genus of bean, *Phaseolus vulgaris*, was introduced from the New World in the sixteenth century, and the tastier haricot, plus all French beans and the scarlet runner, derive from that source. The fashion for fresh peas was also about to take firmer hold of the gentry and smart Londoners, urging them to get fresh peas to the table before anyone else in spring. Garden peas and broad beans began to feature ever more often in gossip about food, and Westmacott in 1694 described large garden beans with bacon as a constant treat in season at country houses. The modest East Sussex shopkeeper, Thomas Turner, was paying someone to plant broad beans in his vegetable garden in the mid-eighteenth century, and reckoned to eat the same fresh green beans (though not many peas) regularly as a matter of course.[149]

Scientific interest in pulses, surging noticeably from the 1620s, is best illustrated in John Parkinson's *Theatrum Botanicum*, in which he devoted a whole chapter to them, and showed that new varieties of beans were one of his particular passions. He was familiar with some that had been brought from Brazil, Africa, the East and West Indies, and Virginia; he also noted that people on the Cornish coast gathered new sorts every year, for they were driven by the wind from America, and were found 'floating in the waters', or were 'raked from under the sands of the shore'. Parkinson actually paid a Frenchman, Guillaume Boel, to search out and send him more varieties from Europe, on which errand Boel went to Spain and Portugal. Boel's reports prompted Parkinson to comment in passing on the way local people often neglected these plants until a curious searcher turned up to pry out their treasures; this was, and is, a universal truth.[150]

By the 1650s all this effort produced results that were mirrored in the Hartlib correspondence. William Coles commented on the fact that even the better sort were now eating broad beans, and the list of varieties named in print lengthened. Sugar peas were one of the discoveries that delighted people in the West Midlands, and when Christopher Merrett in 1666 listed in a book of his all the varieties of peas that he knew, the owner of one copy inserted a facing page adding more. Westmacott, in 1694, settled for the husbandman's simple labelling of peas by five different colours (though adding maple peas separately), and told the story of one grower in Milwich, Staffordshire, sowing some great white garden runcival peas that spread so bountifully, he sold them to neighbours for ten shillings a bushel. Was it a coincidence then that in 1698 peas and beans were being tithed in Cheadle, no more than seven miles from Milwich (and nowhere else in Staffordshire), signifying that there the garden cultivation of pulses was developing on a commercial scale? Westmacott cut short his remarks on pulses, claiming that everyone knew the profit they yielded; and that view chimed with the impressions formed by Pehr Kalm when roaming over Essex and Hertfordshire in 1748: he was struck by the Englishman's great liking for peas in summer, the large extent of beans growing in the fields in Essex that were sent to market in London, and the dominance of the Windsor bean. At the end of the eighteenth century, the spread of beans in the Kent fields was described as something happening 'of late years in the Home Counties', the favourites being the Windsor, the long pod and the mazagon (this was the variety that had come from Africa). The most productive bean in Essex was identified as the tick bean, always selling at a superior price. So gossip contrived to depict a competitive market for beans, though it comes as a disappointment that pulses did not manage to occupy an ever-larger place in English diet. As we have seen, they were ousted by potatoes, so easily grown, such heavy croppers, and using far less fuel than pulses in the cooking.[151]

Gardeners took up another challenge in the eighteenth century: to lengthen the growing season and give their customers fresh vegetables that shortened winter. Some remarkable achievements were claimed by the professional gardeners in country houses, who used hotbeds to produce lamb's lettuce and other green plants as early as February. But ordinary folk made do with storing their cabbages and roots in rooms and cellars, while pickling gave them another method of preserving vegetables that was not beyond their resources if they had some storage space. That story has been told in earlier chapters, and requires no elaboration here, beyond emphasis on the superlative success achieved in pickling cucumbers. It belongs in the category of a fad or fashion, for the phase passed. Pickled cucumbers do not enjoy the same favour nowadays.[152]

The adventurous spirit shown in the seventeenth century towards new foods started a longer-lasting story in the case of mushrooms. People had learned long ago to avoid fungi and mushrooms, so it was a surprise in the mid-seventeenth century when some Englishmen picked up a different attitude on the Continent of Europe, and came home praising the tastiness of mushrooms. Some were alarmingly sanguine in their remarks about them, but others uttered cautionary warnings, reporting the disasters which they knew had befallen others. Tobias Venner, a Somerset physician who made himself available in Bath every spring and autumn, belonged to the cautious school, and in 1620 thought that only 'fantastical people' favoured mushrooms. In the 1650s they were still under suspicion, but not everywhere. John Beale dubbed them 'wholesome and toothsome', and Robert May introduced them into recipes in his 1660 book (was he perhaps deliberately cloaking them in one meat dish by calling them champignons?). By the early years of the eighteenth century, they were being deliberately cultivated in France and Holland, covered with mats to continue all winter, and the English were urged to do likewise.[153]

In the midst of this wide range of plants at the disposal of all, each locality had its favourite vegetables which grew best in that area. Beans were said not to be suitable to the soils in three administrative hundreds of mid-Devon, and so were not much grown there. Instead, they exploited their garlic, which grew wild; in 1600 Norden described its fame in Stratton Hundred in Cornwall, from where it was sold into other counties. Other plants that found their ideal habitat produced the dishes that have become celebrated for their local provenance, and are still recorded in our cookery books, such as sorrel soup, using the sorrel that grows wild on the acid soils of west Herefordshire meadows; the nettle pudding of Pendle in Lancashire; and the herb pudding of north-west England, using bistort or Easter-ledge leaves (also called Easter-mangiant, i.e. *Polygonum bistorta*). When insisting on the multitude of herbs used in food, moreover, we should commemorate the old lady of Staveley who used bistort, but also added a hundred other herbs to her pudding; she became a Westmorland legend.[154]

A host of examples could be cited of unexpected uses for vegetable plants and herbs, like strawberry leaves and violet leaves in salads and in cooling drinks. We have to envisage a variety of flavours known to our ancestors that totally contradict the standard statement that our forebears in the early modern period ate dull, monotonous food. It is true that some London citizens were already in the sixteenth century losing touch with their country roots, as Stubbes alleged, but it could not have been said of the majority of the English, even in 1760.[155]

Enthusiasm for vegetables, not surprisingly, fostered a gentle movement in favour of vegetarian diets. We have noticed this in its most extreme form in the correspondence of John Beale of Herefordshire. He became almost fanatical, and cannot have been easy to live with. He firmly proclaimed in the 1650s his belief that 'roots, herbs, pulse, etc., (which is the ancient food of all heroes) do preserve our health, wit, and spirits more clear and serene than flesh and blood'. So he had planted kidney beans, and his children (but not his servants) were fed on these and were better served, he thought, than with 50 lambs or kids. Let us hope that they agreed with their father. In general, vegetarianism remained a gentle current of opinion running through this period, while not recruiting many extreme devotees, apart from Thomas Tryon. It waited for another turn of the wheel to win stronger support in the 1870s to 1890s, and still more nowadays.[156]

While vegetarianism was far from sweeping the board in this period, the transformation of vegetables and herbs as foodstuffs and the role they played in diet can, nevertheless, be fairly accounted a near-revolution. But it did not maintain its verve and momentum after 1760; it petered out as urban populations increased at the expense of those living in the country. Work in industry deprived them of access to the countryside, and of time to spend on gathering food for free. People lost touch with their country roots and peasant traditions, and vegetables at the table of ordinary folk dwindled away to no more than a poor shadow of their past performance. Henry Phillips, writing a *History of Cultivated Vegetables* in 1827 named many vegetables – borage, burnet, fennel, caraway, mangetout peas, saffron and sorrel – that were now neglected. A gloomier picture still was conjured up in the 1870s by a lecturer in Manchester, who hoped to improve vegetable consumption by education, but her hearers told her a very different tale: all they could ever buy, they said, was shabby cabbage leaves with leeks, cut-up sprouts and parsley, sold in a mixed bag to go into soup.[157]

FRUIT

The place of fruit in diet underwent a similar transformation to that of vegetables and herbs in the period between 1500 and 1760. While we resist the notion of calling it yet another revolution, we can readily discern spurts of activity, followed by pauses. Another such pattern can be charted twice over since 1880, one spurt starting in the 1880s and petering out in the 1920s; another, bringing in much foreign fruit, and much scientific knowledge on the question of a good diet that includes fruit, which has been under way since the 1960s. Each was qualitatively different from the other, and thus we must also characterize events in the early modern period. Attitudes to fruit emerged from a unique combination of several trends, a deep scientific curiosity about botany and the classification of plants, widespread explorations overseas that rallied the enthusiasm of seafarers and botanists to discover new plants, plus a fashion for gardening and display among the well-to-do. It was all enlivened and empowered by European correspondence, the publication of books, and diverse other contacts with foreign food cultures. A maturing food market offered strong commercial incentives.

We can point out some of the landmarks along the way. Thomas Elyot, an early English author on food in a printed book, was telling his readers in 1541 that fruit had once been man's chief food, coming before cereals, but men's bodies had changed and it was now harmful, engendering ill humours and causing putrefying fevers. But not long after, a changing viewpoint became evident when artists began to use fruit (and vegetables and other foods as well) in arresting paintings of still life. It became a rich branch of art that is beginning to be studied more deliberately by historians, though they have yet to link it with current horticultural and food history, rather than emphasizing the classical associations and the moralizing and sexual connotations of fruit and vegetables. Among the very first painters of still life was an Italian lady, Fede Galizia, who was born in 1578 and died in 1630. Her paintings, mainly of fruit, but also including a few vegetables, were brought together in 1989 in a volume published in Italy. An exhibition of Spanish still life in London in 1995 was a more splendid reminder of this phase in art and food history, celebrating in particular the acknowledged Spanish master, Juan Sanchez Cotán (1560–1627). A reviewer of the catalogue and exhibition asked himself what motivated this new choice of subject, wondering if it was 'a desire to celebrate divine creation in its humblest manifestations'. The historian of food must offer another answer, directing attention instead to the profound impression that must have been made on contemporaries in the sixteenth century by the appearance in their markets of improved fruits. Gillian Riley's volume on the Italian writer Castelvetro is a richly illustrated text on this theme, showing paintings of fruit from Italy and Holland, plainly conveying the same delight, and convincing us that the artists truthfully painted what they saw; around 1600 fruit was becoming a qualitatively different food from what it had been in 1541.[158]

In 1500 people had an abundance of wild fruit trees in the hedgerows, and they would almost certainly have regarded that supply as plentiful at their standard of expectation. In due season they looked for wild cherries, plums, damsons and bullace, apples, pears, quinces, medlars and sloes; in the woodlands, they collected strawberries, whortleberries and other berries that were regionally varied – like the berries of the service or chequer tree. Service trees were a speciality of Kent and Sussex, and after long neglect, they are now attracting attention to ensure that we treasure the survivors, and do not heedlessly cut them down.

People recognized that wild fruits flourished more readily in some districts than in others, more in the south than in the north, and whenever they listed particular counties, they named first and foremost Kent, Surrey and Sussex; and Herefordshire, Worcestershire and Gloucestershire. Somerset and Devon should have been named in the same breath but were usually overlooked. One of Hartlib's informants in the mid-seventeenth century told him that plums and damson trees in the hedgerows of Surrey and Kent paid a great part of the locals' rent. Apart from hedgerow trees, some were tended with more than ordinary care in the orchards of monasteries and great houses, and their special status was clearly known to the connoisseurs as we may judge when Henry VIII, building Nonsuch Palace, appropriated the fruit trees of Syon Abbey after the dissolution of the monasteries.[159]

Wild fruit was liable to be more or less sour, even though it looked beautiful, but the varieties growing locally were diverse, allowing some fruits to be eaten straight from the tree. Alternatively, honey and later sugar made the sour ones palatable. Country people plainly took pride in some of their local specialities,

as we may judge from the many gifts of pears and apples that were presented to
Henry VIII in the 1530s when he hunted in a particular neighbourhood. The
donors of these gifts were usually described as poor women, but on one occasion
the mayor of Northampton presented the king with a gift of local pears when
he was hunting in Grafton forest, showing the pride that men of higher rank
took in their local produce. In Lancashire they had a local variety of pears called
'pucelles' which the Shuttleworth family in Lancashire found tasty and enjoyable
at their meal table.[160]

In the years between 1620 and 1630, the identification and cultivation of
fruits reached a crescendo of scientific effort and enthusiasm. Our attention
to these years is focused by John Parkinson's careful work of 1629, which
described all the varieties of fruits then known to him, and explaining how he
had hired the Frenchman Guillaume Boel to search out for him more plants in
southern Europe for growing in England; also we note the publication of books
on gardening coming from Yorkshire, not the most favoured of fruit counties,
written by the parson William Lawson in 1618, 1623 and 1626. Equally significant
in our calendar of these years is the new upper-class interest in lifelike paintings,
depicting fruit and vegetables, to adorn grand houses. Sir Nathaniel Bacon, the
grandson of Sir Francis Bacon, attracts attention as the first known painter of still
lifes in England, producing one splendid canvas of a cookmaid with vegetables
and fruit, which was acquired by the Tate Gallery in 1995, and is dated 1620–5.
The artistic influences in his case came most directly from the Low Countries,
where Nathaniel probably received some training from artists like Pieter Aertsen
and Frans Snijders. At the same time, a network of women also comes to the fore
in the neighbourhood. Jane Bacon, Nathaniel's wife, was a correspondent and
good friend of Lucy, Countess of Bedford (already mentioned as a patron of
Castelvetro, who commended to her the Italian way with fruit and vegetables);
both Lucy and Jane attended on Queen Anne of Denmark, James I's queen, while
she cherished a picture at Oatlands Palace of a gardener with son and daughter
selling melons, cabbages, herbs and fruit at market. (Remember also that her
husband, James I, was a greedy eater of cherries, demolishing a whole bowl at
one go.) The clustering of these courtly associations strengthens the suspicion
of a connection between this fruit frenzy and the experience that Prince Charles
brought back from his trip to Madrid in 1623, seeking marriage with the Spanish
Infanta; surely that opened his eyes to the delights of fruit, for the documents
celebrate some glorious banquets. Nor should we overlook the doings of Aletheia
Talbot, Countess of Arundel, building Tart Hall, near St James's Palace, in the
1630s, and installing a gallery of eye-catching fashions that included pictures of
a cook, a fruiterer and others, and fruits including plums, cherries, artichokes
and more. The network of cronies extends more widely still when we discover
that Nathaniel Bacon's associates included the Sackville family at Knole in Kent,

whom he assisted as art adviser. Their enthusiasm for fruit (and vegetables and herbs too) is loudly proclaimed in their archives. In the year 1630, the Sackville family took delivery in their orchard of 15 different varieties of cherry tree (two, three and four rootstocks of some kinds, and 28 of the Flanders cherry). Indeed, the scene on 25 November is vividly before our eyes in a document charging the household account with 12d. for drink that was given to the men who arrived as 'takers up of the trees'. The Sackvilles were plainly intent on improving fruit supplies in the kitchen, and bought in addition six different varieties of pear, plus more with illegible names, but enough to show the distinction they were making between those for eating raw and those for baking. Their grocers' bills also showed that the fruit was not designed for the privileged members of the family alone, but for guests and staff as well, and it continued to arrive into February and March. On 20 February 1631, three lots of 100 pippins were delivered, along with 26 other apples, five lots of a dozen oranges apiece, one lot of six oranges (sometimes oranges were distinguished as 'sweet oranges'), and five lots of lemons, four at a time. One hundred pippins were deposited at the kitchen door in March 1631 and March 1632, pears and apples in October and November, and chestnuts in 1633. In the summer months strawberries and raspberries were taken to Knole every other day in pints and quarts, and an unusually varied assortment arrived from Erasmus Greenway on 1 July 1631, containing dry apricots, dry green apricots, dry gooseberries, dry natural plums, paste of raspberries, green apricots, quinces, oranges, orange chips and candied eryngo. Plainly someone locally was adding value to the fruit and charging accordingly: half a pound of dry green apricots cost 4s., oranges in quarters 5s. and a pound of dry cherries 8s. For the meaning of all these terms we turn to the cookery books of the 1650s, when apricot chips and fruit pastes are explained. To pack them, three dozen boxes featured at the end of the bill, at 18d. a dozen; they were needed to pack fruit pastes when dry and 'so present it to whom you please'. A later writer described the way the French packed their plums in elegant boxes for sale in London shops. He only hinted at the source of those enthusiasms. But at Knole, some confectioners from somewhere had clearly found another cosy niche for similar wares several decades earlier.[161]

The eating of fruit had hitherto been regarded as an agreeable seasonal extra, not as part of a meal but eaten unceremoniously as it was picked off the tree. But by the 1650s, fruit flans were the vogue, served as 'a closing dish' at the table. A mixed collection of theories now prevailed about the value of fruit as a food. It was known to have been eaten in classical times, and by 1600 it was being commended in a half-hearted way. By 1630 opinion was split in two, some advocating it strongly, others still condemning it. Quite realistically, overeating was condemned for causing sickness, and most general references dwelt on the crude juices of fruit, showing that prejudices persisted: Harington deemed raw pears to be poison; William Vaughan in 1617 thought fruit was taken more for wantonness than nourishment; and even in the Civil war period, Cressy Dymock preserved himself from the diseases caused by eating raw fruit by eating good brown bread an hour or two beforehand. He believed that other boys of his age had killed themselves by not taking this precaution.[162]

Dried fruits, the raisins and currants that poured into the country by the fifteenth century (currants from Corinth, raisins from Spain, prunes from France), did not seem to engender the same prejudice, nor did the large imports of oranges and lemons from Spain; they featured in the earliest recipe books. Moreover, around 1600 buyers differentiated between prunes that came from Damascus and from France, and dates that came from Egypt, Judea, Italy and coastal Spain. Citrons were distinguished from lemons, as were also sweet lemons, frequently named in household accounts, though that is a fruit that we no longer seem to know. Pomecitrons were named by Dawson (1597), and said to be larger than a lemon with a thicker rind and less acid. James Hart in 1633 differentiated oranges that were sweet, sour and in between; presumably the bitter ones were the Seville oranges which continue to be indispensable in our marmalade to this day. John Houghton in the mid-1690s thought that nine million oranges were imported each year, of which one quarter were eaten in London. Thus he underlined what a privileged place was London for food.[163]

We can only guess at the rate at which fashion changed perceptions of fruit, for objective comments are hard to find. But Henry VIII must have absorbed some of the food preferences of his Spanish Queen Catherine, and he certainly picked up more at the table of the French king Francis I. All the signs suggest that he insisted on enjoying the same pleasures at home, and thus were foreign gardeners brought to work in the royal orchards and those of the nobility. In December 1611, the Cecil family was paying the handsome wage of seven shillings per week each to its two French gardeners. Cherry trees from Flanders became a craze, followed by apricots, peaches and nectarines. Production swelled in Kent, and then spread out along streams of influence and action into more counties. Already by the end of Elizabeth's reign, the competition of cherry imports from the Netherlands was arousing shrill protests from English gardeners selling their home-grown ones. When we ask which classes of English people enjoyed these new fruits, then clearly the gentry ate the best quality and the largest variety. Robert Cecil ate fruit immoderately, we are told by a contemporary. But ordinary folk in town and countryside also shared in the bounteous, seasonal harvest. Robert Loder was a gentleman farmer in Berkshire but no specialist fruit grower; his principal crops were cereals. But he had a handsome harvest in 1620 of cherries weighing 6,402lbs, and when he hired women to pick his cherries, he could not stop them eating them. He counted his profits from the farm so carefully that he even included a guess at the total they had eaten from the trees. And, of course, his own family ate their share. He sold the rest at the market, earning in 1620 a profit of £20.[164]

Plainly, many local people of all classes were enjoying more and better-tasting fruit. Indeed, fruit impinged sufficiently on contemporaries to persuade them, as Arthur Standish reported in 1613, that its great plenty caused a fall in demand for meat; it was certainly a possible outcome whenever the weather was unusually hot. Moufet's views (or his editor's?) in favour of fruit were influenced by the fact that many people in other Continents and indeed in parts of Europe had been seen to feed 'wholly or principally of fruit'; and the same view swayed others in England by the 1650s. The recipe books show the cooks positively glorying in their fruit recipes. One cookery book, representing a composite work of 'persons of quality', overflowed with luscious recipes for Lady Gray's cream of quodlings and cream of apricots, the author's quodling pie (of apples mixed with cream and rosewater), and Lady Butler's preserve of apricots or white plums. The jigsaw of clues to this feast of fruit must also find a place for the altruistic gentleman, Sir Edmund Sawyer near Windsor, reported by Hartlib (in 1653) making it his mission to plant fruit trees freely in hedges. John Evelyn after 1660 expected legislation to order the planting of two or three fruit trees per acre, and although this did not happen, it is found among some manorial by-laws, as, for example, in Ombersley, Worcestershire, requiring tenants to plant four fruit trees for every one cut down.[165]

Seventeenth-century documents from all counties supply a host of references to 'new orchards'. By the 1650s contemporaries were noticing not just new orchards, but whole fields of fruit trees as a new feature in the landscape. By the end of the seventeenth century, when John Houghton advertised houses for sale in his news-sheet, it is noticeable how many properties around London, and conspicuously in Isleworth and Edmonton, included orchards 'walled about', and boasting an abundance of good fruit. A witness of the scene in Isleworth in 1724 claimed that several hundred acres had been converted to fruit in the past 60 years, that is, since the Restoration.[166]

Some attributed the spread of orchards after 1660 to the good advice of the Frenchman, Sieur Le Gendre, who had written *The French Gardener* that had been translated into English in 1660, but, as we have seen, many currents were flowing, all carrying the same ideas to fruition. The preservation of fruit became a routine. Instructions filled many pages in the cookery books, so that fruit could appear at meal tables in every month of the year. Fruit-eating gradually became a qualitatively different experience, not everywhere equally, of course, but entering into the diet of all classes.[167]

The commonest fruit were apples, of which innumerable varieties were grown, far exceeding those that we can buy nowadays, and each known for its distinctive flavour, its best use in cooking, and its long or short lasting qualities. By keeping them in barrels in dry sand, Nicholas Blundell in Lancashire enjoyed eating his in late March; he described in his diary opening a barrel on 22 March 1703, and finding his apples very firm and sound. Many had a speck of 'faided' [sic], but few were rotten. Pears similarly were extremely varied. Both were used to make drink, and both cider and perry underwent the most careful experiments to produce a commercial cider and perry that successfully found a good market locally and also in London.[168]

We have already noted the veritable craze for cherries that developed in the period 1610–20. James I admitted eating a whole bowlful at one go. The neighbours around Belvoir castle seem to have learned how much their lady loved cherries, judging by the baskets that were brought to her and noted in the household accounts in 1611. Vicar Rowse's daughter brought one batch, walking four and a half miles from her home in Saltby to deliver them; Vicar Rowse sent another lot nine days later. Incidentally, he was only one of many parsons who became keen gardeners in these years, passing on their enthusiasm to the next generation during the Civil Wars. Further north, cherries were growing successfully in Lancashire in 1617, as Thomas Walmsley's household accounts make clear.[169]

Other fruits that featured alongside the cherries arrived in domestic gardens by various routes. People wanting to tend strawberries were urged to dig them up in the woodland and transplant them at home. Richard Taverner advised those who wanted to grow apple trees to enquire of the women at the market who sold apple pies, from whom, presumably, they would cadge the pips, or even perhaps cuttings. Growing fruit was not something for the rich alone; it called for an interest in gardening, but not for money. Thus fruit turns up in large quantities in rubbish tips at archaeological sites. Plums were eaten by the sailors and/or soldiers on the Mary Rose, which sank in Southampton Water in July 1545; 100 plum stones were found among the archaeological remains. Gerard claimed to have 60 different varieties of plum in his London garden. Peaches, nectarines and apricots became familiar fruits in gentlemen's orchards, and in the case of apricots leave us with an unexplained mystery, since they continued so plentiful in certain places into the late nineteenth century.[170]

Apricots were being acclimatized in gardens in the sixteenth century by being planted against sheltering walls, since on standard trees the apricots did not always ripen. Gervase Markham in 1613 knew of a pentice constructed along a six- to seven-foot wall, which overshadowed the wall and enabled the branches to bear plentifully. Some growers were already well satisfied with their progress. Sir Arthur Throckmorton, Raleigh's brother-in-law, joyfully ate 'a very ripe apricot out of my garden' on 13 July 1610. In the same year, neighbours brought apricots in July to the Duke of Rutland. Dr Hart in 1633 in Northampton deemed the apricot far better than the peach because it ripened successfully and was more firm and solid. All the cooks who wrote cookbooks in the 1650s were using apricots – Jos. Cooper, cook to Charles I, gave four apricot recipes; Lord Ruthin took considerable trouble with his cold dessert of apricots; and his wife gave rules for preserving them. After the Restoration William Temple even grew the trees as standards and considered them the best fruits he had, though in selecting the most satisfactory variety he chose the Brussels apricot, which was good for preserving when green, before the stone had developed. This may mean that he preferred his apricots pickled; he also claimed for himself the fame of having first brought that variety to England. However, his taste was evidently shared by others, for in a long list of the fruit trees growing in the Bishop of Durham's orchard at Glynde Place in Sussex in 1754, four of the apricots were of the same variety. Two more at Glynde were called 'orange apricots', and were planted with a south-west aspect, and another two, so-called 'masculine apricots', were given a north-eastern aspect, their fruit apparently ripening in mid-July, but not in bounteous quantity. But apricots grown on espaliers could make a memorable sight, plainly, for Thomas Hitt, publishing an instructive book on fruit in 1755, illustrated the apricot tree with ten horizontal branches spaced one foot apart on both sides of the main stem; he had served as gardener to the Manners family and Lord Robert Bertie at Chislehurst in Kent. We might be inclined to assume from all this that apricots were only acclimatized south of the Trent; but that would not be correct. In 1778 Lady Irwin at Temple Newsam, near Leeds, ordered ten dozen apricot trees from Dunhill's nurseries (the firm that was more famous at this time for its liquorice and Pontefract cakes).[171]

The recipe books after 1660 gave priority to recipes for apricots in a fruit dessert, and certainly not for pickling; they were used by Anne Blencowe in 1694 in the most matter-of-fact way; and her crystallized apricots sound delicious. A most vivid image of home-grown fruit on the way to market was given in the *Spectator* in August 1712 when Richard Steele described his early morning journey down the Thames amid a cheerful crowd of young women grouped on one of ten apricot boats depositing their cargo at Strand Bridge for Covent Garden. In the 1770s seven or eight varieties were being listed in the textbooks, and Henry Phillips in 1821 called the apricot 'one of our wall fruits in highest esteem'. Somehow, we have lost a precious fruit of our own growing since then, and that in the last century and a half. From Kidlington in Oxfordshire 6,000 dozen apricots were being sent each year to Covent Garden market in the early part of the nineteenth century; and Thorverton in Devon was a village famous within living memory for its apricots. Why and how have the varieties that plainly suited our climate been lost?[172]

As with vegetables, the success of fruit growing encouraged bolder experiments by keen gardeners to extend the growing season of their fruits. Glasses were fitted over melon beds in 1678 in the Earl of Cardigan's garden at Ampthill,

Bedfordshire. Nets were slung over cherry trees to protect the fruit from birds. Among the most sophisticated projects for ripening fruit more readily was that of the Geneva-born mathematician, Nicholas Fatio de Duillier, who became a Fellow of the Royal Society, and published in 1699 a treatise on *Fruit Walls Improved*, advocating sloping walls to capture more efficiently the radiation of the sun. He dedicated it to Wriothesley Russell, heir to the Duke of Bedford, who entered into his inheritance in 1700. Curving walls were already known for this purpose, but not sloping walls. The Russells do not appear to have adopted the idea, but Stephen Switzer claimed that the Duke of Devonshire and the Duke of Rutland did, both building sloping walls on their estates. Expense was evidently no obstacle to the richest fruit enthusiasts.[173]

Nut trees were routinely present alongside fruit trees in the early modern orchard, and this nourishment should never be omitted when calculating the content of English people's diet. The nuts most often eaten were filberts, hazel nuts, chestnuts and walnuts, walnuts being especially valued both for pickling when young, and to eat as a dessert when ripened. Filberts and walnuts were actually tithed at Great Driffield in Yorkshire in 1595, suggesting that even then people harvested more than they needed for household use.[174]

We have earlier described the virtual craze for planting walnuts in the early seventeenth century, and although that excessive zeal moderated over time, it was still responsible for continued plantings. The rectory at Beckley in Oxfordshire in 1659 possessed not one or two walnut trees but a whole walnut tree orchard; and in 1682 the record shows the incumbent then having 14 walnut trees and ten chestnuts, and planting yet more walnuts – 11 trees by the dairy, and another two in the deer yard. In 1709, as far north as Little Crosby in Lancashire, Nicholas Blundell was another keen grower, planting some 132 walnut trees in 1709. We still find avenues of these trees growing on some old estates, like Londesborough in East Yorkshire, and in that particular instance we know that they were planted at this very time.[175]

After walnuts came chestnuts, mostly eaten as sweetmeats, but by 1700, according to John Houghton, eaten also with stewed meat and in pies – a lesson from the French, he said. The English had abandoned the attempt to grow almonds, because they did not ripen. So the Almond Tree Cottages in Kent must tell a story of hopes frustrated. Instead, almonds were imported on a large scale, and the recipe books show how they were used to make macaroons, marzipan, and many sauces.[176]

Thus fruit and nuts settled into the English diet and moved into a secure place at the table. Horatio Busoni from Italy had noticed among his impressions of England in 1618 that fruit was not eaten sedately at meal times; rather, people ate it in the street, like goats, he said. Some theorists commended it at the beginning of the meal, some at the end. But already by the 1650s the anonymous author of one cookbook very firmly served her fruit tart as 'a closing dish'. It had been fairly usual among writers to insist that fruit be cooked or preserved in some way rather than being eaten raw. But that point ceased to be laboured when making fruit pastes, purées and syrups, and bottling fruit became routine kitchen procedures.[177]

One of our journalists recently claimed to know people who were too proud to take their food from the hedgerows. Such sentiments are born of an age when the threat of starvation in our country is unknown. It was totally alien to thinking in the early modern period. The free larder that opened at the door was nature's blessing on all. Rich men graciously received the hedgerow harvest from their humbler neighbours. People ate almost everything in sight in their own neighbourhoods, and although they did not know it, wild fruits gave them rich doses of vitamin C. The scarlet hips of the dog rose are so rich in anti-scorbutic minerals that they run off the scale in the measurements of Violet Plimmer; indeed, the wild fruits are often much richer in vitamin C than cultivated plants. But we have to allow for very considerable local differences in people's access to fruit throughout our period, and more noticeably as people moved into towns.[178]

The workhouse diets recorded by Frederick Eden included 'garden stuff', but no one mentioned the serving of apple puddings or pies. So fruit was not yet taken for granted at mealtimes by all, although apples were undoubtedly the commonest available. Some counties grew far more than others. Townsmen found far more on sale in their markets than some villagers could pick or buy; and Londoners, as always, had the best supply of all, for women tirelessly carried much to market from the suburbs. Engravings from the 1680s onwards of pedlars crying their fruit in London vividly depict the trouble-free opportunities for eating fruit that came the way of Londoners; the gardeners in Kent, Essex, Middlesex and Surrey, after all, were no more than a tolerable walking distance away. So when Frederick Eden surveyed the scene at Ealing, he was told of 250 market gardens in the neighbourhood, from which women, mostly Welsh, walked to London, often twice a day, with their fruit baskets. Moreover, by that date transport by road and river had advanced to the point where Henry Scott, gardener at Weybridge, could issue his trade card in 1754 boasting of the Chertsey coach that carried his fruit every day in season to London, while the Weybridge boats served him twice a week. Fruit was thus generously available to the middle classes in London. We can also reasonably guess at a spasmodic supply of fruit in provincial towns, dependent on the efforts and produce of local merchants, while home-grown treats in good seasons were counted on by country people. In the face of the documentary record, it is difficult to resist labelling these developments as a 'fruit revolution'.[179]

DRINKS

We enjoy a great variety of drinks these days, but there is no doubt that people had an even greater choice of flavours in the early modern period, when every family made at least some of its own drink, exploiting the local resources and mingling ingredients according to family traditions and preferences. If they had further money to spare, they could buy more from the vintners, brewers, alewives and tapsters, who attracted customers by displaying their own originality with yet more flavours. Anne Wilson cites John Taylor being astonished by a Manchester man who had nine different ales on his table, flavoured with hyssop, sage, wormwood, rosemary, betony and scurvy grass. Among these, we already know sage ale, for that was not just one man's idiosyncrasy but a general favourite for drinking in May; and according to John Parkinson, costmary was an added refinement – in other words, when making drink, no one could resist extra personal touches.[180]

A most satisfying, close look at drinks of all kinds is given in Anne Wilson's book on *Food and Drink in Britain* (1973), making another such account superfluous. But some further reflections are prompted by other reading, lighting up dark corners of the same scene. A lively discussion took place in the early modern period about how, when, and why to drink. Among physicians, a debate centred on the virtues of drink versus food, and they could not reach agreement on whether to take a morning draught of liquid when rising, and if so, what liquid one should drink. The argument continued on whether to start or end a meal with drink, and whether to drink at bedtime. James Hart, the Northampton physician, wrote a discursive piece in 1633 starting from first principles, and constructing an image of the stomach like a pot, having meat boiling inside it, and requiring moisture to stop it from going dry. For concoction to proceed, the stomach had to have periods of rest, and so one of his rules was that one should not drink between meals.[181]

WATER

Which liquids were good and which bad was the next topic, and on this Hart had learned some lessons the hard way when travelling in France. After drinking cold water in the heat of summer, he had succumbed to a single, then a double tertian fever, and was sick for a quarter of a year. In the end, he took six months fully to recover. Yet it is not at all clear from his account that he suspected the water to be the culprit, though in then listing different sources of good water, he did not go far wrong. He put rainwater first, and spring water or good river water next, 'correcting' the last by boiling it, and boiling away a third or a half. Some people then strained the water through a linen cloth before adding wine vinegar and perhaps honey and sugar as well. (The women were always the ones blamed for adding sweetness.) Hart held the view that the poor should be drinking more water and not resorting to strong drink that cost money; this went along with a belief that many honourable ladies drank little but water and enjoyed perfect health – an interesting insight into some drinking habits of the well-to-do that one would not expect. Thus he conjures up a picture of much pure water to hand, a state of affairs that was evidently true in Cornwall where, Cogan alleged, the poorer sort seldom drank anything but water and were strong of body. The fact that the parson at St Just near Mawes in Cornwall in 1620 had a cistern of water on his glebe land may point us to the source of one parson's clean drinking water.[182]

Hart seemed not to confront water problems in towns, though his own town, Northampton, was a populous place; he was sure that the lead pipes to conduct the water were perfectly safe. But the quality of water had become an issue of more concern by the 1670s, and in 1674 the Earl of Rutland on several occasions had water fetched for him from Quarndon in Derbyshire, which has a medicinal spring; and a reference in 1675 to his fetching water from 'the spaw' presumably referred to another such journey. In 1681 some of Worcester's drinking water was also evidently suspect (or in short supply, perhaps?), and people fetched it from the river on horseback in leather bags, and sold it. Baskerville, reporting this, had never seen the like except in Ely. But in the later eighteenth century the same problem weighed on Liverpool, giving sailors' wives the chance to turn an honest penny by fetching it in carts from two miles away. It may be that clean water supplies became in the second half of the seventeenth century a noticeably more pressing problem than before.[183]

Only once have I ever alighted on a clear statement by labourers of their drinking habits, and that was in 1616 in a dispute in Lincolnshire in the Isle of Axholme about the use of mills in Epworth and Belton. Several labourers had no corn of their own and only ground meal for brewing at the mill when they had money to buy any. Otherwise they bought 'small drink' for themselves and their families. The thatcher of Epworth was most specific of all: when he had money, he bought drink, and when he had no money, he, his wife and five children, he said, were forced to drink water.[184]

ALE, BEER AND CIDER

Probate inventories and contemporary observers' comments make clear how much brewing went on in the home to the very end of our period. When bread troughs were missing from the list of personal possessions at death, brewing equipment was still conspicuous. That is the strong impression conveyed, for example, by inventories from Northamptonshire between the 1660s and

1690s. Brewhouses were common on farms, and maltmills, maltquerns and malting vessels were everywhere. In Gloucester in 1682 it was the town's policy to encourage home brewing by not allowing any public brewers, a ruling that Baskerville applauded when he visited. In Hertfordshire, Prussian visitors in 1765–6 formed the impression that practically every household there still made its own beer. That was likely and not surprising for it was barley-growing country, and the river Lea ran conveniently through it, carrying large quantities of barley to London; everything conspired to encourage barley-brewing in that part of the kingdom. John Ellman senior, giving evidence to a committee of the House of Commons in 1821, testified to the same situation in Glynde in East Sussex until at least 1776: every man in the parish brewed his own beer. But a dramatic turnaround had occurred by 1830 when William Cobbett asserted that not a single man could afford to do it. That was a change wrought in one lifetime. In the West Riding of Yorkshire, however, where the country people were said to live chiefly by clothing, people in the 1630s bought all their drink, and scarce anyone brewed any. Elsewhere in Yorkshire in the 1760s foreign visitors were struck by another unexpected feature of local life: they saw ale everywhere and little beer (adding irrelevantly that they thought Scottish ale was better than the English). In Cheshire and Gloucestershire, on the other hand, where the Prussians stayed in farmhouses, cider was the everyday drink. Local differences were legion, and class differences too: small beer was always the drink of the poor, and was also found in workhouses.[185]

Gervase Markham underlined the fact that brewing was women's work, and so the most detailed accounts of methods came from them, though they passed into print through the menfolk. For example, Kent was apple-growing country, where Prussian visitors described the very good cider they tasted at Dr Lamb's farm. The occasion of their visit gave Mrs Lamb her chance to speak up, when usually the women remained silent or out of sight. She was doubtless serving the cider, they questioned her, and she told them exactly how she made it. That very human scene was reminiscent of one enacted 200 years earlier when Mrs William Harrison insisted on telling her husband exactly how she brewed beer, not allowing him to gloss over the details, as he would have preferred, when writing his *Description of England*. She made sure that he wrote it all down, thus unknowingly commemorating her own prowess in print for ever more. Our Prussians, incidentally, hoped to get hold of the recipe for porter, a beer that was very popular at that time in London, having been introduced in the 1720s, but it was kept a closely guarded secret, and while the whole purpose of their visit to England had been to discover all the industrial and farming know-how of the English, this secret was withheld from them.[186]

When focusing attention on London, the most conspicuous evidence by the end of the eighteenth century concerns the growth of commercial breweries, and encourages the notion that they had taken over the bulk of beer-brewing. It is a good illustration of the way a London-centred view of food and drink distorts the national situation. London's breweries were growing into large operations – Whitbreads was already one of the leaders – and a Polish reporter in 1785 conjured up the impressive scene in Chiswell Street, London, where three coppers, encased in stonework with iron hoops, were in action; great granaries were stored with malt and hops; pumps, powered by horses, fed the water; and immense reservoirs cooled the beer in underground cisterns. Other urban centres were developing their breweries on a similar but more modest scale, while still adding their own individuality to the general drinking scene.[187]

Houghton in 1727 knew that some brewers liked beans and peas to be malted with their barley, and he may have been reporting on a London practice. But since the majority of drinking English people still lived in the countryside, we may be sure that they were more adventurous still. Around Pontefract where they grew liquorice, even perhaps in London too, we have to allow for a drink of liquorice boiled in water, 'fermented with barm and tunned up', which John Parkinson said in 1640 was 'much used nowadays' instead of ale or beer. His remark hinted at a growing fashion; it is tempting to see it starting around 1620 when we find the lady in charge of the Shuttleworth family's housekeeping in Lancashire buying 200 liquorice plants in October 1618, and four pounds of liquorice in March 1620. This, with the four pounds of sugar bought at Colne at the same time, could well have signified an intention to make liquorice drinks, or was it perhaps comfits? (After all, the family was simultaneously picking up other modish ideas, and buying sweetmeats from Thomas Leaver, the comfit maker in London.) Flavoured ales mentioned in 1654 by Lord Ruthin had mace, oil of nutmegs, or a roasted orange pricked with cloves added to them. Cider and perry, well before they became commercially popular drinks in the mid-seventeenth century, were also being differently flavoured by the connoisseurs: Leonard Mascall, who associated with people in Sussex and Kent, told his readers in 1567 to place in their brewing vessels a linen bag containing powder of cloves, mace, cinnamon and ginger to give a pleasant taste. With adventurous drinks still in mind, we should reflect also on the significance of finding in the far north, on Harehope Moor in Northumberland, a trough for making juniper wine, capable of holding 500 gallons.[188]

HERBAL AND DIET DRINKS

Herbal drinks for health were given the name of 'diet drinks', and obtruded more noticeably than before in the literature of the late sixteenth and the whole of the seventeenth century. It was probably a natural progression as recipe books gave more space to fruit, and drinks and cordials could exploit the larger quantities of fruit and sugar then available, which spurred experiments. Some wild potions were being advertised by 1700, like Parker's spirit of scurvy grass, the grass having been gathered astrologically under planetary influences; and a book entitled *A Family Herbal or the Treasure of Health*, promising to show people 'how to preserve their health by their diet', had gone into its second edition in 1693. In the taverns customers were offered the tavernkeeper's own variety of drink, sometimes with his own name attached. 'Salop' was someone's invention, first referred to in print (according to the *Oxford English Dictionary*) in 1728. It became so popular that 'salop-sellers' were touring the London streets in the later eighteenth century, offering this drink, made from an imported Turkish root infused in water or warm milk. Exotic trends nevertheless went along with a sustained taste for the old-fashioned ways of making ale; hence Houghton's remark that the ale of oatmalt was favoured among the gentry and much sold in London.[189]

TEA, CHOCOLATE AND COFFEE

More changes on the drinking scene were wrought by the arrival from abroad of tea, chocolate and coffee, which introduced consumers to caffeine in place of alcohol, and were immediately recognized for their stimulating effects without making anyone drunk. Their medicinal virtues were carefully watched for. Hartlib in his diary noted that tea was used in China and Japan, and cured fumes, indigestion, stone and gout. Dignitaries with names that impressed people in London circles, like Sir Charles Herbert and Lord Newport, were cited in commendation, as well as Mr Waller 'who studies his health as much as any man'. So even though it was then said to taste 'a litle bitterish', tea forged ahead, and from 1664 the East India Company was importing it. It was expensive, costing at first between £6 and £10 for one pound when it arrived at Amsterdam, but had fallen to £3 per pound by 1700, when smuggling from France became a serious business. As late as the 1820s the French were still hoping to naturalize the tea tree in the south of the country, and the English too, since most plant nurseries near London were said to have some for sale. But foreign trade met the demand, and regular tea-drinking was well illustrated in Thomas Turner's diary between 1754 and 1765. This modest Sussex shopkeeper routinely drank it in the afternoon, ignoring, if he ever knew of it, the fierce denunciation of it by Jonas Hanway, who was convinced that men were losing their stature and comeliness and women their beauty as a result of drinking it.[190]

Chocolate from the New World was being advertised as a drink in 1657, and John Houghton in 1701 reported the contents of a detailed treatise by Dr Henry Stubbe, a learned physician who had lived in Jamaica. By then it had spread 'prodigiously' in Europe, said Houghton, and was the subject of much trial and analysis. It had already found most favour with the Spaniards, a state of affairs that persists to this day; they had become addicted to it, said Houghton, and it was 'the sustenance of families'. But after some 50 years in England, chocolate houses were closing down, whereas tea and coffee had become firmly established. Stubbe's writing, incidentally, alerts us to the contrast in habit of taking hot drinks rather than cold. Tea, coffee and chocolate all demanded hot water, whereas wine, ale, beer, milk, whey, buttermilk and water were all usually drunk cold, except in winter. Plainly, these novelties imposed a change on one kitchen routine.[191]

Coffee was known to Francis Bacon in England as a Turkish drink in 1624, and was seen by John Evelyn being drunk in Balliol College, Oxford in 1637. Its arrival is more usually dated to 1650–2 when coffee houses opened in Oxford and London. We have an unusually precise account of its arrival in London in a report by John Houghton in 1701; and as his story is not well known, and yet its details are thoroughly plausible, it is worth reprinting in full.

> One Rastall, whom I knew, and within these few days I saw, went to Leghorn in 1651 and there found a coffee house. To the same house of merchandize, where this Rastall was, came Mr Daniel Edwards, a merchant from Smyrna [where coffee had been used immemorially] who brought with him a Greek servant named Pasqua, anno 1652, who made his coffee which he drank two or three dishes at a time twice or thrice a day. [A different account by a painstaking researcher, Henry Phillips, gave Pasqua's name as Pasqua Rossee, and described him as a Ragusan-Greek servant.] That year [Edwards] came overland to England and married the daughter of Alderman Hodges, who lived in Walbrook, and there with delight they drank coffee together, and this Edwards was the first I can learn brought the use of coffee hither, except it was the famous inventor of the circulation of the blood, Dr Harvey, who some say did frequently use it.[192]
>
> After this Edwards set up Pasqua for a coffee man in a shed in the churchyard in St Michael Cornhill, which is now a scrivener's brave house, where having great custom, the ale sellers petitioned the Lord Mayor against him as being no freeman. This made Alderman Hodges join his coachman, Bowman who was free, Pasqua's partner, and thus Mr Rastall found them in 1654. But Pasqua for some misdemeanour was forced to run the country, and Bowman by his trade and a contribution of 1,000 sixpences turned the shed to a house. Bowman's apprentices were first John Painter, then Humphry, from whose wife I had this account. How long this drink has been in the world is hard to say, but the English edition of Tavernier's *Travels* says it had been in use but twenty years, although the author says six score years. I am informed that Dr Beveridge has an Arabick book that says a hermit drank it and called it 'bun'. This is the best history I can learn of the original of coffee and coffee houses, may others give better.[193]

In a later number of his newsletter Houghton gave a chemical analysis of coffee, and having a taste for figures, he added the quantity consumed in England and its value. He claimed to have made his calculation in the summer of 1700, and now in May, 1701, 'by reason of the cheapness of coffee', sales had increased by half as much again – a surprising statement since we do not expect to find coffee being dubbed cheap at this time. Had the introduction of coffee in 1697 had some effect?[194]

New hot drinks from the 1650s onwards set up a demand for drinking vessels to match, and splendid examples are found in probate inventories. They were conspicuous among the possessions of Worcestershire gentry, whose probate inventories, listing their possessions at death, are conveniently assembled in one volume of references for the whole county. Gentry simply had to have designated coffee, tea and chocolate cups, starting to acquire them between the 1680s and 1710s; when Sir James Rushout, baronet, died at Northwick Park in Blockley in 1705, my Lady Rushout's dressing room had '6 choquelet cups and saucers' and '5 china choquelet cups with feet' in her dressing room.[195]

WINES AND SPIRITS

Wines in great variety were readily bought in towns everywhere, and Holinshed writing in the 1570s thought the English had the greatest array of any country even though they produced none themselves. But he did not complain of excessive drunkenness at that time, suggesting moderation as the standard, and explaining the practice, in noblemen's houses at least, of not putting drink in a large vessel on the table but rather waiting for individuals to call for a drink; then, after they had drunk, the glass was removed by the servant, and put back into the cupboard, so discouraging 'idle tippling'. If this was common practice, then we can understand the change wrought under Dutch influence by the end of the century.[196]

A first book about wines by William Turner, the botanist, in 1568 was significantly concerned not with their origins and flavours but to defend white Rhenish wines against the charge of causing kidney and bladder stones. Stones were an extremely common complaint, prompting many experiments by individuals into ways of dissolving them. Turner described himself in 1550 as 'every day more and more vexed with the stone', and repeated complaints by others thread their way to the end of the period. Dr Theophilus Lobb, giving his advice on diet for the poor, described his own pain and many experiments in a treatise in 1739. Since they included many trials with fruits, we may wonder how much of the interest in making wine from English fruits, which grew noticeably in the second half of the seventeenth century, stemmed from hopes of a remedy for this suffering. Enthusiasm for fruit wines is most appreciatively described by William Westmacott, not a Londoner but a physician of Newcastle-under-Lyme, shedding light on the Staffordshire scene. He wrote optimistically in 1694 of 'plenty and variety' in food and drink in general, and of raspberries being manured in many gardens, grown from slips, offsets and suckers by 'lovers of fruit'. He did not underline the health virtues of fruit wines but did pay warm tribute to 'the female artists' striving to excel and outdo one another with their different wine recipes.[197]

DISTILLATION

The growing interest in domestic distillation has already been described above, and the publication of John Partridge's *Treasurie of Commodious Conceites* in 1584 (and later editions) is a landmark in that story. He gave to wives and maids thoroughly sensible instructions for gathering the herbs, not washing them but simply wiping them, and using a clean still. Distilling equipment became a regular purchase by the gentry, and sometimes the menfolk showed as much interest as the women. Armagil Waad, a projector with a finger in many pies (and a luxuriously furnished house in Hampstead in 1568), was abreast of all the latest fads and fashions, and had three books on distillation in his impressive library. But clearly a qualitative change was taking place in the practices and the scale of distillation in the early seventeenth century, as parliamentary debates in 1621 bear witness. Quarrels developed between distillers, apothecaries and grocers, and the incorporation of the Company of Distillers in London in 1638 marked another stage in the commercial development of distilling, even while many ordinary housewives used the same skill to produce medicines for their families and neighbours. People continued to experiment with drawing spirits from vegetables, herbs and fruit, resulting in an application for a patent in 1699 for distilling from turnips, carrots and parsnips that may not be unconnected with Westmacott's earlier reference in 1694 to a turnip cider 'being cunningly imposed on us'. The opening of the distillers' trade to all between 1690 and 1703 then produced the most dramatic change, turning gin drinking into a scourge that was not curbed until a sufficiently heavy excise was levied on home-made and imported spirits from the early 1780s.[198]

DRUNKENNESS

Drunkenness was a running theme throughout the early modern period, but public concern varied in intensity; rising, falling, and rising again. In the 1540s Andrew Boorde was more offended by heavy drinking in the Netherlands than in England, and in 1560 Levinus Lemnius considered that the English did not drink heavily. The same view was expressed by Henry Peacham in 1622 looking back to the years 1560–70 when it was rare to see a drunk man. But by 1633 things had changed, and James Hart described drunkenness as a sin once upon a time seen only at night, but now common in the daytime too. People reeling up and down the streets had formerly been assumed to be beggars – hence the saying, 'drunk as a beggar' was a common phrase. But now gentry had assumed it 'as a prerogative to grace their gentility'. Hart had strong Puritan views, and launched into a fierce attack on wantonness in taverns, alehouses, playhouses and whorehouses, ending by deploring, as did many of his contemporaries, the habit of drinking people's healths. It had become a fashion, introduced from the Netherlands, whereby convivial meetings became a veritable merry-go-round for drinking the individual healths of everyone present. Drunkenness may have declined during the Civil War and Interregnum; it was certainly discouraged by a beer duty in 1643, but Anne Wilson refers in her book on food to an increase of drunkenness at the Restoration; and a whole treatise on drunkenness and the drinking of healths focused on the problem in 1685. In the year 2005, as I write, we have sharp experience of what it means to see alternating phases of more and less drinking of alcohol.[199]

By way of a conclusion to the long list of drinks on offer at the end of our period, we can enumerate one middle-class couple's daily routine of drinkings as a spur to the search for more. The Hasteds of Kent were the grandparents of Edward Hasted, the historian of Kent. Grandfather Joseph, who died in 1732, was a chief painter-stainer at Chatham dockyard. The daily drinking routine of Joseph and his wife was recorded as follows: mead for breakfast; no mention of drink at dinner, but for Joseph it is likely to have been the strong beer that he himself brewed with great pride and always aged for several years; they drank tea at four; and elder wine after supper, which was made by his wife. In other words, the bulk of the drink in the Hasted household was still home-made.[200]

CONDIMENTS: SPICES, SALT, PEPPER, SUGAR AND SAUCES

Condiments, the many flavoursome additions that go into food to make it tastier than before, or somehow rescue it from dullness, have a lively history in our period for several different reasons. In the first place, the spices of the East began to arrive in much larger quantities than before, and almost certainly people's experience of their flavours was constantly extended as different local sources overseas were tapped. At the same time home-grown plants for flavouring were more carefully scrutinized by the botanists and publicly discussed, thus spreading information and interest in their use, and inducing more people to bring them in from wild places and grow them in their gardens. The supply of salt also underwent changes, by evaporation in salterns, which moved to new places as old ones were flooded, and by the mining of larger quantities of rock salt. The qualities and flavours of all these condiments featured in discussion in print, and Prussian visitors in the 1760s were obviously impressed by the Englishmen's concern for flavour, when, for example, they refused to feed clover to dairy cows because it spoiled the taste of the cheese and butter. Writers on food constantly underlined differences in the taste and texture of meats that resulted from the feed given to the animals and the salting procedures.

We should also heed the observation of Tom Stobart, an experienced mountaineer who climbed in some of the remotest parts of the world in the 1960s and 1970s: he had shared his food with many poor peasants living a simple life, and in his view, 'It is peasant cooking which makes the greatest use of herbs and spices.' By spices in that context, he meant not the flavourings that are imported and bought from a shop, but roots, plants and berries found locally. Stobart's remark for me lights up a basic truth about human beings everywhere. Food and drink are the basic necessities of life, everyone wants them to be palatable, and people ingeniously use the resources that lie around them to make them so. Living the life of a wanderer in deserts and on mountains (including Everest), Stobart learned how to eat pleasurably. 'I ... would never in these days', he wrote, 'think of setting out for any really wild place without some herbs in screws of paper and a knob of garlic in my pocket.'[201]

Innumerable plants, to which we nowadays pay no heed, were used in the past for flavouring. Maud Grieve's *Modern Herbal* astonishes with its many columns of information on the distinctive flavours and varied uses of herbs that we still have growing wild, but which lie neglected. A herb grower who had a commercial garden in Kent in the 1920s and 1930s, Margaret Brownlow, used to make a point of looking for these neglected plants in the vicinity of old ruined houses and in old church walls. 'When visiting ancient buildings, castles, abbeys, and churches where there have been gardens for many centuries', she wrote, 'it is interesting to see which herbs appear to be naturalized on the crumbling walls or in the vicinity.' She found pellitory of the wall, greater celandine, periwinkles and deadly nightshade (the latter growing abundantly in Knole Park, round Knole House). All these plants had medicinal uses, pellitory (a pyrethrum) for toothache, greater celandine for its orange juice to squeeze on warts, and deadly nightshade as a liniment against gout. But she was also seeking herbs for everyday food. She found ivy-leaved toadflax (then known as *Linaria cymbalaria*, now *Cymbalaria muralis*), whose leaves were used in salads, festooning the church wall of St Nicholas, Sevenoaks. At Beaulieu Abbey, she found hyssop and savory naturalized in the old walls: 'If you have forgotten the cucumber on your picnic', she wrote, 'then pick wild salad burnet.'[202]

Contemporary use of herbs is vouched for by the seventeenth-century botanist William Coles, who firmly asserted that there was not a day when the cook did not need herbs. He knew this well enough since he was constantly in the fields himself identifying wild plants and watching the country people gathering them; for them it was a routine, for example, to pick nettles in spring to put in pottage and purify the blood. Robert May's cookbook (1660) shows him using three to six herbs in one dish, whether it was camomile, pennyroyal, sage, mint, rosemary, thyme, sweet marjoram, savory, balm, parsley, fennel seed or occasionally horseradish root. The quantities used were never stated. But the past use of herbs in England was recaptured for me by a Persian lady, when she described how her mother, visiting her in England, threw out all the dried herbs in small jars in her kitchen, saying that they were scraps not worth keeping. In Persia she was accustomed to using half a kilo of herbs in one meal.[203]

Herbs also went into drinks. Lord Howard of Naworth in 1640 paid his brewer 12d. for bags in which to put herbs 'in my lord's beer'. Robert May put into one posset thyme, blessed thistle, camomile, mint, and marigold flowers. In short, our documents draw attention to herbs at every turn, and it is impossible to separate their medicinal from their culinary use.[204]

Purslane frequently appears in our documents, and evidently persisted in use as a common food in Cambridgeshire into the nineteenth century, for a recipe for spring soup included purslane along with sorrel, chervil and parsley. Purslane (which also has the less endearing name of pigweed) is a pleasant salad herb when young, and was used as a pot herb when older; its thick stems were also pickled in salt and vinegar for winter salads. The Countess of Kent recommended pickling purslane, and one of the Dering family in Kent sowed it in his garden, along with thyme, parsley and blessed thistle. Such repetitious references to the same herbs begin to hint at a standard repertoire lying beneath the quirky preferences of individuals.[205]

Purslane has been deservedly noticed again in recent years as a salad herb, reviving what was once upon a time routinely eaten as a 'cleansing' anti-scorbutic greenstuff. Historians who criticize diets of the past for their lack of vitamin C should pay heed to these many plants growing wild and cultivated in gardens. A nutritionist's analysis of the recipes in books that relied on herbs for flavouring could considerably lengthen the list of plants combating scurvy. Sorrel was another such plant, well known to John Evelyn as an anti-scorbutic, and according to Thomas Moufet regularly used in a sauce with pork, as its acidity contrasted with the fattiness of the meat; the leaves too were pleasantly acidic in salad.[206]

While one cannot make any quantitative statements about the consumption of herbs in early modern diets, contemporaries make it crystal clear that they ate innumerable plants and believed in their ability to promote health. Also they were aware of changing fashions over the course of time. Botanists were continually bringing in from abroad entirely new plants, or new varieties of familiar plants: a French variety of sorrel is said to have been introduced in 1596, for example, and this was preferred in soup because of its larger succulent leaves. We have already noted also the common opinion that wild plants had stronger flavours than the cultivated versions, but since cultivation in a garden was such a convenience, the loss of flavour had to be accepted.[207]

Two of the commonest home-grown flavourings were pickled broom buds and mustard. Interest in the broom bud is reflected in the Plantaganet family taking its name from the broom plant (*Planta genista*). The buds look like capers and were universally used to give a piquant flavouring when pickled. Gerard gave one recipe for pickling them, Elinor Fettiplace another, and the Countess of Kent in 1653 yet another. Much later still, Dr Lobb took it for granted that the poor pickled them.[208]

The other much used home-grown flavouring was mustard. John Evelyn in *Acetaria* (1699) called it an approved anti-scorbutic, and Tewkesbury was the celebrated place where it grew wild. But Wakefield was another place, mentioned by Cogan, and, in fact, it was a common wild plant all over the kingdom; this meant that, when sold, it cost only twopence three-farthings a pound compared with four shillings a pound for pepper. It even became an export in the early seventeenth century from the Lincolnshire port of Boston, which suggests that by then it was already being grown as a cultivated crop; it was certainly grown in the fens in the eighteenth century, and the idea of exporting it could easily have come to an immigrant Dutchman seeing it growing readily on the newly drained land in East Anglia.[209]

Mustard sauce was regarded as essential with venison and features as the prime sauce in Robert May's recipes for meat and fish in 1660. He also gave a recipe for making mustard loaves so that you could carry a small cake of it in your pocket, and have it ready for use at any time. To make it, you added honey, cinnamon, and vinegar to the mustard and dried it in the sun or in the oven. Mustard is said to have been used before pepper was imported, and since it thrives to this day, it can be said to have one of the longest recorded histories of any flavouring in England.[210]

Home-grown flavourings did not, however, preside over an uncontested field in the early modern period. Certainly, they were free to all in the fields, hedgerows and woods, but this made them commonplace; they had none of the glamour surrounding expensive foreign imports. When spices from the East arrived in England as early as the twelfth century, they served at once to distinguish the food of the rich from that of ordinary folk. At first their exotic flavourings served only kings and nobility, but in the course of the fourteenth and fifteenth centuries they became more generally familiar, at least by name. The modest provincial port of Sandwich in Kent, admittedly lying conveniently on a main trading route from the Mediterranean to the Netherlands, was already landing cargoes that contained cloves, mace, ginger, cinnamon, cumin, aniseed and galingale.[211]

Nevertheless, spices continued to be considered expensive through the sixteenth century, and at some tables they were. A bill of £29 was paid for spices for dinners served in one law term only to the Lords sitting in Star Chamber; and a yet higher charge of £39 17s. 10d. was paid in 1605 for spices for 15 days in Michaelmas term. We may guess that ordinary folk buying in provincial markets were much more prudent, affording an ounce of flavouring only for special occasions, or, like the clown in Shakespeare's *Winter's Tale*, cadging a special favour from a friend, when he expected to be given a touch of ginger. But the high cost of spices remained a talking point: William Cholmeley in 1553 bewailed their rise in price and the fact that 'we seek them so greedily', though he was actually writing when prices were hard hit by monetary inflation, not by merchants' conspiracies. William Harrison noted in 1577 the rising cost of spices, but greedy demand was still conspicuous when Philip Stubbes in *The Anatomie of Abuses* (1583) exclaimed at those who had scarce £40 p.a. to spend but lashed out £10–20 on spices. Two documents emanating from the Office of the Spicery in Queen Elizabeth's household suggest some alarm at the expense of spices in 1582, for they presented a comparison of spice costs between two (unspecified) years. The results, in fact, showed not consistently rising prices but substantial variations; the prices of currants had halved from 6d. to 3d. per pound, raisins of the sun from 4d. to 2½d, and prunes from 4d. to 2d. Mace had fallen from 14s. 6d. to 12s. the pound, and cinnamon from 5s. to 4s. 6d. But cloves had risen substantially from 6s. 5d. a pound to 8s. 8d., and nutmegs from 5s. 6d. to 7s. The accountant finished up with the verdict that the increase of prices in sugar, cloves and nutmegs had amounted to £189, but the total cost of spices was less by £145 because of the 'reasonable prices' of other spices: in all honesty, he might have owned up to the pronounced fall in the cost of some items. Prices may have shown less fluctuation thereafter, for they ceased to be anxiously debated after about 1610. Robert Loder, a gentleman farmer in Berkshire, bought his for cheapness in London, while the Shuttleworths of Lancashire bought theirs in Manchester, once in York, and once at least had pepper from a pedlar; that purchase looked like an act of charity rather than a practical necessity since they paid over the odds for it, at fourpence per ounce instead of the usual threepence. That was in 1601, whereas by 1616–17 others were paying only twopence halfpenny an ounce. By the 1660s yeomen farmers' wives often had their own spice mortars, and people took spices so much for granted by 1736 that Bradley in his book entitled *The Country Housewife* printed a letter from someone urging readers when going into the country for the summer to take a supply of 27 such items with them, starting with nutmegs, mace, cinnamon, cloves, pepper and ginger. Otherwise they would find themselves going a mile or two to buy them.[212]

The trend of spice prices over the long term suggests a considerable fall after about 1600. In the case of pepper this is attributed to the fact that the trading monopoly of the Portuguese was broken by the Dutch and English East India Companies thrusting their way into the trade. But if one were catering for large numbers of people in the sixteenth century, spices could look distinctly expensive: at Lord Leicester's banquet in Oxford in 1570 cloves and mace together cost 9s. 2d. for 11½ ounces. Seven ounces of cinnamon cost 4s. 1d., which was 7d. an ounce, whereas in the Howard of Naworth account book, dated some 40 to 60 years later, cinnamon cost only twopence three farthings an ounce at the cheapest rate (3s. 8d. per lb) or fourpence an ounce at the dearest (5s. 4d. per lb). Prices were falling and more spices arrived in modest provincial ports. Cargoes containing mace, aniseed and cinnamon were landed in Boston, Lincolnshire, in the early seventeenth century, though in small quantities of 25lbs or less, not in hundredweights: one load in 1618 contained 12lbs of mace, 12lbs of cloves, 24lbs of nutmegs and 24lbs of ginger. But by 1633 James Hart, the Northampton physician, calmly accepted all these spices as part of a healthy, medicinally sound diet. John Houghton in his fortnightly broadsheet took spices as his subject in August 1700 and wrote dispiritedly about the Dutch dominating a trade in food and medicinal ingredients that he evidently expected to be readily available. High prices were still the cause of complaint, and, as an economy, Houghton urged the use of Jamaica pepper, cardamoms and grains of paradise in place of cloves. When discussing nutmegs and mace he considered that 'the use of these spices almost everybody knows', and having explained to his readers what the trees looked like and where they grew, he offered his readers a picture of them at one shilling apiece. They were being put on sale by the Keeper of Rarities belonging to the Royal Society at Gresham College. In 1750 Farmer Ellis expected his country housewives in Hertfordshire to put cinnamon, cloves and nutmeg into their currant cakes as a matter of course.[213]

Dissident voices against the use of spices in place of home-grown plants rumbled on gently throughout the early modern period, as one might expect, given the lively work of botanists in identifying home-grown herbs and locating their favoured habitats. The mutterings were not confined to England but sounded all over western Europe. It was voiced by the Frenchman, Symphorien Champier, and by Konrad Heresbach, a resident of Cleves, who lamented the extravagance of importing spices from abroad when everyman had satisfactory 'remedies' growing in his garden. Still, everyone knew that the well-to-do favoured expensive things, so among that class spices remained much more desirable. The traditionalists like James Hart (1633) deplored the zest for 'outlandish' spices, when the countryside was brimming over with 'excellent aromatical simples'; moreover, imported spices often arrived rotten, worm-eaten and lacking in virtue, he said – a lively reminder of the practicalities of daily life in the kitchen.[214]

A more careful reading of references to spices in our documents would almost certainly reveal changes in their ranking over two and a half centuries. Cloves and mace seem often to have been mixed together, also cinnamon with ginger. One change of taste may lie behind the fact that cumin was noticeable in the cargoes arriving in Sandwich in 1302–3, whereas it appeared only once in the London port book of 1567–8, bringing one and a half hundredweight from Antwerp. Alan

Davidson's *Encyclopaedia of Food* claims that cumin lost ground to caraway, and that, after all, was a herb that was grown in England. In our own day we have seen a similar rise and fall of individual spices as cumin, coriander and root ginger have risen in estimation and availability, while cloves have declined, and we rarely use mace.[215]

SALT

Salt was the first, essential flavouring in food, and was discerningly discussed by writers throughout the early modern period. We are sensitive nowadays to the difference between refined, packeted salt and sea salt but do not differentiate much beyond that. Discrimination was far more perceptive in the past, for the salting trough was a prominent item in the domestic quarters of most houses. Any and every family, however modest, might at some time own a sheep or a pig, or catch fish in the river; so meat and fish covered with salt lay regularly in the trough, usually for two bouts of salting, one lasting two to three weeks, and the second six to eight weeks, before it was hung up to dry; and people were very finicky about judging the effects of different kinds of salt on different meats and fish. In Devon and Cornwall they did not think English salt from the brine springs could cure pilchards, and so they relied always on French sea salt. Houghton's enquiries made him realize that housewives noticed many differences between salts, and shopped accordingly.[216]

Depending on the source, salt had different grades of whiteness, different strengths, and suited different needs. Rock salt was whitest and was the kind put on the table. The other kind was sea salt, evaporated in salterns round the coast; and if it was evaporated in France in the Bay of Bourgneuf, it was known as bay salt, and was regularly imported in small cargoes from La Rochelle. Many salt-laden vessels hailed from Suffolk, Essex and Kent; and it is bay salt that features prominently in the London port book for the year 1567–8. But 100 years later the bulk of imported sea salt came not from France but from Spain. Much other salt also came from Newcastle, and that had been evaporated in salterns nearby, using the local coal; the Newcastle port books showed much of it then being exported coastwise.[217]

Yet other salterns lay around the coast. The Lincolnshire coast had them, and some of these are said to have been ruined by the great floods of 1571. But that is too general a statement. Some doubtless were abandoned, but others were newly created in the early seventeenth century when marshland was taken in elsewhere as soon as storms shifted the tides and built up fresh stretches of land for reclamation. No salterns necessarily lasted a long time; rather, local people seized on moments of opportunity. One Lincolnshire document of the early seventeenth century said that the accession of James I caused much salt to be imported from

Scotland, and so people gave up evaporating it on the Lincolnshire coast. That statement appears to be partly confirmed in the Boston port books of 1601–40, for already in 1602 salt was coming almost every month of the year from Kirkcaldy on the Firth of Forth in Fife. But the trade went on only until about 1605. Then salt resumed from Amsterdam and ports in Spain and France, and Scottish salt faded away, until by 1640 it had disappeared. Wherever cattle grazing was a paramount speciality in coastal areas, we can be sure that local people seized the chance to evaporate some sea salt if only for local needs; and on the Hampshire coast this activity was still considerable in 1750, since navy victuallers were persistent and reliable buyers of salt for preserving meat on sea voyages.[218]

The alternative to sea salt, being rock salt from the brine springs of Nantwich, Droitwich and Northwich in Cheshire and Worcestershire, had been exploited all through the Middle Ages. More intense activity is implied in the fifteenth century when pumps were introduced into brine pits, and further advances were made in the sixteenth and seventeenth centuries when iron pans were used for boiling the brine, and coal, rather than wood, became the main fuel. Greater output is indicated by the estimate that 1,500 tons of salt were produced at Droitwich in 1400 and 3,000 tons in the second half of the seventeenth century, when, incidentally, Droitwich was growing in size and elegance. It is a great misfortune that the Salters' Company records were lost in a fire, for they would surely have told an intriguing story of enlarged economic opportunities at this time; many gentry families living in the vicinity of the salters' routes sent their sons as apprentices to the Salters' Company in London. It was a conspicuous centre for new trades in the early seventeenth century, a fact that seems to reflect something of the dynamism at this time in meat-salting and related consumer demands.[219]

Since salt was absolutely indispensable in food, and strong opinions were held on its different qualities, illuminating discussions about it are recorded, some in the *Philosophical Transactions of the Royal Society* after 1660, emphasizing its use for different purposes. Bay salt was coarse and dark, but sweet; because of its impurities it cost in the fourteenth to fifteenth centuries between half and two-thirds the price of white salt. It was thought best for curing meats as it penetrated the flesh better. It was even thought by Thomas Moufet, a physician, after all, with a keen eye for such things, to make the flesh of soldiers, sailors and country labourers firmer than that of 'ordinary citizens and dainty gentlemen', since so much hanged beef, salt bacon and salt fish, he said, featured in their diet. Rock salt was different, more searching than French salt and when used to preserve meat it gave a more fiery taste. One writer to the Royal Society had noticed this when eating powdered (i.e. dried) meat on board a Dutch vessel, which he thought was probably preserved with French salt. He seemed to think that rock salt did not normally reach the west country (he probably meant by this the south-west), but during the Dutch war it did, and people complained that it made their meat too salty. The same author also explained the meaning of grey salt; it was grey because it was swept up from the floors of the brine pits and included dirt from the floor; it was sold at half the rate of white salt, and was bought by poor people to salt their bacon and coarse cheese.[220]

An especially careful writer on salt and a Fellow of the Royal Society was John Collins, going to considerable trouble to get reliable information when he wrote *A Discourse on Salt* in 1682. From the saltworks in Cheshire, clod salt dug out from the bottom of the pans was evidently the strongest and was used for salting bacon and neats' tongues. This way the bacon was redder and the fat ate firm, but it was too strong for salting beef, for it took away much of the sweetness of the meat. The same salt was also the kind that women favoured when making cheese. Sea salt from Portsea in Hampshire, on the other hand, was good for making meat red and for pickling samphire. At the same time, experiments were being tried with salt for other purposes, like preserving globe artichokes, laying them on a mat upside down and covering them with salt. Passing comments like this conjure up a vivid picture of continuous trials and innovations in food that might or might not succeed. Robert May distinguished in his cookbook between salt (i.e. rock salt) and bay salt, and used bay salt to boil lobsters. But we can be sure that every single housewife had her own whims, of which we glimpse only one in Farmer Ellis's wife, who reckoned on pickling pork with one part bay salt and two parts rock salt.[221]

Like spices, salt seems to have been subject to sharp fluctuations in price, largely because of the competition between different European countries and the hazards when war disrupted trade routes. Thus Henry Robinson in 1641 argued for England's salterns to be cherished since home-produced salt was protected from these perils, but no politicians bothered to promote that policy. At a more practical level in the home, salt had to be carefully kept out of the damp, and some houses on the North Yorkshire moors still display the sensible solution that was found in the dales, of building a saltbox into the thickness of the stone wall close to the fire, often with the spice cupboard immediately above it. Both were lit by an opposite window, and were handily at waist height for the cook to reach in quickly for a handful; some good examples of these stone boxes have finished up built into garden walls.[222]

PEPPER

In comparison with salt, writers on food paid little attention in print to the kinds of pepper they used or its quality. Cooks normally used three kinds, white, black and long pepper, and since it all came from abroad, they did not perhaps have the chance to hold too many firm opinions. Nevertheless, one physician, Walter Bayley, did see fit to write a treatise on it, *A Short Discourse of the Three Kinds of*

Pepper in Common Use, published in 1588, and he was a distinguished personage, being Regius Professor of Medicine at Oxford, and a personal physician to Queen Elizabeth. There must be some significance in such a personage discussing pepper, though he did not reveal it to his readers. He simply dealt with erroneous opinions about the two different shrubs supplying white and black pepper and the tree that yielded long pepper; he then concentrated on the diseases for which pepper was relied on for a cure.[223]

Massive quantities of pepper were imported. In 1565 a national total was officially valued at £27,000, the bulk of it coming to London from Antwerp. When the London portbook for 1567–8 is closely examined, it presents an intriguing mystery concerning one of the importers: what was Sir John York doing with 10,000lbs of pepper, brought in for him in 1567–8? He was master of the mint, assay master, and member of the Russia Company. Did pepper have some industrial use, or did he fancy exporting it? It may be that the history of pepper deserves closer investigation. In the kitchen, however, James Hart, the physician, claimed that the most used kind was black pepper; white was thought hotter, and long pepper was hottest of all, but was least used. He protested strongly at the large amounts tipped into pigeon pies, enough to set fire to the stomach, he said; plainly, it was a habit associated with this particular dish, 'a preposterous kind of cookery commonly used', he said. Other writers passed over the whole subject in silence.[224]

VINEGAR

Vinegar was another extremely important ingredient in food with innumerable possible flavours according to the fruits or plants inserted in the liquid. We are only nowadays recovering an interest in the varieties that are possible, having recently seen the wide sale of balsamic vinegar from Italy, and a wider use of chilli peppers and home-grown herbs put into ordinary wine or malt vinegar. Verjuice was the basic liquid, a slightly fermented juice of sour green apples, preferably crab apples, for which, as a modern substitute, Hilary Spurling has recommended lemon juice. In practice, different households followed many different routines when laying in a store. On Lord Howard's estate at Naworth, for example, the basic verjuice was not always made in the kitchen, but was sometimes bought from dealers, including the wine merchant. But in the Rutland household at Belvoir castle (in 1592 and 1602) they followed a strenuous routine in October, getting their verjuice (for the whole year?), by hiring one woman for seven days to pick the crabs at 3d. a day and then getting three men to work for seven days at stamping the crabs at 5d. a day. Farmer Ellis in Hertfordshire deliberately grew crab apple trees on his land for the same purpose, and so, probably, did many other farmers. Then there were many alternative ways of adding a further distinctive flavouring: Moufet suggested cloves or gillyflowers; Gervase Markham favoured rose petals, as did Robert May, who also used elderberries; Farmer Ellis used raisins, gooseberries or apples with pears. In fact almost any well-flavoured herb or fruit served. It was, of course, a laborious business and one can understand why May gave ways of making it more quickly. In a hurry, you hastened fermentation by putting in some sour leaven, and plunging in a hot steel, presumably to start the yeast fermenting. You then stoppered it and left it in the sun. For yet greater quickness, you put wine in a sealed pot and in a double boiler cooked it half an hour till it went sour. May had other methods still, including the use of corrupt wine. He also had an ingenious way of making dried pellets of vinegar, using blackberries dried for their solid matter, to which you added vinegar. You then dropped the pellet in wine when you wanted just a touch of vinegar. This idea of carrying a vinegar pellet around with you was not unusual, for Markham also offered a recipe. It shows how serious was the desire to eat nicely flavoured food in all circumstances, and it colours our interpretation of all the imports of cider vinegar into the Lincolnshire port of Boston in the 1630s, coming from Calais and the Netherlands; one or more connoisseurs of food in the neighbourhood were expected to buy.[225]

OIL

Discrimination in food tastes is scattered like pepper all through the documents of the early modern period, introducing many subtleties into the discussion of food qualities, which we are unable to explain. The trouble taken by the gentry to get salad oil, for example, suggests that it was another item of food that varied greatly in quality, and the gentry were very finicky about it. The Shuttleworths of Lancashire deemed it necessary to send to London for both vinegar and salad oil, and when we see the Howards of Naworth in their accounts distinguishing between frying oil and salad oil, we get another glimpse of different qualities, for both at that date must have come from olives. Rapeseed oil did not come into use until about 1660 and then was most readily available only on the eastern side of England among people living near rape mills. After that it was seized on by the opportunists for pickling cucumbers on a large scale, when they became a great fashion. Oil continued in the early eighteenth century to be a food item that was traded in many dubious qualities, as Richard Bradley explained. He thought it was the reason why many people did not like oil on food; it was so difficult to get good oil in England, he claimed; Mr Crosse, a Genoese merchant in Katherine Street, off the Strand, sold the best.[226]

GARLIC

Prejudices against garlic were another feature of the food scene throughout this period. They were hinted at in recipe books in remarks about including garlic 'if liked' or only rubbing a bowl with garlic and then throwing it away. It was not a common flavouring, and the prejudice against it shines through an entry in the diary of Hartlib in 1653 welcoming the news that one Maining, a scrivener over against the Old Exchange, had a way of removing 'the stink from garlic' so that it was a great dish in his house. He had learned how to do it 'from some that lived in Barbary', and the method was also used in Persia. It is possible that a more refined chronological and cooking history for garlic could be uncovered.[227]

SAUCES

The stoutest prejudices of the period surrounded a more considerable innovation in food flavourings, namely sauces. The word was without sin at the beginning of our period. After all, melted butter was sometimes described as a sauce, and it could be sharpened with vinegar. It was innocent stuff that could be further flavoured with herbs, like wild garlic or sorrel; as those were indigenous plants, no one raised any objections to them. Mustard sauce was another thoroughly acceptable flavouring that used an English plant, and green sauce could use a great mix of sweet herbs (betony, mint and basil being Henry Buttes's suggestion).[228]

But the word 'sauce' became clouded in a fog of prejudices when people showed a liking for other sauces, using unfamiliar ingredients, that were labelled foreign. Henry Buttes, without any signs of prejudice in 1599, claimed that condiments were most exquisitely devised by the Italians, and made the better part of their diet. A year later, in 1598, *Epulario or the Italian Banquet* was translated from the Italian and published, and that proposed many unusual sauces using fruits like cherries, mulberries and barberries; it may well have been this work that triggered the dissemination of news about sauces of a new kind and stirred up the first adverse opinions. A strong dislike for sauces became a convention, and the word itself became a synonym for other changes in cooking style, including the serving of more numerous dishes at the table. We cannot blame Varenne (1653) for suggesting anything especially elaborate by way of a French style with sauces, but we can guess that some cooks, put on their mettle by the news of adventurous French sauces, did devise unusual concoctions. At all events, the topic became highly sensitive and remained so; into the eighteenth century it was still possible in the north to hear references to 'pernicious sauces'.[229]

SUGAR

Sugar is another condiment with a lively history in the early modern period. Honey was the traditional sweetener, but it is surprisingly inconspicuous in English farming records and cookery books. Sometimes it was enjoyed as wild honey: that, at least, is a reasonable interpretation of the entry in Lord Howard of Naworth's account book when 6d. was paid to widow Hetherton in 1619 for 'finding honey'. Some inhabitants of woodland kept hives, like the charcoal burner of Sir William Petre who sold honey to his master; he of all people was most likely to spot the wild bees in the course of his work. But the ownership of hives does not feature among the possessions of the gentry and nobility, so it is likely that humble country folk were the principal beekeepers, supplying some to the market, while keeping their hives mainly for their own use and helping out their neighbours. A gentlewoman like Elinor Fettiplace seemed to use honey freely in drinks and fermentations, but it may not have been plentiful enough to meet all demands. Sugar undoubtedly broadened the scope for enjoying fruits grown in England that were not always particularly sweet.[230]

The arrival of sugar in bulk as an item of trade in the early modern period opened a new era, and writers were soon claiming that sugar had ousted honey. That is likely to have been one of the many views of food that was slanted from London. It then went along with the opinion that sugar was a healthier food than honey. In the north, however, honey remained at home. William Lawson in Yorkshire knew the value of bees among the fruit trees in an orchard and underlined their great profit. A longer chronology in sugar history is soberly illuminated for us by looking first to southern Spain, in Moorish hands until 1492, where Spanish historians tell us that sugar was not a familiar food until about 1475, and became more familiar only in the sixteenth century. That surely is the English story too, which the London port book of 1567–8 implies. It shows few cargoes arriving in London with sugar – about five that year – and carrying modest quantities, of 16½cwt on one occasion, 397cwt on another, and 150lbs of Genoa treacle on another. It does not convey a picture of gluttonous consumption at the beginning of Elizabeth's reign. Holinshed, c. 1577, referred to sugarbread as one of many outlandish confections indulged in by the gentry, suggesting indirectly that only then were sugar confections becoming a conceit of professionals making comfits and sugar loaves.[231]

In the provinces, the Boston port book suggests a more regular and frequent trade from Amsterdam into eastern England from about 1612 onwards, bringing white sugar, then refined sugar in 1616, and muscovado sugar in 1617, but still in small amounts of one to two hundredweight. In 1633 molasses came from Calais, along with some refined sugar (½cwt), and in 1639 refined sugar came from Rotterdam. Sugar refining was making progress in the Netherlands by this time, as it did also in London. So down in Devon, where sugar also arrived by a different route, the Reynell family increased its consumption from 24lbs in 1629 to 40lbs in 1631. It was a standard jibe to attribute the demand to the womenfolk rather then the men.[232]

The general view is that the sugar trade was mounting in northern Europe because the Dutch and English companies were nudging their way into the trade. Thus among the better off everywhere, and particularly in towns, the taste for sugar conjured comfit makers into existence, exploiting a willingness among the well-to-do to pay large sums for such things. Mrs Saul was paid £40 for 'a bankett of sweetmeats' on the Earl of Rutland's account in 1614, making Sir William Petre's expenditure of 26s. 8d. on comfits in Elizabeth's reign look quite modest. But costs went up as comfits became routine, and the account book of Sir William Smyth of Hill Hall, Theydon Mount in Essex, shows him in December 1633 paying a bill of £13 10s to the comfit maker, whereas he might spend only 14s. on salt salmon and four great eels, and 1s. 6d. on a barrel of oysters. This expenditure occurred when Sir Thomas's wife was about to give birth, and it was not the only occasion in families at this time when husbands made an effort to procure a dainty food, no matter what the expense, for their wives.[233]

Comfit makers appeared as an occupational group in the 1570s to 1590s and they were usually aliens. Balthaser Sans, i.e. Sanchez, 50 years old in the 1571 *Return of Aliens*, was one such, having been in England since 1547 and having married an Englishwoman. He became a most successful confectioner, having come from Jerez de la Frontera, and then made a great fortune in London; in his will in 1596 he left £300 to provide an annual income for the French poorhouse, and he also left £640 to build an almshouse in Tottenham. The almshouse accommodated eight almsfolk, either men or women, and Sanchez died on 24 August 1600. The almshouse stood until it was demolished in 1925. John Lewes, an alien listed in 1583, was another confectioner from Spain, who came to England 'for conscience'; Conrade Reynoldes, yet another, had come from Brabant, and was in England in 1555. They were pioneers of a new, and almost certainly lucrative, profession.[234]

The first use of the word 'comfitmaker' is given in the *Oxford English Dictionary* as 1594, citing Hugh Platt. But the word 'comfit' dates from much earlier: in the 1330s it was applied to gingerbread confections, and the verb 'to comfit' simply meant to preserve or pickle something (it could be in vinegar). A comfit became in the sixteenth century a sweetmeat of fruit coated in sugar, and the elaborate making of them is described in detail by Richard Bradley in 1736, when he expected the kernel of the comfit to be a caraway, coriander seed or aniseed, and it was a time-consuming operation.[235]

Norwich admitted its first comfit maker as a freeman, Isaac Grandage, in 1604, having recorded its first sugar maker, Nicholas Reading, in 1573. The inventory of John Benton, dated 1685, shows all the equipment for moulding sugar and making sugar plate. By then sugar sculpture had been carried into another world of emblematic artistry at which we can only wonder. Italy had led the way in all this, Giambologna's atelier supplying in the late sixteenth and early seventeenth centuries sugar sculptures for Medici weddings in Florence that made fantastic spectacles. Some pale imitations are described by Victor Morgan in Norwich on their Guild Day.[236]

One would expect physicians to look less favourably on sugar than the confectioners, and Dr James Hart in 1633 brought some highly relevant professional experience to bear in his pronouncements. He acknowledged the higher esteem in which sugar was held when compared with honey, but the fact remained that, eaten immoderately, it rotted the teeth. He had even watched a worse fate threatening a young clerk living with a lawyer in Paris in 1607: he had got hold of the key to his mistress's cupboard of sweetmeats and feasted on them till he fell so sick, he could scarce stand on his legs. The doctors had great ado in restoring him to health. Hart added a further significant reflection on the method used to whiten sugar. The lees of lime were added to the sugar, and he believed that that was one of the main causes of so many dying of consumption in London, as reported in the Weekly Bills of Mortality. The craze for sugary confections swept on, however. Hart was living in the years when it was the height of fashion to indulge in these luxuries. A spirit of moderation seems to have returned by the end of the seventeenth century, and sugar became another condiment among many, though it greatly assisted the preservation of fruit for food in winter. In that regard, it was highly significant in diversifying winter diets.[237]

For the historian, condiments prove to be a conduit in the early modern period for the expression of many subtle statements and opinions about diet. Although they were the lesser items, they prompted remarks concerning some current assumptions that would otherwise have remained unknown. For example, more than one herb was known, at least to some people, as a defence against scurvy, and was consumed accordingly; the weaker flavours of some garden-cultivated plants was generally recognized, and must check our tendency to assume that the picking of wild plants always meant an inferior meal for the poor when compared with the more refined, cultivated plants eaten by the rich. Food snobbery was a powerful factor shaping the food scene, but it did not necessarily always advantage the rich. In some instances the poor must have enjoyed superior flavours and enjoyed better nourishment than the rich by eating wild foods that they got for free. Good oil, as opposed to bad oil, was the privilege of the rich when it came from Spain and they could afford the price, but we have to look askance when contemplating the increasing use of rapeseed oil. When white sugar was the rich man's choice, thinking he was paying for the best, his family was far worse off than the poor, who, when they could afford it at all, bought brown sugar that had not been whitened with lime. So when surveying the full array of condiments used in the early modern period, whether traditional, modified or newfangled, we cannot settle on a firmly optimistic or pessimistic final verdict about improvements in diet. Innumerable refinements altered food and flavours, but they brought both gains and losses to all classes.

10

Conclusion

Food history is a slippery subject that resists the historian's urge to generalize. All people eat food, but they make their own individual choices. So how often do we read these days about a major change that is alleged to have taken place in contemporary diet, and we smile indulgently, knowing that it has not touched our family?

Food history is probably best likened to tides of the sea regularly washing gently over the shore, and gradually depositing silts here and there that build up a new shoreline, until it rises high enough to constitute a major change on the map; in various ways, the hinterland will then also be affected. At the same time stronger spring tides rise and fall, making a more dramatic impact, and it is those that register most effectively in the record. But it is individuals who regularly keep the gentler changes strongest in memory, having watched their impact on their own intimates and in their own locality.

Using this metaphor to illuminate food history, we know how historians have wielded the sharp tools of their trade to identify the phases that wrought major, long-term changes in food patterns, while individuals, drawing on the experience of one lifetime, recall comparatively small innovations and losses. Selecting for a present-day example food changes in my lifetime, I pick on the avocado and pasta; I did not encounter an avocado until the early 1960s, whereas now they are commonplace. In the 1920s to 1940s I never ate pasta, and so the food habits that were formed in my childhood mean that I do not often use pasta in the kitchen, whereas it is a routine food to a younger generation. They likewise take avocados for granted. Turning to the early modern period, we can guess that among individual choices of memorable new foods some people would probably have named veal, skirret and eryngo, or, late in the period, perhaps apple turnovers and a new way with pastry. Among their losses, they themselves remind us repeatedly of their loss of buttermilk and whey. Such reflections spring from the attempt to reconstruct the changes in food patterns that touched people most nearly in the period 1500 to 1760. The larger changes call for the longer perspective of the historian, and these must be the ones to emphasize most in a conclusion. They have turned out to be rather different from those that were expected.

One would naturally look for the chief changes in food patterns among farmyard meats and cereals, since they are regarded as the staple foods. We do, indeed, notice the considerable impact of meat pickling in place of salting and drying, and the expanding supply of veal; we also underline the production of more wheat for bread. But these improvements were less conspicuous, and in the long term almost certainly less significant than the changes affecting four other food categories, namely, the expanding supply of bird meat; of butter and cheese; of vegetables and herbs; and of fruit, when once sugar added the possibility of using it in jams and jellies, preserving fruit for winter use, and serving fruit regularly as an attractive sweet course at dinner.

For some decades in the second half of the twentieth century, food historians chose to concentrate their research on counting, or guessing at, changes in the food calories that people consumed in the past. In contrast, this study has approached the subject from a different angle, listening to people of the time talking and writing about their food, as well, of course, as reading their recipe books. The resulting picture introduces an increasing variety of foods, springing from other economic and cultural developments that mingled many influences. Among them, we have noted principally: the profound effects of the Civil War on dairying; the role of the Dutch in stimulating the trapping and sale of wild birds for food; the zeal of botanists, pursuing their scientific enquiries, finding and acclimatizing new vegetables and fruits, and spurring the interest in experimental cooking. All the developments named above deserve closer investigation since large generalities pass over the fine points in the story that left an indelible memory on the experience of contemporaries.

In exploring their history here, it has proved helpful to divide the long period of 260 years into shorter phases, and to look separately at different foods, in order to identify more clearly the distinctive experiences of single generations. But in relation to some foods, it was single decades that made a much stronger impact on opinion and some people's practices than half centuries; thus we have highlighted the 1590s for cabbages and roots, the 1620s for fruit, the 1650s for beans, and, at a guess for the present, the 1710s for pickled meat. Otherwise, by wandering over longer periods of time, we miss the drama of the story as contemporaries experienced it. Some historians, for example, are happy to put into one sentence the salting and the pickling of meat as though they went together. But for centuries they did not. In the seventeenth century, the meat-preserving routine involved only salting, for which the salting trough was essential. Pickling was new in the early eighteenth century; one can imagine someone in Kent, where pickling first took hold, being quite startled in, say, 1750, to walk into a house and find a salting trough still in place. By then it had usually been thrown out. In the same way with other foods, we can identify changing perceptions between one half century and another. The 1620s have emerged as a period of dramatic changes in some people's perceptions of fruit, particularly in London and the south-east. Refining viewpoints further, we can imagine, on the basis of domestic greengrocers' bills reaching Knole House in Sevenoaks, how the inmates savoured and discussed eryngo in the 1620s, whereas in Northumberland it may well have been totally unknown. Other evidence presented here suggests that between 1570 and 1670 people perceived cheese, butter and wildfowl in totally fresh terms, and similarly pastry, and apple pies that ate 'exceeding short', between 1670 and 1770.

Another insight has been gained by seeing the great advantages that Londoners enjoyed in the food market compared with everyone else. Other large towns that were also ports, like Southampton, came close to enjoying the same advantages. But we have to be cautious when citing the writings about food that emanated from London before assuming that their descriptions applied over the rest of the kingdom. Nevertheless, we must marvel at how opportunist were food merchants in carrying food by water and land to out-of-the-way places, and we have underlined the need to know the changing social geography of the kingdom, in order to explain how food luxuries infiltrated more effectively the districts where more than just a few gentry lived.

At the same time as we focus on the landmarks in food history, we should be aware of the many conventions that were being established in the background and quietly altering the food scene. Among significant changes were the facilities for trade, inland and from overseas; they took more and more people into the markets and shops to buy food rather than relying on home-grown or locally grown food. Once upon a time, some food had been received as payment in kind, or through neighbourly exchanges or gifts. It is more than likely, as people moved to work in towns, that some of those practices fell away. We know also that while the food merchants expanded choice in some directions, especially by bringing in foods from abroad, in other directions they reduced choice, as in the case of the millers ceasing to sell to villagers small quantities of their favourite bread flour; they preferred instead to deal with wholesalers. Doubtless, purchasers also made changing demands on their food suppliers as they experienced new flavours, or absorbed scraps of medical knowledge about foods that promoted health. That last element going into the pot is hardly explored here, and awaits a better-qualified medical scholar. But it concerns changing food demands that were much influenced by the spread of information through cheap literature; John Houghton's news-sheet and many of his advertisements open a window on that scene. But more could clearly be learned from closer reading of the local newspapers, for by 1760 physicians and others were offering advice on food and recipes in cheap print.

Fads and fashions find a place on this canvas, for contemporaries were sometimes eloquent about them. Usually they explained the fads as fancies for rare and expensive foods that caught the rich and would then trickle down to the middle classes. But basically, all fads and fashions sprang from a desire for fresh flavours, and they could affect all classes. The subject has a regional dimension, which challenges local historians to discover more. The use of candied eryngo in Cornwall in 1600, for example, suggests that its consumption had a different chronology and class history from eryngo in Essex and London. Similarly, we can be sure that many other subtle changes took place in local, and class-biased, menus that diners at any food table would have discussed with far deeper knowledge than we can uncover; some that were known to upper-class cooks are momentarily revealed in the books of three royal chefs between 1700 and 1725, but we seek more examples.

Between 1500, when the body of public knowledge about food was minimal, and 1760, when news-sheets like John Houghton's were reaching people scattered all over the kingdom, gentle tides of information gradually spread more knowledge about current food practices. We are brought up short at one milestone in 1754 when Sarah Jackson issued her cheap, serialized pages of recipes signalling the spread of standard instructions that reached quite ordinary housewives in Chatham as well as London. That trend plainly strengthened thereafter, for Eliza Melroe in his book in 1798 cited recipes taken from the *London Evening Post* of 27 October 1795 and the *Gentleman's Magazine* (undated). Along the way, information had been passing to readers of the middling sort, through a rising number of recipe books published after 1650. The standardization of recipes was beginning, and has been most effectively illustrated recently by David Porter, examining the recipe book of Lady Fanshawe. This was compiled between 1651 and 1678, and was augmented when it was passed to her daughter, until her additions ended about 1708. David Porter named 17 recipes that were virtually word-for-word copies of recipes in John Evelyn's cookery book, others were given by Sir Kenelm Digby, and others by named relations and friends. Thus, we can understand how more and more people learned how to make better pastry without using eggs, and how to make deliciously flavoured apple pies. We can safely assume that many other dishes were improved as the womenfolk read recipes in print for fruit drinks, ragouts, fricassées and fools.[1]

Discussion in the 1650s in the Hartlib circle gave a rare glimpse of animated gossip about food that built up on a still more scientific foundation after 1660, and made good use of cheap news-sheets to reach a wider public. We caught sight of an incipient bean revolution that allowed beans to be upgraded from food for animals and the poor to acceptable food for all. It moved gently forward as the food markets slipped into a higher gear in the second half of the seventeenth century, though it stalled when potatoes took centre stage, and surged ahead after 1760. That was an opportunity for putting more cheap protein into diet that was sadly lost. But all change represents both gains and losses. The fading interest in beans is the downside of the food story, in which historians usually concentrate more optimistically on the coming of the potato. Certainly, by then more quantity and variety were being offered all round, and what is also significant is how many food items were sold at a wider range of prices, bringing some within the purses of more poor people. At the other end of the social scale, we light up colourful evidence of food refinements that persuaded people to acquire fancy dishes and drinking vessels in which to serve their fruit, and tea, and chocolate.

Finally, surveying the broad history of food over this long period, we read afresh the judgement of Eliza Melroe, the naval man with a medical background, who showed by far the most astute observation of anyone into local customs when writing his book on food in 1798. 'If we look twenty to thirty years back, the system of living has almost undergone a total change,' he wrote. Having explored not 20 but more than 200 years, we are surely entitled to be more forceful still.

Notes

Notes to Introduction

1 Ellis (2000), pp. 85–7; Moufet (1655), p. 88; Furnivall (1868), p. xci; Standish (1613), p. 34; Cobbett (at great length on this subject), (1926), pp. 14ff., especially p. 21.

2 Melroe (1798), p. 43. For a similar account of continual changes in Italian diet, see Freedman (2003), p. 36 (a book review).

3 Baker (1983); Courteney (1997), p. 35.

4 Hasted (1797), III, p. 277.

5 J. S. (1684); Padulosi (2000), pp. 43, 45.

6 Lister (1995), p. 16.

7 Cohen (1997), p. 15; Hawkes (2000b); Ananthaswamy (2004), pp. 12–13; Powicke (1926), p. 22.

8 A good example of a gentleman's wearying pattern of travel is contained in Sir Arthur Throckmorton's diary, deposited in Canterbury Cathedral Archives.

9 See Melroe (offering an appreciative account of tasty puddings and dumplings associated especially with the diets of Essex, Suffolk, and Norfolk), op. cit., pp. 31–33; Thirsk (1992), p. 19.

10 Stewart (1999), p. 67.

11 Best (1986), p. 8. Some notion of the convenience or otherwise of shops and markets in London is conjured up in M. J. Power's reading of Stow's *Survey of London* (Power (2000), pp. 38–43).

12 Ellis, op. cit., *passim*; Melroe, op. cit., pp. 75–89. On recipes in cheap print after 1700, see especially Sarah Jackson, *The Director* (1754), which seems to have come out originally in weekly parts.

13 Moufet (1655), p. 218. Some significant changes were reported in 2004 in the mineral content of our fruit and vegetables over the last 60 years that add another dimension to our consideration of changing flavours (Leake (2004), p. 6).

14 Wood, Watkins and Wood (1983), p. 39.

15 May (1994), p. 152; Defoe (1928), I, p. 59.

16 Orlebar (1879), p. 53.

17 Ellis, op. cit., p. 53. See also Hartley (1975), p. vi.

18 Gibb (1994), pp. 975–7; Wilson, F. M. (1967), p. 40.

19 For example, see Read and Manjón (1978), pp. 80, 166; Cass (1957), pp. 267–8; Gomiscek, 1989, p. 122–3.

Notes to Chapter 1: Setting the Scene before 1500

1   Eisenstein (1983), pp. 13–17.
2   Dyer (1983), pp. 206–9; (1989), pp. 56, 59.
3   Dyer (1983), pp. 193, 207–9; (1989), p. 61; Currie (1991), pp. 97–107.
4   Dyer (1983), pp. 213–4; Witney (2000), pp. 213, 218, 168. The barley bread on the arch-bishop's estates was the food given for agricultural tasks and to lowly cotlanders. When the archbishop was staying, jobs on the manor for his personal comfort earned wheaten bread.
5   Dyer (1989), pp. 63–4, 158; (1988), p. 25; (1983), p. 195.
6   Dyer (1983), pp. 63–4; Labarge (1961), pp. 493, 496, 500; Hanham (1985), p. 313.
7   Thirsk (1997), p. 9.
8   Dyer, op. cit., p. 195.
9   Harrison (1994), p. 264; Harvey (1981), p. 115. In studying my own village of Hadlow, Kent, in 1460, I am tantalized by a field name, 'herberys', for land that had already been turned over to meadow, whereas its name hints at a former existence as a well-tended garden of herbs and flowers. Since this land lay near Tonbridge Castle, which was the resort of many kings and courtiers in the thirteenth and fourteenth centuries, it is not preposterous to envisage some high-quality gardening that faded away, supporting Harrison's chronology. (Thirsk *et al.* (2006).)
10 Saffron Walden Museum, n.d., p. 2; Holmes (1987), pp. 22–3; *AHEW*, III (1991), p. 260; BL, Add. MS. 5880, f. 186b.
11 Harvey, op. cit., pp. 118, 120, 125, 160; (1972), p. 145.
12 Harvey (1981), pp. 74ff.
13 Ibid., pp. 78, 4, 86–7.
14 Ibid., pp. 86, 121.
15 Dyer (1987), pp. 156–8; Harvey, op. cit., pp. 121, 72–3.
16 Labarge, op. cit., pp. 493–4; Harvey, op. cit., pp. 127, 79–80.
17 Harvey, op. cit., pp. 94–5, 121, 170, 122.
18 De Coca Castañer (2001), pp. 161, 165, 167.
19 I am extremely grateful to Dr Bridgett Jones for the sight of her transcripts of Sandwich customs accounts and receipts. The following remarks are based on NA, SC 6/894/25; 895/14 and 15; 896/1–15; E122/124/5, 12.
20 I thank Prof. Christopher Dyer for drawing my attention to the similar Devon and Cornwall records. See Kowaleski (1993), pp. 25–6; (2001), p. 38.

Notes to Chapter 2: The Food Scene Captured in Print, 1500–50

1   Oxford (1913), pp. 1, 3; the book on carving was reprinted in EETS, 1868.
2   Westbury (1963), pp. xii–xiii; Mennell (1985), p. 69; Elyot (1539); Mary Ella Milham (1998).
3   *DNB* and *ODNB*, under Sir Thomas Elyot.
4   Elyot (1541) (the edition used here, though an earlier one is dated 1539), pp. 8r, 10–11v, 15, 16r, 23, 27v, 28v, 32v, 34r, 41–2.

5   Nairn and Pevsner (1965), p. 479; Furnivall (1870), pp. 40–4, 47, 36–7, 20–2, 14–15, 56.

6   Furnivall, op. cit., pp. 96, 228, 244, 242, 300, 277.

7   Ibid., pp. 89, 286–7, 127, 252–3, 206, 75.

8   Ibid., pp. 206, 137, 185.

9   Ibid., p. 123.

10 Ibid., pp. 150–1, 149, 198, 202, 147, 163, 190, 270.

11 Ibid., pp. 147, 149, 157, 266.

12 Ibid., p. 126.

13 Ibid., pp. 160, 167, 176, 189, 195, 196, 200, 282–3, 267, 283, 285.

14 Ibid., pp. 278–82.

15 Ibid., pp. 255, 257, 148, 149, 156, 255, 257, 126, 256.

16 Ibid., pp. 251, 248, 250, 252.

17 Hales (1543), n.p.; Thirsk (1997), pp. 31–2; Nicolas (1827), pp. 8, 10, 11, 218, 220, 224, 232 and *passim*.

18 Hales, op. cit., n.p.; Lamond (1954), p. xl.

19 Hales, op. cit., n.p.

20 Nicolas, op. cit., pp. 7, xviii, 12, 279, 271, 276, xv, 1, 3, 8.

21 *Encyclopaedia Britannica*, 11th edn (1910–11), XXI, p. 361; Furnivall, op. cit., p. 269; L.& P. Hen. VIII, vol. 6, 549 (no. 1381); Nicolas, op. cit., p. 275, 280; HMC Rutland, IV, 1905, p. 460; personal communication from Prof. Hassell Smith.

22 Nicolas, op. cit., pp. 14, 258, 4, 5, 6, 248, 337, 12.

23 Ibid., pp. 2, 3, 300, 15, 4, 12, 346, 10.

24 Ibid., pp. 45, 141, 147, 10, 15, xxxii, 309, 264.

25 Ibid., pp. 16, 252, 258, 265, 256, 264, 274.

26 Ibid., pp. 79, 12, 16, 277, 3, 49; *AHEW*, I, 231.

27 HMC Rutland, IV, 1905, pp. 262, 268, 281, 312, 292, 302, 312, 291, 324.

28 Ibid., pp. 290, 296, 312.

29 Furnivall, op. cit., pp. 274–5, 270, 154; BL, Royal MS. 7, CXVI, ff. 100ff.; Carew (1723), 31r.

30 Harvey (1981), p. 164.

31 Mead (1967), p. 100; Harvey, op. cit., p. 177; Furnivall, op. cit., p. 187.

32 Mead, op. cit., p. 117.

33 Vives (1959), pp. 32–5, 80–3; Watson (1970), pp. 26–33, 117–22. The banquet dialogue, on pp. 88–96 in Vives (in Spanish) and on pp. 132–49 in Watson (in English), contains an illuminating discussion on bread.

Notes to Chapter 3: The Widening World of Food, 1550–1600

1   Emden (1948), p. 25; Harington (1607), f. B2v.

2   Buttes (1599), f. 38r; Thirsk (1997), p. 54; Vaughan (1617), p. 92; Parkinson (1656), p. 468; Moufet (1746), p. 190.

3   Webster (1979), pp. 301–3, 327; (1982), pp. 4–7 and *passim*.

4   Hester (1575), *passim*; (1582), *passim*; Thirsk (1985), pp. 265–6; Platt (1594 and 1948), *passim*.

5 Byrne (1949), p. 67.

6 Moufet (1655), pp. 238, 184, 160; Thick (1992), *passim*.

7 Appleby (1979), p. 100; HMC Rutland, IV, 1905, pp. 373, 387, 391, 360; Lancs. RO, Shuttleworth MSS.

8 Dietz (1972), nos. 291, 45, 46, 710, 154, 463, 277, 760, 5, 261, 110, 207, 78, 233, 244, 291 and *passim*.

9 Furnivall (1870), p. 273; Moufet, op. cit., pp. 58, 217; Grieve (1984), p. 144. The use of olive oil in food, especially in salads, is a puzzle. No discussion of the use of oils in cooking appears amid the medicinal advice. Its use in food seems to have been uncommon and perhaps eccentric at this time, though it was sometimes used in stews. When mentioned at all in household accounts, it was likely to be a special purchase or gift of what was called 'salad oil'. See Harland, I (1856), pp. 59, 177. Cardinal Wolsey received a barrel of salad oil as a gift from the Comptroller of (the port of?) Poole in June 1529 (L&P Hen. VIII, IV, no. 2546). A singular reference to salad oil in Henry VIII's Privy Purse Expenses, 1529–32, seems to prepare us for an appreciation of olive oil in salads; after all, Henry was still married to Catherine of Aragon. But the context obliges us to interpret it differently. On 20 December 1529 a boat was hired to fetch a pottle of salad oil for the king; the boat hire cost 10d., and the salad oil 2s. 4d. But at the same time a bottle and rushes were bought to burn with the oil, 3d. Was it simply required, on a whim, to give off a pleasing smell? Before this, olive oil had usually been mentioned in connection with the processing of cloth. Some 30 years later, in the 1560s, early experiments began in growing rapeseed for oil, but its purpose was again industrial, for use in the cloth industry (Nicolas (1827), p. 12).

10 Twyne (1583), *passim*; BL catalogue, under Twyne; Webster (1979), pp. 306, 310, 320–1.

11 BL catalogue, under Platina; Westbury (1963), pp. xiii–xiv.

12 Alexis of Piemount (1558); Gratarolus (1574); Newton (1580), 4–5v, 14v, 28v, 32v; Anon, *Epulario* (1598), f. E1, Dr; Thick (1992), p. 44; Stobart (1972), Introduction, esp. p. 19.

13 Hester (1579), *passim*; Gratarolus (1564), *passim*.

14 Partridge (1584); Oxford (1913), pp. 4–5.

15 Slack (1992), pp. 2–3; Palliser (1974), 57–62; Appleby (1979), p. 114 (though the Cambridge population data are weighted towards southern England); Thick (1989), *passim*; Platt (1596); Gardiner (1892 (1599)), pp. 241–2.

16 Vaughan (1617), pp. 111–12.

17 Harrison, ed. Edelen (1994), *passim*.

18 Ibid., pp. 133–9.

19 Ibid., p. 126.

20 Langton (1550), *passim*; Moufet, op. cit., p. 44.

21 Harrison, op. cit., pp. 128, 131, 144.

22 Ibid., pp. 140, 123–4.

23 Ibid., p. 126.

24 Ibid., pp. 126, 251.

25 Simon (1959), pp. 58, 63, 70; HMC Rutland, IV, 1905, 436, 428.

26 Tawney and Power (1924), I, p. 299.

27 Dowe (1588), *passim*. I wish to thank Dr Jane Whittle warmly for drawing my attention to this dairy book on the website of the Henry E. Huntington library. It was originally

published as an annexe to *The Householders Philosophie ... first written in Italian by ... Torquato Tasso and now translated by T. K.* I had long searched for it in vain. The British Library copy does not contain the dairy book, as it had doubtless been taken out and 'read to pieces'.

28 Dowe, op. cit., *passim*. For another sign of contemporary interest in dairying in the Hampshire basin and on the chalk downlands, see R. W. Chell, *Agriculture and Rural Society in Hampshire, c.* 1600, unpublished MPhil thesis, Leicester University (1975), Table 5, Fig. 3, pp. 73–4; also Thirsk, *AHEW*, IV (1967), pp. 67, 69.

29 Denney (1960), pp. 38–9; Dowe, op. cit., 1588, f.C1v; *AHEW*, V, i (1994), p. 318 (map); Hants. probate invs. misc.

30 Harrison, op. cit., p. 264.

31 Ibid., p. 265.

32 Buttes (1599), ff. 11r, E3v, E2v, E5r; Moufet, op. cit., p. 186.

33 Webster (1979), p. 326; Hester (1575), *passim*. I warmly thank Dr Marguerite Dupree for obtaining for me a copy of this work, which is in Glasgow University Library, Special Collections, Ferguson, Af-f54. On pickled cucumbers, see Chapter 6.

34 Harland, I (1856), p. 61: HMC Rutland, IV, 1905, 303, 319; Partridge (1600), ff. D1r–v.

35 Gutch (1781), pp. 4–11.

36 Harrison, op. cit., pp. 115, 116.

37 Ibid., p. 260.

38 Raines (1853), pp. 12, 20, 38; Harland, op. cit., pp. 25, 26, 52, 33, 37, 141, 145.

39 Simon (1959), p. 3; HMC Rutland, IV, 1904, 390, 429.

40 Harland, op. cit., pp. 25, 26, 27, 44, 63, 64 and *passim*; Raines, op. cit., pp. 38, 48, 56; Carrington (1894), pp. 65, 77. I thank Prof. David Hey for drawing my attention to this archive. For buttermilk and a soup of cold milk of Lancashire, see Cogan (1584), pp. 158, 201.

41 Harland, op. cit., pp. 57, 64, 51, 72.

42 Ibid., pp. 48, 60, 12, 20, 38, 41, 42. Hemp cloth was the usual material for wrapping meat for carriage. (See Harland, op. cit., p. 20.) Eighteen yards were bought for the Earl of Rutland 'going to camp' (HMC Rutland, IV, 1904, 360). Woodcocks were relished in all countryside having woodland patches, bracken and bramble (see the Vernons at Haddon Hall, Derbyshire, and in Carrington, op. cit., pp. 62, 74, 82–4); they were eaten whole with the entrails and were said to have an exquisite taste, much superior to partridge. Shakespeare was familiar with catching them in a spring trap rather than a net (see Harland, IV (1858), pp. 115–16).

43 HMC Rutland IV, 1904, 392; Harland, III (1858), pp. 521–2; I (1856), pp. 25, 44, 10, 7, 64, 105; IV (1858), pp. 990–1. Moufet reckoned the best places for catching smelt were Kew, Brentford and West Chester (1655, pp. 187–8).

44 Raines, op. cit., p. 2; Harland, I (1856), pp. 54, 76; HMC Rutland IV, 1904, 440.

45 Harland, op. cit., pp. 29, 64; Raines, op. cit., p. x. In contrast, at Haddon Hall, Derbyshire, the Vernons bought their ale from alewives, one at Bakewell and one running the local inn (Carrington, op. cit., pp. 72–3).

46 Harland, op. cit., pp. 53, 61.

47 Ibid., pp. 21, 53, 72, 177.

48 Ibid., pp. 59, 70, 89, 109, 113.

49   Ibid., pp. 46, 47, 48, 54, 78, 44, 50.
50   Ibid., pp. 62, 67, 103, 115, 82, 50, 64, 108; Harland, III (1858), p. 564.
51   Warde (1558), *Epistle to Lord Russell, Earl of Bedford.*
52   Ibid., ff. 9r, 1v–2v, 62v–66r.
53   Anon. (1585), *passim.*
54   Anon. (1588), *passim.*
55   Ibid.; BBC *Food Programme*, Radio 4, 15 February 2004.
56   Partridge (1584), ff. Aivff, Avi, D1r, G2r, and *passim.*
57   Peachey (1992 (1594)), *passim.* The prices of spices varied somewhat, as one might expect,
      given their different transport costs and the middlemen involved. These prices are taken
      from Gutch (1781) (1570), and Lancs. RO, Shuttleworth household accounts, 1609–10 and
      1617.
58   Peachey, op. cit., p. 6 and *passim.*
59   Ibid., p. 4.
60   Ibid., pp. 22, 25, 28–31, 33.
61   Ibid., pp. 38, 55–6, 61.
62   Dawson (1996) (1597), pp. 41, 69.
63   Ibid., pp. 14, 35, 32, 39–41, 69, 53, 27, 24, and *passim*; Vives (1959), p. 37.
64   Dawson, op. cit., pp. 62, 75, 65, 34.
65   Ibid., pp. 49, 35; Tawney and Power (1924), III, p. 52.
66   Dawson, op. cit., p. 78.
67   Ibid., pp. 70, 71, 127, 135ff.

Notes to Chapter 4: Science and the Search for Food, 1600–40

1   Thirsk (1978), p. 88; Hoskins (1964), pp. 37, 38; *AHEW*, IV, 621.
2   Larkin and Hughes (1973), pp. 161, 163, 189, 200–1, 237–8, 251; Hoskins, op. cit., p. 46.
      For anxiety about cereal supplies and food prices in April and September 1608 around
      Portsmouth and Southampton, see NA, SP 14/32/12; CSPD 1603–10, 458; *AHEW*, IV, 233;
      ODNB, under Arthur Standish; Standish (1611), *passim.*
3   Larkin and Hughes, op. cit., pp. 285–6; Hoskins, op. cit., p. 46.
4   CSPD 1619–23, 91, 124, 129, 130, 140, 413, 405, 397, 460, 498, 288 (the original texts
      contain considerably more detail: see NA SP14/ 112/ 91; 113/17, 21, 26, 90; 122/118; 131/78,
      30; 130/107; 138/74); Larkin and Hughes, op. cit., pp. 521 fn. 1, 522; Appleby (1978), pp. 95,
      121–7, 147, 151–5.
5   CSPD, 1625–6, 107, 132; *AHEW*, IV, 1967, 633. The index of grain prices shows them at a very
      high level from 1621 to 1625, surging again in 1628 and 1629, and reaching an exceptional
      level in 1630. The index of grain prices, at 666 in 1621, reached 1064 in 1630. NA SP 16/177/52;
      CSPD 1629–31, 356, 389, 393–4, 445, 557, 550; *AHEW*, IV, 1967, 850; Hart (1633), pp. 23,
      29, 84, though Palliser on Staffordshire does not notice any crisis in 1630 (1974, p. 64).
6   Appleby, op. cit., p. 155; CSPD 1619–23, 397, 490, 495; CSPD 1629–31, 546–7, 550; CSPD
      1611–18, 488.
7   NA SP16/182/38; CSPD 1637–8, 433 (or more fully in NA SP16/390/66).

8   CSPD 1619–23, 455 (or more fully in NA SP14/133/52).

9   NA SP 16/175/81.

10 CSPD 1619–23, 470, 544; CSPD, 1629–31, 420.

11 *AHEW*, IV (1967), 821; CSPD 1625–49, Addenda, 583 (the price index of all grains was 1031 in 1637, compared with 752 in the year before and 762 in the year after); CSPD, 1640, 97; Macfarlane (1976), p. 185.

12 Standish (1612), 39; CSPD 1637–8, *passim*; Slack (1992), 15.

13 Vaughan (1600), *passim*; (1617), Chapter 1 and pp. 111–12.

14 Markham (1621), *passim*.

15 Vaughan (1630), pp. 4, 8, 9, 10. (It is not absolutely certain that Vaughan went to Newfoundland. The ODNB writer on Vaughan thinks not. Also it is not certain that he met Lessius and Cornaro personally; they may have corresponded.) Compare Hart (1633), p. 34, who believed that more people perished in his day through intemperance, meaning excessive eating and drinking, than by the sword. This statement exactly repeats that of Robert Burton in *The Anatomy of Melancholy*, 1926 (1621), p. 258.

16 Vaughan referred approvingly to Queen Elizabeth's moderate eating habits (1630, pp. 43–4). Vaughan's father and grandfather had both died at about 56 years of age, that being considered then to be a thoroughly reasonable age (Ibid., Epistle Dedicatory). On Ferrar, see *ODNB*. James Hart had read Lessius and Cornaro, for he criticized their unduly meagre food ration (1633, p. 35). For present-day theories on the same lines, see a food regime called Calorie Restriction (CR), started in 1935 in the US, nowadays commanding followers who expect to live for 130 years.

17 Folkingham (1623), pp. 11–12, 18, 43; (1628), Dedicatory Epistle. The interest in improving water at this time went along with a concern for the quality of water for domestic use. See also Capp (1994), pp. 110–12 on John Taylor. Folkingham wrote yet another work (1622) on shorthand writing.

18 An odd interpolation in Vaughan's work of 1630, *The Newlanders Cure* (pp. 48–50), told the gentry to stop engrossing land so greedily, live on a smaller income, and distribute the surplus to the poor. They would be more contented than when preoccupied with 'matters of worldly profit', and their stomachs would shrink.

19 Vaughan (1617), p. 4; Hart (1633), p. 142.

20 Riley (1989), pp. 18–20.

21 Ibid., *passim*; Newton (1580), f. 74v.

22 Parkinson (1629), Epistle to the Reader, and *passim*; (1640), *passim*.

23 *ODNB*, under John Parkinson.

24 Parkinson (1629), pp. 470, 500.

25 Ibid., pp. 494, 484, 491; Parkinson (1640), II, 1068–9, 1064. Monks or bastard rhubarb was also called garden patience (Grieve (1984), p. 680).

26 Parkinson (1629), pp. 490, 470, 504; Hearn (2005), *passim*; *ODNB*, under Sir Nathaniel Bacon; NA, SP16/14/34; Martínez Llopis (1989), 246–8; Thirsk (1997), pp. 200–2; Antrobus (1997), *passim*; Spencer (1993), *passim*.

27 Partridge (1584), f. Aii; Hart, op. cit., p. 45; Parkinson, op. cit., pp. 518–20; Thirsk, op. cit., pp. 31–2.

28 Parkinson, op. cit., pp. 470–1, 525, 466, 490.

29   Ibid., pp. 473, 465, 524–5.

30   Ibid., pp. 494, 495, 498, 516–8, 496, 491, 477, 513.

31   Ibid., pp. 502, 470, 508, 526, 466, 510.

32   Ibid., pp. 463–9, 486, 498, 508 and *passim*.

33   Ibid., pp. 553, 554; Landsberg (1995), p. 47 (showing a plan of Wilton, Wilts., *c*. 1565). Robert Loder, a gentleman farmer in Harwell, Berkshire, had a plentiful crop of apples, pears, cherries and walnuts from his orchard, but makes no reference to grapes, 1606–20 (Fussell (1936), *passim*).

34   Parkinson, op. cit., pp. 567–75; on the cornelian cherry, see *Reader's Digest* (1981), p. 142. This is possibly the fruit described as cherries on the tables of rich men in the later Middle Ages.

35   Parkinson, op. cit., pp. 575–9.

36   Ibid., pp. 579–80.

37   Ibid., pp. 580–83.

38   Ibid., pp. 586–9.

39   Ibid., pp. 590–94.

40   Ibid., pp. 589–90.

41   Ibid., pp. 557–61; Grieve (1985), pp. 82–4.

42   Parkinson, op. cit., pp. 562, 594ff., 583–4; Dietz (1972), pp. 13, 14, 33, 35. These prices are taken from Gutch (1781), and the Shuttleworth MSS., in Lancs. RO, Preston. It is noteworthy that a port book of Boston, Lincs. between 1601 and 1640, shows only one occasion when almonds were delivered there – 24lbs. in 1617, and they came on a boat sailing from Rotterdam (Hinton (1956), 141).

43   *DNB* and *ODNB*, under James Hart; Hart (1633), pp. 87, 12, 2, 9–10, 163, 190.

44   Ibid., pp. 23, 84, 142–4.

45   Ibid., Dedication, pp. 50, 53, 54.

46   Ibid., pp. 71, 42, 43, 44ff., 71ff., 94ff., 109ff.

47   Ibid., pp. 128–37.

48   Ibid., pp. 97, 205, 60, 66.

49   Ibid., pp. 73, 77, 80, 81, 86–7.

50   Ibid., pp. 45, 102, 56.

51   Platt (1602), nos. 15, 11 and *passim*.

52   Murrell (1617a), Dedication and *passim*; (1617b), Dedication; (1621), *passim*.

53   See *DNB* and *ODNB* under Elizabeth Grey, Countess of Kent.

54   Rothschild (1906), pp. 198–9. A forthcoming book on the Spanish marriage may offer insights into new food flavours cultivated by the English thereafter, for much feasting attended Prince Charles's visit to Madrid (Alexander Samson, ed. (2006), *The Spanish Match: Prince Charles's Journey to Madrid, 1623*).

55   Information in correspondence with Prof. Hassell Smith on the Townshend family.

56   Harland, I (1856), p. 171.

57   Ibid., pp. 170, 156, 158, 141, 160, 171, 198, 148, 159, 173.

58   Ibid., pp. 141, 145, 166, 142, 173, 169, 143.

59   Ibid., pp. 176, 177, 181, 179, 180, 182, 188, 203, 207, 198, 200. The full scale of the family's dietary changes is not exactly represented in the printed edition of the Shuttleworth

Accounts that are used here, as the editor ceased to transcribe everything from September 1594.

60   Ibid., pp. 188, 212–13, 223, 226, 229; II, 239, 242, 240, 248.

61   Hartland, I, pp. 191, 197, 213–14; II, pp. 236, 249, 240, 247, 250, 252; I, pp. 201–3, 218, 226, 229.

62   Rothschild (1906), pp. 198–9.

63   Ibid., pp. 199ff.

64   Hollander (1961), 42–5.

65   *DNB* and *ODNB* under Robert Herrick; Martin (1965), pp. 171, 242, 126–7, 200, 229–31, 101–2, 124, 173, 363. See also the poem entitled 'The Country Life, to the honoured Mr Endymion Porter, Groom of the Bed-chamber to His Majesty'. This man was immersed in the dubious moneymaking of the times (ibid., pp. 229–31).

66   Ibid., pp. 101–2.

67   Ibid., pp. 124, 127, 173, 200, 363; Gould (1919), p. 166.

68   Gittings (1960), p. 3 and *passim*; Best (1986), *passim*.

69   Ibid., pp. 74, xvi–xix, lvi–lviii, 85, 92, 110.

70   Ibid., pp. xxv, xxvii.

71   Ibid., pp. xxxvi–xxxvii; Harland, op. cit., p. 134.

72   Best, op. cit., p. xxxix.

73   Ibid., pp. 167, xlvi; Woodward (1984), p. 23; Grey (1653), p. 6.

74   Best, op. cit., p. 60.

75   NA SP16/14/34 (the date 1625 for the cider project is pencilled in in a modern hand); Standish (1612), p. 36; Hart's comment that 'our age has ways of preserving fruit in autumn' suggests some recognition of its novelty (1633, p. 172).

76   Standish, op. cit., p. 36.

77   Woodcroft (1969), pp. 137, 249, 277, 583; Collins (1682), p. 147.

78   Folger MSS, V: b246. On Richard Brome, see Kaufmann (1961), *passim*, and Shaw (1980), *passim*.

Notes to Chapter 5: War and a Renewed Search for Food, 1640–60

1   Sheffield University Library, Hartlib MS, 70/2/7B.

2   CSPD 1650, 109, 572, 600, 604, 561, 603, 567. Dutch cheese was also imported for the army, sometimes as much as 200 tons (CSPD 1649–50, 454; CSPD 1650, 568, 603).

3   Hartlib MSS, 70/2/7B.

4   Hartlib, *Ephemerides* (1648), O–P7; Hartlib MSS, 70/2/7B–8A, 52/65A–66B, 70/2/7A.

5   For a sample of Josselin's comments, see T&C, 48–52, but for a fuller account see his diary: Macfarlane (1976), *passim*.

6   The Hartlib MSS, including Hartlib's diary, *Ephemerides*, are in Sheffield University Library, and the whole archive is available on a CD-ROM.

7   Hartlib MSS, 51/82A, 92A; *Ephemerides* (1649), H–J3, F–G2; Ellis (2000 (1750)), pp. 89–90, 304, 484 (the Hertfordshire cherry was praised in *A General Dictionary of Husbandry* (1779, Bath), because it ripened when others were finished, at the end of July and beginning

of August); Hartlib MSS, 82/2/65B; 28/2/22A; *Ephemerides* (1648), T–S1, S–T8; (1651), Z–Z1.

8   Hartlib, *Ephemerides* (1653), EE–EE5; Hartlib MS. 8/61.

9   Ibid., 29/5/52A; 31/17/11A; 70/1/1A and 5A–B; 57/3/8/1A–8B; Boyle, VI, 85. (Robert Payne described the same or a similar scheme in his *Brief Description of Ireland* (1589), 15–16. Did he get it from Slegger?) For breeding rabbits in hutches, see Hartlib MSS, 67/5/2–4; Hartlib, *Ephemerides* (1651), A–B6.

10   Ibid., 62/24/1A–2B; Speed (1659), p. 101.

11   Hartlib MSS, 51/86B, 90B, 91A; 66/23/1; 64/14/1–3; 51/63–4; 64/14/1–3; *Ephemerides* (1653), FF–FF4. John Beale was living at Stretton Grandison, north-west of Ledbury, Herefordshire, in 1658 and in Yeovil, Somerset in 1662. For his life story, see *ODNB*.

12   Hartlib MSS, C66/22A–B; *Ephemerides* (1652), CC–CC5; MSS, 62/20A; 65/18/1A–2B; 31/14/3B and 2A; Kalm (1892), p. 163; T&C, 1972, 496–500.

13   *DNB* and *ODNB* under William Coles; Henrey (1975), I, pp. 88–90.

14   Harvey (1972), *passim*; Coles (1657), p. 33; Thirsk (1997), p. 60; *AHEW*, V, ii, 1985, 303.

15   Carrichter (1652). The earliest copy of Carrichter in the British Library is dated 1575; it passed through many editions, of which the British Library has six between 1575 and 1597 and six more between 1615 and 1652. A 1739 edition (BL callmark 957 k 34) shows how little was then known of Carrichter's history, beyond the fact that he was a learned man; he wrote other books that have disappeared. His real name was Barth Rinckingen.

16   Hartlib MSS 13/292–3.

17   T&C, 80; *Phil. Trans. of Royal Society*, X, XI, XII, no.116, July 26, 1675, 361; Thirsk (1983), pp. 307–9; Moufet (1655), p. 289. Moufet's (or more likely Bennet's) words are close to those of Ralph Austen in 1653 stressing the value of 'orchard fruits for health and long life' (Austen, 1653a, pp. 24–7).

18   Ruthin (1639); Ruthin (1654), Preface.

19   Grey (1653); *DNB* and *ODNB* under Elizabeth Grey. She is reputed to have married John Selden after her husband's death. He certainly lived with her under the same roof, and she left him £40,000 of her fortune.

20   Ruthin (1654), p. 3; Ruthin (1639), pp. 46–8; Anon. (1653), *Ladies Companion*, 33.

21   Grey, op. cit., p. 71, in contrast with Ruthin (1654), pp. 181, 184; Cooper (1654), pp. 45–6.

22   Hart (1633), p. 97; Grey, op. cit., pp. 36–7, 34; Anon. (1653), pp. 9–10.

23   Cooper, op. cit., p. 128.

24   Woodcroft (1969), pp. 277, 351, 516.

25   Hart, op. cit., pp. 71, 74.

26   Ruthin (1654), p. 207; Grey, op. cit., pp. 74, 93; Anon. (1653), pp. 55, 56–8; Anon. (1658), p. 46.

27   Grey, op. cit., p. 73; Cooper, op. cit., pp. 87–90.

28   Dawson (1996), pp. 79–80; Lancs. RO., Walmsley MSS, DD pt 1/1, ff. 48, 59, 66, 84, 94 (January 1614–December 1615); Hart, op. cit., p. 171.

29   Anon. (1653), pp. 38, 41, 59, 73; Anon. (1658), pp. 74–80; Anon. (1652), 27–8.

30   Spurling (1987), pp. 80, 115, 117–22. Spurling gives bisket recipes for 1604 without yeast, and likens the results to sponge fingers and macaroons.

31 Grey, op. cit., pp. 93–4; Ruthin, op. cit., pp. 199–200; Cooper, op. cit., pp. 67–72. See also Anon. (1653), p. 16.

32 Cooper, op. cit., pp. 3, 30, 33, 45, 76, 98; Anon. (1658), pp. 19–20, 27; Hartlib MS 62/25/1–4. John Evelyn's *Letters* show a note from John Beale in 1664 propounding mushrooms as wholesome and toothsome food (Evelyn, *Letters*, f.45 (3 October 1664)). I thank Dr Mayling Stubbs for this reference.

33 Cooper, op. cit., pp. 21, 22, 36, 35, 109–10, 42, 66–7, 75, 13, 15, 19, 57, 71, 98, 2, 68, 185–6, 16.

34 Varenne (2001), pp. ix–xi and *passim*; Mennell (1985), 71–5, 89.

35 Varenne, op. cit., pp. 9, 184ff, 63, 49, 101, 192ff, 78 and *passim*.

36 For the earlier discussion of Thomas Moufet's work, see Chapter 4.

37 Moufet (1655), pp. 215, 216, 22687.

38 Ibid., pp. 42–4, 79, 82, 264–7.

39 Cromwell (n.d. (1664)), pp. 83, 3, 75.

40 Ibid., pp. 39, 71, 44–7, 36, 37.

41 Ibid., pp. 1, 15, 17–18, 72, 83.

42 Ibid., pp. 64, 57, 58, 61, 79, 53, 54, 52, 80, 38–9; Anon. (1658), p. 43.

43 Cromwell, op. cit., pp. 50, 80–81, 47, 77, 42, 45, 51, 59, 61, 62, 71, 78.

44 Ibid., p. 63.

45 Coles (1657), p. 18 and *passim*.

46 *DNB* and *ODNB*, under William Coles and John French; Coles, op. cit., pp. 119, 31, 113; Coles (1656), pp. 50, 120–21; see also Henrey (1975), I, pp. 88ff.

47 Coles (1657), Chapters CLXXV, CLXV, CLXXXI, XCVII, p. 33 (some page numbering is missing in this work, hence the references to chapters); Grieve (1984), p. 82.

48 Coles, op. cit., pp. 261, 263, Chapter CCLV, pp. 34, 136–9, 172–3, 272, Chapters CCLI, CCLXVII.

49 Ibid., Chapter CCLXXI.

50 BL, Thomason Tract, E572 (16). (This text is also on the CD-ROM of the Hartlib Archive, numbered Hartlib MS, 57/4/1A–12B.)

51 BL, Thomason Tract, E572 (16).

52 Standish (1612), p. 36; *Phil. Trans.*, X, XI, XII, no. 116, 361, 26 July, 1675.

53 Hartlib MS, 13/292–3; Hartlib, *Ephemerides* (1650), K–L4; (1655), 25–25–2.

54 Coles, op. cit., p. 377; Grieve, op. cit., p. 642; Coles (1656), pp. 48–9.

55 Coles (1657), p. 13, Chapter CXXXI, pp. 38–9. Moufet's remarks on rampions suggest that this was another relish that had been lately introduced from Germany, though whether this was Moufet's or Bennet's observation is not clear (Moufet (1655), p. 227).

56 Moufet is also illuminating on the eating of a variety of meats, but the reader is again left with the suspicion that Bennet had altered Moufet's text in line with changing current opinion. See Moufet, op. cit., pp. 262ff. For Higford, see Higford (1658), p. 15.

57 Ellis (2002) (1750), p. 128; Hartlib MSS, 52/97A–102B. On sauces, Moufet is also instructive (op. cit., pp. 253ff). The recipe books of the 1650s show several variants for cheesecake, some including breadcrumbs with flour in the cheese filling, some including rosewater for a luxury fragrance, but all adding currants.

58 Hartlib MSS, 67/23/11–13.

Notes to Chapter 6: Food in a Quickening Commercial World, 1660–1700

1 Houghton, ed. Bradley, II, 3 (3/1/1695/6), referring to an earlier discussion in Houghton, no. 9 (19/10/1682), proving the prohibition of Irish cattle to be good for England.

2 *Phil. Trans.*, X–XII, no. 116 (26 July 1675), 364–5; Royal Society, Domestic MSS, V, 63 (23 June 1664). Dr John Pell (1611–85) also talked to the Royal Society about grain storage methods in Zürich; he had been employed as a diplomat by Cromwell in Switzerland (see *DNB* and *ODNB*).

3 Wood (1984), p. 22; Locke, ed. De Beer, II (1976), pp. 608–9.

4 Locke, op. cit., pp. 52–4, 508, 513, 54; HMC Rutland, IV, 1905, 549, 552, 548; Blencowe (1925), p. 6. Among the continuous themes running on from the Interregnum was spa water, on which John French had written a book in 1652 (*The Yorkshire Spaw*) as well as a book on distillation in 1651 (*The Art of Distillation*). French, moreover, was the uncle of William Coles, noted in Chapter 5 as a leading botanist and expert on herbs.

5 On John Collins, deemed a mathematician, see *DNB* and *ODNB*.

6 Collins (1682), pp. 120, 147ff.

7 Digby (1910), entitled in full *The Closet of Sir Kenelm Digby Knight Opened*; see also *DNB* and *ODNB*; Anon. (1652), p. 26.

8 Digby, op. cit., pp. 121ff., 133, 134, 127, 123, 142, 146.

9 Ibid., p. 138; *London's Charity Enlarged*, BL, Thomason Tract, E 598 (4), 17.

10 Digby, op. cit., pp. 221, 216–18, 221–2. On marchpane, compare Dawson's Elizabethan recipe in Dawson (1996), pp. 117–8. For Houghton's recipes for seed and plum cake, see Houghton, I, no. 91 (27/4/1694), and for caraway seed cake, Stitt (1957), p. 113.

11 Houghton in Bradley (1727–8), I, 409. Tryon also thought it very nourishing, see Tryon (1685), p. 63; Digby, op. cit., p. 228; Rabisha (1661), pp. 206, 97.

12 Digby, op. cit., pp. 157, 156, 215.

13 Ibid., pp. 186, 202, 127.

14 Ibid., pp. 8–83. See also C. Anne Wilson (1973), p. 403, on mead and metheglin and their revived popularity after the Restoration.

15 Houghton in Bradley, IV (1728), 112–13 (9/11/1682); Rabisha, op. cit., p. 19; Digby, op. cit., p. 205; Thick (1998), p. 27.

16 Collins, op. cit., pp. 121–3; Digby, op. cit., pp. 159, 211, 212; Ellis (2000), pp. 98ff.

17 Digby, op. cit., pp. 228–33.

18 Collins, op. cit., pp. 127–8; Evelyn (1699), Appendix; May, 1994, p. 368.

19 For an example of questionnaires in vogue at this time, see Royal Society, Domestic MSS, V, 65; Houghton, I (1692), nos. 40, 57. On the Shetland islands, starting with Faroe, see Houghton, IV 1696, nos. 578–581 (August–September, 1703). People were living on Hirta (ten families), but not on Burra; nothing was said about Soay. On Sir Robert Moray, see *DNB* and *ODNB*.

20 Houghton plainly admired Hartlib as a pioneer in spreading information: Houghton in Bradley, II 459, III 334–5; IV 5; Houghton (1694) I, no. 93 (11/5/1694). See also: IV no. 435 (22/11/1700); Houghton in Bradley, IV 32–3 (8/9/1681); Houghton II 166 (4/10/1695); I 93 (11/5/1694).

21 Houghton in Bradley, IV (1728), 113–14; III, 10 (15/3/1700).

22 Houghton, I, no. 60 (22/9/1693); nos. 32–5 (10/3/1693–31/3/1693), 37 (14/4/1693), 91 (27/4/1694); Houghton in Bradley (1727–8), I, pp. 105ff.

23 Houghton, II, nos. 124 (14/12/1694), 126 (28/12/1694); III, 224 (13/11/1696).

24 Houghton, IV, nos. 444–50 (24/1/1701–7/3/1701), 304 (20/5/1698), 404 (19/4/1700); I, no. 242 (19/3/1697); also IV, no. 422 (23/8/1700).

25 Houghton, IV, no. 429 (11/10/ 1700); CSPD, 1697, 178, 431, 443; Houghton, III, no. 253, (4/6/1697).

26 Houghton, III, no. 209ff. (31/7/1696).

27 T&C, 175–6.

28 Houghton, II, nos. 104 (27/7/1694), 107 (17/8/1694), 111 (14/9/1694), 113 (28/9/1694); Houghton in Bradley, I (1727), 388, 390.

29 Houghton in Bradley, II (1727), 461–2; Houghton, IV, no. 386 (15/12/1699); II, nos. 129 (18/1/ 1695), 156 (26/7/1695), 136 (8/3/1695), 126 (28/12/1694).

30 Houghton, IV, no. 386 (15/12/1699), and in slightly different words, emphasizing how gratefully the Cromwellian soldiers ate them in the early 1650s, in Houghton in Bradley (1727), II, 468.

31 Digby, op. cit., p. 114; Collins, op. cit., pp. 114–5; Royal Society, Domestic MSS, V, 60.

32 Stitt, op. cit., pp. 95, 166; Houghton, IV, no. 386 (15/12/1699); Blencowe, op. cit., p. 24.

33 Rabisha, op. cit., p. 150; Woolley (1664), p. 86.

34 Houghton, IV, no. 382 (17/11, 1699); Beale Correspondence, 23 July 1666, f. 53 (I thank Dr Mayling Stubbs for this reference). The English translation of Thévenot was published in 1687. Its second volume on Persia had a chapter on diet and drink, but the author died before finishing the text on China. I thank Professor Gillian Thompson for finding this book in Canada and giving me the information on its chapter headings.

35 Powicke (1926), p. 22; Houghton in Bradley, I, 238ff.; IV, 137.

36 Temple (1903), pp. 118, 110.

37 Thick, op. cit., p. 39; Evelyn, op. cit., pp. 123, 124.

38 Tryon (1684), Part 1 passim; Tryon (1705), pp. 26ff.; Gordon (1871), passim; Thirsk (1997), pp. 200–1; Thomas (1984), pp. 291–2; Spencer (1993), 206–9. Tryon's recipes have been reprinted by Anne O'Connell, including his 'Bill of Fare of Seventy-Five Noble Dishes', in PPC, 74, 2003, 45–58.

39 Hartlib, Ephemerides (1653), part 3, 28/2/67B; Tillinghast (1678), passim; Stitt (1957), p. 168. This last contains a list of all cookery books in the Bedfordshire Record Office; they are dated 1660, 1682, 1691, c. 1700, 1702, 1711 and later.

40 Rabisha, op. cit., Dedication to the Reader.

41 Stitt, op. cit., p. 168.

42 Ibid., pp. 166–7.

43 A proclamation in January 1664 'to restrain' the eating of flesh in Lent and on fish days attempted to uphold old conventions. (Canney and Knott (1970), no. 1740) Evelyn, op. cit., p. 143.

44 Woolley (1664), pp. 76, 77, 83, 75; Rabisha, op. cit., pp. 80ff., 192, 19; Stitt, op. cit., pp. 166–7, passim; Blencowe, op. cit., p. 19.

45 Rabisha, op. cit., p. 24; Woolley, op. cit., pp. 43, 25, 47–8; Collins, op. cit., pp. 152, 140.

46 Woodcroft, op. cit., pp. 454, 609; Rabisha, op. cit., Book III; Collins, op. cit., pp. 123ff.

47   The first *OED* reference to the word 'pâté' dates from 1706 and meant something quite different, a sort of small pie, made of marchpain (marzipan) and filled with sweetmeats. The first reference to a savoury pâté, i.e. oyster pâté, is dated 1813. (Blencowe, op. cit., pp. 5, 21, 15; Houghton, II, no. 167 (11/10/1695); Stitt, op. cit., p. 156.)

48   Rabisha, op. cit., p. 45; Woolley (1675), p. 145.

49   Evelyn, op. cit., pp. 138–9; Rabisha, op. cit., pp. 247ff; Woolley, op. cit., pages unnumbered.

50   May (1994), pp. 162–3.

51   Ibid., pp. 158ff.; Rabisha, op. cit., pp. 96–7 (for Rabisha's seasonal differences, see the bills of fare and Epistle to the Reader); Woolley, op. cit., p. 21.

52   La Quintinie, *The Compleat Gard'ner*, translated by John Evelyn in 1693, was regarded as the supreme authority.

53   Blencowe, op. cit., pp. 18, 34–5; Avery (1922), p. 12.

54   Blencowe, op. cit., pp. 21, 23.

55   Ibid., p. 35; Stitt, op. cit., pp. 104, 105, 135, 167, 166, 113; HMC Rutland, IV, 1905, 544–7; May, op. cit., p. 238.

56   May, op. cit., Preface to Master Cooks; Anon. (1652), p. 26.

57   May, op. cit., pp. 77–8, 94–5; Langham (1633), p. 125 and *passim*; How (1650), *passim*; Merrett (1666), *passim*.

58   Langham, op. cit., pp. 123–5; Merrett, op. cit., pp. 15, 91, 103.

59   Bryant (1783), pp. 60–1; Merrett, op. cit., p. 115; Grieve (1984), p. 756; Houghton, II, no. 127 (4/1/1695), no. 128 (11/1/1695); Collins, op. cit., pp. 131, 134.

60   May, op. cit., pp. 151, 154–6; Langham, op. cit., p. 123; Grieve, op. cit., p. 570; Merrett, op. cit., p. 41.

61   Lowthorp (1716), II, 837.

62   Langham, op. cit., pp. 227ff., 125, 678; Grieve, op. cit., pp. 408, 771–2; Merrett, op. cit., p. 87; How, op. cit., p. 75.

63   Merrett, op. cit., p. 106; Grieve, op. cit., pp. 671–2; Thirsk, op. cit., p. 71; Colville (1904), *passim*.

64   Merrett, op. cit., pp. 115, 24; Ellis, 2000, pp. 251ff.

65   May, op. cit., pp. 430ff. Note that the editor (p. 19) says that May used many of Varenne's egg recipes; Houghton, II, no. 167 (11/10/1695).

66   May, op. cit., pp. 189, 177ff.

67   Clarke (1677), p. 156. I wish to thank Professor Anne Laurence for this reference.

68   Houghton in Bradley, 1727–8, II, 459; IV, 5; Houghton, IV, nos. 386 (15/12/99), 382 (17/11/1699); Celia Fiennes, cited in Dyer (2000), in Clark, ed. (2000), p. 435.

69   Best, 1986, p. xxxvi; Houghton, IV, no. 529 (11/9/1702), no. 544 (25/12/1702); GLC Record Office, Probate inventory, M1, 1678, 78; Digby op. cit., p. 200; May, op. cit., p. 3; Houghton, no. 440 (27/12/1700); Westmacott (1694), p. 198, cited in Grieve, op. cit., p. 797; Cooper (1654), pp. 110–11.

70   Digby, op. cit., pp. 16–96; Cardigan (1951), pp. 112, 119.

Notes to Chapter 7: On the Edge of the Next Food World, 1700–60

1   Ellis (2000), pp. 85–7; Bradley (1980) (1736), II, pp. 127–8.

2   Pearce (1970), *passim*.

3   Bradley, op. cit., II, p. 105.

4   Wilson, C. Anne (1973), p. 49; Anon. (1779), I, under Beans; Hartlib MS, CD-ROM Index under Beans and Peas, e.g. 62/24/1A; Bradley, op. cit., p. 13.

5   Wilson, op. cit., p. 46; *Tusser Redivivus* (1710), no. VIII, 12; Stern (1976), pp. 70, 74–6.

6   Colville (1904), pp. xxxvii, 28, 54, 2, 5, 12, 52, 55, 68, 17–18, 22, 19, 26, 27, 30.

7   Ibid., p. xxxvii.

8   Cheyne (1724), pp. xiv, 28–9, 32–3; see *DNB* and *ODNB* under George Cheyne for his varied career.

9   Cheyne, op. cit., pp. 38–9, 49, 55; Bradley, op. cit., pp. 98ff.

10   Vaisey (1984), pp. 93–5.

11   *DNB* and *ODNB* under Theophilus Lobb.

12   Lobb's diet for the poor was first printed in his *Medicinal Letters* (1763). For *Primitive Cookery*, see Anon. (1767).

13   Ibid., pp. 5–6 and *passim*; Terry (1665), pp. 358–65.

14   Anon. (1767), pp. 1–6.

15   *The Times, T2,* 19 November 2002, pp. 6–7.

16   Royal Society, Domestic MS V, 60 (20 March 1662).

17   Moffat (2000), pp. 13–15 and *passim*. I warmly thank Dr Moffat for making this article known to me. It is worth noting that Englishmen as well as Scotsmen were reading the classical writers diligently for wisdom on good husbandry. See especially Bradley (1725), p. 172, mentioning bitter vetch, though only to recommend it as a crop on poor ground.

18   Houghton, IV, 580–1 (3/9/1703 and 10/9/1703).

19   Ellis, op. cit., pp. 94–5, 120, 126, 455–6; see also *Tusser Redivivus,* bringing Tusser up to date, and remarking that harvesters at work expected a full diet: *Tusser Redivivus* (1710), no. VIII, 4.

20   Ellis, op. cit., pp. 64, 251, 66–9, 92.

21   Ibid., pp. 251–2, 259–60.

22   Ibid., pp. 71–76.

23   Ibid., pp. 69–70, 81–2.

24   Ibid., pp. 82, 78; see also plum cake, made twice a week for harvest men, and dumplings (Ibid., pp. 128, 284); see also the same statement in *Tusser Redivivus* (1710), no. VIII, 9, and Kalm (1892), p. 326.

25   Ellis, op. cit., p. 97.

26   Ibid., pp. 98–109, 157–69; *Tusser Redivivus* (1710), XII, 5; Lamb (1710), p. 2.

27   Ellis, op. cit., p. 99.

28   *Tusser Redivivus* (1710), XII, 5.

29   Carter (1736), pp. 71ff.; Ellis, op. cit., pp. 165–9.

30   Mortimer (1707), p. 184; Ellis, op. cit., p. 82.

31   Ahmed (2002), pp. 51, 61; Harrison (1994), p. 133; Wilson, op. cit., pp. 202, 245; Ellis, op. cit., p. 263 ; Coles (1657), Chapter CCLXXI.

32 For many references to foodstuffs and the comments of foreigners to Hartlib, see his diary, *Ephemerides*, June–December 1648, 31/22/24Bff.

33 Carrichter (1652), pp. 252–3. I am dependent on the British Library copies of Carrichter for my knowledge of this book. A 1652 edition from Nuremberg in the BL contains the manuscript notes of a reader.

34 Parkinson (1640), II, p. 1058; Hartlib MSS, 28/2/73B; 52/18B; 52/19B; *Kelly's Directory of Herefordshire*, 1934; *DNB* under Jonathan Swift; Hartlib MSS, 52/19B; 55/2/1A–7B; also 64/17/1A–6B; Coles, op. cit., Chapter CCLXXI on peas; Chapters CCXXXVI, CI on beans; Moufet (1655), p. 233.

35 On interest in pulses, see Hartlib MS 52/19B; on John Thomas, see NA, SP 18/221/75; on other pea varieties and the sugar pea, see Worlidge (1970) (1704); *Tusser Redivivus*, X, 10; Ellis, op. cit., pp. 290–3.

36 Worlidge (1675), 37–8; as nitrogen fixers, see *Encyclopaedia Britannica*, 11th edn, vol. VIII under Dietetics, also showing that 22.5% of beans and 24.6% of peas consist of protein; Ellis, op. cit., p. 307; Anon. (1779), under Beans; Hale (1756), p. 389; Kalm (1892), p. 382.

37 The nobility had, of course long since enjoyed fresh peas, see HMC Rutland, IV (1905), 355, showing my lord, the earl of Rutland, on campaign in Scotland being brought buttered peas; Thick (1998), p. 36; Worlidge, op. cit., pp. 37–8, 149, 150. (According to Ellis in *Chiltern and Vale Farming* (1745, p. 219), the blue pea was best for culinary use); Mortimer (1707), pp. 106ff.; Houghton, IV, no. 382 (17/11/1699).

38 Kalm, op. cit., pp. 15–16, 42, 44, 91, 382, 369, 353, 383, 414, 217, 253; Ellis, op. cit., pp. 98, 293, 298.

39 Blundell (1968), p. 231. In Anon. (1779) *The General Dictionary of Husbandry* under Beans, it was taken for granted that the beans would be grown in frames or hotbeds; Thick, op. cit., p. 37; Anon. (1767), 30–1, 50–2.

40 Hale, op. cit., pp. 389–402. (For more on beans, see Philip Miller (1724), under Beans); Kalm, op. cit., p. 91.

41 La Varenne (2001), pp. 27–9, 101–2, 124, 129, 135–7, 190, 214; May (1994), pp. 77–8, 94, 245, 421–2.

42 Smith, Robert (1725), pp. 1, 4, 6, 11, 128–9; Howard (1726), pp. 36–7, 89, 94, 158–9; Carter (1736), pp. 2, 11, 145, 147–8, 151. Peas soup seemed to be a standard first course when a guest at other people's tables (see Stitt, op. cit., pp. 166–7), while a recipe in the same work (p. 142) clearly denoted dried peas. See also Kettilby (1728), p. 9, on separating old peas from new, but this may have been a finicky distinction between fresh, but old, and fresh young peas. The old ones had to be boiled longer, offering us everyday cooks a lesson in the careful cookery of the past. Melroe's economical pease pudding in 1798 used mashed potato to extend it; evidently potatoes were cheaper than peas. More on potatoes follows below. Also, according to Melroe (1798), split peas were more expensive than whole peas (pp. 39, 41).

43 Cleland (1755), pp. 3, 5, 11–14, 17; Ellis, op. cit., pp. 290–3, 298, 307; Thick, op. cit., pp. 36–7; Vaisey (1984), 131–2; Anon. (1767), 30–1, 50–2.

44 Stonhouse's recipes had been first published in the *Northampton Mercury* on 28 November 1757, but reached a much wider public when printed in December of the same year in the

Universal Magazine of Knowledge and Pleasure, XXI, 268–71. On Stonhouse, see also *DNB*, *ODNB*, and *Life of the Rev. Sir James Stonhouse, bart., MD* (1844) (no author named, but W. A. Greenhill wrote the Preface).

45 Bradley (1729), pp. 11–12.

46 Parkinson (1629), Chapter XLIX; Houghton in Bradley, II, 468; Bradley, op. cit., p. 16.

47 *VCH Essex*, II, 474 ff.; CJ, XVII, 4 May 1713.

48 I thank Professor Eric Evans for this tithe information, based on the Dean and Chapter Muniments in the Lichfield Joint RO (it is a rough and ready indicator only of tithes paid); Borthwick Institute, Tithe cause papers, Dean and Chapter of York, 1730, no. 5 for Misterton, Notts.; report of Prussian visitors to English farms, 1765–6, in author's possession; *AHEW*, V(i) (1984), 64, 23, 373–4, 156, 79, 70, 302; Billingsley (1798), 115; Turner (1978), *passim*.

49 Kalm, op. cit., pp. 14, 165; Ellis, op. cit., pp. 293–5.

50 Ibid., pp. 83, 293–6.

51 Smith, op. cit., Preface.

52 Ibid., pp. 8, 3–4; Howard, op. cit., pp. 33–5, 59–60.

53 Kalm, op. cit., pp. 326, 172; Luard (1986), 284, explains ragu as a meat sauce.

54 Kalm, op. cit., p. 373.

55 Smith, op. cit., pp. 117, 212, 120ff.; Howard, op. cit., p. 82.

56 Smith, op. cit., p. 134; Howard, op. cit., pp. 84–5.

57 Smith, op. cit., pp. 137–8, 142, 144.

58 Ibid., pp. 42ff., 134.

59 Ibid., pp. 123ff., 77; Howard, op. cit., pp. 87ff.; Bradley (1980) (1736), I, pp. 117ff.

60 Howard, op. cit., pp. 1–3; Smith, op. cit., pp. 194, 126.

61 Ibid., pp. 181, 204ff.,110, 213; Switzer (1727), vii–ix.

62 Smith, op. cit., pp. 155ff., 215, 216, 162, 190; Thomas Turner's diary underlines the almost ritual status of afternoon tea (Vaisey, op. cit., *passim*).

63 Smith, op. cit., pp. 159, 160, 182; Howard, op. cit., p. 74.

64 Kalm, op. cit., p. 16; Howard (1726), 63–4.

65 Lamb (1710), *passim*.

66 Stitt, op. cit., *passim*.

67 Kettilby, op. cit., *passim*.

68 Stitt, op. cit., *passim*.

69 Ibid., pp. 130ff., 166ff.; Blundell, op. cit., p. 154.

70 Cleland, op. cit., pp. 3, 14, 7, 136, 153 and *passim*.

71 Jackson's book is listed with its full title in Oxford (1913), p. 86.

72 Duhamel du Monceau (1754).

73 Bradley (1729), pp. 160–1; Ellis, op. cit., pp. 84–7. William Ellis published a version of the poem that differed slightly from that published by the author himself in 1724. Welsted had written it in 1704, when he was a boy leaving Westminster School; presumably he was depicting the apple pie cooked there. Welsted regarded it as a trivial piece, but people liked it; it was published by Dr King, who came to be regarded as its author. So Welsted published it in his own collection of poems, to set the record straight, and that is the version printed here. King did not print the last four lines. An edition of *The Works in Verse and Prose of*

Leonard Welsted, esq., was then published by John Nichols in 1787, and 'Apple-Pye' was the first poem in the book. Nichols included information on Welsted's life and family: he became a clerk in ordinary at the Office of Ordnance in the Tower of London. Ellis had another interest in apples, in a particular variety called the parsnip apple, which grew in his neighbourhood. It was sweet enough to require no sugar in cooking, and he offered young trees to customers (Ellis, op. cit., pp. 87–8).

Notes to Chapter 8: *Regional and Social Patterns of Diet*

1. Ernle (1961), p. 83; Best (1986), p. 8; Bamborough (1959), p. 45; Malpica Cuello (2001), pp. 151–68; Thirsk (1992), p. 24.
2. Bradley (1729a), pp. 21–3.
3. Scot (1576), p. 8, gives evidence of very early hops in Kent.
4. Elder (1985), p. 58; Emmison (1964), p. 95.
5. Gray (1995), *passim*. The following account of Cornish diet is based on Cornwall RO, probate inventories, glebe terriers, manorial surveys, and Carew (1723), pp. 19ff., Rowse (1941) and Whetter (1991). On fish, see also a rich account in Fox, 2001.
6. For a rare glimpse of goats, see especially Dyer (2004), *passim*.
7. For the large quantity of oats, see John Dyer's inventory at Probus in June 1667, showing 10 acres wheat, 10 acres barley, 15 acres oats; and a yeoman, Christopher Mynard of Lancells, in 1643 having 6 acres of wheat, 3 acres of barley and 16 acres of oats; oats are also conspicuous in Wyatt (1997); Carew, op. cit., p. 20.
8. Carew, op. cit., p. 19. The fashion for candied eryngo is described in *VCH Essex*, II, 1907, 371–2, and attributed to an apothecary of Colchester finding the plant on the seashore in Essex, and making it renowned for medical use by 1621. His apprentice was of Dutch refugee origins, and so the idea in Essex may have come from the Netherlands. It is, however, likely that eryngo was candied independently in Cornwall and earlier, for Carew was writing about it in 1602. See also Grieve (1984), pp. 407–9, who believed it was used long before this and was known for its anti-scorbutic virtues.
9. Carew, op. cit., p. 19.
10. Ibid., pp. 24–5.
11. Furnivall (1870), pp. 125–6; Ernle, op. cit., p. 126. By 1795, when barley bread in Cornwall had plainly displaced oatbread, it was said that people preferred barley bread to wheat bread. See Davies (1977), p. 32, footnote.
12. Pounds (1984), pp. 133, 138–9.
13. Elder, op. cit., pp. 20–21.
14. Ibid., pp. 27, 32, 30; Ambler and Watkinson (1987), *passim*.
15. Elder, op. cit., pp. 36, 35, 28.
16. Ambler and Watkinson, op. cit., pp. 60, 61.
17. Elder, op. cit., pp. 59, 60.
18. Ibid., pp. 94, 100, 57–8.
19. *AHEW*, V(i), 1984, 60–63, 69; *AHEW*, IV (1967), 85–9; Russell (1986), pp. 122, 138; Thirsk (1984), p. 208.

20 Lancs. RO, Probate Inventories, *passim*, especially that of Thos Ayscough, of Farington in Penwortham, husbandman, 20 June 1615.

21 Wilson, C. Anne (1994), pp. 38–65; Westmorland County Federation of Women's Institutes (1937), *passim*; Linton (1864), p. 34.

22 Wilson, op. cit., p. 61; Bosanquet (1989), pp. 44–5, 31; Greenwell (1860), pp. 268, 219–21.

23 *DNB* and *ODNB* under Moufet; Cheshire Probate Inventories, *passim*.

24 Thirsk (2000), *passim*; Short (1984), *passim*.

25 Hampshire Probate Inventories, *passim*. (One widowed lady, Joan Currington of Minstead, 5 November 1599, had 34 beehives and gave kindly names to her two cows, Patch and Cherry). See also Wordie (1984), *passim*.

26 Malpica Cuello, op. cit., p. 161; Roberts and Parker (1992), pp. 22–3, 30, 34–6, 67, 84–5, 115, 255, 267, 288, 306, 82, 176, 23–8, 56, 169, 343, 408, 206, 252ff., 48ff, 108, 171–3, 84–5, 298, 218, 219, 173, 363, 240, 394.

27 Ibid., pp. 179, 287, 229, 209, 348, 177, 220, 282, 244; NA, SC6/895/5 and 15; HMC Rutland IV, 1905,460; CKS U269/A 526. I wish to thank Dr Todd Gray for letting me use his transcripts of these Countess of Bath's accounts.

28 For Ben Jonson's poem 'To Penshurst', see Hollander (1961), pp. 42–5; John Rylands Univ. Lib., Tatton 347a, 3 March 1656/7.

29 Thirsk (1997), 139; CCA, Throckmorton Diary, vols. II–III; information kindly communicated by Professor Hassell Smith.

30 Havinden (1998–9), p. 70; Blackwood (2001), p. 150; for a Scottish example, see Tay Valley Family History Society (1994), pp. 2, 24, esp. Isabella Findlay, 1864–1950; Anderson (1971), p. 154; Anon. (1653), *The Ladies Companion, passim*.

31 CKS, De Lisle MSS, U1475/A28/2; Cromwell (1664), p. 78; Grey (1653), pp. 5–6.

32 Anon. (1652), p. 26.

33 See, for example, CKS, De Lisle MSS, U1475/A27/5/1, A27/6, A27/5/3, A28/2, A28/5.

34 Harrison (1994), p. 131; Bower (1991), p. 59; Ellis (2000), pp. 120–9.

35 HMC Rutland, IV, 422; Gutch (1781), pp. 10, 7; Bateson (1966), pp. 6–7.

36 CCA, Throckmorton, Diary, II, 131; Ornsby (1878), 95; Moufet (1655), pp. 147–8.

37 Gray, op. cit., pp. 62, 48, and *passim*

38 Anon. (1585), *passim*.

39 Anderson, op. cit., pp. 246–7.

40 Duncombe (1991), p. 992; Linnell (1932), pp. 12–14, 19–20.

41 Moufet, op. cit., pp. 32, 65, 70, 154.

42 Eden (1928), p. 151.

43 Ibid., pp. 309, 317, 204.

44 Ibid., pp. 321, 323, 208–9, 241, 259.

45 Ibid., p. 204; Davies, op. cit., pp. 33–4.

46 Eden, op. cit., pp. 269, 133, 184, 296.

47 Ibid., pp. 103–4, 131, 346, 354, 290, 105, 333, 102.

48 Ibid., pp. 215, 333, 341, 352–3, 172, 335.

49 Ibid., pp. 184, 213, 288, 231, 210, 212, 105.

50 Ibid., pp. 107, 225, 266, 251, 113, 281.

51 Ibid., pp. 295, 301, 106, 225, 212, 199.

52 Ibid., pp. 210, 173, 199.

53 Ibid., pp. 172, 169, 196.

54 Ibid., pp. 260, 273, 306, 317, 129, 195, 198, 199, 162, 323, 301, 315, 176, 320, 196.

55 Ibid., pp. 268, 208, 142, 145, 169, 141, 211, 170, 161–2, 263.

56 Ibid., pp. 224, 196, 199, 201, 205. A Society of Industry had been set up in Rutland in 1785 to help the poor get back on their feet, and domestic industries were introduced to enable the poor to live without relief. A philanthropic spirit was somewhere at work in the county: the poor house was called the House of Protection to present to the old and sick a different image from the norm. Ibid., pp. 288–92, 321, 274–5, 240.

57 Ibid., pp. 102–3, 129, 136, 210, 147, 187, 333.

58 BL, Add. MS. 35128.

59 Eden, op. cit., pp. 168, 332, 210, 164, 182.

60 Ibid., pp. 206, 207, 235, 297, 312, 313.

61 Ibid., pp. 211, 323, 309, 333, 319–20, 107, 157.

62 Ibid., pp. 107, 323, 208, 304.

63 Ibid., p. 106.

64 Ibid., pp. 224, 100–8, 235, 189, 177.

65 Garnier (1895), p. 197, citing Eden, *State of the Poor* (1797), II, ch. 2.

66 Tay Valley Family History Society (1994), pp. 14–16, 65.

67 Westmorland County Federation of WIs (1937), *passim*; the series of county cookbooks by Pippa Gomar, Sarah Gomar and Molly Perham (1988–9). See, for example, Molly Perham (1989a), pp. 5–8; (1989b), pp. 5, 7–9, 14, 59, 79; (1989c), pp. 6, 15.

68 Carew (1811), p. 183; Orlebar (1879), p. 47; Melroe (1798), p. 43.

Notes to Chapter 9: A Closer Look at some Foods

Bread
1 CKS, Drb/Pwr, vol 2, f.231c.

2 Vives (1959 and 1970), *passim*; Ayrton (1980), p. 497.

3 Houghton, I, no. 90 (20/4/1694); Percival (1943), 17.

4 David (1979), pp. 89–93, 299–300, 98.

5 Fitzherbert (1523), pp. 40–1; Markham (1613), Chapter V, p. 17.

6 Best (1986), pp. 209–11; see also Edlin (1805), 59ff; David, op. cit., pp. 90–1; Maurizio (1916), Chapter 8 (this chapter is extremely informative on the variety of bread-raising agents used all over the European Continent); Ellis (2000), 58–9.

7 David, op. cit., pp. 98, 90–1; Maurizio (1932), 513–14; Emmison (1964), p. 45; Ornsby (1878), p. 97; Tryon (1685), 54–5.

8 David, op. cit., pp. 99, 101; Edlin, op. cit., pp. 59–63.

9 Baskerville (1893), Appendix II, 303; Goodacre (1994), pp. 165–7, 60.

10 White (2000), 63–4, 104ff.

The Meat of Farmyard Animals and Rabbits
11 Rye (1865), p. 70.

12 Rothschild (1906), p. 111, citing Earle, *Microcosmography*.

13 Martin (1956), p. 101.

14 Clark, R. (1995–6), pp. 15ff.

15 Moufet (1655), p. 372; Cogan (1584), pp. 113, 115; also Vaughan (1630), p. 3, saying beef made the English courageous, undaunted in perils; *TED*, III, 51; Woodward (1984), p. 23.

16 *AHEW*, V (ii) (1985), pp. 445–6; Haldane (1952), pp. 26–7, 36–7; Bonser (1970), p. 28–9, 128.

17 Wilson, C. A. (1994), pp. 51–2; Newton, T. (1574), pp. 44ff.; Buttes (1599), ff. 1–1v; Hart (1633), p. 71; Byrne (1949), p. 69; Houghton, II, nos. 106, 108, 109, 113 (1694).

18 Moufet, op. cit., pp. 60–1.

19 Vives (1970), p. 37; May (1994), pp. 3, 4, 8, 12, 65, 102, 103, 137, 211; Beeton (1861), p. 295.

20 Hartley, Dorothy (1975), 90–1; Cromwell (1664), p. 47.

21 Hart, op. cit., p. 75; May, op. cit., pp. 97–112; Houghton, II, nos. 127, 128 (4, 11 January 1695).

22 Raines (1853), pp. 37, 40–41, 48 (for veal being eaten in great households only on festive occasions in the 14th century, see Woolgar, 1995, 21); T & C, 182–3.

23 T & C, 175–6; Ellis (2000), pp. 431–8; Beeton, op. cit., pp. 401–36.

24 Vaughan (1600), p. 15; Moufet, op. cit., p. 62; Weatherill (1990), p. 145 and *passim*; Hope (1987), pp. 156–7, 216; Geddes (1994), p. 47.

25 Goodacre (1994), pp. 123ff.; Moorhouse (1956), pp. 14–19.

26 Buttes, op. cit., f. 14v; Hart, op. cit., pp. 71–2.

27 Broad and Hoyle (1997), pp. xii, 50ff.; Markham (1623), pp. 128–9; Blith (1653), p. 165.

28 Lancs. RO., Probate inventories of Furness, Lancs.; Everitt, *AHEW*, IV (1967), p. 416.

29 T&C, 402; Thirsk (1978), p. 91.

30 Sheail (1971), pp. 17–18; Dyer (1989), p. 59; Thirsk (1957), pp. 93, 95, 164; Thirsk (1997), pp. 11, 53–4; Moufet (1655), p. 77; Wilson, C. A. (1973), pp. 108–11.

31 Hammer (1999), p. 59; Cromwell, op. cit., pp. 65–6; May, op. cit., pp. 45, 46, 61, 62, 81; Bradley (1727–8), IV, p. 142.

32 Jackson (1754), pp. 100, 104, and recipes nos. 16, 17, 19.

33 Houghton, II, no.109 (31/8/1694).

34 Hart, op. cit., p. 71; Collins (1682), 5–6; Fetlar Community Enterprises (1987), pp. 7–8.

35 BL, Sloane MS, 2189, f.127 (for which reference I thank Mr Malcolm Thick); Wilson, C. A., op. cit., pp. 105, 134–5; Houghton, II, no. 167 (11/10/1695); May, op. cit., pp. 228.

36 Ellis (2000), pp. 98–109; for another careful recipe for pickled pork, see Stitt (1957), p. 162.

37 Mrs Cromwell had a recipe for cooking beef and then putting it in pickle in a sealed barrel: this could have been the germ of the idea for raw meat pickling (Cromwell, op. cit., pp. 55–6); Mortimer (1707), p. 184; *Tusser Redivivus* (1710), p. 237; Bradley (1980) (1736), Glossary, p. 65; Melroe (1798), pp. 30–1; Kettilby (1728), p. 19; Cleland (1755), Chapter III and pp. 107ff.

38 Houghton, II, no. 167 (11/10/1695); Ellis, op. cit., p. 289.

39 Beeton, op. cit., p. 306. Elinor Fettiplace was not much interested in sauces, but May used them for roast veal (one with claret), for red deer, for pork, roast pigeons and game, a French sauce for goose, one for duck, and for pork in the Spanish fashion (May, op. cit., pp. 151–4, 196).

40 Harrington, Pearson and Rose (2000), pp. 455, 457, 459. The significance of this unusual information about ovens is not discussed by the editor.

41 Peachey (1992) (1594), pp. 5ff.; Ambler and Watkinson (1987), *passim*; Ellis, op. cit., p. 311.

42 Schofield (1994), pp. 52, 185 and *passim*; Thirsk (1978), pp. 13, 34, 54–5.

43 Mandrou (1961), p. 966.

44 Spufford, forthcoming; *AHEW*, V, ii (1985), p. 385, citing Bradley (1729), p. 37.

45 Linnell (1932), pp. 12–14.

Eggs and Bird Meat, Farm-fed and Wild

46 For a wildfowler's equipment, see Norfolk RO, Raynham, 408. I thank Prof. Hassell Smith warmly for this unusual document, listing the nets of Edmund Daber of Coxford (5m. SW of Fakenham) for trapping many different wild birds; they were sold at his death, and significantly were bought by Sir Roger Townsend. On wildfowling generally, see Markham (1621).

47 Harrison, ed. Edelen (1994), p. 317.

48 Estienne and Liébault (1602), pp. 40–2; Mascall (1581), f. Lr.

49 Mascall, op. cit., Epistle to Reader.

50 Le Choyselat (1951), *passim*.

51 *AHEW*, IV (1967), p. 44.

52 T&C (1972), p. 167.

53 Harland, I (1856), pp. 49, 114 (for an example of tithed eggs, see Ornsby (1878), p. 88); Gutch (1781), p. 5. Cf. also Harvey, B. (1993), p. 61, fn 85, showing the purchase by Westminster Abbey of some 82,000 eggs in 32 weeks in 1491–2 (some 250 per week).

54 Shewring (1699), p. 24; Ellis (2000), pp. 228–30.

55 Gutch, op. cit., pp. 6–7; Simon (1959), p. 57.

56 Hart (1633), pp. 77–8; Moufet (1655), pp. 42–4, 83; Gray (1995), pp. 96, 98, 103 and *passim*; Ruthin (1654), p. 203; Anon. (1658), p. 31; Bradley, Rose M. (1912), p. 88; Digby (1910), pp. 229–30; Ellis, op. cit., pp. 216–17.

57 Rham (1850), under Poultry; Cox (1730), under Dorking, Surrey (Cox named Dorking as the largest market for poultry in England); Ellis, op. cit., pp. 211–17.

58 Wilson, C.A. (1973), pp. 128–9; *AHEW*, IV (1967), pp. 194, 44, 123; Gutch, op. cit., pp. 1–3, 7; Harrison, ed. Edelen, op. cit., p. 317; Ellis, op. cit., pp. 220–2, 218.

59 Mascall, op. cit., np; Moufet, op. cit., p. 87; Boston RO, Whaplode Acre book (10 March, 18 Chas. I, 1642).

60 Defoe (1928), I, p. 59; Bradley (1980) (1736), p. 126; Ellis, op. cit., p. 225.

61 Bradley, op. cit., p. 163.

62 Probate inventories, misc.; *AHEW*, IV (1967), p. 194.

63 Ellis, op. cit., pp. 223–6; Bradley, op. cit., pp. 163–4.

64 Furnivall (1870), p. 167; Moufet, op. cit., p. 88; Harington (1607), np; Hammer (1999), pp. 660–1; Gutch, op. cit., p. 7; Peachey (1992) (1594), p. 9.

65 Standish (1611), pp. 25ff. (note that different impressions of Standish's treatise show different page numbers); Ellis, op. cit., pp. 222–3.

66 CSPD, 1623–5, pp. 188, 200, 211; *ODNB* under Standish.

67 Wentworth-Day (1970), pp. 116–18, 129–30.

68   Shewring, op. cit., pp. 60, 61.

69   Emmison (1964), pp. 89ff; Gutch, op. cit., p. 10; Mascall, op. cit., np; Byrne (1949), p. 69; Gray, op. cit., pp. 52, 74, 77–9.

70   Markham, op. cit., Chapters III, VI, VIII.

71   Bradley, op. cit., p. 18.

72   Markham, op. cit., *passim*; Worlidge (1970) (1675), pp. 248–50.

73   Standish (1612), pp. 25–6; Woodward (1984), pp. 114–16.

74   Prof. Hassell Smith, personal communication; Estienne and Liébault, op. cit., p. 45; HMC Rutland IV, 1905, 460, 470.

75   Hartlib Papers on CD-ROM, 29/5/52A; 26/44A–B; 31/17/11A–B; 62/24/1A–2B; 70/1/1A; 70/5A–B; Powell and Jenkinson (1938), p. 71.

76   Worlidge, op. cit., pp. 167, 165; Hartlib Papers on CD-ROM, 62/3/1A–2B; Blome, *Britannia*, 225, cited in Short (1982), p. 19.

77   Shewring, op. cit., *passim*. It is possible that poultry-keeping featured much more often in magazines.

78   Dawson (1996), pp. 9ff. for other wildfowl recipes.

79   Bradley (1727–8), IV, pp. 112–13.

80   Peachey, op. cit., *passim*.

81   Dawson, op. cit., pp. 34, 24; Peachey, op. cit., p. 20.

82   May (1994), pp. 214–16; Stitt (1957), pp. 166–7; Cleland (1755), pp. 83, 93, 96–8, 101, 109; Jackson (1754), *passim*.

83   Elder (1985), p. 61.

Fish

84   Small (2002), pp. 34–7.

85   Wilson, C.A. (1973), pp. 31, 46; Bradley (1980 (1736)), II, pp. 162–3.

86   Dent (1877), p. 140; BL Add. MS, 34218, f.38v; CKS S/MN A21; Thirsk, *AHR* (1953), p. 23.

87   Gutch (1781), pp. 1–3; Dietz (1972), *passim*; Harrison, ed. Edelen (1994), pp. 322–3.

88   Rowse (1964), p. 294.

89   Hants. RO, Jervoise of Herriard Collection, Sherfield MSS, 44 M69/L48/13. I gratefully acknowledge permission to cite this document.

90   Moufet (1655), p. 184.

91   Rye (1865), pp. 249–50; Harrison, ed. Edelen, op. cit., p. 321.

92   Bradley, op. cit., II, pp. 129; Houghton (1727–8), IV, nos. 543, 544 (18 and 25/12/1702); Moufet, op. cit., p. 157.

93   Ornsby (1878), 261–2, 343, xlvii; Prior (1982), p. 60.

94   Moufet, op. cit., pp. 142–3, 155, 158, 149, 164, 165, 167.

95   Houghton, op. cit., no. 545 (1/1/1702); Moufet, op. cit., pp. 154, 167, 169, 165, 170–2.

96   Harrison, ed. Edelen, op. cit., p. 322; Taverner (1601), pp. 7–8, 10–11, 14; Cooper (1654), p. 38; Woodcroft (1969), pp. 454, 609.

97   Contrary to Taverner's statement, one Sidney family document about Penshurst (1567–82) does show the stocking of a new pond: CKS U1500 E35 (I thank Lord De Lisle for permission to cite this document); May (1994), pp. 301–18; Collins (1682), *passim*.

98   Wilson, C.A., op. cit., p. 46; Cobbett (1967), p. 475.

Dairy Foods
99   Ellis (2000), p. 439; Thomas (1996), p. 98; *AHEW*, IV (1967), p. 495.
100   Harrison (1994), p. 51. (In 1985 an unusual find was made, buried among silver coins at Castle Farm, Breckenbrough, near Thirsk in North Yorkshire, of a receipt for cheese supplied to the Royalist army by the farmer. *The Times*, 26 September 1985.) CSPD 1650, pp. 109, 501, 572; 1651, 537, 559, 563, 571. One document about cheese for the forces in Ireland describes it as 'being of special use for field service' (CSPD 1649–50, p. 211). Blith's phrase about 'poor men's pursuits' was used in an edition of his *Whole Art of Husbandry*, which is in the Bodleian Library, whereas copies in the British Library do not show it.
101   PRO SP14/140/78; *AHEW*, V(ii) (1985), p. 361; Pepys (1924), p. 745; Larwood (1881), pp. 61–2, 71, 121.
102   Furnivall (1877–82), p. 49; Northeast (2001), p. 10. In the 1860s, Creeting St Peter was still a small village of family farmers, where the land was 'much subdivided', a description signifying a layout of land that encouraged dairying as an occupation.
103   For Dowe's account, see Chapter 3 above.
104   HMC Rutland, IV, 1905, 441; Latham and Matthews (1983), pp. 175, 184, 222, 260, 534; *AHEW*, IV (1967), p. xxxv; Garnier (1895), p. 207; Markham (1986), pp. 174–5; Ellis, op. cit., p. 406; Melroe (1798), p. 44.
105   Saxby (1932), pp. 166ff.; Best (1986), p. xlvi.
106   Furnivall (1870), p. 267.
107   Hart (1633), p. 208; Spencer (2002), p. 123; also Spurling (1987), pp. 116, 158–9; Wilson, C.A. (1973), pp. 146, 348; Gutch (1781), pp. 1–3, 5; May (1994), p. 261.
108   Armstrong (1946), p. 11. I thank Professor Mauro Ambrosoli warmly for identifying Francesco Cappello.
109   Worlidge (1970) (1704), under Butter; see also Thomas Turner's diary, in Vaisey (1984), *passim*.
110   Furnivall, op. cit., pp. 147, 339–40, 149, 157; Buttes (1599), f. N4r.; Best, op. cit., p. 174; Thirsk (1957), p. 117; Hartlib MSS, *Ephemerides*, 1655, 25-25-2.
111   Garnier (1895), p. 208, citing John Houghton in the 1690s. Butter went rancid sooner if the buttermilk was not wholly removed (*Encyclopaedia Britannica*, 11th edn, VII, pp. 750–52).
112   Moufet (1655), p. 129; Coles (1657), Chapter 251; Melroe, op. cit., p. 33. See also O'Connell (2003), analysing 75 recipes of the vegetarian, Thomas Tryon, showing butter used on vegetables, and the bread served separately. Only once, in recipe 13, is there a reference to 'bread, or bread and butter'. On Misson, see Thick (1998), p. 27.
113   Phillips (1958–9), p. 62; Digby (1910), pp. 209–10.
114   Garnier, op. cit., p. 208 (this informant, Russell Garnier, had lived for eight years next door to a Lancashire farmer who made it this last way, yet confessed that he had never had the curiosity to taste it!); Ellis, op. cit., pp. 230–2, 392–3.
115   Cromwell, n.d. (1664), p. 36.
116   Ruthin (1654), pp. 195–6; Houghton (1727–8), IV, 163, 178, 398; Ellis, op. cit., pp. 403, 401; also against clover in Somerset cheese, see Ellis, op. cit., pp. 394–7, 414; Hartlib,

Ephemerides, 1652, CC–CC2; Houghton, op. cit., II, pp. 373–4; Prussian account from German archives in author's possession; Pearce (1970), p. 9.

117 Hinton (1956), pp. 213, 216, 249; Hartlib, *Ephemerides*, KK–KK6-7; Pearce, op. cit., *passim*.

118 Moufet, op. cit., p. 133; May, op. cit., pp. 356, 379; Venner (1620), pp. 9, 92; Hart, op. cit., p. 209; Gratarolus (1574), p. 60; Harington (1607), f. B2; Buttes, op. cit., f. N7r.

119 Vinet (1607), pp. 533–5.

120 Cheshire cheeses were first mentioned in 1430, and in a period requiring alternative agricultural strategies they hint perhaps at the way small farmers, who still predominated in the area in 1760, turned more deliberately to dairying. The same situation is suggested in Arden, Warwickshire; *VCH* Oxon, X (1972), pp. 6, 52–4; Thirsk (1997), pp. 8–9; Watkins (1989), *passim*; Emmison (1964), p. 37–9; Cheke (1959), p. 90.

121 Palmer (1982), p. 24; Anon. (1598), *passim*; Riley (1989), pp. 28, 63, 74, 105, 106, 138; Furnivall, op. cit., p. 160; Hart, op. cit., p. 208.

122 Furnivall, op. cit., p. 126; Venner, op. cit., p. 92; Wilson, C.A. (1994), p. 56.

123 Ellis, op. cit., pp. 122–6.

124 Gutch, op. cit., pp. 4–11; Hartley and Ingilby (1968), p. 13.

125 Hartlib MSS, 33/1/34A–34B. Mrs Hill evidently farmed on the Ryelands, so she may have been a Worcestershire or Herefordshire woman.

126 On Cheshire cheese, see especially Foster (1998), *passim*; CSPD 1654, 388.

127 Hartlib, *Ephemerides*, KK–KK6-7; Hartlib MSS 28/2/65B, 25/1A–B; Ornsby (1878), p. 84; Gibson (1895), pp. 146, 178; Bradley (1729b).

128 Cheshire RO, DAR A/65/2; Slack (1975), pp. 111–12.

129 Cardigan (1951), p. 119. (Women's specialities are neatly summarized by the fact that Lord Ailesbury always got his butter, cream, eggs and pigeons from Goody Hanscomb and Goody Beal: Cardigan (1951), pp. 111–12.) *AHEW*, V(i) (1984), pp. 329–31; *VCH* Leics., II (1954), pp. 232–3.

130 An account by Prussian visitors to England in 1765–6, from the German archives, in the author's possession.

131 Broad (1980), pp. 77–89, esp. 88.

132 Elyot (1541), f. 34r; Thirsk (1978), pp. 91, 95; *AHEW*, V(ii) (1985), pp. 336–7; Eden (1928), pp. 113, 129ff., 210, 225, 295, 281, 105; Houghton, op. cit., II, nos. 147–56, 165; Spencer, op. cit., p. 296ff.

Vegetables and Herbs
133 Peachey (1992) (1594), p. 6; Buttes (1599), f. G7v–G8r; Speed (1659), p. 144.

134 Webber (1968), pp. 20ff.; White (2000), p. 113; Coles (1656), p. 49; Grieve (1984), pp. 500–1.

135 The point of Ellis's story was that a woman picked one herb by mistake, and it seemed to have poisoned her sow (2000, p. 185); Coles, op. cit., Chapter XXXIII, p. 119.

136 Harvey (1972), pp. 14ff; Rye (1865), pp. 204, fn 39; L&P, Henry VIII, III, part 2, 1408 (no. 3375): CSPD, 1547–80, 29.

137 Northcote (1912), p. 30; BL, Lansdowne MS, 81/48; NA, E190/185/6; Simon (1959), p. 59.

138   Similarly, nowadays concern is shown for the loss of the fragrance of flowers. See Leake (1997).

139   Dewar (1964), pp. 142–3, 148; Coles, op. cit., p. 120.

140   Hughes (1967), p. xxvii; Hart (1633), p. 56. (For a recent scientific evaluation of sage in improving memory, see *New Scientist*, vol. 148, no. 1999 (14/10/1995), 10; also *The Times*, 12 March 2000, 11; Dewar, op. cit., pp. 132–3; Harington (1624), np; Northcote, op. cit., p. 33.)

141   Burton (1926), I, p. 252.

142   Lawson (1982a), pp. 11–19; Moufet (1655), pp. 216–17; Grieve, op. cit., pp. 143–5.

143   Speed, op. cit., p. 101; Tawney and Power (1924), III, p. 41; Norwich RO, Walsingham MSS XVII/2, De Grey Letter Book, *c.* 1620–1 (I thank Professors Derek Hirst and Paul Slack for this reference); Hartlib MSS, 31/22/24B; Locke, ed. De Beer (1976), I, p. 609; ibid., II, p. 684; (1978), III, pp. 53, 504, 508, 513; CKS, U269/A474.

144   Bradley (1980) (1736), pp. 123, 70; Moufet, op. cit., p. 227 (Lawrence Hills initiated an enquiry into surviving rampions in 1980, see *The Times*, Letters, 24 December 1980); Parkinson (1629), pp. 489–90.

145   Buttes, op. cit., f. H7r; Parkinson, op. cit., Chapter XXXVII, p. 469; Harvey, John (1981), p. 164; Columella's words were influential on cabbage, see Forster and Heffner (1945), vol. III (and Columella, Book X), and faith in cabbage lasted long. See Phillips (1827), I, pp. 106–8, on the country people's enduring belief in the common cabbage 'to prevent occasion for the medicines used in the shops'; Simon, op. cit., p. 55.

146   Gray (1996), p. 33; Locke, ed. De Beer (1978), III, pp. 53–4; Switzer (1727), p. 376.

147   Parkinson, op. cit., pp. 498, 469–70; Harrison, ed. Edelen (1984), p. 129. (Sweet cicely, with lovage and costmary, were named by E. S. Rohde in 1931 as being rarely seen growing, and not being offered for sale in any catalogues, but now, in 2005–6, interest in lovage and sweet cicely, at least, has returned: Rohde (1931), pp. 154–5); Coles, op. cit., p. 87. (On purslane, it is interesting to read Cobbett's denunciation of it as 'a mischievous weed eaten by Frenchmen and pigs when they can get nothing else' (Cobbett (1838), p. 127), whereas it was commended in 1994 for its alpha-linolenic acid, thus explaining why the Cretans have the second lowest rate of heart attacks (*New Scientist*, 18 June 1994, 8)); CKS, U269, 474; Cooper (1654), pp. 110–11; Grieve, op. cit., p. 797.

148   Somerset RO, DD/SP, 1691.

149   Moufet, op. cit., p. 234; Ahmed (2002), p. 61; De Rougemont (1989), p. 55 (dating the introduction of this bean genus into Spain to 1594); Westmacott (1694), p. 22; Vaisey (1984), pp. 1, 7 and *passim*.

150   Parkinson (1640), II, pp. 1054ff.

151   Coles, op. cit., p., 141; Hartlib MS, 52/18A–19B; Merrett (1666), p. 94; Westmacott, op. cit., pp. 157–8; I thank Professor E. Evans for the information about tithe payments, taken from the tithe returns in the Lichfield Joint RO, which I compare with evidence of tithes from Warwickshire glebe terriers in Barratt (1955 and 1971), *passim*; Kalm (1892), pp. 353, 382, 91; Banister (1799), pp. 106ff. It is instructive to read in December 2004 in the *Yorkshire Post* (Benson, p. 18) of the success of John and Lorraine Cooling of Hall Farm, Sharlston, near Wakefield, in being judged the nation's top bean growers, but the beans go to Egypt where they are 'a vital part of Egyptian diet, providing a much needed source of protein as well

as essential minerals'. The potato crop growing in fields in 1801 was still modest in many counties; potatoes were more noticeable in kitchen gardens. Turner (1978), p. 227 and *passim*.

152 Kalm, op. cit., p. 311.

153 Newton (1580), f. 74v; Hart (1633), p. 47; Venner (1620), p. 135; Evelyn-Beale correspondence (I thank Dr Mayling Stubbs for this reference); May (1994), 102, 397; Switzer, op. cit., p. 373; Bradley (1980) (1736), Glossary, pp. 62–3.

154 Gray (1992), p. 40; Roberson (1941), p. 460; Perham (1989b), p. 5; Gomar, Ann (1988), p. 44; Gomar, Pippa, n.d., p. 34; Westmorland County Federation of Women's Institutes (1937), pp. 75–6; Grieve, op. cit., pp. 105–7.

155 Northcote, op. cit., p. 99; Furnivall (1877–82) (1583), p. 103.

156 Hartlib MS 62/24/1A. An Italian writer, summing up Italian experience in 1743, said that he thought vegetarianism was then returning to favour among Italian physicians; his work was translated into English in 1745. Thus were fads and fashions recognized. Cocchi (1745), p. 90.

157 Phillips (1827), *passim*; Thirsk (1997), p. 173.

Fruit

158 Elyot (1541), p. 23; Caroli (1991), *passim*; Jordan and Cherry (1995), *passim*; Snell (1995), p. 19; Riley (1989), *passim*.

159 McGrath (1948), p. 211.

160 Nicolas (1827), p. xv, and *passim*; Harland, I (1856), p. 59 (13 August 1590).

161 Parkinson (1629), *passim*; Lawson (2003), *passim* (one of Lawson's books was actually entitled *A New Orchard and Garden*); Hearn (2005), *passim*; Peck (2005), pp. 210, 220, and authorities cited therein; *ODNB* under Sir Nathaniel Bacon; CKS, U269/A474. For an early reference to fruit pastes, see Dawson (1996), pp. 73, 77; for plum paste and barberry paste to go into galley pots, see Anon. (1653), pp. 34–5; for pippin paste to counterfeit plums, and gift boxes, see Ruthin (1654), pp. 28, 30–1; for gift boxes, see also Grey (1653), p. 28; Ruthin, op. cit., p. 31; for apricot chips, see Cooper (1654), pp. 163–4.

162 Anon. (1653), p. 49; Vaughan (1617), p. 95; Hartlib, *Ephemerides*, 1649, J-3.

163 Buttes (1599), 11r, E3v; Nicolas, op. cit., pp. 6, 92; Phillips (1958–9), p. 64; Dawson, op. cit., pp. 102–3; (Barnaby Googe had described pomecitrons as 'citrons, very round and great': *OED*); Ruthin, op. cit., p. 33; Hart, op. cit., pp. 67–8; Houghton, IV, no. 401 (29/3/1700).

164 Thirsk (1997), p. 32; HMC, Salisbury MSS, XXIV, 202; Goodman (1839), p. 46; Fussell (1936), pp. 148–9, 185.

165 Standish (1612), p. 36; Moufet (1655), p. 194; Anon. (1653), pp. 13, 25–6, 31–7; Hartlib, *Ephemerides*, 1653, 28/2/70B; Evelyn (1664), p. 2; Large (1980), 40–1.

166 Thirsk, op. cit., pp. 56, 282, fn.35; Austen (1653a), p. 28 and *passim*; Blith (1653), p. 126; Houghton, II, no. 182; III, nos. 196, 246; *VCH* Middlesex, III, 116.

167 *Phil. Trans.*, X, 303 (26 April 1675); Ruthin, op. cit., p. 4–5, 17, 199.

168 Blundell (1968), p. 202.

169 HMC, Rutland IV, 1905, 471, 476; George (1991), p. 187.

170 Taverner (1928 (1600)), p. 21; information displayed at an exhibition at the National Fruit Collection, Brogdale, Kent.

171 Coles (1656), Chapter 171; Markham (1613), p. 129; Rowse (1964), p. 282; HMC, Rutland, IV, 1905, 476; Hart (1633), p. 64; Cooper, op. cit., pp. 163–6; Ruthin, op. cit., p. 8; Grey, op. cit., p. 31; Temple (1903), p. 9; East Sussex RO, Glynde MS, 914; Hitt (1768), Plate IV; Chartres (2004), p. 131.

172 Blencowe (1925), p. 9; Addison, Steele and others, nd., pp. 208–10; Phillips (1821), p. 30; Stapleton (1893), p. 169; Hoskins (1972), p. 494.

173 Cardigan (1951), p. 112; Kidwell (1983), pp. 405, 406, 413.

174 Information kindly given me by the late Dr Addy; NA, C78/592/13.

175 Blundell, op. cit., p. 202.

176 Houghton (1727–8), IV, p. 440 (27/12/1700), 434 (15/11/1700).

177 CSP Venetian, 1617–19, 319; Anon. (1653), p. 49; Hart, op. cit., p. 59.

178 Plimmer (1935), p. 57.

179 Shesgreen (1990), *passim*; Eden (1928), p. 240; Henrey (1986), p. 232.

Drinks

180 Wilson (1973), p. 388; Parkinson (1629), p. 478.

181 Hart (1633), pp. 113, 115, 109.

182 Ibid., pp. 112, 116–7, 124, 185; Cogan (1584), p. 26; Cornwall RO, Glebe terriers.

183 HMC Rutland IV, 1905, 549, 552; T&C, 405; Scarfe (1995), p. 81.

184 NA, E134, 14 Jas.I, Hil. 6.

185 Baskerville (1893), p. 295; typescript of report of Prussian visitors to English farms, 1766, from German archives, in author's possession; Brandon (2003), p. 193; CSPD 1637–8, vol. 390, no. 66; Scarfe (1988), p. 208. See also Sambrook (1996), *passim*.

186 Best (1986), p. 180; Prussian Report, 1766, p. 150; Harrison, ed. Edelen (1994), pp. 135–9; on porter, an almost black beer, heavily hopped, and left for a long period to ferment, see Wilson, op. cit., p. 386.

187 Wilson, op. cit., pp. 384–5; Scarfe (1995), pp. 223–6.

188 Houghton in Bradley (1727), IV, p. 67; according to Westmacott (1694, p. 22), beans and peas in beer made the beer 'smile at you', making it more volatile and clear; Parkinson (1640), p. 472; Harland, II (Chetham XLI) (1856), pp. 234, 239–40; Ruthin (1654), pp. 215–16; Mascall (1569), p. 76; BL, Add. MS 37616, 410.

189 See, for example, Vaughan, referring in 1600 to 'a wholesome ordinary drink' which became 'a diet drink' when he wrote in 1617. Vaughan (1617), pp. 37, 52–3; Houghton, I, 69 (24/11/1693), 90 (20/4/1694) and ff. I thank Dr John Broad for the reference to 'salop'; see also Wilson, op. cit., pp. 214–15. On oats in ale, see Westmacott, op. cit., pp. 22–3, and Houghton, IV, 304 (20/5/1698).

190 Smith, S.D. (2001), p. 245; Phillips (1827), II, pp. 292–310; Hartlib, *Ephemerides* (1657), 51-51-8; Wilson, op. cit., p. 411; Vaisey (1984), *passim*. For a bibliography of recent writing on these three new drinks, see Clark (2000), p. 222, fn. 119.

191 Wilson, op. cit., pp. 408–11; Houghton, IV, 443 (17/1/1701), 444 (24/1/1701), 450 (7/3/1701).

192 Wilson, op. cit., p. 405; Phillips (1821), pp. 109–18; Houghton, IV, 458 (2/5/1701).

193 For slightly different details from Houghton's description, and a reference to a first account by Houghton in the *Philosophical Transactions of the Royal Society*, see Smith, op. cit., pp. 245ff.

194 Houghton, IV, 460 (16/5/1701), III, 242 (19/3/1697) and ff.; Wilson, op. cit., pp. 405–6.

195 Wanklyn (1998), p. 296 and *passim*.

196 Holinshed (1913), pp. 63, 66, 61.

197 Turner (1568), *passim*; Westmacott, op. cit., pp. 26–7.

198 Anon. (1600), ff. D1r.ff; *ODNB* under Armagil Waad; NA, E159/357, no.532; Notestein, Relf and Simpson (1935), IV, 108; VII, 77ff.; Woodcroft (1969), p. 182, also p. 491; Westmacott, op. cit., p. 9; Wilson, op. cit., pp. 396–9.

199 Furnivall (1870), pp. 149, 156–7, 337; Rye (1865), pp. 79, 194; Hart, op. cit., pp. 128–37; Wilson, op. cit., p. 399; Scrivener (1685), *passim*.

200 Cooke (1904), pp. 267–94.

Condiments

201 Stobart (1972), pp. 14, 15, 19.

202 Brownlow (1978), pp. 20–1.

203 Coles (1657), *passim*; Coles (1656), p. 49; May (1994), *passim*; BBC Radio Talk, 31 December 1996.

204 Ornsby (1878), p. 359. See also the Howard accounts (ibid., p. 163), for 'setwell roots' or 'heal all' (valerian), for which Howard paid 6d. According to Maud Grieve, the same herb was also used as a spice, but Howard may have been obsessive about herbs for health; it is used to promote sleep. Grieve writes at length on its uses (1984, pp. 824–9); David (1970), p. 10.

205 Grieve, op. cit., pp. 660–1.

206 Purslane is carefully cultivated as a food plant in Holland and elsewhere on the Continent. Violet Plimmer, writing in 1935 on salads and herbs, thought 'a revival of the theory and practice of the herbalist is urgently called for so that the free gifts in the hedgerows and fields are not wasted' (Plimmer (1935), p. 102); Moufet (1655), p. 69; Grieve, op. cit., p. 753.

207 Grieve, op. cit., pp. 752–4.

208 The full name for broom is *Genista scoparius*. Richard II's tomb in Westminster abbey bears as his heraldic device a broom plant with empty buds; Grieve, op. cit., pp. 125–6; Ornsby, op. cit., p. 94; Spurling (1987), pp. 112, 103; Grey (1653), p. 19; Lobb (1767), pp. 73–4.

209 Grieve, op. cit., p. 567; Cogan (1584), p. 167; Hinton (1956), pp. 71, 105 (mustard was exported from Boston to Amsterdam in 1612 and again in 1615); Darby (1956), p. 164; Thirsk (1957), p. 225.

210 May, op. cit., p. 157.

211 I wish to thank Dr Bridgett Jones for the sight of her transcripts of customs records for Sandwich, NA, E121/124/6 (1302–3); SC 6/894/22–30 (1298–1347); SC 6/895/1–23 (1351–1439).

212 Simon (1959), pp. 59, 70; Tawney and Power (1924), III, pp. 145–6; Furnivall (1877–82), p. 105; Harrison, ed. Edelen (1994), p. 116; NA, SP 12/153/71 (a forward estimate of spice costs for 1589 was also made, showing the anticipated prices: NA, SP 12/225/76); Fussell (1936), p. 153; Harland, I (1856), pp. 5, 12, 62, 67, 82, 103, 134; Bradley (1980) (1736), part II, pp. 161–2.

213 Wake (1979), pp. 388–9; Gutch (1781), II, p. 9; Ornsby, op. cit., pp. lxxv ff; Hart (1633), pp. 94 ff.; Houghton, IV, nos. 420 (9/8/1700), 421 (16/8/1700), 422 (23/8/1700); Ellis (2000), p. 128.

214 Hart, op. cit., p. 102.

215 Dietz (1972), no. 710; Davidson (1999), p. 233. Harland, I (Chetham, XXXV) (1856), p. 134. For a glimpse of a travelling salesmen in spices, see White (2000, p. 77), mentioning a probate inventory of Thomas Gryssop, chapman of York, dated 7 October 1446, and showing his stock of cloves, mace, galingale, ginger, pepper, saunders, cinnamon powder, sugar and saffron.

216 Collins (1682), p. 121; for alternative ways, see ibid., pp. 121ff., 152; Houghton, III, no. 215 (11/9/1696). Houghton's account of English salt ran on in his Newsletters from issue number 210 to 215.

217 Houghton, III, no. 210 (7/8/1696).

218 Wilson (1973), p. 39; Hinton, op. cit., pp. 5–7; Lloyd (1967), p. 91.

219 Thirsk (1997), pp. 112, 141.

220 Lowthorp (1716), II, p. 359.

221 Collins (1682), pp. 9–10, 129, 124, 140; Houghton (1692), III, no. 215 (11/9/1696); Ellis, op. cit., p. 104.

222 Robinson (1641), p. 19; Frank (1970), np.

223 Bayley (1588), *passim*.

224 Dietz, op. cit., no. 298; Hart, op. cit., pp. 100, 78.

225 Spurling, op. cit., p. 95; HMC Rutland, IV, 1905, 404, 440; Ellis, op. cit., pp. 313–14; Moufet, op. cit., p. 156; Best (1986), pp. 133–4; May, op. cit., pp. 154–6, 400.

226 Harland, I (1856), p. 59; Ornsby, op. cit., p. 135; May, op. cit., p. 369; Bradley (1980) (1736), p. 96.

227 The reserved words used in recommending garlic in recipes have been cited above. For Hartlib's note, see Hartlib, *Ephemerides* (1653), part 3, 28/2/67B.

228 So described by John Parkinson (1629), p. 521; Hart, op. cit., p. 50; see also Parkinson, op. cit., pp. 470, 486 on sorrel; Buttes (1599), f. 2v.

229 Ibid., f. 3r; Stubbes's remark in 1583 is an early reference to a multitude of curious sauces and of dishes, when at one time one or two dishes were thought sufficient; Furnivall, op. cit., p. 69; Hunt (1996), p. 147.

230 Ornsby (1878), pp. 87–8; Emmison (1964), p. 64; Spurling, op. cit., *passim*.

231 Lawson (1982b), p. 58; Dietz, op. cit., nos. 154, 291, 591; Holinshed (1913), p. 63.

232 Gray (1995), *passim*.

233 HMC Rutland, IV, 1905, 500; Emmison, op. cit., p. 45; Folger Library MS, V, b 246. (Smyth was nephew and heir of Sir Thomas Smyth, 1513–77.)

234 Sanchez had been a member of the French church (Pettegree (1986), pp. 297, 304). David Avery's notes about Sanchez say that he came late in life to Tottenham from London, and lived at the 'George and Vulture' (see *Newsletter of the Edmonton Hundred Historical Society*, June 2002, citing Avery (1963)). See also Jordan (1960), p. 145. I wish to thank Dr Lien Lu for the references to comfit makers. See also Kirk and Kirk (1900–1908), II, pp. 83, 90, 355; I, p. 391.

235 Bradley (1980) (1736), II, pp. 43–8.

236 Morgan (1996), *passim*; Millican (1934), pp. 38, 123. I wish to thank Dr Victor Morgan for this reference.

237 Hart, op. cit., pp. 95–7.

Notes to Chapter 10: Conclusion

1 Melroe (1798), pp. 62–3, 43; Potter (2006), pp. 19, 21, 25, 27–9. Lady Fanshawe is named in Chapter 6 above for her ingenuity in fattening poultry in a fortnight by keeping a candle burning in their coop all night to keep them eating. For an attractive view both pictorially and in printed text of the expanding range of fancy foods from the sixteenth into the later seventeenth century, see Caton (1999), *passim.*

Bibliography

The place of publication is London in all cases where not otherwise stated.

Addison, Joseph, Richard Steele, and others (n.d.), *Spectator*, ed. G. Gregory Smith.

Ahmed, Anne (2002), *A Proper Newe Booke of Cokerye*, Margaret Parker's Cookery Book. Cambridge: Corpus Christi College.

Alexis of Piemount (1558), *The Secretes of the Reverende Maister Alexis of Piemount*, trans. William Warde.

Alsop, James (1980), 'John Le Leu, alias Wolf, French arboriculturist at the Tudor court: precursor of later Huguenot gardeners', *Proceedings*, Huguenot Society of London, XXXIII (4).

Ambler, R. W., B. Watkinson and L. Watkinson (1987), *Farmers and Fishermen. The Probate Inventories of the Ancient Parish of Clee, South Humberside, 1536–1742*. Hull.

Ananthaswamy, A. (2004), 'Eat less and keep disease at bay', *New Scientist*, 24 April.

Anderson, Jay A. (1971), 'A Solid Sufficiency: An Ethnography of Yeoman Foodways in Stuart England'. PhD thesis: University of Pennsylvania.

Anon. (1585), *The Widowes Treasure, Plentifully Furnished with Sundrie Precious and Approved Secretes in Physicke and Chirurgery for the Health and Pleasure of Mankinde*.

Anon. (1588), *The Good Hous-Wives Treasurie, beeing a verye Necessarie Booke Instructing to the Dressing of Meates. Hereunto is also Annexed Sundrie Holsome Medicines for Divers Diseases*.

Anon. (1598), *Epulario or The Italian Banquet, wherein is showed the Maner how to Dress and Prepare all Kind of Flesh, Foules or Fishes … Translated out of the Italian into English*.

Anon. (1652), *A Hermeticall Banquet Drest by a Spagiricall Cook; for the Better Preservation of the Microcosme*.

Anon. (1653), *The Ladies Companion, or a Table Furnished with Sundry Sorts of Pies and Tarts … by Persons of Quality whose Names are Mentioned*.

Anon. (1658), *Archimagirus Anglo-Gallicus: or Excellent and Approved Receipts and Experiments in Cookery … Copied from a Choice Manuscript of Sir Theodore Mayerne, Knight, Physician to the Late King Charles*.

Anon. (1704), *Dictionarium Rusticum et Urbanicum*.

Anon. (1767), *Primitive Cookery or the Kitchen Garden Display'd* (in BL, Tracts on Cookery, 1699–1808, Call mark: 1037 e 41) (1–7).

Anon. (1779), *A General Dictionary of Husbandry, Planting and Gardening … by the Editors of the Farmers' Magazine*, vols I and II. Bath.

Antrobus, Derek (1997), *A Guiltless Feast*. Salford: Salford City Council.

Appleby, Andrew B. (1973), 'Disease or famine? Mortality in Cumberland and Westmorland, 1580–1640', *EcHR*, 2nd Ser., XXVI (3).

— (1978), *Famine in Tudor and Stuart England*. Liverpool.

— (1979), 'Diet in sixteenth-century England: sources, problems, possibilities', in Charles Webster (ed.), *Health, Medicine and Mortality in the Sixteenth Century*. Cambridge.

Archer, R. E. and S. Walker (eds) (1995), *Rulers and Ruled in Late Medieval England: Essays presented to Gerald Harriss*.

Armstrong, Edward A. (1946), *Shakespeare's Imagination*.

Atkinson, F. (1960–62), 'Oatmeal in northern England', Gwerin, III.

Austen, Ralph (1653a), *The Spirituall Use of an Orchard; or Garden of Fruit-Trees*.

— (1653b), *A Treatise of Fruit-Trees*. Oxford.

Avery, David (1963), 'Poverty and philanthropy in Tottenham in the sixteenth and seventeenth centuries'. Occasional Paper 4: Edmonton Hundred Historical Society.

Avery, Susanna (1922) (1685), *A Plain Plantain: Country Dishes and Herbal Cures from a Seventeenth-Century Household MS Receipt Book, arranged ... by Russell George Alexander*. Ditchling, Sussex.

Ayrton, E. (1980), *English Provincial Cooking*.

Baker, Hugh D. R. (1983), 'The rituals of the table', *The Times Literary Supplement*, 24 June.

Bamborough, J. B. (1959), *Ben Jonson*. Writers and their Works, no. 112. Bibliographical series of British Council Supplements to 'British Book News'.

Banister, John (1799), *A Synopsis of Husbandry, being Cursory Observations in the Several Branches of Rural Oeconomy*.

Barclay, W. (1616), *Icon Animarum*.

Barley, M. W. (1987), *The English Farmhouse and Cottage*.

Barratt, D. M. (ed.) (1955) (1971), 'Ecclesiastical Terriers of Warwickshire Parishes'. Dugdale Society, XXII, XXVII.

Baskerville, T. (1893), 'Thomas Baskerville's Journeys in England temp. Car. II', HMC, 13th Report, Appendix II.

Bateson, F. W. (1966), *Brill: A Short History*.

Batho, G. R. (ed.) (1962), 'The household papers of Henry Percy, Ninth Earl of Northumberland (1563–1632)', Camden Soc., 3rd Ser., XCIII.

Bayley, Walter (1588), *A Short Discourse of the Three Kinds of Pepper in Common Use*.

Beeton, Isabella (1861), *The Book of Household Management*.

Bell, Susan and Derwent May (1999), 'Eurocratic red tape stops French from hunting the bunting', *The Times*, 5 March.

Beltrán, María Helena Roxo (1997), 'Sixteenth century books of distillation and materia medica' in G. Emptoz and P. A. Pastraña (eds), 'Between the Natural and the Artificial', Proceedings of the Twentieth International Congress of the History of Science, vol. II (20–26 July). Liège.

Benson, Robert (2004), 'Beans bring a second success for top growers', *Yorkshire Post*, 4 December, p. 18.

Best, Michael R. (ed.) (1986), Gervase Markham, *The English Housewife*. Montreal and Kingston, London.

Billingsley, John (1798), *General View of the Agriculture of the County of Somerset*. Bath.

Birch, T. (ed.) (1772), *The Works of the Honourable Robert Boyle*, 2nd edn, VI.

Blackwood, Gordon (2001), *Tudor and Stuart Suffolk*. Lancaster.

Blencowe, Ann (1925) (1694), *The Receipt Book of Mrs Ann Blencowe*.

Blith, Walter (1653), *The English Improver Improved, or The Survey of Husbandry Surveyed*.

Blundell, Nicholas (1968) (1970) (1972), ed. J. J. Bagley, *The Great Diurnal of Nicholas Blundell of Little Crosby, Lancs.*, I (1702); II (1712–19); III (1720–28). Record Society of Lancashire and Cheshire, vols 110, 112, 114.

Blythman, Joanna (1996), 'Shop horror' and 'Spilt milk', *BBC Good Food Magazine*, August.

Bonser, K. J., *The Drovers, Who they Were, and Where they Went*.

Bo(o)rde, Andrew, see Furnivall, F.J. (1870).

Bosanquet, Rosalie E. (1989), *In the Troublesome Times. Memories of Old Northumberland, Collected by the Cambo Women's Institutes*, Stocksfield, Northumberland.

Bower, Jacqueline (1991), 'Probate accounts as a source for Kentish early modern economic and social history', *AC*, CIX.

Bradley, Rose M. (1912), *The English Housewife in the Seventeenth and Eighteenth Centuries*.

Bradley, Richard (1725), *A Survey of the Ancient Husbandry and Gardening, Collected from Cato, Varro, Columella, Virgil and Others*.

— (1727a), *The Country Gentleman and Farmer's Monthly Director*, 2nd edn.

— (1727–8), A Collection of Letters for the Improvement of Husbandry and Trade, 4 vols. (Cited in Notes as Houghton, in Bradley.)

— (1729a), *A Philosophical Enquiry into the Late Severe Winter, the Scarcity and Dearness of Provisions and the Occasion of the Distemper Raging in Several Remote Parts of England*.

— (1729b), *The Gentleman and Farmer's Guide for the Increase and Improvement of Cattle*.

— (1980) (1736), *The Country Housewife and Lady's Director*.

Brandon, Peter (2003), *The Kent and Sussex Weald*. Chichester.

Bright, Timothy (1580), *A Treatise wherein is Declared the Sufficiencie of English Medicines*.

Broad, John (1980), 'Alternate husbandry and permanent pasture in the Midlands, 1650–1800', *AHR*, 28 (ii).

— (2004), *Transforming English Rural Society: The Verneys and the Claydons, 1600–1820*, Cambridge Studies in Population: Economy and Society in Past Time, 30. Cambridge.

Broad, John and Richard Hoyle (1997), *Bernwood: The Life and Afterlife of a Forest*, Harris Paper 2. Lancaster.

Brownlow, Margaret (1978), *Herbs and the Fragrant Garden*, 3rd edn.

Bryant, Charles (1783), *Flora Diaetetica; or History of Esculent Plants, both Domestic and Foreign*.

Burton, Robert (1926) (1621), *The Anatomy of Melancholy*, I.

Buttes, Henry (1599), *Dyets Dry Dinner, Consisting of 8 Several Courses*.

Byrne, Muriel St Clare (1949), *The Elizabethan Home: Discovered in Two Dialogues by Claudius Hollyband and Peter Erondell*.

— (1981), *The Lisle Letters*, 6 vols. Chicago.

Canney, Margaret and David Knott (1970), *Catalogue of the Goldsmiths' Library of Economic Literature.* Cambridge.

Capp, Bernard (1994), *The World of John Taylor, the Water-Poet, 1578–1653.* Oxford.

Cardigan, Earl of (1951), 'Domestic expenses of a nobleman's household, 1678', Beds. Hist. Rec. Soc., XXXII.

Carew, Richard (1723 (recte 1769)) *The Survey of Cornwall:* Penzance.

— (1811), *The Survey of Cornwall,* Plymouth.

Carlé, María del Carmen (1977), 'Notas para el estudio de la alimentación en la baja Edad Media', *Cuadernos de Historia de España,* LXI–LXII, Buenos Aires.

Caroli, Flavio (1991), *Fede Galizia,* 2nd edn. Turin.

Carrichter, Bartholomaeus (1652), *Kraüter und Arztenenbuchs,* Nüremberg (BL 546 b 17); also 1739, Tübingen (BL 957 k 34).

Carrington, W. A. (1894), 'Selections from the steward's accounts preserved at Haddon Hall, for the years 1549 and 1554', *Jnl Derbys Archaeolog. and Nat. Hist. Soc.,* XVI.

Carter, Charles (1736), *The Compleat City and Country Cook: or Accomplish'd Housewife,* 2nd edn.

Cass, Elizabeth (1957), *Spanish Cooking.*

Chalklin, C.W., see Palliser, David.

Caton, Mary Anne (1999), *Fooles and Fricassees: Food in Shakespeare's England.* Washington, DC.

Chartres, John (2004), 'A special crop and its markets in the eighteenth century: the case of Pontefract liquorice', in R. W. Hoyle (ed.), *People, Landscape and Alternative Agriculture: Essays for Joan Thirsk.*

Cheke, Val (1959), *The Story of Cheesemaking in Britain.*

Cherry, Peter, see Jordan, W.B.

Cheyne, George (1724), *An Essay of Health and Long Life.*

Child, Mrs (1835) (1832), *The Frugal Housewife, dedicated to Those who are not Ashamed of Economy,* 15th edn.

Church, Rocke, 1612, An Olde Thrift Newly Revived.

Clark, Peter (ed.) (2000), *The Cambridge Urban History of Britain,* vol. II, 1540–1840. Cambridge.

Clark, Ros (1995–6), 'The butcher, the baker, the candlestickmaker … A study of occupations in Spalding in 1642', *Lincolnshire Past and Present,* no. 22, Winter.

Clarke, Samuel (1677), *A Looking Glass for Good Women to Dress Themselves by* (reprinted 1683 in S. Clarke, *The Lives of Sundry Eminent Persons in this Later Age*).

Cleland, Elizabeth (1755), *A New and Easy Method of Cookery.* Edinburgh.

Cobbett, W. (1838), *The English Gardener.*

— (1926) (1821), *Cottage Economy.*

— (1967), *Rural Rides.* Penguin.

Cocchi of Mugello, Antonio (1745), *The Pythagorean Diet of Vegetables Only Conducive to the Preservation of Health and the Cure of Diseases.*

Cogan, Thomas (1584), *The Haven of Health.*

Cohen, Philip (1997), 'Another reason to diet', *New Scientist,* 8 Nov.

Coles, William (1656), *The Art of Simpling.*

— (1657), *Adam in Eden.*

Collins, E. J. T. (1975), 'Dietary change and cereal consumption in Britain in the nineteenth century', *AHR* 23 (ii).

Collins, John (1682), *Salt and Fishery: A Discourse Thereof.*

Colville, James (ed.) (1904), *Letters of John Cockburn of Ormistoun (1727–44)*, Scottish Historical Society, 45.

Cooke, R. (1904), 'Anecdotes of the Hasted family', *Archaeologia Cantiana*, XXVI.

Cooper, Derek (1998), 'Good food, good ingredients', *Saga*, Jan.

Cooper, Joseph (1654), *The Art of Cookery Refin'd and Augmented.*

Copley, Esther (1849), *Cottage Cookery.*

Coppock, Heather C. (n.d.), *The Saffron Crocus in Cherry Hinton and other Areas of Cambridgeshire.* Cherry Hinton.

Courteney, Hazel (1997), 'What's the alternative?', *The Sunday Times*, 2 February and 28 December.

— (2000), 'Vital elements', *The Sunday Times*, 29 October.

Cox, Francis (1575), *Treatise of the Making and Use of Divers Oils, Unguents, Emplasters, and Distilled Waters.*

Cox, T. (1730), *Magna Britannia.*

Croker, T. Crofton (ed.) (1837), *The Tour of M. de la Boullaye le Gouz in Ireland, AD. 1644.*

Cromwell, Joan (n.d.) (1664), *Mrs Cromwell's Cookery Book.* Cambridgeshire Libraries.

Crosby, Alan (1997), 'Oats in the Lancashire diet (1750–1850)', *Lancaster University CNWRS Regional Bulletin*, CNWRS, NS, 11.

Crossley, A. and others (1972), *VCH* Oxon, X, Oxford.

Cuello, Antonio Malpica (ed.) (2001), *Navegación Marítima del Mediterráneo al Atlántico.* Granada, Spain.

Culpeper, Nicholas (1656), *Health for the Rich and Poor by Diet without Physick.*

— (*c.* 1816), *The British Herbal and Family Physician.* Halifax.

Currie, Christopher K. (1991), 'The early history of the carp and its economic significance in England', *AHR*, 39(ii).

Darby, H. C. (1956), *The Draining of the Fens.* Cambridge.

David, Elizabeth (1970), *Spices, Salt and Aromatics in the English Kitchen.*

— (1979), *English Bread and Yeast Cookery.*

Davidson, Alan (1999), *The Oxford Companion to Food.* Oxford.

Davies, David (1977) (1795), *The Case of Labourers in Husbandry Stated and Considered.*

Dawson, Thomas (1996) (1596–7), ed. Maggie Black, *The Good Housewife's Jewel.* Lewes, Sussex.

De Coca Castañer, Jose Enrique Lopez (2001), 'Granada y la ruta de Poniente: el tráfico de frutos secos (siglos XIV y XV)' in Antonio Malpica Cuello (ed.), *Navegación Marítima del Mediterráneo al Atlántico.* Granada.

Defoe, Daniel (1928), *A Tour through the Whole Island of Great Britain.* Everyman Library.

de la Quintinie, Jean (1693), trans. John Evelyn, *The Compleat Gard'ner.*

de la Varenne, François Pierre (2001) (1653), *The French Cook, Englished by I. D. G.* Lewes, Sussex.

Denney, A. H. (1960), *The Sibton Abbey Estates. Select Documents, 1325–1509*, Suffolk Records Society, II.

Dent, Emma (1877), *Annals of Winchcombe and Sudeley.*

De Rougemont, G. M. (1989), *A Field Guide to the Crops of Britain and Europe.*

Dewar, Mary (1964), *Sir Thos. Smith: A Tudor Intellectual in Office.*

Dietz, Brian (ed.) (1972), *The Port and Trade of Early Elizabethan London. Documents,* London Record Society, VIII.

Digby, Sir Kenelm (1910) (1669), ed. Anne Macdonell, *The Closet of Sir Kenelm Digby Knight Opened.*

Dowe, Bartholomew (1588), *A Dairie Booke for Good Huswives* ... Website of Henry E. Huntington Library and Art Gallery, and UMI Collection, Early English Books, 1641–1700, 1241:15.

Driver, Christopher (ed.) (1997), *John Evelyn Cook: The Manuscript Receipt Book of John Evelyn.* Totnes, Devon.

Duhamel Du Monceau, Henri L. (1754), *Traité de la Conservation des Grains et en particulier de Froment.* Paris.

Duncombe, W. G. (1991), *Stuart Yeomen of the Darent Valley,* KAS, Kent Records, NS, I.

Dyer, Alan (2000), 'Small market towns, 1540–1700', in Peter Clark (ed.), *The Cambridge Urban History of Britain,* II, 1540–1840. Cambridge.

Dyer, Christopher (1983), 'English diet in the later Middle Ages', in T. H. Aston with others (eds), *Social Relations and Ideas: Essays in Honour of R. H. Hilton.* Cambridge.

— (1987), 'Jardins et vergers en Angleterre au moyen âge' in *Jardins et Vergers en Europe Occidentale (VIIIe–XVIII Siècles),* Flaran, 9.

— (1988), 'Changes in diet in the late Middle Ages: the case of the harvest workers', *AHR,* 36 (i).

— (1989), *Standards of Living in the Later Middle Ages: Social Change in England, c. 1200–1520.* Cambridge.

— (2004), 'Alternative agriculture: goats in medieval England', in R. W. Hoyle (ed.), *People, Landscape, and Alternative Agriculture, AHR,* Supplement Series, 3.

Earle, John (1628), *Micro-cosmographie.*

Eden, Sir Frederick Morton (1797), *The State of the Poor, or An History of the Labouring Classes in England from the Conquest to the Present* ... *with Parochial Reports.*

— (1928), *The State of the Poor,* abridged and edited by A. G. L. Rogers.

Edlin, A. (1805), *A Treatise on the Art of Bread-making.*

Eisenstein, Elizabeth (1983), *The Printing Revolution in Early Modern Europe.* Cambridge.

Elder, Eileen (1985), *Lincolnshire Country Food.* Scunthorpe.

Elliott, Valerie (2000), 'Alarm raised over "junk diet" children', *The Times,* 2 June.

Ellis, William (1745), *Chiltern and Vale Farming.*

— (2000) (1750), *The Country Housewife's Family Companion.* Totnes, Devon.

Elyot, Sir Thomas (1539/1541), *The Castell of Health,* corrected and in some places augmented by the first author thereof.

— n.d. (*c.* 1907/8), ed. Foster Watson, *The Boke named the Governour.* Everyman.

Emden, C. S. (1948), 'Thomas Cogan (154?–1607), a doctor writing on diet', in Emden, *Oriel Papers.* Oxford.

Emmison, F. G. (1964), *Tudor Food and Pastimes.*

Encyclopaedia Britannica (1910–11), 11th edn. Cambridge.

Ernle, Lord (1961 edn), *English Farming Past and Present.*

Evelyn, John (1664), *Sylva ... to which is annexed Pomona.*

— (1699), *Acetaria.*

Estienne, Charles and Jean Liébault (1602), *L'Agriculture et Maison Rustique.* Rouen.

Fetlar Community Enterprises (1987), *Fetlar's Favourite Recipes.* Fetlar, Shetland.

Fitzharberts (*sic*), John (1598), *Booke of Husbandrie.*

Fitzherbert, John (1523), *The Boke of Husbandrie.*

Folkingham, W. (1623), *Panala ala Catholica, or a Compound Ale.*

— (1628), *Panala Medica vel Sanitatis et Longae Vitatis Alumna Catholica: the Fruitfull and Frugall Nourse of Sound Health and Long Life.*

Forster, E. S. and E. H. Heffner (eds) (1945), *Columella*, III.

Forster, John (1664), *England's Happiness Increased ... by a Plantation of ... Potatoes.*

Forsyth, Hazel (1999), *London Eats Out: 500 Years of Capital Dining.*

Foster, Charles F. (1998), *Cheshire Cheese and Farming in the North West in the 17th and 18th Centuries.* Northwich, Cheshire.

Fox, Harold (2001), *The Evolution of the Fishing Village: Landscape and Society along the South Devon Coast, 1086–1550.* Oxford: Leicester Explorations in Local History, I.

Frank, Bertram (1970), *Saltboxes of the North Yorks Moors.* Ryedale Folk Museum, Hutton Le Hole, reprinted from *The Dalesman*, December.

Freedman, Paul (2003), 'Best in white', *The Times Literary Supplement*, 12 December.

Fuller, Thomas (1987), ed. Richard Barber, *Fuller's Worthies.* Folio Society.

Furnivall, F. J. (ed.) (1868), *Early English Meals and Manners*, EETS, Original Ser., 32.

— (1870), *The Fyrst Boke of the Introduction of Knowledge made by Andrew Borde of Physycke Doctor: A Compendyous Regyment or a Dyetary of Helth*, EETS, ES, 10.

— (1877–82), *Phillip Stubbes's Anatomy of the Abuses in England in Shakspere's Youth, AD 1583*, New Shakespere Soc., Ser. VI, nos. 4, 6.

Fussell, G. E. (ed.) (1936), *Robert Loder's Farm Accounts, 1610–20*, Camden Society, Third Ser., LIII.

Gardiner, Richard, of Shrewsbury (1603) (1599), *Profitable Instructions for the Manuring, Sowing and Planting of Kitchen Gardens very Profitable for the Commonweal and Greatly for the Help and Comfort of Poor People.*

— (1892), 'Richard Gardiner's "Profitable Instructions" (1603)', Trans. Salop. Archaeolog. & Nat. Hist. Soc., Series II, IV.

Garnier, Russell M. (1895), *Annals of the British Peasantry.*

Geddes, Olive M. (1994), *The Laird's Kitchen.* Edinburgh.

George, David (ed.) (1991), *Records of Early English Drama: Lancashire.*

Gerard, John (1596), *Catalogus Arborum, Fruticum ac Plantarum.*

— (1597), *The Herball, or Generall Historie of Plantes.*

— (1998), ed. Marcus Woodward, *John Gerard's Historie of Plants.* Twickenham.

Gibb, H. A. R. (1994), *The Travels of Ibn Battuta, AD 1325–54*, vol. IV, Hakluyt Soc., 2nd Ser. 178.

Gibson, Revd T. Ellison (1895), *Blundell's Diary, comprising Selections from the Diary of Nicholas Blundell, Esq., from 1702–28.* Liverpool.

Gittings, Robert (1960), *Shakespeare's Rival.*

Gomar, Ann (1988), *Lancashire Country Recipes.* Horsham, Sussex.

Gomar, Pippa (n.d.), *Cumberland and Westmorland Country Recipes.* Horsham, Sussex.

— (1988), *Warwickshire Country Recipes.* Horsham, Sussex.

Gomišček, Toní (1989), 'The regional dish: Slovenian ravioli', *Slow Food Manifesto* (The Magazine of the Slow Food Movement), no. 2.

Goodacre, John (1994), *The Transformation of a Peasant Economy: Townspeople and Villagers in the Lutterworth Area, 1500–1700*. Aldershot.

Goodman, Godfrey (1839), ed. John S. Brewer, *The Court of King James the First*.

Gordon, Alexander (1871), 'A Pythagorean of the seventeenth century', paper read to Liverpool Literary and Philosophical Society, 3 April.

Gosse, Edmund (1913), *Seventeenth-Century Studies*.

Gould, S. Baring (1919), *Devon*, 5th edn.

Graham, William (1770), *The Art of Making Wine from Fruits, Flowers, and Herbs, and All the Native Growth of Great Britain*.

Gratarolus, Gulielmus (1574), trans. Thos. Newton, *A Direction for the Health of Magistrates and Studentes*.

Gray, Todd (ed.) (1992), *Harvest Failure in Cornwall and Devon: the Book of Orders and the Corn Surveys of 1623 and 1630–31*, Sources of Cornish History, I, Institute of Cornish Studies.

— (1995), *Devon Household Accounts, 1627–59, Part I, Sir Richard and Lady Lucy Reynell of Forde (and others)*, Devon and Cornwall Record Society, NS, 38.

— (1996), *Devon Household Accounts, 1627–59, Part II, Henry, Fifth Earl of Bath, and Rachel, Countess of Bath, 1637–55*, Devon and Cornwall Record Society, NS, 39.

Greenwell, W. (1860), *Wills and Inventories from the Registry of Durham*, Part II, Surtees Society, XXXVIII.

Grey, Eliz., Countess of Kent (1653), *A Choice Manuall of Rare and Select Secrets in Physick and Chyrurgery* (2nd edn) and *A True Gentlewoman's Delight, Wherein is Contained All Manner of Cookery*.

Grieve, Maud (1984) *A Modern Herbal*.

Griffiths, Elizabeth (ed.) (2002), *William Windham's Green Book, 1673–1688*, Norfolk Record Society, LXVI.

Groves, Barry (2003), 'William Banting: the father of the low-carbohydrate diet', *PPC*, 72.

Gutch, J. (1781), *Collectanea Curiosa*, II. Oxford.

Haldane, A. R. B. (1952), *The Drove Roads of Scotland*.

Hale, Thomas (1756), *A Compleat Body of Husbandry*.

Hales, John (1543), *The Preceptes of the Excelllent Clerke and Grave Philosopher, Plutarche, for the Preservacion of Good Healthe*.

Hammer, Carl I. (1999), 'A hearty meal? The prison diets of Cranmer and Latimer', *Sixteenth Century Journal*, XXX (3).

Hanham, Alison (1985), *The Celys and their World. An English Merchant Family of the Fifteenth Century*. Cambridge.

Harington, Sir John (1607), *The Englishman's Doctor or The Schoole of Salerne or Physical Observations for the Perfect Preserving of the Body of Man in Continuall Health*.

— (1624), *The Englishman's Doctor, or The School of Salerne*.

Harland, John (ed.) (1856–8), *The House and Farm Accounts of the Shuttleworths of Gawthorpe Hall in the County of Lancaster from Sept. 1582 to Oct. 1621*, four parts, Chetham Society: Part I (XXXV), Part II (XLI), Part III (XLIII), Part IV (XLVI).

Harley, David (1998), 'James Hart of Northampton and the Calvinist critique of priest-physicians: an unpublished polemic of the early 1620s', *Medical History*, 42.

Harrington, Duncan (ed.), Sarah Pearson and Susan Rose (2000), *Kent Hearth Tax Assessment, Lady Day, 1664*, British Record Soc., 116, and KAS, XXIX.

Harrison, William (1994), (ed.) Georges Edelen, The Description of England: The Classic Contemporary Account of Tudor Social Life. Washington and New York.

Hart, James (1633), *Klinike or the Diet of the Diseased.*

Hartley, Dorothy (1975), *Food in England.*

Hartley, Marie and Joan Ingilby (1968), *Life and Tradition in the Yorkshire Dales.*

Harvey, Barbara (1993), *Living and Dying in England, 1100–1540.* Oxford.

Harvey, John (1972), 'Mediaeval plantsmanship in England: the culture of rosemary', *Garden History*, I (i).

— (1981), *Mediaeval Gardens.*

— (1984), 'Vegetables in the Middle Ages', *Garden History*, XII (ii).

Hasted, Edward (1797), *The History and Topographical Survey of the County of Kent.* Canterbury.

Havinden, Michael (1998–9), 'The increase and distribution of the resident gentry of Somerset, 1500–1623', *Southern History* 20/21.

Hawkes, Nigel (2000), 'Fast food blamed for rise in asthma', *The Times*, 22 August.

— (2000b), 'Eat less for a longer life', *The Times*, 25 November.

Hearn, Karen (2005), *Nathaniel Bacon: Artist, Gentleman and Gardener.*

Henisch, Bridget A. (1976), *Fast and Feast: Food in Medieval Society.* Pennsylvania and London.

Henrey, Blanche (1975), *British Botanical and Horticultural Literature before 1800*, 3 vols. Oxford.

— (1986), ed. A. O. Chater, *No Ordinary Gardener: Thomas Knowlton, 1691–1781.*

Herrick, Robert (1965), ed. L. C. Martin, *The Poems of Robert Herrick.*

Hester, John (1575), *The True and Perfect Order to Distill Oyles out of all Maner of Spices, Seedes, Rootes and Gummes.*

— (1579), *A Joyfull Jewell, Contayning … Orders, Preservatives … for the Plague.*

— (1582), *A Compendium of the Rationall Secretes of the Worthie Knight and Most Excellent Doctour of Phisicke and Chirurgerie, Leonardo Phioravante Bolognese.*

Hey, D. (2000), 'Moorlands', in Joan Thirsk (ed.), *The English Rural Landscape.* Oxford.

Higford, William (1808) (1658), ed. Clement Barksdale, 'Institutions or Advice to His Grandson', *Harleian Miscellany*, 9.

Hinton, R. W. K. (1956), *The Port Books of Boston, 1601–40*, Lincoln Record Society, 50.

Historical Manuscripts Commission (1905), *The Manuscripts of His Grace, the Duke of Rutland, KG*, preserved at Belvoir Castle, vol. IV.

Hitt, Thomas (1768), *A Treatise of Fruit Trees*, 3rd edn.

Holinshed, Raphael (1913), *England in the Sixteenth Century.*

Hollander, John (1961), *Ben Jonson.* New York.

Holmes, Clare Patricia (1987), *Economic Activity in Saffron Walden between Sixteenth and Eighteenth Centuries.*

Hope, Annette (1987), *A Caledonian Feast.* Edinburgh.

Hoskins, W. G. (1964), 'Harvest fluctuations and English economic history, 1480–1619', *AHR*, XII (i).

— (1972), *Devon (A New Survey of England)*. Newton Abbot.

Houghton, John (1681), *A Collection of Letters for the Improvement of Husbandry and Trade*.

— (1692), *A Collection for Improvement of Husbandry and Trade*, 4 vols. Republished 1969 by Gregg International, Farnborough, Hants.

— (1727–8), *A Collection for the Improvement of Husbandry and Trade, Revised and Republished by Richard Bradley*, 4 vols. (Cited in text as Houghton in Bradley.)

How, William (1650), *Phytologia Britannica*.

Howard, Henry (1726), *England's Newest Way in All Sorts of Cookery, Pastry, and all Pickles that are Fit to be Used*, 5th edn.

Howell, James (1903), *Familiar Letters*, 3 vols.

Hoyle, R. W. and C. J. Spencer (2006), 'The Slaidburn poor pasture: changing configurations of popular politics in the eighteenth- and early nineteenth-century village', *Social History*, 31 (2).

Hudleston, C. Roy (1958), *Naworth Estate and Household Accounts, 1648–1660*, Surtees Society, CLXVIII.

Hughes, Charles (ed.) (1967), *Shakespeare's Europe … being Unpublished Chapters of Fynes Moryson's Itinerary (1617)*, 2nd edn. New York.

Hughes, P. L. and J. F. Larkin (1969a), *Tudor Royal Proclamations: II, The Later Tudors (1553–1587)*. New Haven and London.

— (1969b), *Tudor Royal Proclamations: III, The Later Tudors (1588–1603)*, New Haven and London.

Hurst, J. D. (1992), *Savouring the Past: The Droitwich Salt Industry*. Archaeology Section, Hereford and Worcester County Council.

Hunt, Margaret R. (1996), *The Middling Sort: Commerce, Gender and the Family in England, 1680–1780*. Berkeley, USA.

Jackson, Sarah (1754), *The Director: or Young Woman's Best Companion … a Book Necessary for All Families*.

Johnston, James F. W. (1863), *Elements of Agricultural Chemistry and Geology*. Edinburgh and London.

Jordan, W. B. and Peter Cherry (1995), *Spanish Still Life from Velázquez to Goya*. London: National Gallery.

Jordan, W. K. (1960), *The Charities of London, 1480–1660*.

J. S. (1684), *The Storehouse of Nature* (BL, 546 g 33).

Kalm, Pehr (1892), *Kalm's Account of his Visit to England on his Way to America in 1748*, trans. Joseph Lucas.

Kaplan, Steven L. (1996), *The Bakers of Paris and the Bread Question (1700–1775)*. Durham, NC, USA.

— (1997), 'Breadways', *Food and Foodways*, 7 (i).

Kaufmann, R. J. (1961), *Richard Brome, Caroline Playwright*. New York.

Keating, Shela (2002), 'The go-between', *The Times Magazine*, 23 November.

Kettilby, Mary (1728), *A Collection of above Three Hundred Receipts in Cookery, Physic, and Surgery … by Several Hands*, 4th edn.

Kidwell, Peggy (1983), 'Nicholas Fatio de Duillier and fruit walls improved: Natural philosophy, solar radiation, and gardening in late seventeenth-century England', *Agricultural History*, 57, part 4.

Kiple, K. F. and K. C. Ornelas (2000), *The Cambridge World History of Food*, I. Cambridge.

Kirk, R. E. G. and E. F. Kirk (1900–8), *Returns of Aliens Dwelling in the City and Suburbs of London*, 2 vols. Huguenot Society Publications, 10.

Kleiner, Kurt (1996), 'Life, liberty and the pursuit of vegetables', *New Scientist*, no. 2012, 13 January.

Kowaleski, Marianne (ed.) (1993), *The Local Customs Accounts of the Port of Exeter, 1266–1321*, Devon and Cornwall Record Society, 36.

— (ed.) (2001), *The Havener's Accounts of the Earldom and Duchy of Cornwall, 1356*, Devon and Cornwall Record Society, 44.

Labarge, Margaret Wade (1961), 'Eleanor de Montfort's household rolls', *History Today*, XI (7).

Lacey, Richard W. (1994), *Hard to Swallow: A Brief History of Food*, Cambridge.

Lamb, Patrick (1710), *Royal Cookery or the Complete Court-Cook*.

Lamond, Elizabeth (ed.) (1954), *A Discourse of the Commonweal of this Realm of England*. Cambridge.

Langham, William (1633), *The Garden of Health*, 2nd edn.

Langton, Christopher (1550?), *An Introduction into Phisycke wyth an Universal Dyet*.

Landsberg, Sylvia (1995), *The Medieval Garden*.

Lansberry, H. C. F. (ed.) (1988), *Sevenoaks Wills and Inventories in the Reign of Charles II*, KAS, Kent Records, XXV.

Larkin, J. F. and Paul L. Hughes (1973), *Stuart Royal Proclamations, I, Royal Proclamations of King James I, 1603–1625*. Oxford.

Larwood, Jacob (1881), *The Story of the London Parks*.

Latham, Robert and William Matthews (1983), *The Diary of Samuel Pepys*, IX, 1668–9.

La Varenne, François Pierre (2001) (1653), *The French Cook*, Introduction by P. and M. Hyman. Lewes, E. Sussex.

Lawson, William (1982a) (1617), *The Countrie Housewifes Garden*. New York.

— (1982b (1618)), *A New Orchard and Garden*. New York.

— (2003), ed. M.Thick, *A New Orchard and Garden*. Totnes.

Leake, Jonathan (1997), 'Official: flowers are losing their scent', *The Sunday Times*, 16 February.

— (2002), 'Dentists blacklist tooth-rot apples', *The Sunday Times*, 10 February.

— (2004), 'It's not the fruit it used to be', *The Sunday Times*, 8 February.

le Choyselat, Prudent (1951), *The Discours Oeconomique of Prudent Choyselat*, Preface by H. A. D. Neville. Reading.

Lennard, R. V. (1932–4), 'English agriculture under Charles II: the evidence of the Royal Society's "Enquiries"', *EcHR*, IV.

Linnell, Revd. J. E. (1932), *Old Oak: The Story of a Forest Village*.

Linton, E. Lynn (1864), *The Lake Country*.

Lister, Sam (1995), 'A diet rich in beans', *The Times*, 15 September.

Lloyd, A. T. (1967), 'The salterns of the Lymington area', *Proc. Hants. Field Club*, XXIV.

Lobb, Theophilus (1739), *A Treatise on Dissolvents of the Stone; and on Curing the Stone and Gout by Aliment*.

— (1767), 'Advice to the poor with regard to diet', in Anon., *Primitive Cookery or the Kitchen Garden Display'd*.

Locke, John (1976–89) ed. E. S. de Beer, *The Correspondence of John Locke*, 8 vols. Oxford.

Lodge, Eleanour (ed.) (1927), *The Account Book of a Kentish Estate, 1616–1704, Records of Social and Economic History*, VI, British Academy.

Lowthorp, John (1716), *Philosophical Transactions of the Royal Society*, II.

Luard, Elisabeth (1986), *European Peasant Cookery: The Rich Tradition*.

Luard, Nicholas (1982), *Andalucía: A Portrait of Southern Spain*.

Lyons, N., ed. (1984), *The Farmworker in North-west Lincolnshire*, 2 vols. Scunthorpe.

M., W. (1655), *The Queen's Closet Opened*. (BL: Thomason Tracts, E1519)

Macfarlane, Alan (1976), *The Diary of Ralph Josselin, 1616–83*, British Academy, *Records of Social and Economic History*, NS, III.

McGrath, P. V. (1948), 'The Marketing of Food, Fodder and Livestock in the London Area in the Seventeenth Century'. MA thesis: University of London.

McLean, Teresa (1989), *Medieval English Gardens*.

McTaggart, Lynne (2000), 'Doctor's handwritings', *Ecologist*, 30 (4), June.

Malpica Cuello, Antonio (ed.) (2001), *Navegación Marítima del Mediterráneo al Atlántico*. Granada, Spain.

Mandrou, Robert (1961), 'Vie matérielle et comportements biologiques', Annales ESC, 16e année, 5.

Markham, Gervase (1613), *The English Husbandman*.

— (1621), *Hunger's Prevention, or The Whole Art of Fowling by Water and Land*.

— (1623), *Cheap and Good Husbandry*.

— (1931) (1675), *Office of a Housewife*.

Martinez Llopis, Manuel M. (1989), *Historia de la Gastronomía Española*. Madrid.

Mascall, Leonard (1569), *A Booke of the Art and Maner how to Plante and Graffe*.

— (1581), *The Husbandlye Ordring and Governmente of Poultrie*.

Maurizio, Adam (1916), *Die Getreide-nahrung im Wandel der Zeiten*. Zürich.

— (1932), *Histoire de l'Alimentation*, Paris.

May, Robert (1994) (1660), *The Accomplisht Cook or the Art and Mystery of Cookery*. Totnes.

Mead, William E. (1967), *The English Medieval Feast*.

Melroe, Eliza (1798), *An Economical and New Method of Cookery … adapted to the Necessity of the Times, Equally in all Ranks of Society*.

Mennell, Stephen (1985), *All Manners of Food: Eating and Taste in England and France from the Middle Ages to the Present*. Oxford.

Merrett, Christopher (1666), *Pinax Rerum Naturalium*.

Meyer-Renschhausen, Elisabeth (1991), 'The porridge debate: grain, nutrition and forgotten food preparation techniques', *Food and Foodways*, 5 (1).

Middleton, John (1734), ed. Henry Howard, *Five Hundred New Receipts in Cookery, Pastry, Preserving, Conserving, Pickling*.

Miller, Philip (1724), *The Gardener and Florist's Dictionary*.

Millican, Percy (comp.) (1934), *The Register of the Freemen of Norwich, 1548–1713*. Norwich.

Milham, Mary Ella (ed. and trans.) (1998), *Platina: On Right Pleasure and Good Health*, Medieval and Renaissance Texts and Studies, 178. Tempe, Arizona.

Moffat, Brian (2000), 'A marvellous plant? The place of the heath pea in the Scottish ethnobotanical tradition', *Folio*, National Library of Scotland, 1, Autumn.

Moorhouse, Sydney (1956), 'Herdwick sheep of the Lake counties', *Wool Knowledge*, III, 12.

Morgan, Victor (1996), 'Perambulating and consumable emblems: the Norwich evidence', in Peter M. Daly and Daniel Russell (eds), *Deviceful Settings: the English Renaissance Emblem and its Contexts*. New York: Studies in the Emblem.

Mortimer, John (1707), *The Whole Art of Husbandry*.

Moufet, Thomas (1746) (1655) *Health's Improvement … corrected and enlarged by Christopher Bennet*.

Murrell, John (1617a), *A New Booke of Cookerie*.

— (1617b), *A Daily Exercise for Ladies and Gentlewomen*.

— (1621), *A Delightfull Daily Exercise for Ladies and Gentlewomen*.

Nairn, Ian and Nikolaus Pevsner (1965), The Buildings of England Series. Sussex.

Newman, Karen (1996), 'Sundry letters, worldly goods: the Lisle letters and Renaissance studies', *Journal of Medieval and Early Modern Studies*, 26 (1).

Newton, Thos (1580), *Approved Medicines and Cordiall Receiptes, with the Natures, Qualities and Operations of Sundry Simples*.

Nicolas, Nicholas Harris (ed.) (1827), *The Privy Purse Expences of King Henry the Eighth from November 1529 to December 1532*.

Northcote, Lady Rosalind (1912), *The Book of Herbs*, 2nd edn.

Northeast, Peter (2001), *Wills of the Archdeaconry of Sudbury, 1439–74*, I, Suffolk Records Society, 44.

Notestein, W., F. H. Relf and H. Simpson (1935), *Commons Debates, 1621*. New Haven.

Nuttall, Nick (2000), 'Importing out-of-season fruit adds to global warming', *The Times*, 11 November.

O'Connell, Anne (2003), 'Thomas Tryon's *A Bill of Fare of Seventy Five Noble Dishes*', *PPC*, 74.

Ornsby, George (1878), *Selections from the Household Books of the Lord William Howard of Naworth Castle*, Surtees Society, 68.

Owen, Richard (2000), 'A slow death for fast food', *The Times*, 27 October.

Oxford, Arnold W. (1913), *English Cookery Books to the Year 1850*. Oxford.

Padulosi, Stefano (2000), 'Ripe for revival – opinion interview', *New Scientist*, 2 September.

Page, William (ed.) (1907), *VCH Essex*, II.

Palliser, David (1974), 'Dearth and disease in Staffordshire, 1540–1670', in C. W. Chalklin and M. A. Havinden (eds) (1974), *Rural Change and Urban Growth, 1500–1800*.

Palmer, María del Carmen Simón (1982), *La Alimentación y sus Circunstancias en el Real Alcázar de Madrid*, Serie Estudios, no. 2. Instituto de Estudios Madrileños, Madrid.

Parkinson, John (1629 edn), *Paradisi in Sole Paradisus Terrestris*.

— (1656 edn), *Paradisi in Sole Paradisus Terrestris*, 2nd impression, corrected and enlarged.

— (1640), *Theatrum Botanicum: The Theater of Plants*.

Partridge, John (1584), *The Treasurie of Commodious Conceites and Hidden Secrets Commonly Called the Good Huswives Closet of Provision for the Health of Her Household.*

Payne, Robert (1589), *A Briefe Description of Ireland made in this Yeare, 1589.*

Peachey, Stuart, ed. (1992) (1594), *The Good Huswifes Handmaide for the Kitchin.* Bristol: Historical Cookery Books Series.

Pearce, D. (1970), 'Yarm and the butter trade', Cleveland and Teesside Local History Society, 9.

Peck, Linda Levy (2005), *Consuming Splendor: Society and Culture in Seventeenth-Century England.* Cambridge.

Percival, John (1943), *Wheat in Great Britain.*

Pepys, Samuel (1924), ed. G. Gregory Smith, *The Diary of Samuel Pepys.*

Perham, Molly (1989a), *Gloucestershire Country Recipes.* Horsham.

— (1989b), *Herefordshire and Worcestershire Country Recipes.* Horsham.

— (1989c), *Wiltshire Country Recipes.* Horsham.

Pettegree, Andrew (1986), *Foreign Protestant Communities in Sixteenth-Century London.* Oxford.

Phillips, A. P. (1958–9), 'The diet of the Savile household in the seventeenth century', Trans. Thoroton Society of Notts., 62–3.

Phillips, Henry (1821), *Pomarium Britannicum*, 2nd edn.

— (1827), *A History of Cultivated Plants.*

Philotheus Physiologus (i.e. Thomas Tryon) (1684), *Friendly Advice to the Gentlemen-Planters of the East and West Indies.*

Platt, Hugh (1594), *The Jewell House of Art and Nature.*

— (1596), *Sundrie New and Artificall Remedies against Famine.*

— (1602), *Delightes for Ladies.*

Plimmer, Violet G. (1935), *Food Values at a Glance.*

Potter, David (2006), 'The Household Receipt Book of Ann, Lady Fanshawe', *PPC*, 80.

Pounds, N. J. G. (1984), *The Parliamentary Survey of the Duchy of Cornwall*, Part II, Devon and Cornwall Record Society, NS, 27.

Powell, Dorothy L. and Hilary Jenkinson (1938), *The Order Books and the Sessions Rolls, Easter 1663–Epiphany 1666*, Surrey Record Soc., XXXIX.

Power, M. J. (2000), 'John Stow and his London', in R. C. Richardson (ed.), *The Changing Face of English Local History.* Aldershot.

Powicke, F. J. (1926), *The Reverend Richard Baxter's Last Treatise*, Reprint of the *Bulletin of the John Rylands Library*, 10 (1). Manchester.

Prior, Mary (1982), *Fisher Row: Fishermen, Bargemen and Canal Boatmen in Oxford, 1500–1900.* Oxford.

Rabisha, Will (1661), *The Whole Body of Cookery Dissected.*

Raines, Revd. F. R. (ed.) (1853), *The Derby Household Books: Comprising an Account of the Household Regulations and Expenses of Edward and Henry, Third and Fifth Earls of Derby.* Chetham Soc., XXXI.

Ray, Elizabeth (ed.) (1974), *The Best of Eliza Acton.* Penguin Books.

Read, Jan and Maite Manjón (1978), *Flavours of Spain: A Gastronomic Journey.*

Reader's Digest (1981), *Field Guide to the Trees and Shrubs of Britain.*

Rham, Revd. W. L. (1850), *The Dictionary of the Farm.*

Rickard, Gillian (1995), *Vagrants, Gypsies and 'Travellers' in Kent, 1572–1948.* Canterbury.

Riley, Gillian (1989), *The Fruit, Herbs, and Vegetables of Italy. Giacomo Castelvetro.*

Roach, F. A. (1985), *Cultivated Fruits of Britain: Their Origin and History.*

Roberson, B. S. (1941), *Cornwall. The Land of Britain*, Part 91.

Roberts, Edward and Karen Parker (eds) (1992), *Southampton Probate Inventories, 1447–1575*, 2 vols, Southampton Record Series, XXXIV and XXXV.

Robinson, Henry (1641), *England's Safety in Trade's Increase.*

Rohde, E. S. (1931), *The Scented Garden.*

Rosener, Werner (1994), *The Peasantry of Europe.*

Rothschild, J. A. de (1906), *Shakespeare and his Day.*

Rowse, A. L. (1941), *Tudor Cornwall: Portrait of a Society.*

— (1964), *Raleigh and the Throckmortons.*

Russell, Nicholas (1986), *Like Engend'ring Like: Heredity and Animal Breeding in Early Modern England.* Cambridge.

Ruthin, Lord (1639), *The Ladies Cabinet Opened.*

— (1654), *The Ladies Cabinet Enlarged and Opened.*

Rycraft, Anne (2000), 'Can we tell what people ate in late medieval York?', in Eileen White (ed.), *Feeding a City: The Provision of Food from Roman Times to the Beginning of the Twentieth Century.* Totnes.

Rye, William B. (1865), *England as seen by Foreigners.*

S., J. (1684), *The Storehouse of Nature* (BL: 546g33).

Saffron Walden Museum (n.d.), *The Saffron Crocus*, Museum Leaflet, no. 13.

Salter, Elizabeth (2000), 'Early puberty', Letter to the Editor, *The Times*, 22 June.

Sambrook, Pamela (1996), *Country House Brewing, 1500–1900.*

Sams, Craig, 'Healthy diet', Letter to the Editor, *The Times*, 23 August.

Saxby, Jessie M. E. (1932), *Shetland Traditional Lore.* Edinburgh.

Scarfe, Norman (1988), *A Frenchman's Year in Suffolk (1784).* Suffolk Records Soc., XXX.

— (1995), *Innocent Espionage.* Woodbridge.

Schofield, John (1994), *Medieval London Houses.* New Haven and London.

Scot, Reynolde (1576), *A Perfite Platforme of a Hoppe Garden.*

Scrivener, M. (1685), *A Treatise against Drunkenness ... especially that of Drinking Healths.*

Sharrock, Robert (1660), *The History of the Propagation and Improvement of Vegetables.*

Shaw, Catherine M. (1980), *Richard Brome.* Boston, USA.

Sheail, John (1971), *Rabbits and their History.* Newton Abbot.

Sheppard, R. and E. Newton (1957), *The Story of Bread.*

Sherman, Sandra (2002), 'An Eden on a plate', *PPC*, no. 69.

Shesgreen, Sean (1990), *The Criers and Hawkers of London.* Stanford, CA, USA.

Shewring, Adam (1699), *The Plain Dealing Poulterer* (in BL, Tracts on Cookery, 1699–1808, no. 1, call mark 1037 e 41).

Short, B. M. (1984), 'The South-East: Kent, Surrey, and Sussex', in *AHEW*, V, i, Cambridge.

— (1982), 'The art and craft of chicken cramming: poultry in the Weald of Sussex, 1850–1950', *AHR*, 30 (1).

Simon, André (1959), *The Star Chamber Dinner Accounts ... provided for the Lords of the Privy Council in the Star Chamber, Westminster, during the Reigns of Queen Elizabeth I and King James I*, Wine and Food Society.

Slack, Paul (1975), *Poverty in Early-Stuart Salisbury*, Wiltshire Record Series, XXXI.

— (1992), 'Dearth and social policy in early modern England', *Social History of Medicine*, 5.

Small, Meredith F. (2002), 'The happy fat', *New Scientist*, 24 August.

Smith, Brian (1964), *A History of Malvern*. Leicester.

Smith, E. (1729), *The Compleat Housewife*.

Smith, R. E. F. and David Christian (1984), *Bread and Salt*. Cambridge.

Smith, Robert (1725), *Court Cookery: or the Compleat English Cook*, 2nd edn.

Smith, S. D. (2001), 'The early diffusion of coffee drinking in England', in M. Tuchscherer (ed.), *Le Commerce du Café*. Cairo.

Snell, Robert (1995), 'A quince, a cabbage and a cucumber', *The Times Literary Supplement* (17 March).

Speed, Adam (1659), *Adam out of Eden*.

Spencer, Colin (1993), *The Heretic's Feast: A History of Vegetarianism*.

— (2002), *British Food: An Extraordinary Thousand Years of History*.

Spurling, Hilary (1987), *Elinor Fettiplace's Receipt Book: Elizabethan Country House Cooking*.

Standish, Arthur (1611), *The Commons Complaint, wherein is contained Two Special Grievances*.

— (1612), *The Commons Complaint ... newly corrected and augmented*.

— (1613), *New Directions of Experience to the Commons Complaint ... for the Planting of Timber and Firewood*.

Stapleton, Mrs Bryan (1893), *Three Oxfordshire Parishes*, Oxfordshire History Society, 24.

Stern, Walter M. (1976), 'Fish marketing in London in the first half of the eighteenth century', in D. C. Coleman and A. H. John (eds), *Trade, Government and Economy in Pre-Industrial England*.

Stewart, Chris (1999), *Driving over Lemons: An Optimist in Andalucía*.

Stitt, Bette (ed.) (1957), *Diana Astry's Recipe Book, c. 1700*, Bedfordshire Historical Record Society, XXXVII.

Stobart, Tom (1972), *Herbs, Spices and Flavourings*.

Stone, David (2003), 'The productivity and management of sheep in late medieval England', *AHR*, 51 (1).

Stonhouse, Sir James (1844), *Life of the Rev. Sir James Stonhouse, bart, MD, with Extracts from his Tracts and Correspondence*. Oxford.

Studd, Helen (2000), 'Junk food blamed for huge rise in diabetes', *The Times*, 6 November.

Sullivan, Bernard (2000), 'Some stories of wheat flour and bread from original documents', *Lincolnshire Past and Present*, 41, Autumn.

Switzer, Stephen (1727), *The Practical Kitchen Gardener*.

Taverner, J. (1928 (1600)), *Certaine Experiments concerning Fish and Fruite ...* Manchester.

Tawney, R. H. and Eileen Power (1924), *Tudor Economic Documents*, 3 vols.

Tay Valley Family History Society (1994), *Granny's Cookbook*. Dundee.

Temple, William (1903), *Essays of Sir William Temple*. Selection with an Introduction by J. A. Nicklin.

Terry, Edward (1665), *A Relation of Sir Thomas Roe's Voyage into the East Indies.*

Thick, Malcolm (1989), 'Roots and other garden vegetables in the diet of Londoners, *c.* 1550–1650, and some responses to harvest failures in the 1590s', Paper given at the Oxford Food Symposium.

— (1990), 'Root crops and the feeding of London's poor in the late sixteenth and early seventeenth centuries', in *English Rural Society, 1500–1800: Essays in Honour of Joan Thirsk*. Cambridge.

— (1992), 'Sir Hugh Platt's promotion of pasta as a victual for seamen', *PPC*, 40, March.

— (1998), *The Neat House Gardens: Early Market Gardening Around London*. Totnes.

Thirsk, Joan (1953), 'The Isle of Axholme before Vermuyden', *AHR*, I.

— (1957), *English Peasant Farming: The Agrarian History of Lincolnshire from Tudor to Recent Times.*

— (1978), *Economic Policy and Projects: The Development of a Consumer Society in Early Modern England*. Oxford.

— (1983), 'Plough and pen: agricultural writers in the seventeenth century', in T. H. Aston and others (eds.), *Social Relations and Ideas: Essays in Honour of R. H. Hilton*. Cambridge.

— (1985), 'Forest, field and garden: landscape and economies', in John F. Andrewes (ed.), *William Shakespeare: His World, his Work, his Influence*, vol. I. New York.

— (1990), 'The fashioning of the Tudor-Stuart gentry', *Bulletin*, John Rylands University Library of Manchester, 72 (1).

— (1992), 'Making a fresh start: sixteenth-century agriculture and the classical inspiration', in Michael Leslie and Timothy Raylor (eds), *Culture and Cultivation in Early Modern England: Writing and the Land*. Leicester and London.

— (1997), *Alternative Agriculture: A History from the Black Death to the Present Day.* Oxford.

— (2000), 'Agriculture in Kent, 1500–1640', in M. Zell, *Early Modern Kent, 1540–1640*. Woodbridge.

Thirsk, Joan and J. P. Cooper (1972), *Seventeenth-Century Economic Documents*. Oxford.

Thirsk, Joan and others (2006), *Hadlow: Life, Land and People in a Wealden Parish, 1460–1600*. E-book, www.kentarchaeology.ac.

Thomas, Keith (1996), *Man and the Natural World: Changing Attitudes in England, 1500–1800.*

Tillinghast, Mary (1678), *Rare and Excellent Receipts.*

Tryon, Thomas (1684), *Friendly Advice to the Gentlemen Planters of the East and West Indies.*

— (1685), *The Good Housewife made a Doctor.*

— (1684), see Philotheus Physiologus.

— (1705), *Some Memoirs of the Life of Mr Tho. Tryon … written by Himself.*

Tuchscherer, Michel (ed.) (2001), *Le Commerce du Café avant l'Ère des Plantations Coloniales*. Cairo.

Turner, Michael (ed.) (1978), 'The 1801 Crop Returns for England'. Typescript, Institute of Historical Research, London.

Turner, William (1568), *A New Boke of the Nature and Properties of all Wines that are Commonly Used Here in England.*

Tusser Redivivus, with Notes by Daniel Hilman (1710).

Twyne, Thomas (1583), *The Schoolemaster or Teacher of Table Phylosophie.*

Tyssen-Amherst, A. M. (1894), 'A fifteenth-century treatise on gardening', *Archaeologia*, 54.

Ude, Louis Eustache (1813), *The French Cook.*

Vaisey, David (ed.) (1984), *The Diary of Thomas Turner (1754–65).* Oxford.

Vaughan, William (1600), *Naturall and Artificiall Directions for Health, Derived from the Best Philosophers as Well Moderne … as Ancient.*

— (1608), *The Golden Grove.*

— (1617), *Directions for Health both Natural and Artificiall … Newly Enriched with Large Additions by the Author*, 5th edn.

— (1630), *The Newlanders Cure.*

Venner, Tobias (1620), *Via Recta ad Vitam Longam.*

Victoria County History of England, *Middlesex*, III (1962, ed. R. B. Pugh).

Vinet, Elie (1607), *La Maison Champestre et Agriculture d'Elie Vinet.* Paris.

Vives, Juan Luis (1959), *Diálogos*, 4th edn. Madrid.

Wake, C. H. H. (1979), 'The changing pattern of Europe's pepper and spice imports, *ca.* 1400–1700', *Journal of European Economic History*, 8 (2).

Walter, John and Roger Schofield (1989), *Famine, Disease and the Social Order in Early Modern Society.* Cambridge.

Wanklyn, Malcolm (ed.) (1998), *Inventories of Worcestershire Landed Gentry, 1537–1786*, Worcesterhire Historical Society, NS, 16.

Warde, William (1607), *God's Arrowes or Two Sermons concerning the Visitation of God by the Pestilence.*

Watkins, Andrew (1989), 'Cattle grazing in the Forest of Arden in the later Middle Ages', *AHR*, 37 (1).

Watson, Foster (ed. and trans.) (1970), *Tudor School-boy Life: The Dialogues of Juan Luis Vives.* London.

Weatherill, Lorna (ed.) (1990), *The Account Book of Richard Latham, (1724–1767)*, British Academy, Records of Social and Economic History, NS, 15.

Webb, Jeremy (2000), 'Let them eat caju', *New Scientist*, 2 September.

Webber, Ronald (1968), *The Early Horticulturists*, Newton Abbot.

Webster, Charles (1979), 'Alchemical and Paracelsian medicine', in Charles Webster (ed.), *Health, Medicine, and Mortality in the Sixteenth Century.* Cambridge.

— (1982), 'Paracelsus and demons: science as a synthesis of popular belief', in papers of a conference on *Scienze Credenze Occulte Livelli di Cultura*, ed. Leo S. Olschki, Florence.

Welsted, Leonard (1787), ed. John Nichols, *The Works in Verse and Prose of Leonard Welsted, Esq.*

Wentworth-Day, J. (1970), *A History of the Fens*, East Ardsley, Wakefield.

Westbury, Lord (R. M. T. Bethell) (1963), *Handlist of Italian Cookery Books.* Florence.

Westmacott, William (1694), *Historia Vegetabilium Sacra.*

Westmorland County Federation of Women's Institutes (1937), *Westmorland Cookery Book*. Penrith.

Whetter, James (1991), *Cornwall in the Seventeenth Century*. Gorran, St Austell, Cornwall.

White, Eileen (ed.) (2000), *Feeding a City: The Provision of Food from Roman Times to the Beginning of the Twentieth Century*. Totnes.

Whiteman, Anne (ed.) (1986), *The Compton Census of 1676*, British Academy, Records of Social and Economic History, X.

Wilkinson, Paul (1997), 'How chivalry died in Roses battle', *The Times*, 17 October.

Williams, Clare (1979), *Thomas Platter's Travels in England, 1599*.

Wilson, C. Anne (1973), *Food and Drink in Britain*.

— (1994), *Traditional Food East and West of the Pennines*. Stroud.

Wilson, Francesca M. (1967), *Rebel Daughter of a Country House: The Life of Eglantyne Jebb, Founder of the Save the Children Fund*.

Witney, Kenneth (ed.) (2000), *The Survey of Archbishop Pecham's Kentish Manors, 1283–5*, Kent Records, Kent Archaeological Society, XXVIII.

W. M. (1655), *The Queen's Closet Opened*.

Women's Institutes, National Federation of (1948), *Traditional Fare of England and Wales*.

Wood, B. A., Charles Watkins and C. A. Wood (eds.) (1983), *Life at Laxton, c. 1880–1903, The Childhood Memories of Edith Hickson*. Nottingham.

Wood, Neal (1984), *John Locke and Agrarian Capitalism*. Berkeley and Los Angeles.

Woodcroft, Bennet (1969), *Alphabetical Index of Patentees of Inventions, 1617–1852*.

Woodward, Donald (ed.) (1984), *The Farming and Memorandum Books of Henry Best of Elmswell, 1642*, British Academy, Records of Social and Economic History, NS, VIII.

Woolgar, C. M. (1995), 'Diet and consumption in gentry and noble households: a case study from around the Wash', in R. E. Archer and S. Walker, *Rulers and Ruled in Late Medieval England*.

— (1999), *The Great Household in Late Medieval England*. New Haven, USA.

Woolley, Hannah (1664), *The Cook's Guide: or Rare Receipts for Cookery*.

— (1675), *The Gentlewoman's Cabinet Unlocked*, 7th impression.

— (2001) (1675), *The Gentlewoman's Companion or, A Guide to the Female Sex*, Introduction by Caterina Albano. Totnes.

Wordie, J. R. (1984), 'The South: Oxfordshire, Buckinghamshire, Berkshire, Wiltshire, and Hampshire' in *AHEW*, V, i.

Worlidge, John (1970) (1675), *Systema Agriculturae: The Mystery of Husbandry Discovered*.

— (1970) (1704), *Dictionarium Rusticum et Urbanicum*. Los Angeles.

Wyatt, Peter (ed.) (1997), *The Uffculme Wills and Inventories, Sixteenth to Eighteenth Centuries*, Devon and Cornwall Record Soc., NS, 40.

Index

CPSIA information can be obtained at www.ICGtesting.com
Printed in the USA
LVOW09s0637170616

492917LV00010B/13/P